Wi-Fi 7

Gang Cheng • Zhihong Qian • Yiming Jiang •
Zhijie Yang • Thirumurthy Rajamanickam

Wi-Fi 7

Principles, Technology, and Applications

Gang Cheng
Broadband Device BU
Nokia
Shanghai, China

Zhihong Qian
Broadband Device BU
Nokia
Shanghai, China

Yiming Jiang
Broadband Device BU
Nokia
Shanghai, China

Zhijie Yang
Broadband Device BU
Nokia
Shanghai, China

Thirumurthy Rajamanickam
Broadband Device BU
Nokia
Raleigh, NC, USA

ISBN 978-981-97-9025-8 ISBN 978-981-97-9026-5 (eBook)
https://doi.org/10.1007/978-981-97-9026-5

Jointly published with Tsinghua University Press

This Springer imprint is published by the registered company Springer Nature Singapore Pte Ltd.
The registered company address is: 152 Beach Road, #21-01/04 Gateway East, Singapore 189721, Singapore

Foreword I

Wi-Fi has become an invisible thread woven into the fabric of our daily lives. It allows us to connect to the Internet instantly, fueling everything from our morning news scroll to late-night video chats. We work, learn, and enjoy entertainment, all thanks to this seamless connection. Wi-Fi's influence stretches far beyond simple browsing—it is the backbone of smart home devices, facilitating remote work and even influencing how we socialize. Wi-Fi 7 is a revolutionary technology that unlocks a new level of speed, reliability, and responsiveness. Imagine downloading massive files in seconds, streaming ultra-high-definition video without any interruptions, and enjoying lag-free online gaming—all at the same time.

Head of Nokia Wi-Fi, Broadband Devices Business Unit, Nokia, Los Angeles, CA, USA

Justin Doucette

Foreword

Foreword II

After more than two decades since its introduction, Wi-Fi is taking a giant leap forward to meet the growing household needs for communications. Wi-Fi 7 triples the throughput of its predecessor and offers many new features, including support for applications, such as virtual reality, low-latency gaming, and high-quality streaming. This book provides a holistic insight into the new standard, making it a highly recommended read for both interested consumers and technical experts alike.

Business Finland China, Trade and Innovation Consul, Head of Innovation, China, Shanghai, China

Mika Klemettinen, PHD

Foreword III

Wi-Fi has established itself as the most successful short-range wireless communication technology, achieving data transfer rates of more than 30 Gbps with the latest Wi-Fi 7 specification. Over the past decades, Wi-Fi technology has rapidly evolved, incorporating concepts from 3GPP technology while maintaining simplicity and cost-effectiveness in network design. This book, authored by experts with profound knowledge and extensive engineering experience in Wi-Fi technologies, serves as a comprehensive and detailed reference on the state-of-the-art Wi-Fi 7 technology. It provides a systematic overview and in-depth insights that are typically gained from practical product development and deployment. This makes it an invaluable resource for both industry professionals and enthusiasts seeking to understand the intricacies and advancements of Wi-Fi 7.

Professor, George Mason University,
IEEE Fellow, Washington, DC, USA

Zhengdao Wang

Foreword IV

Wi-Fi 7, also known as IEEE 802.11be, is the latest generation of Wi-Fi technology, offering significant improvements over its predecessors in terms of throughput, capacity, latency, efficiency, and security. This book covers a wide range of topics, including the standard evolution, underlying principles, defining features, and practical implementation strategies. A large number of examples and case studies are presented to illustrate the design philosophy and methodology, making the complex technology easy to understand.

Whether you are an engineer developing Wi-Fi products, a technology enthusiast, a university student, or simply someone curious about how Wi-Fi works, it is highly recommended to take this book as a comprehensive guide to the ever-evolving Wi-Fi standards.

Principal Engineer, Amazon, IEEE Fellow, AAIA Fellow, San Diego, CA, USA

Pengfei Xia

Preface

In the ubiquitous Internet era nowadays, Wi-Fi is the most successful indoor wireless connectivity technology. Given its extensive commercialization, it is common for many to perceive Wi-Fi technology as having reached its peak maturity. Even professionals within the communications and computer industries may assume that there is little untapped potential left in Wi-Fi technology.

The reality is that Wi-Fi technology has been evolving at a steady pace, nearly twice as fast as mobile communication, with each new generation of Wi-Fi technology significantly uplifting user experiences. Since the introduction of the first Wi-Fi standard in 1997, new standards have emerged approximately every four to five years, each bringing significant improvements in physical data rates. Starting from an initial speed of 2 Mbps, these rates have progressively increased to 54 Mbps, then to 600 Mbps, and now surpass 30 Gbps with the latest Wi-Fi 7 standard.

In offices, Wi-Fi has become an essential infrastructure, and at home, it has become as indispensable as water, electricity, and gas for people's daily lives.

According to a Wi-Fi Alliance report, the global economic value of Wi-Fi was estimated at $3.3 trillion in 2021 and is expected to grow to $4.9 trillion by 2025. This growth is driven by the increasing demand for data-intensive real-time applications, the digital transformation of enterprise communication, and the availability of new 6 GHz spectrum, which has been authorized by many countries and regions. After more than two decades of technological development and standard evolution, Wi-Fi has become one of the economic engines of the digital economy today.

The newest Wi-Fi standard, defined by the IEEE as 802.11be and branded Wi-Fi 7 by the Wi-Fi Alliance, represents the next generation of wireless connectivity. Prior to it, Wi-Fi 6 was widely adopted by telecom operators, router manufacturers, and smart device makers soon after the Wi-Fi Alliance established the certification testing standard in 2019.

As the next generation of Wi-Fi technology, Wi-Fi 7 aims to deliver ultra-high bandwidth and ultra-high performance, with more technological innovations and breakthroughs. The theoretical rate of Wi-Fi 7 exceeds 30 Gbps, more than three times that of Wi-Fi 6, and also exceeds the peak rate of 5G mobile communication.

The latest Wi-Fi 7 specification has recently been ratified by the IEEE. The new handsets have been equipped with the Wi-Fi 7 technology, and millions of devices with the upgraded Wi-Fi capability are expected to hit the market, similar to the trend seen with every predecessor Wi-Fi standards release. Uncontroversially, Wi-Fi 7 will dominate short-range communication in home networks, enterprise wireless offices, and public Wi-Fi applications in the next years before Wi-Fi 8 takes over. Its ultra-high performance will facilitate various high-bandwidth latency-sensitive services, such as ultra-high definition video, online gaming, and virtual reality.

There are few books on the market about the principles and design practices of Wi-Fi product development. This book fills that gap, serving as a comprehensive professional resource across industries regarding Wi-Fi 7 key technologies, Wi-Fi 7 product development, and Wi-Fi 7 business applications, such as the integration of new Wi-Fi technology with 5G mobile networks, etc. This book also helps those interested in Wi-Fi technology to understand the technical concepts and principles behind remote learning, home entertainment, and other life experiences.

This book is divided into two main parts.

The first part starts with the basic concepts and principles of Wi-Fi technology and then delves into the key technologies and standard changes that Wi-Fi 6 and Wi-Fi 7 bring, respectively, providing readers an in-depth understanding of various aspects of Wi-Fi 7.

The second part discusses product development and testing methods based on Wi-Fi 7, explores utilizing Wi-Fi 7 applications in different industry or home scenarios, as well as the convergence of Wi-Fi 7 and 5G mobile technologies. At the end, this book provides a forecast on Wi-Fi technology trends and the changes it will bring to the public in the future.

This book features an in-depth introduction to Wi-Fi 7 technology, as well as new product development and the Wi-Fi monetization applications of service providers.

The authors are Cheng Gang, Qian Zhihong, Jiang Yiming, Thirumurthy Rajamanickam, while Yang Zhijie is one of the original authors of the Chinese edition, which was published in September 2023. Compared with the Chinese edition, many chapters have undergone extensive revisions, encompassing a meticulous refinement of Wi-Fi principles, the incorporation of the newest advancements in Wi-Fi 7 technology, and the adoption of a more systematic and precise approach to illustrate cutting-edge technologies.

Chapters 1, 2, and 3 were written by Qian Zhihong and Cheng Gang.
Chapter 4 was written by Jiang Yiming, Thirumurthy Rajamanickam, and Cheng Gang.
Chapters 5 and 8 were written by Cheng Gang and Thirumurthy Rajamanickam.
Chapters 6 and 7 were written by Thirumurthy Rajamanickam and Cheng Gang.
Cheng Gang served as the overall editor for this English edition.

It is challenging for a single book to cover all the points of an ever-evolving digital landscape. If the readers find any flaws or have any comments, please do not hesitate to reach out to us.

Shanghai, China — Gang Cheng
Shanghai, China — Zhihong Qian
Shanghai, China — Yiming Jiang
Shanghai, China — Zhijie Yang
Raleigh, NC, USA — Thirumurthy Rajamanickam

Contents

1 Overview on Wi-Fi Technology 1
1.1 Wi-Fi Specification and Evolution 1
1.1.1 Wireless LAN Transmission Technology 2
1.1.2 Continuous Evolution of IEEE 802.11 Standards 5
1.2 Basic Concepts and Typical Features of Wi-Fi 9
1.2.1 Basic Concepts and Terminologies 10
1.2.2 Introduction to Wi-Fi Physical Layer Technologies 17
1.2.3 Standards of Wi-Fi Physical Layer 39
1.2.4 Standards of Wi-Fi MAC Layer 46
1.2.5 Wi-Fi Media Access Mechanism 56
1.2.6 Wi-Fi Network Discovery, Authentication, and Association 66
1.2.7 Power Saving Mode Supported by Wi-Fi 70
1.3 Summary 76
References 77

2 Wi-Fi 6 Technology Bringing High Efficiency 79
2.1 Wi-Fi 6 Technology Overview 79
2.1.1 Limitations of Legacy Wi-Fi Technology 80
2.1.2 Wi-Fi 6 New Characteristics 83
2.2 Wi-Fi 6 Key Technologies 84
2.2.1 Technology Overview 85
2.2.2 Orthogonal Frequency Division Multiple Access (OFDMA) 87
2.2.3 Enhanced MIMO Technology in Wi-Fi 6 97
2.2.4 Enhanced Power Saving in Wi-Fi 6 103
2.2.5 Spatial Reuse Technology to Improve Spectrum Efficiency 116
2.2.6 Multiple BSSID Technology to Support Multi-BSS Scenario 122

2.2.7 Preamble Puncturing Accommodating Noncontiguous Channels 128
2.3 Updates of Physical Layer and MAC Layer for Wi-Fi 6 130
2.3.1 Wi-Fi 6 Physical Layer Technology 131
2.3.2 New Physical Layer Data Unit Frame Format 138
2.3.3 New Trigger Frame in Wi-Fi 6 144
2.3.4 Dual Carrier Modulation for Data Transmission 147
2.4 Wi-Fi 6E: Extension into the 6 GHz Band 149
2.4.1 Planning and Development of 6 GHz Channels 150
2.4.2 Optimized Discovery and Connection Procedure on the 6 GHz Band 153
2.5 Summary 157
References 158

3 Wi-Fi 7 Principles and Innovations 159
3.1 Wi-Fi 7 Technical Overview 159
3.1.1 Wi-Fi 7 Technical Characteristics 160
3.1.2 Development Timeline of Wi-Fi 7 Standard 168
3.2 Wi-Fi 7 Key Technologies 169
3.2.1 Overview on Wi-Fi 7 Innovation 169
3.2.2 New Multiple Link Device (MLD) Introduced from Wi-Fi 7 169
3.2.3 Multi-Link Operation Offering High Efficient Data Transmission 179
3.2.4 Discovery, Authentication, and Association Procedure of MLD 196
3.2.5 Multiple Resource Unit Further Enhancing Spectrum Efficiency 203
3.2.6 MU-MIMO Technology Update in Wi-Fi 7 213
3.2.7 Low Latency Technology in Wi-Fi 7 216
3.2.8 Enhanced Peer-to-Peer Communication 228
3.3 Emergency Preparedness Communications Services 243
3.3.1 Feature Procedure of New Service 244
3.3.2 Service Setup Approaches with Parameters 246
3.4 The Updates on Physical Layer by Wi-Fi 7 247
3.4.1 New 4 K-QAM Modulation 247
3.4.2 320 MHz Channel Bandwidth 250
3.4.3 Wi-Fi 7 New Physical Layer Data Unit Frame Format 251
3.5 The Security Evolution for Wi-Fi 7 254
3.5.1 Typical Wi-Fi Security Standards 255
3.5.2 Key Features in Wi-Fi Security 257
3.5.3 WPA3: Latest Wi-Fi Security Standard 266
3.5.4 Updates on the Security Protocols in Wi-Fi 7 271
3.6 Mesh Networking with Wi-Fi 7 277
3.6.1 Overview on Wi-Fi Multi-AP Technology 279

3.6.2 Mesh Networking Update with Wi-Fi 7 Support 288
3.7 Summary 293
References 295

4 Wi-Fi 7 Product Development and Test Methods 297
4.1 Overview of Wi-Fi 7 Product Development 297
4.1.1 Wi-Fi 7 Product Definition and Specifications 298
4.1.2 Wi-Fi 7 Product Development Process 305
4.2 Wi-Fi 7 AP Product Software Development 310
4.2.1 Software Architecture for Wi-Fi 7 AP Products 310
4.2.2 Wi-Fi 7 Connection Management 318
4.2.3 Wi-Fi 7 Data Forwarding 325
4.2.4 Wi-Fi 7 Performance Optimization 332
4.2.5 Wi-Fi 7 Wireless Channel Management 341
4.2.6 Wi-Fi 7 EasyMesh Network 347
4.2.7 Wi-Fi 7 Network Management 363
4.3 Wi-Fi 7 AP Product Testing 370
4.3.1 Wi-Fi 7 Performance Testing 370
4.3.2 Wi-Fi 7 Key Technologies Test 379
4.4 Summary 388
References 389

5 Wi-Fi Industry Alliance Promoting Technologies and Products 391
5.1 The Success of Wi-Fi Alliance in the Age of Technology 391
5.1.1 Wi-Fi Alliance Testing and Certification Methods 393
5.1.2 Certification Specifications Developed by Wi-Fi Alliance 394
5.1.3 Wi-Fi Alliance Certification for QoS Management 394
5.2 Contribution of Wireless Broadband Alliance to Wi-Fi Industry 397
5.2.1 Wireless Broadband Alliance Working Groups and Task Groups 398
5.2.2 Promote the Development of Wi-Fi Sensing Technology 398
5.3 Contribution of Broadband Forum to Wi-Fi Management 400
5.3.1 Support TR-069 Protocol for Broadband Network Devices 401
5.3.2 TR-369 Protocol for All Aspects of Home Network Management 402
References 403

6 Wi-Fi 7 Technology Applications and Experience Upgrades 405
6.1 Enhancing Entertainment Experiences in the Comfort of Your Home 405
6.1.1 Exploring AR/VR User Experience and Advancements in Wi-Fi Technology 405

6.1.2 Wi-Fi 7 Technology Supporting Ultra HD Video Services 410
6.1.3 Elevating Home Wi-Fi Technology: Enhancing the Experience 414
6.2 Wi-Fi 7 Applications in Various Industries 419
6.2.1 Wi-Fi Applications in Educational Multimedia Classrooms 419
6.2.2 Wi-Fi Network Challenges in High-Density Stadium Settings 422
6.2.3 Wi-Fi Network Design for Hotel Buildings: Meeting Modern Guest Connectivity Needs 424
6.2.4 Wi-Fi Usage in Enterprise Offices: Enhancing Workplace Efficiency 429
References 432

7 Convergence of Wi-Fi 7 and Mobile 5G Technology 435
7.1 Technology Comparison Between Wi-Fi 7 and Mobile 5G 435
7.2 The Continuous Integration of Wi-Fi Networks and Mobile 5G 438
7.2.1 3GPP Convergence Standard Evolution with Wi-Fi Technology Support 440
7.2.2 5G Network Slicing Requirements Incorporating with Wi-Fi Technology 444
7.3 Application Scenarios for Wi-Fi Network and 5G Convergence 451
7.3.1 Types of Scenarios Applied by 5G and Wi-Fi Network Convergence 451
7.3.2 Application Examples of Convergence Network 451
7.3.3 The Future of 5G and Wi-Fi Network Convergence Evolution 454
References 455

8 Outlook for Wi-Fi Technology Development 457
8.1 Turning on Ultra-High Broadband Networks 457
8.2 Looking Ahead to Key Technologies of Next-Generation Wi-Fi 459
8.2.1 Upgrades to Traditional Key Technologies 459
8.2.2 Evolution of New Key Technologies 461
8.3 Conclusion 464
References 464

Abbreviations

AAD	Additional authentication data
AC	Access category
Ack	Acknowledge
AC_BK	AC background
AC_BE	AC best effort
AC_VI	AC video
AC_VO	AC voice
ACS	Auto configuration server
AFC	Automated frequency coordination system
AIFS	Arbitration interframe space
AIFSN	Arbitration interframe space number
AI/ML SIG	Artificial Intelligence Machine Learning Special Interest Group
A-MPDU	Aggregate MPDU
AID	Association identifier
A-MSDU	Aggregate MSDU
AP	Access point
AR	Augmented reality
ASK	Amplitude shift keying
ATL	Authorized test laboratory
BA	Block Ack
BAR	Block Ack Request
BBF	Broadband forum
BCC	Binary convolutional code
BFRP	Beamforming Report Poll
BQR	Bandwidth Query Report
BQRP	Bandwidth Query Report Poll
BSRP	Buffer Status Report Poll
BSS	Basic service set
b-TWT	Broadcast TWT

C-BA	Compressed Block Ack
CBC-MAC	Cipher-block chaining message authentication code
CBR	Constant bit rate
CCA	Clear channel assessment
CCA-ED	CCA-energy detection
CCA-PD	CCA-packet detection
CCMP	CTR with CBC-MAC protocol
CEPT	Confederation of European Posts and Telecommunications
CM	Cable modem
CPE	Customer premise equipment
CRC	Cyclic redundancy check
CSI	Channel state information
CSMA/CA	Carrier sense multiple access/collision avoidance
CTR	Counter mode
CW	Contention window
CWmin	Minimum contention window
CWmax	Maximum contention window
DA	Destination address
DBPSK	Differential binary phase shift keying
DC	Direct current subcarriers
DCM	Dual carrier modulation
DFS	Dynamic frequency selection
DHCP	Dynamic host configuration protocol
DHKE	Diffie–Hellman key exchange
DIFS	Distributed coordination function interframe space
DL	Down link
D-MIMO	Distributed-MIMO
DQPSK	Differential quadrature phase shift keying
DS	Distributed system
DSCP	Differentiated services code point
DSL	Digital subscriber line
DSSS	Direct sequence spread spectrum
DTIM	Delivery traffic indication map
EAPOL	Extensible authentication protocol over LAN
EAP-TTLS	EAP-tunneled transport layer security
eMBB	Enhanced mobile broadband
ECWmin	Exponent form of CWmin
ECWmax	Exponent form of CWmax
EDCA	Enhanced distributed channel access
EHT	Extremely high throughput
EIFS	Extended interframe space
EIRP	Effective isotropic radiated power
EPCS	Emergency preparedness communications services

ESS	Extended service set
ETSI	European Telecommunications Standards Institute
EVM	Error vector magnitude
FAGF	Fixed access gateway function
FCC	Federal Communications Commission
FDM	Frequency division multiplexing
FEM	Front-end module
FN	Fragment number
FT	Fast transition
GC	Group client
GI	Guard interval
GMK	Group master key
GO	Group owner
GTK	Group transient key
HE	High efficiency
HT	High throughput
IEEE	Institute of Electrical and Electronics Engineers
IFS	Interframe space
IPsec	Internet protocol security
ISI	Intersymbol interference
ISM	Industrial scientific medical
i-TWT	Individual TWT
LAN	Local area network
LDPC	Low density parity check
LLC	Logical link control
L-LTF	Legacy long training field
L-SIG	Legacy signal
L-STF	Legacy short training field
LTF	Long training field
KCK	EAPOL-key confirmation key
KEK	EAPOL-key Encryption Key
MAC	Medium access control
M-BA	Multi-STA Block Ack
MBSSID	Multiple-BSSID
MCS	Modulation and coding scheme
MIC	Message integrity code
MIMO	Multiple input multiple output
MLD	Multiple link device
mMTC	Massive machine type of communication
MPDU	MAC layer protocol data unit
MQTT	Message queuing telemetry transport
MRU	Multiple resource unit
MSCS	Mirrored stream classification service

MSDU	MAC service data unit
MSK	Master session key
MTP	Message transfer protocol
MU-MIMO	Multiuser-multiple input multiple output
N3IWF	Non-3GPP interworking function
NAV	Network allocation vector
NDP	Null data PPDU
NDPA	Null data PPDU announcement
NFRP	NDP Feedback Report Poll
OBSS	Overlapping basic service sets
OFDM	Orthogonal frequency division multiplexing
OFDMA	Orthogonal frequency division multiple access
OPS	Opportunistic power saving
OSI	Open systems interconnection reference model
P2P	Peer-to-peer
PAR	Project authorization request
PE	Packet extension
PIFS	Priority interframe space
PMK	Pairwise master key
PON	Passive optical network
PPDU	Physical layer protocol data unit
PSD	Power spectral density
PSDU	Physical service data unit
PSK	Phase shift keying
PS-POLL	Power Saving Poll
PTK	Pairwise transient key
QAM	Quadrature amplitude modulation
QoS	Quality of service
QPSK	Quadrature phase shift keying
RA	Receiver address
RAN	Radio access network
RF	Radio frequency
RG	Residential gateway
RNR	Reduced neighbor report
RSSI	Received signal strength indication
RTS/CTS	Request to send/clear to send
RA-RU	Random access resource unit
RCE	Relative constellation error
RSNE	Robust security network element
RU	Resource unit
RVR	Rate vs range
r-TWT	Restricted target wakeup time
SÁ	Source address

SAE Simultaneous authentication of equals
SCS Stream classification service
SDK Software development kit
SG Study group
SGI Short guard interval
SIFS Short interframe space
SN Sequence number
SNR Signal-to-noise ratio
SR Spatial reuse
SSID Service set identifier
STA Station
STBC Space time block code
STF Short training field
SU-MIMO Single-user MIMO
TA Transmitter address
TBTT Target beacon transmit time
TDLS Tunneled direct link setup
TG Task group
TKIP Temporal key integrity protocol
TID Traffic identifier
TIM Traffic indication map
TXS TXOP sharing
TWT Target wake time
TPC Transmission power control
TXOP Transmission opportunity
UHDTV Ultra-high definition television
UHR SG Ultra High Reliability Study Group
UL Up link
UORA UL OFDMA-based random access
uRLLC Ultra-reliable low latency communications
USP User services platform
VBR Variable bit rate
VBSS Virtualized BSS
VHT Very high throughput
VR Virtual reality
XR Extended reality
WBA Wireless broadband alliance
WECA Wireless Ethernet Compatibility Alliance
WEP Wired equivalent privacy
WFA Wi-Fi alliance
Wi-Fi Wireless-fidelity
WSC Wi-Fi simple configuration
WLAN Wireless local area network

WMN	Wireless mesh network
WMM	Wi-Fi multimedia
WPA	Wi-Fi protected access
3GPP	The Third Generation Partnership Project

Chapter 1
Overview on Wi-Fi Technology

Abstract Over the past two decades, Wi-Fi technology has demonstrated its highly viable nature through rapid iteration. Approximately every 5 years, a new generation of Wi-Fi specification is ratified and quickly becomes dominant in the market. Such evolution is primarily driven by the growing bandwidth capabilities of the broadband access technologies, the widespread adoption of Wi-Fi based smart devices, and the emergence of various new services in the wireless network environment. Wi-Fi has already become an indispensable part of our daily life. This chapter serves as an introduction to the evolution of Wi-Fi standards and the overall landscape of Wi-Fi technology. It aims to provide fundamental knowledge to readers who may not be familiar with Wi-Fi technology, ensuring they gain a basic understanding of its principles and development, including both Physical Layer (PHY) and Medium Access Control (MAC) specifications. With this foundation, readers will be better prepared to comprehend and grasp the advancements and potential of Wi-Fi 6 and Wi-Fi 7, which are discussed in the following chapters.

1.1 Wi-Fi Specification and Evolution

Different from the cellular communication that transmits voice and data through base stations and mobile core networks, which provides coverage over a wider area, Wi-Fi operates as a wireless Local Area Network (WLAN) technology and has a smaller coverage area. For example, a typical Wi-Fi router has a coverage area of up to 100 meters or less. This limited coverage is suitable for providing wireless connectivity within a localized area, such as a home, office, or public hotspot.

To enable wireless connectivity within such limited coverage area, Wi-Fi technology has two main objectives:

To enable wireless communication: Wi-Fi technology uses radio waves to transmit data wirelessly in the form of binary bit streams. It allows devices to establish a wireless connection and communicate with each other without the need for physical wired connections.

G. Cheng et al., *Wi-Fi 7*, https://doi.org/10.1007/978-981-97-9026-5_1

To create a network infrastructure: Wi-Fi technology provides the means to establish a network infrastructure within a limited coverage area mentioned above which allows Wi-Fi-enabled devices to connect to the network, share data, and communicate with each other.

Wi-Fi is a widely used WLAN technology, so let us start with a brief introduction to wireless LAN technology first.

1.1.1 Wireless LAN Transmission Technology

The terms "Wi-Fi" and "WLAN" are often used interchangeably, but Wireless LAN (WLAN) is a generic term that refers to any local area network (LAN) employing wireless communication instead of physical cables to connect devices. It encompasses various wireless technologies utilized for local network connections and can be regarded as an extension or alternative to a LAN, providing wireless connectivity to devices within its coverage area.

When introducing WLAN, it is important to understand the transmission of electromagnetic waves. The electromagnetic waves are affected by various environmental factors such as free space path loss, reflection, scattering, refraction, and diffraction. A wireless signal may reach the receiver through multiple paths with different propagation delays and losses, which is known as **Multipath Effect**.

Since Wi-Fi is typically used for indoor scenarios, Multipath Effect is a major concern in Wi-Fi technology design. The walls, furniture, and even the movement of people or pets in an indoor environment can affect the propagation path and cause the loss, reflection, and diffraction of the Wi-Fi signals. As shown in Fig. 1.1, when a

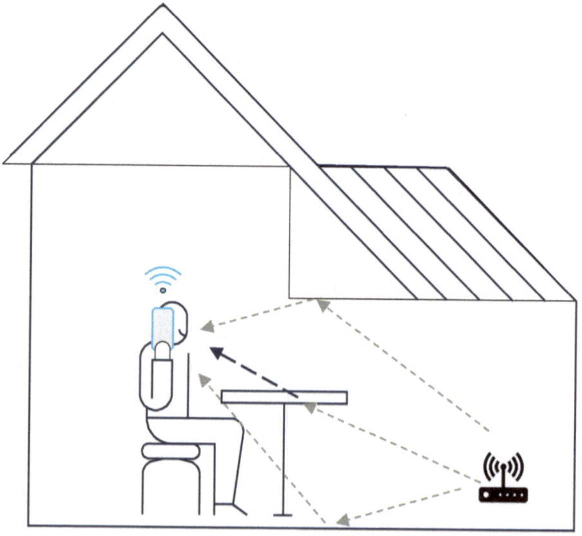

Fig. 1.1 Wi-Fi signal transmission at indoor environment

Wi-Fi signal is transmitted from a wireless router, it can reach the receiver through multiple paths, including both direct and indirect paths. The indirect path can occur when the signal reflects off walls, furniture, or other objects in the environment. These paths can introduce different delays and phase shift to the signal. As these different paths converge at the receiver, they superimpose on each other, and the superimposition of paths with different phases can distort the original Wi-Fi signal. These distortions can manifest as amplitude variations, phase distortions, or even complete signal loss in certain regions. This can lead to degraded signal quality, reduced data rates, and increased error rates in the wireless communication.

The electromagnetic waves used in wireless communication are also susceptible to the interference from other signals operating in the same frequency bands. This interference can come from other wireless devices or networks operating nearby. To address these specific issues, the wireless LAN must establish an effective, reliable, and secure wireless communication system for the local area network connectivity.

1.1.1.1 The Origin of Wireless Local Area Networks

One of the earliest WLAN, Additive Links On-line Hawaii Area network (ALOHAnet) [1] shown in Fig. 1.2, is a computer network system built at the University of Hawaii in June 1971. ALOHAnet demonstrated data communication over a shared wireless medium via the **Random Access Method** [2].

Based on the Random Access Protocol, the ALOHAnet has a simple control of the data transmission [2]. The procedure is as follows:

(1) When a remote device needs to transmit message, it builds data into "packets" and directly broadcasts them over the shared wireless network. It is worth noting

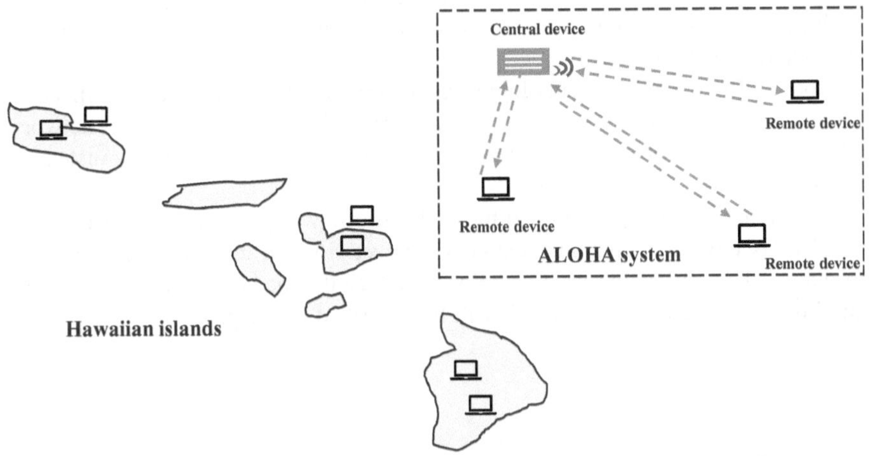

Fig. 1.2 ALOHAnet, one of the earliest WLAN

that each remote device transmits packets in a completely unsynchronized manner.

(2) When the central device, acting as the receiver, gets a packet without error, it will reply with an acknowledgment.

(3) After sending out a packet, the remote device waits for a certain amount of time for an acknowledgment. If it does not receive the response, it will continue retransmitting the packet until a successful acknowledgment is received or the process is terminated.

(4) If two devices in the network send data frames simultaneously over the wireless medium, a collision occurs. This will trigger a retransmission from both devices, because they do not receive an acknowledgment within the given time.

The Random Access mechanism ensures that multiple users are equally prioritized to access the wireless medium. This mechanism is the basis of 802.11 Wi-Fi networks. The Sect. 1.2 will introduce how Wi-Fi avoids collisions before sending data.

The development of Wi-Fi technology began in the 1990s with the aim of providing an efficient communication approach between devices in short-range wireless local area networks (LANs). The fundamental principle of Wi-Fi is to establish wireless connectivity standards that enable devices to communicate within a limited geographical area. In contrast to LAN for a short-distance local communication, the Wide Area Network (WAN) is for long-haul public communication, covering vast geographical areas from a few miles to thousands of miles, by utilizing various transmission methods such as optical fiber, microwave, satellite communications, and third Generation Partnership Project (3GPP) cellular communication.

Being a WAN technology versus a LAN technology, the 3GPP cellular technology and the Wi-Fi technology are completely different in terms of network topology, control and management mechanism, target user scenarios, frequency bands, and Quality of Service (QoS) requirements. However, Wi-Fi technology has incorporated certain features from 3GPP, such as OFDMA (Orthogonal Frequency Division Multiple Access), MU-MIMO (Multi-User Multiple-Input Multiple-Output) to enhance its capabilities.

Both 3GPP and Wi-Fi technologies can be utilized in an end-to-end application. For example, 3GPP can be used as a WAN connection option for a Wi-Fi network, allowing Wi-Fi devices to connect to the internet via cellular networks instead of relying solely on a fixed network.

Additionally, Wi-Fi can offload the 3GPP traffic when a terminal moves within the WLAN coverage, enabling seamless connectivity and improving network performance. This offloading process helps to reduce the load on the cellular network and improve the user experience. It will be described in Chap. 7.

1.1.1.2 The Frequency Band Used by the Wireless LAN

The Wi-Fi operates at the special frequency bands which are called the Industrial, Scientific, and Medical (ISM) bands in the electromagnetic wave spectrum.

The ISM bands are a set of unlicensed bands reserved for industrial, scientific, and medical applications. These bands vary per country or region and do not require a specific license from the radio regulatory agency. However, they are subject to transmission power limits defined by each country's regulations.

The ISM bands have evolved over time based on the frequency band strategic planning of each country. The initial 802.11 standard by IEEE chose the 2.4 GHz ISM band for Wi-Fi operations. Later, the 5 GHz band was also added to provide additional frequency options. More recently, the use of 6 GHz band was approved by certain countries and regions as a new ISM band to support higher bandwidth and performance for Wi-Fi 6E and Wi-Fi 7, which will be introduced in subsequent Chaps. 2 and 3.

Table 1.1 shows the ISM bands and the applicable services included in ITU-T 2020 Radio regulation [3], where fixed networks refer to the communications based on the wired cables, such as fiber, coax line, or twisted line. Since Wi-Fi routers are usually connected to the Internet through Ethernet cables or fiber optics, in the communications industry, Wi-Fi is regarded as an extension of fixed networks. But it is important to note again that Wi-Fi itself is a wireless technology that enables devices to connect to a network without the need for physical cables.

The unlicensed ISM Band has played a crucial role in the success of Wi-Fi technology. However, since other technologies like Bluetooth, ZigBee devices, cordless phones, and more can use the same ISM band, there is a potential for spectrum resource conflicts when these devices are in close proximity to a Wi-Fi network.

The widespread adoption and deployment of Wi-Fi have put strain on the limited wireless resources available within Wi-Fi bands. Interference from neighboring Wi-Fi networks operating on the same or adjacent channels can significantly impact the performance and reliability of Wi-Fi connection, especially for applications that require high network performance. To address these challenges, each new iteration of the Wi-Fi standards considers the need to reduce interference between Wi-Fi devices and optimize the utilization of shared wireless media.

1.1.2 Continuous Evolution of IEEE 802.11 Standards

The Wi-Fi standards are the iterations of the IEEE 802.11 series of specifications. The letter suffixes after 802.11 indicate different versions and specifications within series, such as 802.11a and 802.11b.

After IEEE ratifies a new 802.11 standard, Wi-Fi Alliance offers the corresponding certification programs for Wi-Fi devices based on those standards.

Table 1.1 ISM band for unlicensed use

Frequency range	Central frequency	Applicability	Approved service
6.765 MHz ~ 6.795 MHz	6.78 MHz	Subject to local acceptance	Fixed network or mobile services
13.553 MHz ~ 13.567 MHz	13.56 MHz	Worldwide	Fixed network or mobile services, excluding aviation use
26.957 MHz ~ 27.283 MHz	27.12 MHz	Worldwide	Fixed network or mobile services, excluding aviation use
40.66 MHz ~ 40.7 MHz	40.68 MHz	Worldwide	Fixed network or mobile services, satellite services, etc
433.05 MHz ~ 434.79 MHz	433.92 MHz	Region 1 (subject to local acceptance)	Amateur radio, etc
902 MHz ~ 928 MHz	915 MHz	Region 2 (subject to local acceptance)	Fixed network or mobile services, excluding aviation use
2.4 GHz ~ 2.5 GHz	2.45 GHz	Worldwide	Fixed network or mobile service, amateur &and amateur-satellite service
5.725 GHz ~ 5.875 GHz	5.8 GHz	Worldwide	Fixed network or mobile service, amateur and amateur-satellite service
24 GHz ~ 24.25 GHz	24.125 GHz	Worldwide	Amateur and amateur-satellite service, satellite earth exploration service
61 GHz ~ 61.5 GHz	61.25 GHz	Subject to local acceptance	Fixed network or mobile services, satellite services, etc
122 GHz ~ 123 GHz	122.5 GHz	Subject to local acceptance	Satellite-related services, fixed network or mobile services, space-related services, etc
244 GHz ~ 246 GHz	245 GHz	Subject to local acceptance	Radio services, radio astronomy applications, amateur and amateur-satellite service

Note 1: Region 1 includes Europe, the Soviet Union, Africa, Mongolia, the western Persian Gulf region, etc. Region 2 includes the Americas (including Greenland) and parts of the Pacific Islands region

Note 2: In Table 1.1, 2.4 GHz and 5.8 GHz bands are commonly used by Wi-Fi. In some countries and regions, there are additional frequency ranges (5.15 GHz to 5.35 GHz and 5.47 GHz to 5.725 GHz) that are designated for ISM applications. These extended 5 GHz bands are often used for Wi-Fi communication as well, providing more channels and options for wireless networking

The certification tests ensure that the devices comply with the specified standards and are interoperable with other Wi-Fi devices. If a device passes the tests, the manufacturers are granted permission to use the corresponding Wi-Fi certification logo [4] on their commercial products, as indicated in Fig. 1.3. This logo signifies to

Fig. 1.3 The logo of Wi-Fi Alliance (left) and the Wi-Fi certification logo (right)

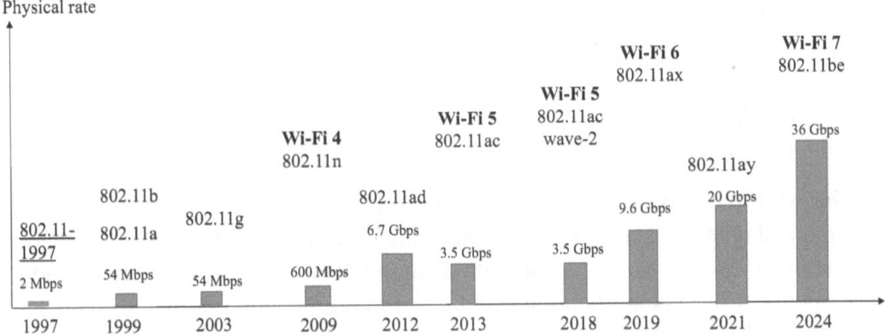

Fig. 1.4 Evolution of the Wi-Fi standards

consumers that the device has met the required standards for Wi-Fi compatibility and interoperability.

In 2019, the 802.11ax was ratified by IEEE. In an effort to simplify the naming and make it easier for consumers to understand the different generations of Wi-Fi technology, Wi-Fi Alliance introduced a new naming scheme. Instead of referring to the IEEE 802.11 standards by their letter suffixes such as 802.11ax, 802.11ac, and 802.11n, Wi-Fi Alliance introduced a numerical naming convention. That is, Wi-Fi Alliance named 802.11ax as Wi-Fi 6, 802.11ac as Wi-Fi 5, and 802.11n as Wi-Fi 4.

Figure 1.4 shows the evolution of IEEE 802.11 specifications from 1997 to 2024.

(1) The first generation of Wi-Fi specification defined by IEEE was the **802.11 standard in 1997**, defining the data transmission on the 2.4 GHz ISM band at a data rate of 2 Mbps. It was primarily used for low-speed data collection scenarios, such as wireless barcode scanners in warehouse and manufacturing environments. This initial version of Wi-Fi laid the foundation for the development and expansion of wireless networking technology.

(2) In 1999, the IEEE ratified **802.11b** and **802.11a** standards. The 802.11b operates in the same 2.4 GHz band as the 802.11-1997 standard, and it supports multiple data rates at 11 Mbps, 5.5 Mbps, 2 Mbps, and 1 Mbps with various modulation schemes. The 802.11a standard was developed with the intention of replacing

802.11b standard for commercial deployment. It operates in the 5 GHz frequency band, capable to support data transmission rates up to 54 Mbps and covering the transmission distance of 10 ~ 100 m. However, due to the lack of authorization for unlicensed services in the 5 GHz in most regions at that time, the industry did not widely adopt the 802.11a standard. The 802.11b, which uses the unlicensed 2.4 GHz band, quickly became the mainstream Wi-Fi standard.

(3) In 2003, the **802.11g** standard was released, which is backward compatible with 802.11a and 802.11b standard. The 802.11g supports the same transmission rates as 802.11a, up to 54 Mbps. However, unlike 802.11a, which operates in the 5 GHz, the 802.11g standard uses the 2.4 GHz band, the same as 802.11b. The introduction of 802.11g increased the adoption of Wi-Fi technology, as it offered higher speeds and better compatibility with existing devices.

(4) In 2009, the **802.11n** standard was ratified, offering a maximum physical data transmission of 600 Mbps physical rate, which represents a significant leap in the data transmission rate of WLAN technology. By operating in both 2.4 GHz and 5 GHz frequency bands, Wi-Fi devices with the adoption of the 802.11n standard began to utilize multi-antenna technology.

The Multiple Input Multiple Output (MIMO) leverages multiple antennas to transmit and receive data at the same time, which can significantly improve spectrum utilization and performance. Another innovation introduced by the 802.11n standard is the concept of channel bonding. The 802.11a/b/g supports 20 MHz bandwidth, while 802.11n supports to combine two 20 MHz subchannels to a channel of 40 MHz bandwidth, doubling the data rate.

The 802.11n standard is a key milestone on the Wi-Fi evolution path, enabling the high-bandwidth and high-performance wireless LAN and leading to the wide adoption of Wi-Fi technology around the world.

(5) In 2013, the **802.11ac** was approved. In addition to supporting 20 MHz and 40 MHz channel bandwidth, 802.11ac also supports 80 MHz and optional 160 MHz bandwidth. Operating at the 5 GHz frequency band, the 802.11ac standard is capable of achieving a data rate of up to 1 Gbp. Moreover, the 802.11ac also incorporates multi-antenna MIMO technology.

In 2016, the Wi-Fi Alliance ratified the 802.11ac wave 2, adding more features such as Multiple User Multiple Input Multiple Output (MU-MIMO) technology and support for up to 8 spatial streams.

(6) The **802.11ax** standard was ratified in 2019 and subsequently marketed as Wi-Fi 6 by the Wi-Fi Alliance. The focus of Wi-Fi 6 is on enhancing performance and service quality in high-density Wi-Fi environment. In 2020, following the approval of 6 GHz frequency band by US Federal Communications Commission (FCC) for Wi-Fi communication, the Wi-Fi Alliance designated devices compliant with the Wi-Fi 6 standard that operate on the 6 GHz band as Wi-Fi **6E**. Starting with Wi-Fi 6E, Wi-Fi can operate on three frequency bands: 2.4 GHz, 5 GHz, and 6 GHz.

Table 1.2 IEEE 802.11 standards

802.11 Standard	Release time	Frequency (GHz)	Bandwidth (MHz)	Data rate (Mbps)	Modulation
802.11-1997	June 1997	2.4	22	1, 2	DSSS, FHSS
802.11b	Sept 1999	2.4	22	1, 2, 5.5, 11	DSSS
802.11a	Sept 1999	5	20	6, 9, 12, 18, 24, 36, 48, 54	OFDM
802.11g	June 2003	2.4	20	6, 9, 12, 18, 24, 36, 48, 54	OFDM
802.11n (Wi-Fi 4)	Oct 2009	2.4, 5	20, 40	Up to 600 Mbps	OFDM
802.11ad	Dec 2012	60	2160	Up to 6.7 Gbps	OFDM
802.11ac (Wi-Fi 5)	Dec 2013	5	20, 40, 80, 160 (optional)	Up to 6.9 Gbps	OFDM
802.11ax (Wi-Fi 6)	Jan 2019	2.4, 5	20, 40, 80, 160	Up to 9.6 Gbps	OFDMA
802.11ay	Dec 2021	60	2160, 4320, 6480, 8640	Up to 20 Gbps	OFDM
802.11be (Wi-Fi 7)	2024	2.4, 5, 6	20, 40, 80, 160, 320	Up to 36 Gbps	OFDMA

(7) Up to 2024, IEEE is finalizing the **802.11be**, the Wi-Fi 7 standard which is the focus of this book.

It should be noted that the 802.11 standards encompass not only the Wi-Fi standards, but also other standards such as 802.11ad, 802.11ay, and others. The 802.11ad and 802.11ay standards define the data transmission operating at 60 GHz millimeter wave band. Similar to Wi-Fi, WiGig band, defined by the Wireless Gigabit Alliance (WFA), encompasses products compliant with the 802.11ad/ay standards. Operating at the 60 GHz band, the WiGig is capable of providing a very high data rate. However, due to its limited ability to penetrate obstacles, the WiGig is primarily utilized for line-of-sight applications.

Table 1.2 shows the release time and the characteristics of the IEEE 802.11 standards.

1.2 Basic Concepts and Typical Features of Wi-Fi

Since the introduction of IEEE 802.11a/b standard, Wi-Fi has continuously evolved by incorporating and embracing novel technologies, updating both the physical layer and MAC layer to accommodate high performance of Wi-Fi networks. Despite these advancements, the fundamental Wi-Fi network topology and random access mechanisms have remained constant. The newly defined Wi-Fi standards are meticulously designed to be backward compatible with previous specifications, thereby ensuring that the latest generation Wi-Fi routers can support older Wi-Fi devices. This compatibility guarantees users a seamless upgrade process when transitioning their Wi-Fi networks to newer standards.

This section provides an overview of the essential concepts, principles, and key features of Wi-Fi network to help the readers prepare for understanding Wi-Fi 7 standard in upcoming chapters. Here's a breakdown of this section:

- Wi-Fi network topology and its components.
- Core concepts of the Wi-Fi physical layer, including spectrum allocation, channels, coding and modulation techniques, multi-antenna technologies, data rates, and the structure of physical layer frames.
- The fundamentals of the Wi-Fi MAC layer, detailing the three types of MAC layer frames and their respective formats.
- The principle of Wi-Fi wireless medium access, along with the Wi-Fi connection establishment process.
- Wi-Fi power-saving mechanism.

1.2.1 Basic Concepts and Terminologies

1.2.1.1 The Components of a Home Wi-Fi Network

Before diving into the specifics of Wi-Fi technologies, let's first examine the fundamental components that make up a typical home network, as illustrated in Fig. 1.5.

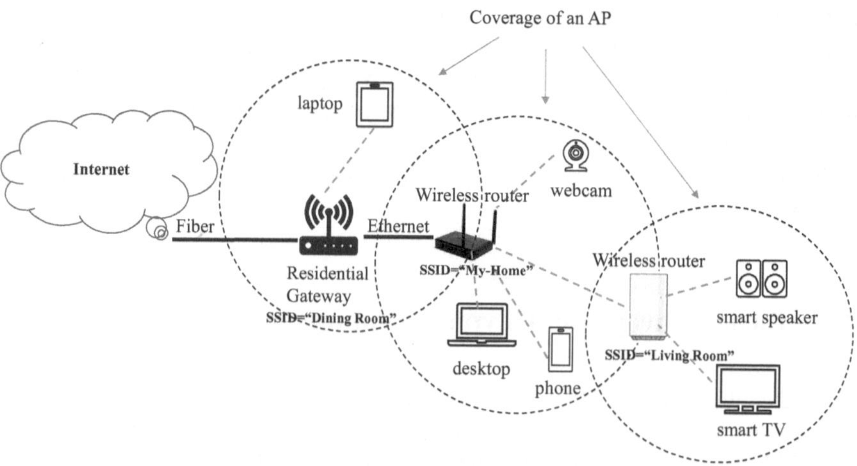

Fig. 1.5 An example of a home network

In Fig. 1.5, all devices are equipped with Wi-Fi functionality, including the home gateway installed for fiber broadband access, wireless routers connected to the home gateway, as well as computers, smartphones, webcams, smart TVs, and smart speakers that link to the home gateway or wireless routers via Wi-Fi.

The home gateway is typically installed by the communication service provider (CSP) as part of their broadband access provision. Depending on the specific access technology employed, this gateway terminates either a fiber optic cable, twisted pair line, or coaxial cable, ultimately delivering Ethernet wired connectivity or wireless Wi-Fi access to the array of devices within the residence.

The wireless routers are either furnished by operators or independently acquired by the end-users. To establish an internet connection, these routers must be interconnected with the home gateway. Also known as Wi-Fi access points (APs), wireless routers serve as the pivotal element providing Wi-Fi access services to a diverse range of devices. It's noteworthy that many contemporary residential gateways incorporate integrated wireless router capabilities, thereby also functioning as integral access points within the Wi-Fi network.

The Service Set Identifier (SSID), which is the unique identifier for an Access Point (AP), is visibly printed on the device label and can be customized through the device's web interface. When end-users seek to connect to a Wi-Fi network, they will find the SSIDs of nearby networks listed in their available WLAN options of handset or computers. For instance, the SSID might denote "Dining Room" for the residential gateway or "My-Home" and "Living Room" for separate wireless routers. It's worth noting that the maximum character length of an SSID does not exceed 32 octets.

Wi-Fi-enabled devices, referred to as stations (**STAs**), connect to either a wireless router or a home gateway in order to gain access to the internet. In the context of a Wi-Fi network architecture, it is essential to understand that a wireless LAN essentially comprises an Access Point (AP) which acts as the central hub, and one or multiple STAs that are interconnected to this AP, thus enabling seamless data transmission within the network.

1.2.1.2 Terminology and Concepts of Wi-Fi Network

Next, let us delve deeper into the intricacies of the Wi-Fi network by exploring its various terminologies as illustrated in Fig. 1.6. Besides access points (AP), stations (STA), and service set identifier (SSID), there exist other integral components of the network, such as the Basic Service Set (**BSS**) and the Extended Service Set (**ESS**). The Distributed System (DS) and the Portal also play crucial roles in the seamless operation of the Wi-Fi network [5].

The Basic Service Set (BSS) constitutes a fundamental unit of a wireless LAN, featuring an AP and multiple associated STAs. In the confines of a BSS network, the AP plays a pivotal role in managing the flow of data traffic not only between the internet and connected STAs but also facilitating intercommunication among the STAs themselves. Within a confined geographical space, it's common to

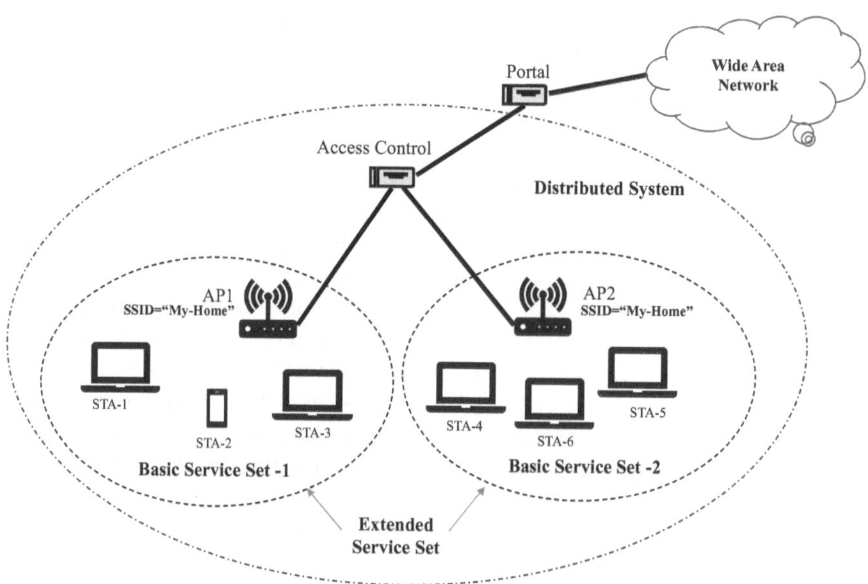

Fig. 1.6 Wi-Fi network terminologies

have multiple overlapping BSSs. To uniquely identify each BSS and prevent confusion, the IEEE has established a 48-bit MAC address known as the Basic Service Set Identifier (**BSSID**). This identifier serves as a distinguishing factor among different BSS networks within close proximity.

An Extended Service Set (**ESS**) functions as an interconnected of a BSS. It is composed of multiple BSS networks, typically two or more, which all bear the same SSID, thereby creating a unified Wi-Fi domain. The AP devices within this ESS are interconnected either through wired backhaul links or wireless mesh networking which in turn extends overall Wi-Fi coverage area to provide seamless connectivity.

The ESS is commonly implemented in public spaces, residential communities, corporates environments, etc. Because the APs within an ESS broadcast the same SSID, STAs do not require manual intervention to switch between Wi-Fi networks while roaming within the ESS coverage area. Instead, they automatically connect to the nearest APs, ensuring seamless connectivity as user move around.

The Distribution System (DS) refers to a network architecture that interfaces one or multiple WLANs and LANs. Within a corporate Wi-Fi network, the DS encompasses an interconnected array of wireless routers, mobile devices, and switches. When the DS assumes the form of a single BSS network, the DS service is typically implemented on the AP node, which serves as the primary point of connection for mobile devices. Conversely, in an ESS network configuration, the DS service is integrated within a central node or an Access control mechanism that efficiently forwards data for multiple APs.

The Portal acts as a logical interface between the Wi-Fi network and Wide Area Network (WAN), thus it serves to translate frame formats between the 802.11

protocol and other protocols, for example, converting from 802.11 Wi-Fi protocol to G.987 XGS PON in case of a 10G FTTH uplink connection. General speaking, a distributed system employs only one such logical portal.

1.2.1.3 Essential Wi-Fi Features

Let's begin with a general overview of the Wi-Fi technologies shown in Fig. 1.7. There are various ways to approach the understanding of Wi-Fi:

When we viewed through the lens of IEEE 802.11 standards, Wi-Fi technology essentially encompasses the physical layer and the data link layer. To gain a comprehensive understanding of how a Wi-Fi network functions, it is crucial to comprehend the Wi-Fi frequency bands and channels, how Wi-Fi devices compete for shared wireless media, and how APs and STAs establish connections. From the perspective of Wi-Fi devices, key technologies include data transmission using multiple antennas and support for Wi-Fi power-saving mode.

The IEEE 802.11 standards will be discussed in detail in the following sections. For now, this section provides a high-level overview of how the Wi-Fi network and its devices operate.

1. **Wi-Fi Data Transmission**

Wi-Fi uses electromagnetic waves and operates at the ISM bands 2.4 GHz, 5 GHz, or 6 GHz, which fall within the microwave frequency band, as illustrated in Fig. 1.8.

The Wi-Fi band is not solely occupied by a single Wi-Fi device, instead it is divided into multiple channels, similar to lanes on a highway. Wi-Fi devices transmit data on their designated channels. The AP selects the least interference-prone working channel, and all STAs in the BSS must operate on the same channel to communicate with the AP. In case the AP switches to another channel, it informs all STAs in the BSS to switch to the same channel.

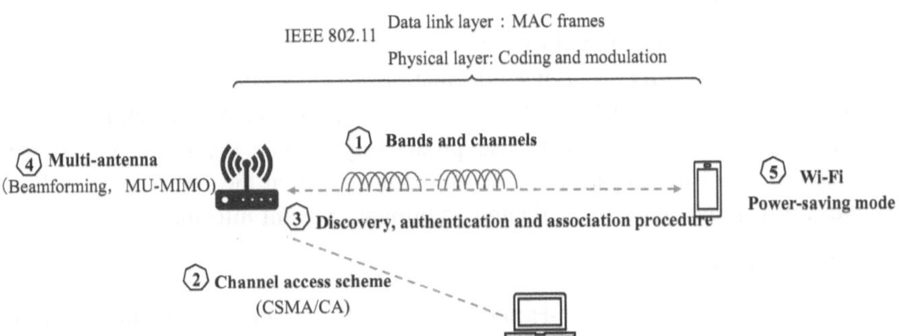

Fig. 1.7 Wi-Fi key technologies

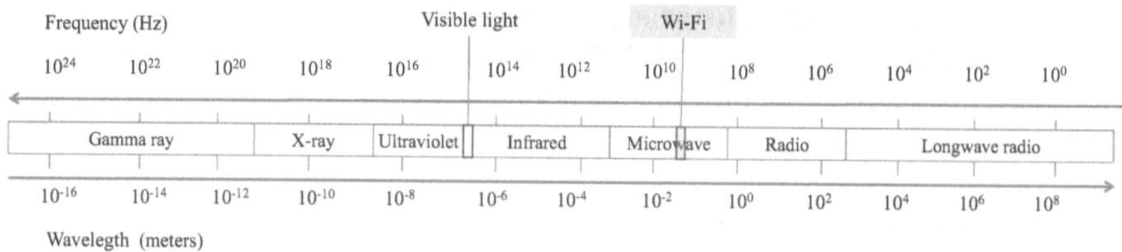

Fig. 1.8 The electromagnetic spectrum

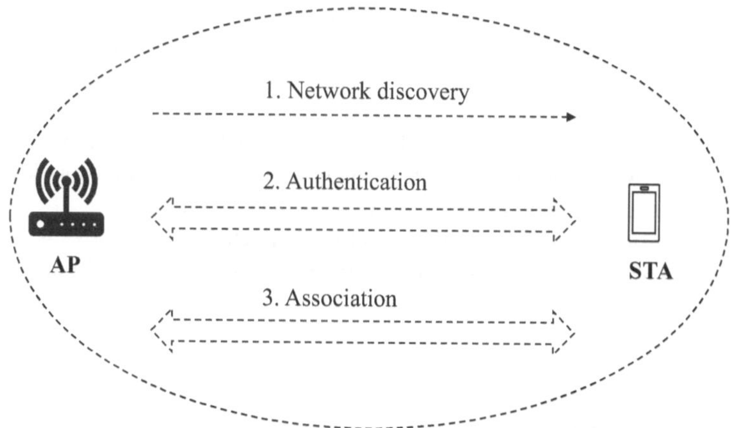

Fig. 1.9 Procedure of an STA connects to the AP

2. **Discovery, Authentication, and Association Mechanisms Between APs and Stations**

The AP is the central controller of the BSS and processes the data frames between the uplink and the stations. All the stations must connect to the AP to transmit or receive data frames. The procedure for a Wi-Fi STA connecting to the AP includes network discovery, authentication, and association, as illustrated in Fig. 1.9.

(1) **Network Discovery**

The AP periodically announces its presence by broadcasting Beacon frames, which contain the SSID and other information. Upon receipt of this message, the mobile phone displays the SSID "My-Home" within its WLAN search list.

Alternatively, the station can also proactively initiate the network discovery procedure by transmitting a Probe Request frame. When the AP receives a Probe Request, it responds with its SSID and additional relevant information.

(2) **Authentication**

When the user selects "My-Home" SSID on the mobile phone and enters the password, the mobile phone then sends an Authentication Request to the AP to authenticate itself as a valid 802.11 device and gain permission to join the network.

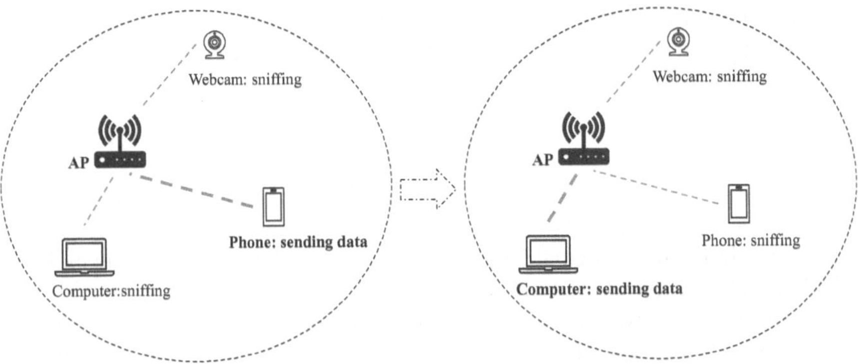

Fig. 1.10 An example of multiple Wi-Fi devices competing for channel access

(3) **Association**

Upon successful authentication, the mobile phone subsequently sends an Association Request to establish an association with the AP. Throughout this authentication and association process, the AP serves as the pivotal entity, ultimately determining whether or not to permit the station to join the BSS.

(4) **Encryption Key Negotiation**

After the successful completion of authentication and association process, the mobile phone joins the BSS. The AP verifies the SSID password from the STA and if they are valid, the AP and the STA negotiate the encryption keys for the encrypting of data frames.

After the key exchange procedure completes, the STA begins data transmission with the AP.

3. **Channel Access Scheme**

Wi-Fi is based on random access to the wireless medium. The AP and stations work on same channel for data communication. If multiple devices try to send data at same time, collision occurs. Therefore, before sending data, the AP or stations need to obtain the access to the wireless medium. In case the channel is occupied by other devices, only after the current data transmission completes, other devices can compete for access to the wireless medium.

The channel access scheme of Wi-Fi technology is called Carrier Sense Multiple Access with Collision Avoidance (CSMA/CA) mechanism. An example is shown in Fig. 1.10 for illustration purpose:

- While the mobile phone is transmitting data frames, the webcam and computer detects the Wi-Fi signal in the wireless channel, and they wait for transmission by sensing the channel for idleness.
- When the phone finishes the transmission, the channel becomes idle, then the webcam and the computer start a random timer respectively.

- The computer times out first, so it gets access to the wireless medium and starts transmitting data. The webcam resets its timer and continues to sense the channel along with the phone which is now also idle.

4. **MIMO Technology**

Most AP devices have multiple antennas to provide a robust coverage and decent performance. These antennas can be either visible, known as external antennas, or invisible, referred to as internal antennas, or a combination of both. Some high-end APs boast up to eight or even more antennas.

Due to size and weight constraints, the stations typically have few antennas compared with the APs. Nevertheless, some stations may have multiple antennas to accommodate high-data rate services.

The industry uses the form like 2 × 2, 4 × 4, or etc. to indicate the number of the antennas on a device, where the two numbers represent the transmitting and receiving antennas respectively. The Wi-Fi antenna design is typically half-duplex, meaning the same antennas are used for transmitting and receiving at different times.

When a device supports multiple bands, the industry uses the form like 2 × 2 + 4 × 4, 2 × 2 + 4 × 4 + 4 × 4 and etc., to indicate the number of antennas on each band. For a dual-band Wi-Fi 5 device, if it's indicated as 2 × 2 + 4 × 4, it means that the device has 2 antennas on 2.4 GHz and 4 antennas on 5 GHz band.

The Multiple Input Multiple Output (MIMO) is a form of multi-antenna communication that aims to enhance spectral efficiency via spatial stream multiplexing, that is, achieved by simultaneously transmitting independent data streams, or utilizing spatial diversity by transmitting redundant data to enhance link reliability. There are three primary MIMO topologies, as shown in Fig. 1.11.

- Single-User MIMO (SU-MIMO): The transmitter simultaneously sends data to a receiver through multiple antennas.
- Multi-User MIMO (MU-MIMO): The transmitter simultaneously sends data streams to multiple receivers through multiple antennas.
- Beamforming: The signal is transmitted towards the target device using an array of antennas, which are designed with the phase of the signal at each antenna being slightly altered, in order to achieve a higher signal-to-noise ratio (SNR) in the desired direction versus the SNR achieved with omnidirectional signals.

5. **Power Saving Mode**

The energy efficiency is a key concern for the Wi-Fi terminals powered by batteries, such as mobile phones, webcams, and many smart mobile devices. The IEEE 802.11 specification defines the messages and processing mechanism of Wi-Fi power-saving mode, as illustrated in Fig. 1.12.

The power saving technology allows the device to periodically enter a doze state to conserve power. The AP buffers data for stations in power-saving mode to ensure that their downstream data is not lost, and the stations periodically wake up to check if there is buffered data for them. If there is, they retrieve it in a timely manner.

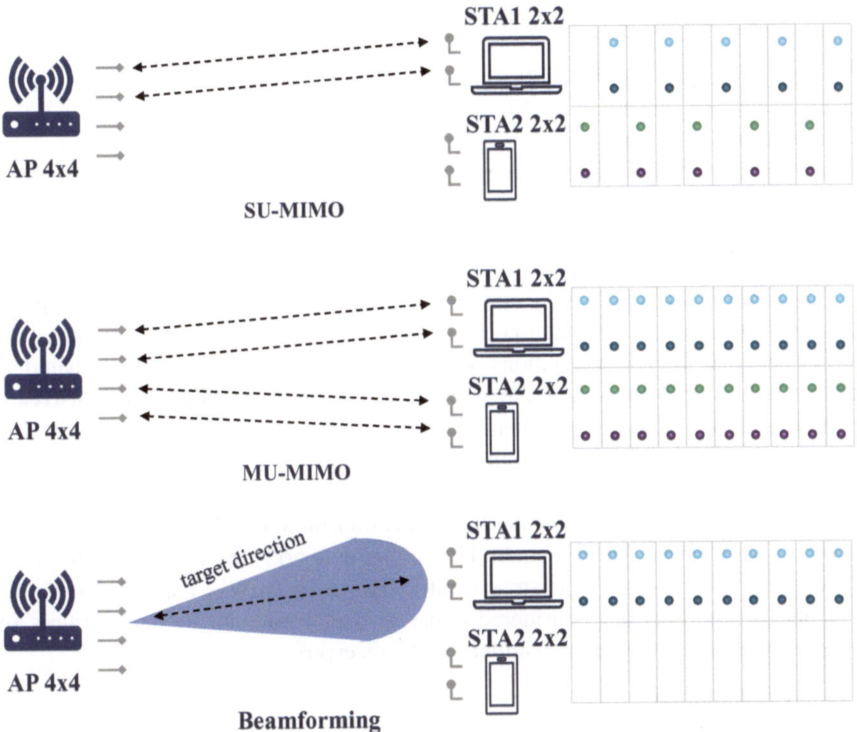

Fig. 1.11 Wi-Fi MIMO topologies

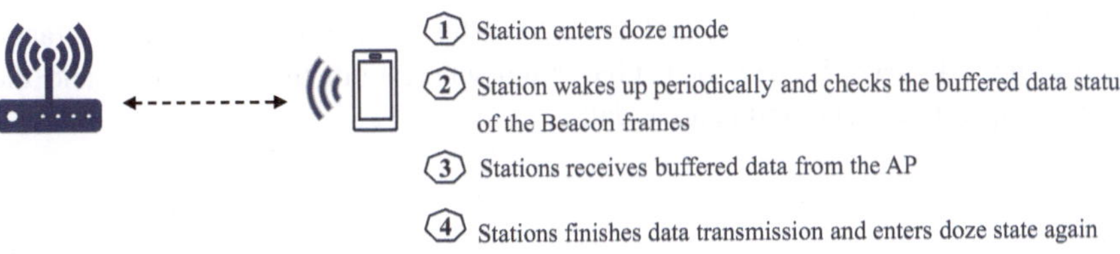

Fig. 1.12 Power saving mode of the stations

The subsequent sections will delve into the practical implementation of these key technologies through Wi-Fi physical layer and data link protocols.

1.2.2 Introduction to Wi-Fi Physical Layer Technologies

This section provides an overview of the principles of Wi-Fi communication system, including the concepts of Wi-Fi physical layer, spectrum and channels, coding and modulation schemes, as well as the MIMO technology.

1.2.2.1 Wi-Fi Communication System

Wi-Fi is a form of short-range digital signal communication technology that utilizes radio waves to transmit data. Similar to other communication systems, a Wi-Fi communication system involves processes such as information encoding and decoding, encryption and decryption, channel coding and decoding, as well as signal modulation and demodulation. These processes are indicated in Fig. 1.13.

1. **The Transmitter and the Receiver**

The information source is the initiator of the data communication, and the target is the destination of the information transmitted by the communication system. In a Wi-Fi network, the AP and stations serve as transmitters or as receivers. When data is transmitted from the AP to the stations, it is called **downlink** or **downstream** communication. Conversely, when data is sent from the stations to the AP, it is called **uplink** or **upstream** communication.

The AP forwards data between the upper-layer network and the stations, for example, streaming video from the Internet is transmitted to the wireless router AP and then sent by the AP to a smart TV. In real networks, there are typically more downstream traffic than the upstream traffic. However, in Wi-Fi specifications, the AP and the stations are considered equal in data communication, regardless of whether they are acting as transmitters or the receivers.

2. **Wi-Fi Channel**

A channel in the context of a Wi-Fi communication system represents the medium through which the signal is transmitted from the transmitter to the receiver. This medium is essentially the free air for a Wi-Fi network.

In Wi-Fi technology, a channel typically refers to a specific frequency range within the 2.4 GHz, 5 GHz, or 6 GHz band where both the transmitter and the receiver operate to send and receive data.

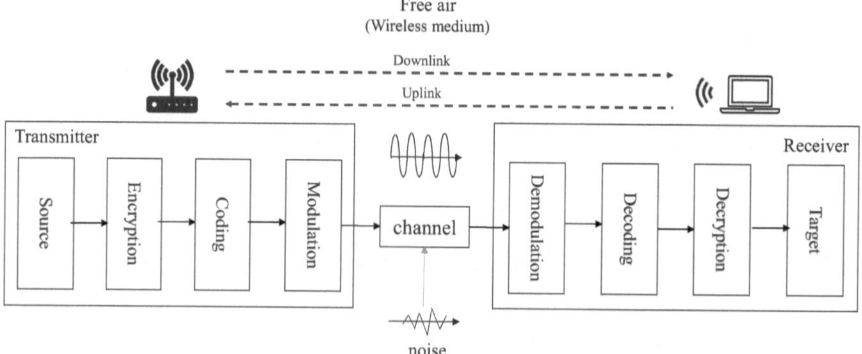

Fig. 1.13 Wi-Fi communication system

Wi-Fi channels are characterized by multipath transmission and time variability. Multipath transmission, as previously explained, involves an electromagnetic wave signal that, after being refracted, reflected, or diffracted along different paths, reaches to the receiver. The actual signal received by the receiver is the composite of the signal from all these paths. Furthermore, the characteristics of the Wi-Fi channel change over time due to various factors, such as the movement of the people and the pets, interference from neighboring networks, changes in the humidity levels, and so forth. This inherent dynamic nature makes Wi-Fi channels time-variable.

3. **Noise of Wi-Fi Channels**

The noise in a wireless channel is interference that affects the signal, such as the noise caused by internal circuit of Wi-Fi devices or external sources, such as interference from a microwave oven operating at the 2.4 GHz frequency band.

The Signal-to-Noise Ratio (SNR) quantifies the comparison between the amplitude of the desired signal and the background noise level. This metric is used to gauge the quality and condition of the communication channel.

4. **Coding and Decoding**

Wi-Fi signals are susceptible to distortion due to the noises in wireless channels. To enhance the resistance against interference and thus ensure reliable communication, Wi-Fi transmitters encode the signals before transmission. Subsequently, the Wi-Fi receiver decodes the received signal, detects and corrects any errors present, thereby restoring the original signal. Among the coding techniques commonly employed by Wi-Fi standards are Binary Convolutional Code (BCC) and Low Density Parity Check (LDPC).

5. **Encryption and Decryption**

The Wi-Fi signal is transmitted through open space, and the information can potentially be intercepted by other devices that share the same wireless medium. To ensure the information security, the data need to be encrypted before transmission. In other words, the original signal is transformed according to a specific algorithm, making it unintelligible if intercepted. At the receiver end, the encrypted information is restored using the same algorithm. The keys are essential for both encryption and decryption using this algorithm.

In the Wi-Fi communication system, common encryption methods include Wired Equivalent Privacy (WEP) and Wi-Fi Protected Access (WPA). With the evolution of Wi-Fi standards, there have been three generations of WPA encryption: WPA, WPA2, and WPA3. The Wi-Fi security principle and the innovation introduced in Wi-Fi 7 will be described in Chap. 3.

6. **Modulation and Demodulation**

Like other wireless communication technologies, the transmission and reception of Wi-Fi signals requires a process of modulation and demodulation. The amplitude, frequency, or phase of the Wi-Fi carrier signal is modulated by the baseband signals, which contain the original information. The receiver demodulates these signals to retrieve the baseband signals.

In this context, Amplitude Shift Keying (ASK) is the modulation technique where the amplitude of the carrier signal is varied in accordance with the baseband information. Conversely, when the phase of the carrier is manipulated to represent the data, the method used is known as Phase Shift Keying (PSK). When both the amplitude and phase are simultaneously modulated for increased spectral efficiency and higher data rates, the modulation scheme adopted is Quadrature Amplitude Modulation (QAM), which combines ASK and PSK principles in a single coherent framework.

Additionally, it's worth noting that Wi-Fi standards have evolved over time to utilize advanced forms of QAM, such as 256-QAM and even higher-order modulation schemes in the latest standard, to achieve greater throughput and improved performance in congested wireless environments.

1.2.2.2 The Physical Layer Basics

In order to standardize and streamline the interconnection of diverse computer networks worldwide, the International Organization for Standardization (ISO) developed a comprehensive framework known as the seven-layer Open Systems Interconnection Reference Model (OSI/RM, or OSI).

This OSI model, from its foundational to the most abstract layer, comprises the following: the physical layer, which deals with the transmission and reception of raw bit streams over a physical medium; followed by the data link layer, further divided into two sub-layers—logical link control (LLC) and media access control (MAC); then comes the network layer responsible for addressing and routing; the transport layer ensuring end-to-end data transfer reliability; subsequently, the session layer manages communication sessions between applications; the presentation layer is concerned with data representation and encryption/decryption; finally, the application layer supports direct interaction with software applications.

Wi-Fi technology particularly emphasizes the functionality and protocols at the media access control layer (MAC) and the physical layer within the OSI model. These layers are critical for Wi-Fi's operation, as they govern how devices gain access to the shared wireless medium and transmit data packets in an efficient and reliable manner, as depicted in Fig. 1.14.

In the OSI model, data is encapsulated in packets at each layer, which are composed of two primary components: a header and a payload. The header section serves to include protocol version identification along with control information specific to that particular layer's function. For instance, when data reaches the network layer, an Internet Protocol (IP) header is appended to it. This IP header contains crucial addressing details necessary for routers to forward IP packets across different networks correctly. It includes source and destination IP addresses, as well as other fields used for routing decisions and ensuring reliable packet transmission.

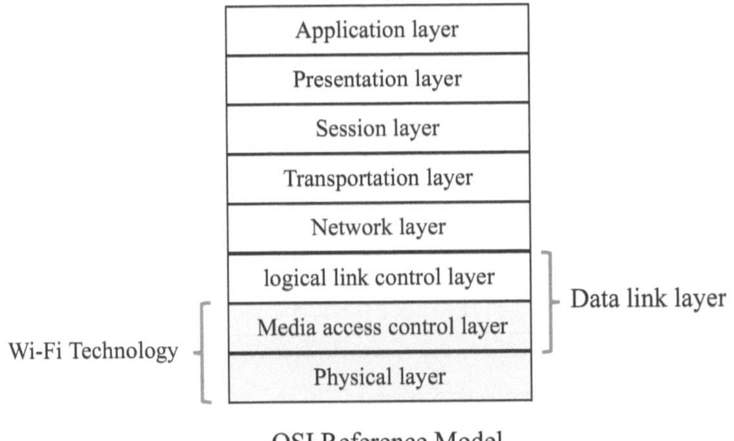

Fig. 1.14 Wi-Fi in the OSI reference model

IP Packet	IP Header	Payload	
PPDU	Preamble	Header	MPDU

Fig. 1.15 Comparison of IP packet format and PPDU frame format

The data unit that is handled and processed by the Wi-Fi physical layer, commonly referred to as the Physical Layer Protocol Data Unit (PPDU), consists of three integral segments: the physical layer preamble, the header, and the payload, as shown in Fig. 1.15.

The preamble serves a critical function, enabling the receiver to detect and synchronize with the incoming Wi-Fi signal. It also facilitates an estimation of the wireless channel characteristics, such as signal strength and noise conditions, which are essential for reliable communication.

The frame header contains vital coding modulation parameters that the receiver uses to accurately demodulate and decode the received signal. This information ensures that the transmitted data can be interpreted correctly at the receiving end.

Finally, the payload encapsulates the actual data being transferred and is termed as the MAC layer Protocol Data Unit (MPDU) or, equivalently, the Physical Service Data Unit (PSDU). This part of the PPDU carries the user data or control information destined for higher layers in the network stack, particularly the Media Access Control (MAC) layer.

The process of data transmission and reception in the context of Wi-Fi physical layer frames is depicted in Fig. 1.16. At the transmitting end, the physical layer receives the MPDU from the MAC layer Subsequently, it encapsulates into a PPDU by appending the necessary preamble and the header information. Once the PPDU is

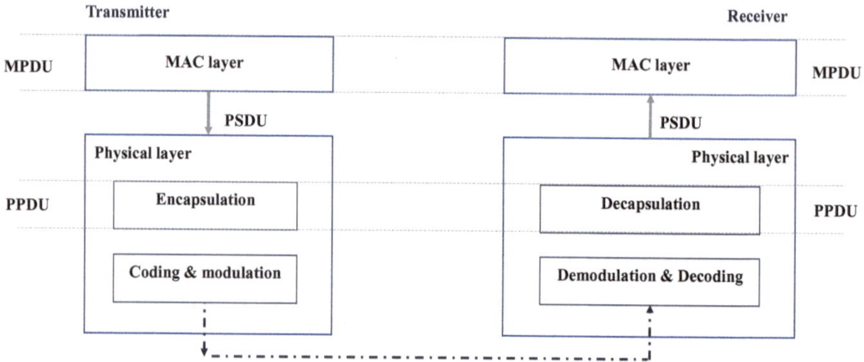

Fig. 1.16 Wi-Fi physical layer data processing

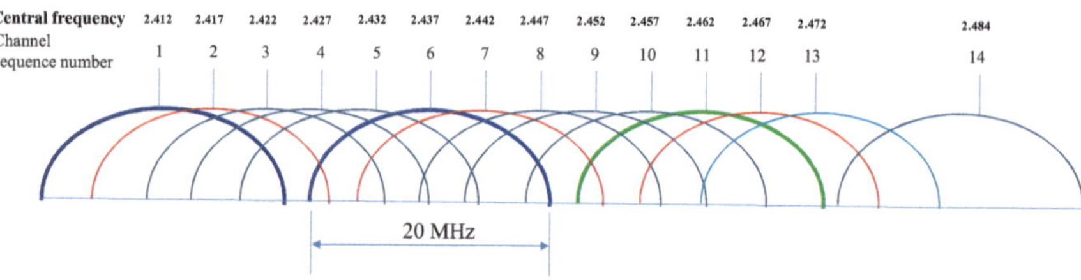

Fig. 1.17 2.4 GHz spectrum and channel division

formed, it undergoes encoding to ensure error detection and correction capabilities, followed by modulation, which transforms the digital data into an analog signal suitable for wireless transmission. This modulated PPDU is then transmitted over the wireless channel to reach its intended recipient.

On the receiving side, the reverse process occurs: The signal is received from the wireless channel, demodulated back into digital form, decoded to recover the original data, and stripped of the preamble and header to retrieve the MPDU for further processing at the MAC layer and above.

Before the advent of Wi-Fi 6, earlier Wi-Fi standards utilized ISM bands at 2.4 GHz and 5 GHz for wireless communication. In the following section, we will delve into the spectrum allocation and channel division within these two frequency bands.

1.2.2.3 Wi-Fi 2.4 GHz Spectrum and the Channels

Each country has its own definition of Wi-Fi channels according to its 2.4 GHz spectrum resources. For example, in Japan, the 2.4 GHz frequency range is divided into 14 channels, ranging from 2.412 GHz to 2.484 GHz, as illustrated in Fig. 1.17.

The frequency at the top shows the center frequency at which each channel operates, with a spacing of 5 MHz between adjacent channels. For example, Channel

1 operates at a center frequency of 2.412 GHz, whereas channel 14 operates at a center frequency 2.484 GHz. Each individual channel has a bandwidth of 20 MHz, visually represented by the semicircular arc in the figure. As indicated in the spectrum, there are only four non-overlapping channels, namely, channel 1, 6, 11, and sometimes 14 (depending on regional regulations). The signal transmitted on these four channels do not interfere with each other.

The 2.4 GHz ISM band for China and Europe is defined as 2.412 ~ 2.472 GHz, which includes 13 channels in total. In the United States, however, only 11 channels are available in the range of 2.412 ~ 2.462 GHz.

The 2.4 GHz is a heavily utilized frequency range where numerous devices operate, not just Wi-Fi devices, and also non-Wi-Fi devices such as microwave ovens, Bluetooth devices, and various Internet of Things (IoT) devices that employ technologies like ZigBee. This shared occupancy leads to significant interference within the 2.4 GHz spectrum, which in turn has a notable impact on the user experience of Wi-Fi connections, often resulting in slower speeds or reduced reliability. Moreover, with the limited bandwidth capacity, the channel allocation becomes less flexible and may struggle to meet the burgeoning demand for high-speed and high-bandwidth applications.

1.2.2.4 Wi-Fi 5 GHz Spectrum and the Channels

As Wi-Fi technology gains increasing attention, many governments approved the 5 GHz band for unlicensed ISM band use [6]. The 5 GHz band offers a greater number of non-overlapping channels compared with 2.4 GHz band.

- **Europe and Japan:** The allocated frequency bands are 5.15 GHz to 5.35 GHz (commonly referred to as the lower 5.1 GHz band) and 5.47 GHz to 5.725 GHz (referred to as the upper 5.4 GHz band), which are divided into 19 channels 20 MHz channels in total.
- **China**: The allocated frequency bands are also 5.15 GHz to 5.35 GHz (lower 5.1 GHz band) and 5.725 GHz to 5.85 GHz (upper 5.8 GHz band). In the 5.8 GHz band, there is a total bandwidth of 125 MHz, divided into 5 channels, with channel numbers 149, 153, 157, 161, and 165, each having a bandwidth of 20 MHz.
- **United States**: The allocated frequency bands include 5.1 GHz, 5.4 GHz, and 5.8 GHz band. The channel division within these bands may differ slightly from other countries; however, they do share some common channel assignments.

The specific channel division for each band is shown in Fig. 1.18.

Among the 5 GHz frequency bands, the ranges of 5.25 GHz to 5.35 GHz and 5.47 GHz to 5.725 GHz are globally recognized as U-NII (Unlicensed National Information Infrastructure) bands defined by FCC. AP routers operating in these U-NII bands must have the capability to detect radar signals and support Dynamic Frequency Selection (DFS). Additionally, they may optionally support Transmission Power Control (TPC). Upon detecting a radar signal on the current channel, the AP is

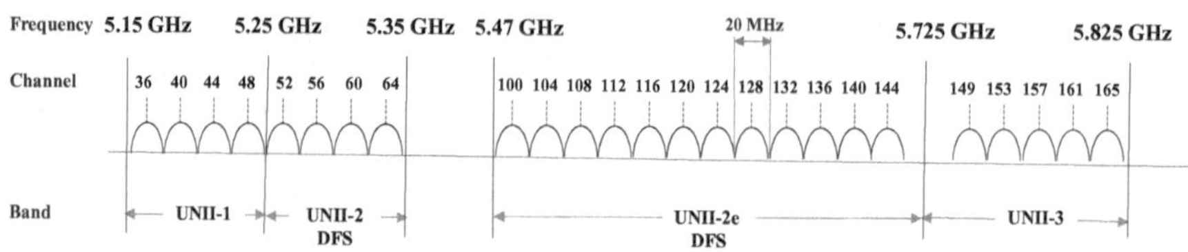

Fig. 1.18 5 GHz spectrum and channel division

Table 1.3 EIRP of 5 GHz band defined by ETSI

	EIRP (maximum transmission power) (dBm)	
Frequency range (MHz)	Support TPC	Do not support TPC
5150 ~ 5250	23	23
5250 ~ 5350	23	20
5470 ~ 5725	30	27

required to promptly switch to another channel and regulate its transmission power to ensure no interference with the radar system.

As previously stated, the Wi-Fi devices are mandated to adhere to global or local regulatory specification concerning transmission power over ISM bands. Regulatory bodies such as FCC or European Telecommunication Standards Institute (ETSI) establish the Effective Isotropic Radiated Power (EIRP) levels per bands and channels. The EIRP essentially represents the maximum transmission power from a device, which comprises the conducted power combined with the antenna Gain.

Table 1.3 [7] provides an illustration of the EIRP defined by ETSI. For devices supporting TPC, ETSI permits them to transmit at higher power levels, but only under the condition that no interference with radar signals occurs. This means that TPC-enabled devices can dynamically adjust their transmission power to ensure they do not disrupt radar operations while maximizing their own signal strength within the allowed limits.

1.2.2.5 Wi-Fi Channel Bonding

The adjacent non-overlapping channels can be bundled together to create a wider channel, which doubles the transmission rate and provides a higher throughput. For example, two adjacent 20 MHz channels can be combined into a 40 MHz bandwidth channel, or two adjacent 40 MHz/80 MHz channels can form a single 80 MHz/ 160 MHz bandwidth channel. As indicated in Fig. 1.19, the channel 1, 6, and 11 are not overlapping in the 2.4 GHz spectrum, so two of these channels can be bundled together to form a 40 MHz channel.

Regarding to the 5 GHz band, there are a total of 25 non-overlapping 20 MHz channels available for the devices that comply with the FCC. These channels can be combined into 12 channels of 40 MHz, or 6 channels of 80 MHz, or 2 channels of 160 MHz, as illustrated in Fig. 1.20.

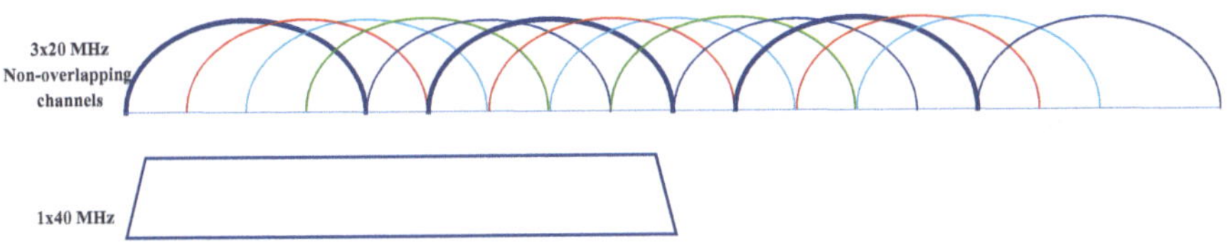

Fig. 1.19 Wi-Fi channel bonding in 2.4 GHz

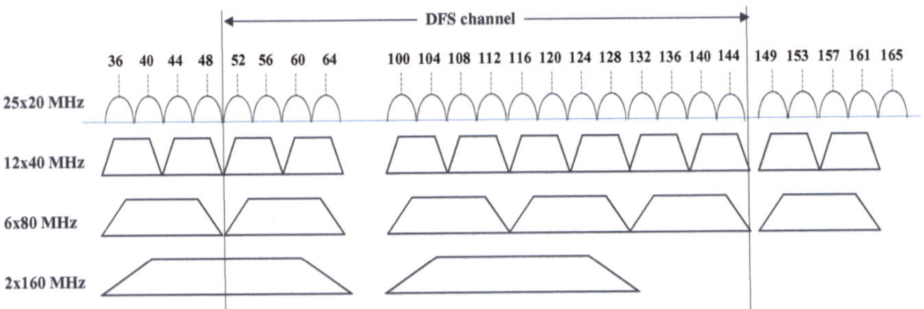

Fig. 1.20 Wi-Fi channel bonding in 5 GHz

Many countries do not open the 5.47–5.725 GHz band to Wi-Fi services, so there is only one 160 MHz Wi-Fi channel available for these countries. In order to maximize the available bandwidth, the 802.11 standard allows two noncontiguous 80 MHz channels to operate in an 80 MHz + 80 MHz mode.

In the IEEE 802.11 standard, a 40 MHz channel consists of two adjacent 20 MHz subchannels, with one serving as the primary subchannel and the other as secondary. Similarly, an 80 MHz channel consists of four consecutive 20 MHz channels, with one of the two 40 MHz subchannels being the primary subchannel and the other one being secondary. Within the primary 40 MHz subchannel, one of the 20 MHz subchannels is designated as the primary 20 MHz subchannel, and the other one serves as secondary. The AP determines which 20 MHz channel is the primary.

In case interference is detected on the secondary subchannel, the AP can revert to 20 MHz channel mode. If the interference is on the primary subchannel, the AP marks the channel as busy and holds off data transmission till it becomes idle.

As illustrated in Fig. 1.21, there are protection intervals between the 20 MHz subchannels, which are designed to reduce signal interference between adjacent subchannels. When two adjacent 20 MHz channels are bundled, the protection interval between subchannels can be utilized for data transmission. Consequently, the effective bandwidth at 40 MHz is greater than the sum of the bandwidths of the two individual 20 MHz subchannels.

The channel bonding technology represents a significant progression in Wi-Fi standards, enabling enhanced bandwidth and high data transfer rates. However, numerous devices, particularly low-speed Internet of Things (IoT) devices, do not support this feature as their minimal data transmission requirements can be adequately met by a 20 MHz channel width.

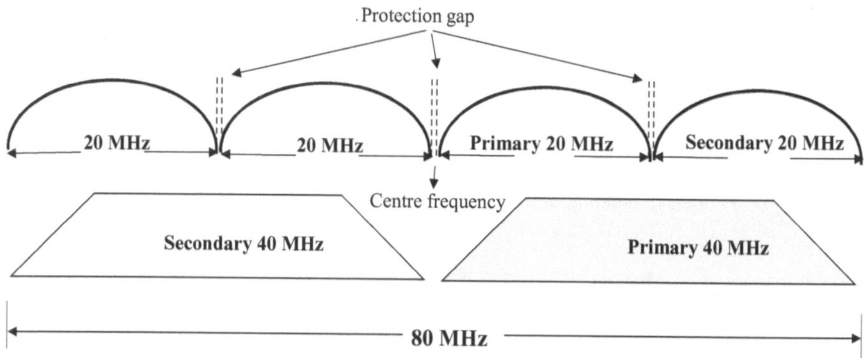

Fig. 1.21 Channel bonding of an 80 MHz channel

Crucially, Wi-Fi management or control frames must be received by all STAs connected to the AP. To guarantee that even those devices which do not support channel bonding can still receive these critical frames, they are transmitted over the primary 20 MHz subchannel.

1.2.2.6 Competition on the Bundled Channel

In a scenario where a Basic Service Set (BSS) operates on an aggregated 80 MHz bandwidth channel, if a STA sends data to the AP on the primary 20 MHz channel and another STA sends data on the secondary 40 MHz channel simultaneously, the AP might not be able to reliably distinguish between these asynchronously transmitted signals.

Accordingly, the 802.11 standard mandates that in order to utilize a bandwidth greater than 20 MHz, the AP or any STA must successfully contend for wireless media resources across all constituent subchannels. The entire bundled channel can be used only when contention is won on all of its component 20 MHz subchannels simultaneously. If a device fails to gain access to one or more of the 20 MHz subchannels, it can only send data on the remaining consecutive subchannels, which must contain the primary 20 MHz or the primary 40 MHz channel.

Take the example of Fig. 1.21, consider a STA attempting to acquire the access to all four 20 MHz subchannels. If the STA does not compete successfully on the first 20 MHz subchannel, under prior Wi-Fi standards up to and including Wi-Fi 6 (802.11ax), the STA can only send data on the primary 40 MHz channel which is composed of the last two consecutive 20 MHz subchannels. It's important to note that before Wi-Fi 7, bundling the last three 20 MHz subchannels into a 60 MHz channel was not supported.

However, in case a device does not succeed in acquiring the primary 20 MHz subchannel, but only obtain the other non-consecutive channels, according to the previous description, the device would be unable to send any data across those fragmented channels. The exact behavior in such scenarios may vary depending on the specific Wi-Fi standard and implementation details, which will be elaborated further in Chap. 3.

1.2.2.7 Coding and Modulation

The maximum data transmission rate depends on the bandwidth and the signal-to-noise ratio. For Wi-Fi communication, the channel bandwidth is limited. For example, the maximum channel bandwidth for the 2.4 GHz band is 40 MHz, and the maximum channel bandwidth for the 5 GHz band is 160 MHz. Therefore, the challenge in enhancing Wi-Fi transmission efficiency lies in dealing with the interference from other wireless signals and Bit Error Rate (BER) caused by multipath transmission in indoor environments. Every new generation of Wi-Fi standards focus on improving channel coding and modulation, aiming to reduce the Bit Error Rate effectively and enhance data rates within the constraints of the limited channel bandwidth.

1. **Wi-Fi Channel Coding**

The coding efficiency is measured by the portion of effective information in the entire encoded information, represented by k/n. For each k bits of information, the encoder generates n bits of data, where n-k bits are redundant data. The higher k/n, the higher coding efficiency.

The Wi-Fi channel coding technology has evolved from Spread Spectrum Communication coding scheme to Error Correction Coding (ECC), achieving higher coding efficiency and automatic error correction of digital signals. Figure 1.22 shows the evolution of the coding scheme up to Wi-Fi 5.

The early Wi-Fi specification 802.11b adopted Direct Sequence Spread Spectrum (DSSS), which utilizes high bitrate spread spectrum code sequences to expand the spectrum of the signal at the transmitter end. At the receiver, the same spread spectrum code sequence is utilized to despread the spread spectrum signal to restore the original information.

Assuming the effective information is k bits, and an encoding sequence of length n is produced after encoding. If m is the spread spectrum code length, then $n = m \times k$ and coding efficiency $R = k/n$. Therefore, the bitrate of spread spectrum communication $R = k / (m \times k) = 1/m$. As shown in Fig. 1.22, the coding efficiency of

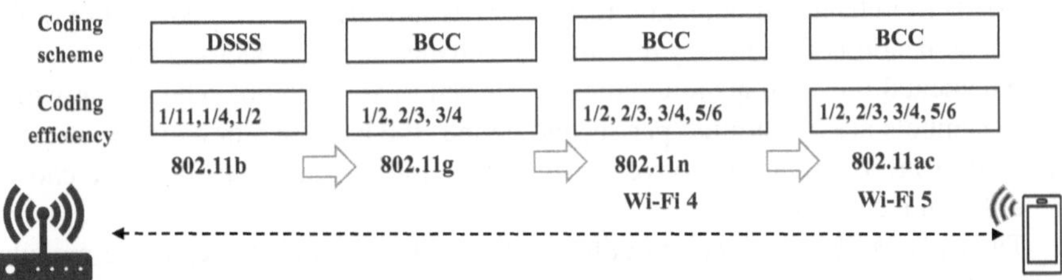

Fig. 1.22 Wi-Fi coding scheme evolution

802.11b is 1/11, 1/4, and 1/2. Spread Spectrum Communication coding is powerful in addressing the high noise environment and providing low bit error rates.

To enhance the reliability and coding efficiency, following the 802.11g, Wi-Fi physical layer technology adopted Error Correction Coding scheme which is capable of correcting errors during the transmission of digital signals.

The Error Correction Coding can be divided into two categories: Block code and Convolutional code. 802.11g, 802.11n, and 802.11ac standards utilize Binary Convolutional Code (BCC), while the Wi-Fi 6802.11ax has shifted to Low Density Parity Check (LDPC), which is a type of Block code.

Block Code The information is segmented and divided into multiple non-correlated blocks, with redundant bits appended to each block for the purpose of error detection or correction. Well-known block codes include Parity Check code, Hamming code, and many others.

The LDPC code chosen by Wi-Fi 6 is widely used in deep space communication, optical communication, 4G/5G wireless communication, and future 6G mobile communication. It offers the benefits of high performance, close to the Shannon limit, low decoding complexity at the receiver, flexible structure, short decoding delay, and high throughput.

Convolutional Code Instead of dividing the information into blocks and encoding them separately, the information is fed to the encoder as a continuous stream of data bits. The encoder generates streams of data bits through the sliding application of functions. The encoded stream depends on not only the current input but also on previous inputs stored in memory.

Thus, while block codes provide error correction through fixed-length blocks and added redundancy, convolutional codes offer an alternative method by creating a time-correlated sequence of encoded bits, allowing for more efficient and flexible error correction in real-time communication systems such as wireless communications or satellite transmissions.

The coding efficiency of Wi-Fi's channel coding is continuously improved along with the evolution of new specifications. As indicated in Fig. 1.22, the coding efficiency of 802.11n and 802.11ac can reach up to 5/6, representing a significant improvement over 802.11g and 802.11b.

2. **Wi-Fi Modulation**

The Wi-Fi channel modulation technology is primarily concerned with optimizing the utilization of frequency resources to enhance signal capacity. In this context, a fundamental unit of transmitted data is referred to as a symbol. The rate at which these symbols are transmitted per second defines the baud rate or symbol rate. The amount of information bits conveyed by each symbol is determined by the chosen modulation technique.

The early Wi-Fi specification utilized Phase Shift Keying (PSK) as the modulation scheme, meaning that the phase of the carrier signals is modulated by the information "1" or "0." Specifically, the 802.11b standard employed the modulation

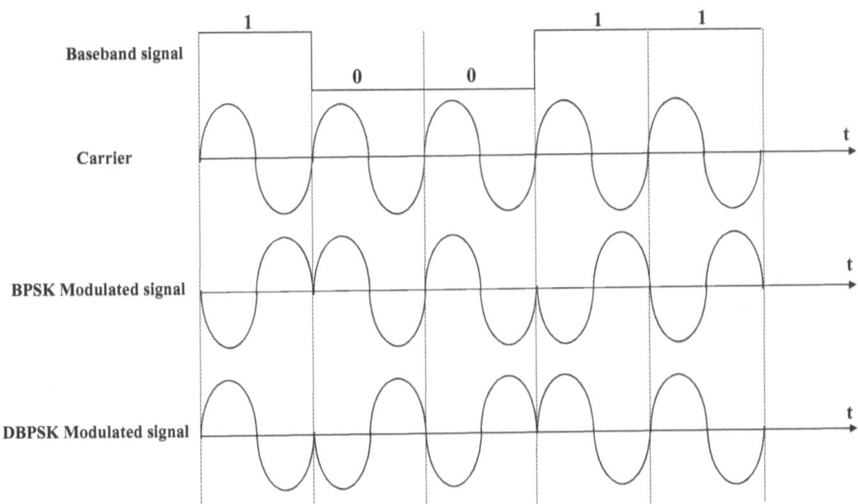

Fig. 1.23 BPSK and DBPSK modulation

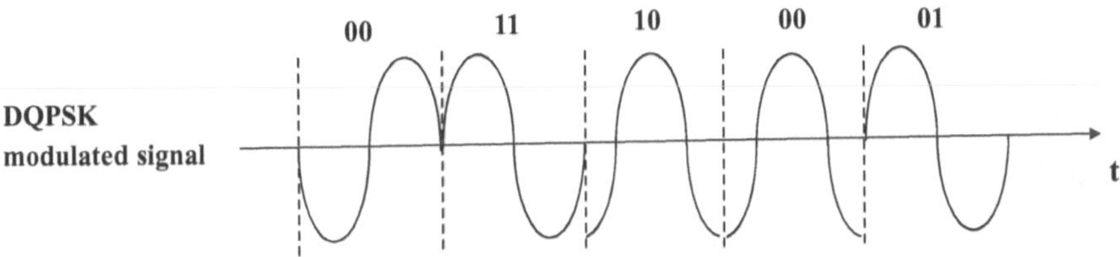

Fig. 1.24 DQPSK modulation

schemes of Differential Binary Phase Shift Keying (DBPSK) and Differential Quadrature Phase Shift Keying (DQPSK).

BPSK stands for Binary Phase Shift Keying. It means that the phase of the carrier signal is controlled by a binary digital signal, with 0 and 1 corresponding to phase 0 and π respectively. Figure 1.23 shows the waveform of a modulated signal based on BPSK. In this figure, each cycle of the modulated signal represents a binary information of 0 or 1. A phase of 0 represents the number 0, while a phase of π represents the number 1. As for DBPSK, if the binary information of the symbol is not the same as the preceding one, such as changing from 0 to 1 or from 1 to 0, the phase of carrier is reversed. Each symbol of BPSK or DBPSK carries 1 bit of information.

The Quadrature Phase Shift Keying (QPSK) is also known as four-phase Phase Shift Keying (4PSK) modulation, which utilizes four phases to represent 00, 01, 10, 11. The DQPSK is based on QPSK. Similar to the DBPSK, the carrier phase is determined by the difference of the digital information of the current symbol versus the preceding one, as indicated in Fig. 1.24. Each DQPSK symbol carries two bits of information.

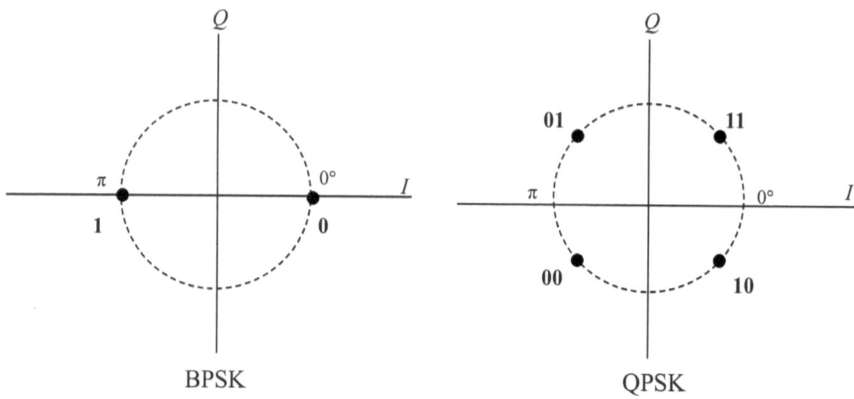

Fig. 1.25 Constellation diagram

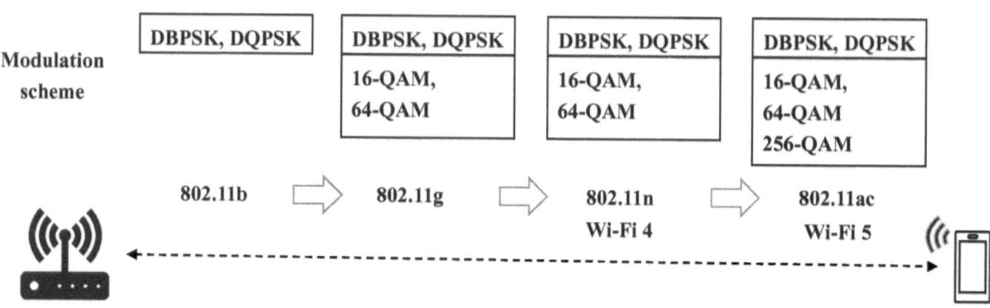

Fig. 1.26 Wi-Fi modulation schemes

Constellation diagram serves as an intuitive visual representation that describes the mapping between the modulated signals and their corresponding digital information. As shown in Fig. 1.25, the phases 0 radians and π radians of BPSK respectively correspond to the digital bits 0 and 1. In contrast, QPSK utilizes four distinct phases separated by a 90° interval each to represent the bit pairs 00, 01, 10, and 11. In the constellation diagram, the horizontal axis represents the in-phase (I) component of signal, and the vertical axis represents the quadrature (Q) component.

The Phase Shift Keying modulation is indeed straightforward but may not be the most efficient in terms of spectral efficiency. Figure 1.26 outlines the progression of the modulation schemes before the advent of Wi-Fi 5. Beginning with 802.11g, the Wi-Fi standards began employing Quadrature Amplitude Modulation (QAM), a hybrid approach that integrates both amplitude and phase modulation. With QAM, a single symbol can carry data amounts corresponding to 4 bits, 6 bits, or 8 bits, often denoted as 16-QAM, 64-QAM, and 256-QAM respectively. Specifically, 16-QAM processes four bits at once, resulting in 16 (2^4) distinct combination possibilities.

Constellation diagram is also used to illustrate the mapping between symbols and their corresponding digital information in the QAM modulation. As illustrated in Fig. 1.27, in a 16-QAM constellation, each symbol embodies 4 bits of information,

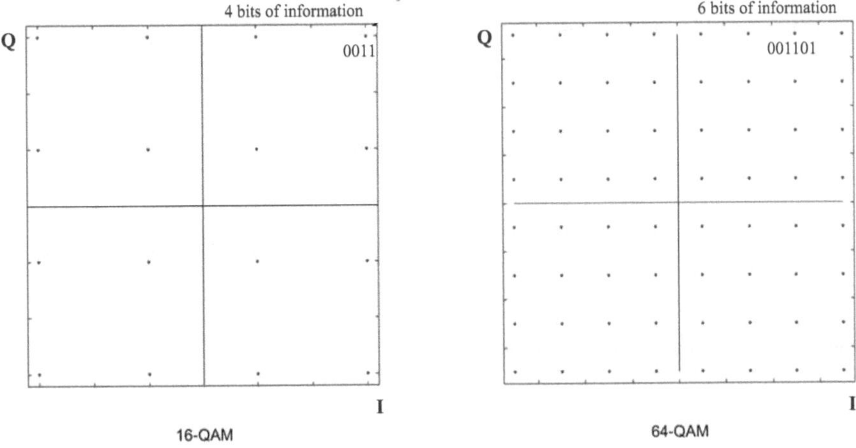

Fig. 1.27 Constellation diagrams of 16-QAM and 64-QAM

while in 64-QAM configuration, each symbol represents 6 bits of information. In the case of Wi-Fi 5, or 802.11ac, it supports 256-QAM, that is, each symbol carries 8 bits of information. This results in a modulation efficiency that is either four or eight times more than that of 802.11b, thereby enhancing the data transmission rate up to four times over 802.11b due to the utilization of this sophisticated modulation technique.

3. **Orthogonal Frequency Division Multiplexing (OFDM)**

Orthogonal Frequency Division Multiplexing (OFDM) is the modulation technique employed in the Wi-Fi standards. The Wi-Fi channels are partitioned into many subcarriers of equal bandwidth and period, yet with overlapping spectrum, where these subcarriers are orthogonal to one another, thus ensuring they do not interfere with each other.

In contrast, traditional Frequency Division Multiplexing (FDM) splits the data stream into multiple low-rate bit streams, modulates each through on separate subcarriers, and transmits them concurrently. As shown in Fig. 1.28, a distinct frequency gap exists between two subcarriers to prevent mutual interference, which consequently results in lower spectrum utilization. However, OFDM technology enables the subcarriers to overlap with each other without causing interference. This characteristic allows for more subcarriers within the same bandwidth as in FDM, thereby enabling OFDM to utilize the spectrum in a significantly more efficient manner.

4. **Multipath Propagation**

In a real -world environment, the electromagnetic waves propagate through the air and undergo various phenomena when encountering different types of objects. Upon contact with these surfaces, the waves may refract or reflect eventually

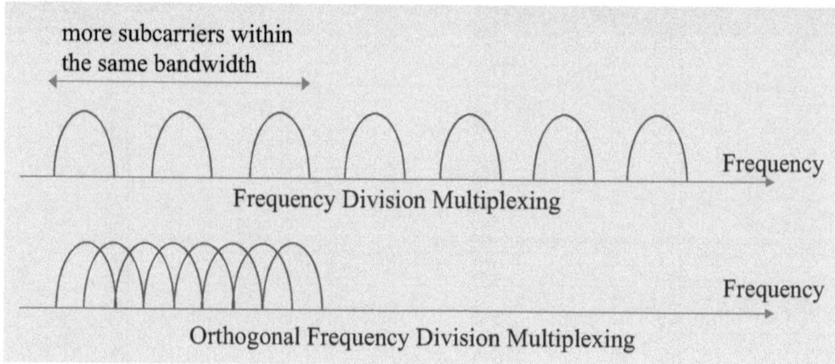

Fig. 1.28 Channel utilization of FDM and OFDM

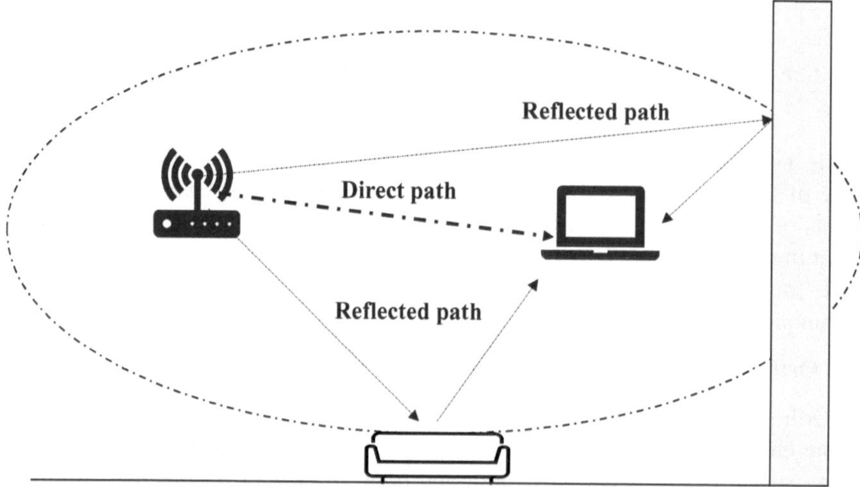

Fig. 1.29 Multipath propagation

reaching their destination via multiple paths. This complex phenomenon is known as multipath propagation as visually depicted in Fig. 1.29.

In a Wi-Fi transmission, a series of OFDM symbols are included. When multipath propagation occurs, the same OFDM symbol can traverse different paths and reach the receiver at disparate intervals. This means that the energy from the initial OFDM symbol on path 2 might overlap with the second OFDM symbol arriving via path 1, potentially causing the receiver to incorrectly decode the signal. This phenomenon is referred to as Inter Symbol Interference (ISI) as illustrated in Fig. 1.30.

To address Inter Symbol Interference, an idle period known as Guard Interval (GI), is inserted between consecutive OFDM symbols. If the duration of the guard interval exceeds the maximum possible delay of the OFDM symbol caused by multipath propagation, the tail end of the preceding symbol would fall entirely within this interval, thereby preventing interference with the next OFDM symbol.

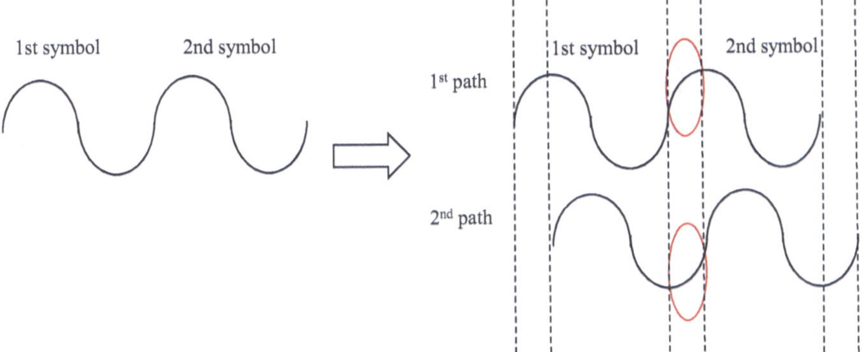

Fig. 1.30 Inter symbol interference

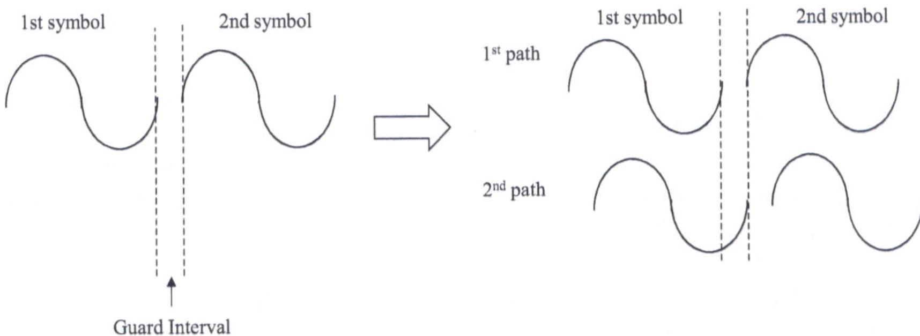

Fig. 1.31 OFDM symbol with the guard interval

As shown in Fig. 1.31, the guard interval can effectively mitigate the issue of inter-symbol interference.

The 802.11g defines a guard interval of 800 ns, which effectively eliminates the inter-symbol interference in indoor environments. However, large guard intervals can lead to a reduction in data transmission efficiency. Recognizing this trade-off, the subsequent 802.11n introduces a Short Guard Interval (SGI) option, reducing the interval to 400 ns, which helps to balance the anti-interference introduced by the multipath propagation and the transmission rate in most scenarios. By using SGI, 802.11n devices can achieve higher data rates while still coping effectively with potential ISI issues.

1.2.2.8 Multiple-Input Multiple-Output (MIMO)

Multiple-input multiple-output technology (MIMO) is an advanced method to transmit signals through multiple antennas at both the transmitter and receiver ends. It improves the SNR and signal capacity without requiring additional bandwidth. The

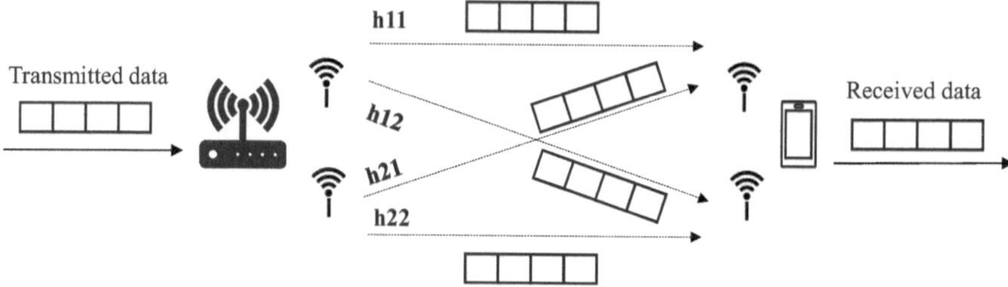

Fig. 1.32 Spatial diversity

MIMO technology can be categorized into three main types: Spatial Diversity, Spatial Multiplexing, and Beamforming.

- **Spatial Diversity:** It is a technique in which the same data is transmitted through multiple antennas to reduce the bit error rate and improve the channel reliability. This approach can help to mitigate the effects of signal fading and interference, thereby increasing the overall robustness of the wireless communication system.
- **Spatial Multiplexing:** On the other hand, this is a technique in which different data is transmitted simultaneously through multiple antennas to improve the channel capacity. By transmitting multiple data streams over the same frequency band, spatial multiplexing can significantly increase the overall data throughput of the system without requiring additional bandwidth.
- **Beamforming:** A technique in which the transmitter adjusts the amplitude and the phase of the signals through multiple antennas to focus on the combined signal towards a specific direction, rather than spreading the signal in all directions. This approach can help to increase the signal strength at the receiver and reduce interference from other sources. At the receiver, signals from multiple antennas are collected and weighted to obtain a better signal quality.

This subsection focuses on elucidating the concepts of Spatial Diversity and Spatial Multiplexing, and we will delve into beamforming techniques in the subsequent subsection.

1. **Spatial Diversity**

Figure 1.32 is an example of data transmission through multiple antennas with Spatial Diversity technology. In this scenario, the raw data is simultaneously sent through two distinct transmitting antennas. Concurrently, the signal is received by a pair of receiving antennas. Upon reception, the receiver can adopt one of two strategies: It may choose to select the stronger among the two for decoding, or it may opt to synthesize both signals as maximal ratio combining, thereby achieving an improved Signal-to-Noise Ratio (SNR).

The Wi-Fi channel is a time-varying system with many factors leading to signal degradation, such as transmission loss, station roaming, multipath propagation, and the influence of the Doppler effect. This is referred to as fading. The channel fading brings the challenge to the modulation technique. Spatial Diversity addresses the

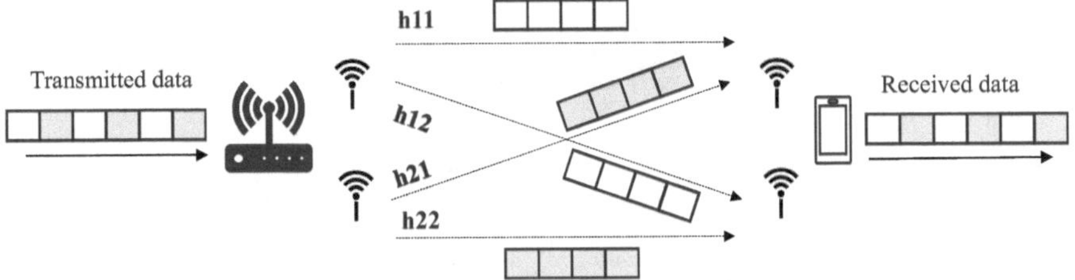

Fig. 1.33 2 × 2 Spatial multiplexing MIMO

channel fading problem through multi-antenna technology, also known as anti-fading technology.

There are two types of Spatial Diversity:

- **Receive Diversity:** Given that the same information is received through multiple antennas, if the distance between the antennas is greater than half a wavelength, the receiving paths have independent fading characteristics, ensuring that the signal is uncorrelated. This means the receiver receives a replica of the signal on each antenna. It can select the strongest signal or synthesize the signals before demodulation. The difference of the received signal strength between the Spatial Diversity antennas and a single antenna represents the gain of Receive Diversity. It is directly related to the number of receiving antennas.
- **Transmit Diversity:** The transmitter sends signals through multiple antennas, with the antennas designed to experience independent channel fading. The receiver experiences a higher signal-to-noise ratio across multiple fading channels. The Transmit Diversity Gain is measured by the difference of received signal strength between transmitter antennas and a single antenna.

The Delay Diversity is a form of Transmit Diversity where the replicas of the signal are transmitted on multiple antennas at different time to achieve additional gains. Although Delay Diversity is relatively straightforward, it introduces delays.

Another implementation of Transmit Diversity is Space-Time Block Code (STBC) based Diversity, that is, data is encoded using a Space-Time Block Code (STBC) and transmitted from two or more antennas. The signal vectors transmitted by multiple antennas are orthogonal to each other, ensuring that the signals do not interfere with each other. By utilizing STBC technology in a system with M transmit antennas and N receive antennas, the maximum diversity gain achieved is M × N. Figure 1.32 provides an example of 2 × 2 MIMO spatial diversity.

2. **Spatial Multiplexing**

The transmitter sends different data to the wireless channel through the multiple antennas, and correspondingly, the receiver receives these distinct data streams via its own set of antennas. This process boosts the transmission capacity by leveraging a technique known as Spatial Multiplexing. As shown in Fig. 1.33, a MIMO system

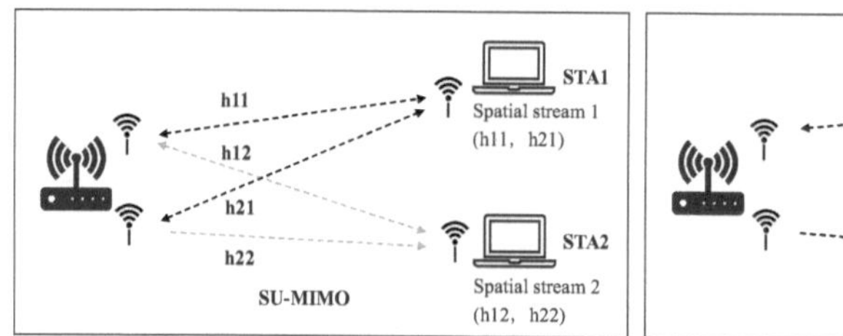

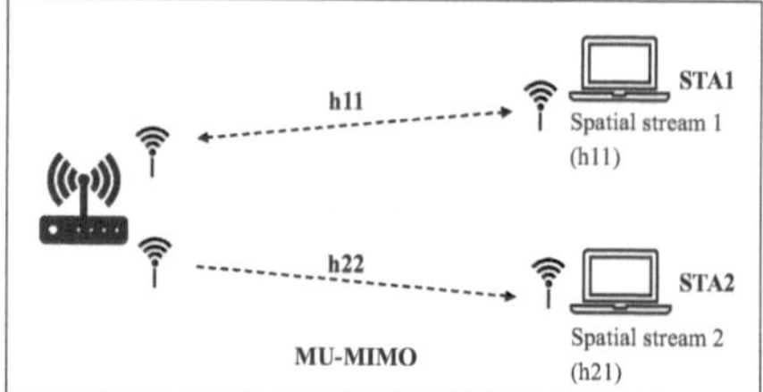

Fig. 1.34 SU-MIMO and MU-MIMO

composed of two transmitting antennas and two receiving antennas effectively doubles the transmission rate versus a single-antenna system.

According to the number of the receivers, MIMO systems can be categorized into Single User MIMO (SU-MIMO) and Multi-User MIMO (MU-MIMO). In SU-MIMO data transmission, the communication is directed towards a single receiver equipped with multiple antennas at any given time. On the other hand, MU-MIMO allows for simultaneous transmission to multiple receivers, each potentially having one or more antennas.

In a MU-MIMO communication network, the transmitter concurrently sends different data streams to several distinct receivers, thereby efficiently utilizing the available channel resources. This capability enhances the overall channel capacity and reduces the latency as multiple users can be served in parallel, rather than sequentially.

3. **MU-MIMO**

The downlink MU-MIMO technology was first introduced in the 802.11ac standard, where an AP transmits data simultaneously to multiple stations. In the downlink direction, the AP initiates the sounding process to collect the channel feedback from each STA and constructs a transmit channel response matrix. The data on each transmitting antenna is adjusted using the matrix to ensure no interference between the multiple spatial streams, allowing each STA to only receive its own data.

Supporting uplink MU-MIMO is more complex. This requires strict control on the transmission rate, power, time synchronization, and other parameters across multiple STAs. Due to its complexity, Wi-Fi 5 did not include support for uplink MU-MIMO mode until Wi-Fi 6.

Figure 1.34 provides an example of two spatial streams to demonstrate the difference between SU-MIMO and MU-MIMO.

In a SU-MIMO communication, the channel feedback (h11, h21) or (h12, h22) are known by both the AP and the STAss. Therefore, the sounding process is not required. The STA resolves data streams on different antennas based on the known channel feedback.

The MU-MIMO system is designed in such a way that STA1 does not receive any signal from path h21, and STA2 does not receive any signal from path h12. The transmitter initiates the Sounding process to establish the channel response matrix before sending signals, minimize the power on these paths, and improve the signal-to-noise ratio of the receivers, so that the receivers can obtain their own information without additional channel information.

If an AP only obtains the information for one of the channels, it is referred to as Single User Sounding (SU-sounding). If multiple channel information is obtained at the same time, it is called Multiple Users Sounding (MU-sounding).

1.2.2.9 Beamforming

Traditionally, access points are equipped with omnidirectional antennas, which emit energy equally in all directions. Wi-Fi signals are transmitted through these omnidirectional antennas to the surrounding in the form of electromagnetic waves. Within the Wi-Fi signal coverage area, devices can communicate with each other. However, if a STA is located far away from the AP or there are significant obstacles between them, the signal quality can degrade, leading to disconnections from the Basic Service Set (BSS).

As shown in Fig. 1.35a, there is an obstacle between STA1 and AP, and STA2 is at the edge of AP's signal coverage. The Wi-Fi signal strength received by STA1 or STA2 is weak, resulting in a low Wi-Fi data transmission rate. Given that each country has strict limits on the maximum transmit power of Wi-Fi devices, simply increasing the transmit power cannot enhance coverage.

Starting with the Wi-Fi 5, beamforming technology was introduced to improve Wi-Fi coverage. The principle behind this is that, in the case of a multi-antenna transmitter, the device adjusts the amplitude and phase of the radiated signal to concentrate the signal energy in a desired direction. The beamforming technology can expand the Wi-Fi coverage, increase the signal-to-noise ratio, reduce interference in other directions, and improve the throughputs. As shown in Fig. 1.35b, the AP beamforms in the direction of STA1 or STA2.

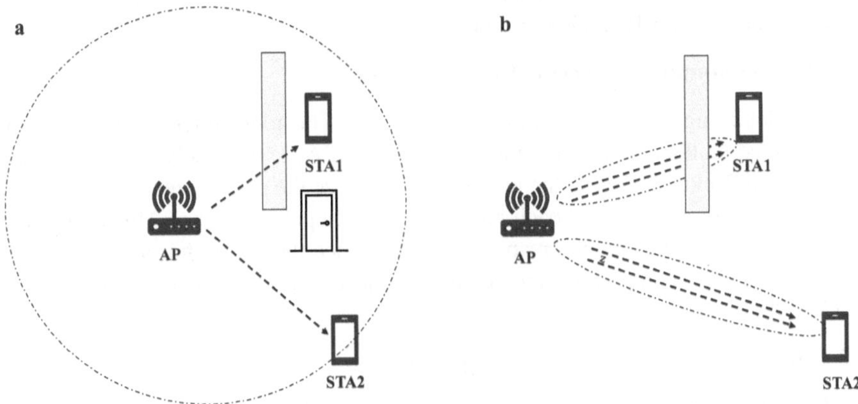

Fig. 1.35 (**a**) Omnidirectional antenna, (**b**) beamforming

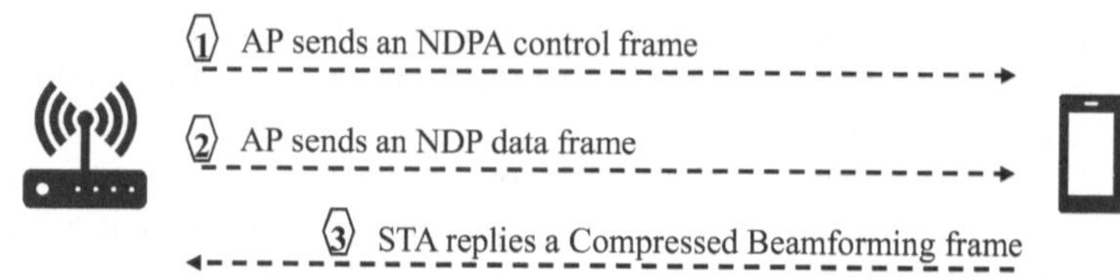

Fig. 1.36 Channel sounding process of a single-user

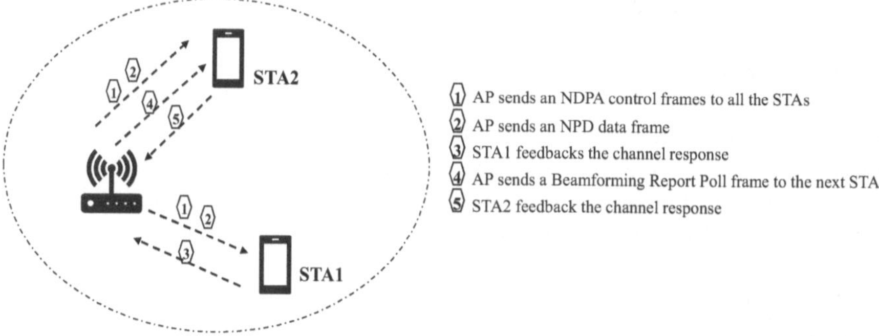

Fig. 1.37 Channel sounding process of multiple users

In order to focus the signal towards a specific direction, it is necessary to obtain channel information from receiver's feedback and then process the transmitted signal accordingly before the transmission. This is the Sounding technology mentioned earlier in the section of MIMO.

The device that sends data through beamforming technology is called the beamformer, and the device that receives the beamforming data is called the Beamformee. Both Beamformer and Beamformee use Channel State Information (CSI) in the physical layer header to implement the Sounding process. The Sounding process for single user and multi-user is slightly different. Now, let us proceed to describe the Wi-Fi 5 Beamforming process.

1. **Channel Sounding Process of a Single User**

The Sounding process is shown in Fig. 1.36. The transmitter sends a control frame called Null Data Packet Announcement (NDPA) to the receiver. It then sends a Null Data Packet (NDP) so the receiver can analyze the channel response between each transmitter antenna and each receiving antenna per subcarrier. This allows the receiver to obtain the channel response matrix. Since the matrix has a large dimension, the receiver compresses and sends it in the Compressed Beamforming frame back to the transmitter.

2. **The Channel Sounding of Multiple Users**

The channel sounding process involves a transmitter and multiple receivers as shown in Fig. 1.37.

(1) The transmitter broadcasts a Null Data Packet Announcement (NDPA) frame to the BSS.
(2) The transmitter sends a Null Data Packet (NDP) for the receivers to analyze the channel response per subcarrier between each transmitter antenna and each receiving antenna.
(3) The first receiver indicated by the NDPA sends a Compressed Beamforming frame to feed back the channel response.
(4) The transmitter processes the feedback from the first receiver. It then sends a Beamforming Report Poll to the second receiver to query the channel response.
(5) The second receiver sends a Compressed Beamforming frame. Once all receivers have provided the feedback, the transmitter completes the entire Sounding process.
(6) The transmitter generates a channel response matrix based on the feedback from all the receivers. It then then transforms the data with the matrix and sends them to the receivers respectively. This accomplishes beamforming.

In addition, the receivers can process the signals in specific directions by weighting and synthesizing the signals from multiple antennas to achieve better signal quality in preferred directions. This is called receive beamforming. However, due to the complexity of implementing this technology on the receivers, the 802.11ac protocol only defines the transmit beamforming technology and not the receive beamforming technology.

1.2.3 Standards of Wi-Fi Physical Layer

The continuous evolution of the Wi-Fi physical layer is primarily driven by the quest to enhance transmission speeds, achieved through advancements in channel coding and modulation schemes, increasing channel bandwidth, and multiplying the number of simultaneous spatial streams, among other improvements.

Moreover, with each new Wi-Fi standard, a key consideration is maintaining compatibility with previous specifications. This ensures that newer generation devices can seamlessly interoperate with already existing equipment. The backward compatibility feature plays a pivotal role in facilitating smooth transitions to new standards, fostering widespread adoption, and ultimately contributing to the commercial triumph of Wi-Fi technology.

In the upcoming subsection, we will delve into the methods for calculating Wi-Fi transmission rates and outline the structure of the Wi-Fi physical layer frame format.

1.2.3.1 Wi-Fi Transmission Rate

Under the ideal conditions, theoretical maximum transmission rate for Wi-Fi can be calculated as Eq. 1.1:

$$data\ rate = \frac{\substack{number\ of\ information\ bits\ per\ symbol \times coding\ efficiency \\ \times number\ of\ data\ subcarriers \times number\ of\ spatial\ streams}}{a\ symbol\ period} \tag{1.1}$$

In Wi-Fi communications, the parameters are illustrated as below:

- **The number of information bits per symbol** represents how many bits are effectively conveyed by symbol on a subcarrier. When this value is divided by the symbol period, it gives us the number of bits transmitted in each unit time.
- **The coding efficiency**, on the other hand, refers to the proportion of actual data content to the total encoded data within a frame. This measures how much of the encoded data is useful payload as opposed to overhead for error correction and synchronization purposes.
- **The number of data subcarriers** denotes the count of effective subcarriers carrying data within the channel bandwidth that are utilized for transmitting data; they do not include the guard bands or null subcarriers which are used to separate channels or provide interference protection.
- **The number of spatial streams** reflects the gain from the MIMO transmission technology. More antennas, more spatial streams, and higher the transmission rate. A higher number of antennas equates to more spatial streams, allowing for parallel data streams to be transmitted and received simultaneously, thus increasing the overall transmission rate.

In the realm of Wi-Fi communications, a symbol can be likened to a delivery truck on a digital highway, carrying bits from the transmitter to the receiver.

The number of bits per symbol represents the cargo capacity of each truck; the more bits a symbol can carry, the more information it transmits in a single transmission cycle.

The number of data subcarriers corresponds to the number of lanes on this highway; having more subcarriers means that more symbols can be transmitted simultaneously within the channel bandwidth, thereby increasing the overall throughput.

Spatial streams are akin to multiple layers or tiers of highways stacked one above the other. Each layer can independently transport its own set of trucks (symbols), thus allowing for a dramatic increase in the total amount of data that can be transmitted at once. Now, with these parameters, let's proceed to calculate the transmission rates for different Wi-Fi standards by considering their modulation schemes, channel bandwidth, number of data subcarriers, coding efficiency, and the number of spatial streams available.

1. **The Number of Information Bits Per Symbol**

The number of information bits per symbol is determined by the modulation order or level. According to the channel modulation mode in the previous section, for a 16-QAM, each symbol encodes 4 bits of data. For a higher order 64-QAM, every symbol can carry 6 bits of information. The mapping of QAM modulation levels and

Table 1.4 QAM modulation level for Wi-Fi standards

Wi-Fi standards	802.11g	802.11n	802.11ac
QAM modulation level	64-QAM	64-QAM	256-QAM
The number of bits per symbol	6	6	8

Table 1.5 Coding efficiency of different Wi-Fi standards

Coding and modulation	802.11b (DSSS)	802.11a/g	802.11n	802.11ac
DBPSK	1/11			
DQPSK	1/11			
DQPSK	1/4			
DQPSK	1/2			
DBPSK		1/2	1/2	1/2
DQPSK		1/2	1/2	1/2
DQPSK		3/4	3/4	3/4
16-QAM		1/2	1/2	1/2
16-QAM		3/4	3/4	3/4
64-QAM		2/3	2/3	2/3
64-QAM		3/4	3/4	3/4
64-QAM		5/6	5/6	5/6
256-QAM				3/4
256-QAM				5/6

their corresponding number of bits per symbol across different Wi-Fi standards are shown in Table 1.4.

2. **Coding Efficiency**

The coding efficiency is commonly represented as a ratio k/n, where "k" represents the number of bits carrying actual or effective information content, and "n" is the total number of bits generated after encoding. For every "k" bit of useful data, the encoder creates a frame of "n" bits, with the difference (n-k) being redundant information added for channel error detection and correction purposes.

A higher value of k/n signifies a more efficient transmission because it implies that a larger proportion of the transmitted bits are dedicated to conveying the original message rather than error protection. This directly impacts the overall throughput and reliability of the communication system. Table 1.5 provides an overview of the coding efficiencies achieved under different Wi-Fi standards.

3. **The Number of Data Subcarriers**

The number of data subcarriers refers to the quantity of orthogonal frequency carriers within a channel that are specifically assigned for transmitting user data. This excludes any null subcarriers, which serve as guard bands or spectral gaps to prevent interference between adjacent channels, and pilot subcarriers, used for channel estimation, synchronization, and phase/frequency offset correction.

Table 1.6 Channel bandwidth and data subcarriers

Wi-Fi standards	802.11a/b/g	802.11n	802.11ac
Channel bandwidth (MHz)	20	40	80
Data subcarriers	52	108	234

Table 1.7 The number of spatial streams of Wi-Fi standards

Wi-Fi standard	802.11a/b/g	802.11n	802.11ac
Spatial streams	1	4	8

The relationship between channel bandwidth and the number of data subcarriers is direct and proportional. As the channel bandwidth increases, it allows for more subcarriers to be packed within the available spectrum. Table 1.6 lists the channel bandwidth and the number of data subcarriers under different Wi-Fi standards before Wi-Fi 5.

4. **Symbol Period**

The symbol period in Wi-Fi communication consists of two primary components: the time required to transmit a single symbol, and the guard interval inserted between two adjacent symbols in order to mitigate the effects of inter-symbol interference.

In Wi-Fi standards prior to Wi-Fi 6 a standard symbol duration was defined as 3.2 μs. To address potential interference issues, two types of guard intervals were introduced—a short guard interval of 0.4 μs and a long guard interval of 0.8 μs, so it makes the symbol period 3.6 μs or 4 μs.

5. **The Number of Spatial Streams**

The number of spatial streams in Wi-Fi technology refers to concurrent data paths that can be transmitted over multiple antennas simultaneously. From 802.11b/g to 802.11ac, the maximum number of spatial streams increases from 1 to 8, as shown in Table 1.7. These enhancements allow for much higher data rates by transmitting multiple data streams at the same time over different spatial channels within the wireless medium.

6. **Examples on the Calculation of Wi-Fi Transmission Rate**

Take 802.11n and 802.11ac as examples, the ideal maximum transmission rate can be obtained from Eq. 1.1, as shown in Table 1.8.

1.2.3.2 Wi-Fi Physical Layer PPDU Frame Format

A PPDU frame consists of three fields: the preamble, the header, and the payload MPDU, as shown in Fig. 1.38. The preamble is used for Wi-Fi signal detection and estimation of the channel characteristics, etc. Meanwhile the frame header contains coding and modulation information used by the receiver to demodulate and decode

Table 1.8 Theoretical maximum transmission rate of 802.11n and 802.11ac

Wi-Fi standard	802.11n	802.11ac
Number of spatial streams	4	8
Information bits per symbol	6	8
Coding efficiency	5/6	5/6
Number of data subcarriers	108 (40 MHz)	234 (80 MHz)
Symbol period (μs)	3.2 μs +0.4 μs short guard interval	3.2 μs + 0.4 μs short guard interval
Maximum data rate (Mbps)	**600**	**3466**

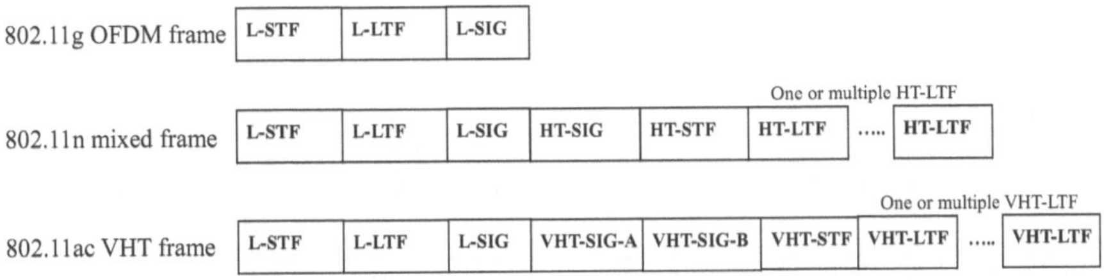

802.11g OFDM frame: L-STF | L-LTF | L-SIG

One or multiple HT-LTF

802.11n mixed frame: L-STF | L-LTF | L-SIG | HT-SIG | HT-STF | HT-LTF | ..... | HT-LTF

One or multiple VHT-LTF

802.11ac VHT frame: L-STF | L-LTF | L-SIG | VHT-SIG-A | VHT-SIG-B | VHT-STF | VHT-LTF | ..... | VHT-LTF

Fig. 1.38 Preamble of Wi-Fi standards

the signal. The evolution of the physical layer modulation, channel bandwidth, spatial streams, and other factors affects the definition of the preamble and the header.

It's important to note that devices compliant with older Wi-Fi standards cannot interpret the new preamble field. For example, devices that support the 802.11g standard cannot interpret the preamble defined by 802.11n. Therefore, the protocol mandates that the new Wi-Fi standard must support the preamble of the old Wi-Fi standard, for interoperability with the old devices.

1. **The Evolution of PPDU**

As shown in Table 1.9, the Wi-Fi standard supports a physical layer format that is compatible with the old standard. For example, the physical layer frame defined by the 802.11n is compatible with the 802.11g, enabling the Wi-Fi devices that are compliant to the new standard and are able to communicate with legacy devices in the same Wi-Fi network. In the IEEE standard, 802.11n is also referred to as High Throughput (HT), while 802.11ac is called Very High Throughput (VHT). The physical layer format is accordingly designated with the terms HT and VHT.

Figure 1.38 shows the examples of the preamble field of 802.11g, 802.11n, and 802.11ac standards.

The 802.11g preamble field contains three parts, namely, the Legacy Short Training Field (L-STF), the Legacy Long Training Field (L-LTF), and the Legacy

Table 1.9 PPDU frame formats

Wi-Fi standard	Frame format
802.11b	Format 1: 144 bits long preamble, for early Wi-Fi standards of 1Mbps/2Mbps devices
	Format 2: 72 bits short preamble, for 2Mbps or above Wi-Fi devices
802.11g	Format 1 and 2: long and short PPDU compatible to 802.11b
	Format 3: OFDM frame with new preamble and header
802.11n	Format 1: OFDM frame compatible to 802.11g
	Format 2: mixed frame compatible to 802.11g and containing HT header defined by 802.11n
	Format 3: frame contains HT header defined by 802.11n
802.11ac	VHT frame: compatible to the 3 formats of 802.11n, and supporting MIMO

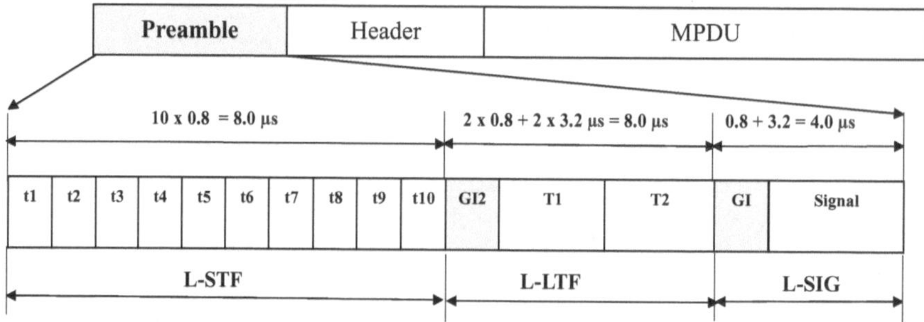

Fig. 1.39 Legacy preamble

Signal (L-SIG) field. The preamble of 802.11n consists of two parts: the 802.11g legacy preamble and the newly defined preamble.

As shown in Fig. 1.39, the first three fields of the 802.11n preamble are the same L-STF, L-LTF, and L-SIG as 802.11g, followed by the newly defined HT-SIG, HT-STF, and HT-LTF fields. Similarly, the 802.11ac preamble has the same structure but upgrades the HT subfields by the VHT fields.

The preamble of 802.11n and 802.11ac consist of either one or multiple HT-LTF or VHT-LTF subfields, which are utilized for channel fading estimation. This is relevant to the number of spatial streams.

When the number of the spatial stream is one or even, the preamble contains the same number of HT-LTF or VHT-LTF subfields. If the number of spatial streams n is odd and more than two, the preamble contains n + 1 HT-LTF or VHT-LTF subfields. For example, if there are three spatial streams, the preamble has 4 HT-LTF or 4 VHT-LTF subfields. In addition, for 802.11ac, if the PPDU is for multiple STAs, the preamble needs to contain the VHT-SIG-B field which indicates the spatial stream allocation information of each STA.

2. **The Legacy Preamble**

The 802.11g preamble is the legacy standard which the subsequent standards are required to be compatible with. The L-STF and the L-LTF are the short and the long training subfields, respectively, used for frame identification and synchronization.

As shown in Fig. 1.39, L-STF contains 10 repetitions of a "short training sequence" (t1 ~ t10), each with a duration of 0.8 μs, so a total duration of 8 μs. The L-LTF subfield is constructed by 2 repetitions of a "long training sequence" (T1, T2), each with a duration of 3.2 μs, plus a double GI (GI2), resulting in a total of 8 μs. The L-SIG has a duration of 4.0 μs and serves as the signal subfield indicating the data rate, frame length in unit of octets, and parity information. A Guard Interval (GI) is inserted between the fields for protection.

The legacy preamble serves several crucial purposes:

(1) **Wi-Fi signal detection:** The receiver identifies the presence of a Wi-Fi signal by analyzing the training sequence within the Long Short Training Field (L-STF) subfield. This helps to distinguish Wi-Fi signals from other radio frequency noise or interference.
(2) **Automatic gain control (AGC)**: To ensure proper signal reception, the receiver adjusts its gain based on the strength of the received L-STF signal. It measures the signal attenuation and equalizes the amplitude to an appropriate level for further processing.
(3) **Synchronization**: The receiver synchronizes its clock with that of the transmitter using timing information obtained from the L-STF field. This synchronization is critical for accurate sampling and reduces decoding errors.
(4) **Frequency offset estimation**: Due to factors such as Doppler shift, the carrier frequency can deviate during transmission. The L-STF and Long Training Field (L-LTF) sections are used to estimate and correct both coarse and fine frequency offsets.
(5) **Channel estimation:** The receiver continually assesses channel conditions through the L-LTF subfield. By measuring the signal's attenuation and delay over time, it estimates the channel response, which is essential for proper demodulation and decoding.
(6) **Transmission duration estimation:** Based on the data rate and PPDU length indicated in L-SIG subfield, the devices can estimate how long the current Wi-Fi transmission occupies the wireless medium. This allows them to set an appropriate backoff period before attempting their own transmissions to avoid collisions and maintain efficient use of the shared channel resources.

3. **HT and VHT Preambles**

The new Wi-Fi technologies introduce more parameters and control functions in the physical layer, so the standards define the new preamble subfields accordingly.

Table 1.10 describes the HT-LSF, HT-LTF, and HT-SIG subfields of the 802.11n (High Throughput, HT) preamble, and the VHT-LSF, VHT-LTF, and VHT-SIG subfields of the 802.11ac (Very High Throughput, VHT) preamble.

Table 1.10 New preamble subfields defined by 802.11n and 802.11ac

Wi-Fi standard	Subfield	Description	Purpose
802.11n	HT-SIG	HT signal	Provides information such as data rate, coding, modulation, bandwidth, the number of MIMO streams, and etc
	HT-STF	HT short training sequence	Used for automatic gain control estimation of the MIMO system
	HT-LTF	HT long training sequence	Used for the channel estimation for the MIMO system. The number of HT-LTF subfields equals to the number of the spatial streams. Wi-Fi 4 allows maximum 4 spatial streams, so the maximum number of HT-LTFs is 4
802.11ac	VHT-SIG	VHT signal	It includes two subfields: VHT-SIG-A and VHT-SIG-B. The VHT-SIG-A is similar to HT-SIG which indicates the information such as data rate, coding, modulation, bandwidth, the number of MIMO streams, and the number of spatial streams for each user in case of a MU-MIMO communication. The VHT-SIG-B provides the downlink frame length and data rate for each user in case of a MU-MIMO communication
	VHT-STF	VHT short training sequence	Similar to the HT-STF, the VHT-STF facilitates the estimation for automatic gain control up to 80 MHz bandwidth.
	VHT-LTF	VHT long training sequence	Similar to HT-LTF, VHT-LTF supports to estimate the channel characteristics up to 8 spatial streams

1.2.4 Standards of Wi-Fi MAC Layer

The 802.11 Data Link layer consists of a generic Logical Link Control (LLC) sublayer, which is responsible for receiving and processing Ethernet data packets, as well as an 802.11 specific Media Access Control (MAC) sublayer focusing on the wireless medium processing, including the transmission and reception of data, as well as controlling and managing the transmissions, such as access control, link state management, and device power state management, etc.

1.2.4.1 Data Transmission

Figure 1.40 shows how data frame is processed at the MAC layer.

The process on the transmitter side can be outlined as following:

(1) The LLC sublayer adds an Ethernet header to construct a MAC Service Data Unit (MSDU) and forwards it to the MAC layer.

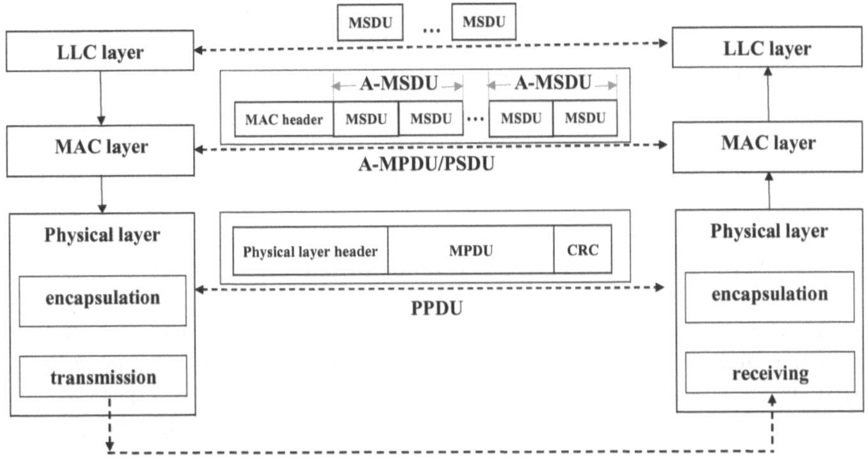

Fig. 1.40 Data processing at Wi-Fi MAC layer

(2) The MAC layer then has the capability to concatenate multiple MSDUs to form a larger unit, known as the Aggregate MAC Service Data Unit (Aggregate MSDU, A-MSDU).
(3) Subsequently, the MAC layer adds a MAC header to the MSDU or A-MSDU, encapsulating it into a MAC Protocol Data Unit (MPDU). If multiple MPDUs are combined, they form an Aggregate MAC Protocol Data Unit (Aggregate MPDU, A-MPDU). Both MPDU and A-MPDU are also referred to as Physical layer Service Data Unit (PSDU) in the physical layer.
(4) Finally, the physical layer appends a preamble, Cyclic Redundancy Check (CRC), etc. to the PSDU, thereby constructing a Physical layer Protocol Data Unit (PPDU), which is then transmitted.

On the receiver side, the MAC layer receives either MPDU or A-MPDU, decapsulates them to restore the original MSDUs or A-MSDUs, and subsequently delivers these units to the LLC layer for further processing.

1.2.4.2 Control and Management of MAC Layer

The AP or the STA utilize the control frame to regulate the access to the wireless media. Management frame, on the other hand, are employed for network management interactions between the AP and the STA or among STAs themselves, such as in processes like BSS discovery, authentication, and association.

Upon receiving instructions from higher layers, the MAC layer of a transmitting device generates the corresponding management frames and control frames and transmits them through the physical layer.

Conversely, upon reception, the MAC layer of a receiving device captures these control or management frame, and converts them to the management control messages, and relays them up to the upper layer for further processing.

This section delves into the frame format of the MAC layer, detailing the structure of data frames, the control frame and management frame, as well as the concepts related to the data transmission and reception procedures.

1.2.4.3 Wi-Fi MAC Layer MPDU Frame Format

As previously introduced, an 802.11 frame is composed of the physical layer preamble and the header, followed by the payload MPDU originating from the MAC layer. The structure of MPDU frame format is shown in Fig. 1.41 [5].

The MPDU frame has the subfields such as the Frame Control, the duration required for MAC frame transmission, identification, address information, and etc.

The description and purpose of the frame control subfields as listed in Table 1.11.

Besides the frame control field, other fields of the MPDU frame are illustrated in Table 1.12.

1.2.4.4 Frame Types of 802.11 MAC Layer

The 802.11 MAC layer defines three types of MPDU frames, namely, management frames, control frames, and data frames, to achieve the communication between wireless devices.

1. **Management Frame**

Management frames are employed for network management interactions between the AP and the STA or among STAs themselves, such as in processes like BSS discovery, authentication, and association.

The 802.11 specifies the following management frames as shown in Table 1.13.

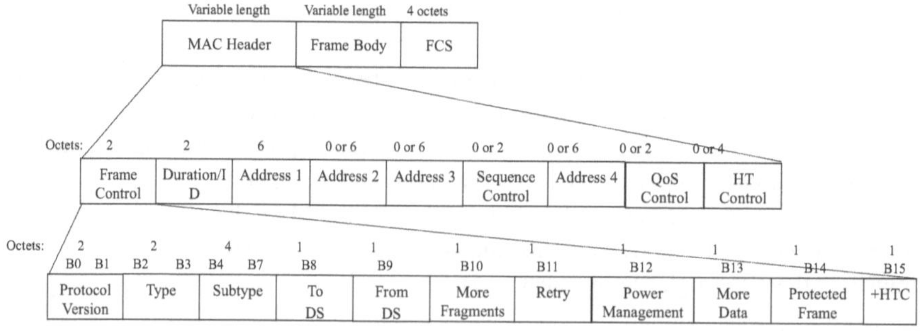

Fig. 1.41 802.11 MPDU frame format

Table 1.11 The subfields of frame control field

Subfield	Bits	Description and purpose
Protocol version	B0, B1	Indicates the version of the MAC layer protocol, usually set to 0
Type	B2, B3	Indicates the type of frame: 00—a management frame; 01—a control frame; 10—a data frame; 11—an extended frame
Subtype	B4-B7	Indicates the subtypes
To DS and from DS	B8, B9	Indicates the direction of frame transmission: 00—direct communication between STAs; 10—the data is from STA to AP; 01—the data is from AP to STA, or from a STA in a mesh BSS with a 3-address MAC header; 11—the data from a STA in a mesh BSS with a 4-address MAC header
More fragment	B10	Indicates whether there is a fragment: 1—there is more data or management frames to follow; 0–otherwise
Retry	B11	Indicates whether it is a retransmitted frame: 1—the data or management frame is a retransmission of a previous frame with the same content; 0—not a retransmission
Power management	B12	Indicates the power management mode of the STA: 1—the STA will enter power-saving mode; 0—the STA will be in active mode
More data	B13	Indicates whether there are buffered data for the STA: 1—the AP has buffered data to the STA. This indicator can be used as both unicast and multicast data; 0—no buffered data
Protected frame	B14	Indicates whether it is encrypted: 1—the frame is encrypted; 0—the frame is not encrypted. If the MPDU does not contain user data, such as NDP frames used for probing purpose, no encryption required. For such cases this subfield is 0
+HTC	B15	This subfield indicates: 1—the MAC header contains an HT control field if it's a management frame or a QoS data frame; or the frame being transferred using the Strictly Ordered service if it's a non-QoS data frame. Otherwise, it is set to 0

According to the receiver address information, the management frame can be categorized as unicast, multicast, and broadcast management frame, as shown in Table 1.14.

Table 1.12 Description of the fields of MPDU

Field	Octet	Description and purpose
Duration/ID	2	Indicates the duration or the identification of a frame: If it indicates the time: B15 is 0, and B0 ~ B14 indicates the duration (in milliseconds) of the current and all subsequent frames (except for PS-POLL frames). If it indicates the identification: B15 and B14 are both 1, B0 ~ B13 represents the ID assigned to the STA after association to the AP indicated by the PS-POLL frame, which is called Association Identifier (AID). The AID ranges from 1 to 8191. The PS-POLL frames will be introduced in Sect. 1.2.7
Address1, address2, address3, address4	0 or 6	These address fields are BSSID, Source Address (SÁ), Destination Address (DA), Transmitter Address (TA), and Receiver Address (RA). Not all types of frames use these addresses. The RA can be multicast addresses or unicast addresses. If all bits of RA are 1, it indicates a broadcast address
Sequence control	0 or 2	The sequence control field consists of a 12-digit Sequence Number (SN) and a 4-bit Fragment Number (FN). SN is used to indicate the order of the MPDU frames, and FN is used to indicate the number of the fragments of a MSDU. The receiver reorders and filters the duplicate frames based on SN and PN. The control frame does not contain this field
QoS control	0 or 2	This QoS control field is used in the MAC header of QoS data frames, composed of traffic identifier (TID) subfield, end of service period (ESOP) subfield, etc
HT control	0 or 4	This is a new field added in the 802.11n amendment. This control field is used for link adaptation, TxBF, the Reverse Direction Protocol, etc
Frame body	Variable length	Contains the data information to be transmitted
FCS	4	It contains a 32-bit cyclic redundancy check for error detection and correction of data frames

2. **Control Frame**

Control frames are used by an AP or an STA to control the access of wireless media. Table 1.15 describes the types of the control frames and the respective purposes.

3. **Data Frame**

Depending on the type of service, the data transmitted in the network has different Quality of Service (QoS) requirements. For example, voice service is more sensitive to the latency, so when the voice services and the other data services are transmitted at the same time, the voice services shall be handled with high priority.

The MAC layer handles the data frames from highest priority to lowest. The Traffic Identifier (TID) field of the data frame is used to indicate the service priority.

Table 1.13 Management frames

Management frame	Initiator	Purpose
Beacon frame	AP	An AP periodically broadcasts beacon frames to announce its presence
Probe request frame	STA	An STA sends probe request frames to discover the network
Probe response frame	AP	An AP sends a probe response frame to respond to the probe request frame, with the AP capability information, robust security network (RSN) information, etc
Authentication request frame	STA	An STA initiates an authentication request to an AP
Authentication response frame	AP	An AP sends an authentication response frame to an STA in response to the STA's authentication request.
Association request frame	STA	An STA initiates an association request frame to an AP, which is used to illustrate the capabilities of the STA, RSN information, etc
Association response frame	AP	An AP responds to an STA according to its capability set, with the result of successful or unsuccessful. If successful, the station will be assigned with an Association ID
Disassociation frame	AP or STA	An AP or an STA sends the disassociation frame to disconnects the association with the other party
Reassociation request frame	STA	Used when an STA associated to one AP desires to associate to another AP connecting to the same ESS. It can also be used if an STA leaves the BSS for a short duration and wants to rejoin the BSS
Reassociation response frame	AP	Response from AP to STA for reassociation request
Action frame	AP or STA	For special purposes. For example, in block Ack negotiation, the initiator sends an ADDBA request action frame, and the receiver sends an ADDBA response action frame.

Table 1.14 Management frames based on the receiver address

Management frame	Initiator	MAC address	Purpose
Unicast	AP or STA	The 48th bit of the destination address is 0	The AP sends a management frame to a specific STA, or the STA sends a management frame to the AP
Multicast	AP	The 48th bit of the destination address is 1	The AP sends a management frame to the STAs in a specific group
Broadcast	AP	All the bits of the destination address are 1	The AP sends a management frame to all STAs

If a data frame contains a TID field, it is referred to as a QoS data frame, and vice versa, it's called a non-QoS data frame. At the MAC layer, the data services are categorized into eight levels of priority, denoted by TID 0 ~ 7.

Table 1.15 Types of control frames

Control frame	Initiator	Description and purpose
Request To Send (RTS) frame	AP or STA	An AP or an STA sends a request to the receiver indicating that it will send data frames, at the same time detects whether there is a collision. If no CTS response received, the transmitter repeats sending the same RTS frame
Clear To Send (CTS) frame	AP or STA	After an AP or an STA receives the RTS, it responds with the CTS frame to allow the receiver to send data. The other devices planning to send frames receive the CTS, then pause the backoff counter, and reset the wait time based on the duration subfield carried in the CTS. Through the RTS/CTS interaction, the transmitter obtains the access to the media
Acknowledge (Ack) frame and Block Ack (BA) frame	AP or STA	The receiver sends an acknowledgment frame to the transmitter to confirm receiving the data frames, where the Ack frame is used to acknowledge the non-aggregated MPDU, and the BA frame is used for the aggregation frame A-MPDU
Block Ack Request (BAR) frame	AP or STA	After the transmitter sends the A-MPDU, if it doesn't receive the BA frame from the receiver, it can retransmit the entire A-MPDU, or send a BAR frame. The BAR frame requests the receiver to feedback the status of the latest A-MPDU. Compared with a retransmission of the entire A-MPDU, the BAR occupies a smaller wireless resource
Power Saving Poll (PS-POLL) frame	STA	When a STA wakes up from power-saving mode, and learns that the AP has buffered unicast data for it, the STA sends a PS-POLL frame to request the AP to send the buffered data
VHT Null Data Packet Announcement (VHT NDPA) frame	AP	A beamformer sends a VHT NDPA to the beamformee in order to initiate the channel information query procedure
Beamforming report poll frame	AP	A beamformer polls multiple beamformees to report the channel information one by one as part of the sounding process

In the context of Wi-Fi's Quality of Service (QoS) mechanisms, the 802.11 standard defines four access categories (AC) to manage different types of traffic and their respective priorities when accessing the wireless channel: AC Background (AC_BK), AC Best Effort (AC_BE), Video (AC_VI), and Voice (AC_VO), of which AC_VO has the highest priority, followed by AC-VI, then AC_BE, and AC_BK. The higher priority data has the privilege to access the radio resources, as indicated in Table 1.16.

Table 1.17 lists the types of data frames based on if it contains TID.

Table 1.16 The mapping between the traffic type and the radio access category

Traffic type	Radio access category	Description
1 Background (BK)	1 (AC_BK)	Background
2 (Default level)	1 (AC_BK)	Default level if the service data does not indicate a priority
0 (Best effort, BE)	2 (AC_BE)	Best effort
3 (Excellent effort)	2 (AC_BE)	Best effort
4 (Controlled load)	3 (AC_VI)	Video
5 (Video, VI)	3 (AC_VI)	Video
6 (Voice, VO)	4 (AC_VO)	Voice
7 (Network control)	4 (AC_VO)	Voice

Note: For "Traffic Type" and "Radio Access Category", the higher number, the higher priority.

Table 1.17 Types of data frames

Data frame	Purpose
Non-QoS data	A data frame that does not contain TID information. In case of the legacy 802.11b/g device which doesn't support QoS data, the transmitter and the receiver must use non-QoS data frames.
Non-QoS null	A data frame that does not contain any data payload, used for query purpose. For example, the AP sends a null frame to query the buffering status of each STA. STA can also send NULL to the AP to obtain the buffered data frame
QoS data	A data frame containing TID information. The devices of 802.11n or the successor Wi-Fi standards use QoS data to transmit data
QoS null	A QoS data frame that does not contain any data payload. It has same function as the non-QoS Null data frame

1.2.4.5 Data Transmission of MAC Layer

The Wi-Fi MAC layer data transmission is based on an acknowledgement mechanism, which means that after the transmitter sends a frame, the receiver replies with a status frame based on the types of the received frame.

- If the transmitter sends a data frame or management frame, the receiver sends an ACK frame for acknowledgement.
- If the transmitter sends a control frame, such as an RTS frame, the receiver responds with a CTS frame, and then the data frame transmission starts.

The duration of a complete transmission of a data frame or a management frame is called a Transmission Opportunity (TXOP).

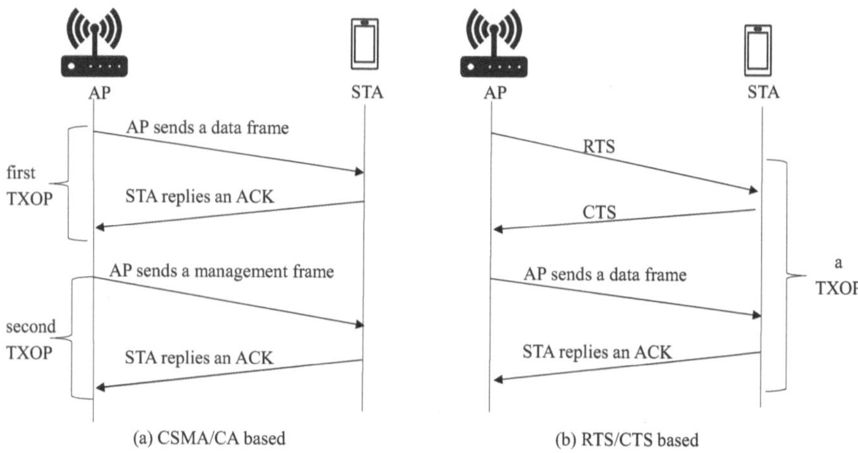

Fig. 1.42 Transmission opportunity based on CSMA/CA and RTS/CTS

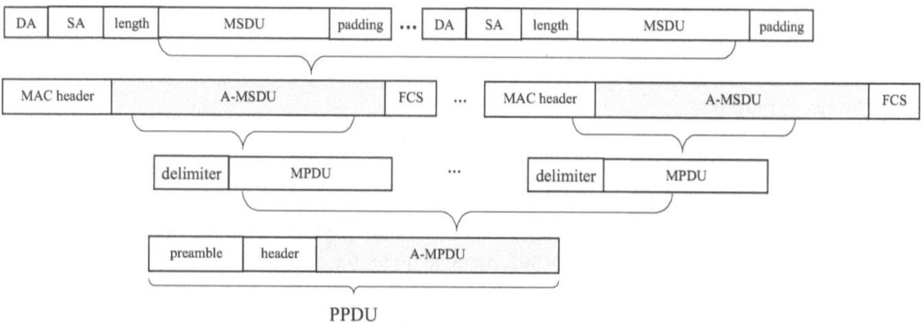

Fig. 1.43 PPDU composed by A-MSDU and A-MPDU

There are two ways of obtaining an TXOP, as illustrated in Fig. 1.42: The device competes for the access to the channel using the traditional CSMA/CA mechanism; or the device preemptively acquires the channel with the interaction of RTS/CTS control frames. The RTS/CTS don't contain the data information. The RTS/CTS control frames and the following data frames create an effective TXOP.

In practice, developers can choose either mechanism based on the length of the MPDU. For example, if the MPDU has more than 1500 octets (the maximum length of an MSDU), it's more efficient to select the RTS/CTS mechanism so that more data can be sent in a TXOP with only a small overhead for transmitting the control frames.

As shown in Fig. 1.43, the CSMA/CA mode is efficient for addressing the case of transmitting one data frame. However, if the transmitter has a large amount of data, it requires frequently preemption of the channel to obtain sufficient TXOPs and accomplishes data transmission.

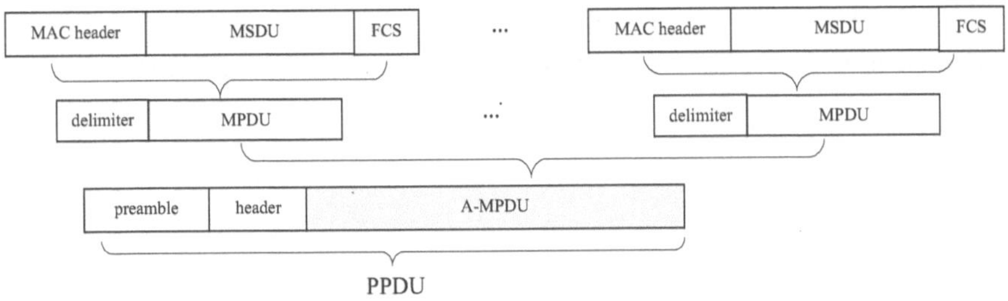

Fig. 1.44 PPDU composed by multiple MSDUs

In order to improve performance, the MAC layer supports the aggregation of data frames, which combines multiple data frames into one "big data frame" for transmission. Figure 1.43 shows the two modes of frame aggregation: A-MSDU and A-MPDU [5].

Both A-MPDU and A-MSDU are frame aggregation technique that combines multiple frames into a single frame transmission. It shall be noted that the aggregated MPDUs do not need to have the same destination address and the data payload of each MPDU is encrypted separately by using the individual dynamic encryption keys between the AP and each STA. On the contrary, only the MSDUs with same destination can be aggregated in a single frame, and they are encrypted by using the same dynamic encryption key.

1. **A-MSDU**

A-MSDU is formed by aggregating multiple MSDUs into a larger frame, with the original MSDUs becoming the subframe of the A-MSDU. If the MSDUs are Ethernet packets, each Ethernet headers are translated into 802.11 MAC headers, and an FCS is added at the end of the A-MSDU.

The A-MSDU technology reduces the number of MAC data frames, which in turn reduces the overhead of the MAC frame headers. This reduction in overhead also leads to a decrease in the overhead of the 802.11 physical layer preamble. As a result, A-MSDU improves the efficiency of data transmission by allowing more data to be sent in a single transmission, reducing the overall overhead and increasing throughput.

2. **A-MPDU**

Similarly, MPDU aggregation involves aggregating multiple 802.11 MPDUs to form an A-MPDU. The original MPDU becomes a subframe of the A-MPDU, and each subframe has a 4-octet delimiter at the front, and a padding of a 0 ~ 3 octets appended to make the subframe a multiple of 4 octets in length.

The PPDU is composed by an A-MPDU, a preamble and a header, instead of multiple preambles and headers for each MPDU. In this way, the overhead of the physical layer is reduced, contributing to improved channel utilization.

Figure 1.44 shows how a PPDU is constructed with multiple MSDUs, but not A-MSDUs. A MAC header and an FCS are added respectively to each MSDU to

Table 1.18 Maximum length of A-MSDU和A-MPDU

Wi-Fi standard	A-MSDU	A-MPDU
802.11n	Up to 3839 octets	Up to 65,535 octets
802.11ac	Up to 7935 octets	Up to 4,692,480 octets

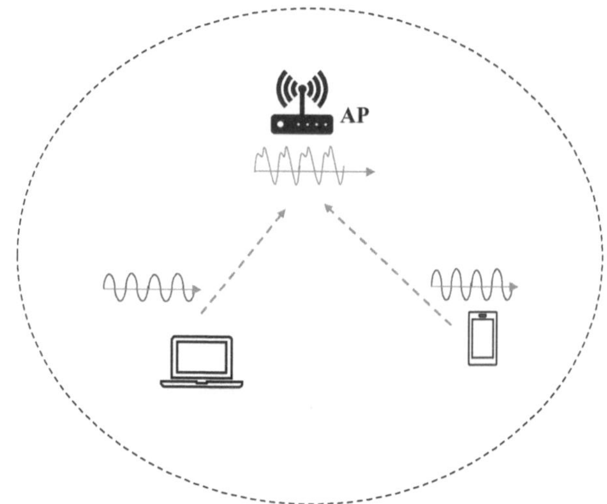

Fig. 1.45 Collision within a BSS

construct a MPDU, and then the MPDUs are aggregated into an A-MPDU with the delimiters in front of each MPDU. By adding a preamble and a header to the A-MPDU, a PPDU is constructed.

The maximum length of A-MSDU and A-MPDU defined by the 802.11n and 802.11ac standards is shown in Table 1.18. In practical Wi-Fi networks, the maximum length is influenced by the Wi-Fi chipsets used in both the transmitter and receiver devices, along with other practical considerations to maintain optimal network performance under varying environmental and application-specific conditions.

1.2.5 Wi-Fi Media Access Mechanism

In a Wi-Fi network, the AP and the STAs transfer the data over the shared wireless medium, which requires the devices to compete for the access to the wireless medium and then start transfer, so to avoid signal collision.

There are two situations in which Wi-Fi signal collision can occur in a Wi-Fi network:

- Collision within a BSS: In this scenario, the AP and the STAs within the same BSS share the wireless channel for data communication. As shown in Fig. 1.45,

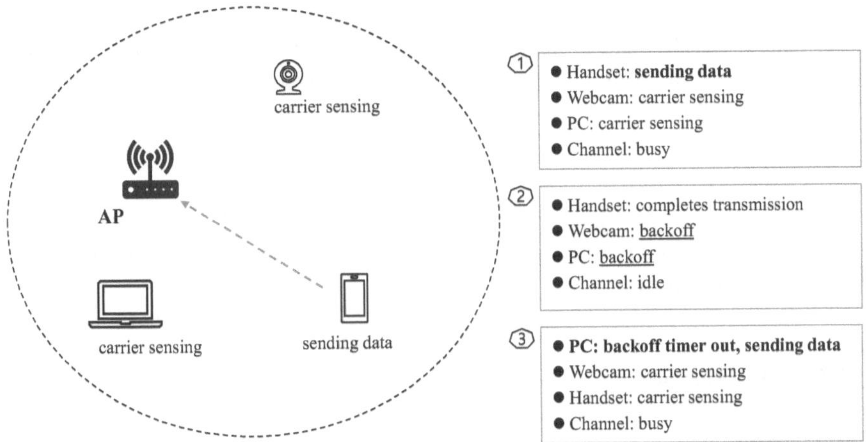

Fig. 1.46 An example of CSMA/CA

when two devices attempt to transmit data on this channel at the same time, the receiver is not able to resolve the superimposed signal, leading to a collision.

- Collision between adjacent BSSs: In the event that a BSS and an adjacent BSS operate on the same channel, collisions can occur if the devices in both BSSs attempt to send data at the same time.

In order to minimize the collisions among multiple STAs in shared wireless media, Wi-Fi defines Carrier Sensing Multiple Access/Collision Avoidance (CSMA/CA), that is, all the devices only send data over the Wi-Fi network when the channel is idle. The device shall listen to the channel and check the busy/idle state of the medium. If the channel is busy, the device defers the transmission. If the channel is idle, the device waits by a random backoff time to compete the access, and if no transmission is detected, it obtains the opportunity to send data to the wireless channel.

The CSMA/CA approach operates on the principle of "listen before talk" mode, which is an asynchronous transmission mechanism. In the example of Fig. 1.46, when the mobile phone sends data, both the webcam and computer are passively listening to the channel and waiting for the next idle window. When the mobile phone completes the transmission, the webcam and the computer then enter into a contention phase where they each wait for a random backoff period before attempting to gain access to the now-idle channel.

The CSMA/CA mechanism involves the following concepts which will be elaborated in the following:

- Carrier sense: Before sending data, the device listens to the wireless medium using the physical carrier sense or virtual carrier sense mechanism.
- Interframe space (IFS): This refers to the interval between the current frame and the subsequent frame.

- Backoff: When two or more devices sense that the channel is idle, each device begins a random backoff timer. The timer is reduced by one unit after each slot period. Once the backoff timer is reduced to zero and the channel remains still idle at that time, the device can transmit data, while the other devices once again enter carrier sensing mode. This backoff mechanism helps minimize collisions among multiple STAs.

The number of interframe spaces, backoff timer, and the duration of the current data transmission determine how long a Wi-Fi device can access the medium using CSMA/CA mechanism.

1.2.5.1 Carrier Sense

Wi-Fi devices determine whether the current channel is busy or idle by detecting the physical carrier and virtual carrier. If either is detected, the medium is regarded as busy.

1. **Physical Carrier Sensing**

The physical carrier sensing serves to detect the busy/idle status of a wireless channel through the physical layer, commonly known as Clear Channel Assessment (CCA). This process can be executed in two distinct manners:

- **CCA-Energy Detection (CCA-ED):** This method is employed to gauge the strength of non-Wi-Fi signals within the target frequency band. If the interference level from devices like Bluetooth headsets, microwave ovens, or any other equipment operating on the same channel surpasses a predefined threshold (which defaults to −62 dBm), the channel is classified as busy.
- **CCA-Packet Detection (CCA-PD):** This mechanism focuses specifically on detecting Wi-Fi interference. When the Wi-Fi preamble is recognized—such as when the L-STF (Long Short Training Field) and L-LTF (Long Training Field) fields are successfully parsed from the received signal—the device measures the intensity of the Wi-Fi signal to decide if the medium is occupied. The default threshold for packet detection is set at −82 dBm.

In both cases, should the energy level of either non-Wi-Fi or Wi-Fi signals exceed their respective thresholds, the wireless medium is considered busy. Conversely, if the energy levels fall below these thresholds, the medium is deemed idle.

2. **Virtual Carrier Sensing**

As the Physical carrier sensing is performed by the physical layer, the Virtual Carrier Sensing is handled by the MAC layer.

The device checks the receiving address of the MPDU. If the RA is not its own MAC address, it means the ongoing data transmission is intended for another device. Based on the duration subfield of the MPDU, the MAC layer sets a countdown timer known as Network Allocation Vector (NAV). When the device attempts to send

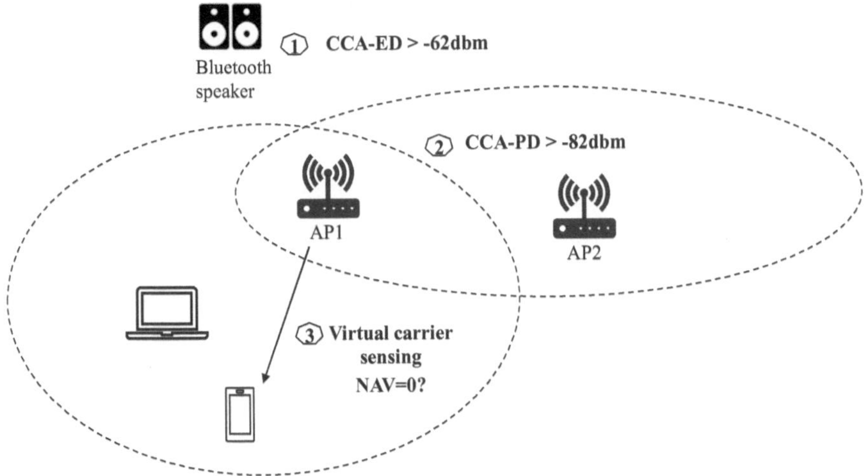

Fig. 1.47 Physical carrier sensing and virtual carrier sensing

data, it checks whether the NAV has reached zero. If it has, the medium is considered idle, otherwise, the medium is considered busy and the device must wait before attempting to send the data.

During the NAV countdown, the device can enter the doze state instead of continuously listening to the channel through CCA, so Virtual Carrier Sensing aids in conserving power consumption of the devices.

Figure 1.47 illustrates how the carrier sensing mechanism works. AP1 detects an interference from a Bluetooth speaker with a signal strength above -62dbm, and another interference from AP2 which signal strength is higher than -82dbm. Consequently, AP1 acknowledges the presence of another Wi-Fi device using the same channel and sets the NAV counter based on the duration of the MPDU sent by AP2. When AP1 attempts to send data, it first checks if NAV counts down to zero. If the NAV timer expires, AP1 can compete for access to the wireless medium.

1.2.5.2 Interframe Space

Interframe Space (IFS) [5] is the interval between the last symbol of the previous frame and the initial symbol of the subsequent frame in a Wi-Fi network. During this period, devices perform Carrier Sensing to determine the busy or idle state of the wireless medium.

To establish different types of IFS, the 802.11 standard defines the Slot Time, which represents a fixed duration that accounts for various factors such as propagation delay, MAC layer processing delay, carrier sensing interval, and the transition time between transmission and reception modes of the Wi-Fi transceiver.

There are two types of slot time value defined in the standard, namely 9 μs short slot time and 20 μs long slot time. It depends on the device capability of both the

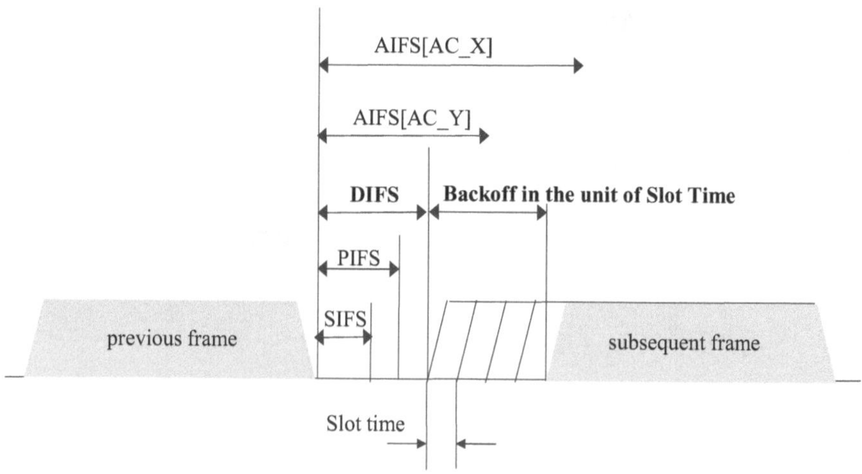

Fig. 1.48 Different interframe space

transmitter and the receiver to choose what slot time applies. The different interframe space in the 802.11 standard are illustrated in Fig. 1.48.

(1) **Short Interframe Space (SIFS)**: It is the shortest interframe interval between consecutive frames and is used for immediate responses in critical operations. It ensures that no other frame transmission can intervene between, for example, a data frame and its corresponding Acknowledgement (ACK) frame, or during the Request To Send (RTS) and Clear To Send (CTS) handshake process.

(2) **Priority Interframe Space (PIFS):** PIFS is utilized when higher-priority access to the wireless medium is required, such as during retransmissions within TXOP period if an STA doesn't receive an ACK or when APs broadcast frames to all STAs. The PIFS duration is slightly longer than SIFS by one Slot Time to allow some level of priority while still maintaining fairness.

$$\mathrm{PIFS} = \mathrm{SIFS} + 1 \times \mathrm{Slot\ Time}$$

(3) **Distributed Coordination Function Interframe Space (DIFS):** DIFS is the interframe space primarily used by Wi-Fi devices to determine whether the channel is idle before initiating a new transmission. When a device senses the medium as idle for a duration equal to DIFS and its backoff counter reaches zero, it can send non-QoS data, management, or control frames. DIFS is somewhat longer than SIFS, providing enough time for potential collisions to be detected and resolved.

$$\mathrm{DIFS} = \mathrm{SIFS} + 2 \times \mathrm{Slot\ Time}$$

(4) **Arbitration Interframe Space (AIFS):** In order to ensure that QoS data frames are handled in priority, the 802.11 protocol defines different AIFS accordingly.

Each Access Category (AC_X), which represents different QoS priorities, has a distinct AIFS value. Higher-priority QoS data frames have shorter AIFS values, thus they get faster access to the medium.

The AIFS value for each AC_X is calculated as SIFS plus a multiple of the Slot Time determined by the Arbitration Interframe Space Number (AIFSN) specific to that AC as indicated in Table 1.20. The minimum AIFS is equal to DIFS, ensuring that even the lowest priority QoS traffic adheres to a certain minimum delay before transmitting.

$$\text{AIFS}[\text{AC\_X}] = \text{SIFS} + \text{AIFSN}[\text{AC\_X}] \times \text{Slot Time}$$

(5) **Extended Interframe Space (EIFS):** EIFS is used when a device encounters a frame with a failed Frame Check Sequence (FCS), indicating that the received data frame was corrupted or damaged during transmission. In this scenario, instead of immediately contending for the channel after DIFS or AIFS, the receiving device remains silent for an EIFS interval to allow the transmitter to potentially retransmit the faulty frame.

If the wireless medium is idle at the end of EIFS, the device can then send the data frame directly without waiting for any existing NAV countdown to zero. The EIFS is calculated as follows:

$$\text{EIFS} = \text{SIFS} + \text{DIFS} + \text{time to transmit an ACK frame (for non-QoS data)}$$

or

$$\text{EIFS} = \text{SIFS} + \text{AIFS}[\text{AC\_X}] + \text{time to transmit an ACK frame (for QoS data)}$$

1.2.5.3 Random Backoff

The random backoff window is a dynamic quiet period that Wi-Fi devices utilize before attempting to transmit frames. Unlike IFS intervals which are fixed and determined by the type of frame being transmitted, the random backoff window varies among devices based on a randomly selected value.

The basic procedure of random backoff is described as below:

(1) When AP or a STA sense that the wireless channel has been idle for at least an IFS duration (e.g., DIFS), it selects a random number within a contention window (CW). This CW size initially starts small but can grow after each unsuccessful transmission attempt to reduce congestion and collisions.
(2) The STA then begins a countdown from this randomly chosen value. While counting down, the device continuously listens to the channel to ensure that it remains idle.
(3) If another Wi-Fi signal is detected during the countdown, the STA suspends its countdown immediately and waits until the medium becomes idle again. After

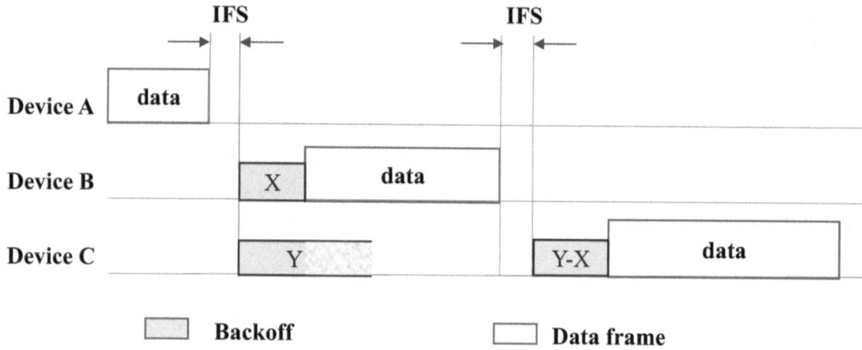

Fig. 1.49 Example of backoff mechanism

the channel clears, it waits for another IFS interval before restarting the countdown.

(4) Once the countdown reaches zero without any new transmissions occurring, the STA gains permission to send its own data frame.

This backoff mechanism ensures that multiple STAs competing for access to the shared medium do not transmit simultaneously, thereby reducing collision probability. Each STA's randomized backoff time contributes to the fair and efficient distribution of airtime among all contenders.

An example is shown in Fig. 1.49. Suppose Device A is currently transmitting a data frame, Devices B and C are also ready to transmit but must wait until Device A finishes and the channel becomes idle.

After Device A completes its transmission, both Devices B and C listen for an Interframe Space (IFS), indicating that the medium has been quiet long enough to attempt a transmission. They then each randomly select a backoff window duration—let's say Device B selects X microseconds and Device C selects Y microseconds, where Y > X.

When Device B countdown reaches zero first, and it still detects no other activity on the channel, Device B begins transmitting its data frame to the AP. During this period, Device C detects the transmission from Device B within its own backoff window, so it pauses its countdown to avoid collision.

Once Device B completes its transmission, the channel becomes idle again. At this point, Device C waits for another IFS interval, ensuring the channel is indeed clear. It then resumes its countdown, but not from the original Y value; rather, it subtracts the difference between Y and X (Y—X) because it already counted down by X microseconds before pausing. When Device C's adjusted countdown hits zero, it sends its data frame to the AP.

The range of the backoff timer value is referred to as the backoff window, which is represented in the unit of Slot Time to denote the size of the backoff window. When a device's random backoff window is small, it tends to gain channel access more readily; however, this also increases the likelihood that multiple devices will randomly select the same backoff time within the smaller window, thereby leading to a higher probability of collisions. On the contrary, when a device has a larger random backoff window, the chance of conflicting backoff times among multiple devices decreases, but this comes with the trade-off of potentially decreased throughput due to extended waiting periods for devices, causing performance degradation.

In order to balance the selection of backoff window sizes and to efficiently utilize wireless medium resources, the 802.11 standard defines a specific algorithm for choosing the random backoff window accordingly.

(1) **Contention Window (CW):**

The backoff window can be represented as the range [0, CW], within which a device randomly selects a value to serve as its initial backoff time.

(2) **Automatic Adjustment of the Contention Window:**

The device sends data frames after its backoff timer counts down to zero. However, if it doesn't receive the acknowledgment, it assumes that a collision has occurred, indicating that other devices were simultaneously transmitting on the same channel. Consequently, the contention window expands in a binary exponential manner; the device resets its initial backoff value within a doubled interval and restarts the countdown until the data is successfully transmitted.

Due to the exponential growth of the contention window size, there is a high probability that devices will randomly select large backoff windows, leading to extended waiting periods, which are not conducive to promptly acquiring channel resources and transmitting data.

Therefore, the 802.11 standard imposes the upper and lower limits on the contention window size, namely, Maximum Contention Window (CWmax), and Minimum Contention Window (CWmin), respectively, thus confining the range to [CWmin, CWmax].

The initial value of CW equals to Cwmin. Following a transmission failure due to collision, the contention window is reset to $CW = 2 \times CW + 1$, and $CW \leq CWmax$.

After a successful transmission, namely, the ACK frame is successfully received, CW is reset back to Cwmin, repeating this cycle.

An example is shown in Fig. 1.50. When a STA sends a video stream to an AP, the default range of CW is [7,15] (refer to the AC_VI entries in Table 1.20). Hence the initial value of CW is 7, corresponding to a random backoff window of [0,7]. Upon the first failed transmission and subsequent first retransmission attempt, the CW is reset as 15, resulting in a new backoff window of [0,15], with CW now at its maximum, CWmax. If the first retransmission also fails, and a second retransmission starts, the CW remains at its maximum of 15. Upon a successful retransmission, the CW is then reset back to 7.

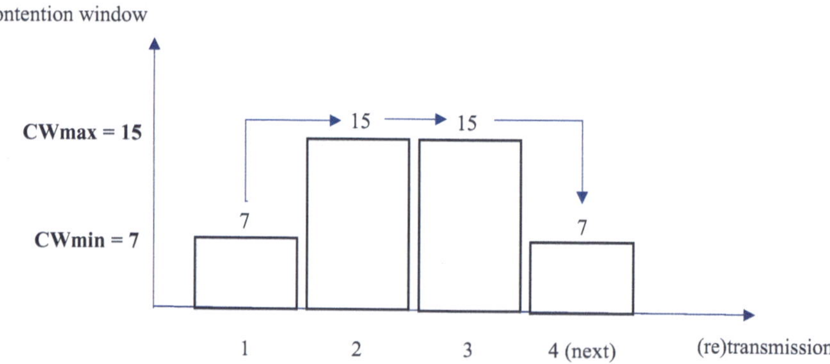

Fig. 1.50 Contention window

1.2.5.4 EDCA Parameters for QoS Data

To enhance the transmission quality of QoS data and ensure that latency sensitive QoS data, such as voice and video data, are prioritized for transmission, the 802.11 standard introduces an Enhanced Distributed Channel Access (EDCA) mechanism. This mechanism defines distinct wireless medium access parameters for different priority levels of QoS data, known as EDCA parameters, which QoS data uses to access wireless medium resources according to their respective interframe spaces, backoff windows, and other EDCA parameters.

As described in Table 1.16, the EDCA framework specifies four different Access Categories (ACs), namely, AC_BK, AC_BE, AC_VI, and AC_VO, each corresponding respectively to background data flows (BK), best-effort data flows (BE), video data flows (VI), and voice data flows (VO).

The EDCA parameters include the Arbitrated Interframe Space Number (AIFSN), Exponent form of CWmin (ECWmin), Exponent form of CWmax (ECWmax), and Transmission Opportunity Limit (TXOP Limit), which are described in Table 1.19.

The default EDCA parameters for 802.11b/g and 802.11n are shown in Table 1.20, from which it can be seen that higher priority QoS data is assigned EDCA parameters that are more conducive to gaining access to the channel.

1.2.5.5 An Example of the Backoff Mechanism

Figure 1.51 shows an example of multiple devices competing the medium with backoff mechanism. The procedure is as follows:

(1) **Multi-Device Backoff in the Presence of Collision**: When devices B, C, and D attempt to send data and detect that Device A is currently transmitting. Device B, C, and D set the NAV based on the Duration/ID field of the data frame sent by A. They continue monitoring the state of the wireless mediums. After Device A

Table 1.19 EDCA parameters

EDCA parameters	Number of bits	Description
Arbitrated Interframe Space Number (AIFSN)	8	The IFI of the QoS Data frame is an SIFS interval plus the number of slot time defined by AIFSN. The minimum AIFSN is 2
Exponent form of CWmin (ECWmin)	4	CWmin = (2ECWmin −1) CWmin is a non-negative integer, in the unit of Slot Time. When ECWmin is 0, CWmin is defined as 32,767
Exponent form of CWmax (ECWmax)	4	CWmax = (2ECWmax −1), CWmax is a non-negative integer, in the unit of Slot Time. When ECWmax is 0, CWmax is a defined as 32,767
Transmission Opportunity Limit (TXOP Limit)	16	The TXOP Limit refers to the duration of time that a device maintains continuous control over the wireless medium for data transmission, including both the transmission time for the device's data as well as the response time required by the receiving end The TXOP Limit is a non-negative integer measured in units of 32 μs. The data transmission shall not exceed the TXOP limit. When the TXOP limit of a QoS data queue is set to 0, the queue can send the fragmented PPDU frames within a TXOP after the queue obtains a TXOP.

Table 1.20 The default EDCA parameters for the QoS data frames

Access categories	ECWmin	ECWmax	AIFSN	TXOP limit	
				802.11b/g (non OFDM)	802.11n (OFDM)
AC_BK	aCWmin*	aCWmax*	7	0	0
AC_BE	aCWmin	aCWmax	3	0	0
AC_VI	(aCWmin +1)/2 -1	aCWmin	2	6.016 ms	3.008 ms
AC_VO	(aCWmin +1)/4 -1	(aCWmin +1)/2 -1	2	3.264 ms	1.504 ms

Note: *aCWmin and aCWmax are configurable, with default value 15 and 1023 respectively.

completes the frame transmission, Device B, C, and D wait for another DIFS interval, then start a random backoff timer and count down respectively.

(2) **Data Transmission During Idle Detection**: When the device's backoff timer expires and it detects that wireless medium is idle, it begins sending its data. At this point, devices B and D stop the countdown and reset the NAV according to the Duration/ID field of the data frame sent by C, restarting carrier sensing.

(3) **Re-backoff Timing Following a Collision**: After Device C completes the transmission, Devices B and D wait for another DIFS interval, then resume the backoff timer countdown. Now Device E also joins the competition for the

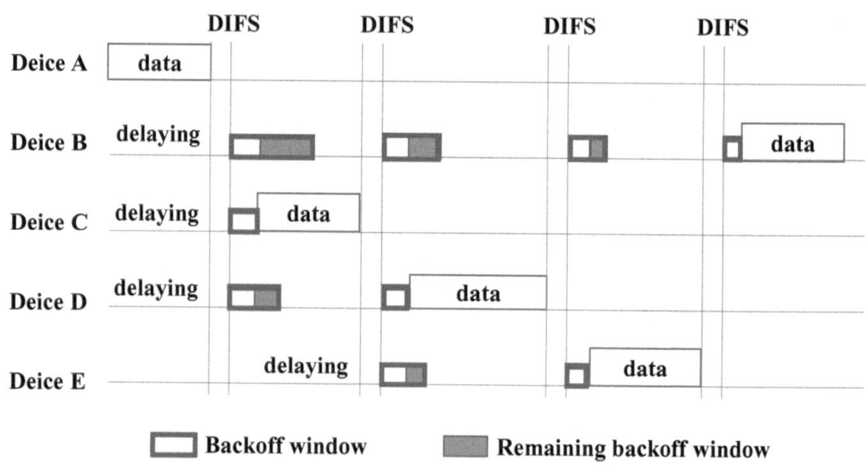

Fig. 1.51 An example of multiple devices competing the channel

wireless medium, and it sets a random backoff timer and starts the countdown as well.

(4) **Data Transmission Upon Further Idle Detection**: Device D countdowns to 0, and since the wireless medium is idle so it can send data frame immediately. Similarly, Device E and Device B send data after they successful obtain the access the channel via the backoff process.

1.2.6 Wi-Fi Network Discovery, Authentication, and Association

When a Wi-Fi device joins a BSS, that is, when the device establishes a connection with an AP, both parties must undergo network discovery, authentication, and association, and a four-way authentication frame exchange procedure. Conversely, when a device disconnects from the AP, it goes through a disassociation and deauthentication procedure.

1.2.6.1 Network Discovery

According to the 802.11 standard, devices must discover neighboring AP by employing either passive scanning or active scanning mode, as shown in Fig. 1.52.

The Passive Scan Mode This involves a device being in a listening state where it passively captures AP beacon frames. These beacon frames, periodically transmitted by APs, contain their capabilities and essential information such as maximum

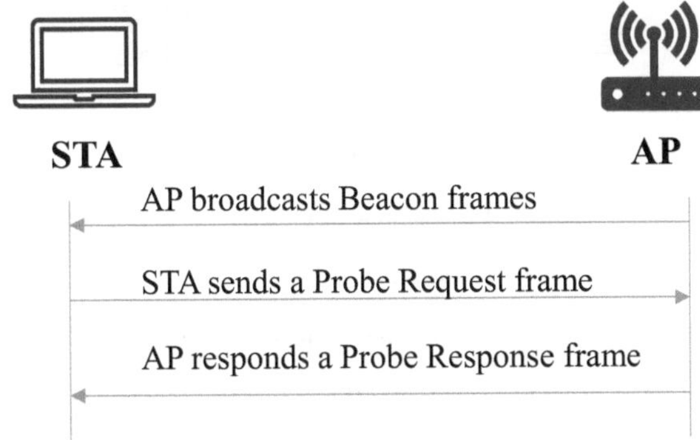

Fig. 1.52 Wi-Fi Network Discovery

supported bandwidth, highest data rates, and operating channels. When a device receives a beacon frame, it becomes aware of the presence of an AP.

The Active Scan Mode The STA sends a Probe Request frame which carries the SSID information of the intended AP. Upon receipt of a STA's Probe Request frame, the AP assesses whether the included SSID matches its own SSID. If the SSID matches, or the Probe Request frame carries a non-specified SSID, the AP sends a Probe Response on its operational channel.

Comparing with the passive scan mode, the active scan mode allows for faster detection of APs. Both the Probe Request and Response frames can be sent as unicast frames, targeting a specific recipient, or as broadcast frames, intended for all recipients within range.

1.2.6.2 Authentication

After a STA discovers an AP, it must complete a mutual connection process consisting of authentication, association, and a four-way frame exchange for encryption key negotiation, as shown in Fig. 1.53.

The authentication phase primarily involves the exchange of authentication information between both parties to prevent unauthorized devices from joining the network.

The association process focuses on the interchange of capability sets, wherein the AP assigns an identifier to the associated STA.

The four-way frame exchange processes are the handshake between the AP and the STA to negotiate a set of peer encryption keys, which will subsequently be used for encryption and decryption during the data transmission process.

The 802.11 defines three types of authentication methods: Open System authentication, Shared Key authentication and fast BSS transition authentication. The first two are used when a STA connects with an AP within a BSS, and the third is employed for switching connections between APs within an ESS.

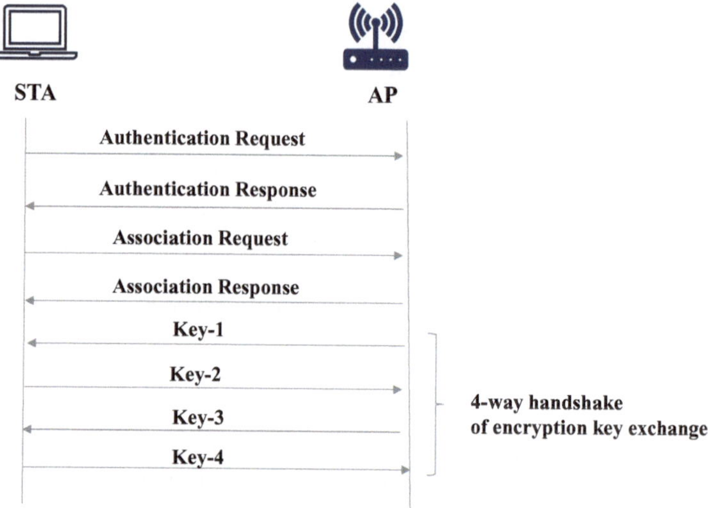

Fig. 1.53 Wi-Fi Network authentication, association, and 4-way handshake procedure

```
v IEEE 802.11 Wireless Management
  v Fixed parameters (6 bytes)
      Authentication Algorithm: Open System (0)
      Authentication SEQ: 0x0001
      Status code: Successful (0x0000)
```

Fig. 1.54 Authentication request frame format

```
v IEEE 802.11 Wireless Management
  v Fixed parameters (6 bytes)
      Authentication Algorithm: Open System (0)
      Authentication SEQ: 0x0002
      Status code: Successful (0x0000)
```

Fig. 1.55 Authentication response frame format

When a STA sends an Authentication Request frame to the AP, upon receiving this request, the AP responds with an Authentication Response frame, which includes a status field set to "successful" if it's a valid 802.11 connection. An example of the Authentication Request and Response frames of the Open System Authentication is shown in Figs. 1.54 and 1.55.

- **Authentication Request**: The authentication mode is Open System, the authentication sequence number is 0x0001, and the status is successful.

- **Authentication Response:** The authentication method is also the open system mode, and the sequence number increases by 1 on top of the sequence number of the Authentication Request.

1.2.6.3 Association

The association process primarily involves the exchange of capability information between the AP and the STA. Upon successful completion of this connection, both parties adjust parameters such as transmission rates, number of spatial streams, and other settings based on each other's supported capabilities to facilitate data reception and transmission.

Upon a successful authentication, the STA sends an Association Request frame to the AP. This frame contains information defined by 802.11 standards, which includes the supported data rates of the STA, maximum aggregation levels for A-MSDU and A-MPDU frames, MIMO capability, as well as the listen interval used for receiving buffered data in power saving mode.

Upon receiving the Association Request from the STA, the AP responds with an Association Response frame. This frame contains status code indicating whether the association was successful, along with the AP's supported data rates, its own maximum aggregation levels for A-MSDU and A-MPDU frames, MIMO capability, and the Association ID assigned by the AP to the STA.

1.2.6.4 The Four-Way Encryption Key Exchange Process

The key exchange process is primarily used for both the sending and receiving parties to negotiate a set of keying information based on specific key algorithms, which are then utilized during communication to encrypt and decrypt data transmitted over the channel. The purpose of this process is to prevent the Wi-Fi communication from the eavesdropping and ensure the security and privacy of user data.

In a home Wi-Fi network, before connecting to an AP, users are required to enter the password matching the SSID credential of the AP. During the encryption key exchange process, AP and STA first negotiate a shared key based on the password of the AP, then each append their own generated random numbers and send it to the other to generate a unique set of temporary authentication keys. The details of the four-way handshake for encryption key exchange will be covered in Chap. 3.

1.2.6.5 Disconnect

As illustrated in Fig. 1.56, the STA disconnects from the AP by undergoing the disassociation and the deauthentication process between itself and the AP. Afterwards, the STA can discover a new AP and subsequently go through

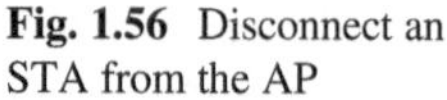

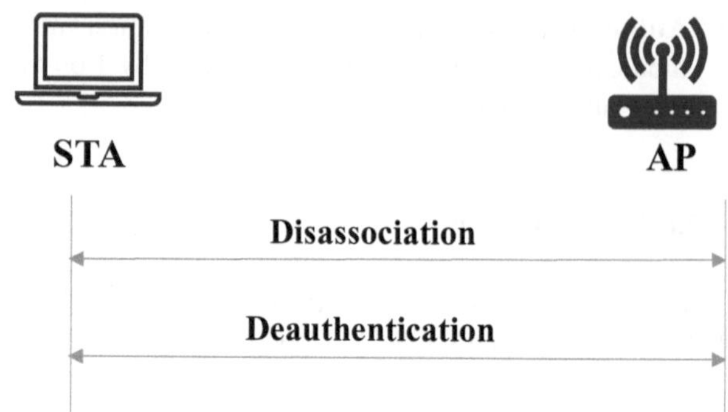

Fig. 1.56 Disconnect an STA from the AP

authentication, association, and key exchange procedure to set up the connection with the newly found AP.

1.2.7 Power Saving Mode Supported by Wi-Fi

APs are typically powered by a power source, whereas STAs may be battery powered. For example, the video surveillance cameras, and VR/AR headsets, etc. With limited energy in the battery, STAs often enter power-saving modes to conserve power. The power management mechanism in Wi-Fi power-saving mode refers to the process where an AP temporarily catches data for a STA that is in a power-saving state, and the STA periodically wakes up to retrieve this buffered data.

To support this management mechanism, message exchanges between the AP and STA are required. Specifically, the AP communicates the status of data buffering in its beacon frames to the STA, while the STA sends query messages to fetch cached data from the AP. Simultaneously, the STA needs to maintain time synchronization with the AP, ensuring it can periodically wake up from its doze state to receive the AP's beacon frames.

As illustrated in Fig. 1.57, the Wi-Fi power-saving mode encompasses several key technical aspects:

(1) **Network Timing synchronization:** The STA periodically receives beacon frames sent by AP to synchronize the timing between the STA and the AP, thereby wakes up at the negotiated time in order to receive the buffered data.
(2) **STA retrieving Buffered Data:** The STA checks whether there is any buffered data based on the status information carried within the beacon frames, and if there is, then it sends a query message to obtain the buffered data promptly from the AP.
(3) **Power-saving mode management**: STA need to maintain the awake mode and the power-saving mode and informs the AP of the current mode in time.

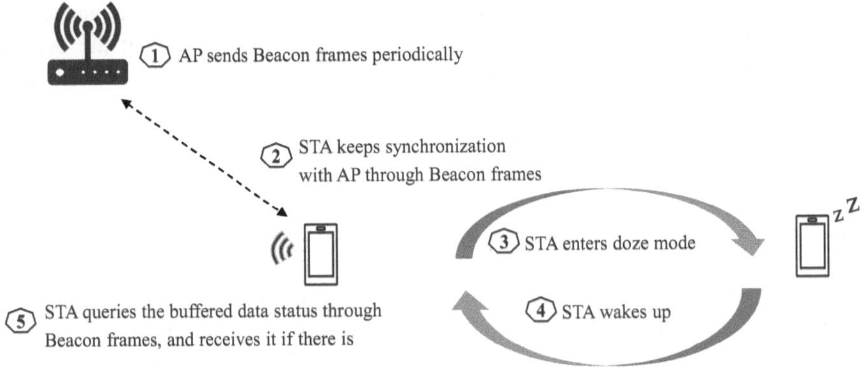

Fig. 1.57 Wi-Fi power saving mode

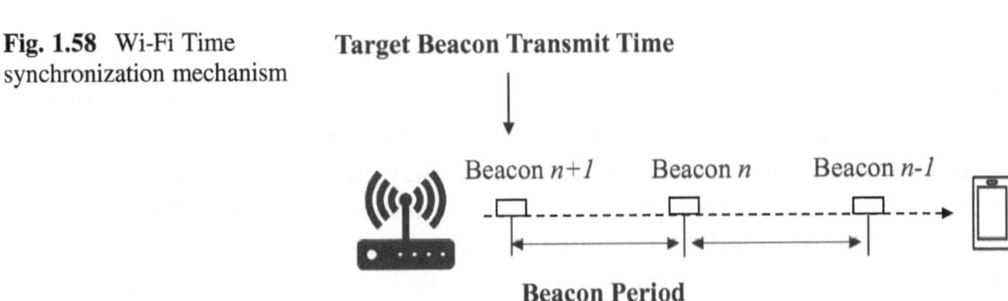

Fig. 1.58 Wi-Fi Time synchronization mechanism

1.2.7.1 Timing Synchronization Mechanism

The 802.11 standard stipulates that STA must periodically receive and synchronize its time with the beacon frames transmitted by AP so as to ensure the consistency of time across all devices in the same BSS network. There are two relevant terms in the context: the beacon interval and the Target Beacon Transmit Time (TBTT).

As shown in Fig. 1.58, the beacon interval refers to the period between the consecutive beacon frames being sent out. Within the Timing Synchronization Function (TSF) field of the Beacon frame, the time is defined as when the first data symbol is sent by the antenna.

To ensure that the TSF value is accurate, the AP calibrates the delay on the transmission path, such as the delay from the MAC layer to PHY layer. This calibration process ensures that the timing synchronization is precise among all STAs within the BSS.

The Target Beacon Transmit Time (TBTT) refers to the specific moment which the beacon frame is scheduled for transmission. The APs must prioritize the beacon frame over other frames, ensuring that the beacon frame is transmitted at each predetermined TBTT. Despite potential delays caused by the shared Wi-Fi wireless medium and network congestion, the subsequent beacon frame shall be sent at its planned TBTT.

To successfully receive the beacon frames, the STA wakes up in advance and waits for the beacon frame at the designated TBTT. Upon receiving the beacon frame, the STA synchronizes its time based on the information within and calculates the subsequent TBTT. If STA detects no indication of buffered data in the beacon frame, it will return to a low-power doze state until the next TBTT.

1.2.7.2 Traffic Indication Map

When a STA enters power-saving mode, the AP temporarily buffers the data for it until the STA wakes up and queries the data. Nevertheless, the buffer capacity is limited, so if the buffered data exceeds the buffer size, the subsequent incoming data will be discarded.

As shown in Fig. 1.59, 802.11 defines Traffic Indication Map (TIM) and Delivery Traffic Indication Map (DTIM), which are used respectively to indicate the status of buffered unicast data and multicast data. The buffered unicast data refers to that with a specific STA receiving address, while buffered multicast data refers to multicast data or broadcast data packets addressed to a multicast address.

In practice, TIM informs STAs whether they have buffered unicast frames waiting at the AP, whereas DTIM serves as an announcement to all power-saving STAs that there is multicast or broadcast data awaiting them when they wake up. This way, STAs can efficiently manage their wake-up periods and retrieve their data without missing out due to buffer overflow.

1. **Traffic Indication Map (TIM)**

Figure 1.59 shows that the Traffic Indication Map field which appears in every beacon frame sent by the AP, indicates whether there are buffered unicast data packets for the STAs.

TIM contains the subfields such as the length, DTIM count, period, and Partial Virtual Bitmap. Each bit in the Partial Virtual Bitmap corresponds to the buffered state of an STA, represented by the STA's Association ID. If a bit is 1, it signifies that the AP has unicast buffered data for the STA. As the example shown in Fig. 1.60, the Partial Virtual Bitmap is $0x04 = 2^2$, which means the AP has buffered message for the STA with AID = 0x02 in power-saving mode.

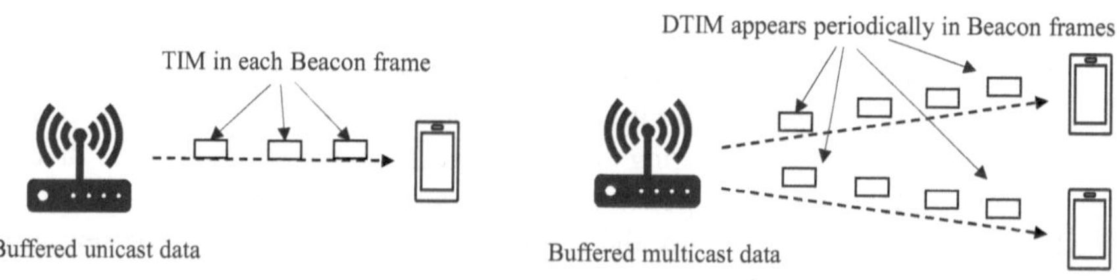

Fig. 1.59 Traffic indication map of unicast and multicast data

```
∨ Tag: Traffic Indication Map (TIM): DTIM 1 of 0 bitmap
    Tag Number: Traffic Indication Map (TIM) (5)
    Tag length: 4
    DTIM count: 1
    DTIM period: 3
  ∨ Bitmap control: 0x00
      .... ...0 = Multicast: False
      0000 000. = Bitmap Offset: 0x00
    Partial Virtual Bitmap: 04
    Association ID: 0x02
```

Fig. 1.60 Example of TIM field

```
∨ Tag: Traffic Indication Map (TIM): DTIM 0 of 1 bitmap
    Tag Number: Traffic Indication Map (TIM) (5)
    Tag length: 4
    DTIM count: 0
    DTIM period: 3
  ∨ Bitmap control: 0x01
      .... ...1 = Multicast: True
      0000 000. = Bitmap Offset: 0x00
    Partial Virtual Bitmap: 04
    Association ID: 0x02
```

Fig. 1.61 Example of DTIM field

2. **Delivery Traffic Indication Map (DTIM)**

The DTIM is a special type of TIM. In addition to the Partial Virtual Bitmap to indicate the buffered status for each individual STA, it has another bit to indicate whether there is a buffered multicast data available.

While the regular TIM is included in every Beacon frame, the DTIM appears periodically in beacon frames, as indicated by the DTIM count and DTIM period subfields when it appears.

As shown in Fig. 1.61, the DTIM count field is 0, indicating that it is a DTIM; The DTIM period is 3, which means that the next DTIM is to be sent in 3 beacon periods.

If the AP has buffered both multicast and unicast data, the AP prioritizes buffered multicast data. The buffered unicast data must wait until the multicast data transmission is completed. This prioritization ensures that multicast traffic, which is typically intended for multiple recipients, is delivered without delay, while unicast traffic, which is specific to individual clients, may experience a slight delay if there is multicast data being transmitted.

Before a STA joins a BSS, it listens to the Beacon frames or Probe response frame in order to obtain the Beacon Period and DTIM Period. It also sets the listen interval to inform the AP how often it receives beacon frames.

DTIM period = Beacon Period × DTIM period configured by the AP
Listen interval = Beacon Period × number in the Association Request from the STA

When the STA is idle, it does not need to listen and receive beacons at every TBTT, but only receive beacons at its own listen interval. It checks whether there is buffered data through the TIM or DTIM fields of the beacon frames. If there is buffered data, it follows the procedure of receiving buffered data. If not, the STA continues to doze and waits for the next listen interval. By this power-saving management, the STA achieves the energy efficiency.

The AP decides the timeout of buffered data according to the listen interval of each STA. If the buffered data has not been sent to the STA after the timeout period, the AP can discard buffered data.

1.2.7.3 Power-Saving Mode Management

The power consumption is critical concern for the mobile devices such as smart phones, tablets, and video cameras. How to manage the operation mode effectively, or more specifically, how to send and receive Wi-Fi data when these devices are in power-saving mode, constitutes an essential aspect of the Wi-Fi standard. Subsequently, we will delve into the power-saving management procedure.

1. **The Operation States and Power Mode**

According to the 802.11 standard, STAs operate in two primary states: Awake and Doze, which correspond respectively to the Active mode and Power Save (PS) mode for power management purposes. The relationship between these operation states and power modes is detailed in Table 1.21. The STA reports its current operating state to the AP through the power management field within either data frame or management frame.

When an STA reports "active mode" to the AP, it indicates that the STA is ready and able to receive data. The AP can then transmit data directly to the STA, with the understanding that the STA remains awake for this purpose.

However, when an STA reports "power-saving mode" to the AP, the AP cannot send data directly to the STA. At this point, the STA may alternate between being awake and in a doze state automatically. If the STA is awake during its power-saving mode, it can proactively query the AP for any buffered data and subsequently receive it. Conversely, if the STA is in the doze state, it will not actively receive any data as it conserves energy by suspending its wireless communication activities, as shown in Fig. 1.62.

Table 1.21 Power mode and operation mode

Power mode	Operation state
Active	Awake
Power saving	Awake or doze

Fig. 1.62 Comparison of STA operation modes

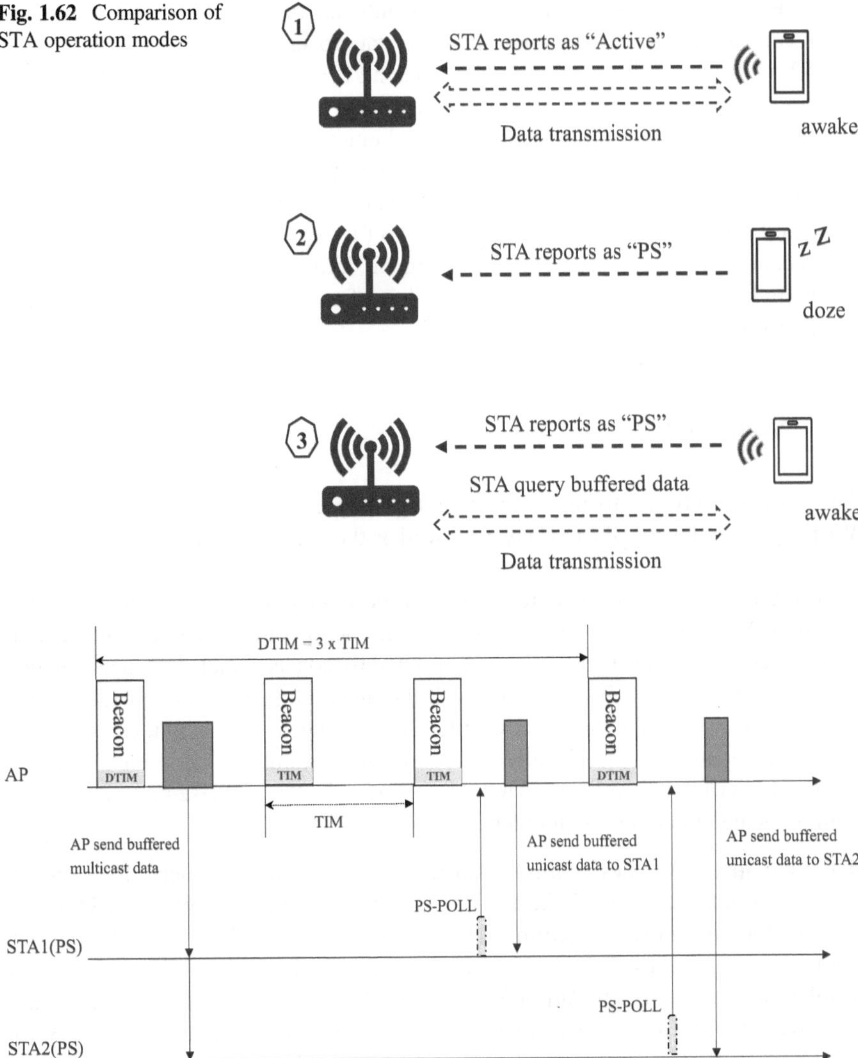

Fig. 1.63 STA obtain buffered data from AP

2. **Example of STA Query for Buffered Data**

Figure 1.63 gives an example of how the AP and the STAs handled the buffered unicast and multicast data, where DTIM is assumed to be equal to 3 TIM periods.

(1) STA1 and STA2 are both in power-saving mode and wake up before the TBTT. They receive the beacon frame, where DTIM Partial Virtual Bitmap indicates that the AP has buffered multicast frames but no buffered unicast frames for either of them.

(2) Both STA1 and STA2 remain awake until all buffered multicast frames are received once done, they enter the doze state to save energy.
(3) STA1 wakes up at the TBTT of the second beacon frame, receives the beacon frame, and discovers that its corresponding bit in Partial Virtual Bitmap is set in the TIM field, indicating there's buffered unicast data for it. In response, STA1 sends a PS-POLL frame to request the buffered data. Upon receiving the PS-POLL frame, the AP sends the unicast data frames to STA1.
(4) Similarly, STA2 wakes up at the next TBTT, receives the beacon frame of the second DTIM, finds its corresponding bit indicator is set, and subsequently completes the querying and transmission of unicast data in the same manner as STA1.

1.3 Summary

This chapter delves into the fundamental principles and the key technologies of Wi-Fi Physical layer and MAC layer, as well as the Wi-Fi standards predating Wi-Fi 6.

These concepts form the core foundation necessary for understanding the more advanced Wi-Fi 6 and Wi-Fi 7 technologies in the upcoming chapters. The continuous success of Wi-Fi standards is underpinned by consistent advancements on both the physical and MAC layers, along with the inherent backward compatibility that ensures new Wi-Fi standards can seamlessly integrate with legacy devices.

This compatibility significantly streamlines the commercial adoption process for the newer Wi-Fi standards, allowing APs/STAs adhering to these new standards to communicate effectively with older devices.

The Principle of Wi-Fi Communication A Wi-Fi network is essentially a wireless network composed of Wi-Fi Access Points (APs) and multiple Stations (STAs), all sharing the unlicensed spectrum. The establishment of Wi-Fi connections and communication relies on the premise that individual devices gain access to the wireless medium through Carrier Sense Multiple Access with Collision Avoidance (CSMA/CA). The definition and interaction of management frames within the Wi-Fi MAC protocol stack are primarily based on this mechanism, and the performance and efficiency of Wi-Fi communications are closely tied to how these devices compete for access to the wireless medium.

Key Technologies of the Physical Layer To begin with, a fundamental understanding of the standard definitions for spectrum and channels is crucial, as these are the prerequisite conditions and central concepts underpinning Wi-Fi communications. Subsequently, in order to continually enhance performance on the Wi-Fi physical layer, 802.11 standards have introduced Quadrature Amplitude Modulation (QAM) technology for modulation techniques, Orthogonal Frequency Division Multiplexing (OFDM) for channel modulation and multiplexing, and Multi-Input Multi-Output (MIMO) technology that supports multiple antennas. In the subsequent on Wi-Fi 6 and Wi-Fi 7 technologies, it will be evident that the specifications for QAM, OFDM, and MIMO will continue to evolve and play an increasingly significant role in boosting the performance of newer Wi-Fi advancements.

Key Technologies of the MAC Layer The management frame, control frame, and data frame are defined to streamline the management and communication processes between Wi-Fi APs and STAs. Wi-Fi devices leverage management frames like Beacon, Probe Request /Response, Association Request/Response, Authentication Request/Response, and Action frames to accomplish network discovery, authentication, and association. Control frames such as RTS/CTS, acknowledge frame, Power Saving Poll, are employed to enable AP/STA to acquire control over the wireless medium and data communications effectively. The MAC layer defines EDCA for different access categories of data frames, allowing for the application of various backoff parameters, including Interframe Space, to manage Quality of Service (QoS) efficiently.

This chapter concludes with an introduction to the concept of time synchronization in Wi-Fi networks and power-saving mode management mechanism. These concepts serve as instructive insights for Wi-Fi developers during product design and testing phases.

References

1. University of Hawai'i College of Engineering. ALOHAnet. Retrieved from https://www.eng.hawaii.edu/about/history/alohanet/. Accessed 6 Aug 2024
2. Fall Joint Computer Conference (1970) The ALOHA System—Another alternative for computer communications
3. Radio Regulations (2020) Retrieved from https://www.itu.int/en/publications/ITU-R/pages/publications.aspx?parent=R-REG-RR-2020&media=electronic
4. Wi-Fi Alliance. https://www.wi-fi.org/certification. Accessed 6 Aug 2024
5. IEEE (2020) IEEE Standard for Information Technology—Telecommunications and Information Exchange between Systems – Local and Metropolitan Area Networks—Specific Requirements – Part 11: Wireless LAN Medium Access Control (MAC) and Physical Layer (PHY) Specifications (Revision of IEEE Std 802.11-2016). IEEE Std 802.11-2020. pp. 1–4379. doi: https://doi.org/10.1109/IEEESTD.2021.9363693
6. Ho QD, Tweed D, Le-Ngoc T (2017) Long Term Evolution in Unlicensed Bands [Internet]. SpringerBriefs in Electrical and Computer Engineering. Springer International Publishing; 2017. Available from: https://doi.org/10.1007/978-3-319-47346-8
7. ETSI EN 301 893 V1.8.1 (2015) Broadband radio access networks (BRAN); 5 GHz high performance RLAN; Harmonized EN covering the essential requirements of article 3.2 of the R&TTE Directive. European Telecommunications Standards Institute Std., 2015

Chapter 2
Wi-Fi 6 Technology Bringing High Efficiency

Abstract A vast array of new Wi-Fi devices emerges every year, facilitating short-range wireless communication, entertainment, online education, home office work, and smart home applications. However, the congestion in the 2.4 GHz and 5 GHz bands is becoming increasingly evident due to the limited number of available Wi-Fi channels. When numerous Wi-Fi devices compete for these scarce channel resources, collisions occur, severely degrading network performance and compromising the user experience. The Wi-Fi 6 standard, officially ratified in 2019, specifically aims to enhance performance and improve service quality, with a primary focus on addressing the challenges posed by high-density environments. Through this chapter, readers will gain insights into the evolutionary advancements in the Wi-Fi 6 Physical Layer and Medium Access Control specification, uncovering how this technology effectively enables a higher number of concurrent connections and sustains optimal performance levels in densely populated scenarios. This exploration encompasses the pivotal Wi-Fi 6 innovations, detailed new changes in the Wi-Fi 6 specification, and the introduction of support for the 6 GHz spectrum, which is known as Wi-Fi 6E.

2.1 Wi-Fi 6 Technology Overview

Wi-Fi devices gain access to the wireless medium through Carrier Sensing Multiple Access/Collision Avoidance (CSMA/CA). When a Wi-Fi device acquires the wireless medium and starts data transmission, other devices must wait and can only compete for media access when the channel is free again. If there are multiple Wi-Fi devices in the BSS, there can be significant network congestion and transmission delays due to the traditional CSMA/CA mechanism.

The Wi-Fi standards prior to Wi-Fi 6 primarily concentrated on boosting the data transmission rate between an AP and a single STA; however, with Wi-Fi 6, the standards pivot to address not only the performance of individual devices but also holistic network efficiency. Wi-Fi 6 technology corresponds to the IEEE 802.11ax standard, which is known as High Efficiency (HE). The name indicates that the essence of the Wi-Fi 6 standard lies in enhancing spectrum efficiency, which is

G. Cheng et al., *Wi-Fi 7*, https://doi.org/10.1007/978-981-97-9026-5_2

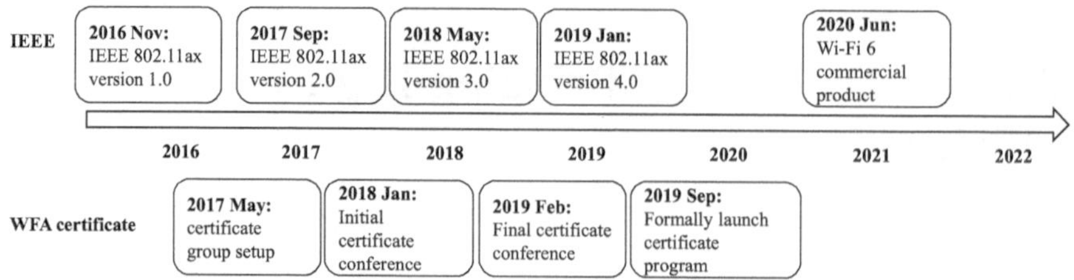

Fig. 2.1 Wi-Fi 6 history for IEEE standard and Wi-Fi Alliance certificate

distinct from the Wi-Fi 5 (802.11ac), which focused on Very High Throughput, and from Wi-Fi 7 (802.11be), which emphasizes on Extremely High Throughput.

Figure 2.1 shows the timeline of the standard definition of IEEE 802.11ax and Wi-Fi Alliance certification standard for Wi-Fi 6.

In March 2013, IEEE established the 802.11ax working group and kicked off research and definition. In November 2016, IEEE released version 1.0 of the 802.11ax standard, and then, in January 2019, ratified version 4.0 as the final version of the Wi-Fi 6 standard.

In May 2017, Wi-Fi Alliance established the Wi-Fi 6 certification test team, which began certifying Wi-Fi 6 products in September 2019. Since 2020, Wi-Fi 6 devices have boomed in the market as the new generation of Wi-Fi products.

In 2020, the Wi-Fi Alliance announced Wi-Fi 6E, which extends Wi-Fi 6 technology from the 2.4 GHz and 5 GHz bands to the 6 GHz band. **E** stands for Extended. Accordingly, new Wi-Fi 6E APs and STAs can support up to three frequency bands.

In April 2020, the Federal Communications Commission (FCC) took the lead in opening up 1200 MHz of the 6 GHz band for 802.11ax-and-up Wi-Fi devices. The European Conference of Postal and Telecommunications Administrations (CEPT) followed the FCC by announcing that 480 MHz of the lower 6 GHz band is allocated for Wi-Fi in European Union member states. Subsequently, more than 30 countries, such as Canada, Brazil, South Korea, and the United Arab Emirates, also announced that they would open the 6 GHz band for Wi-Fi 6E, while the other countries or regions are assessing whether to reserve the 6 GHz band as a licensed band for the evolution of cellular communication or as an unlicensed band for Wi-Fi communications.

2.1.1 Limitations of Legacy Wi-Fi Technology

In the last decade, with the widespread adoption of smartphones and smart homes, coupled with a strong demand for home offices, the number of Wi-Fi devices per household has been increasing rapidly year over year. As illustrated in Fig. 2.2, there are numerous types of Wi-Fi devices in a Wi-Fi network, such as tablets, smartphones, network printers, webcams, smart TVs, smart speakers, smart

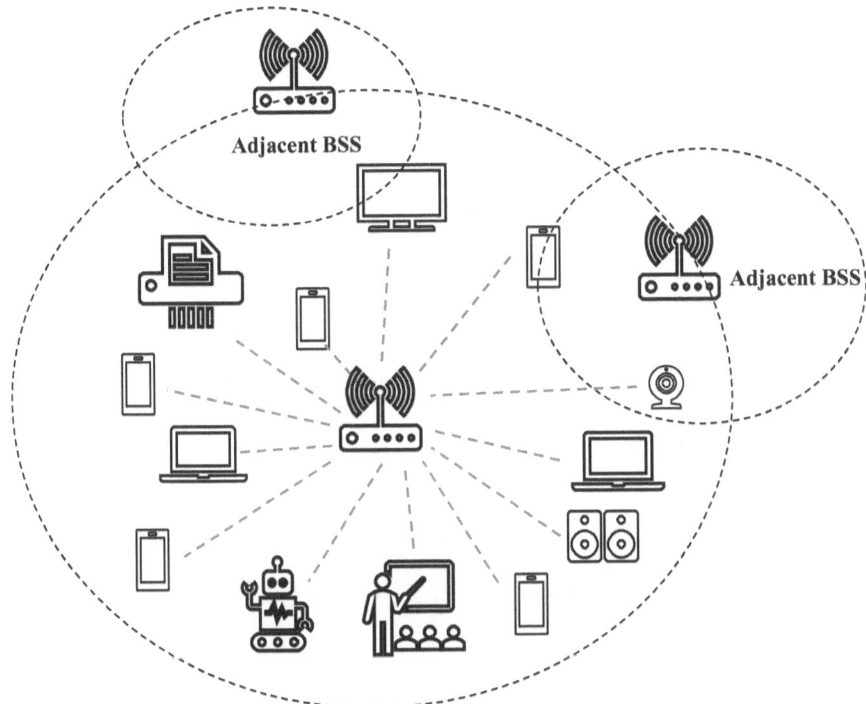

Fig. 2.2 High density of Wi-Fi connection

doorbells, VR/AR glasses, etc. These devices have a wide range of requirements for data transmission. Video-streaming devices demand high-speed real-time transmission, whereas for smart home devices, the data rate is relatively low but power efficiency is crucial. The Wi-Fi 6 standard offers the technologies to facilitate such high-density Wi-Fi networks and improve performance to meet these varying needs.

The Wi-Fi hotspot has become a popular public service in urban areas, particularly at locations like airports and stadiums, as well as for small-medium enterprises like coffee shops. People often connect their smartphones to Wi-Fi hotspots to take advantage of the low-cost, high-performance connection for web browsing, audio and video entertainment, and video calls. However, the increasingly frequent Wi-Fi connections and heavy traffic pose challenges to Wi-Fi networks. As many people may have observed, even when the Wi-Fi signal displayed on the phone indicates a good connection, they might experience intermittent disconnections, video buffering, or slow data speeds.

As illustrated in the lab simulation results in Fig. 2.3, the actual Wi-Fi throughput diminishes as the number of connected Wi-Fi terminals increases.

With 5 Wi-Fi stations connected to an AP, the downlink rate reaches 300 Mbps, while the uplink rate is at 280 Mbps. However, as the number of stations reaches 30, the performance decreases significantly, with the downlink rate falling by more than 15% and the uplink rate dropping by over 70%. Furthermore, if the number of

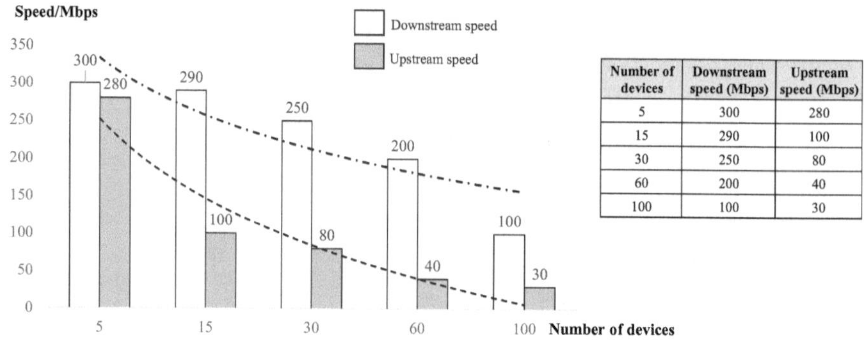

Number of devices	Downstream speed (Mbps)	Upstream speed (Mbps)
5	300	280
15	290	100
30	250	80
60	200	40
100	100	30

Fig. 2.3 Throughput decreases with more Wi-Fi stations connected

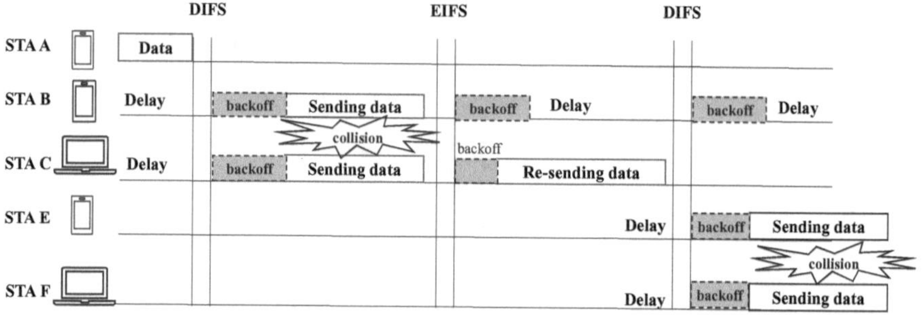

Fig. 2.4 Collision for Wi-Fi device in the random back-off time

devices increases to 60 and even 100, the performance deterioration becomes even more pronounced.

In summary, the higher the number of connected Wi-Fi stations, the lower the overall throughput.

The root cause lies in the CSMA/CA mechanism, which was introduced in Chap. 1. Both the AP and the STAs listen to the wireless medium before transmitting data to avoid collisions. If the channel is occupied, the transmitter waits until the current transmission is over; once the channel is idle, the transmitter waits for a specified interframe interval and a randomly generated backoff time. If the medium remains idle during this period, data transmission commences.

The random backoff mechanism allows devices to independently set their backoff times. When there are only a few Wi-Fi devices present, the likelihood of different devices selecting the same backoff time is low. However, as the number of Wi-Fi devices increases, the probability of choosing identical backoff times rises, leading to a higher frequency of collisions as the devices attempt to send data. This, in turn, causes significant degradation in throughput.

Figure 2.4 illustrates an example of a collision that occurred due to the random selection of the same backoff timer by chance.

(1) When STA B and STA C are about to send data to the AP, they listen to the channel and sense that STA A is sending data.
(2) STA B and STA C wait until STA A completes its data transmission.
(3) Following the conclusion of STA A's data transmission, STA B and STA C wait for a DIFS interval. Subsequently, both stations select a random backoff timer, but coincidentally, they end up choosing the same backoff duration.
(4) Once the backoff counters expire, STA B and STA C simultaneously send packets to the AP, resulting in signal interference. The AP is unable to demodulate and decode the corrupted signal, consequently failing to send an ACK back to STA B and STA C.
(5) As a result, STA B and STA C must wait for an EIFS interval before selecting a new backoff timer. They will attempt to send the packets after the backoff counter clears again.
(6) STA C's timer expires first, allowing it to complete the data retransmission and receive the ACK. STA B detects the wireless medium is busy after its timer expires, so it must wait until the current transmission is over. Meanwhile, STA E and STA F also have data to transmit but must wait for the medium to become available.
(7) Following a DIFS interval, STA B, E, and F initiate their random timers to compete for the channel. However, STA E and STA F coincidentally select the same timer, resulting in interference between their data frames and a failed transmission.

In this example, STA B and STA C select the same backoff window, resulting in data conflicts. During this period, the wireless medium remains unutilized, leading to a decrease in throughput. Similarly, STA E and STA F set the same backoff window. The higher the number of devices at a Wi-Fi BSS, the greater the chances of collisions.

To enhance Wi-Fi performance in high-density scenarios, Wi-Fi 6 introduces an improved wireless medium access mechanism as part of the new Wi-Fi standard.

2.1.2 Wi-Fi 6 New Characteristics

The Wi-Fi 6 standard aims to improve spectrum utilization and Wi-Fi performance in high-density scenarios. Wi-Fi 6 is characterized by high rate, high concurrency, low latency, and low power consumption.

(1) **High rate**

Wi-Fi 6 supports a higher-order modulation of 1024-QAM, where each symbol represents 10 bits, that is, $2^{10} = 1024$. Thanks to 1024-QAM modulation and other bandwidth-boosting technologies, Wi-Fi 6 can reach a maximum physical rate of 9.6 Gbps, representing a 39% increase compared to Wi-Fi 5.

(2) **High concurrency**

Before Wi-Fi 6, devices accessed the channel exclusively, meaning that at any given moment, when a device transmitted data, it occupied the entire channel, preventing other devices from sharing it.

Wi-Fi 6, however, splits the channel in the spectrum into subcarriers, which can be grouped into resource units (RUs) of different sizes. This allows Wi-Fi devices to transmit data simultaneously within their allocated RUs. This new technology, known as Orthogonal Frequency Division Multiple Access (OFDMA), significantly enhances spectrum utilization.

(3) **Low latency**

With its enhanced physical rate capability and support for concurrent transmissions, Wi-Fi 6 reduces both transmission time and delays. In addition, Wi-Fi 6 introduces Spatial Reuse (SR) technology and BSS coloring, which are designed for scenarios with Overlapping Basic Service Sets (OBSS). This technology enables APs and STAs within overlapping BSSs to discern interference from their own BSS or neighboring BSS, thereby allowing them to transmit efficiently without impacting other BSSs. The implementation of BSS Coloring significantly reduces data transmission delays in environments with a high density of deployed APs.

(4) **Low power consumption**

Wi-Fi 6 defines Target Wake Time (TWT) to decrease power consumption for devices requiring infrequent, low-rate data transmission, such as IoT devices. The AP and the STA negotiate a wake-up service cycle, during which the AP allocates the STA to one of the TWT groups with a matching service cycle. The TWT mechanism effectively reduces the number of devices waking up and competing for the wireless medium simultaneously. Through this work/doze status management, the power efficiency and battery life of stations can be significantly improved.

Finally, with the allocation of the 6 GHz band to Wi-Fi communications in various regions, Wi-Fi 6E and subsequent Wi-Fi standards have a clean band to offer higher performance and serve high-speed LAN applications effectively.

The pertinent Wi-Fi 6 technologies are outlined in Table 2.1 [1] and will be elaborated upon in the upcoming sections.

2.2 Wi-Fi 6 Key Technologies

The Wi-Fi 6 standard leverages technology from adjacent domains. For instance, the Orthogonal Frequency Division Multiple Access (OFDMA) technology originates from cellular communications. Additionally, it strengthens and expands legacy Wi-Fi technology to meet higher specifications. For example, QAM modulation has evolved from 256-QAM to a more advanced 1024-QAM level, while

Table 2.1 Wi-Fi 6 key specifications

Type	Domain technology	Wi-Fi 6	Standards prior to Wi-Fi 6
Physical layer	Modulation	1024-QAM	256-QAM (Wi-Fi 5)
	OFDM symbol	12.8 μs	3.2 μs
	Guard Interval (GI)	0.8 μs (5% overheads), 1.6 μs (10% overheads), 3.2 μs (20% overheads)	0.4 μs(10% overheads), 0.8 μs(20% overheads)
	Number of streams with MIMO	8	4 (Wi-Fi 4) 8 (Wi-Fi 5)
	Current users with MIMO	8	4
	Channel bandwidth	40 MHz on 2.4 GHz 160 MHz on 5 GHz/6GHz	40 MHz on 2.4 GHz (Wi-Fi 4 and Wi-Fi 5) 80 MHz (mandatory) and 160 MHz (optional) on 5 GHz (Wi-Fi 5)
	Maximum physical layer data rate	9.6 Gbps	6.9 Gbps
MAC	Channel access mechanism	CSMA/CA Trigger frame	CSMA/CA
	Multiuser concurrent transmission	Uplink/Downlink MU-MIMO OFDMA	Downlink MU-MIMO (Wi-Fi 5)
	A-MPDU	256	64
	Anti-interference	SR/BSS coloring (Two NAVs), Dynamic CCA-PD threshold	NAV, RTS/CTS, static CCA-PD threshold

MU-MIMO has been extended to encompass both upstream and downstream, as opposed to only downstream in Wi-Fi 5.

To accommodate these advancements, the Wi-Fi 6 standard introduces updates to the frame format, control mechanisms, and management procedures of both the physical layer and Medium Access Control (MAC) layer, which will be detailed in Sect. 2.3.

2.2.1 Technology Overview

The key technologies of Wi-Fi 6 and their maximum specifications are depicted in Fig. 2.5 [2–4].

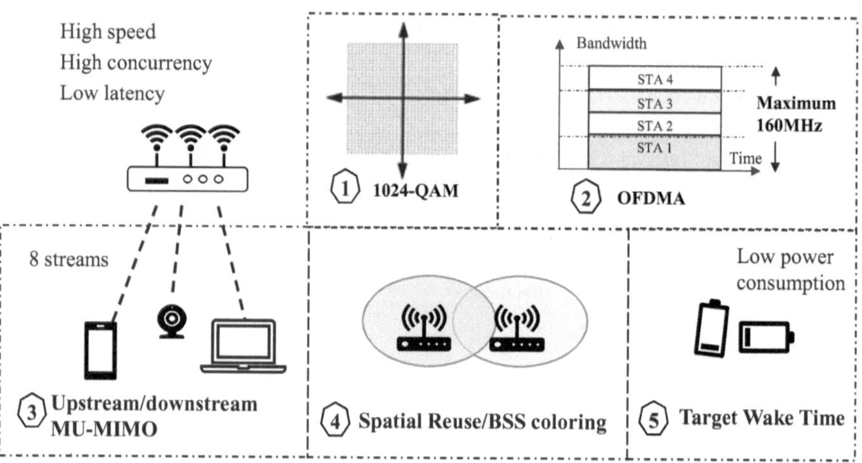

Fig. 2.5 Wi-Fi 6 key technology

(1) **1024-QAM**

The evolution of modulation technology has always been a crucial aspect of every generation of Wi-Fi standards.

Wi-Fi 5 supports a maximum modulation level of 256-QAM, with each OFDM symbol carrying 8 bits of data, i.e., $2^8 = 256$. In contrast, Wi-Fi 6 supports up to 1024-QAM, allowing each OFDM symbol to carry 10 bits of data, that is, $2^{10} = 1024$. Thanks to this new modulation scheme, Wi-Fi 6 enhances the maximum transmission rate by a factor of 1.25.

(2) **OFDMA**

Prior to Wi-Fi 6, the Wi-Fi standards employed OFDM modulation, meaning when a Wi-Fi device transmits data, it occupies all the subcarriers of the entire channel at a given time.

OFDMA is a multiple access technology based on OFDM. Unlike its predecessor, OFDMA subdivides the channel's subcarriers and allocates them to one or several Wi-Fi stations concurrently. This allows STAs to transmit and receive data simultaneously without causing mutual interference. Consequently, OFDMA significantly enhances spectrum efficiency, enabling concurrent transmissions and minimizing delays within the constraints of limited channel resources.

(3) **Upstream and downstream MU-MIMO**

MU-MIMO was introduced in Wi-Fi 5 but was limited to downstream traffic only. In Wi-Fi 5, the AP can send up to four or eight spatial streams to different Wi-Fi STAs simultaneously. However, Wi-Fi 6 MU-MIMO extends this capability by defining up to eight spatial streams for both upstream and downstream traffic. This means that Wi-Fi 6 APs are now capable of receiving the upstream spatial streams from multiple STAs simultaneously, enabling bidirectional concurrent data transmission and further improving channel utilization.

(4) **Spatial reuse and BSS coloring**

With the increasing proliferation of Wi-Fi devices in residential environments, there has been a significant rise in the deployment of APs, leading to the formation of multiple BSSs in adjacent households. As a result, electromagnetic wave signals emanating from neighboring BSSs have the potential to cause interference with Wi-Fi devices within individual households. Such interference can ultimately affect the efficiency and quality of data transmission, deteriorating the overall performance of the Wi-Fi network. According to the Wi-Fi CSMA/CA mechanism, when an AP or STA detects another device sending data in the channel, it backs off and waits for the channel to become idle. When the AP or STA receives data frames from the air, it parses the MAC header to identify and receive the data intended for itself, while discarding the rest. The more interference in the BSS, the more overhead is required to process irrelevant frames. To improve performance in high-density BSS scenarios, Wi-Fi 6 introduced Spatial Reuse technology. The AP or STA detects a Wi-Fi signal on the operating channel from an adjacent BSS and compares the signal strength to a specific threshold. If it is below the threshold, it is considered non-interfering, allowing the device to send data in the wireless medium.

BSS coloring technology differentiates between BSSs by assigning a unique BSS coloring field in the frame header of the physical layer. Wi-Fi devices receiving data from different BSSs can determine, at the physical layer, whether the data is from their own BSS or from an adjacent BSS without processing it at the MAC layer.

Spatial Reuse and BSS Coloring improve channel utilization and reduce delays in overlapping BSS scenarios.

(5) **Power saving and Target Wake Time**

Wi-Fi 5 supports the STA power saving mode, which allows the STA to wake up from the doze state periodically, query the buffer data status from Beacon frames, and receive the data.

The Wi-Fi 6 Target Wake Time (TWT), based on the IEEE 802.11ah standard, defines a mechanism for APs to negotiate with STAs on service cycles. STAs can be grouped into different wake-doze cycles, thereby reducing the number of devices waking up simultaneously and competing for the wireless medium. The TWT technology provides advanced management for power saving mode, extending the battery life of STAs.

Next, we will detail how these key technologies function in Wi-Fi 6.

2.2.2 *Orthogonal Frequency Division Multiple Access (OFDMA)*

As the simulation result in Fig. 2.3 demonstrates, when a large number of Wi-Fi STAs are connected to an AP, the contention among the STAs significantly reduces the Wi-Fi channel utilization due to inherent characteristics of the CSMA/CA mechanism. To address this issue and enhance spectrum utilization as well as network performance in high-density Wi-Fi scenarios, OFDMA has been introduced.

OFDMA is rooted in Multiple Access Multiplexing, where spectrum resources are dynamically divided and allocated among multiple users, enabling concurrent data transmission by several users.

Specifically, OFDMA is built upon Frequency Division Multiplexing, which involves dividing the spectrum into many nonoverlapping subcarriers. These subcarriers are then assembled into units known as Resource Units (RU). The AP dynamically allocates these RUs to different STAs.

In the downlink direction, RUs carry the data destined for different STAs; conversely, in the uplink direction, RUs transport data from the STAs back to the AP.

Figure 2.6 illustrates the difference between OFDM and OFDMA when considering simultaneous communication between multiple STAs. In OFDM mode, transmission must occur sequentially. However, in OFDMA mode, STAs can send data simultaneously over different RUs, reducing the overall transmission time compared to OFDM. The OFDMA technology enables the AP to allocate granular channel resources to multiple Wi-Fi STAs, thereby realizing a highly efficient data transmission mechanism.

As shown in Fig. 2.6, each of the Wi-Fi 5 STAs occupies the entire channel when transmitting. Therefore, only one STA is allowed to transmit at any one time, even if it is transmitting a small data frame.

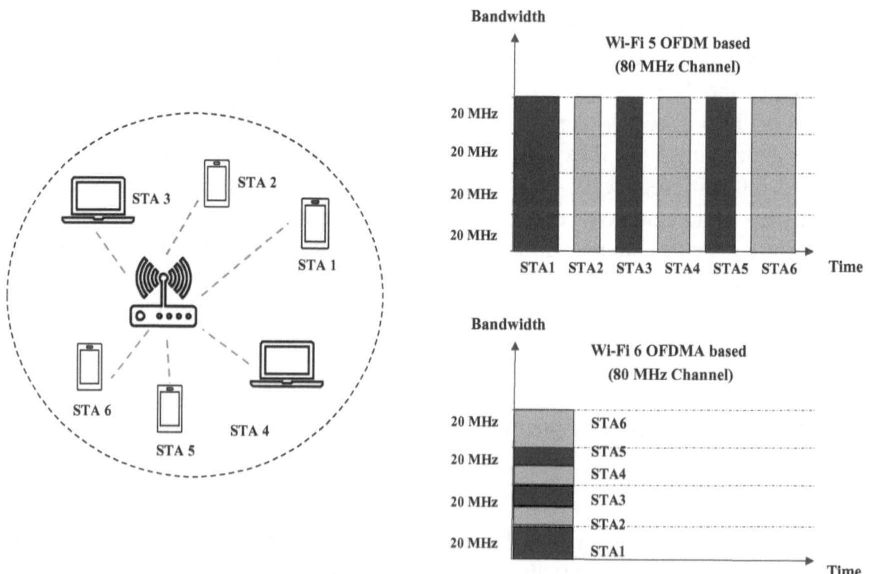

Fig. 2.6 Data transmission of OFDM-based mode and OFDMA-based mode

In comparison, the Wi-Fi 6 STAs share the wireless medium and are allowed to transmit data at the same time, each occupying a different frequency range of the channel. In environments with high-density Wi-Fi terminals, the OFDMA technology significantly improves channel utilization, enhances the performance of the entire network, and reduces latency and collisions.

In this section, we will discuss the OFDMA technology in terms of RU division, uplink and downlink channel access mode, MPDU aggregation, and BlockACK.

Depending on whether the AP specifies the RU for each STA, the OFDMA-based uplink supports AP-specified RU division and random RU division.

2.2.2.1 RU Division

The RU consists of multiple consecutive orthogonal subcarriers, each with a bandwidth of 78.125KHz, which are also referred to as tones. For example, a 20 MHz channel can be divided into 9 RUs, with each RU consisting of 26 subcarriers. Alternatively, the channel can be divided into RUs of a combination of different sizes, such as 26, 52, or 106 subcarriers. It's also possible to represent the entire channel as a single RU containing all 242 subcarriers, as indicated in Fig. 2.7 [2, 3].

There are three types of subcarriers:

(1) **Data subcarrier:** These subcarriers transmit user data information.
(2) **Pilot subcarrier:** They carry both phase and frequency information for physical layer modulation and demodulation processes. The receiver uses the pilot subcarrier to estimate and correct phase and frequency offsets.

An RU is composed of a combination of pilot subcarriers and data subcarriers. RU configurations consisting of 26, 52, 106, and 242 subcarriers are respectively termed as 26-tone RU, 52-tone RU, 106-tone RU, and 242-tone RU. Table 2.2 [2]

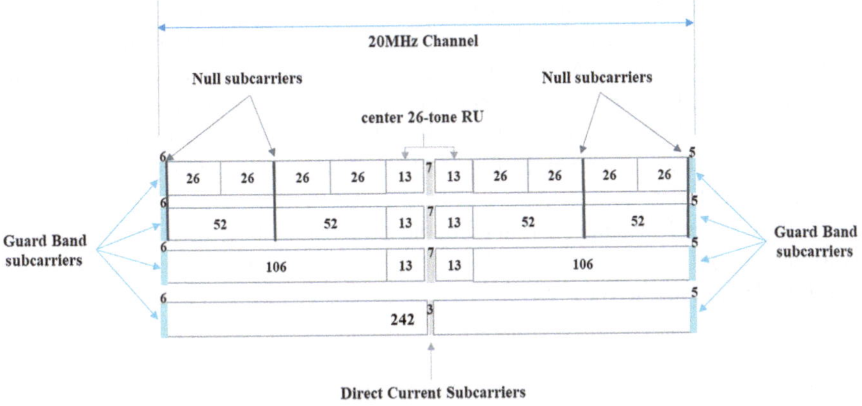

Fig. 2.7 Subcarrier and resource unit of a 20 MHz channel

Table 2.2 RU type with data subcarriers and pilot subcarriers

RU type	Number of data subcarriers	Number of pilot subcarriers
26-tone	24	2
52-tone	48	4
106-tone	102	4
242-tone	234	8
484-tone	468	16
996-tone	980	16
2 × 996-tone	980 × 2	16 × 2

Table 2.3 Number of RUs of different sizes

RU type	20 MHz	40 MHz	80 MHz	80 + 80 MHz or 160 MHz
26-tone RU	9	18	37	74
52-tone RU	4	8	16	32
106-tone RU	2	4	8	16
242-tone RU	1	2	4	8
484-tone RU	N/A	1	2	4
996-tone RU	N/A	N/A	1	2
2 × 996 tone RU	N/A	N/A	N/A	1

outlines the number of data subcarriers and pilot subcarriers present within each type of RU.

(3) **Unused subcarriers:** This includes Null Subcarriers, Direct Current Subcarriers (DC), and Guard Band subcarriers. These particular subcarriers are not utilized for data transmission; instead, their role is pivotal in mitigating interference between subcarriers, diminishing the signal's peak-to-average power ratio for Wi-Fi power amplifiers, and in preventing inter-channel interference.

In accordance with Wi-Fi 6 standards, each STA can only be assigned one tone RU at any given time. For a channel with a 160 MHz bandwidth, it is possible to assign up to 74 26-tone RUs, allowing for simultaneous data transmission across multiple STAs. When the AP assigns an RU to an STA, it is required to inform the STA of both the RU type and its specific location within the channel.

Table 2.3 [2, 3] shows the number of RUs for different channel bandwidths.

Taking 80 MHz as an example, Fig. 2.8 [2] indicates some possible combinations of various RU types.

As we can see from Figs. 2.7 and 2.8, the simplest method of frequency division is to allocate all subcarriers as a whole to a single user. This is referred to as the non-OFDMA mode in Wi-Fi 6.

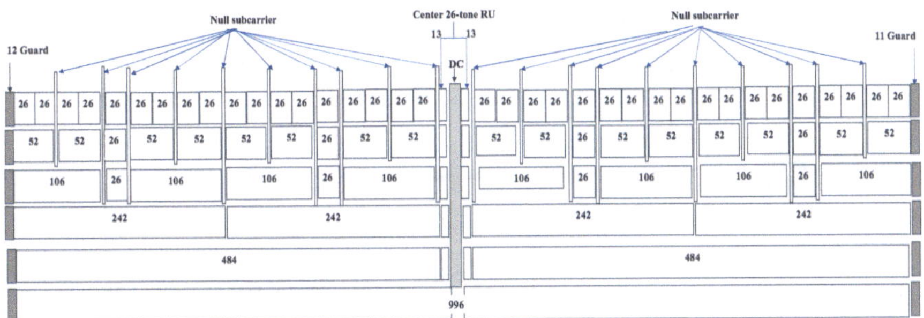

Fig. 2.8 Number of RUs of different sizes in an 80 MHz channel

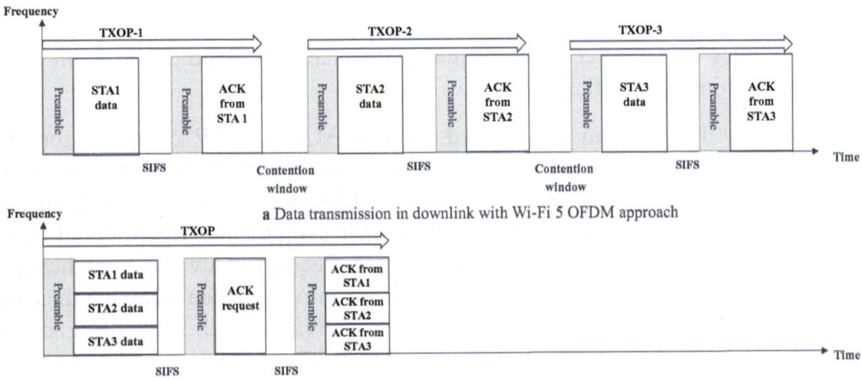

a Data transmission in downlink with Wi-Fi 5 OFDM approach

b Data transmission in downlink with Wi-Fi 6 OFDMA approach

Fig. 2.9 (**a**) Data transmission in downlink with Wi-Fi 5 OFDM approach, (**b**) data transmission in downlink with Wi-Fi 6 OFDMA approach

2.2.2.2 Uplink and Downlink OFDMA-Based Channel Access Mode

1. **Downlink Data Transmission**

The AP transmits data to multiple STAs using different resource units within the same transmission period, improving data throughput and reducing waiting times and collisions.

Figure 2.9 shows the difference between a Wi-Fi 5 downlink data transmission utilizing OFDM and a Wi-Fi 6 transmission employing OFDMA technology.

Downlink Data Transmission Based on OFDM When the AP sends downstream data to three STAs, it must compete for the wireless medium at least three times. Only after each successful competition, it can obtain the Transmission Opportunity (TXOP) to send data. In a high-density Wi-Fi environment, collisions from STAs and adjacent BSSs can affect the success rate of the AP. The AP may need to attempt

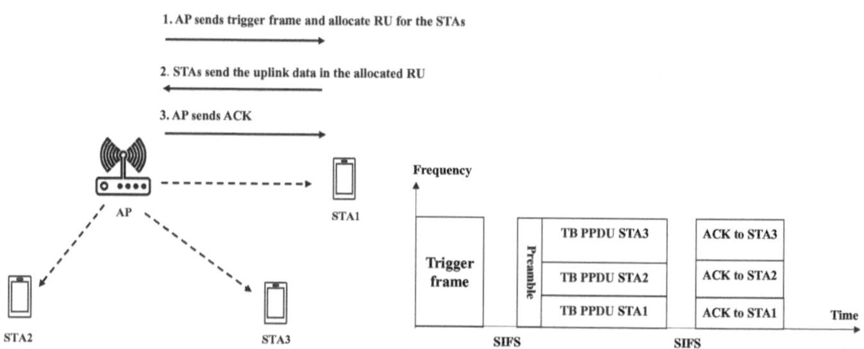

Fig. 2.10 Data transmission in uplink direction with Trigger Frame

multiple times before successfully acquiring the channel to send downstream data, thereby resulting in significant delays.

Downlink Data Transmission Based on OFDMA The AP competes for the wireless medium using CSMA/CA. Once it is successful, it can simultaneously send downstream data to three STAs using multiple RUs. In the preamble of the data frame, the AP informs the STAs about their assigned RU location and type. Following an SIFS, the AP sends a multiuser ACK Request to three STAs, indicating the RU information for each STA to respond with an ACK. Upon receiving the data frame, each STA waits for its designated SIFS interval and subsequently sends an ACK frame back to the AP through the RU that was assigned to it, respectively.

2. **Uplink Data Transmission**

The AP obtains the TXOP and shares it for uplink transmission by coordinating multiple STAs to send upstream data using different resource units within the same transmission period.

The OFDMA-based uplink access is illustrated in Fig. 2.10. Initially, the AP sends a control frame containing RU information to inform the STAs about the RU type and the allocation for each of them. This special control frame is known as the *Trigger Frame*. The duration/ID field of the Trigger frame specifies the TXOP period available for the STAs. Upon receiving the Trigger Frame, the STAs send upstream data in their allocated RUs following an SIFS interval. The AP receives the upstream data from multiple STAs and, after another SIFS interval, responds with an ACK message. The acknowledgment can take the form of either the traditional Compressed Block Ack (C-BA) or the Multiuser Block Ack (M-BA) method defined in Wi-Fi 6. The C-BA and M-BA will be introduced in the next section.

This Trigger-frame-based TXOP sharing mechanism eliminates the overhead for STAs to compete for and back off from using the same channel, therefore reducing the waiting delays and collisions of the STAs.

In high-density Wi-Fi networks, the adoption of OFDMA-based uplink and downlink channel access methods enables concurrent transmissions among multiple

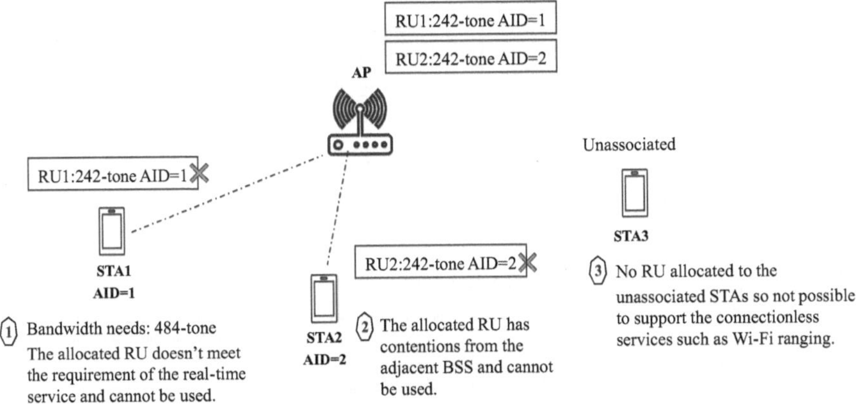

Fig. 2.11 Limitations for the RU allocation

devices. This mechanism not only minimizes contention between Access Points (APs) and Stations (STAs) for the shared channel but also effectively decreases the likelihood of packet collisions. As a result, these enhancements lead to a significant boost in channel utilization efficiency and, consequently, a marked improvement in overall network performance.

3. **Uplink OFDMA-Based Random Access**

The AP employs a Trigger Frame to assign RU resources to various STAs, effectively scheduling their upstream data transmissions, thus representing a noteworthy improvement over the standard CSMA/CA channel access protocol. However, there exist potential limitations, illustrated by the three cases presented in Fig. 2.11.

(1) **The allocated RU does not fulfill the service requirements**

In the given example, STA1 requires a bandwidth of 484-tone to transmit a file; however, due to a lack of real-time buffer status information, the AP assigns it a smaller 242-tone RU. As a result, the AP is unable to allocate the appropriate RU type that would meet the actual, immediate bandwidth requirements for the service being provided to STA1.

(2) **The allocated RU has collisions**

In environments where multiple BSSs coexist, the AP and the STAs might perceive different busy/idle states of the wireless medium due to varying interference impacts from adjacent BSSs. The greater the distance between the AP and the STAs, the higher the probabilities of inconsistency. For example, in Fig. 2.12, the AP fails to detect signals on the channel and, therefore, judges that RU1 and RU2 are idle. However, STA2 detects a data transmission on RU2, which is deemed busy due to interference from another BSS. Consequently, STA2 cannot send uplink data even though the resource unit has been allocated.

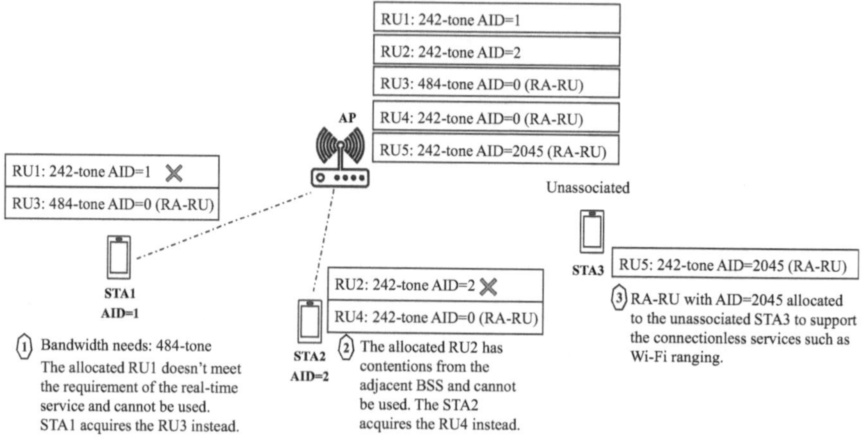

Fig. 2.12 Upstream OFDMA random access

(3) **Do not support the connectionless applications with the unassociated STAs**

According to the Wi-Fi standard, only after an STA establishes a connection with the AP and obtains an Association Identifier (AID), the AP can allocate the RUs to the STA through the Trigger Frame. However, certain applications like Wi-Fi ranging, do not necessitate the STA to form a connection with the AP. In these cases, the AP and the unassociated STA can still gather direction and distance information from each other via frame interaction. Despite this, under the OFDMA-based channel access scheme, no RUs are allocated to unassociated STA, which prevents them from engaging in interactions with the AP to facilitate ranging services.

To address the above issues, Wi-Fi 6 defines the Uplink OFDMA-based Random Access (UORA). This mechanism involves the AP reserving a Random Access Resource Unit (RA-RU) in the Trigger Frame. Consequently, an unassociated STA can utilize the RA-RU to transmit upstream data whenever necessary.

Figure 2.12 provides an example of how RA-RUs are allocated to address the three issues in the OFDMA-based access.

To differentiate the RA-RUs for various purposes, the AP assigns unique AIDs to each. As illustrated in Fig. 2.12, the AP allocates three RA-RUs in the Trigger Frame. The first RA-RU is assigned AID 2045, signifying that it is reserved exclusively for the unassociated STA; the remaining two RA-RU have AIDs set to 0, indicating that they are available only to STAs that have already established a connection with the AP.

(1) **Acquire RA-RU based on service requirements:** STA1 requires a 996-tone RU to fulfill its service requirements, so it secures RU3 and sends upstream data.
(2) **Acquire RA-RU based on channel state:** STA2 has an RU allocated by the AP but detects that RU2 is busy. Since there are RA-RUs indicated in the Trigger frame, STA2 acquires RU4 and sends data.

(3) **Acquire RA-RU by an unassociated STA:** STA3 acquires RU5, which is assigned AID 2045, to interact with the AP without an established connection.

To minimize collisions when multiple STAs compete for RA-RUs, Wi-Fi 6 specifies the following backoff mechanism:

(1) **Setting the backoff timer:** Each STA that intends to compete for an RA-RU first obtains the backoff range [*0, m*] from the AP. The STA then selects a random value within this range to be its backoff window and waits for a Trigger frame. The value "*m*" is determined by the AP device's vendor.
(2) **Backoff ends and STA obtains an RA-RU:** Upon receiving the Trigger Frame, the STA compares its current backoff counter with the number of RA-RUs. Suppose the Trigger Frame includes ***n*** RA-RUs. If ***n*** is greater than or equal to the current backoff counter ***k***, the STA acquires an RA-RU and resets the counter.
(3) **Recalculating the backoff counter:** If ***n*** is less than the current backoff value ***k***, the STA recalculates the backoff window to **[0, *k*-*n*]**. The STA then waits for the subsequent Trigger Frame and repeats step 3 till ***n*** is greater than or equal to ***k***. At this point, as described in step 2, the STA secures the RA-RU.

2.2.2.3 Multi-TID A-MPDU and BlockAck

As introduced in Chap. 1, A-MPDU technology aggregates multiple MAC layer data frames into a physical layer frame, known as a PPDU, and subsequently transmits it during a TXOP period. This A-MPDU technology substantially boosts throughput, decreases latency, and enhances channel utilization.

Prior to Wi-Fi 6, A-MPDU could only concatenate MAC layer data frames of the same priority. Consequently, when an AP or STA sent data frames with varying QoS levels, the data corresponding to different QoS were aggregated in separate PPDUs and transmitted independently in distinct TXOPs.

To accommodate A-MPDU functionality in mixed QoS scenarios, Wi-Fi 6 brings the Multi-Traffic Identifier (Multi-TID) A-MPDU. That is, the transmitter aggregates data frames of different QoS, such as voice data and video stream data, into a single A-MPDU for transmission.

Figure 2.13 illustrates the difference between A-MPDU and Multi-TID A-MPDU. In A-MPDU transmission, the device must complete the voice transmission in the first TXOP and then compete for the wireless medium again for video streaming. However, with Multi-TID A-MPDU transmission, both voice and video data are aggregated and transmitted within the same TXOP, eliminating the need for separate transmissions and reducing contention on the wireless medium.

Wi-Fi 6 defines two types of BlockAck frames for multi-TID A-MPDU transmissions: the multi-TID BlockAck and the Multi-STA multi-TID BlockAck. The application scenarios for these two BlockAck frames are detailed as follows.

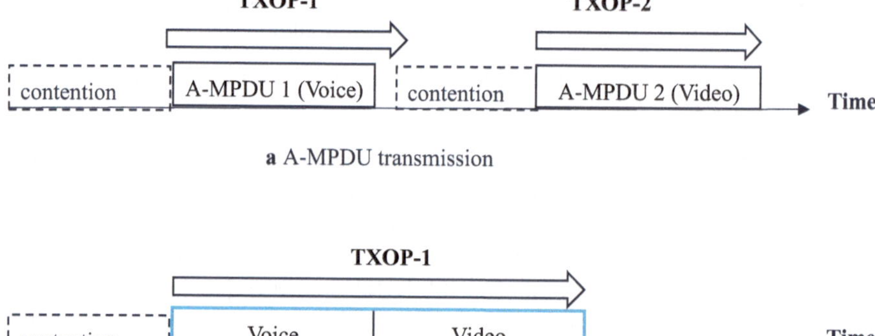

Fig. 2.13 (**a**) A-MPDU transmission, (**b**) multi-TID A-MPDU transmission

1. **Multi-TID BlockAck Frame**

The multi-TID BlockACK is an aggregated acknowledgment frame that corresponds to a multi-TID A-MPDU frame. As depicted in Fig. 2.15a, when a device transmits a multi-TID A-MPDU, the receiver responds with a multi-TID BlockACK frame, consolidating the acknowledgments for each individual service flow.

Figure 2.14b illustrates another scenario involving multiple STAs, in which STA1 and STA2 aggregate voice and video traffic, sending A-MPDU1 and A-MPDU2 on RU1 and RU2, respectively. Following an SIFS, the AP transmits multi-TID BlockACK frames on RU1 and RU2 to acknowledge STA1 and STA2, respectively.

2. **Multi-STA Multi-TID BlockACK Frame**

In the second scenario, the multi-STA multi-TID BlockACK frame, also referred to as the multi-STA BlockACK frame (M-BA), can be utilized as an alternative. As depicted in Fig. 2.15, each STA aggregates the service flows of different QoS into a single A-MPDU and sends this multi-TID A-MPDU to the AP using the allocated RU within the same transmission period. The AP then sends an M-BA frame, which contains acknowledgments for each STA and each service flow. STA1 and STA2 retrieve the ACK fields corresponding to the specific data subframes of their respective A-MPDUs.

When a Multi-STA BlockACK frame contains only acknowledgments for only one user, it functions in the same way as a multi-TID BlockACK frame. Consequently, both multi-TID BlockACK frames and multi-STA BlockACK frames are applicable to scenarios involving either single-user or multiuser transmissions in multi-TID scenarios. The choice of implementation can be made by the AP device vendor based on their preferred strategy or design.

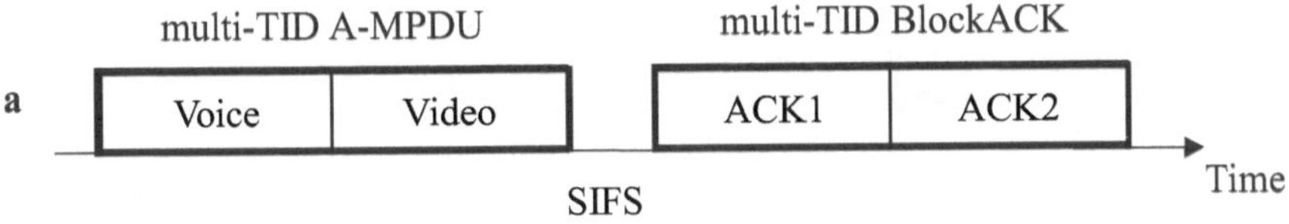

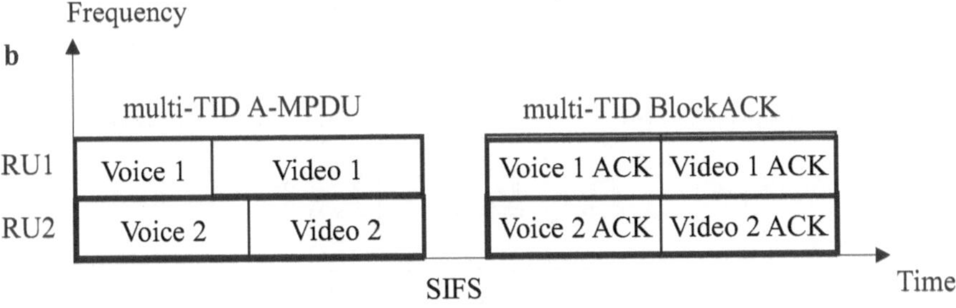

Fig. 2.14 (**a**) Multi-TID A-MPDU from a single STA, (**b**) multi-TID A-MPDU from multiple STAs

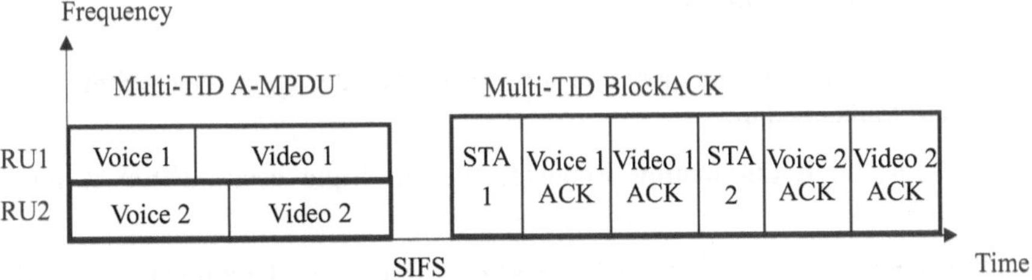

Fig. 2.15 Multi-STA BlockACK structure and example

2.2.3 Enhanced MIMO Technology in Wi-Fi 6

The Wi-Fi 6 standard enhances MIMO technology on top of Wi-Fi 5 by accommodating a greater number of MU-MIMO in both uplink and downlink directions. It also introduces a more efficient channel sounding procedure. Furthermore, Wi-Fi 6 combines frequency and spatial multiplexing by integrating OFDMA with MU-MIMO, which allows for more efficient utilization of the wireless medium, as illustrated in Fig. 2.16.

(1) **High spatial multiplexing capability**

The Wi-Fi 5 standard defines MU-MIMO support for up to four users and a maximum of eight spatial streams, but these are limited to downlink transmissions only. In contrast, as illustrated in Fig. 2.16a, Wi-Fi 6 extends this capability to support up to eight users and eight spatial streams for both uplink and downlink communications. This increased spatial multiplexing capacity enhances the

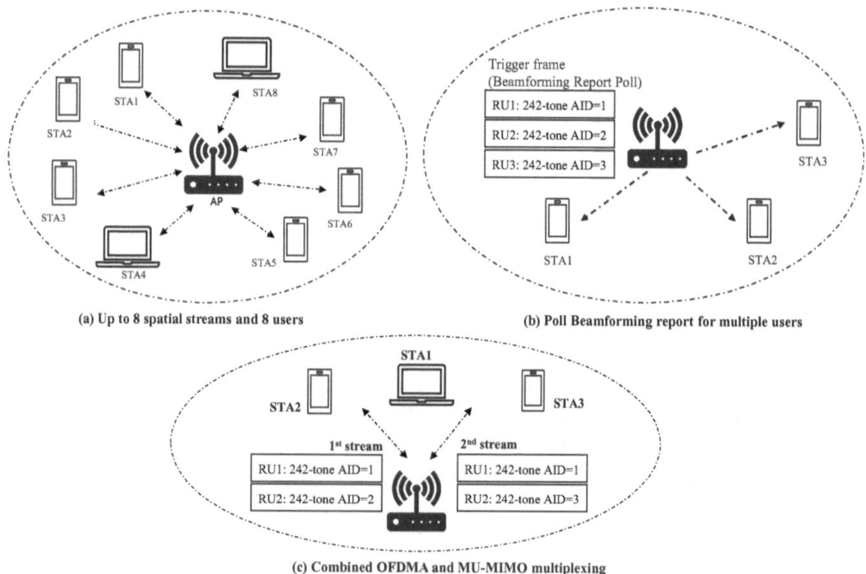

Fig. 2.16 The enhanced MIMO in Wi-Fi 6

network's ability to handle more concurrent users and decreases their waiting times for access to the medium.

(2) **Polling the Beamforming Reports from multiple users within a single command**

The channel sounding process in a Wi-Fi 5 AP involves the following steps: the AP broadcasts a VHT Null Data Packet Announcement, followed by sending a null data packet to each Beamformee to measure the channel response. Subsequently, the AP sends a Beamforming Report Poll (BFRP) to each Beamformee in turn to query the channel information.

In the Wi-Fi 6 standard, the AP does not send BFRP to each Beamformee individually. Instead, it sends a Trigger frame of Beamforming Report Poll type to solicit the necessary reports and assigns different RUs to the Beamformees. The Beamformees then respond with their channel states to the AP using the assigned RUs, respectively. This enhanced sounding process is exemplified in Fig. 2.16b. Obviously, the Wi-Fi 6 method of Beamforming Report Poll is more efficient than the Wi-Fi 5 approach.

(3) **A combined frequency and spatial multiplexing with OFDMA and MU-MIMO technologies**

OFDMA and MU-MIMO are technologies that enable multiuser multiplexing in the frequency domain and spatial domain, respectively. The Wi-Fi 6 standard facilitates the combination of these two technologies, providing a more flexible and efficient method to support the multiple user scenarios. Each spatial stream operates independently, containing the RUs allocated to different STAs. Each STA sends and receives data through its own RU from the corresponding spatial stream, as depicted in Fig. 2.16c.

The remainder of this section will delve into more detail on Wi-Fi 6 uplink and downlink MU-MIMO, enhanced Beamforming channel sounding, and the integrated uses of OFDMA and MU-MIMO.

2.2.3.1 Wi-Fi 6 Uplink and Downlink MU-MIMO

The Beamformer obtains channel characteristics through the channel sounding procedure and accordingly adjusts the transmitted signal prior to transmission. This capability empowers the AP to send the signals through multiple antennas, directing them toward specific directions.

MU-MIMO in Wi-Fi 5 is applicable only to downlink transmission, meaning that the AP transmits downstream data to multiple STAs simultaneously through multiple spatial streams over the same channel. In Wi-Fi 6, MU-MIMO capability is extended to the upstream direction, allowing the AP to receive upstream data from multiple STAs simultaneously through different spatial streams on the same channel. Given that the number of spatial streams adds complexity to real-world implementation, Wi-Fi 6 defines up to eight spatial streams for MU-MIMO and allows up to four spatial streams per STA.

Downlink MU-MIMO and uplink MU-MIMO have distinct procedures for obtaining the channel characteristics and for communicating spatial stream information.

1. **The Channel Response Matrix**

Figure 2.17 shows an example of both downlink MU-MIMO and uplink MU-MIMO, where the AP communicates with STA1 and STA2 simultaneously using two spatial streams in both the downlink and uplink directions.

In Fig. 2.17a, the AP gathers the channel response from each Beamformee through the channel sounding process and then constructs a channel response matrix. The channel characteristic reported by STA1 is H1 = {h11, h21}; that is, STA1 receives two spatial streams from the AP via the h11 and h21 paths. The data received on the h11 path is the intended signal for STA1, while the spatial stream on the h21 path constitutes interference.

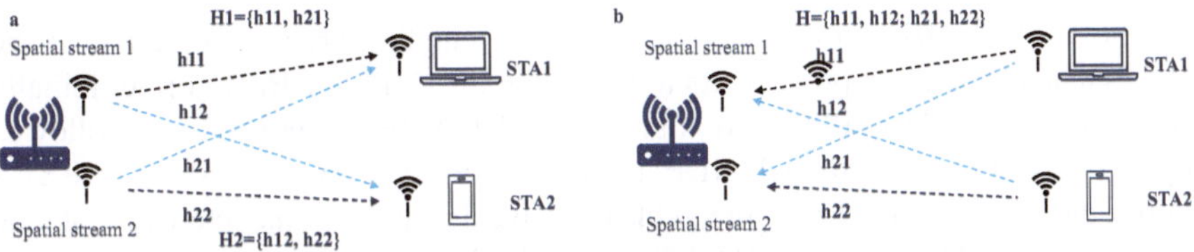

Fig. 2.17 (**a**) Downlink MU-MIMO, (**b**) uplink MU-MIMO

Similarly, the channel response matrix for STA2 is H2 = {h12, h22}, where the spatial stream on the h22 path represents the desired data, and the spatial stream on the h12 path is considered interference.

After the AP receives the Compressed Beamforming reports from STA1 and STA2, it processes the signals on each transmit antenna accordingly by reducing the spatial stream energy on the h12 and h21 paths. Ideally, the spatial streams of the h21 and h12 would have zero energy, meaning there would be no interference.

For uplink MU-MIMO, the channel sounding process is not required because the AP can directly obtain the complete channel characteristics from either STA1 or STA2. As illustrated in Fig. 2.17b, the AP uses the channel response matrix H = {h11, h12; h21, h22} to process the received spatial streams sent by STA1 and STA2, thereby retrieving the uplink data.

2. **Spatial Stream Location Indication**

During the downlink MU-MIMO procedure, the AP sends data to multiple users in the HE MU PPDU format, where the HE-SIG-B field of the preamble contains the details of the spatial stream information, such as the MU-MIMO allocation and RU division for each user. The STAs adjust their demodulation rates, decoding modes, and other physical layer parameters based on the HE-SIG-B field, then receive and decode the downstream data. The Wi-Fi 6 PPDU frame format will be discussed in Sect. 2.3.2.

Regarding the uplink MU-MIMO procedure, the AP first sends a Trigger Frame, which contains the spatial stream allocation and the RU information for each STA. Subsequently, multiple STAs transmit upstream data simultaneously according to the information specified in the Trigger Frame.

2.2.3.2 Enhanced Beamforming Channel Sounding

The channel sounding technology of Wi-Fi 6 is known as HE channel sounding, which is an enhancement over the VHT channel sounding used in Wi-Fi 5. Wi-Fi 6 channel sounding operates in two modes, depending on whether the AP sends a Trigger Frame to allocate the RU resources: non-trigger mode and trigger mode. Non-trigger mode is used when the AP initiates the channel sounding process with a single Beamformee. In contrast, the trigger mode is used when the channel sounding process involves multiple Beamformees.

1. **Non-trigger Mode**

The Wi-Fi 6 HE non-trigger mode channel sounding process is similar to the VHT channel sounding process. As illustrated in Fig. 2.18, the Beamformer initially sends an HE Null Data PPDU Announcement (HE NDPA) control frame, followed by an HE Null Data PPDU (HE NDP) to the STA. Both the Wi-Fi 6 AP and the STA utilize the HE-LTF field of the preamble to derive the channel characteristics, akin to how they would use the VHT-LTF field in Wi-Fi 5 for the same purpose.

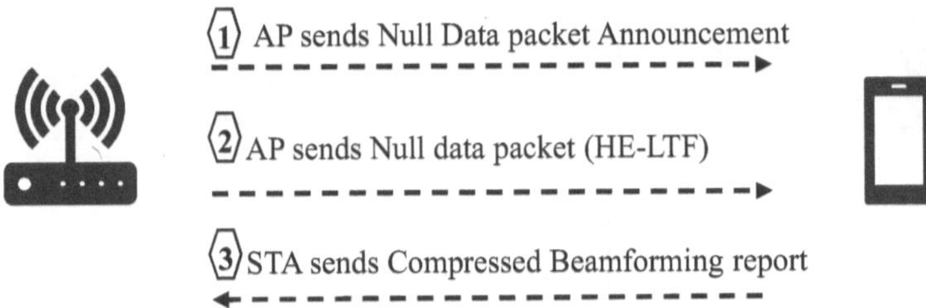

Fig. 2.18 The non-trigger sounding process

Subsequently, the STA sends an HE Compressed Beamforming report to the AP, which helps in constructing the channel response matrix.

2. **Trigger Mode**

To cater to multiuser scenarios, Wi-Fi 6 introduces a trigger mode channel sounding procedure. As depicted in Fig. 2.19, following the transmission of an HE NDPA and an HE NDP by the AP, it sends a Trigger frame of Beamforming Report Poll (BFRP) type, embedding RU division information for the STAs. Subsequently, each STA responds with an HE Compressed Beamforming frame, providing their individual channel responses to the AP within the designated RUs during the same transmission period.

The trigger mode channel sounding process mitigates the overhead associated with polling Beamforming reports from multiple Beamformees, thus enhancing channel utilization more efficiently than in Wi-Fi 5.

2.2.3.3 Combined OFDMA and MU-MIMO Mode

The OFDMA technology represents frequency domain multiplexing, whereas the MIMO technology embodies spatial multiplexing using multiple antennas. The Wi-Fi 6 standard integrates both multiplexing technologies, MU-MIMO and OFDMA, meaning that the AP can allocate OFDMA RUs across each spatial stream to concurrently transmit data to multiple users for both upstream and downstream traffic.

Figure 2.20 illustrates the four multiuser access methods incorporated in Wi-Fi 6:

- Figure (**a**) depicts multiuser access utilizing Time Division Multiplexing (TDM), which operates on the foundation of Carrier Sensing Multiple Access/Collision Avoidance (CSMA/CA). This represents the conventional multiplexing technique inherent in legacy Wi-Fi standards.
- Figure (**b**) demonstrates Spatial Multiplexing based on Multiuser MIMO (MU-MIMO), a multiplexing technology that was introduced in Wi-Fi 5, enabling simultaneous data transmission to multiple users by leveraging spatial diversity.

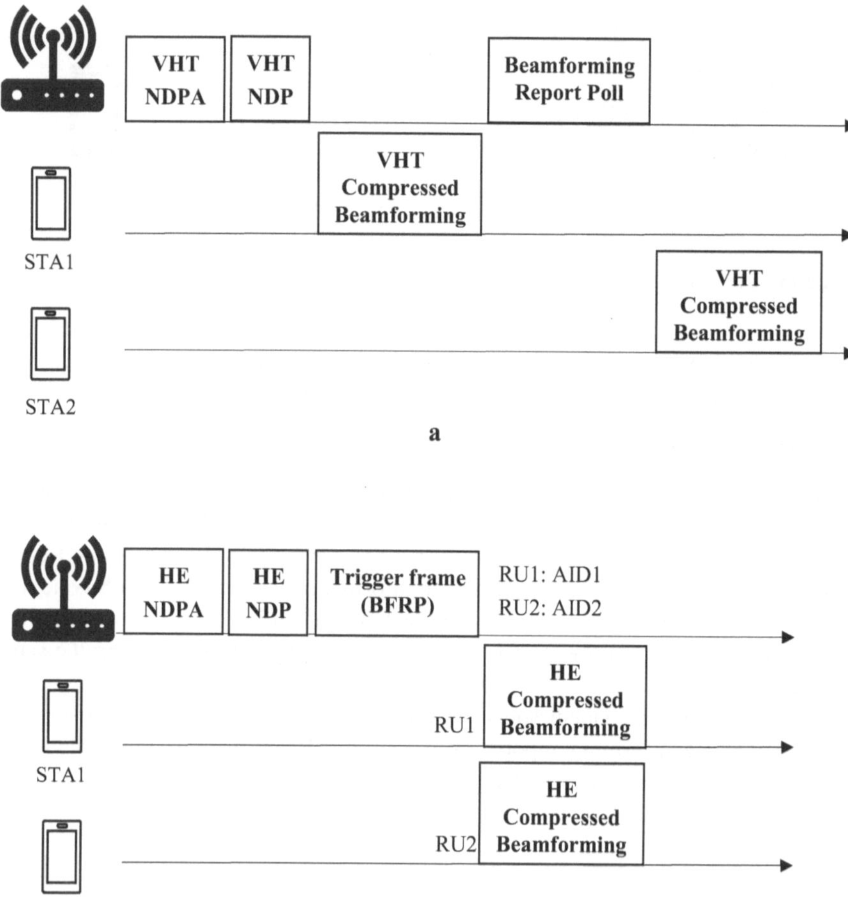

Fig. 2.19 (**a**) Wi-Fi 5 VHT channel sounding, (**b**) Wi-Fi 6 EH Trigger-mode channel sounding

- Figure (**c**) presents the OFDMA introduced in Wi-Fi 6, where multiple users are multiplexed across different frequency divisions, thereby dividing the spectrum in the frequency domain for concurrent communication.
- Figure (**d**) illustrates the hybrid mode combining MU-MIMO and OFDMA in a multi-antenna Wi-Fi 6 setup. This innovative approach merges the multiplexing capabilities of both spatial and frequency domains, allowing for increased efficiency and improved user experience in dense networks.

Figure 2.21 shows an example of MU-MIMO and OFDMA hybrid mode operation. The AP simultaneously transmits two spatial streams. The first spatial stream is divided into RUs that are individually assigned to STA1, STA2, STA3, and STA4.

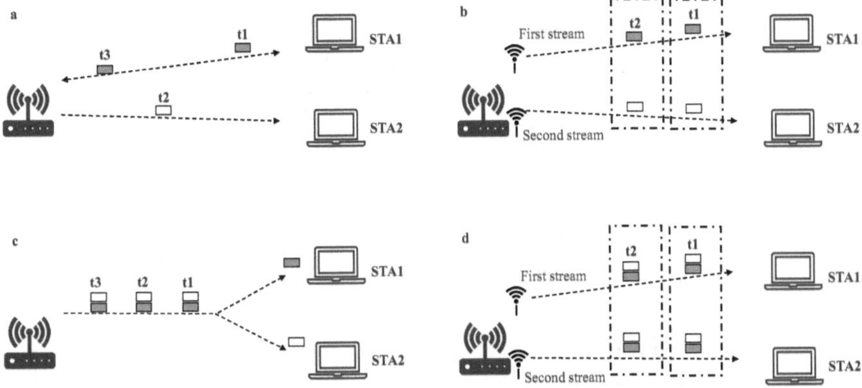

Fig. 2.20 (**a**) Time Division Multiplexing based on CSMA/CA, (**b**) spatial multiplexing based on MU-MIMO, (**c**) frequency division multiplexing based on OFDMA, and (**d**) MU-MIMO and OFDMA hybrid mode

Concurrently, the second stream serves STA5, STA6, and STA4 again, with dedicated RUs allocated to each station.

In OFDMA and MIMO hybrid mode, the RUs in each spatial stream can be independently allocated to different users; however, it is essential that the allocation of RUs to any given user remains consistent across all spatial streams, both in terms of method and size.

Figure 2.22 provides a more detailed explanation of the RU allocation exemplified in Fig. 2.21. In this instance, the RU allocation pattern for both the first and second spatial streams is identical, consisting of a sequence of 484-tone, 26-tone, 242-tone, and another 242-tone. The RUs can be assigned to the same or different STAs, except for the 26-tone RU. Due to the complexities involved with 26-tone or 52-tone RUs when employing MIMO technology, Wi-Fi 6 defines that only RUs of 106-tone or greater can be utilized for MIMO in the OFDMA and MIMO hybrid mode. In Fig. 2.22, the 26-tone RU is solely allocated to STA2 in the first stream but not allocated in the second stream.

2.2.4 Enhanced Power Saving in Wi-Fi 6

Wi-Fi 6 not only delivers advancements in Wi-Fi performance, characterized by high-speed and low-latency, but also introduces enhanced power-saving features for battery-powered STAs and IoT devices.

In the traditional Wi-Fi power-saving mode, an STA wakes up periodically at the Target Beacon Transmit Time (TBTT), receives the Beacon frame broadcast by the AP, and inspects the TIM/DTIM field in the Beacon frame to determine whether there is any buffered data awaiting it. If there is an indication of buffered

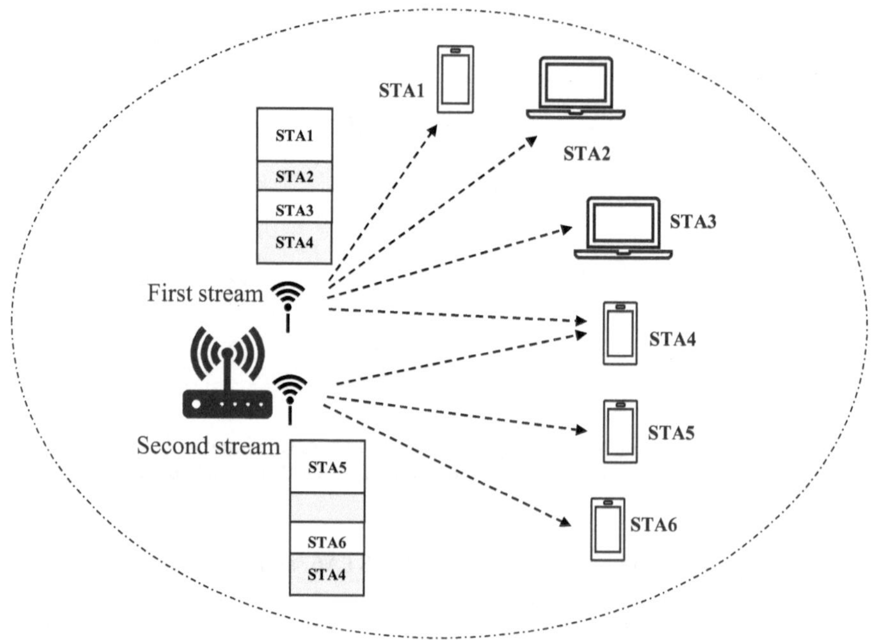

Fig. 2.21 The OFDMA and MIMO hybrid method

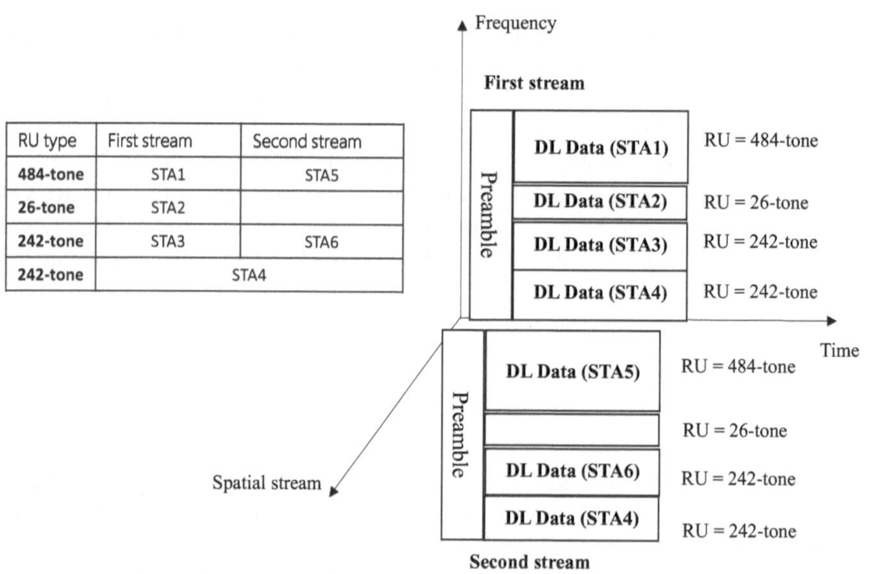

RU type	First stream	Second stream
484-tone	STA1	STA5
26-tone	STA2	
242-tone	STA3	STA6
242-tone	STA4	

Fig. 2.22 An example of RU allocation in OFDMA and MU-MIMO hybrid mode

information, the STA sends a PS-POLL frame to the AP to request the downstream data, after which the AP sends the buffered data frames to the STA. Once the STA concludes the reception process, it returns to its doze state.

Wi-Fi 6 introduces the Target Wake Time (TWT) mechanism, enabling the AP to engage in negotiations with STAs regarding their service periods. This allows the AP to assign STAs to different wake-up groups, thereby minimizing collisions caused by multiple STAs awakening and competing for the wireless medium simultaneously. Compared to the legacy power-saving method, TWT facilitates the negotiation of diverse service cycles, which proves especially beneficial for low-data IoT devices. Figures 2.23 and 2.24 illustrate the differences between the legacy Wi-Fi power-saving mode and the Wi-Fi 6 TWT mode. In the legacy mode, multiple STAs periodically wake up and compete for the wireless medium with the aim of transmitting a PS-POLL frame and receiving buffered data. However, during each Beacon interval, only one device can gain channel access, while the other devices must wait for the next transmit window to compete for channels again before sending their PS-POLL frames. The AP also competes for the wireless medium before it can send the downlink buffered data. In high-density Wi-Fi networks, this approach can lead to inefficient power management, as many STAs may be competing for access when a fixed wake-up cycle occurs.

In TWT mode, the AP negotiates a specific service period with each STA, intentionally staggering their wake-up times. For example, STA1 wakes up at T1, marking the start of its TWT service period (SP). As no other STAs are awake at this moment, STA1 obtains the channel and sends a PS-POLL frame to request any buffered data. The AP then successfully sends the buffered data without any

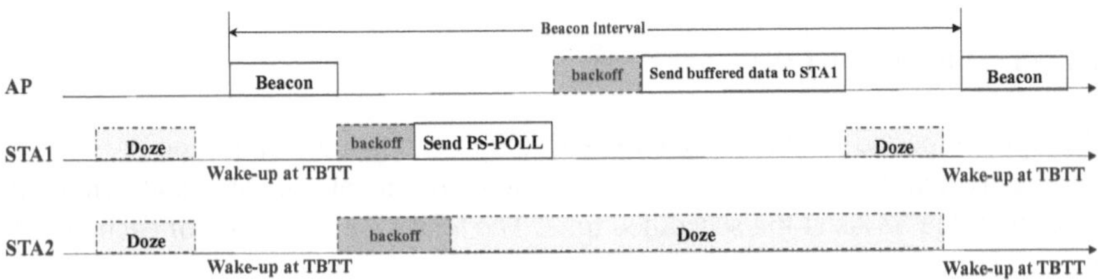

Fig. 2.23 Multiple STAs wake up under legacy power-saving mode

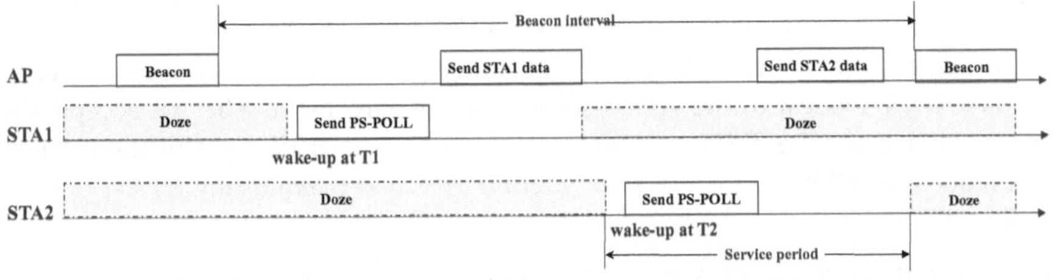

Fig. 2.24 The scheduled service period of multiple STAs in TWT mode

collisions from other STAs. Subsequently, STA2 wakes up at T2 and follows the same procedure.

The TWT technology reduces the additional power consumption that results from channel competition among waking STAs. Moreover, the staggered wake-up schedule enhances channel utilization.

The TWT technology was initially conceived as part of the IEEE 802.11ah protocol, tailored for power-saving in IoT devices operating in frequencies below 1GHz and employing bandwidths of 1 MHz, 2 MHz, 4 MHz, 8 MHz, and up to 16 MHz. In the Wi-Fi 6 standard, TWT has been integrated alongside OFDMA technology, thus enabling it to facilitate multiuser simultaneous upstream data transmission based on Trigger Frame.

In Wi-Fi 6, there are three ways in which the AP negotiates the service period with the STAs: individual-TWT, broadcast-TWT, and Opportunistic Power Saving (OPS).

- **Individual TWT (i-TWT):** Each STA negotiates a unique service period with the AP individually. The STAs wake up at their respective times for data transmission with the AP.
- **Broadcast TWT (b-TWT)**: The AP divides a Beacon interval into multiple service periods designated for TWT groups. Using Beacon frames, the AP broadcasts the TWT group service information. STAs negotiate with the AP to join a TWT group; however, they cannot negotiate specific service periods.
- **Opportunistic Power Saving (OPS):** There is no negotiation process between the AP and the STAs. When the AP sends Beacon frames, it announces the TWT service period for specific STAs, which then wake up during the designated service period.

2.2.4.1 Individual TWT

The service period for Individual TWT (i-TWT) is negotiated between the AP and each individual STA separately. The AP maintains a local timetable and communicates with the STAs at the scheduled time. The STAs are not aware of each other's service periods.

The negotiation between the AP and the STA can occur when the STA is establishing a connection with the BSS through the Association Request frame and Association Response frame, which include i-TWT parameters. The negotiation can also take place after the connection has been established.

As depicted in Fig. 2.25, the STA, as the initiator of the TWT negotiation process, sends a TWT request to the AP to set up a TWT agreement. The AP accepts the request and sends the TWT response. According to the IEEE specification, STAs that request an i-TWT agreement are referred to as TWT-requesting STAs.

The TWT negotiation includes the following parameters:

- **Target Wake Time (TWT)**: This is the time, measured in microseconds, when the TWT-requesting STA is scheduled to wake up for its service period.

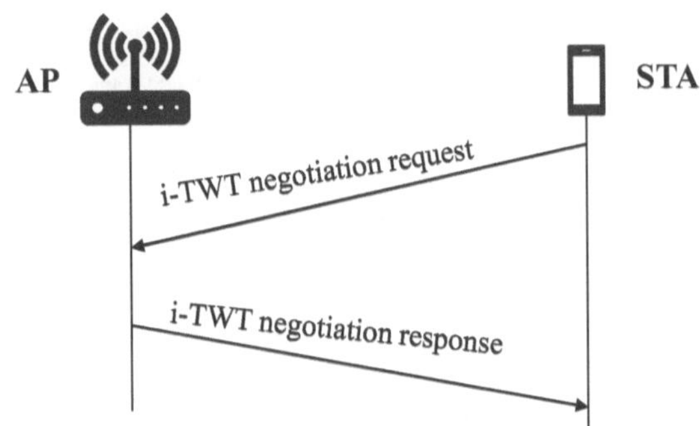

Fig. 2.25 i-TWT negotiation process

- **TWT interval:** This refers to the duration between subsequent TWT sessions. The value is greater than 0 if the TWT is arranged to occur periodically.

1. **i-TWT Operation Mode**

Depending on whether the TWT interval is defined during negotiation, i-TWT operates in two modes: explicit TWT and implicit TWT.

Explicit TWT In this mode, the wake-up interval is nonperiodic. When a TWT-requesting STA awakens, it exchanges data with the AP and receives the start time for the next TWT SP before it enters the doze state.

Explicit TWT operation allows for flexibility to accommodate unexpected service flows. For example, if there is a considerable amount of service data for an STA, the AP can adjust the wake-up schedule to transmit the buffered data to the STA as soon as possible. The drawback is that the negotiation process consumes channel resources each time.

Implicit TWT Here, the wake-up schedule is periodic. When a TWT-requesting STA awakens, it calculates the start time for the next TWT SP based on the TWT Interval, without the need to obtain the TWT SP time from the AP upon each wake-up. With implicit TWT, the TWT interval is typically set to one or multiple Beacon frame intervals.

Implicit TWT operation is well-suited for cyclical service flows where data transmission is predictable and aligns with a fixed schedule. This mode minimizes the use of channel resources for i-TWT negotiation but lacks flexibility and cannot handle burst service flows effectively.

The choice between these modes is at the discretion of the AP vendor and should be made according to the specific requirements of the service.

2. **Channel Access Mode of i-TWT**

The TWT technology enables STAs to wake up at different times, which reduces collisions among them. However, when STAs wake up, they still adhere to the

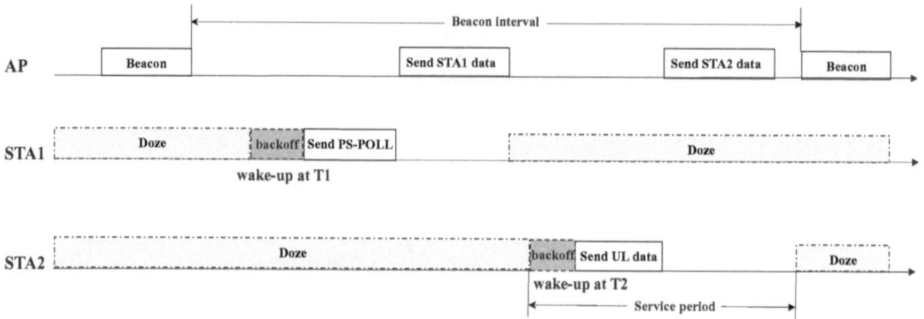

Fig. 2.26 CSMA/CA-based channel access for i-TWT

traditional CSMA/CA method to gain access to the channel, competing with other STAs within the same BSS or managing interference from adjacent BSS.

As for the i-TWT technology, an STA has two methods for accessing the wireless channel after waking up: non-trigger-enabled and trigger-enabled channel access. The non-trigger-enabled mode is the traditional CSMA/CA-based channel access as outlined by the 802.11ah standard.

(1) **CSMA/CA-based channel access**

An STA wakes up and obtains the channel through CSMA/CA. It then either sends uplink data to the AP or transmits a PS-POLL frame to inquire about buffered data, as illustrated in Fig. 2.26.

STA1 wakes up at T1 and secures the channel via CSMA/CA. As it has no data to transmit upstream, it sends a PS-POLL frame and receives buffered data from the AP. Afterwards, STA1 enters a doze state.

STA2 wakes up at T2 and attempts to obtain the channel through CSMA/CA. After sending upstream data and receiving downstream buffered data from the AP, STA 2 goes back into a doze state.

(2) **Trigger-enabled channel access**

When an STA wakes up, it gains access to the channel through CSMA/CA. The AP then sends a Trigger Frame to grant the STA a Transmission Opportunity (TXOP). This approach eliminates the power overhead associated with the STA competing for channel access via CSMA/CA.

Figure 2.27 illustrates an example of how the i-TWT requesting STAs access the channel using a Trigger frame under implicit TWT operation.

In Fig. 2.27, STA1 and STA2 each negotiate an i-TWT service period with the AP, respectively. Upon waking up, each STA is granted a TXOP by the AP, which sends a Trigger frame to facilitate this process. This allows the STA to send upstream data and receive downstream buffered data.

Explicit TWT operation and implicit TWT operation are modes chosen during the i-TWT negotiation phase, typically selected to align with the requirements of the service flow. Conversely, trigger-enabled and non-trigger-enabled modes are

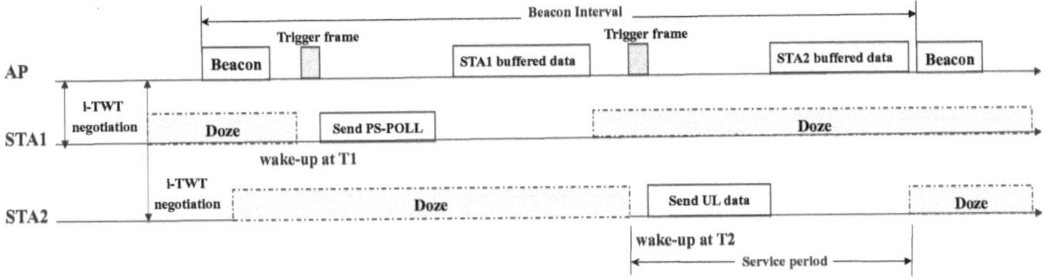

Fig. 2.27 Trigger-enabled channel access for i-TWT

determined within a TWT session. There are no specific rules or guidelines for choosing between CSMA/CA or a Trigger frame for channel access, and it is up to the AP device vendors to decide how i-TWT devices will obtain channel access.

Moreover, there is an additional TWT mode specified during the i-TWT procedure, known as Announced or Unannounced TWT. Announced TWT implies the conventional mode where i-TWT requesting STAs must send a PS-Poll to the AP to request the buffered data. Unannounced TWT, on the other hand, allows the AP to deliver data without waiting for a PS-Poll from the TWT-requesting STA.

2.2.4.2 Broadcast TWT

Broadcast TWT (b-TWT) is a variant of the TWT technology that places STAs into different service groups. In essence, the AP pre-divides the entire transmission period into a number of service periods, each dedicated to a b-TWT group identified by a specific TWT-ID. The AP broadcasts b-TWT service information using the Beacon frame, and an STA can join one of the b-TWT groups either with or without negotiation with the AP. However, STAs are not able to negotiate the service period with the AP. In this context, the STA is referred to as a TWT-scheduled STA, and the AP is known as a TWT Scheduling AP.

Since the b-TWT groups have predefined service periods, the scheduling process is relatively straightforward compared to i-TWT. Additionally, it's possible to schedule multiple devices within the same b-TWT group using OFDMA or MU-MIMO technology, which can significantly reduce waiting time.

As depicted in Fig. 2.28, b-TWT possesses the following characteristics:

- **Fixed service period:** The total service time is the Beacon interval, which is subdivided into multiple service periods. The AP schedules the b-TWT groups periodically.
- **Multiusers in a b-TWT group:** Each service period is allocated to a b-TWT group, which can consist of multiple users. The Wi-Fi 6 AP concurrently schedules upstream and downstream data for these users using OFDMA or MU-MIMO technology.

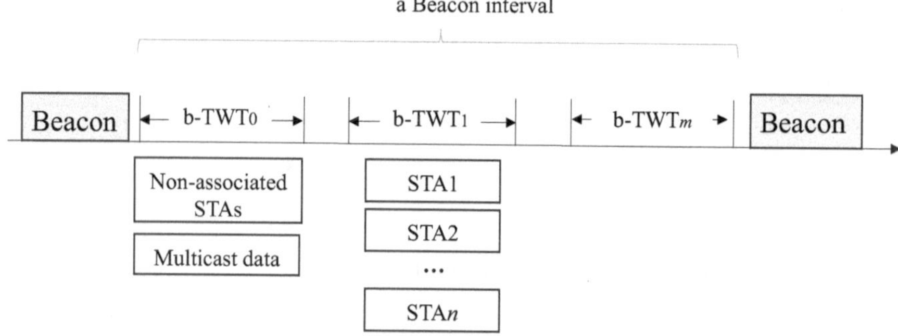

Fig. 2.28 Characteristics of b-TWT

- **Scheduling for nonassociated STAs:** STAs that have not formed a connection with the AP can be scheduled in b-TWT group #0 without negotiation and can utilize the RA-RU for upstream and downstream data transmission.
- **Multicast data transmission in b-TWT:** In b-TWT group #0, the AP is capable of scheduling both unicast data and multicast data transmissions.

The rest of this section will explore b-TWT technology from four aspects: b-TWT group broadcast, joining and leaving a b-TWT group, channel access mode, and b-TWT group #0 for unassociated STAs. Finally, we will discuss two use cases that utilize b-TWT technology.

1. **b-TWT Group Broadcast**

First, the AP takes the interval between two consecutive Beacon frames as a service cycle for scheduling b-TWT devices. It divides the entire cycle into multiple nonoverlapping service periods, with each service period designated for a b-TWT group identified by a unique b-TWT ID. The AP then broadcasts the b-TWT service parameters, which include the start time and duration for each b-TWT ID, within the Beacon frames.

For example, in Fig. 2.29, the AP sets up three b-TWT groups identified as b-TWT #0, b-TWT #1, and b-TWT #2, with their service periods set to 50 ms, 20 ms, and 20 ms, respectively.

To reduce overheads, not all Beacon frames contain b-TWT information. In practice, b-TWT information fields are included in the interleaved Beacon frames. For instance, in the example shown in Fig. 2.29, the b-TWT field is carried only in the first Beacon frame, not the second one.

2. **Join and Withdraw a b-TWT Group**

There are two methods by which an STA can join a b-TWT group: either by initiating the negotiation process itself or by being directly assigned to a b-TWT group by the AP, as depicted in Fig. 2.30.

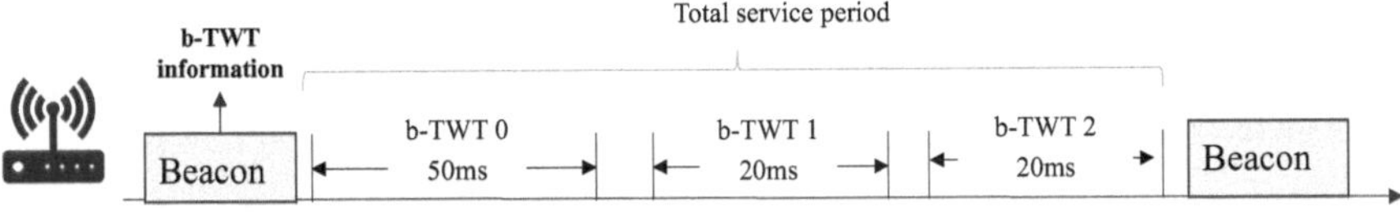

Fig. 2.29 b-TWT service group broadcast

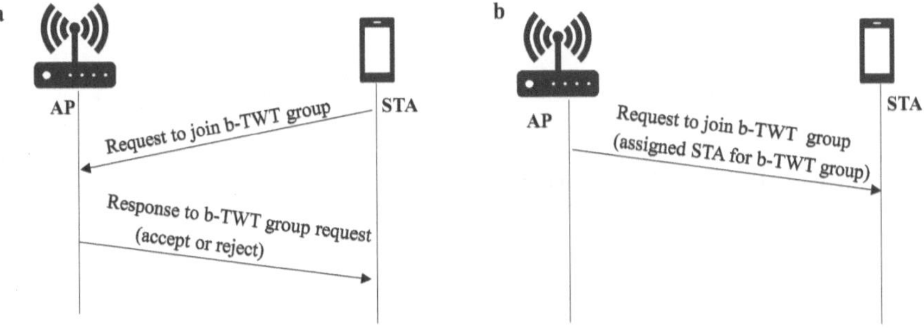

Fig. 2.30 (**a**) The STA initiates the negotiation process, (**b**) the AP assigns the STA to a b-TWT group

- **The STA initiates the negotiation process:** The STA sends a b-TWT request frame to its associated AP to join a b-TWT group. The AP then accepts or rejects the request in the response frame.
- **The AP assigns the STA to a b-TWT group:** The AP assigns an STA to a b-TWT group that is nonzero. Compared to the negotiation method, this method is considered semi-negotiated because it involves fewer frame interactions.

During the b-TWT negotiation process, the response frame from the AP may either allocate service time to the b-TWT group to which the STA is assigned or specify the transmission cycle of the next Beacon frame that will contain the b-TWT parameter set. The STA then parses the service time for the corresponding b-TWT group from this b-TWT information field. The selection of the options will be determined by the AP vendor.

To remove an STA from a b-TWT group, either the STA or the AP sends a TWT Teardown frame, which terminates the STA's membership in the broadcast TWT group.

3. **Channel Access Mode of b-TWT**

The channel access mode of b-TWT is the same as that of i-TWT, either based on CSMA/CA or Trigger frames.

In actual scenarios, multiple STAs may join the same b-TWT group and transmit during the same service period. The Trigger frame-based method can efficiently reduce collisions through frequency multiplexing.

As shown in Fig. 2.31, STA1 and STA2 belong to the same b-TWT group. During the service period, the AP sends a Trigger frame to both STA1 and STA2

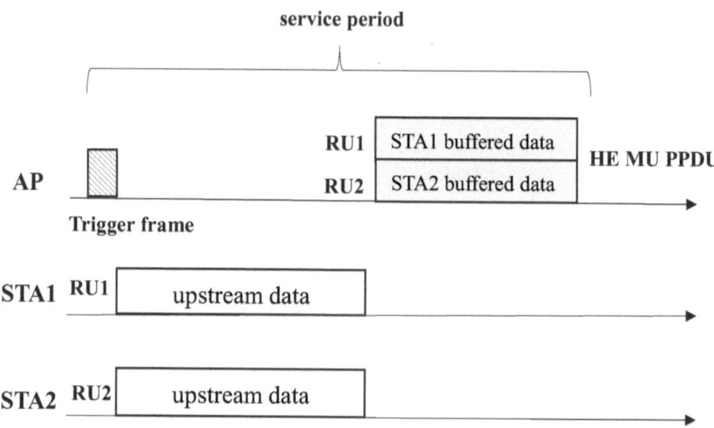

Fig. 2.31 Trigger frame-based b-TWT

with RU allocation information. STA1 and STA2 then send upstream data to the AP on RU1 and RU2, respectively, and receive buffered data from the AP.

4. **b-TWT Group #0 for Unassociated STAs**

The b-TWT group #0 is a special b-TWT group that is utilized for multicast data transmission, and it can be leveraged to facilitate connectionless service for unassociated STAs.

Generally, an STA must establish a connection with an AP before negotiating with the AP to join a b-TWT group. Wi-Fi 6 is capable of supporting connectionless service with unassociated STAs. To support such unassociated STAs in Wi-Fi power-saving mode, these STAs can directly utilize the service period of b-TWT group #0 without undergoing b-TWT negotiation, thereby bypassing the joining or teardown process.

From the AP's perspective, due to the absence of the association and b-TWT negotiation processes, the AP cannot acquire STA information. Therefore, only the RA-RU specified by AID 2045 in the Trigger frame can be utilized by the nonassociated STA.

As illustrated in Fig. 2.32, at the beginning of the service period, the AP sends a Trigger frame carrying RA-RU information. STA1 is not associated with the AP, but it is allowed to send upstream data in RU1, which is AID = 2045. Afterwards, the AP sends downstream data to STA1, thus completing the data interaction with the nonassociated STA.

In case there is multicast downstream data, the AP shall schedule the service period of the b-TWT group#0 right after a Beacon frame that carries the DTIM field. The STAs wake up at the DTIM time to receive the buffered multicast data frames.

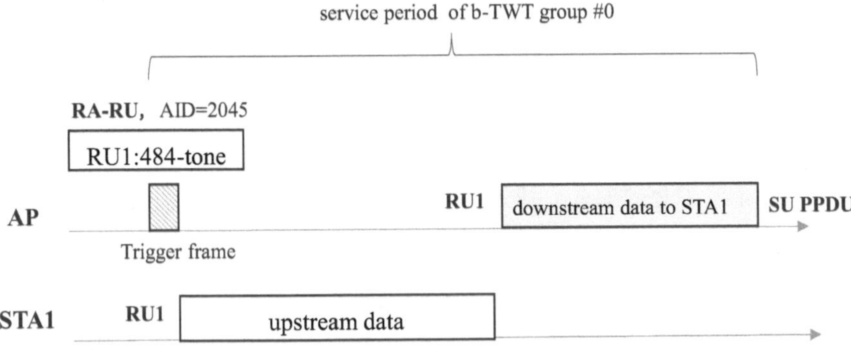

Fig. 2.32 b_TWT 0 group for a nonassociated STA

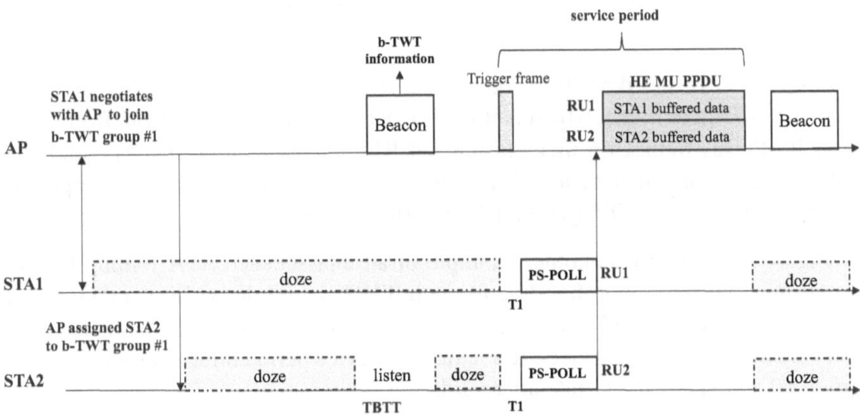

Fig. 2.33 Example of a b-TWT group with 2 STAs

5. **Examples of b-TWT**

Figure 2.33 shows an example of a b-TWT group with two STAs. In this example, STA1 initiates the request and negotiates with the AP to join the b-TWT group, while STA2 is assigned to the group by the AP.

STA1 Initiates the Negotiation Process STA1 sends a b-TWT negotiation request to the AP, which accepts it, allowing STA1 to join b-TWT group #1. The AP informs STA1 that the b-TWT service period is T1. STA1 then enters doze state.

AP Assigns b-TWT Group#1 to STA2 The AP assigns STA2 to b-TWT group #1. The next Beacon frame will carry additional b-TWT parameter set information. STA2 then enters doze state.

Query the Wake Interval Through the Beacon Frame STA2 wakes up at the next TBTT, receives the Beacon frame, and obtains T1 as the service start time for b-TWT group #1. It then enters doze state again.

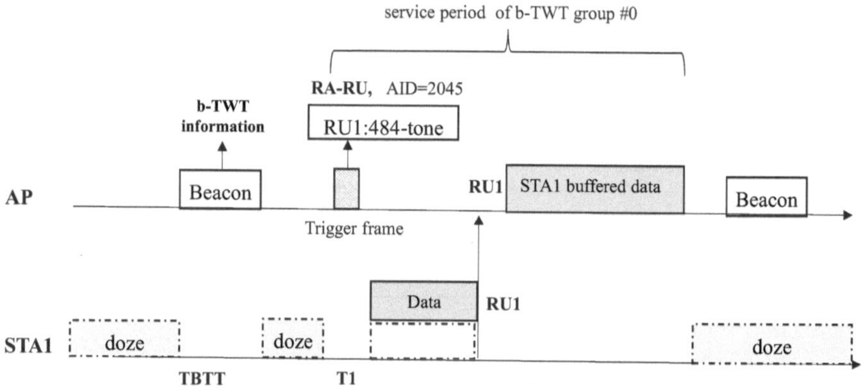

Fig. 2.34 Example of b-TWT group #0 with a nonassociated STA

Channel Access Based on the Trigger Frame STA1 and STA2 wake up at T1 and receive the Trigger frame, which includes the RU allocation information. Both STAs send PS-POLL frames on their designated RUs. Subsequently, the AP sends the buffered downstream data to STA1 and STA2. After receiving their respective buffered data frames, STA1 and STA2 return to doze state.

Figure 2.34 indicates another example of an unassociated STA joining b-TWT group #0. **Establish membership for a b-TWT schedule without negotiation:** STA1 wakes up at TBTT and receives a Beacon frame from the unconnected AP carrying the b-TWT parameters. It obtains the service period information for b-TWT group #0 and enters doze state afterwards.

Channel Access Based on the Trigger Frame STA1 wakes up again before the b-TWT group #0 service period starts and waits for the Trigger frame.

AP Allocates RA-RU for Group #0 The AP broadcasts the Trigger frame with the RA-RU information, and the RA-RU for AID 2045 is reserved for the nonassociated STAs.

STA Competes for RA-RU STA1 acquires the RA-RUs, sends upstream data to the AP, receives the buffered downstream data, and then re-enters doze state.

2.2.4.3 Opportunistic Power Saving (OPS)

The support of OPS in Wi-Fi 6 aims to enhance the scheduling efficiency of the b-TWT#0 group for nonassociated STAs.

One advantage of b-TWT group #0 lies in its reduction of the overhead involved in joining and leaving the b-TWT group. However, a constraint for the AP (Access Point) is its limited control over this group. Nonassociated STAs can directly join b-TWT group #0 without establishing a connection with the AP. Consequently, if

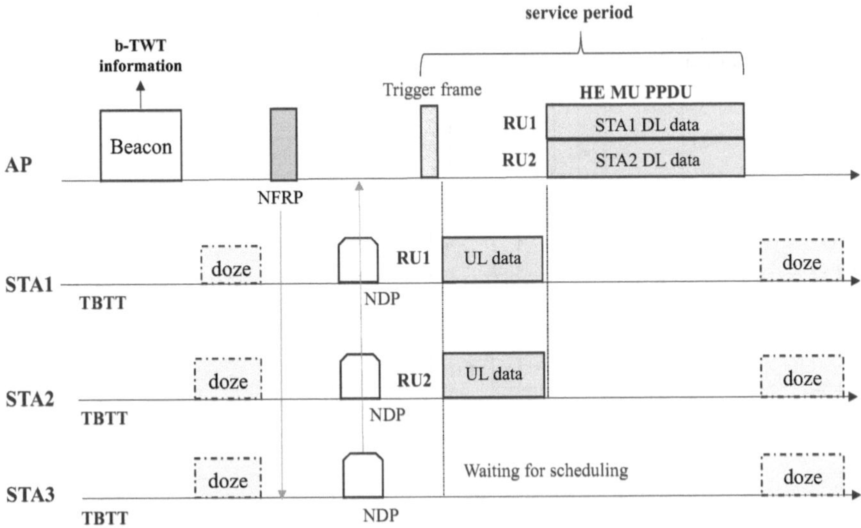

Fig. 2.35 Constraint for b-TWT 0 group scheduling

the number of STAs in group #0 surpasses the AP's scheduling capacity, the AP is unable to schedule these STAs promptly. The unscheduled STAs then have to remain awake until the end of the Beacon period.

In Fig. 2.35, the AP sends a Beacon frame where the TIM field indicates that it has buffered data for STA1, STA2, and STA3. However, since there was no prior negotiation concerning the TWT service cycle, the AP does not know whether these three STAs will indeed wake up during the service period of b-TWT group #0. To address this, the AP sends an NDP Feedback Report Poll (NFRP) Trigger frame to inquire about the current state of the STAs. Simultaneously, it assigns RU1, RU2, and RU3 to STA1, STA2, and STA3, respectively. Subsequently, STA1, STA2, and STA3 respond with NDP frames within their designated RUs.

Due to a large amount of buffered data, the AP can only transmit downstream data to STA1 and STA2 within a single service period. At the onset of the service cycle for b-TWT group #0, the AP sends a Trigger frame and allocates RU1 and RU2 to STA1 and STA2. After the AP receives the upstream data from STA1 and STA2, it then sends them their corresponding buffered downstream data. During the entire service period, STA3 fails to secure an opportunity to transmit; thus, STA3 remains awake until the conclusion of the service time but is unable to transmit any data.

The Opportunistic Power Saving (OPS) eliminates the need for a negotiation process, thereby reducing overhead. At the start of the service period, the AP broadcasts an OPS frame containing a TIM field. Similar to the TIM field in a Beacon frame, each bit of the Partial Virtual Bitmap indicates whether the corresponding STA is scheduled for service in that period. STAs not scheduled enter the doze state and will wake up at the next TBTT to check the TIM field in the OPS frame.

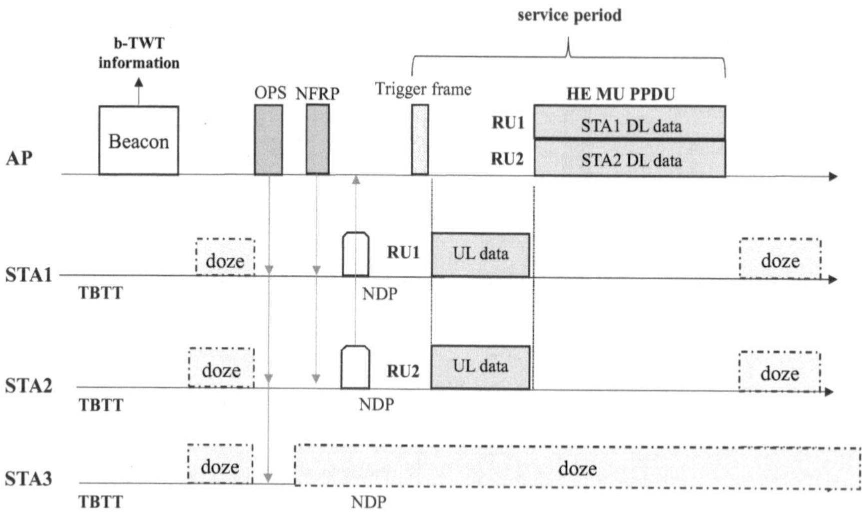

Fig. 2.36 Optimization from OPS for b-TWT 0 group scheduling

As depicted in Fig. 2.36, the TIM within the OPS frame indicates that only STA1 and STA2 are scheduled for the current service period. Consequently, STA1 and STA2 remain awake to engage in data transmission with the AP. STA3, upon learning from the OPS frame that it is not scheduled for this service period, enters the doze state to conserve power saving.

2.2.5 *Spatial Reuse Technology to Improve Spectrum Efficiency*

Wi-Fi 6 aims to optimize performance and service quality in high-density Wi-Fi environments. Two types of high-density Wi-Fi scenarios exist: the first involves a single AP serving a large number of connected stations, while the second scenario involves multiple APs operating simultaneously in a confined space, leading to Overlapping Basic Service Sets (OBSS). In the latter scenario, each BSS operates on its own dedicated channel, enabling APs and STAs from different BSSs to communicate on their respective channels. However, due to the restricted number of channels in the ISM bands, nearby APs may inadvertently select the same operating channel. This results in mutual interference between them, causing devices within different BSSs to defer their transmissions whenever they detect activity from neighboring BSSs.

As shown in Fig. 2.37, BSS1 and BSS2 are operating on the same channel of 2.4 GHz. STA2 is located within the overlapping area of the two BSSs. If STA2 is receiving data from BSS1 and AP2 begins transmitting to STA-3 simultaneously, the

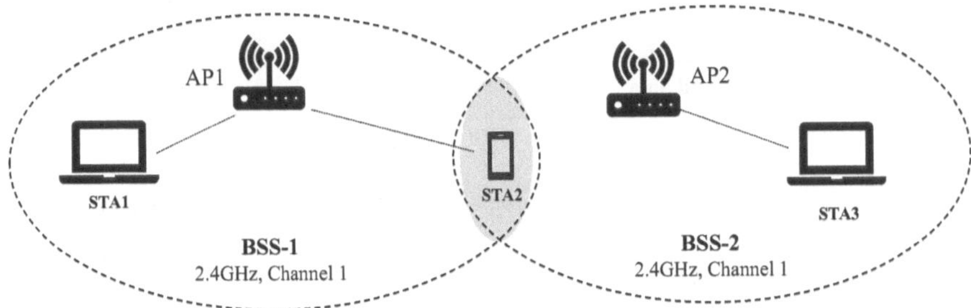

Fig. 2.37 Example of OBSS with the same channel

signals at STA2 may become corrupted. In the OBSS region, the STAs are required to monitor the channel from both BSSs before sending data. An STA can only transmit data frames if it determines that both BSSs are idle. The network performance in the OBSS environment is compromised due to interference from adjacent BSSs.

In Wi-Fi 6, an AP allocates OFDMA resource units to STAs within the same BSS. However, when multiple APs are present, these APs cannot coordinate their resource units' allocation among each other. Consequently, this lack of coordination can lead to collisions within the resource units when BSSs overlap.

To enhance performance and reduce interference in OBSS, Wi-Fi 6 has introduced a new technology known as Spatial Reuse (SR). A new field, called BSS coloring, is defined within the Wi-Fi physical frame to differentiate between various BSSs. When a Wi-Fi device receives data frames, it determines their origin by examining the BSS Coloring field. If the data originate from another BSS and the signal strength is below a certain threshold, the device considers the interference negligible for the OBSS signals. Consequently, the Wi-Fi device is permitted to transmit data. Figure 2.38 illustrates the difference between traditional CSMA/CA and Spatial Reuse in cases where interference from OBSS is detected, but the signal strength remains below the threshold.

In the legacy Wi-Fi network depicted in Fig. 2.38a, when STA2 in BSS2 detects that the channel is occupied, it must delay transmission and wait until the channel becomes idle. It makes no difference whether the usage is due to internal communication within BSS2 or from the adjacent BSS1.

Figure 2.38b depicts the same scenario but with Wi-Fi 6 APs and STAs supporting Spatial Reuse technology. STA2 can determine that the ongoing transmission is from an adjacent BSS by using the BSS coloring field. Since the signal is below the threshold, it is considered to have no interference, allowing STA2 to send data using the current channel. Spatial Reuse can effectively enhance spectrum utilization and performance in scenarios involving overlapping BSSs.

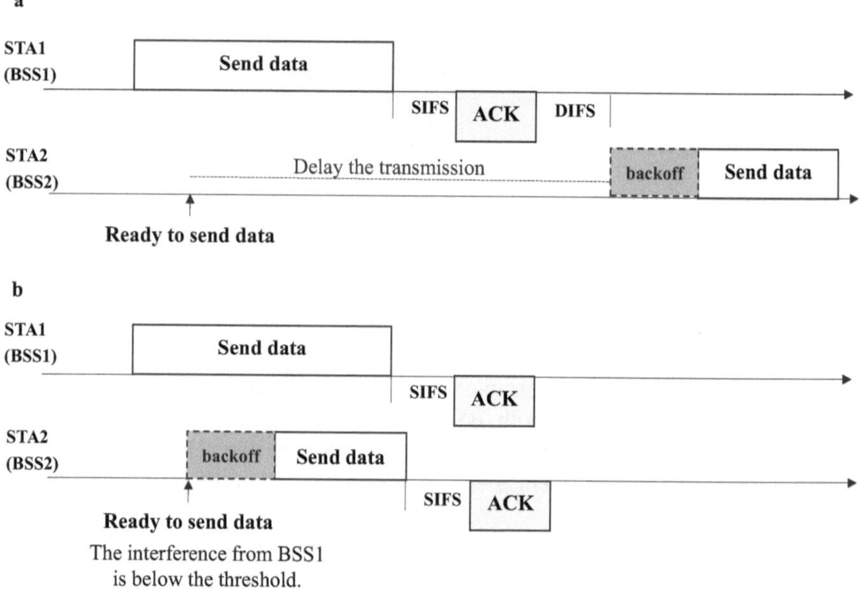

Fig. 2.38 (**a**) Legacy mode, (**b**) Spatial Reuse mode

2.2.5.1 The Workflow of Spatial Reuse

The workflow of Spatial Reuse technology is shown in Fig. 2.39. In addition to the traditional CCA detection, Spatial Reuse technology incorporates an extra procedure, denoted by the dotted line, for determining the source of the signal, checking its strength, and setting the NAV. This extra step is crucial in deciding whether the device can send data or whether it must postpone the transmission and try in the subsequent cycle.

(1) **Determining the source BSS**

The device receives Wi-Fi data frames and examines the BSS coloring in the preamble to ascertain whether they originate from an adjacent BSS or its own BSS and the transmission time of the frame. If the data originates from an adjacent BSS, the device compares its signal strength with a predefined threshold.

(2) **Establishing a dynamic transmit power threshold**

If the signal strength of a data frame from an adjacent BSS falls below the threshold, the device is allowed to transmit data. Ensuring that no interference is inflicted on ongoing data frame transmissions is crucial. Therefore, the device's transmit power must not surpass a threshold dynamically derived from the received signal strength of overlapping BSSs.

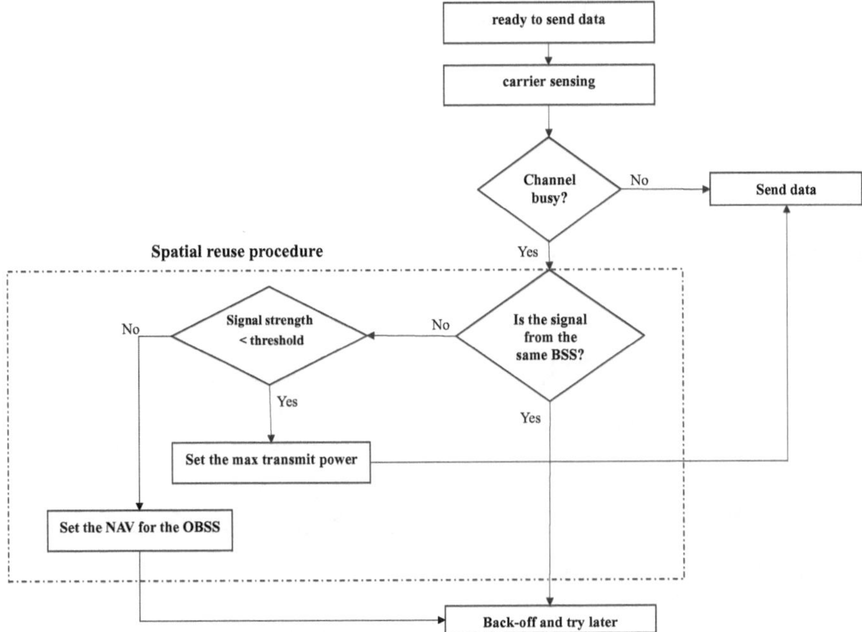

Fig. 2.39 Spatial reuse procedure

(3) **Implementing Network Allocation Vector for OBSSs**

When the signal from an OBSS exceeds the threshold, the device sets two NAVs to track the data transmission durations of its own BSS and the neighboring BSS. Only when both NAVs reach zero does it attempt to access the channel for PPDU transmission.

In the following sections, we will delve into these three aspects in detail.

2.2.5.2 BSS Coloring

The BSS coloring is a special field in the preamble of the physical layer that serves as the identifier of the BSS. When a device receives a frame and compares this field with its own BSS coloring, it can determine whether the physical frame belongs to its own BSS or an OBSS.

Prior to Wi-Fi 6, Wi-Fi devices had to parse the BSSID in the MAC header to determine which BSS the PPDUs came from. With BSS coloring technology, the identifier of the BSS is placed at the physical layer, eliminating the need for MAC layer processing overhead.

The BSS coloring field and the BSSID field within a PPDU are illustrated in Fig. 2.40.

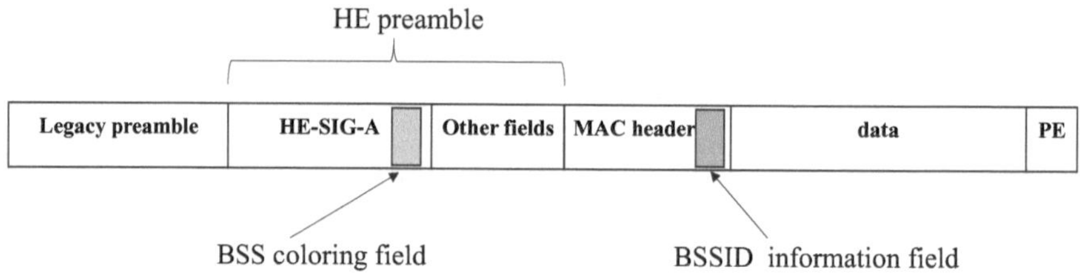

Fig. 2.40 Wi-Fi 6 HE PPDU format

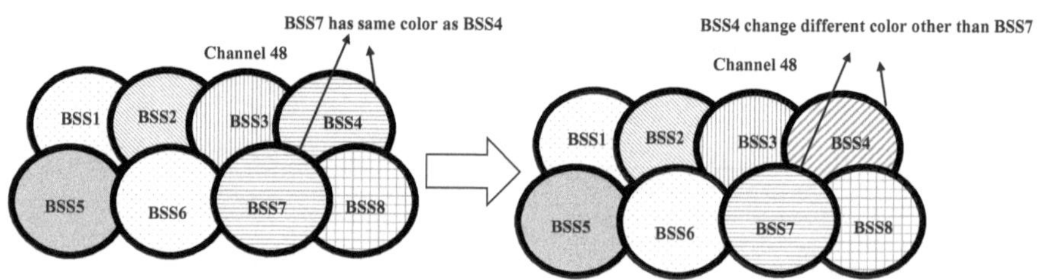

Fig. 2.41 BSS color change process

BSS coloring originated from the 802.11ah standard, where up to 8 BSSs could be identified using a 3-bit field. As Wi-Fi networks have become increasingly crowded, the BSS coloring field was extended to 6 bits in Wi-Fi 6, allowing for up to $2^6 = 64$ BSSs to be tagged.

When an AP begins operating, it first detects the BSS color of nearby APs on the same channel before choosing a distinct BSS color for itself. Each AP communicates its BSS color to other devices by embedding it in Beacon frames or Probe Response frames. Consequently, all STAs within its BSS adhere to the assigned BSS coloring scheme. The HE PPDUs transmitted by an STA include the BSS color learned from the associated AP.

The AP gathers the BSS color of nearby BSSs independently or with assistance from STAs. Due to the different signal coverage between APs and STAs, the AP may not detect BSS colors at greater distances. Therefore, STAs situated in overlapping areas can report the detected BSS colors back to the AP. In the event of a BSS color collision, the AP uses the BSS color change announcement field in the Beacon frame or Probe Response frame to inform the connected STAs to switch to a new BSS color.

As shown in Fig. 2.41, the AP for BSS4 discovers that its BSS color value is the same as that of BSS7. Consequently, the AP initiates the BSS coloring change announcement process to update its BSS color.

2.2.5.3 Set Dynamic Threshold of the Transmit Power

As discussed in Chap. 1, two thresholds are defined for Carrier Sense/Clear Channel Assessment at the physical layer: −62 dBm as the CCA-ED threshold for non-Wi-Fi signals and − 82 dBm as the CCA-PD threshold for Wi-Fi signal strength. At the MAC layer, a Network Allocation Vector (NAV) is used to account for the current PPDU transmission time, according to Virtual Carrier Sensing. If the received signal strength is above these thresholds, as determined by CS/CCA, or if the NAV is not zero, the channel is considered busy.

The Spatial Reuse technology extends these carrier sensing technologies for high-density AP scenarios. This subsection focuses on the physical layer carrier sensing thresholds.

With Spatial Reuse technology, the threshold of CCA-PD is relaxed up to -62 dBm, aligning it with the threshold of CCA-ED, meaning that stronger signals from neighboring BSSs are allowed in Wi-Fi 6 networks.

On the other hand, it is mandated to limit the maximum transmission power in order to prevent interference with the data transmission of neighboring BSSs. According to the Wi-Fi 6 protocol, the equation defining the maximum transmission power is given as Eq. 2.1:

$$\mathbf{TX\_PWR_{max}} = \mathbf{TX\_PWR_{ref}} - (\mathbf{OBSS\_PD_{level}} - \mathbf{OBSS\_PD_{min}}) \tag{2.1}$$

where $\mathbf{TX\_PWR}_{\mathbf{max}}$ is the maximum transmit power, $\mathbf{TX\_PWR}_{\mathbf{ref}}$ is the reference transmission power, which is 21 dBm defined by Wi-Fi 6, $\mathbf{OBSS\_PD}_{\mathbf{level}}$ is the CCA-PD threshold in the range of [−82 dBm, −62 dBm], $\mathbf{OBSS\_PD}_{\mathbf{min}}$ is the lowest CCA-PD threshold, which is −82 dBm.

From this equation, it means that the lower the CCA-PD threshold, the higher the allowed transmit power.

In the example shown in Fig. 2.42, the CCA-PD threshold of STA2 is set to − 74 dBm. When STA2 is ready to transmit data to AP1, it detects that there is a transmission from an OBSS with a signal strength of −76 dBm, which is below the threshold. Therefore, STA2 is allowed to transmit the data with a maximum transmit power calculated as 21 dBm − (−74 dBm + 82 dBm) = 13 dBm.

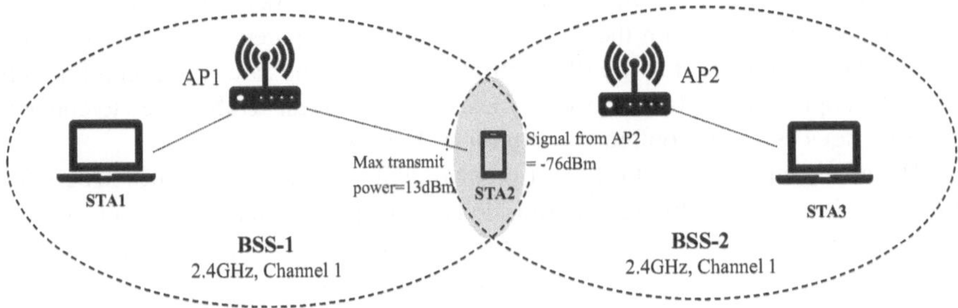

Fig. 2.42 Set the dynamic threshold of the transmit power

According to the Spatial Reuse technology in the Wi-Fi 6 standard, there is another formula for calculating the transmission power under Spatial Reuse, which is unrelated to the signal strength of neighboring BSSs. However, it has the compatibility issues among devices from different vendors. This formula and its challenges are not covered in this book.

2.2.5.4 Set Network Allocation Vector for OBSSs

The Spatial Reuse reinforces the Virtual Carrier sense mechanism by defining two NAVs, aiming to track the transmission duration of the received PPDUs from both its own BSS and a neighboring BSS. The Intra-NAV is employed to record the transmission time of PPDUs within its own BSS, while the other one, referred to as Basic-NAV, serves to count the transmission time of PPDUs originating from a neighboring BSS. If either one is not zero, the medium is considered busy.

If the PPDU being transmitted in the channel originates from the BSS to which it belongs, the device starts the intra-NAV countdown.

When a PPDU being transmitted in the channel comes from a neighboring BSS, the device does not immediately initiate the Basic-NAV. Instead, it first compares the received signal strength with a predefined threshold. If the signal strength exceeds the threshold, the device then sets the Basic-NAV and begins its countdown.

For instance, if the signal strength from a neighboring BSS measures at −58 dBm, which is stronger than the threshold of −62 dBm, then the device should wait until the current transmission from the OBSS has completed. It will then start the Basic-NAV countdown and attempt to access the channel once the counter reaches zero.

2.2.6 Multiple BSSID Technology to Support Multi-BSS Scenario

A Wi-Fi AP can create multiple BSS networks simultaneously, each identified by a unique BSSID.

As shown in Fig. 2.43, the AP creates two BSS networks: one with the SSIDs "Home" and the other with the SSID "Guest". The computers, Web cameras, and family phones connected to the BSS with the SSID "Home" are configured for web browsing, uploading and downloading files, etc. The "Guest" BSS is used to connect visitors' devices and is configured only for web browsing.

The administrator can set different passwords for the BSSs to control access for different devices, set different permissions, and even provide different service qualities through the BSS settings. This gives high flexibility in managing the Wi-Fi network.

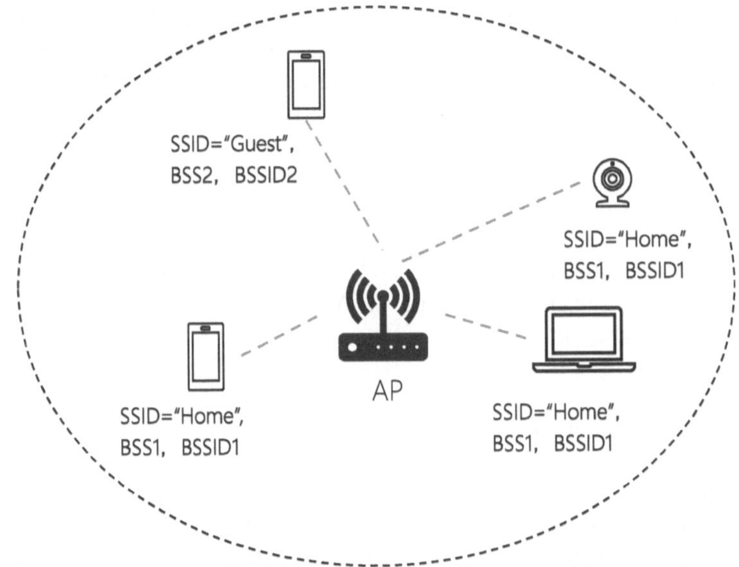

Fig. 2.43 Example of multiple BSS at home

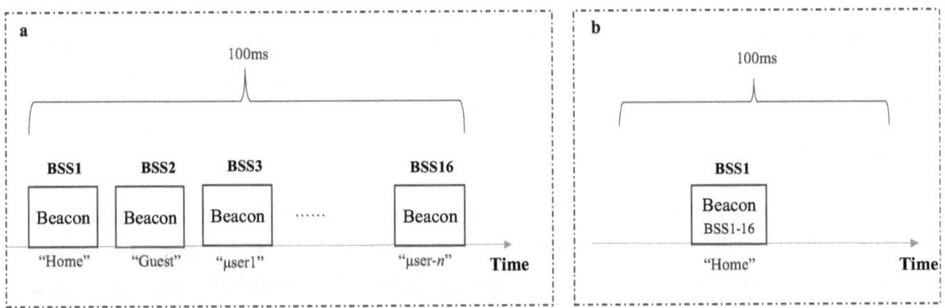

Fig. 2.44 (**a**) Beacon frames under legacy multiple BSSs mode, (**b**) Beacon frames under MBSSID mode

In a multi-BSS scenario, each BSS operates on the same channel simultaneously. Therefore, devices adhere to the CSMA/CA mechanism and must obtain wireless medium resources before transmission. The AP periodically sends Beacon frames for each BSS network. Consequently, the higher the number of BSSs created by an AP, the greater the number of Beacon frames transmitted, leading to increased overhead on the wireless channel.

According to the Wi-Fi 6 certification standard developed by the Wi-Fi Alliance, a Wi-Fi 6 AP can create up to 16 BSSs on each channel, where each BSS has its own SSID, BSSID, and password. In the example shown in Fig. 2.44a, the AP creates 16 BSSs, and each one must periodically broadcast Beacon frames. Assuming all BSSs share the same Beacon period of 100 ms, then every 100 ms/16 = 6.25 ms, a Beacon frame would be transmitted over the channel.

The multiple-BSSID (MBSSID) technology, introduced in Wi-Fi 6, combines the Beacon frames or the Probe Response frames of different BSSs into a single aggregated Beacon or Probe Response frame to improve channel utilization. As indicated in Fig. 2.44b, the Beacon frames from 16 BSSs are combined into a single Beacon frame. This frame is transmitted only once every 100 ms period. Obviously, MBSSID technology decreases the number of Beacon frames and Probe Response frames in the wireless channel, thereby enhancing the efficiency of wireless media use.

MBSSID was initially defined in the 802.11 k specification ratified in 2008. It was later adopted as a mandatory feature in Wi-Fi 6 standard to enhance network efficiency and management.

2.2.6.1 Key Technologies of MBSSID

As shown in Fig. 2.44b, the Beacon frames are combined and transmitted on the "Home" BSS but not on the other BSSs. This BSSID is known as the Transmitted BSSID, while the other BSS contained within the Beacon or Probe Response frame are referred to as non-transmitted BSSIDs. As depicted in Fig. 2.45, BSS1 is the Transmitted BSSID, and BSS2 through BSSn are non-transmitted BSSIDs.

The MBSSID field comprises MBSSID field ID, length, maximum number of BSSIDs, and the parameter sets of the non-transmitted BSSIDs. To further reduce overhead, the MBSSID field is optimized through the use of derived MAC addresses, parameter inheritance, and a unified AID.

1. **The Derived MAC Address**

Each BSS possesses a BSSID, which is a unique 48-bit MAC address. It is defined that the non-transmitted BSSIDs have consecutive MAC addresses following that of the Transmitted BSSID. Consequently, the MBSSID does not need to include all MAC addresses; instead, the MAC address of each non-transmitted BSSID can be calculated based on the transmitted BSSID's MAC address and its index. This approach eliminates redundant information in the MAC addresses of the MBSSID field.

The MAC address for a non-transmitted BSSID can be derived as Eq. 2.2:

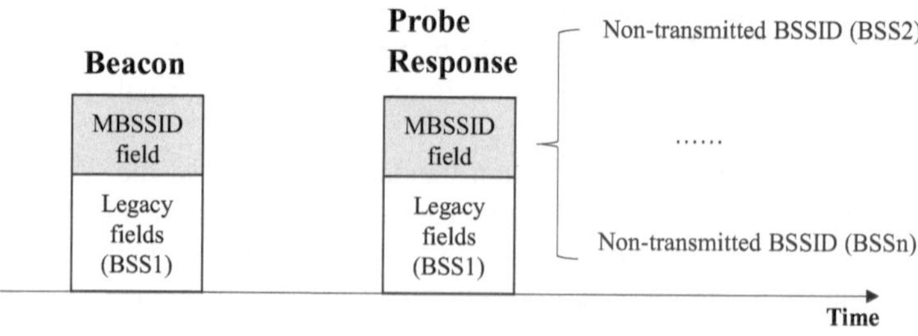

Fig. 2.45 MBSSID transmitted BSSID and non-transmitted BSSID

	BSS1	BSS2	BSS3
MAC address	MAC1	MAC2	MAC3
Channel/Band width	36/80MHz	36/80MHz	36/80MHz
SSID	µser	Guest	Home
Maximum spatial streams	8	8	8

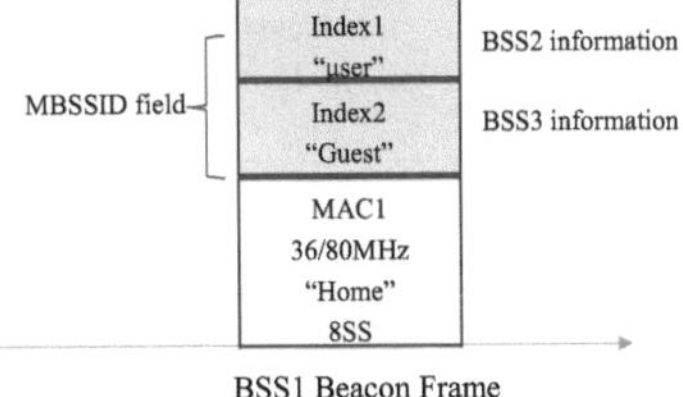

Fig. 2.46 An example of the Beacon frame with the MBSSID field

$$
\begin{aligned}
&A0 - A1 - A2 - A3 - A4 - A5 = \textit{transmitted BSSID MAC address} \\
&B = A5 \ mod \ 2^n \\
&A5(i) = A5\text{–}B + ((B + i) \ mod \ 2^n) \\
&BSSID(i) = A0 - A1 - A2 - A3 - A4 - A5(i)
\end{aligned} \tag{2.2}
$$

where 2^n is the number of BSSIDs, and BSSID(i) is the MAC address of the ith non-transmitted BSSID.

As indicated in Eq. 2.2, only the last byte of the non-transmitted BSSID's MAC address differs from that of the transmitting BSSID's MAC address.

For example, if the MAC address of the transmitting BSSID is 88:b3:62:36:05:5f, and there are up to 16 BSSs created, the MAC address of the fifth non-transmitted BSSID can be calculated as follows:

A0-A1-A2-A3-A4-A5 *= 88:b3:62:36:05:5f, and A5 is 5f*
2^n = 16,
B = 5f ***mod*** *16 = f*
A5(5) = 5f—f + ((f + 5) ***mod*** *16) = 54,*
BSSID (5) = ***A0-A1-A2-A3-A4-A5(5)*** *= 88:b3:62:36:05:54.*

2. **Parameter Inheritance**

Given that the non-transmitted BSSIDs are created on the same channel as the transmitted BSSID, they share the same capabilities, such as the number of antennas and maximum rate. Consequently, it is unnecessary to transmit this duplicate information in the MBSSID field. Therefore, the non-transmitted BSSIDs inherit the physical layer parameters from the transmitted BSSID, including the working channel, bandwidth, maximum physical rate, etc. The MBSSID carries only the unique parameters, such as SSID and encryption method, for the non-transmitted BSSIDs.

For instance, as shown in Fig. 2.46, the AP operates on channel 36 with an 80 MHz channel bandwidth and creates three BSSs: BSS1, BSS2, and BSS3. The Beacon frame sent by BSS1 includes the MBSSID field, which carries the index and SSID for BSS2 and BSS3, while the channel, bandwidth, and other common

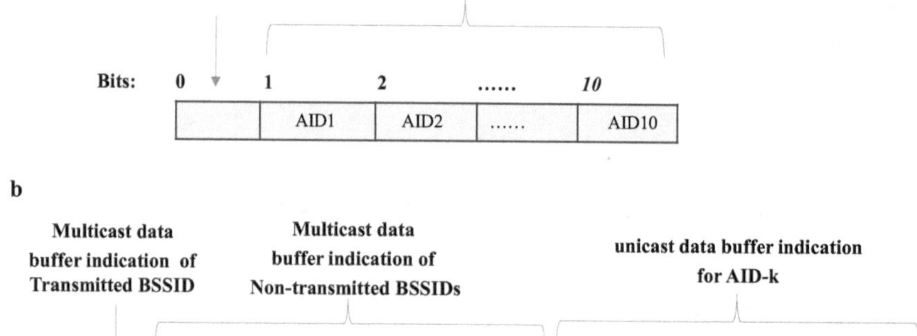

Fig. 2.47 (**a**) Legacy TIM/DTIM bitmap, (**b**) extended TIM/DTIM bitmap in a MBSSID

information are inherited from the parameter set of BSS1. This approach ensures that the MBSSID field does not contain duplicate parameters.

3. **Unified AID**

In the traditional Wi-Fi connection scenario, each STA is allocated a unique AID after it becomes associated with an AP. The AP then uses the TIM/DTIM to indicate the buffered data status for all STAs connected to it. As shown in Fig. 2.47a, bit 0 of the bitmap indicates whether there is multicast buffered data, while the other bits indicate unicast buffered data status for each STA corresponding to their AID.

In Wi-Fi 6, *both* the transmitted BSS and the non-transmitted BSSs allocate unified AIDs to the connected STAs. This *approach* leverages the bitmap of the transmission BSSID. Consequently, the non-transmitted BSSIDs do not *need* to maintain their own bitmaps within the MBSSID *environment.*

The MBSSID extends the bitmap to include both multicast and unicast indications, as shown in Fig. 2.47b.

(1) **Multicast buffer indication**

The first ***n*** bits of the bitmap are utilized to indicate the multicast data buffering status for the different BSSs, where the value of ***n*** represents the maximum number of BSSs that can be supported.

(2) **Unicast buffer indication**

The STAs are allocated a unified AID starting from n + 1. Beginning with bit n + 1, the bitmap indicates the unicast data buffering status for the STAs corresponding to their respective unified AIDs. In the example shown in Fig. 2.47b, the first 16 bits indicate the multicast buffered data status for 16 BSSs. Starting from bit 17, the bitmap represents the unicast data buffering status for the ten STAs with AID ranging from 16 to 25.

2.2.6.2 Other Improvements on Wi-Fi 6 MBSSID

To further minimize overhead, MBSSID is optimized through the use of refined MBSSID or partial MBSSID techniques.

1. **Refined MBSSID**

The refined MBSSID carries only the index of each non-transmitted BSSID, not the complete parameter sets. The difference between the MBSSID and refined MBSSID fields is indicated in Fig. 2.48. If an STA requires the complete parameter set of a non-transmitted BSSID, it sends a Probe Request frame to the AP, specifying the non-transmitted BSSID it wants to retrieve. The AP then delivers the parameter set of the non-transmitted BSSID through a Probe Response frame to the STA.

2. **Partial MBSSID**

As illustrated in Fig. 2.49, the partial MBSSID carries the parameter sets for some of the non-transmitted BSSs, and it requires multiple Beacon frames to transmit the complete MBSSID parameter sets in turn. STAs collect the information for all the non-transmitted BSSIDs information over time.

The use of a partial MBSSID reduces the amount of non-transmitted BSSID information in each Beacon frame, thereby improving the efficiency of communication.

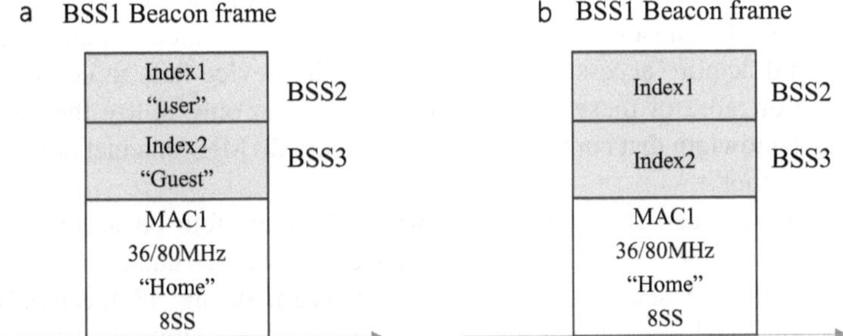

Fig. 2.48 (**a**) Normal MBSSID, (**b**) refined MBSSID

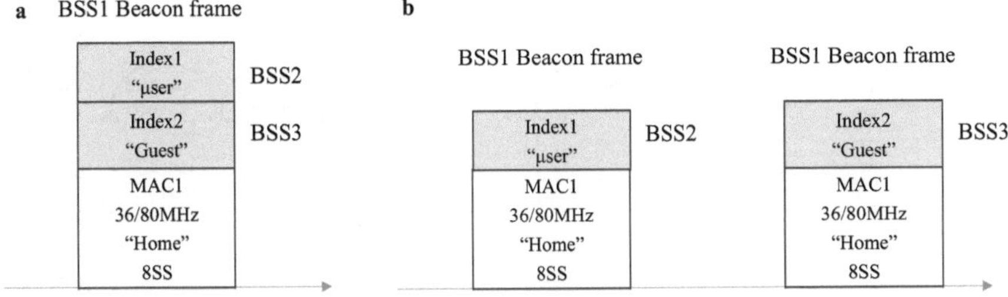

Fig. 2.49 (**a**) Normal MBSSID, (**b**) partial MBSSID

2.2.7 Preamble Puncturing Accommodating Noncontiguous Channels

The Wi-Fi channels can be combined to form a larger bandwidth channel in order to achieve higher throughput. As illustrated in Fig. 2.50a, two adjacent 20 MHz channels are bundled to create a single 40 MHz bandwidth channel, and similarly, two contiguous 40 MHz channels are bundled to form an 80 MHz bandwidth channel. Furthermore, this bundling process can be applied to two adjacent 80 MHz channels to form a 160 MHz bandwidth channel.

In Wi-Fi 6, this mechanism is extended to accommodate noncontiguous channels. Even when a channel is occupied, other channels can still be bundled for data transmission, even if they are not contiguous in the frequency spectrum. As illustrated in Fig. 2.50b, should one of the secondary 20 MHz channels be unavailable, the primary channel and the remaining two 20 MHz channels can still be combined to form a new 60 MHz channel. In both the second and third scenarios, some of the 20 MHz channels are not directly adjacent to the primary channel.

The noncontiguous channels are bundled, or rather, the unavailable channels are effectively bypassed. This technology is referred to as *Preamble Puncturing*, which entails setting the punctured channel's transmission power to a significantly low level so that receivers do not detect signals from that particular channel. Due to its inherent complexity, Wi-Fi 6 APs support Preamble Puncturing only for downstream data transmissions and not for upstream ones.

As described in Sect. 1.2.2, in order to bundle multiple 20 MHz channels, a legacy AP or STA must compete for wireless medium resources on all the 20 MHz channels and acquire access simultaneously. If the device fails to compete for or secure one or more of these 20 MHz channels, it can only utilize the contiguous frequency bandwidth that contains either the primary 20 MHz channel or the primary 40 MHz channel.

An example is depicted in Fig. 2.51, where there are four consecutive 20 MHz channels: channel 36, 40, 44, and 48. In the scenario where channel 44 is occupied, even if a Wi-Fi 5 AP successfully obtains channels 36, 40, and 48, it can only utilize the primary 20 MHz channel 48 for data transmission, thus limiting its bandwidth to just 20 MHz. Conversely, a Wi-Fi 6 AP can apply Preamble Puncturing to channel 44 and bundle together channels 36, 40, and 48 to form a 60 MHz bandwidth channel for data transmission.

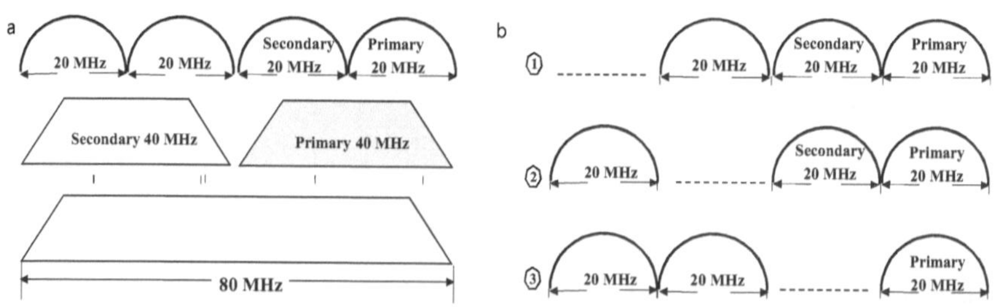

Fig. 2.50 (**a**) Bonding contiguous channels, (**b**) bonding noncontiguous channels

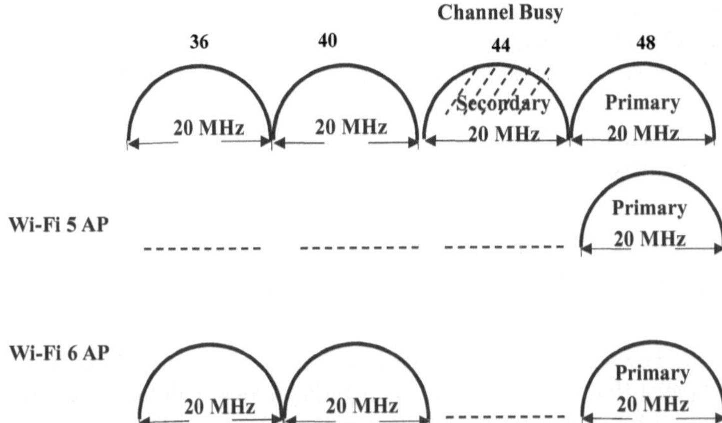

Fig. 2.51 Example of noncontiguous channel bonding

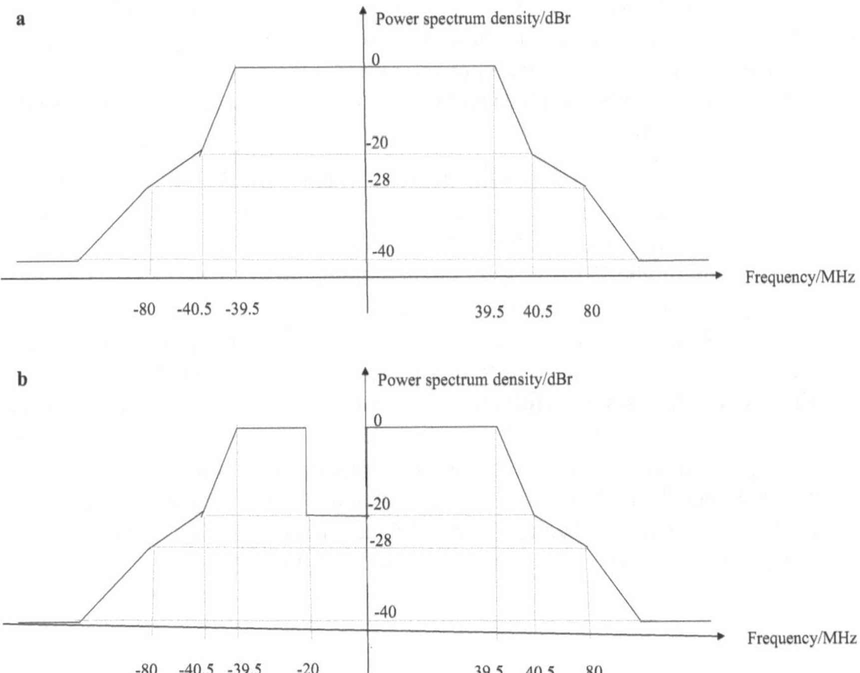

Fig. 2.52 (**a**) PSD of an 80 MHz channel bandwidth, (**b**) PSD of a Preamble Punctured 80 MHz Wi-Fi channel

Figure 2.52a illustrates the transmit power spectrum density (PSD) of a Wi-Fi signal across an 80 MHz channel bandwidth. The power spectrum density remains constant in the range of [−39.5 MHz, 39.5 MHz], while it decreases linearly in the frequency bands [−40.5 MHz, −39.5 MHz] and [39.5 MHz, 40.5 MHz].

Figure 2.52b illustrates the power spectrum density of the Wi-Fi signal in which the signal within the frequency range [−20 MHz, 0] has been punctured. In practical engineering design, filters are not ideal and cannot completely eliminate unwanted signals. In the Wi-Fi 6 standards, it is required that any signal leakage into the punctured channel must be at least 20 dB weaker than the signals in the active or working channels.

2.3 Updates of Physical Layer and MAC Layer for Wi-Fi 6

Most of the key technologies discussed in Sect. 2.2, such as OFDMA, enhanced MIMO, Spatial Reuse, and Preamble Puncturing, along with the 6 GHz frequency band that will be further elaborated upon in Sect. 2.4, are all closely related to the physical layer of Wi-Fi 6 technology.

As indicated in Fig. 2.53, the physical layer of a Wi-Fi 6 device applies channel coding, carrier modulation, and OFDMA RU multiplexing to the data being transmitted. The receiving device, in turn, reverses this process by performing the demodulation and decoding in the opposite order on the reversed signal.

Compared to Wi-Fi 5, the physical layer of Wi-Fi 6 incorporates several significant changes, including:

(1) **Channel coding:** In Wi-Fi 6, Low-density Parity Check (LDPC) coding is used, as opposed to the Binary Convolutional Code utilized in Wi-Fi 5. LDPC reduces decoding complexity and delay, achieving higher throughput.
(2) **Modulation mode:** Wi-Fi 6 supports modulation up to 1024-QAM, where each symbol can carry 10 bits of information, compared to Wi-Fi 5, which supports up to 256-QAM with each symbol carrying 8 bits. Therefore, 1024-QAM offers a 25% improvement in modulation efficiency over the 256-QAM of Wi-Fi 5.
(3) **Frequency division multiplexing:** In Wi-Fi 6, the spectrum is divided into orthogonal subcarriers, which are grouped as RUs that can be dynamically allocated to different STAs for concurrent data transmission. In contrast, Wi-Fi 5 allows each device to occupy the entire channel during data transmission. This method of spectrum utilization in Wi-Fi 6 can effectively improve performance, especially in scenarios with a high density of Wi-Fi STAs.

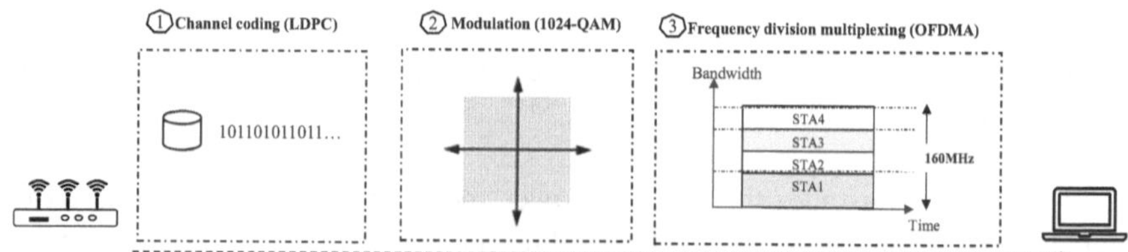

Fig. 2.53 Data transmission in Wi-Fi 6 physical layer

At the MAC layer, the PPDU format has been enhanced to include new preamble fields, as well as the introduction of the HE PPDU frame and Trigger frames. In this section, we will focus on these updates introduced in Wi-Fi 6.

2.3.1 Wi-Fi 6 Physical Layer Technology

2.3.1.1 1024-QAM Modulation

Starting from Wi-Fi 4, different Modulation and Coding Scheme (MCS) have been defined, offering various rates based on coding, modulation, channel bandwidth, and OFDM Guard Interval settings. The evolution of the MCS is illustrated in Fig. 2.54, where the maximum rate refers to the data rate of a single spatial stream.

- **Wi-Fi 4:** Defines 8 MCS rates, with a maximum rate of 150Mbps at MCS 7
- **Wi-Fi 5:** Adds MCS 8 and MCS 9, capable of achieving a maximum rate of 433.3Mbps
- **Wi-Fi 6:** Introduces MCS 10 and MCS 11, with a maximum rate of 600.5Mbps, which is 38.6% higher than Wi-Fi 5

The data rates for MCS 10 and MCS 11 under various channel bandwidths and OFDM Guard interval settings are listed in Table 2.4. If the channel bandwidth is 80 MHz and the Guard Interval is 0.8 μs, the maximum achievable rate is 600.5Mbps with a single spatial stream at MCS 11.

In Wi-Fi communication systems, the performance at the transmitter side is susceptible to influences from design choices in the radio frequency (RF) components, circuit board layout, and implementation methods. This can result

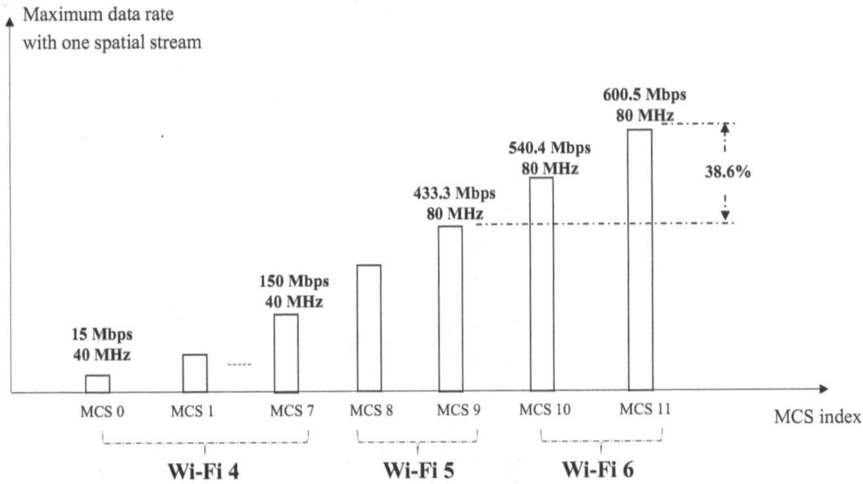

Fig. 2.54 The evolution of MCS along with the Wi-Fi standards

Table 2.4 MCS 10 and MCS 11 introduced in Wi-Fi 6

Data rate at physical layer (Mbps)										Coding	Modulation
Bandwidth	**20 MHz**			**40 MHz**			**80 MHz**				
GI (us)	0.8	1.6	3.2	0.8	1.6	3.2	0.8	1.6	3.2		
MCS 10	129.0	121.9	109.7	258.1	243.4	219.4	540.4	510.4	459.4	3/4	1024-QAM
MCS 11	143.4	135.4	121.9	286.8	270.8	243.8	600.5	567.1	510.4	5/6	1024-QAM

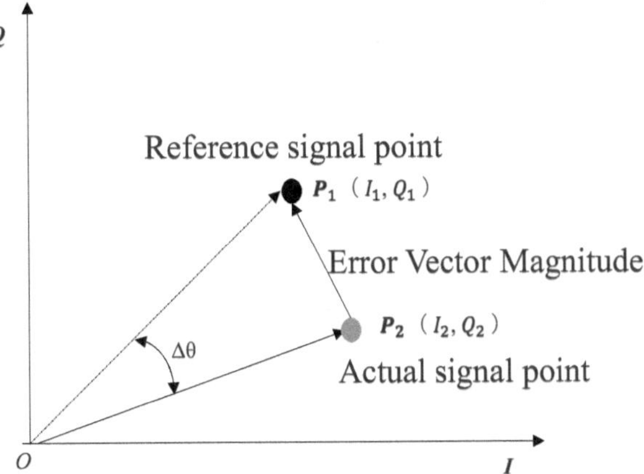

Fig. 2.55 Example of EVM with QPSK modulation

in a certain amount of relative constellation deviation between the ideal constellation points and the actual transmitted points during modulation. This deviation encompasses both amplitude deviation and phase deviation, which in turn introduces a degree of "blurriness" or distortion in the constellation diagram observed at the receiver end.

In practical engineering, Error Vector Magnitude (EVM) or Relative Constellation Error (RCE) is commonly employed to quantify the vector difference between actual constellation points and their ideal counterparts. EVM, in particular, measures the deviation of the actual signal point position from its reference position in terms of a percentage.

The EVM measurement is illustrated in Fig. 2.55. It can be calculated using Eq. 2.3:

$$\mathrm{EVM}(\%) = \frac{\sqrt{(I_2 - I_1)^2 + (Q_2 - Q_1)^2}}{|P_1|} \tag{2.3}$$

EVM is typically employed to measure the average deviation across multiple signal points rather than a single point. Assuming that Qi represents the actual constellation point and Pi denotes its corresponding reference point, the EVM of multiple signals can be calculated using Eq. 2.4:

$$\mathrm{EVM}(\%) = \frac{\sqrt{\sum_{i=1}^{i=k}(Q_i - P_i)^2}}{\sum_{i=1}^{i=k}|P_i|} \tag{2.4}$$

EVM can also be expressed in dB, as shown by Eq. 2.5:

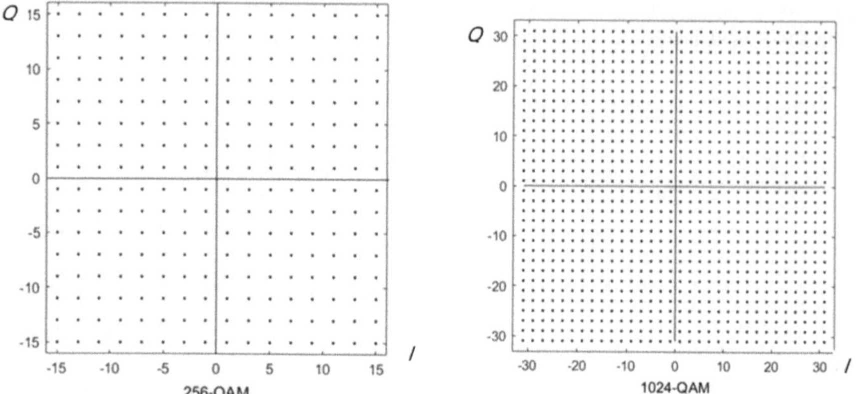

Fig. 2.56 256 QAM and 1024 QAM constellations

$$\text{EVM (dB)} = \mathbf{20} \times \ \mathbf{log} \ \text{EVM}(\%) \tag{2.5}$$

For example, if the EVM of a BPSK modulation system measure −5 dB, according to Eq. 2.5, this corresponds to an EVM (%) of approximately 56%. It's important to note that the higher the EVM value, the worse the performance of the communication system.

Low-order modulation schemes, such as QPSK, demonstrate increased resilience against high EVM levels. In QPSK, there is a single point (often metaphorically referred to as a "star") in each quadrant, with ample distance between them. Consequently, the system can tolerate higher EVM values without affecting the accuracy of its decision-making process.

As illustrated in Fig. 2.56, the distance between stars in a 1024-QAM constellation diagram is reduced by 50% compared to that of a 256-QAM constellation. With increasing modulation order, the tolerance margin diminishes exponentially, which means the decision region contracts correspondingly. It is crucial that the maximum EVM does not exceed this decision zone, as exceeding it would inevitably lead to demodulation errors.

In the Wi-Fi standards, Fig. 2.57 illustrates the minimum EVM required for various modulation methods. For instance, in Wi-Fi 6's 1024-QAM scheme, the maximum permissible EVM level is −35 dB, which corresponds to an EVM of approximately 1.77%. On the other hand, for 256-QAM with MCS 9, the EVM must not exceed -32 dB, translating to an EVM of around 2.5%. It is evident that these specifications demand a higher performance standard at the PHY layer of Wi-Fi 6 devices.

Wi-Fi standard	Modulation	EVM(db)	EVM(%)
Wi-Fi 4	BPSK	-5	56%
Wi-Fi 4	64-QAM	-27	4.4%
Wi-Fi 5	256-QAM	-30	2.5%
Wi-Fi 6	1024-QAM	-35	1.77%

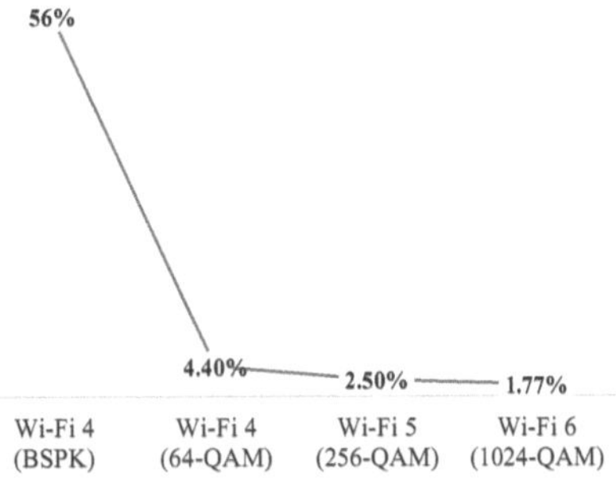

Fig. 2.57 EVM specification for different modulation schemes

2.3.1.2 OFDMA

In Wi-Fi 6, the subcarrier spacing for OFDMA is 78.125 kHz, which is a quarter of the OFDM subcarrier spacing at 312.5 kHz, as illustrated in Fig. 2.58. With the same channel bandwidth, OFDMA mode supports a greater number of subcarriers. For instance, in a 20 MHz channel, the number of data subcarriers for OFDM mode is 52, while in OFDMA, this number increases to 234. This frequency multiplexing in OFDMA provides Wi-Fi 6 with enhanced flexibility for supporting multiple users and high levels of concurrent operations.

1. **Symbol Period**

In the time domain, an OFDM symbol is constructed from multiple orthogonal subcarriers, meaning that it represents the superposition of individual orthogonal subcarriers.

As shown in Fig. 2.59, the orthogonal subcarriers can be expressed as $\{sin(2\pi \times wt), sin(2\pi \times 2wt), sin(2\pi \times 3wt), \ldots, sin(2\pi \times kwt)\}$, where w is the frequency of the first subcarrier, and the spacing between adjacent subcarriers is $\Delta f = w$.

An OFDM symbol period should be selected such that the amplitude of all subcarriers is zero at the same time. The period of the first carrier is T = 1/w, meaning the first subcarrier hits zero amplitude at time T. At this same time T, the amplitude of the kth subcarrier is $\sin(2\pi \times kwT) = \sin(2\pi \times k) = 0$, that is, the kth subcarrier also hits zero amplitude. Therefore, the period T = 1/w is the period at which all subcarriers in the OFDM symbol simultaneously hit zero amplitude.

In summary, the relationship between the subcarrier spacing Δf and the OFDM symbol period can be expressed as Eq. 2.6:

$$\Delta f = \frac{1}{\text{OFDM symbol period}} \tag{2.6}$$

The OFDM and OFDMA subcarrier spacings are 312.5KHz and 78.125KHz, respectively. Accordingly, the OFDM symbol period is 3.2 μs, and the OFDMA symbol period is 12.8 μs according to Eq. 2.6.

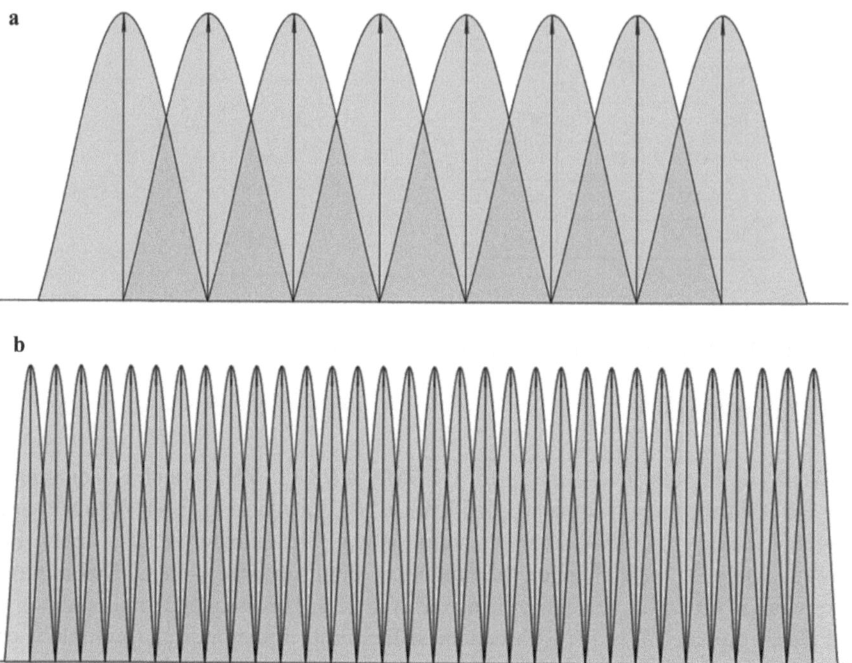

Fig. 2.58 (**a**) Wi-Fi 5 subcarriers with 312.5KHz spacing, (**b**) Wi-Fi 6 subcarriers with 78.125KHz spacing

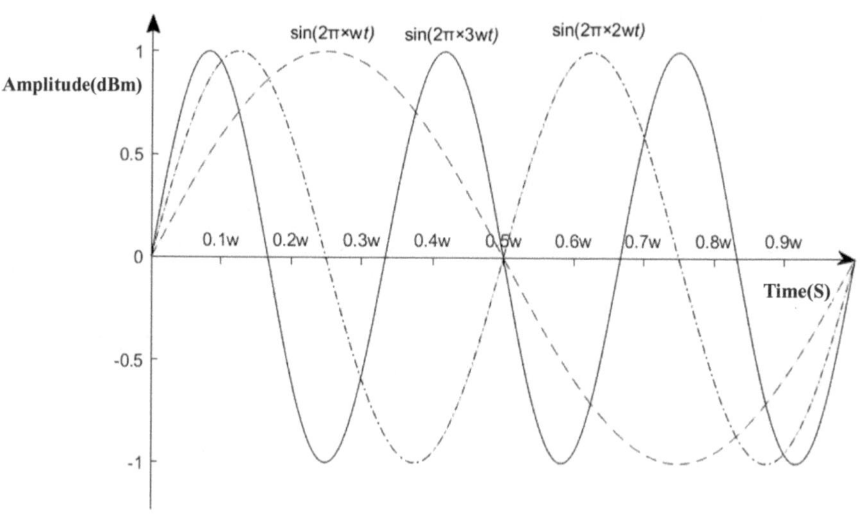

Fig. 2.59 Orthogonal subcarriers of an OFDM symbol

Table 2.5 Wi-Fi 6 GI and the user scenario

GI(μs)	User scenario
0.8	Indoor environment
1.6	Indoor or outdoor environment with notable multipath interference
3.2	Outdoor environment with severe multipath interference.

Table 2.6 Parameters of Wi-Fi 5 OFDM and Wi-Fi 6 OFDMA

Parameters	Wi-Fi 5	Wi-Fi 6
Number of subcarriers in a 20 MHz channel	64	256
Number of data subcarriers in a 20 MHz channel	52	234
Subcarrier spacing	312.5 kHz	78.125 kHz
OFDM symbol period	1/ 312.5 kHz = 3.2 μs	1/ 78.125 kHz = 12.8 μs
SGI	0.4 μs	Not defined
GI	0.8 μs	0.8 μs
2 × GI	Not defined	1.6 μs
4 × GI	Not defined	3.2 μs
Efficiency: OFDM symbol period vs OFDM symbol period plus GI	80%, 89%	80%, 89%, 94%

2. **Guard Interval**

As introduced in Chap. 1, the OFDM Guard interval (GI) was introduced as a means to mitigate the problem of mutual interference between OFDM symbols resulting from multipath transmission. A larger Guard interval improves immunity against interference but also increases overhead.

Before Wi-Fi 6, there were two standard types of Guard interval: the regular 0.8 μs and the shorter 0.4 μs, which could be employed in relatively clean environments. With Wi-Fi 6, the Guard interval has been expanded to include three types, as indicated in Table 2.5. In addition to the conventional 0.8 μs, two new types, 1.6 μs and 3.2 μs, are defined, particularly suited for noisy environment and outdoor environments, where Wi-Fi signals often experience significant variations due to transmission path effects or severe multipath interference. In these scenarios, a longer GI proves helpful in addressing signal overlap and interference across different paths.

The Wi-Fi 6 OFDMA parameters are listed with the Wi-Fi 5 OFDM parameters for comparison in Table 2.6.

Taking the parameters of Wi-Fi 6 into consideration in Eqs. 1–1, we can derive the maximum physical rate achievable under ideal environment for the 5GHz band, as shown in Table 2.7, which is 9.6Gbps.

Table 2.7 Wi-Fi 6 5GHz band theoretical data rate

Wi-Fi 6 parameters	Maximum capacity
Number of spatial streams	8
Number of bits per symbol	10
Symbol efficiency	5/6
Number of data subcarriers (160 MHz channel)	980 × 2 (bandwidth 160 MHz)
Minimum symbol period (μs)	12.8 μs + 0.8 μs
Maximum physical rate (Mbps)	$\frac{10 \times 5/6 \times (980x2) \times 8}{13.6} = 9607$

Table 2.8 Wi-Fi 6 PPDU frame formats

Wi-Fi 6 HE PPDU	HE preamble fields	Use case
HE SU PPDU	HE-SIG-A, HE-STF, HE-LTF and PE	Uplink and downlink of single-user transmission
HE MU PPDU	HE-SIG-A, HE-SIG-B, HE-STF, HE-LTF and PE	Downlink of OFDMA-based multiuser transmission, or uplink and downlink of MU-MIMO
HE TB PPDU	HE-SIG-A, HE-STF, HE-LTF and PE	Uplink of OFDMA-based multiuser transmission
HE ER PPDU	HE-SIG-A, HE-STF, HE-LTF and PE	Long reach transmission

2.3.2 *New Physical Layer Data Unit Frame Format*

With the introduction of new technologies, such as 1024-QAM modulation and OFDMA in the Wi-Fi 6 standard, the preamble fields have been updated accordingly. Moreover, Wi-Fi 6 defines a Packet Extension (PE) field at the end of the physical frame to allow for extra processing delay at the receiver. Consequently, the PPDU frame format has been extended to include these new preamble fields for different scenarios, as shown in Table 2.8.

2.3.2.1 HE Preamble Fields

As shown in Fig. 2.60 [2], the HE preamble fields introduced by Wi-Fi 6 replace the VHT preamble fields used in Wi-Fi 5.

- **HE-SIG-A**: This field is used to indicate Wi-Fi 6 modulation coding, channel bandwidth, spatial reuse, and other parameters.
- **HE-SIG-B**: It serves to specify the location and dimensions of the RUs for multiple STAs.
- **HE-STF and HE-LTF**: These are training sequences employed in the MU-MIMO channel sounding procedure.

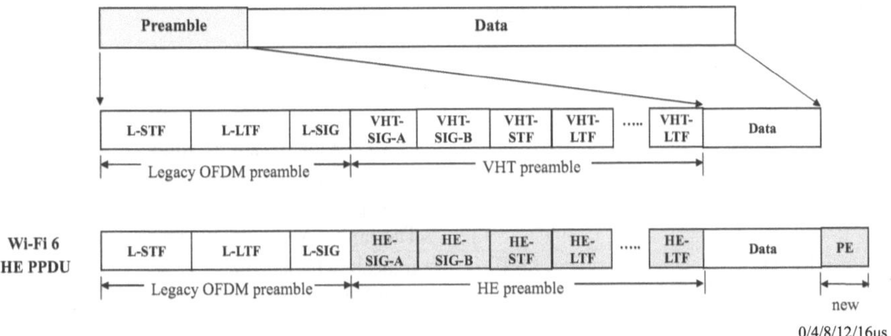

Fig. 2.60 HE PPDU frame format

- **Preamble extension (PE):** This provides an additional processing delay for the receivers. The duration can be configured to 0 μs, 4 μs, 8 μs, 12 μs, or 16 μs, depending on the parameters specified in the preceding fields.

The HE-SIG-A field has a similar definition across different HE PPDUs, although some bits in the same position have different meanings. For example, the meaning of each bit in the HE SIG-A field within the HE MU PPDU is shown in Table 2.9 [2].

The HE-SIG-B field is used by STAs to obtain downstream data based on the RU position and size. It consists of two parts: the common field and the user-specific field, as shown in Fig. 2.61.

(1) **Common field:** This field includes common information, CRC, and tail. It indicates the RU allocation information and the number of MU-MIMO users. It should be noted, however, that the common field is not present in the HE-SIG-B field when there is a full bandwidth MU-MIMO transmission, as there is no RU allocation in such a scenario.
(2) **User-specific field:** This field contains multiple user blocks followed by padding. To reduce overhead, each user block includes information for two users, a CRC, and a tail field. However, if the number of concurrent users is odd, the last user block may contain information for only one user. This field includes details such as MU-MIMO allocation and RU allocation, enabling the STA to decode the payload.

2.3.2.2 HE PPDU Frames

In Wi-Fi 6, four HE PPDU frame formats are defined: HE SU PPDU for single-user uplink and downlink transmission; HE MU PPDU for multiuser uplink and downlink transmission; HE TB PPDU for multiuser uplink transmission; HE ER PPDU for single-user long-distance uplink and downlink transmission. The frame formats are described below.

Table 2.9 HE-SIG-A field in HE MU PPDU

Field	Bit	Usage
UL/DL	B0	Indicate MU PPDU is sent upstream or downstream. 1: MU PPDU is addressed to an AP 0: MU PPDU is addressed to an STA
HE-SIG-B-MCS	B1-B3	Indicate the MCS of HE-SIG-B field The higher MCS, the higher throughput
HE-SIG-B DCM	B4	Indicate whether HW-SIG-B is modulated with Dual Carrier Modulation (DCM). Refer to Sect. 2.3.4 1: HW-SIG-B modulated with DCM 0: HW-SIG-B is not modulated with DCM
BSS color	B5-B10	Indicate BSS color. Refer to Sect. 2.2.5
Spatial reuse	B11-B14	Indicate Spatial Reuse mode. Refer to Sect. 2.2.5
Bandwidth	B15-B17	Indicate the channel bandwidth, such as 20 MHz, 40 MHz, and so on
The number of symbols in HE SIG-B, or the number of MU-MIMO Users	B18-B21	Indicate the number of OFDM symbols in HE SIG-B field. If the channel bandwidth is exclusively allocated to a single STA, this field indicates the number of MU-MIMO users
HE-SIG-B Compression	B22	Indicate the state of HE-SIG-B Common field 1: The Common field in the HE-SIG-B is not present 0: The Common field in the HE-SIG-B is present
GI and HE-LTF Size	B23-B24	Indicate the GI and HE-LTF size
Doppler	B25	Indicate Doppler effect, used by high-speed roaming devices

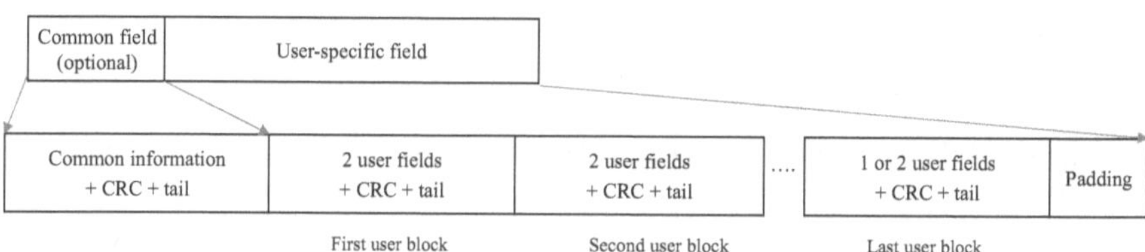

Fig. 2.61 HE-SIG-B field

1. **HE SU PPDU**

HE SU PPDU is used for one-on-one uplink and downlink data transmission between an AP and an STA. The frame format is illustrated in Fig. 2.62 [2]. The number of HE-LTF fields corresponds to the number of spatial streams; for instance, eight spatial streams would necessitate eight HE-LTF fields.

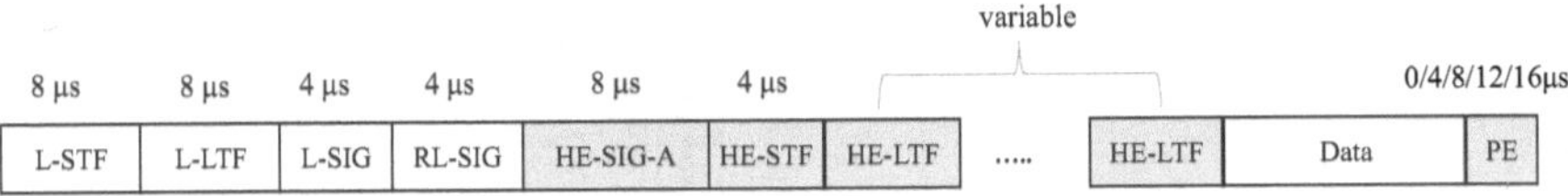

Fig. 2.62 HE SU PPDU frame format

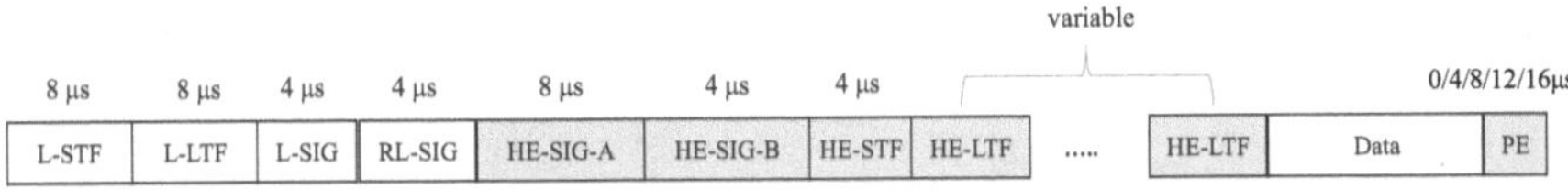

Fig. 2.63 HE MU PPDU frame format

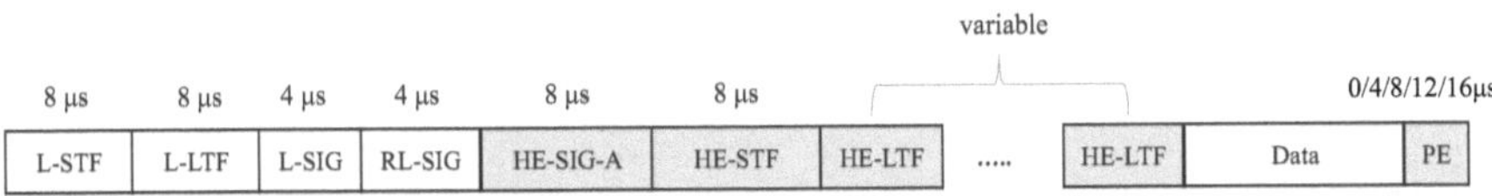

Fig. 2.64 HE TB PPDU frame format

2. **HE MU PPDU**

HE MU PPDU can be used for either single or multiuser downlink transmission based on OFDMA, as well as for uplink and downlink transmission based on MU-MIMO. As shown in Fig. 2.63 [2], the HE MU PPDU differs from the HE SU PPDU by including an additional HE-SIG-B field, which conveys multiuser information.

3. **HE TB PPDU**

HE TB PPDU is utilized for OFDMA-based multiuser uplink transmission, carrying the upstream data of STAs once they have received the Trigger frame from the AP. To ensure that the HE TB PPDU can be accurately parsed across all RUs, it is imperative that STAs maintain consistent parameters within the HE TB PPDU, such as MCS, RSSI, and upstream data length, among others.

The TB PPDU format is shown in Fig. 2.64 [2]. Compared to the HE MU PPDU, the differences are as follows:

- HE TB PPDU does not incorporate the HE SIG-B field, which typically conveys multiuser and RU assignment details. This is because such information has already been encapsulated within the Trigger frame that initiates the uplink transmission.
- In an HE TB PPDU, the HE-STF length is extended from its standard 4 μs to 8 μs. This elongation serves the purpose of providing ample time for collecting HE-STF fields from multiple MU-MIMO users during the channel sounding process, ensuring better synchronization and more accurate channel estimation in the context of multiuser uplink transmission.

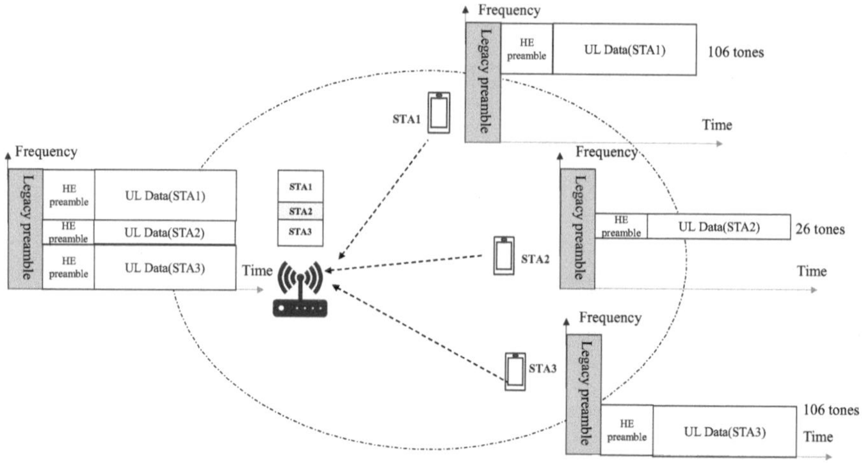

Fig. 2.65 Example of HE TB PPDU transmission between STA and AP

The legacy preamble fields of the HE TB PPDU are aligned in 20 MHz units, ensuring that legacy STAs can recognize the Wi-Fi signal. HE-SIG-A and HE-SIG-B fields are transmitted similarly to legacy preamble fields, meaning that they are broadcast across the entire channel bandwidth; this allows devices that operate solely on the primary 20 MHz, such as low-power IoT devices, to correctly parse the HE signal. However, other HE fields like HE-STF and HE-LTF are transmitted within the allocated RUs, rather than over 20 MHz channels.

Because the AP prescribes the legacy preamble rules in the Trigger frame, ensuring that all legacy preambles from the STAs are identical and sent simultaneously, the STAs can send their legacy preamble across the full 20 MHz channel even when they are allocated an RU narrower than 20 MHz.

If the bandwidth of the allocated RU surpasses 20 MHz, as is the case with a 484-tone RU, for instance, the legacy preamble is sent across both of the corresponding 20 MHz subchannels that make up this wider bandwidth RU.

An example is shown in Fig. 2.65. The BSS operates on a 20 MHz channel, and the AP assigns RUs of 106-tone, 26-tone, and 106-tone to STA1, STA2, and STA3, respectively. The STAs transmit identical legacy preambles across the entire channel, while transmitting other preamble parts and the uplink data on their individual RUs. On the AP side, it receives the same legacy preamble from the 20 MHz channel, as well as the distinct HE fields and UL data on the corresponding RUs.

When an STA receives a non-MU-RTS Trigger frame from an AP, it constructs an HE TB PPDU with the upstream data and sends it on the allocated RU. As shown in Fig. 2.66, if the data is insufficient to fill the size indicated in the Trigger frame, the STA must add a padding field to ensure that HE TB PPDUs from all STAs are of the same length, thereby reducing the complexity for the AP.

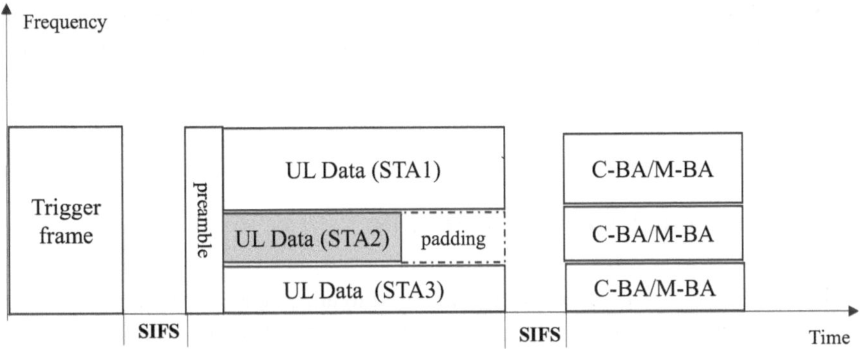

Fig. 2.66 Example of padding field in HE TB PPDU

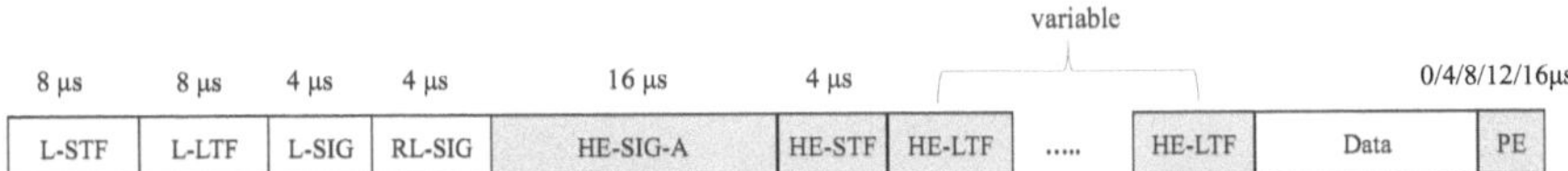

Fig. 2.67 HE ER PPDU frame format

It shall be noted that the padding is added at the end of the MPDU, not at the end of the PPDU. As discussed in Sect. 1.2.4, the MPDU is followed by a checksum; therefore, the padding should be added before the checksum field.

4. **HE ER PPDU**

HE ER PPDU is utilized for long-distance transmission, which inherently implies dealing with weak signals, deep fading conditions, and increased difficulty in demodulation and decoding at the receivers. To ensure reliable communications under such challenging circumstances, the HE ER PPDU adopts MCS0 through MCS2 coding schemes to enhance the transmission power, confines its operational bandwidth to 20 MHz, and exclusively supports 242-tone and 106-tone RU types. HE ER PPDU is employed for one-to-one communications between an AP and STA to address reliability concerns.

The L-STF, L-LTF, HE-STF, and HE-LTF fields are transmitted with an extra 3 dB gain, which helps receivers to decode the preamble and the subsequent data field. Since only the preamble field is transmitted with the increased power and not the other fields of the HE ER PPDU, it does not violate regulatory power limits.

The HE ER PPDU format is illustrated in Fig. 2.67 [2]. Since the preceding fields of HE-SIG-A are transmitted at high power, HE-SIG-A is duplicated to ensure successful decoding by the receiver. Therefore, the HE-SIG-A field has a duration of 16 μs in an HE ER PPDU, while the other fields are the same as those in a HE SU PPDU.

HE ER PPDU requires Automatic Gain Control (AGC) for both the transmitter and the receiver. If a BSS uses the Beacon frames in the HE ER PPDU format, it is called an HE ER BSS. An HE ER BSS has better signal coverage than a standard

BSS. However, STAs that do not support the HE ER PPDU format cannot decode the Beacon frames. As a common engineering practice, the AP typically sets up a standard BSS on the same channel alongside the HE ER BSS to accommodate legacy STAs.

2.3.3 New Trigger Frame in Wi-Fi 6

A Trigger frame is a special control frame used to allocate RUs for uplink transmission. Both basic and special Trigger frames are defined to accommodate various scenarios in Wi-Fi 6, as shown in Table 2.10 [2].

The Trigger frame format is depicted in Fig. 2.68. The MAC header is the same as in the generic frame format. Attention should be directed toward the Common Info field and the User Info List within the Trigger frame.

Table 2.10 Types of Trigger frame

Trigger frame	Type	User scenario
Basic	0	This indicates the RU allocation for multiuser and trigger the STAs to send upstream data
Beamforming Report Poll (BFRP)	1	It is used in the multiuser channel sounding procedure. The AP sends BFRP to simultaneously collect Compressed Beamforming data from multiple users
Multi-User Block Ack Request (MU-BAR)	2	It is used to request BlockACK from multiple users. The AP sends downstream data to the STAs using OFDMA, followed by an MU-BAR. The STAs then respond with BA information in the Rus indicated by the MU-BAR
Multi-User Request to Send (MU-RTS)	3	Used to inform the STAs that the AP will send data frames to multiple users and detect whether there is a collision. The targeted STAs respond by sending a CTS to inform the AP that the RU is available. Meanwhile, other devices set their NAV based on the duration field of the received CTS and initiate a backoff procedure
Buffer Status Report Poll (BSRP)	4	Used to poll the upstream buffer status of STAs. The STAs respond to send BSRP by sending a buffer status report in any subsequent frame to the AP
Groupcast with Retries MU-BAR (GCR MU-BAR)	5	Though similar to MU-BAR, GCR MU-BAR is used exclusively in scenarios where the AP transmits multicast frames with a retransmission function to multiple STAs
Bandwidth Query Report Poll (BQRP)	6	Used to query the channel status from multiple STAs before allocating the Rus for upstream and downstream transmission, in order to avoid the collision with the OBSS
NDP Feedback Report Poll (NFRP)	7	Used to query the STAs in a doze state. If an STA responds to the NFRP, the AP can send buffered data to it.

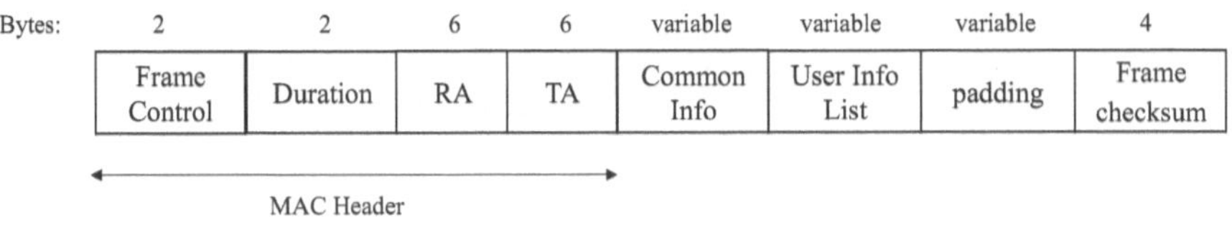

Fig. 2.68 Trigger frame format

Table 2.11 Common Info field

Field	Bit	Definition
Trigger type	B0-B3	Indicate the Trigger frame variant from the seven types presented in Table 2.10
UL length	B4-B15	Indicate the value of the L-SIG LENGTH field of the solicited HE TB PPDU.
CS required	B17	If this subfield is set to 1, it indicates that the STAs specified in the User Info fields should sense the channel state with CCA-ED before deciding whether to respond to the Trigger frame. If it's set to 0, it indicates that the STAs do not need to consider the channel state when determining their response.
UL bandwidth	B18-B19	Indicate the bandwidth in the HE-SIG-A field of the HE TB PPDU.
UL STBC	B26	If this subfield is set to 1, AP requests the STA to use STBC coding for the HE TB PPDU; if it's set to 0, no such request is made.
AP Tx Power	B28-B33	Indicate the transmit power of the Trigger frame. The STAs calculate the path loss using this subfield and the power of the received signals. They then determine the transmit power for UL data to ensure that the PPDUs reach the AP with approximately the same RSSI, enabling the AP to demodulate all HE TB PPDUs correctly.

Note: CCA-ED is used for channel sensing here instead of CCA-PD because the STAs have only a 16us SIFS interval to determine the channel state. In comparison, the legacy preamble requires at least 20us for CCA-PD to ascertain whether it is a Wi-Fi signal

2.3.3.1 Common Info

Some subfields of the Common Info field are defined in Table 2.11 [2].

2.3.3.2 User Info List

The User Info List field comprises zero or more User Info fields, the format of which is illustrated in Fig. 2.69 [2].

The key subfields are shown in Table 2.12 [2].

	B0 B11	B12 B19	B20	B21 B24	B25	B26 B31	B32 B38	B39	
	AID12	RU allocation	UL FEC Coding type	UL MCS	UL DCM	SS allocation/ RA-RU information	UL Target Receive Power	Reserved	Trigger dependent user information
Bytes:	12	8	1	4	1	6	7	1	variable

Fig. 2.69 User info field

Table 2.12 User Info field

Field	Bit	Usage
AID12	B0-B11	0: The User Info field allocates one or more contiguous RA-RUs for associated STAs 1–2007: The User Info field is addressed to an associated STA whose AID is equal to the value in the AID12 subfield 2045: The User Info field allocates one or more contiguous RA-RUs for unassociated STAs 2046: Unallocated RU
RU Allocation	B12-B19	The RU Allocation subfield, in conjunction with the UL BW subfield in the Common Info field, identifies both the size and location of the RU for the AID
UL FEC Coding type	B20	0 means BCC coding 1 means LDPC coding
SS Allocation/RA-RU information	B26-B31	When it's used for Spatial Stream allocation, this field indicates the starting spatial stream and the number of spatial streams When used for RA-RU information, it specifies the number of contiguous RUs allocated to nonassociated STAs
UL Target Receive Power	B32-B38	Indicate the expected signal power of UL data received at the AP

2.3.3.3 The Transmit Power of STA UL Data

Due to the various propagation paths between the AP and the STAs, it is important to manage the power of the uplink signals to ensure they are at the correct level when received by the AP for accurate demodulation and decoding.

The STAs can measure the path loss by comparing the TX power of the AP, as indicated in the Trigger frame, with the actual signal strength received, as shown in Eq. 2–7:

$$\textbf{Path Loss} = \textbf{TX power (AP transmitted)} - \textbf{RSSI (STA received)} \tag{2.7}$$

The AP specifies the target receive RSSI for the UL Data in the User Info field for each STA. Each STA should then calculate its own transmit power according to the path loss and UL Target Receive Power, as shown in Eq. 2–8:

$$\textbf{TX power (STA transmitted)} = \textbf{Path Loss} + \textbf{RSSI (AP received)} \tag{2.8}$$

$$\textbf{Propagation Loss} = \mathbf{32.44} + \mathbf{20lg}\ d(\mathbf{km}) + \mathbf{20lg}\ f(\mathbf{MHz}) \tag{2.9}$$

According to Eq. 2.9, *Propagation Loss* is correlated with distance and frequency. For multiple STAs operating on the same channel, the greater the distance from the AP, the higher the required transmit power.

2.3.4 Dual Carrier Modulation for Data Transmission

Dual Carrier Modulation (DCM) modulates the same information on a pair of subcarriers, resulting in a higher SNR for data transmission. DCM is an optional modulation scheme for the HE-SIG-B and Data fields. DCM is applicable only to HE-MCSs and HE-SIG-B-MCSs with indices 0, 1, 3, and 4. Figure 2.70 depicts one example of DCM mode.

To mitigate mutual interference and resist the effects of the same channel fading patterns, the two subcarriers should not be adjacent but instead maintain a distance from each other in the frequency domain.

As illustrated in Fig. 2.71, a 20 MHz channel bandwidth is divided into 9 RUs of 26-tone size. These RUs are then allocated to multiple STAs based on OFDMA.

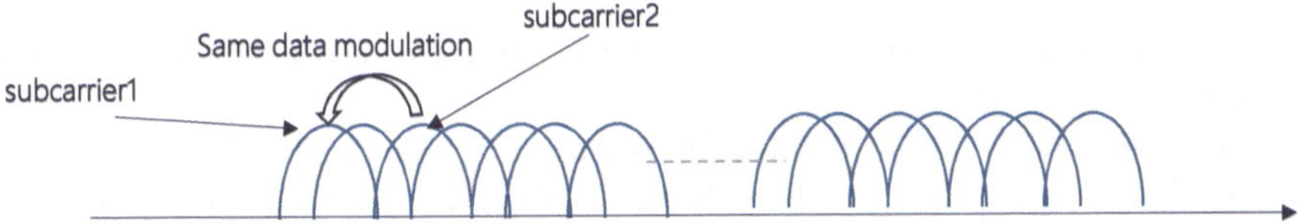

Fig. 2.70 Example of dual-carrier modulation

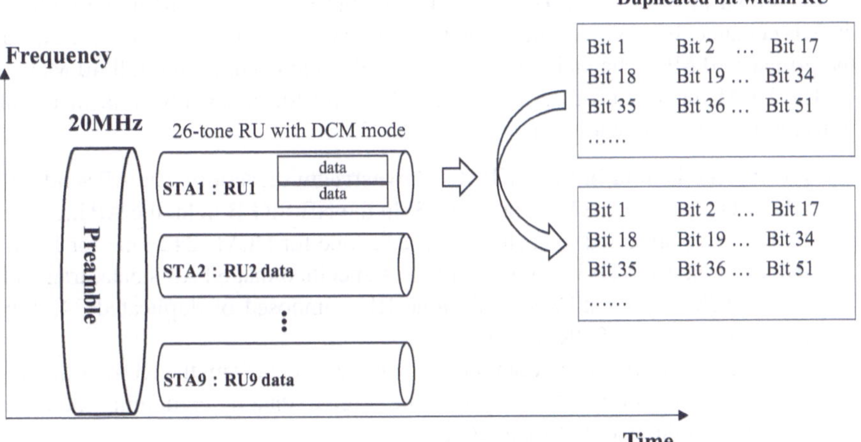

Fig. 2.71 Example of RU allocation under dual-carrier modulation

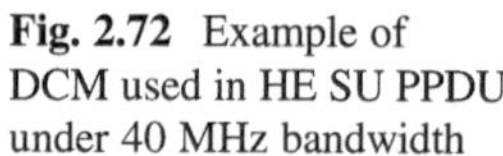

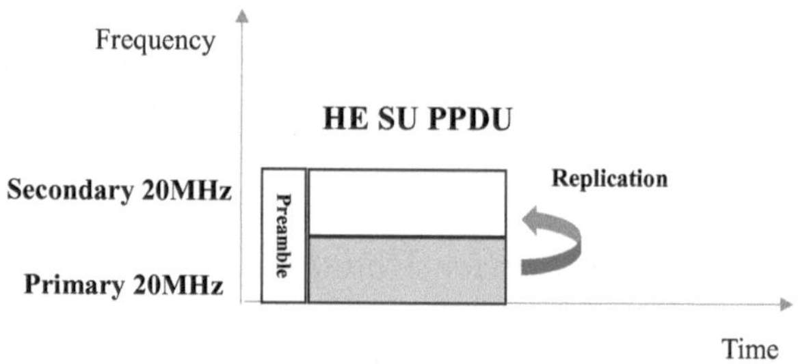

Fig. 2.72 Example of DCM used in HE SU PPDU under 40 MHz bandwidth

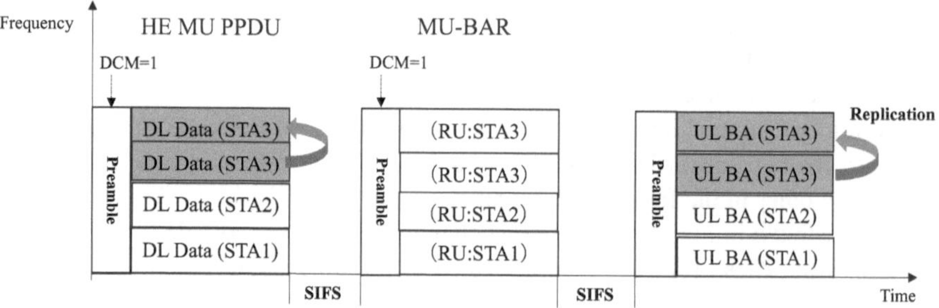

Fig. 2.73 Example of DCM used in upstream and downstream

STA1 supports DCM mode, in which its data is replicated and modulated across the subcarriers within its RU.

The simulation indicates that the DCM can achieve more than 3.5 dB gains in SNR. Therefore, it can be used to improve coverage at the cost of losing half of the capacity. It should be noted that currently, DCM mode is only supported with BSPK, DPSK, and 16-QAM, and not with high-level modulation schemes.

All the HE PPDU frames introduced in Sect. 2.3.2 support DCM mode.

As shown in Fig. 2.72, a HE SU PPDU is transmitted in DCM mode within a 40 MHz channel bandwidth. The secondary 20 MHz channel carries the same data as the primary 20 MHz channel, while the preamble field occupies the full 40 MHz.

The DCM mode can be applied at the RU level for either downlink or uplink transmission. An example is shown in Fig. 2.73.

(1) **The AP sends data in the OFDMA downstream direction:** The AP sends HE MU PPDU to STA1, STA2, and STA3. In the HE-SIG-B field, the AP indicates the RU sizes allocated to each station: 242-tone for STA1, 242-tone for STA2, and 484-tone for STA3. Additionally, it is specified that STA3's data, transmitted in DCM mode, utilizes a 484-tone RU composed of duplicated 242-tone data, enhancing the SNR for STA3.
(2) **STAs receive data:** STAs obtain the downstream data from the RUs. Following the DCM instruction, STA3 recovers the original data by combining the information from the two 242-tone RUs.
(3) **The AP sends the Trigger frame:** The AP sends a MU-BAR trigger frame to all STAs, with the same HE-SIG-B indication regarding the RU sizes and DCM.

Since MU-BAR is a control frame, it is sent on these 20 MHz subchannels using the non-HT PPDU format.

STA sends acknowledgment: STA1 and STA2 send an acknowledgment message in the allocated RUs, respectively. STA3 responds with ACK in both 242-tone RUs, and the ACK information contained within these two RUs is identical.

2.4 Wi-Fi 6E: Extension into the 6 GHz Band

The Wi-Fi Alliance designated Wi-Fi devices that operate in the 6 GHz band as Wi-Fi 6E, with "E" signifying "Extended," indicating an extension of the operational bands from the conventional 2.4 GHz and 5 GHz bands to include the 6 GHz band.

As shown in Fig. 2.74, a Tri-band W-Fi 6E router connects to the terminals across all three frequency bands: 2.4 GHz, 5 GHz, and 6 GHz band. At the 6 GHz band, the AP and the Wi-Fi 6E STA can utilize up to 1200 MHz bandwidth, depending on the regulations in different countries.

Compared with the 2.4 GHz and 5 GHz bands, the 6 GHz band offers the following advantages:

(1) **Higher bandwidth**

Enhanced Bandwidth: Under various regulatory frameworks, the 6 GHz band can provide bandwidth up to 1200 MHz—or, put another way, it can accommodate up to seven contiguous 160 MHz channels. This expanded capacity enables the fulfillment of emerging business needs that require high bandwidth and low latency.

(2) **Higher performance**

The 6 GHz is a pristine frequency band, free of interference generated by legacy Wi-Fi devices operating at lower performance levels and non-Wi-Fi devices utilizing the ISM band. As a result, Wi-Fi discovery processes, association mechanisms, and

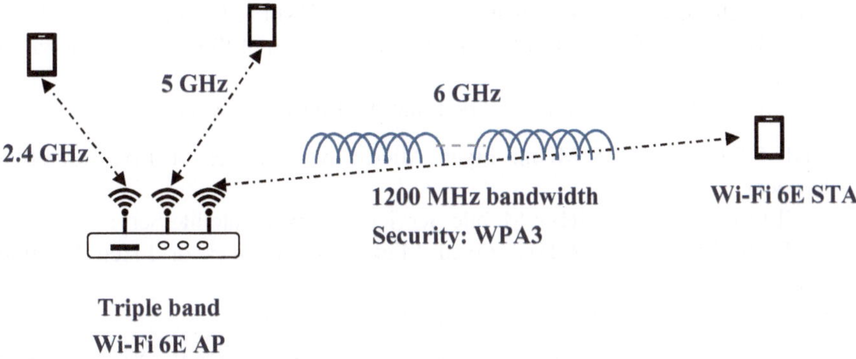

Fig. 2.74 Wi-Fi 6E devices operating at three bands

other management messages are specifically optimized for operation within the 6 GHz band. This optimization leads to higher operational efficiency and improved overall performance of Wi-Fi in this band.

(3) **Enhanced security**

Wi-Fi 6E devices do not need to account for backward compatibility with older devices on the 6 GHz band. This allows for the exclusive implementation of WPA3 encryption across all devices operating at 6 GHz, thereby providing improved security for wireless data transmission over the channel.

In the subsequent sections, we will delve into the new Wi-Fi technologies specifically tailored for the 6 GHz band and further explore the defining characteristics of Wi-Fi 6E.

2.4.1 Planning and Development of 6 GHz Channels

Spectrum is a scarce resource crucial for the development of wireless communications. The success of Wi-Fi technology over the past decades can be largely attributed to the use of unlicensed spectrum.

However, the rapid growth of Wi-Fi networks, along with their coexistence with legacy devices, has pushed the 2.4 GHz and 5 GHz bands close to their capacity limits. Consequently, these bands are struggling to meet the rising demand for high traffic volume and to support emerging wireless applications and services.

The wireless spectrum committees in many countries have decided to expand spectrum resources by opening the 6 GHz band, aiming to unlock the technology's potential.

2.4.1.1 6 GHz Spectrum and Channel Division

The Federal Communications Commission (FCC) took the lead in approving the 6 GHz spectrum as a new unlicensed band for Wi-Fi [5], which ranges from 5.925 GHz to 7.125 GHz and offers a total bandwidth of 1200 MHz, as shown in Fig. 2.75.

The entire 6 GHz spectrum is divided into the following segments:

- UNII-5(5925 to 6425 MHz): Fixed Microwave Services or Fixed Satellite Services
- UNII-6(6425 to 6525 MHz): Mobile Services or Fixed Satellite Services
- UNII-7(6525 to 6825 MHz): Fixed Microwave Services or Fixed Satellite Services
- UNII-8(6875 to 7125 MHz): Fixed Microwave Services

The 6 GHz band, when fully utilized, can be divided into a total of 233 individual channels, including:

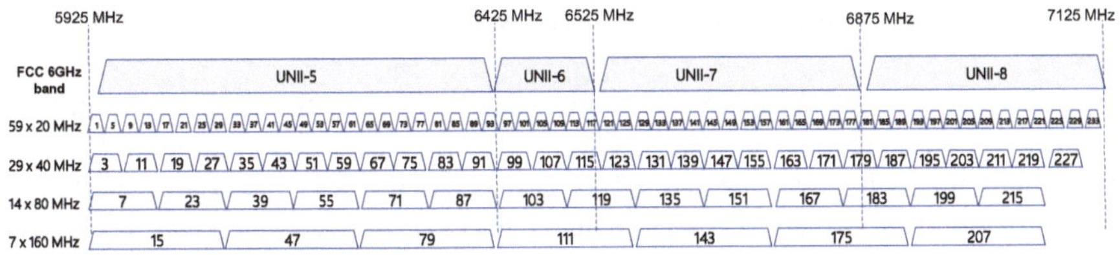

Fig. 2.75 6 GHz channel division defined by FCC

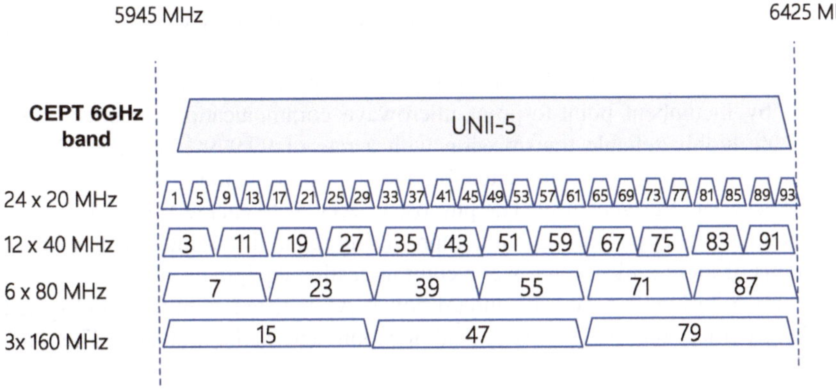

Fig. 2.76 6 GHz channel division defined by CEPT

- 59 nonoverlapping channels with 20 MHz bandwidth
- 29 nonoverlapping channels with 40 MHz bandwidth
- 14 nonoverlapping channels with 80 MHz bandwidth
- 7 nonoverlapping channels with 160 MHz bandwidth

The European Conference on Postal and Telecommunications (CEPT), following the FCC, has proposed opening up the 6 GHz band from 5945 to 6425 MHz for Wi-Fi usage, providing a total bandwidth of 480 MHz. As shown in Fig. 2.76, this segment is divided into 93 channels, including:

- 24 nonoverlapping channels with 20 MHz bandwidth
- 12 nonoverlapping channels with 40 MHz bandwidth
- 6 nonoverlapping channels with 80 MHz bandwidth
- 3 nonoverlapping channels with 160 MHz bandwidth

It should be noted that while these channel configurations are suggested based on the given frequency range, the detailed standard for CEPT's adoption of the 6 GHz band for Wi-Fi use has not yet been officially announced or finalized.

In the subsequent section, we will introduce the detailed specifications for the 6 GHz band as defined by the FCC.

2.4.1.2 Wi-Fi 6E Device Types Defined by FCC

Two distinct types of Wi-Fi 6E AP devices are defined by the FCC based on their transmit power: namely, standard-power APs and low-power indoor APs. The maximum transmit power of the STAs connected to these two types of APs is correspondingly specified. A comprehensive list of device types and their respective maximum transmit powers can be found in Table 2.13.

2.4.1.3 Automated Frequency Coordination Defined by FCC

The UNII-5 and UNII-7 bands within the 6 GHz spectrum have historically been utilized by incumbent point-to-point microwave communication systems, which necessitate highly reliable transmission with a rate of 99.999% to 99.9999%. In 2022, the FCC approved Automated Frequency Coordination (AFC) systems to oversee access to this spectrum. The purpose of AFC is to enable Wi-Fi 6E devices to transmit at higher power without compromising reliability or interfering with the operations of these critical microwave communication equipment.

As shown in Fig. 2.77, each standard-power AP registers with the AFC system via the Internet, reporting its physical location and serial number. The AFC

Table 2.13 Device types defined by FCC

Device type	Working channel	Maximum power (dBm)	Maximum PSD (dBm/MHz)	Channel bandwidth (MHz)/ maximum power (dBm)
Standard-power AP (AFC)	U-NII-5 (5.925 ~ 6.425 GHz) U-NII-7 (6.525 ~ 6.875 GHz)	36	23	320/36 160/36 80/36 40/36 20/36
STAs connected to a standard-power AP		30	17	320/30 160/30 80/30 40/30 20/30
Low-power AP for indoor deployment	U-NII-5 (5.925 ~ 6.425 GHz) U-NII-6 (6.425 ~ 6.575 GHz) U-NII-7 (6.525 ~ 6.875 GHz) U-NII- 8 (6.875 ~ 7.125 GHz)	30	5	320/30 160/27 80/24 40/21 20/18
STAs connected to a low-power AP		24	−1	320/24 160/21 80/18 40/15 20/12

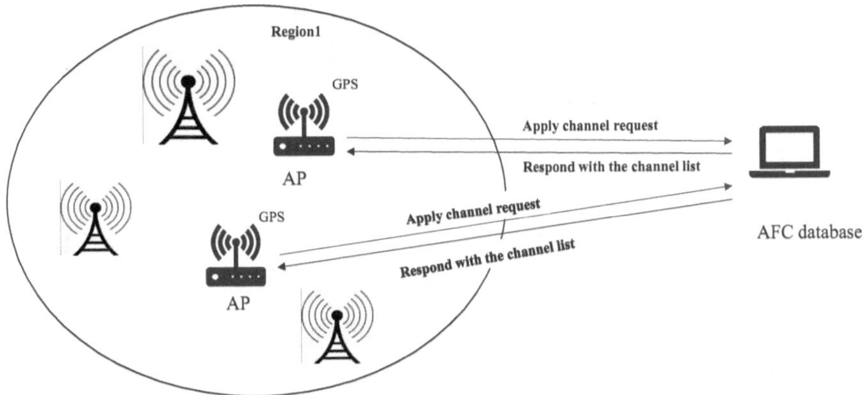

Fig. 2.77 Standard-power AP with AFC system

determines the available frequencies for a given geographic location and then provides the standard-power APs with a list of available channels from which to select.

Low-power APs are typically used for indoor deployment and have limited coverage. These APs, as well as STAs such as notebooks, desktops, smartphones, and IoT devices, can use the entire 6 GHz band for data transmission in the same way as they use 2.4 GHz or 5 GHz band resources, without the need to register with or be coordinated by the AFC system.

According to the FCC's regulations, the maximum transmit power allowed for standard-power APs is 36 dBm, whereas indoor low-power APs must not exceed 30 dBm. To enhance the coverage capabilities of these low-power APs, Dual Carrier Modulation (DCM) is one optional feature described in Sect. 2.3.4, which enables achieving a higher SNR by modulating the same data on two nonadjacent subcarriers within the 6 GHz band.

2.4.2 Optimized Discovery and Connection Procedure on the 6 GHz Band

The 6 GHz band is a new unlicensed spectrum, eliminating the need to consider compatibility with legacy Wi-Fi devices, unlike the 2.4 GHz or 5 GHz bands. Management frames and control frames have been optimized to support both in-band and out-of-band discovery, making Wi-Fi 6E more efficient, reliable, and secure, as shown in Fig. 2.78.

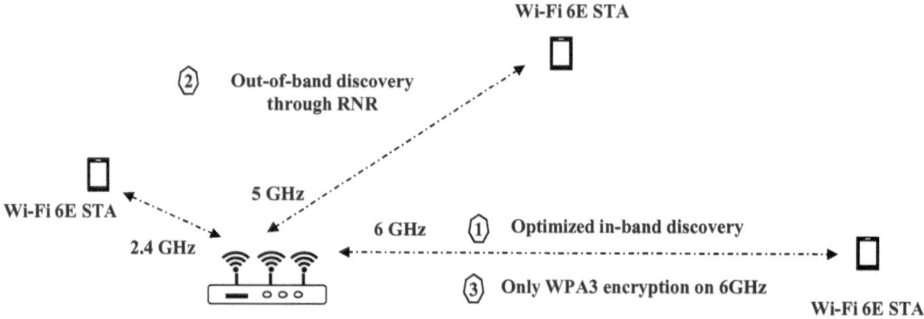

Fig. 2.78 The optimized discovery and connection of Wi-Fi 6E devices

Table 2.14 Probe Request and Response frames on 6 GHz

Index	Rules for Probe Request and Response frames
1	An STA must send Probe Request frames specifying both the SSID and BSSID at 6 GHz, ensuring that only the corresponding AP will respond
2	If an STA has received the Probe Response frame or Beacon frame from an AP, it should not send a Probe Request frame with the same BSSID
3	An STA can only send a Probe Request frame with a specified SSID within every 20 ms
4	An STA can send up to three Probe Request frames with a specified BSSID within every 20 ms
5	An AP broadcasts Probe Response frames. When other STAs on this channel receive these Probe Response frames, then can discover the AP, reducing the need for them to send their own Probe Request frames
6	An AP broadcasts the Probe Response frame every 20ms, even when it doesn't receive Probe Request frames.

2.4.2.1 In-band Discovery on 6 GHz

The in-band discovery procedure in the 6 GHz band is similar to the existing processes in the 2.4 GHz and 5 GHz bands, where an STA discovers an AP through active and passive scanning, utilizing Beacon frames, and exchanging Probe Request and Probe Response frames. However, the absence of legacy devices in the 6 GHz band allows for more efficient in-band discovery.

As detailed in Table 2.14, specific rules for Wi-Fi 6E devices operating in the 6 GHz band enhance discovery efficiency by reducing the number of Probe Request frames and Probe Response frames exchanges.

To improve scanning efficiency and expedite the discovery of APs by STAs, the *Preferred Scanning Channels* method is defined for use in the 6 GHz band. Rather than sequentially scanning all 59 of the 20 MHz channels, an STA can opt to scan every fourth 20 MHz channel. Assuming it takes 20 ms to scan one channel, the Preferred Scanning Channels method would complete the scanning process in 15×20 ms $= 300$ ms, in contrast to the traditional method, which would take 59×20 ms $= 1180$ ms.

2.4.2.2 Out-of-Band Discovery

Wi-Fi 6 employs out-of-band discovery through the use of the *Reduced Neighbor Report (RNR)*. For instance, when an AP supports 2.4 GHz, 5 GHz, and 6 GHz bands, it can convey information about its 6 GHz BSS within Beacon frames or Probe Response frames transmitted in either the 2.4 GHz or 5 GHz BSS.

The RNR encapsulates only the essential data about other bands, such as the operating channel, BSSID, SSID, and the TBTT offset for calculating the periodicity of Beacon frames. With this preliminary information at hand, the STAs can bypass the scanning procedure and tune directly to the correct channel. Subsequently, they can acquire more detailed information from subsequent Beacon frames of the new band.

As illustrated in the example of Fig. 2.79, an AP creates three BSSs with the SSIDs of "Home," "Guest," and "User" on the 2.4 GHz, 5 GHz, and 6 GHz bands, respectively. The corresponding BSSIDs are BSSID-1, BSSID-2, and BSSID-3:

- **BSSID-1:** Operates at channel 4 of the 2.4 GHz with a 20 MHz bandwidth
- **BSSID-2:** Operates at channel 36 of the 5 GHz with an 80 MHz bandwidth
- **BSSID-3:** Operates at channel 233 of the 6 GHz with an 80 MHz bandwidth

The RNR field in Beacon frames carries BSS information of other bands, including the TBTT offset, channel bandwidth, SSID, and BSSID. For instance, an STA working on the 2.4 GHz band can discover BSSID-3 through the RNR field in the Beacon frame of BSSID-1. Subsequently, the STA sends a Probe Request frame on the 6 GHz band and initiates the association and authentication process.

It is important to note that RNR technology differs from MBSSID technology, which was introduced in Sect. 2.2.6. MBSSID pertains to the operation of multiple BSSs on the same frequency band, where parameters from multiple Beacon frames

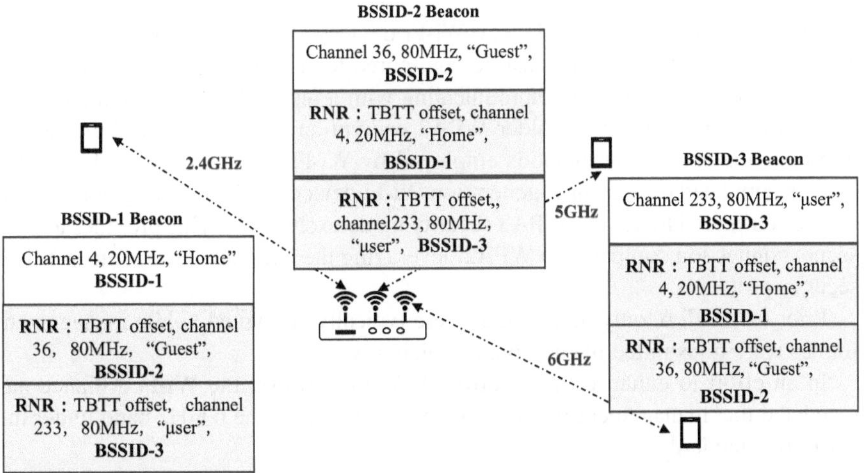

Fig. 2.79 Beacon frames containing RNR field

Table 2.15 MBSSID and RNR

Characteristic	MBSSID	RNR
Band and BSS	Multiple BSSs are created on the same band	Multiple BSSs are created across different bands
Beacon frame and Probe Response frame	Only the transmitted BSSID is allowed to send Beacon frames and Probe Response frames; the non-transmitted BSSIDs are not	Each BSS sends Beacon frames and Probe Response frames on its own operating channel independently
Information carried in the frames	The transmitted BSSID carries all essential parameters of the non-transmitted BSSIDs, while common information can be inherited from the transmitted BSSID	The RNR field conveys only a portion of the information about other BSSs to facilitate rapid discovery, and the STA must acquire the complete information by engaging in an in-band discovery procedure
TBTT offset	The transmitted BSSID and non-transmitted BSSIDs may have different beacon periods, but their TBTT remain synchronized	The beacon periods for different frequency bands can be distinct. Their TBTTs will also vary accordingly

can be aggregated and transmitted in a single-BSS Beacon frame representing a single BSS. In contrast, RNR technology involves transmitting information about BSSs operating on other frequency bands, which is particularly useful for multiband APs. The distinctions between these two technologies are illustrated in Table 2.15.

If a multiband AP creates multiple BSSs across different frequency bands, then both RNR and MBSSID technologies can be employed in tandem to enhance channel utilization.

2.4.2.3 Security Enhancement on 6 GHz

To ensure compatibility with legacy Wi-Fi devices operating in the 2.4 GHz and 5 GHz bands, a Wi-Fi 6 AP must be configured to support both WPA and WPA2 compatibility modes. When communicating with a legacy Wi-Fi terminal, such an AP will default to using the older WPA2 encryption mode. In Sect. 3.5, we will introduce the encryption methods employed by Wi-Fi networks. Since the 6 GHz band is populated only by new generation Wi-Fi devices, APs operating in this band can be configured to use the WPA3 security mode exclusively. This provides a more secure connection compared to WPA2, leveraging the latest advancements in Wi-Fi security protocols.

Prior-to Wi-Fi 6, only data frames were typically encrypted, while management frames were transmitted unencrypted in plain text.

In an effort to enhance the security of Wi-Fi network, the Wi-Fi Alliance has mandated that management frames must be encrypted on the 6 GHz band under the Wi-Fi 6E standard.

2.5 Summary

Wi-Fi 6 is designed with the primary goal of improving Wi-Fi spectrum efficiency and maximizing connection performance, particularly in high-density user environments. In essence, the key technical characteristics of Wi-Fi 6 include high speeds, high concurrency, low latency, and reduced power consumption. Furthermore, the introduction of the new 6 GHz frequency band extends Wi-Fi's bandwidth and boosts its overall high performance to meet the demands of emerging applications and services.

High Speed With *1024-QAM* modulation support, the maximum physical rate of a Wi-Fi 6 device can reach 9.6 Gbps, which is 39% higher than that of Wi-Fi 5. The preamble puncturing technology allows bundling of noncontiguous channels for downlink transmission, effectively improving channel utilization and the transmission rate.

High Concurrency Leveraging *OFDMA* technology, upstream and downstream data from multiple devices can be transmitted simultaneously across distinct subcarriers, reducing the delay for each device waiting for channel access. The Trigger frame serves as an effective way to orchestrate uplink transmission, thereby preventing collisions when multiple users attempt to transmit upstream data concurrently. Moreover, the *multiple-BSSID* technology reduces the overhead of Beacon frames and Probe Response frames when an AP hosts multiple BSSs on the same band, further optimizing channel utilization.

Low Latency Spatial Reuse (SR) and BSS coloring technology are introduced to mitigate interference from adjacent APs operating on the same channel, thereby enabling APs and STAs in overlapping BSS to transmit data with minimal impact on one another, thus reducing latency. Additionally, OFDMA technology facilitates the collection of channel feedback from multiple users within a single transmission period, which decreases the delay associated with the multiuser channel sounding procedure.

Low Power Consumption Wi-Fi 6 incorporates *Target Wake Time (TWT)*, where the AP utilizes i-TWT technology to negotiate individual wake-up intervals with STAs. Moreover, b-TWT technology enables STAs to be grouped into different wake-up cycles. TWT technology reinforces power-saving mechanisms by ensuring that devices are not all competing for the wireless medium simultaneously upon waking up, thereby conserving energy effectively.

New Frequency Band With the advent of Wi-Fi 6, the *6 GHz* band is now available for Wi-Fi communication. As there are no legacy devices operating in this new frequency band, the design does not need to consider backward compatibility with legacy devices. The Probe Request and Response frames have been optimized through in-band or out-of-band discovery processes, enhancing channel utilization. Furthermore, only WPA3 authentication is supported within the 6 GHz band, thereby improving the security of Wi-Fi communications.

Through studying this chapter, readers will gain an understanding of the evolution of Wi-Fi technology and grasp the essential key technologies underlying Wi-Fi 6, which serve as the foundational prerequisites for the subsequent development and advancement of Wi-Fi 7.

References

1. Cheng G (2019) IEEE 802.11ax Key Technologies. Electronic Technology & Software Engineering, (14), 15-18
2. IEEE (2021) IEEE Standard for Information Technology–Telecommunications and Information Exchange between Systems Local and Metropolitan Area Networks–Specific Requirements Part 11: Wireless LAN Medium Access Control (MAC) and Physical Layer (PHY) Specifications Amendment 1: Enhancements for High-Efficiency WLAN. (2021). (Amendment to IEEE Std 802.11-2020). IEEE Std 802.11ax-2021. pp. 1-767. doi: https://doi.org/10.1109/IEEESTD.2021.9442429
3. Deng D-J, Lin Y-P, Yang X, Zhu J, Li Y-B, Luo J, Chen K-C (2017) IEEE 802.11ax: Highly Efficient WLANs for Intelligent Information Infrastructure. IEEE Communications Magazine, December 2017
4. Khorov E, Kiryanov A, Lyakhov A (2015) IEEE 802.11ax: How to build high efficiency WLANs. In Proc. IEEE En T. pp. 77–82. Moscow.
5. FCC (2020) FCC Opens 6 GHz Band to Wi-Fi and Other Unlicensed Uses [online]. Available at: https://www.fcc.gov/document/fcc-opens-6-ghz-band-wi-fi-and-other-unlicensed-uses-0

Chapter 3
Wi-Fi 7 Principles and Innovations

Abstract Wi-Fi 7, known as IEEE 802.11be or Extremely High Throughput (EHT), has built upon the capabilities of Wi-Fi 6, representing a significant leap forward in wireless networking technology. It triples the maximum throughput of its predecessor, which facilitates rapid data transmission and seamless streaming of ultra-high-definition content, among other capabilities. With enhancements such as multi-link operation, 4 K-QAM modulation, and channel bandwidth extending up to 320 MHz, Wi-Fi 7 dramatically enhances network capacity, adeptly handling a high density of devices in homes, offices, and public areas. This chapter aims to familiarize readers with the core tenets of Wi-Fi 7 technology, encompassing key technological advancements and fundamental principles, the evolution of the Physical Layer and Medium Access Control Layers in Wi-Fi 7, as well as updates to security protocols and wireless mesh networking.

3.1 Wi-Fi 7 Technical Overview

Prior to Wi-Fi 6, each iteration of Wi-Fi has consistently focused on increasing bandwidth. However, with Wi-Fi 6, the emphasis shifted to ensuring the performance in dense environments by utilizing technologies such as OFDMA technology to support high performance and concurrent transmission. Wi-Fi 7 technology [1, 2], building upon Wi-Fi 6, enhance both throughput and the concurrent transmissions, comprehensively surpassing the Wi-Fi 6 in the aspects of high bandwidth, massive concurrency, and low latency performance domains.

The main Wi-Fi 7 specification from IEEE was completed by 2023, and the final version has been ready in 2024.To promote the Wi-Fi 7 commercial products, Wi-Fi Alliance has published the Wi-Fi 7 certification specifications by the end of 2023. Figure 3.1 shows the timeline from Wi-Fi 4 to Wi-F 7 standards.

G. Cheng et al., *Wi-Fi 7*, https://doi.org/10.1007/978-981-97-9026-5_3

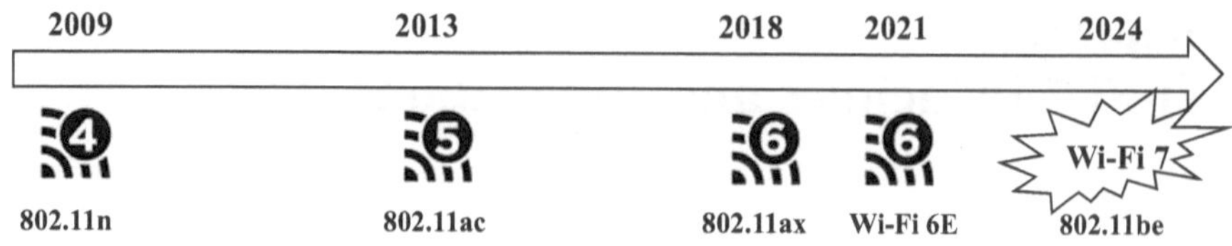

Fig. 3.1 Wi-Fi standard timeline

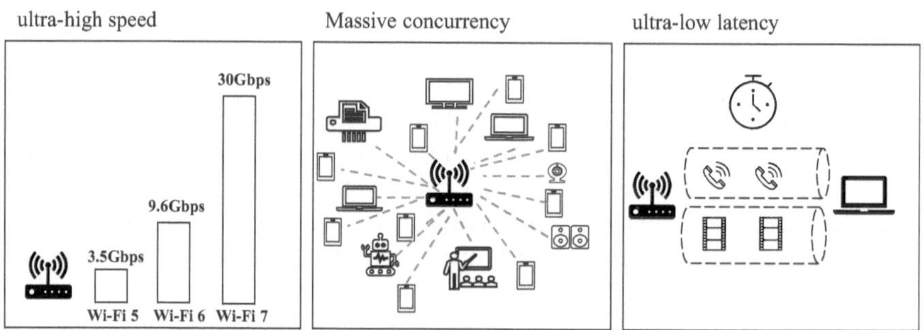

Fig. 3.2 Wi-Fi 7 characteristics

3.1.1 Wi-Fi 7 Technical Characteristics

The Wi-Fi 7 standard is also termed as Extremely High Throughput (EHT), which signifies its capability as a short-range wireless communication technology to achieve exceedingly high data transfer rates. Thus, a prime characteristic of Wi-Fi 7 is its ultra-high speed performance. The maximum rate of Wi-Fi 7 can reach 36 Gbps, which is at least 3 times of maximum rate of 9.6 Gbps for Wi-Fi 6, and 5 times of the maximum rate of 6.9 Gbps for Wi-Fi 5.

While improving the speed, Wi-Fi 7 also enhances its capability to support more concurrent transmission by expanding the channel bandwidth as well as OFDMA Resource Unit allocation. Consequently, the maximum number of simultaneous connections for Wi-Fi 7 doubles that of Wi-Fi 6. Therefore, the massive concurrency of Wi-Fi 7 is a pair of high-performance technical features that coexist with super high speed.

In addition, services such as high-definition video, AR/VR, and online games, not only require high bandwidth, but also demand very low latency to deliver a premium user experience. Wi-Fi 7, as the next-generation high-performance Wi-Fi standard, places a strong emphasis on ultra-low latency as its key technical feature. With Wi-Fi 7, latency can be reduced by 50% or more for real-time QoS services like voice and video.

Figure 3.2 indicates the most important characteristics of Wi-Fi 7, namely, ultra-high speed, massive concurrency, and ultra-low latency.

3.1.1.1 Wi-Fi 7 Ultra-High Speed

Wi-Fi 7 can provide up to 36 Gbps of connectivity for home use, complementing with the 10 Gbps or 25 Gbps fiber broadband access to homes or serving as an extension for mobile 5G. With this high-speed wireless connection, users can enjoy 8 K streaming videos, immersive VR from any corner of their homes.

The ultra-high speed of Wi-Fi 7 benefits from the technologies of channel bandwidth expansion, modulation efficiency improvement, and Multi-Link Operation.

1. **Channel Bandwidth Expansion**

Wi-Fi 7 operates on the 2.4 GHz, 5 GHz, and 6 GHz bands, with the 6 GHz band supporting channels with a maximum bandwidth of **320 MHz.** In comparison, as shown in Fig. 3.3, Wi-Fi 4 technology offers a maximum channel bandwidth of 40 MHz, while Wi-Fi 5 and Wi-Fi 6 support 80 MHz and 160 MHz respectively. With Wi-Fi 7, the maximum channel bandwidth can reach up to 320 MHz on the 6 GHz band.

Figure 3.4 illustrates how data rate varies with the transmission distance at the channel bandwidth of 80 MHz, 160 MHz, and 320 MHz. As the channel bandwidth increases, the data rate also increases. However, as the distance increases, the Wi-Fi signals are attenuated, resulting in a gradual decrease in data rate. Notably, the performance of 320 MHz channels consistently outperforms that of 160 MHz and 80 MHz at various distances. It is important to note that the data rate in the figure is for illustration purpose only. In the real-world deployment, the actual data rate is determined by various factors such as the Wi-Fi AP configuration, transmission

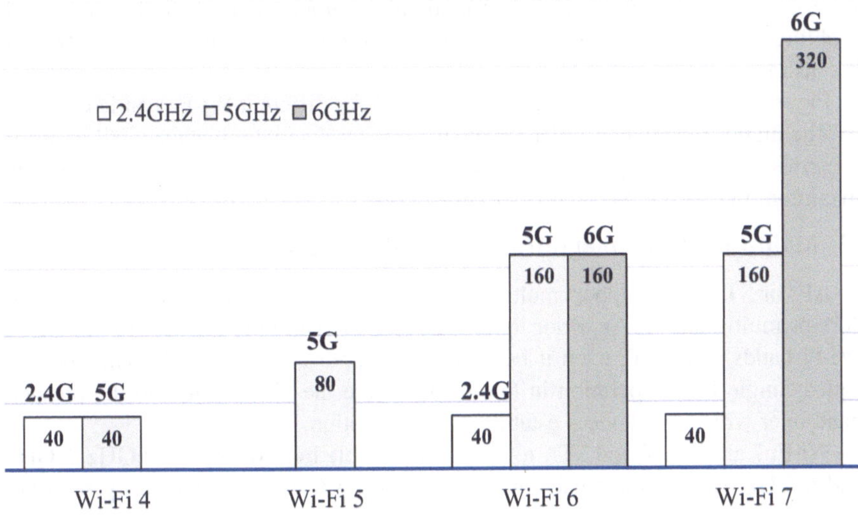

Fig. 3.3 Evolution of Wi-Fi channel bandwidth

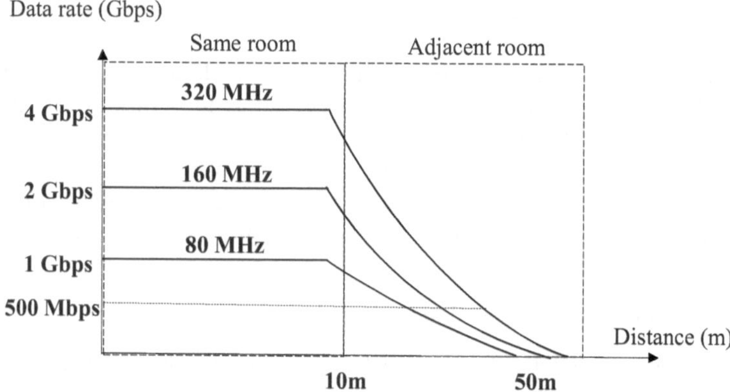

Fig. 3.4 Wi-Fi data rate under different channel bandwidth

environment including the number of Wi-Fi spatial streams, the modulation scheme, and potential obstacles within the home, etc.

2. **Modulation Efficiency Improvement**

Every generation of Wi-Fi technology has introduced advancements in the modulation techniques to increase the transmission rate. Wi-Fi 4, for example, introduced the Quadrature Amplitude Modulation (QAM) which allows each symbol carries up to 6 bits of information, that is, $2^6 = 64$, so it is represented as 64-QAM. With Wi-Fi 5, the modulation scheme was improved to support 256-QAM, enabling each symbol to carry up to 8 bits of information. Similarly, Wi-Fi 6 further enhanced the modulation to 1024-QAM, allowing for 10 bits per symbol. In the case of Wi-Fi 7, the modulation order has been further increased, enabling each symbol to carry up to 12 bits of information, namely, $2^{12} = 4096$, so it's also known as 4 K-QAM.

Figure 3.5 shows the evolution of the QAM for different Wi-Fi standards.

The higher modulation order results in a higher data rate. Each symbol of Wi-Fi 7 carries 12 bits, compared to 10 bits per symbol in Wi-Fi 6. Consequently, the maximum rate of the physical layer is increased by (12-10)/10 = 20%.

3. **Multi-Link Operation (MLO) for Band Aggregation**

APs or STAs that support multiple frequency bands are referred to as multi-band APs or multi-band STAs. Prior to Wi-Fi 7, a STA can only connect to one of the Wi-Fi bands of an AP, even if both devices supported multi-bands. This mode is called Single-Link Operation in this book, where the "link" refers to the physical band over which the devices establish the connection.

Wi-Fi 7 allows AP and STA to establish multiple links over the 2.4 GHz, 5 GHz, and 6 GHz bands. This means that an AP and STA can simultaneously send and

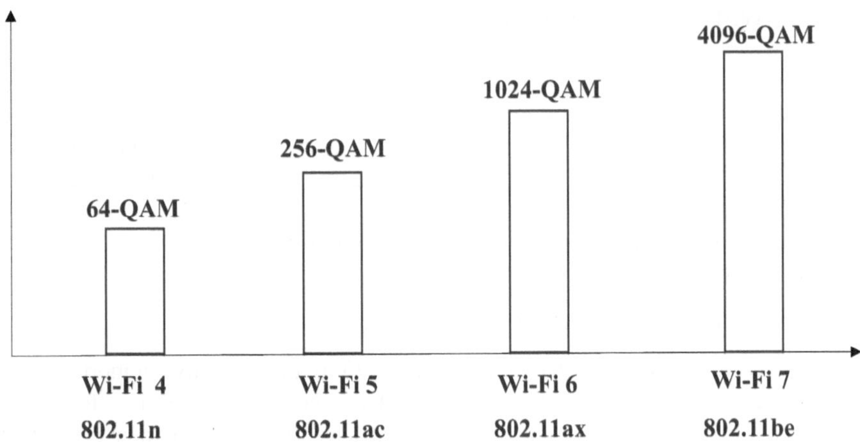

Fig. 3.5 Evolution of Wi-Fi modulation scheme

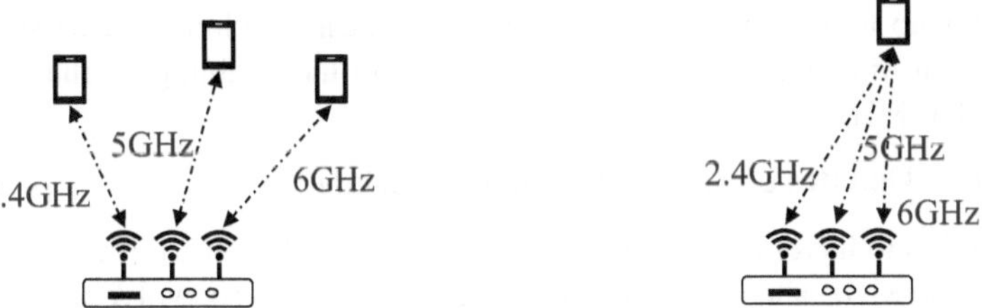

Fig. 3.6 Single-link operation and multi-link operation

receive data across different frequency bands. This mode is defined as Multi-Link Operation (**MLO**) in Wi-Fi 7. Obviously, such band aggregation leads to a much higher throughput than the Single-Link Operation mode.

Figure 3.6 is an illustration of Single-Link Operation and Multi-Link Operation.

Multi-link Operation technology operates somewhat like combining or bundling multiple frequency bands. The channels in the 2.4 GHz, 5 GHz, and 6 GHz bands are bundled for data transmission, thereby increasing the throughput between the AP and the STA. However, it is essential to note that the MLO doesn't simply expand the bandwidth in a conventional sense; instead, it enhances overall network efficiency by utilizing available resources in different bands.

The effects of MLO technology on the data transmission process and link management are complex and multifaceted that will be discussed in greater detail in subsequent sections.

3.1.1.2 Wi-Fi 7 Massive Concurrency

The number of concurrent terminals represents another key performance indicator of Wi-Fi technology. In crowded public areas like stadiums, airports, railway stations, shopping malls, and so on, a large number of people rely on Wi-Fi hotspots to access the Internet. Wi-Fi 7 introduces a massive concurrent capability that benefits high-dense Wi-Fi user scenarios.

Wi-Fi 7 achieves improved concurrent connections through updates to OFDMA and the channel bundling technology.

1. **Wi-Fi 7 Updates on OFDMA**

As previously detailed in Sect. 2.2.2, Wi-Fi 6 theoretically supports up to 74 concurrent transmissions through OFDMA, where each user is allocated a Resource Unit (RU), typically consisting of at least 26-tones, for their individual data transmission.

As illustrated in Fig. 3.7, building upon the foundation of Wi-Fi 6 capabilities, Wi-Fi 7 doubles the theoretical number of concurrent users, thereby enabling support for up to 148 simultaneous users under ideal conditions. This substantial improvement in concurrency is partly attributed to the doubling of channel bandwidth to 320 MHz.

2. **Wi-Fi 7 Updates on Channel Bundling Technology**

In addition to increasing the single channel bandwidth from 20 MHz to 40 MHz, 80 MHz, 160 MHz, and 320 MHz, Wi-Fi standards have also evolved with channel bundling technology to further increase the overall bandwidth. **Wi-Fi 4 and Wi-Fi 5** support the bundling of multiple contiguous 20 MHz channels, with one of these channels designated as the primary subchannel. The bundled channel can be utilized only when all the subchannels are idle. If interference is detected on any of the subchannels, that specific subchannel is excluded from the bundled channel. However, the remaining contiguous subchannels can still function as a bundled channel, provided that the primary subchannel is included. It is essential that the subchannels be contiguous in the spectrum.

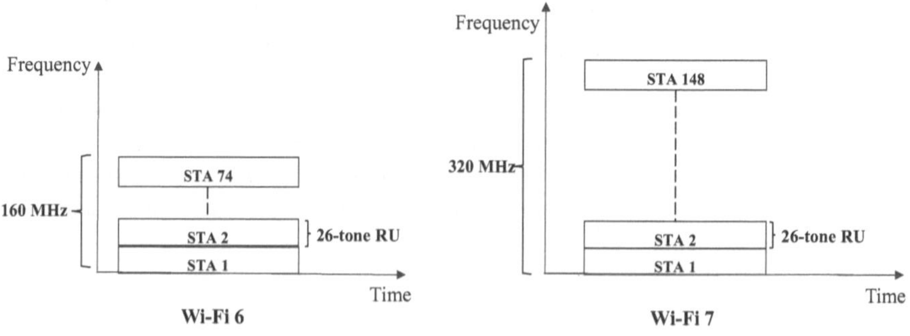

Fig. 3.7 OFDMA concurrent connection

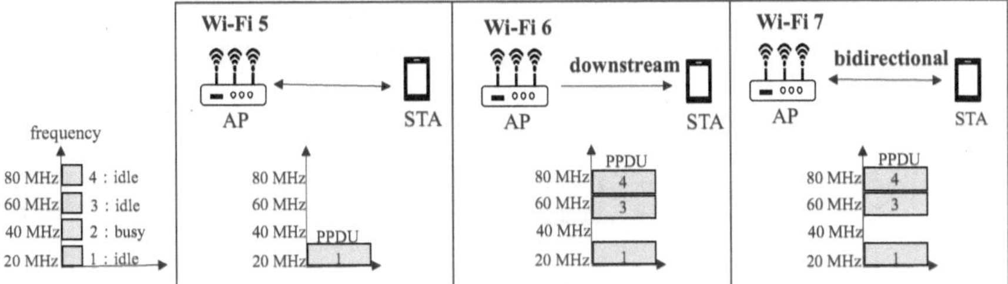

Fig. 3.8 Evolution of channel bundling

Wi-Fi 6 allows to bundle **discontinuous** sub-channels, but this feature is limited to the downstream direction. If interference is detected in the downstream direction on subchannels other than the primary subchannel, the Wi-Fi 6 device will still bundle the remaining channels, even if they are not contiguous in the spectrum. The upstream direction, however, operates similarly to Wi-Fi 4 and Wi-Fi 5.

Wi-Fi 7 supports the **bundling** of the discontinuous channels in both downlink and uplink directions. Moreover, it supports the bundling with the form of RU rather than just 20 MHz channels. Therefore, this increases flexibility in channel bundling options to improve the capacity of concurrent users, expand channel bandwidth and enhance tolerance to interference.

Figure 3.8 shows an example with the different channel bundling technologies. In Wi-Fi 5, only consecutive subchannels can be bundled. Consequently, even if channel #3 and #4 are idle, a Wi-Fi 5 device is not able to bundle them with channel #1. In Wi-Fi 6, the ability to bundle discontinuous channels is introduced but limited to the downlink direction. However, Wi-Fi 7 offers support for bidirectional data transmission and enables the bundling of channel #1, #3, and #4.

3.1.1.3 Wi-Fi 7 Ultra-Low Latency

With the proliferation of delay-sensitive applications like immersive VR, video streaming, and online meetings, low latency becomes critical measure of data transmission technology. Network delay plays an instrumental role in ensuring optimal user experience; For instance, a VR service typically requires latency levels below 5 to 10 milliseconds to deliver an optimal user experience. Any delays or video stutters can severely degrade user service quality. Wi-Fi 7 addresses this need by providing the ultra-low latency capabilities to meet these requests. Ultra-low latency is inherently linked to ultra-high speed and ultra-high concurrency. For example, while Wi-Fi 7 enhances the maximum data transmission rate, it also diminishes the average delays. The multi-concurrency technology enables more users to transmit data simultaneously, thereby reducing both collision and wait time for channel access.

Wi-Fi 7 facilitates mapping traffic with different QoS requirements onto the multiple links through its support for QoS characteristics and restricted TWT

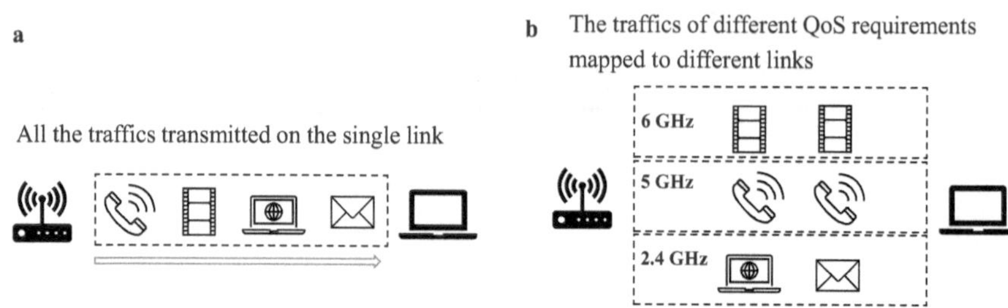

Fig. 3.9 (**a**) Single link of Wi-Fi 6, (**b**) traffic mapping of Wi-Fi 7 multiple links

technology, thus serving the latency-sensitive applications in a more flexible and effective manner.

1. **Traffic Identifier to Link Mapping**

Before the introduction of Wi-Fi 7, multi-band APs and STAs could only establish connections over a single link. All traffics was transmitted sequentially on the same channel, without the ability to prioritize traffic based on QoS requirements. However, with the advent of Wi-Fi 7, AP and STA now have the capability to establish a connection over multiple links and transmit and receive data through them. A Wi-Fi 7 compliant AP with MLO can allocate traffic to different links using Traffic Identifier (TID) to link mapping. This allows for improved management of delays and enhances overall network performance. For instance, latency-sensitive services can be prioritized to transmit on the 6 GHz link, benefiting from lower interference and higher bandwidth, while other services can utilize the 2.4 GHz and 5 GHz. An example is shown as Fig. 3.9, where the video, voice, and Internet services are mapped to different links.

2. **QoS Characteristics**

In the first chapter, we introduced the concept that the legacy Wi-Fi technology categorizes data frames to prioritize traffic: Voice (AC_VO), Video (AC_VI), Best Effort (AC_BE), and Background (AC_BK). Each category corresponds to a queue with different priorities, ensuring that time-sensitive traffic, such as voice and video, is given precedence over less urgent data. This system does not consider the specific latency requirements of each service.

However, Wi-Fi 7 introduces more advanced QoS characteristics that allow for more precise traffic scheduling. In Wi-Fi 7, the AP can identify parameters such as maximum delay, service start and end time, service interval, and maximum packet error rate based for different services. Using this information, AP can then schedule the traffic based on the specific latency requirements of each service. As shown in Fig. 3.10, the traffic is assigned to four priority queues based on predefined rules in legacy Wi-Fi. However, with Wi-Fi 7, the AP can identify various parameters, including the maximum service delay, and utilize them to schedule traffic based on specific latency requirements.

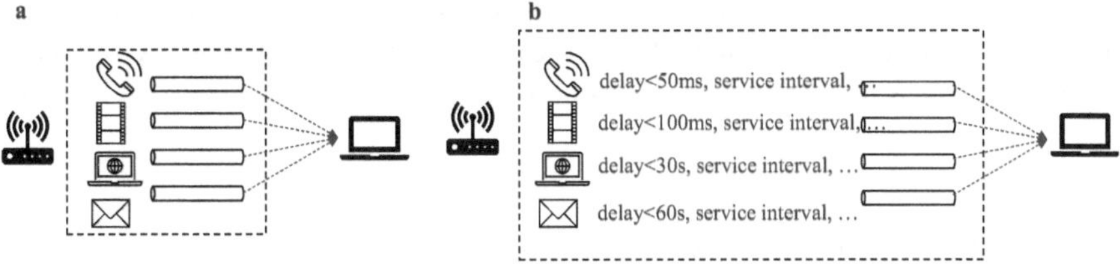

Fig. 3.10 (**a**) Access categories of legacy Wi-Fi, (**b**) QoS characteristics of Wi-Fi 7

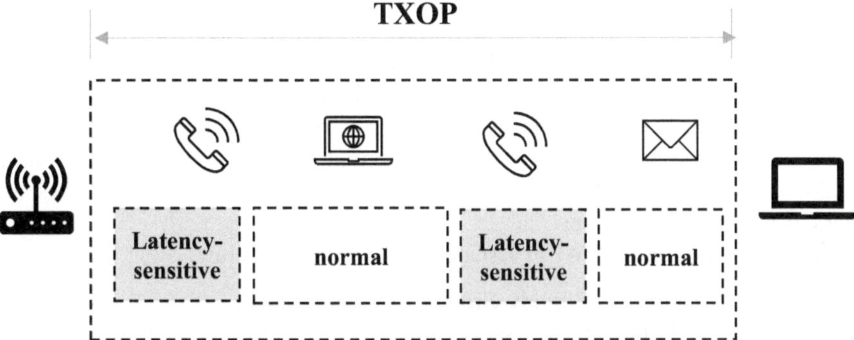

Fig. 3.11 Wi-Fi 7 R-TWT for the latency-sensitive services

For instance, a mobile phone is concurrently running multiple applications with distinct latency requirements. Leveraging the QoS characteristics technology in Wi-Fi 7, Wi-Fi 7 AP can accurately discern and prioritize based on the maximum transmission delay of each individual application. It thereby efficiently schedules the network traffic to ensure seamless synchronization between client applications and the network server, thus guaranteeing an optimized user experience across all applications being used.

3. **Restricted TWT**

In Wi-Fi 6, the introduction broadcast Target Wake Time (b-TWT) technology allows AP to negotiate specific service time with individual STAs. STAs then wake up at these designated times to access channels for data transmission. Building upon b-TWT, Wi-Fi 7 supports restricted Target Wake Time (r-TWT) technology. The AP divides the total service time into multiple service periods, some of which are exclusively allocated to latency-sensitive services. This results in more frequent scheduling of these services, thereby reducing transmission delays. Additionally, the r-TWT technology defines a quiet period during which STAs running non-latency-sensitive services do not compete for the channel. This assures that the AP can prioritize scheduling for latency-sensitive services.

Figure 3.11 illustrates an example of how r-TWT technology prioritizes latency-sensitive services. In this example, the IP telephony service, which requires real-time and low-latency transmission, is given high priority. Wi-Fi 7 AP allocates two dedicated r-TWT service periods specifically for the telephone service, ensuring that its latency requirements are met. This allocation allows the IP telephony service to frequently access the channel and transmit data without compromising on latency.

3.1.2 Development Timeline of Wi-Fi 7 Standard

The timeline for the development and definition of Wi-Fi 7 standard is detailed in Fig. 3.12 [3]. The IEEE Wi-Fi 7 study group was formed in June 2018. The final version of Wi-Fi 7 is planned to be ratified by IEEE in 2024. In parallel, Wi-Fi Alliance took a step forward in 2021 by establishing a dedicated task group for Wi-Fi 7, which has already made the certificate ready by end of 2023.

Similar as the previous generations, there are early birds of the Wi-Fi 7 products appearing in the market in 2023. After the formal approval of the standards from 2024, an increasing number of commercial-grade Wi-Fi 7 APs and STAs are anticipated to hit the shelves.

The key milestones of Wi-Fi 7 standard are described below:

- June 2018: The Wi-Fi 7 Study Group (SG) was formed.
- March 2019: Following the successful approval of the Project Authorization Request (PAR), the EHT Study Group transitioned into a Task Group (TG) with the mandate to formulate and outline the specifications for the Wi-Fi 7 standard.
- September 2020: The Wi-Fi 7 Task Group released draft version 0.1, which outlined the framework of the new standard.
- May 2021: The Wi-Fi 7 Task Group released draft version 1.0, completing the definition of basic functions.
- May 2022: The Wi-Fi 7 Task Group released draft version 2.0 which refined some new features on top of draft 1.0.
- November 2022: The Wi-Fi 7 Task Group released draft version 3.0, which marked the inclusion of some complex features in the standard.
- November 2023: Wi-Fi TG released draft version 4.0.
- Dec 2024: The final version is supposed to be ratified.

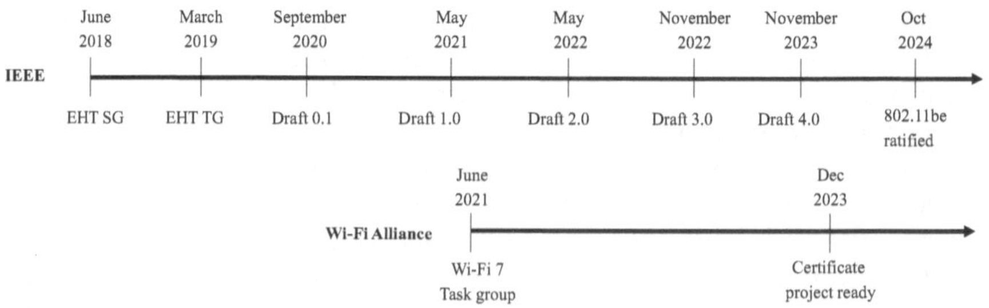

Fig. 3.12 Wi-Fi 7 standard timeline

3.2 Wi-Fi 7 Key Technologies

Wi-Fi 7, or so-called EHT, represents the cutting-edge evolution in Wi-Fi communication technology that emphasizes ultra-high speed, massive concurrency, and ultra-low latency.

The enhancements made at both the Physical Layer (PHY) and Medium Access Control (MAC) layer are pivotal to its groundbreaking advancements. Notably, innovations like Multi-link Operation significantly boost Wi-Fi performance by enabling devices to simultaneously connect and transfer data across multiple frequency bands or channels, thus ensuring a more efficient and seamless user experience.

3.2.1 Overview on Wi-Fi 7 Innovation

In the development and formulation of the Wi-Fi 7 standard, IEEE has identified and outlined numerous critical technologies along with their corresponding technical specifications. To manage complexity and ensure a smooth rollout, these advancements have been strategically planned in two separate waves. However, due to the intricate nature of certain technologies initially intended for the second phase, they have been deferred to the future Wi-Fi 8 standard.

This book primarily focusses on those key technologies finally taken into the last version of the specification, summarized as Table 3.1. Chap. 8 provides a concise overview of some of the key technologies initially planned for the second phase.

Table 3.2 outlines the differences in physical layer and MAC layer specifications between Wi-Fi 7 and Wi-Fi 6.

3.2.2 New Multiple Link Device (MLD) Introduced from Wi-Fi 7

The Wi-Fi 7 device with multi-link operation capability is referred to as Multiple Link Device (MLD), including multi-link AP (AP MLD), and multi-link STA (non-AP MLD).

Figure 3.13 illustrates a generic scenario where a multi-link AP establishes connection with a non-AP MLD and transmits data simultaneously on both links. The AP MLD has two affiliated APs, namely, AP1 and AP2, and the non-AP MLD has two affiliated stations, namely, STA1 and STA2. AP1 and STA1 communicate over Link 1, while AP2 and STA2 communicate over Link 2.

Table 3.1 Key technologies introduced by Wi-Fi 7

Num	Benefit	Solution	Wi-Fi 7 technologies
1	Ultra-high speed	High-order modulation	Support 4096-QAM
2	Ultra-high speed Massive concurrency	Ultra-high bandwidth	320 MHz channel bandwidth in the 6GHz band
3	Ultra-high speed Ultra-low latency	Multi-link operation	Multi-link discovery, authentication and association; Multi-link security; Multi-link Wi-Fi mesh
4	Massive concurrency	Bundle of discontinuous channels	Discontinuous channel bundling for uplink and downlink
5	Massive concurrency	Multi-resource unit bundling	Multi-RU bundling for uplink or downlink; Combined MU-MIMO and multi-RU bundling
6	Ultra-low latency	Recognition of latency-sensitive service	QoS characteristics
7	Ultra-low latency	Channel access scheme for latency-sensitive services	r-TWT
8	Ultra-low latency	Emergency service	Priority access for emergency services

3.2.2.1 Multi-Link Operation Mode

The Multi-link Operation has two transmission modes: **synchronous** and **asynchronous**.

In the multi-link operation's asynchronous mode, each link operates independently. The device acquires a channel on one link, sends and receives data without synchronization with the other links. This means that the device can utilize each link separately and does not require strict alignment or coordination between different links. Each link functions autonomously, allowing for independent data transmission and reception.

On the other hand, in the synchronous mode of multi-link operation, multiple links send and receive data at the same time, and the timing of these links is strictly aligned. The synchronous mode enables coordinated and simultaneous data transmission across multiple links. Multi-link APs and STAs have the flexibility to operate in either asynchronous or synchronous modes, and they can switch between these modes as required.

When the operational channels of two links are spectrally proximate, for example, one link operates on channel 36 in the low portion of the 5 GHz band, while another link runs on channel 100 within the 5 GHz band as well. It is difficult to eliminate the side lobes completely, which could potentially lead to mutual interference. In such

Table 3.2 Comparison of Wi-Fi 7 and Wi-Fi 6 specifications

Layer	Technology	Wi-Fi 7	Wi-Fi 6
Physical layer	Modulation	Up to 4096-QAM	Up to 1024-QAM
	OFDM symbol duration	12.8 μs	12.8 μs
	Guard interval	0.8, 1.6, 3.2 μs (5%, 10%, 20% overhead)	0.8, 1.6, 3.2 μs (5%, 10%, 20% overhead)
	Number of spatial streams	8	8
	Number of MU-MIMO users	8	8
	Channel bandwidth	2.4 GHz band: 40 MHz 5 GHz band: 160 MHz 6 GHz band: 320 MHz	2.4 GHz band: 40 MHz 5 GHz band: 160 MHz 6 GHz band: 160 MHz (Wi-Fi 6E)
	OFDMA concurrent users	148	74
	Maximum data rate	36 Gbps	9.6 Gbps
MAC layer	Channel access scheme	CSMA/CA, Trigger frame	CSMA/CA, Trigger frame
	Multi-user access mode	MU-MIMO, OFDMA	MU-MIMO, OFDMA
	MU-MIMO	Uplink and downlink MU-MIMO	Uplink and downlink MU-MIMO
	A-MPDU	1024	256
	Anti-interference	Supports two NAVs and dynamic CCA-ED threshold, Supports discontinuous channel bundling in both downlink and uplink	Supports two NAVs and dynamic CCA-ED threshold

case scenario, it is recommended that two links function in synchronous operation mode.

When the operating frequencies of the two links are sufficiently separated within the spectrum, they do not interfere with each other. For instance, one link operates in the 2.4 GHz frequency band, while the other link operates in the 5 GHz frequency band. This allows the multi-link device to function in asynchronous operation mode.

Figure 3.14 demonstrates signal interference that occurs in asynchronous operation mode. In this scenario, the device encounters challenges in ensuring reliable data transmission due to spectral overlap between two links.

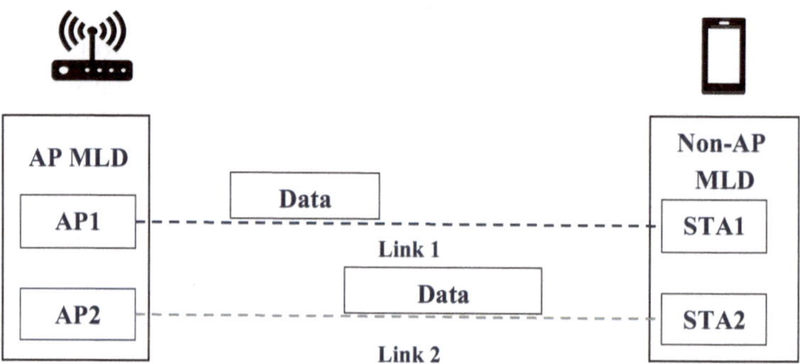

Fig. 3.13 Multi-link connection between AP MLD and non-AP MLD

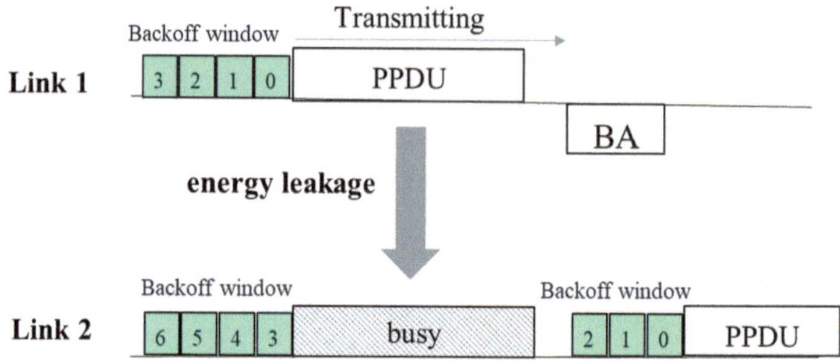

Fig. 3.14 An example of interference between the links of an asynchronous non-AP MLD

A multi-link device plans to transmit data on both links. It initiates random backoff windows on both links and counts down. The link 1 reaches zero first and sends data. However, due to the close spectral proximity of the two links and the incomplete interference removal by the device's filtering circuit, energy from Link 1 leaks into Link 2. This leakage is detected by Link 2, which then interprets it as a busy working channel. Consequently, Link 2 suspends its counter and waits for Link 1's transmission to complete before resuming counting.

In such scenarios, the asynchronous operation mode is proven to be inadequate. Conversely, when the links operate in synchronous mode, communication remains unaffected by interference from the other link.

As indicated in Table 3.3, to minimize design complexity, Wi-Fi 7 specifies that AP MLD always operate in asynchronous multi-link mode. In contrast, the hotspots which equipped with MLD function in synchronous multi-link mode.

For the STAs, under the premise that only one physical link is used for data transmission and reception, it is further divided into single-radio mode and enhanced single-radio mode, depending on whether channel listening is performed on multiple logical links.

Table 3.3 Operation modes of multi-link devices

Index	MLD type	Operation mode	MLO remark
1	AP MLD	Simultaneous transmit and receive multi-link multi-radio (**STR-MLMR**)	Transmit and/or receive data simultaneously on two or more links independently, and they don't interfere with each other
2	AP MLD	Nonsimultaneous transmit and receive multi-link multi-radio (**NSTR-MLMR**)	With transmission synchronized between different links, all links concurrently either transmit or receive at a single time
3	Non-AP MLD	Simultaneous transmit and receive multi-link multi-radio (**STR-MLMR**)	Same as STR-MLMR in AP MLD, it can transmit or receive data simultaneously on two or more links independently
4	Non-AP MLD	Enhanced multi-link multi-radio (**eMLMR**)	The devices support to dynamically reconfigure spatial multiplexing on multiple links
5	Non-AP MLD	Nonsimultaneous transmit and receive multi-link multi-radio (**NSTR-MLMR**)	Same as NSTR-MLMR in AP MLD, all links concurrently either transmit or receive at a single time
6	Non-AP MLD	Multi-link single radio (**MLSR**)	Either transmit or receive over a single link at a time though the devices have multiple links
7	Non-AP MLD	Enhanced multi-link single radio (**eMLSR**)	The devices support to listen to more than one link but only transmit or receive over a single link at a time

Next, we will introduce the multi-link devices defined by the Wi-Fi 7 standard in more detail.

3.2.2.2 Multi-Link Devices Supported by Different Modes

1. **AP MLD with Simultaneous Transmit and Receive Multi-link Multi-radio (STR-MLMR)**

The STR-MLMR AP exemplifies the typical mode of an AP MLD, where it independently sends and receives data across multiple links. This means that the device contends for access on each individual link without requiring inter-link synchronization.

Referring to Fig. 3.15, an AP MLD establishes two separate links with a non-AP MLD. In this setup, as the affiliated AP1 sends data to STA1 on the link 1, simultaneously, the counterpart affiliated AP2 is receiving the data sent by STA2 on the link 2. These two links operate independently and do not require synchronization or interdependence.

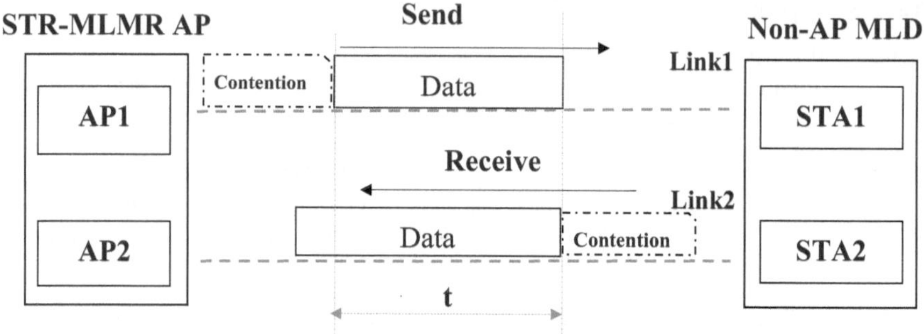

Fig. 3.15 Data transmission between STR-MLMR AP and non-AP MLD

2. **Nonsimultaneous Transmit and Receive (NSTR) Mobile AP MLD**

The NSTR mobile AP MLD is an instance of NSTR-MLMR AP. In this case, the transmission and reception of data on two links are synchronized, meaning that the start time and end time of sending and receiving data are the same. This synchronization ensures that the data transmission and reception occur simultaneously across both links.

The typical application scenario for the NSTR mobile AP MLD is the hotspot of mobile devices, that is, a Wi-Fi 7 mobile phone acts as a Wi-Fi hotspot and establishes two links with a non-AP MLD. The mobile phone, functioning as the AP MLD, is capable of transmitting and receiving data simultaneously on both links, providing high-speed connectivity to multiple devices.

In the NSTR mobile AP MLD setup, there is a primary link and a secondary link. The connection procedure is only required on the primary link. The secondary link is synchronized to the primary link for sending and receiving data. Specifically, the NSTR mobile AP MLD schedules the transmissions of Beacon frames, Probe Response frames, and data frames with group address only on the primary link. This means that these frames are transmitted and received exclusively through the primary link.

Single-link STAs can only connect to the primary link and can send and receive data through it. As shown in Fig. 3.16, the NSTR mobile AP MLD is depicted with two separate links for data transmission: a primary link associated with AP1 and a secondary link connected to AP2. The data frame transmission of AP1 and AP2 are fully synchronized on two links.

3. **STA with Simultaneous Transmit and Receive Multi-link Multi-radio (STR-MLMR)**

The non-AP MLD with STR MLMR is a typical mode of non-AP MLD. Same as STR-MLMR AP, it does not require time synchronization for data transmission on multiple links.

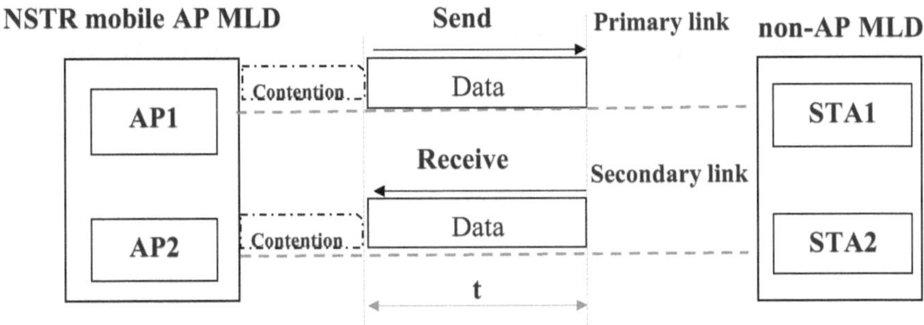

Fig. 3.16 Data transmission on two links between NSTR mobile AP MLD and non-AP MLD

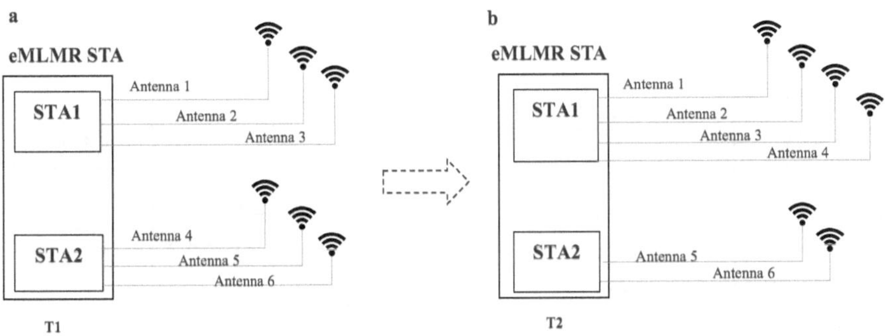

Fig. 3.17 (**a**) Original antenna allocation, (**b**) antenna 4 relocated from link 2 to link 1

4. **STA with Enhanced Multi-link Multi-Radio (eMLMR)**

An eMLMR non-AP MLD is capable of dynamically reconfiguring spatial multiplexing on each link, making it more flexible than non-AP MLDs with a fixed number of antennas on each link.

As shown in Fig. 3.17, an eMLMR STA has six antennas distributed across two links. At T1, the antennas are evenly allocated to two links, with three antennas on each, while at T2, the allocation is changed to four antennas on one link and two on the other, with the fourth antenna from the second link being reassigned to the first link. When an eMLMR STA reconfigures the number of antennas per link, i.e., reconfiguring the spatial streams, it coordinates with the AP MLD in advance to ensure that both parties can update the number of spatial streams and the transmission rate on each link in a timely manner.

5. **STA with Nonsimultaneous Transmit and Receive Multi-link Multi-radio (NSTR-MLMR)**

Just like NSTR MLMR AP, an NSTR-MLMR STA is required to synchronize the links in order to transmit or receive data simultaneously.

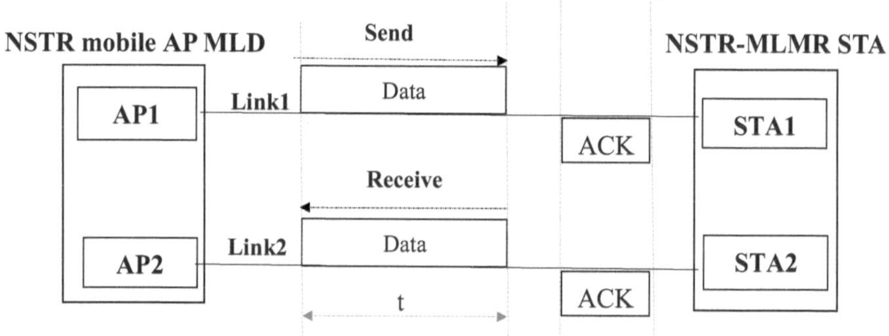

Fig. 3.18 Data transmission between a NSTR mobile AP MLD and a NSTR-MLMR STA

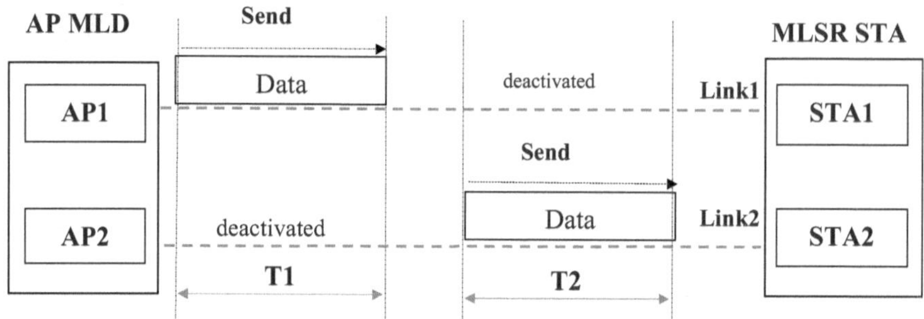

Fig. 3.19 Data transmission between AP MLD and MLSR STA

As depicted in Fig. 3.18, an NSTR mobile AP MLD and an NSTR-MLMR STA establish a connection on two links. AP1 and AP2 transmit data on both links simultaneously and receive acknowledgment frames from STA1 and STA2 at the same time.

6. **STA with Multi-link Single Radio (MLSR)**

An MLSR STA has only one radio interface. However, it establishes multiple links with an AP MLD, transmitting or receiving on one link at a time. Such an MLSR STA has the ability to dynamically select the link with the channel to communicate with the AP MLD without the need to re-establish the connection.

As shown in Fig. 3.19, an AP MLD establishes a connection with an MLSR STA on two links, but only one link is active for transmission at any given time. During the T1 period, AP1 and STA1 communicate on link 1. During the T2 period, the AP MLD and the MLSR STA switch to link 2, and concurrently, AP2 and STA2 start communicating solely on link 2.

An MLSR STA constantly monitors the activity on the link. Upon detecting that the link is busy, the MLSR STA switches to the other link and competes for the channel before sending data. As depicted in Fig. 3.20, an MLSR STA automatically switches to link 2 when the channel of link 1 is busy.

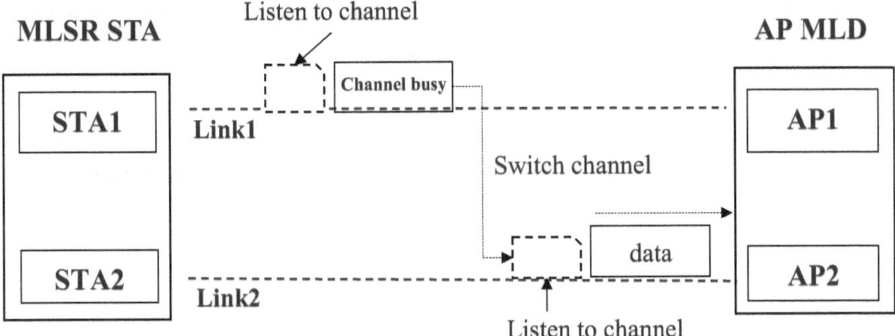

Fig. 3.20 Link transition example of MLSR STA

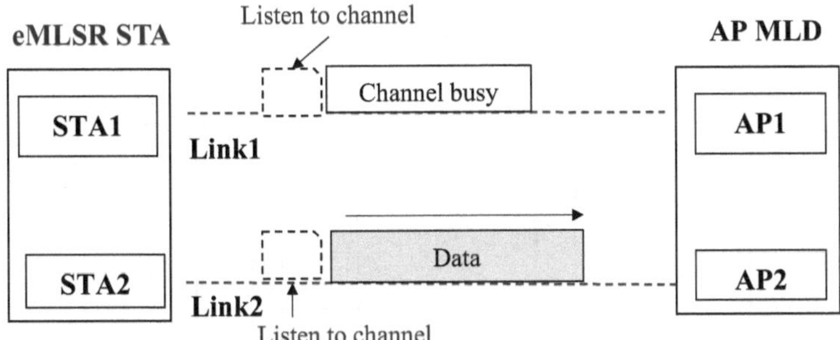

Fig. 3.21 Link selection of eMLSR STA

7. **STA with Enhanced Multi-Link Single Radio (eMLSR)**

Compared with the MLSR STA that listens to the channel first and then decides to switch links, an eMLSR STA has the advantage of supporting simultaneously listening to multiple links. This allows an eMLSR STA to quickly identify an idle link for data transmission, thus reducing the waiting delay associated with listening to multiple channels.

As shown in Fig. 3.21, an eMLSR STA simultaneously listens to the channels on both link 1 and link 2. Since the channel on link 1 is busy, and the channel on link 2 is idle, the eMLSR STA automatically selects the idle channel on link 2 for data transmission.

As shown in Fig. 3.22, the eMLSR STA has two states: channel snooping and data transmission.

Channel Snooping State

For the upstream direction, before an eMLSR STA sends data over the uplink, it conducts listen operation across all its links. To ensure effective reception of both Wi-Fi and non-Wi-Fi signals on each channel, at least one antenna is dedicated to each. Upon detecting that the channel is idle on any of these links, the eMLSR STA transitions into a data transmission mode.

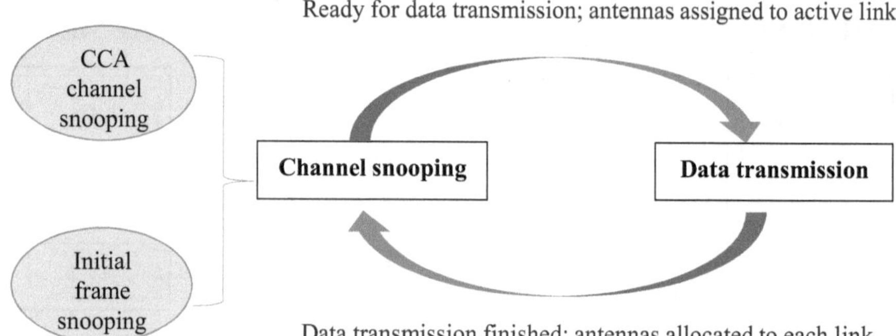

Fig. 3.22 State transition diagram of eMLSR STA

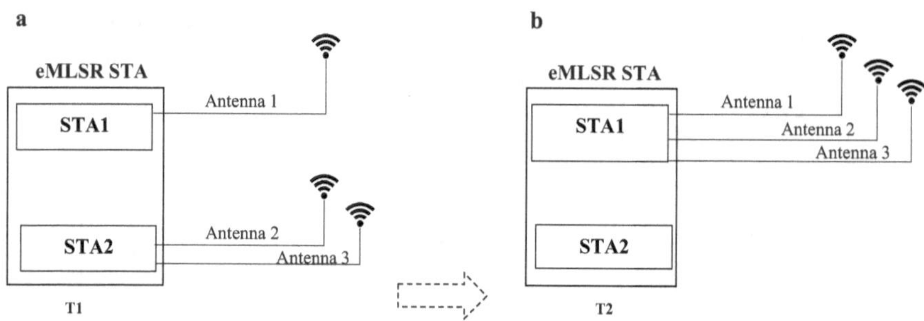

Fig. 3.23 (**a**) Channel snooping, (**b**) data transmission

In the downstream direction, when an eMLSR STA in the channel snooping state receives a specific initial frame sent by the AP MLD, it promptly transitions from the snooping state to the data reception state. Consequently, the eMLSR STA begins receiving the downstream data frames or Trigger frames from the AP MLD.

Data Transmission State

The eMLSR STA possesses the capability to configure its antenna for data transmission to leverage the benefits of a multi-antenna setup, thereby enhancing throughput performance. Following the conclusion of each transmission phase, it promptly reverts to the channel monitoring or snooping state.

During periods when one link is actively engaged in data transmission, the remaining links do not have dedicated antennas for channel snooping, hence they are rendered temporarily inactive state. As shown in Fig. 3.23, an eMLSR STA operating in the channel snooping state assigns a single antenna to STA1 and two antennas to STA2. Both affiliated STAs listen to their respective channels. When STA1 receives the specific initial frame from the AP, so the eMLSR STA reallocates all the antennas to STA1, transitioning into data transmission state. Consequently, downstream data frames are received through STA1.

3.2.3 Multi-Link Operation Offering High Efficient Data Transmission

The Multi-link Operation (MLO) technology, as mentioned, establishes multiple links between an AP MLD and a non-AP MLD for data communication. Compared with traditional single-link connection, the multi-link operation technology offers a more flexible and efficient data transmission, as indicated in Fig. 3.24.

(1) **Load balancing:** MLO devices dynamically adjust the traffic over the links based on the link load situation and the channel conditions, aiming to achieve load balancing over the multiple links.
(2) **Multi-link data aggregation:** MLO devices send or receive data simultaneously on multiple links, increasing the throughput of data transmission.
(3) **Uplink and downlink data transmitted on different links:** MLO devices can distribute data transmission across different links according to their characteristics and available bandwidth. For instance, uplink traffic may be routed through one link while downlink data is transmitted over another link.
(4) **Control frames and data frames transmitted on different links:** Different types of frames are transmitted on different links. For instance, control and management frames may be sent over the 2.4 GHz band because of its wider coverage range, while data frames that demand higher throughput are directed to the 6 GHz band, which typically offers more capacity and less interference.

Multi-link operation technology introduces several updates to the MAC layer architecture, frame transmission and retransmission, the discovery and connection process, link management, and more. In the upcoming subsections, we will delve into the details of the MAC layer architecture enhancements, frames handling, and link management. The comprehensive discovery and connection process for MLO will be introduced in Sect. 3.2.4.

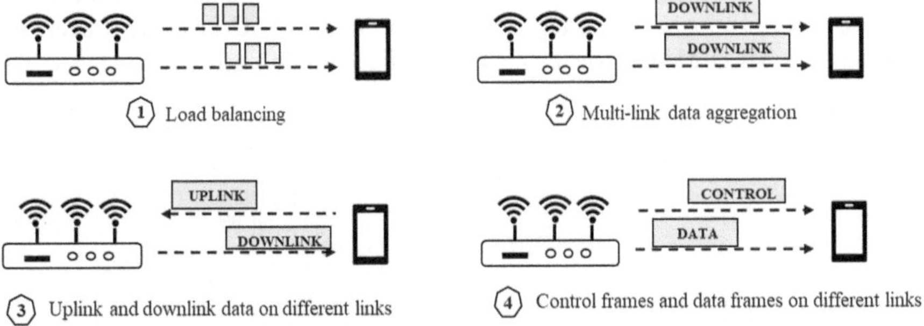

Fig. 3.24 Characteristics of multi-link operation

3.2.3.1 The Updates of MLO on MAC Layer Architecture

Figure 3.25 presents a comparison of the Physical layer and the MAC layer configurations for three types of Wi-Fi AP: a single-band AP, a dual-band AP, and a dual-link Wi-Fi 7 AP MLD respectively.

(1) **Single-band AP**: It possesses both a MAC layer and a physical layer, operating within a single frequency band.
(2) **Dual-band AP:** It operates on two distinct frequency bands, each with its own MAC layer and physical layer, enabling independent operations across both bands.
(3) **Dual-link Wi-Fi 7 AP MLD:** It offers two frequency bands, with independent physical layers but a shared MAC layer. This MAC layer is divided into an upper MAC layer and a lower MAC layer, with the lower MAC layer designated for each individual band. The dual-link AP MLD features a single MLD MAC address but has two lower MAC layer addresses, reflecting its dual-band capabilities.

The upper MAC layer, referred to as the common MAC layer, plays a crucial role in processing data packets. It interfaces with the logical link layer and manages tasks such as MSDU aggregation, frame numbering, encryption, decryption, reordering, etc. Notably, each MLD possesses a unique MLD MAC address at this upper MAC layer.

The lower MAC layer is also referred to as link-dependent MAC layer, is closely aligned with each physical link. It is responsible for handling both data frames and the control frames. For instance, it adds the source and destination addresses of A-MPDU, filters A-MPDU frames, and sends control frames such as RTS/CTS. Each physical link has a unique MAC address at this lower MAC layer, which is referred to as the link MAC address.

AP MLDs are capable of creating multiple BSSs on diverse links and assigning unique BSSIDs to each of them. This allows the AP MLD to establish connections with non-Wi-Fi 7 STAs across any link, as well as engage in multi-link simultaneous data transmission with non-AP MLDs.

As depicted in Fig. 3.26, an AP MLD and a non-AP MLD establish a connection across two distinct links. The process of the data frame encapsulation and data frame parsing process remains consistent with legacy Wi-Fi MAC layer. However, the transmitter's MLD MAC layer manages data transmission across both links. The

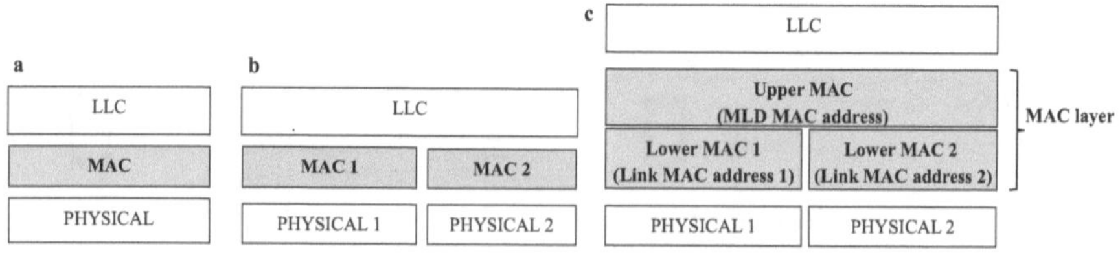

Fig. 3.25 (**a**) Single-band AP, (**b**) dual-band AP, (**c**) Wi-Fi 7 AP MLD

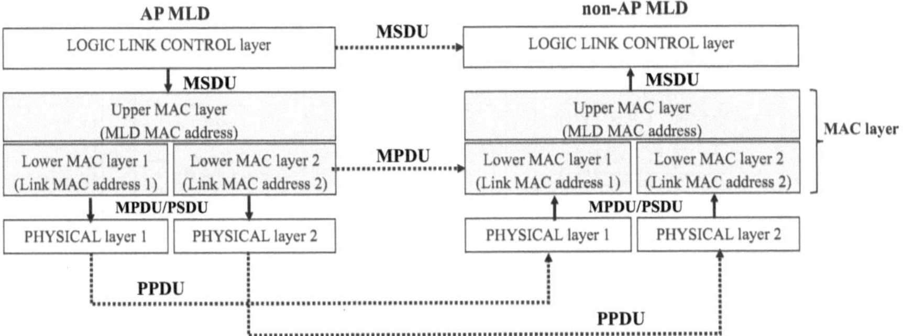

Fig. 3.26 Communication of multi-link devices

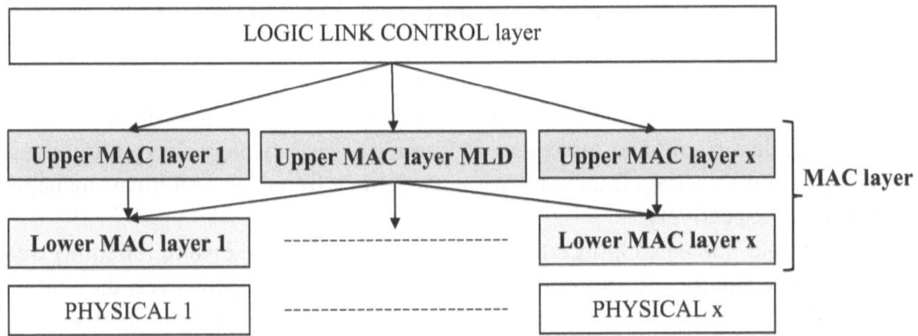

Fig. 3.27 MAC layer of AP MLD

receiver's MLD MAC layer receives data frames from both links, reorders them, and passes them on to the logical link control layer for further processing.

AP MLDs not only interact with non-AP MLDs, but also engage with legacy single-link STAs. To facilitate this, in the Wi-Fi 7 standard, MLD incorporates an upper MAC layer with each link, effectively managing the single-link STAs.

As shown in Fig. 3.27, there are two cases of upper MAC layer in the architecture of AP MLDs.

- **Upper MAC layer for MLD:** A common MAC layer that supports multi-link operations. There is only one upper MAC layer in AP MLD, corresponding to all the low MAC layers. **Upper MAC layer per link:** In an MLD AP, a unique upper MAC layer is created for each link, which establishes a 1:1 correspondence with the lower MAC layer. This configuration is specifically designed to manage connections with legacy single-link STAs.

Figure 3.28 illustrates how a multi-link AP establishes connections on two links with a multi-link STA, while also connecting to a legacy single-link STA. The data is transmitted between the upper MAC layer and lower MAC layers of the multi-link AP, as well as between these layers and the MAC layer of the single-link STA.

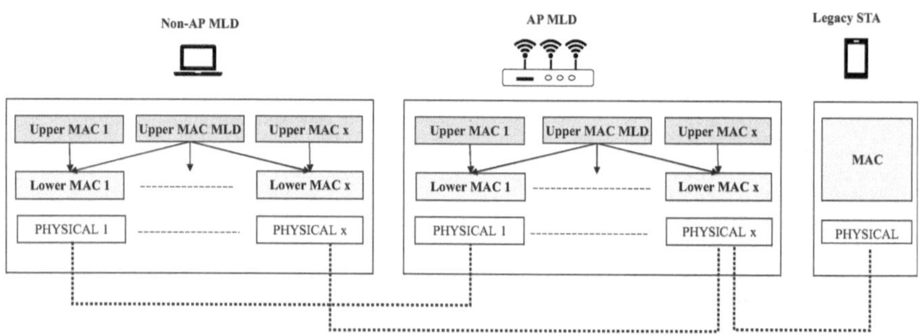

Fig. 3.28 Communication of AP MLD, non-AP MLD and legacy STA

3.2.3.2 Features of Transmitting Wi-Fi Frames Over Multiple Links

In the first chapter, we delved into three types of Wi-Fi frames: data frames, management frames, and control frames. Furthermore, according to the destination address, the data frame and management frame can be subcategorized into unicast data frame, multicast data frame, unicast management frame, and multicast management frame, respectively.

Unicast data frames support retransmission mechanisms to ensure reliability and aggregation techniques for improved transmission efficiency. However, they might arrive at the receiver out-of- sequence due to network congestion, multipath effects, or other transmission irregularities. Consequently, the receiver is responsible for correctly sorting the unicast data frames and subsequently forwarding them to the upper layers for further processing.

Table 3.4 shows how MLO technique handles different types of frames.

When an AP MLD sends multicast data, the receiver may be either a legacy STA or a non-AP MLD. To ensure that all STAs receive the same multicast data frame, the AP MLD replicates the multicast data frame on all links and send them separately. This allows legacy STAs to receive the multicast frame on their respective links, and non-AP MLDs to receive the multicast frame from any link they are connected to or receive multiple copies of the same multicast frame from multiple links. Prior to sending them to the logical link control layer, the non-AP MLD drops any duplicate frames.

As introduced in Chaps. 1 and 2, multiple data frames can be aggregated into an A-MPDU to enhance the channel utilization. However, should there be a transmission failure, these aggregated data frames must be retransmitted individually or as a group, which may result in the frames arriving at the receiver out of their original order. To address this, the transmitter assigns a frame number to each frame before transmission, enabling the receiver to reorder the received frames based on the frame number, discard duplicate data frames, and forward them to the upper layer.

Furthermore, upon receiving an A-MPDU, the receiver sends a Block ACK (BA) to inform the transmitter of the receiving status of each MPDU within the A-MPDU.

Table 3.4 Frame transmission by MLD

Frame type	The source of the frame	Destination address	Retransmission	Multi-link	Typical frame
Data frame	Upper layer	Unicast	Retransmission supported	Transmitted on any of the links	Data frames
		Multicast	Retransmission not supported	Each data frame is replicated and transmitted on all links	Broadcast ARP frames
Control frame	Lower MAC layer	Unicast	Retransmission not supported	Transmitted on the current link	CTS/RTS, ACK, BA frames
Management frame	Upper MAC layer	Unicast	Retransmission supported	Transmitted on any of the links	Association request and response frames, etc
Management frame	Lower MAC layer	Unicast	Retransmission supported	Transmitted on the current link	Probe request and response frames, etc
	Lower MAC layer	Multicast	Retransmission not supported	Transmitted on the current link	Beacon frame

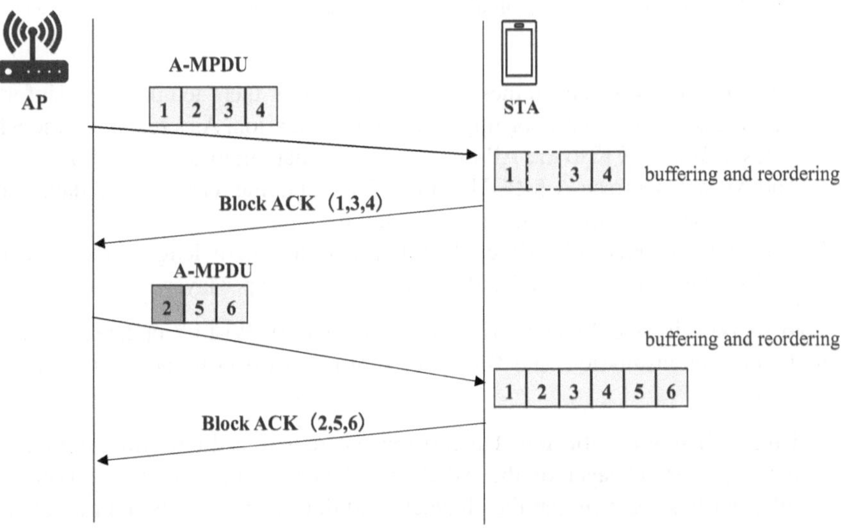

Fig. 3.29 A-MPDU transmission

Figure 3.29 illustrates the procedure of A-MPDU frame transmission.

(1) The AP sends an aggregate frame A-MPDU to the STA containing numbered data frames 1, 2, 3, and 4.

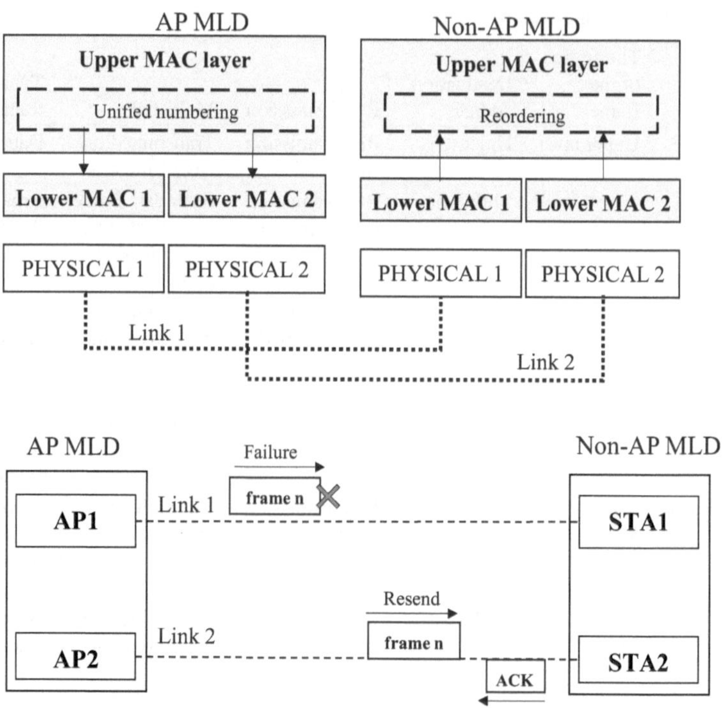

Fig. 3.30 Multi-link transmission with unified numbering, retransmission, and acknowledgement

(2) The STA receives data frames 1, 3, and 4, storing them temporarily. Unfortunately, data frame 2 gets corrupted during transmission. As a response, the STA sends a Block ACK to the AP to acknowledge data frames 1, 3, and 4.
(3) The AP sends a fresh A-MPDU to the STA containing retransmitted data frame 2, along with new frames numbered 5 and 6.
(4) The STA responds with a Block ACK to the AP to acknowledge frames 2, 5, and 6. The frames are reordered and forwarded to the upper layer.

To support the MLO technology, the MAC layer of Wi-Fi 7 updates the frame numbering, retransmission, and Block ACK of unicast data frames as indicated in Fig. 3.30.

(1) **Unified frame numbering:** Unicast frames are assigned uniformly numbers at the upper MAC layer of the MLD and then scheduled for transmission on different links. Given that the channel conditions and transmission rate of each link are inconsistent, the frames received at the receiver through the links may not be in the order of their sequence number. The upper MAC layer of receiver buffers the data frames and reorders them based on the frame numbering, subsequently forwarding them to the upper layer.

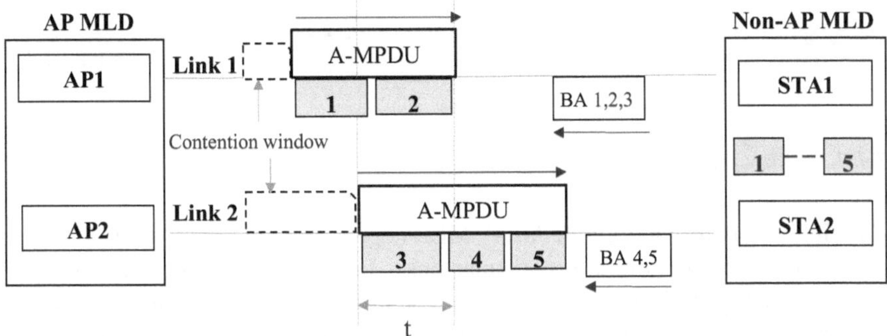

Fig. 3.31 A-MPDU transmission and block ACK of multi-link devices

(2) **Retransmission:** If a data frame transmission fails on one link, it can be retransmitted on the same link or another link, while maintaining the original frame numbering. It is up to the chipset or device manufacturer to determine how to implement the multi-link retransmission mechanism.
(3) **Cross-link Block ACK:** When the receiver receives data frames from multiple links, it will send a separate Block ACK frame on each link, containing bitmap information for both the frames received on the current link and those from other links. The Block ACK information must remain consistent across links. The implementation of cross-link Block ACK is tailored by the manufacturer.

Figure 3.31 illustrates an example of unicast data frames transmitted in A-MPDU and the corresponding Block ACK over multiple links.

The AP MLD establishes connections with the non-AP MLD on both link 1 and link 2. The AP MLD competes for wireless channel resources on two links. Then it sends an A-MPDU containing data frames numbered 1, 2 on link 1, and another A-MPDU containing data frames numbered 3, 4, and 5 on link 2.

After receiving the data frames on both links, the non-AP MLD replies Block ACK frames on each link. Specifically, the Block ACK frame on link 1 serves to confirm the successful reception of frames 1 through 3, while the Block ACK on link 2 acknowledges frames 4 through 5. The data frames from both links are reordered in sequence and forwarded to the upper layer.

3.2.3.3 Management of Multi-Link Operation

Wi-Fi 7 introduces the management of multi-link operations to enhance the QoS of various traffic types on multiple links and improve power saving for mobile terminals.

This management encompasses three key aspects: link and traffic mapping, link state management, and buffered data transmission on multiple links, as indicated in Fig. 3.32.

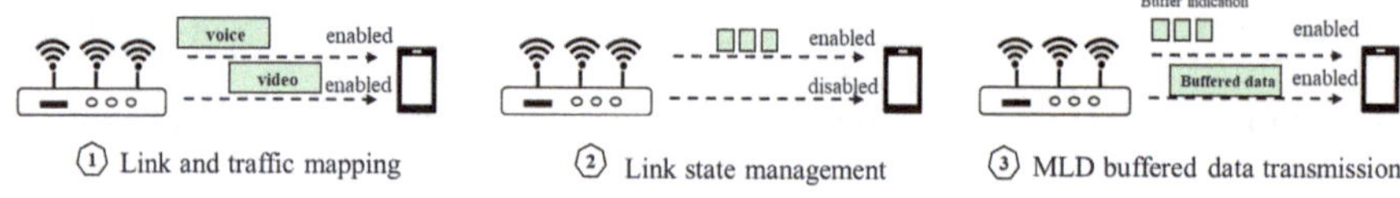

Fig. 3.32 Management of multi-link operation

(1) **Link and traffic mapping:** An AP MLD negotiates with a non-AP MLD to map specific types of traffic to particular links. For instance, latency-sensitive services such as real-time video streaming or VoIP are assigned to the link with the best quality, lowest latency, or maximum available bandwidth, ensuring optimal performance.
(2) **Link state management:** An AP MLD dynamically manages the state of its multiple links. It has the ability to enable or disable individual links based on current network conditions and requirements. By doing so, it can effectively schedule data transmission across multiple links to achieve load balancing, thereby improving overall network efficiency and avoiding congestion on any single link.
(3) **Buffered data transmission for power-saving MLDs**: When non-AP MLD devices are in power-saving mode, they rely on the buffering capabilities of the AP MLD. The AP MLD accumulates data intended for these devices from different links and provides buffer status indications to them. The non-AP MLDs then retrieve their buffered data according to this indication, allowing them to conserve energy without missing critical data packets during their low-power operation phases.

1. **Link and Traffic Mapping**

As introduced in Chap. 1, when an AP or STA receives data frames of different traffic types from the upper layer, the frames will be classified based on the traffic type and placed in priority queues: BE (normal data stream), BK (background stream), VI (video stream), VO (voice stream), with the voice stream having the highest priority.

The data frames of different traffic types can be mapped to the same link or dedicated links. Data of the same traffic type can also be mapped to different links. A link can be enabled or disabled. When a link is disabled, no data transmission is permitted.

Figure 3.33 shows how a non-AP MLD sends different types of data to an AP MLD across multiple links.

- BK and BE types are mapped to link 1.
- BE, VI, and VO are mapped to link 2.
- Link 3 is disabled, so no traffic is allowed on it.

In this example, the non-AP MLD sends data frames of traffic type BK and BE to the AP MLD through link 1, and data frames of type BE, VI, and VO on link 2. The

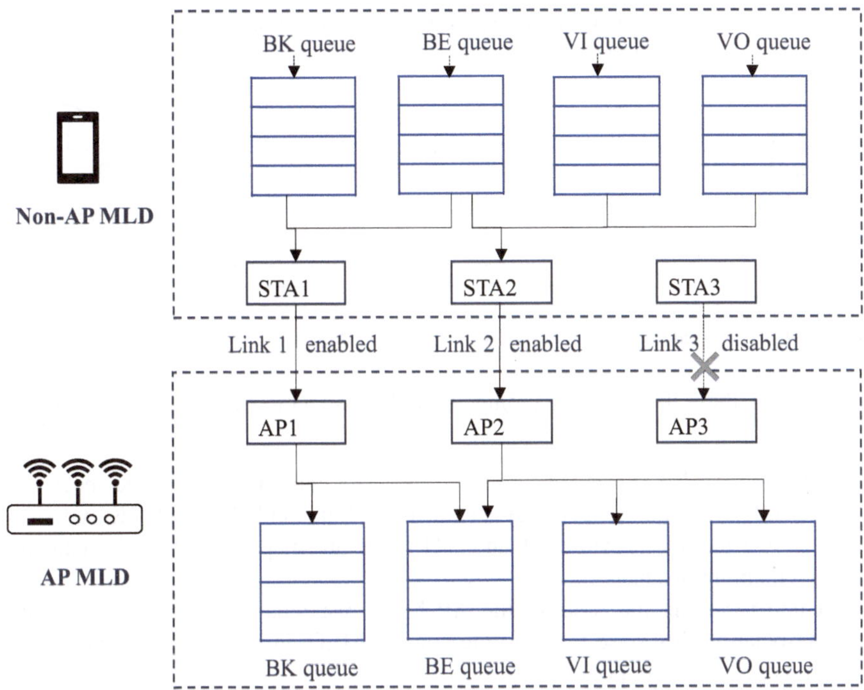

Fig. 3.33 Link and traffic mapping

AP MLD receives these data frames from the respective links and places them in the corresponding queues.

By default, when a link is enabled, it permits all types of traffic, similar to the traditional single-link connection. The AP MLD and the non-AP MLD negotiate to map traffics to the link. There are two methods of negotiation:

(1) **Negotiation Through Multi-link Association Request and Response Frames**

The non-AP MLD initiates the negotiation process by sending a Multi-Link Association Request frame. This frame encapsulates the mapping details between Traffic Identifier (TID) and the desired links for data transmission. By including this information directly in the request, it streamlines the negotiation process, minimizing overhead and saving time.

Upon receipt of the Multi-Link Association Request, the AP MLD responds with a Multi-Link Association Response, accepting or denying the TID-to-link mapping. If the AP chooses to deny the request due to any constraints such as bandwidth limitations or link quality issues, it will include alternative traffic type and link mapping information within its response. The non-AP MLD, upon receiving a denial along with new mapping suggestions, adjusts its request accordingly and resends an updated Multi-Link Association Request based on the feedback from the AP MLD. Figure 3.34 depicts this interaction where an AP MLD and a non-AP MLD are

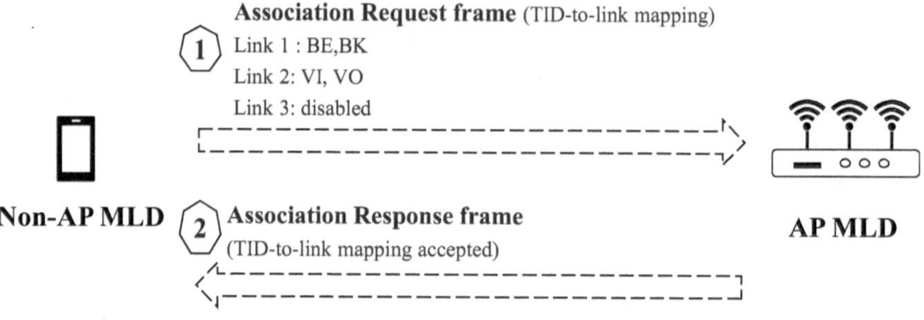

Fig. 3.34 TID-to-link mapping through association procedure

negotiating the TID-to-link mapping through Association Request and Response frames.

(a) The non-AP MLD transmits a multi-link Association Request frame specifying the following mapping policy in the multi-link field: BE and BK types are mapped to link 1, while VI and VO types are mapped to link 2, with link 3 remaining disabled.
(b) Upon receiving the request, the AP MLD responds by sending a multi-link Association Response frame to the non-AP MLD, indicating acceptance of the proposed mapping policy.

After the non-AP MLD successfully negotiates and establishes a multi-link connection with the AP MLD, based on the negotiation results mentioned above, different types of data frames are transmitted on link 1 and link 2 according to the mapping policy. No data is transmitted on link 3, which subsequently enters a dormant state.

(2) **Negotiation Through Action Frame**

Besides the Association Request/Response frames, both the AP MLD and non-AP MLD can utilize Action frames to negotiate the TID-to-link mapping after the initial connection process, or to modify the existing mapping policy dynamically.

The Action Request and Response frames are used to handle unplanned state changes that may occur during data transmission. For instance, when a link transitions from an enabled state to a disabled state, the associated mapping policy needs to be updated, and the data traffic previously assigned to that link shall be redirected to an active link through a renegotiation procedure.

Figure 3.35 shows the mapping policy renegotiation using Action frames. In this scenario, the non-AP MLD and the AP MLD establish a connection with three links, and the initial mapping policy is as follows:

- BK and BE are mapped to link 1.
- VI and VO are mapped to link 2.
- Link 3 is disabled.

TID-to-link	Link 1	Link 2	Link 3
Previous	BE, BK	VI, VO	disabled
New	BE, BK, VI, VO	disabled	disabled

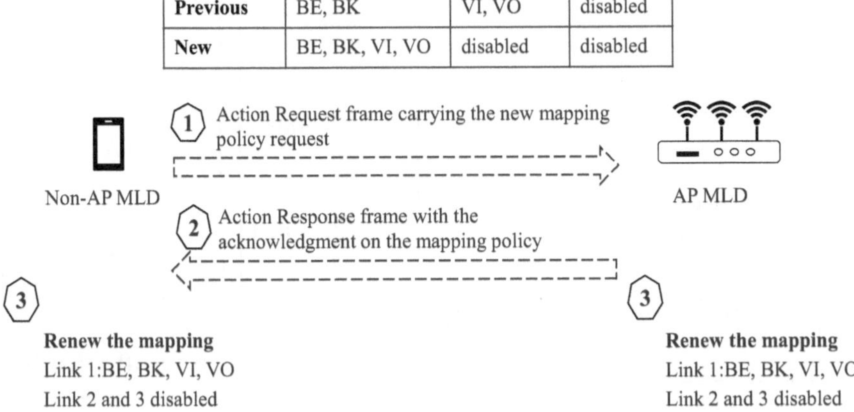

Fig. 3.35 Renegotiate the mapping policy through action frames

To save power, the non-AP MLD can disable link 2 and send an Action frame to initiate renegotiation process. The steps involved in this process are as follows:

(a) The non-AP MLD sends an Action frame, including the new mapping policy, which states that BE, BK, VI, and VO traffics will be bundled to link 1, while link 2 and link 3 will be disabled.
(b) The AP MLD responds with an Action frame, indicating that it accepts the new mapping policy proposed by the non-AP MLD.
(c) After the negotiation is successful, the non-AP MLD sends all types of data on link 1. Additionally, it disables both link 2 and link 3.

2. **Link State Management**

A link can be in either a disabled or an enabled state. According to the mapping policy, unicast data frames or unicast management frames are transmitted exclusively over enabled links. Conversely, disabled links are restricted to transmitting only multicast data frames and multicast management frames; they do not support the transmission of unicast frames. For an AP MLD, the same link may exhibit different states when connecting to distinct non-AP MLD devices. As shown Fig. 3.36, an AP MLD contains three links, connecting to the non-AP MLD-a and non-AP MLD-b.

With respect to the link states for non-AP MLD-a, the first link is enabled while the remaining two links are disabled. In contrast, for non-AP MLD-b, the second and third links are enabled, while the first one is disabled. Consequently, the AP MLD is capable of sending management frames and unicast data frames to non-AP MLD-a via link 1 alone. On the other hand, it can send both management frames and data frames to non-AP MLD-b across link 2 and link 3.

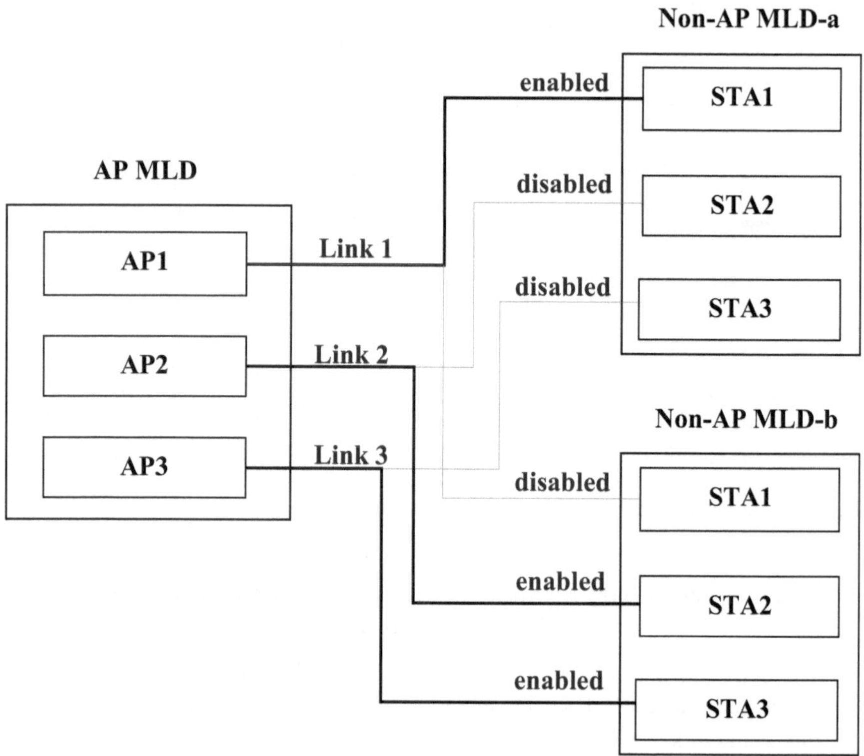

Fig. 3.36 Link state management

The link status can dynamically transition from one state to another. Through the implementation of the link state management, the AP MLD can effectively schedule data transmission between different non-AP MLDs across various links.

Furthermore, when a non-AP MLD has only a minimal amount of data to be transmitted with the AP MLD, the non-AP MLD may opt to activate only a single link, setting the rest to the disabled state in order to conserve energy power. On the other hand, if a non-AP MLD suddenly needs to transmit a large volume of data, it can instantly enable additional or all links without having to re-establish the connection anew. This ensures seamless scalability and adaptability to varying traffic loads while maintaining a stable and efficient communication channel with the AP MLD.

3. **Data Transmission in Power-Saving Mode**

As introduced in Chap. 1, the AP buffers the downstream traffic for STAs in power-saving mode and broadcasts the buffer states through the TIM field in the Beacon frames. When a STA wakes up during TBTT and finds buffered information in the Beacon frame, it sends PS-Poll or QoS Null frames to the AP to retrieve the

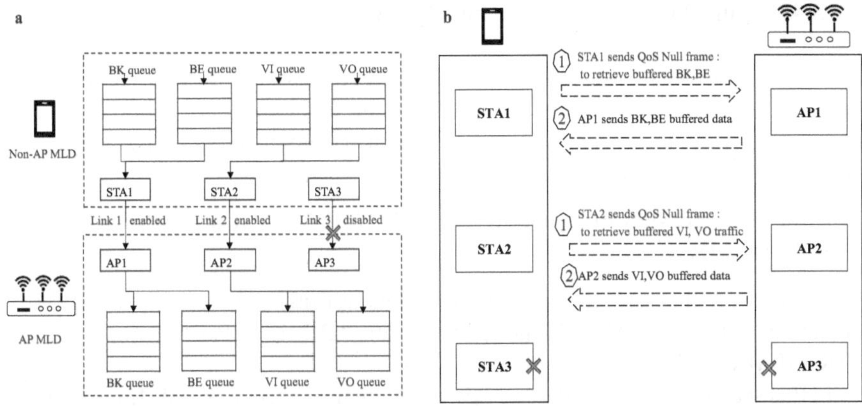

Fig. 3.37 (**a**) Link and traffic mapping, (**b**) non-AP MLD acquires buffered data from different links

buffered frames. In Wi-Fi 7 multi-link operation mode, the handling of buffered data for power-saving STA is as follows:

- The AP MLD sends Beacon frames on each link, with each frame indicating the buffer state for non-AP MLDs and legacy STAs.
- Non-AP MLDs in power-saving mode periodically wake up on only one of the links to receive Beacon frames, while the other links remain in a deep dormant state to save power.
- When a non-AP MLD reads from the Beacon frame that AP MLD has buffered data, it sends a PS-Poll or QoS Null frame on one link which doesn't restrict the traffic type to retrieve the buffered data.
- In case a traffic type is mapped to a specific link, the non-AP MLD can only retrieve buffered data of the traffic type from that specific link, while the buffered data of other types can be obtained from the other links.

As shown in Fig. 3.37, the non-AP MLD and the AP MLD establish a connection on three links. The link and the traffic mapping policy is as follows:

- BK and BE are mapped to link 1.
- VI and VO are mapped to link 2.
- Link 3 is disabled and not used for any traffic type.

The non-AP MLD, in power-saving mode, receives a Beacon frame and finds buffered data for itself. Consequently, it sends a QoS Null frame on link 1 to receive the data frames of BK and BE, and a QoS null frame on link 2 to receive video and voice data.

3.2.3.4 Typical Cases of Multi-Link Operation

Due to the presence of various types of AP MLDs and non-AP MLDs, the multi-link operations between them exhibit distinct behavior. In this section, we will outline the multi-link operation procedure of the five typical combinations of AP MLDs and non-AP MLDs as depicted in Fig. 3.38.

1. **Data Transmission Between an AP MLD STR-MLMR and a Non-AP MLD STR-MLMR**

   Figure 3.39 illustrates the asynchronous data transmission between an AP MLD operating in the STR-MLMR mode and a non-AP MLD also functioning in the STR-MLMR mode.

   In this scenario, the AP MLD competes for channel access on link 1, transmitting data to the non-AP MLD over that link. Subsequently, it receives ACK from the non-AP MLD via the same link 1. Concurrently, but independently, the non-AP MLD competes for the channel access on link 2. It then sends data to the AP MLD using link 2 and receives ACK from the AP MLD also on link 2.

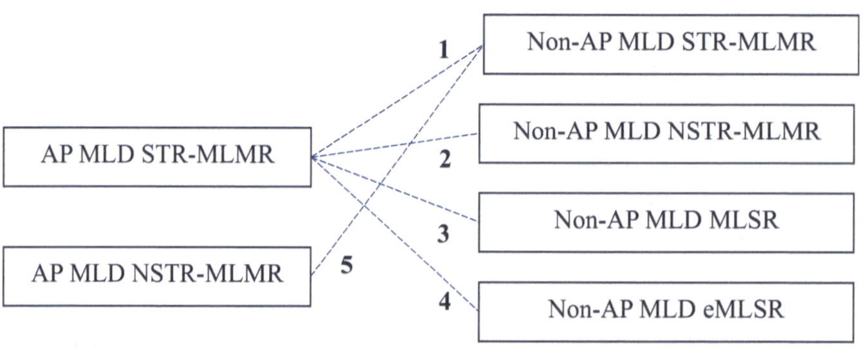

Fig. 3.38 Five typical cases of multi-link operations

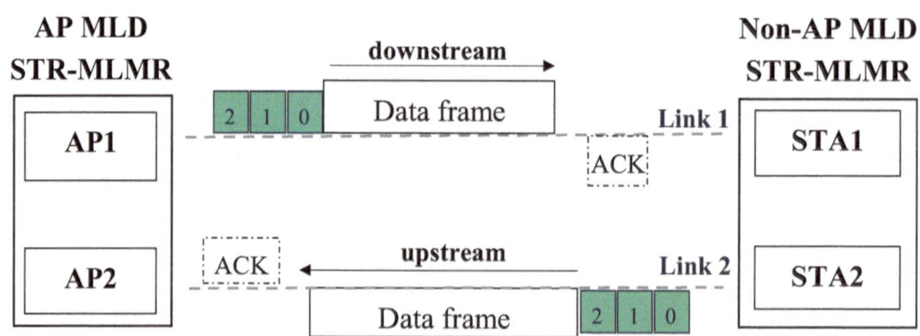

Fig. 3.39 Data transmission between MLDs of STR-MLMR mode

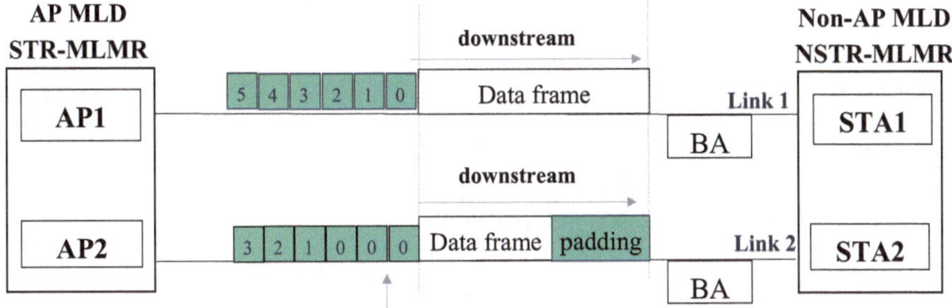

Fig. 3.40 Data transmission between AP MLD and non-AP MLD of NSTR-MLMR mode

Both links operate asynchronously, with each link engaging in separate contention processes, sending and receiving data without influencing or interfering with the other's operations.

2. **Data Transmission Between an AP MLD STR-MLMR and a Non-AP MLD NSTR-MLMR**

The MLDs compete for channel access on different link through CSMA/CS scheme separately. Due to this random backoff process, the exact time when an MLD starts its transmission on any given link can vary. Moreover, the transmission over multiple links may also end at different times due to variations in channel modulation, bandwidth, and frame length.

To achieve synchronization of the transmission start and end time across the links for the non-AP MLD NSTR-MLMR, the Wi-Fi 7 standard defines the following two methods:

- When the backoff window of one link hits 0 and is ready to start transmission, it waits until the backoff windows of all other links also count to 0. This ensures that all links start transmitting simultaneously, achieving synchronization in transmission start time.
- In case where one link finishes transmitting data while other links are still in transmission, padding is added to the end of the PPDU on the finishing link. This padding ensures that the transmission on the finishing link aligns with the transmission on the other links, achieving synchronization in transmission end time.

Figure 3.40 illustrates an example how a non-AP MLD in NSTR-MLMR mode receives data from the multi-links. The AP MLD establishes a connection with the non-AP MLD on both links. The AP MLD begins channel snooping on both links simultaneously, attempting to gain access to the channel. When the backoff countdown on link 2 reaches zero first, it pauses there, waiting until the backoff window on link 1 also expires and reaches zero. Once both backoff windows reach zero, the AP MLD sends data on both links simultaneously. To complete the data transmission with link 1 at the same time, the link 2 adds a padding field at the end of PPDU.

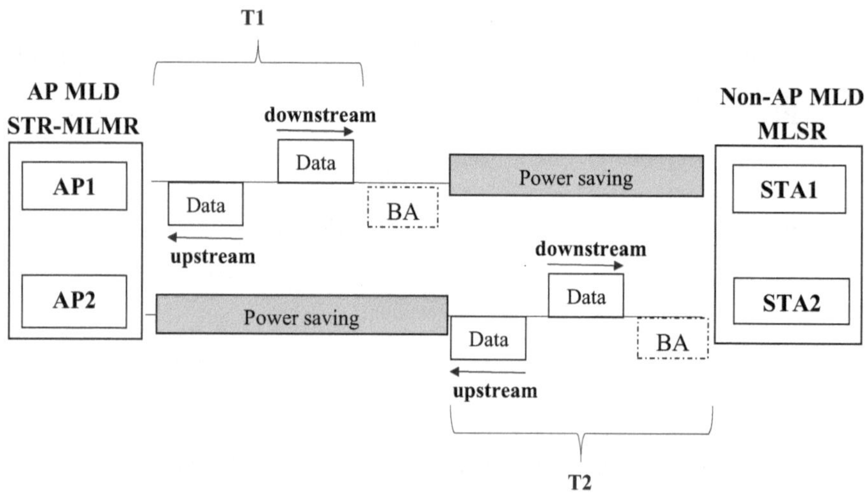

Fig. 3.41 Data transmission between AP MLD and non-AP MLD MLSR

The non-AP MLD receives data on both links and sends Block ACK (BA) frames simultaneously after an SIFS interval.

3. **Data Transmission Between an AP MLD and a Non-AP MLD MLSR**

A non-AP MLD MLSR is capable of transmitting and receiving data on one of the links at a time, but it has the flexibility to switch its working link whenever necessary.

When a non-AP MLD MLSR switches its active link, it communicates this change by embedding information about the current working channel within the MAC header of the transmitted data frames. The AP MLD then reads this information to understand the current link state of the non-AP MLSR. Based on these link states, the AP MLD can select the active links for downlink data transmission.

As in Fig. 3.41, the AP MLD establishes a dual-link connection with a non-AP MLD MLSR. The non-AP MLD MLSR communicates its current link status within the data frames: during T1 time interval, it indicates that link 1 is in operation mode while link 2 is in power-saving mode. Consequently, the AP MLD transmits data to the non-AP MLD on link 1.

Subsequently, at T2 time, the non-AP MLD MLSR updates its status and informs the AP MLD that link 2 has transitioned into active mode, whereas link 1 has shifted to power-saving mode. In response to this change, the AP MLD adjusts its transmission accordingly and begins sending data over link 2.

4. **Data Transmission Between an AP MLD and a Non-AP MLD eMLSR**

Based on non-AP MLD MLSR technology, the enhanced version known as eMLSR supports channel snooping capabilities across all its connected links. It operates in two distinct working modes:

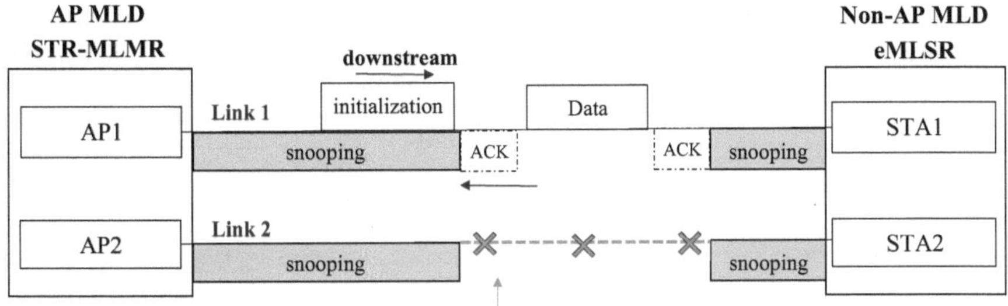

Fig. 3.42 Data transmission between AP MLD and non-AP MLD eMLSR

- **Multi-link simultaneous channel snooping state:** The non-AP MLD eMLSR allocates at least one antenna to each link to snoop the channel state. This allows it to simultaneously listen to and receive initialization frames from any of the connected links.
- **Single-link data interaction state:** The non-AP MLD eMLSR dedicates all its antennas to a single link for data transmission. The antennas are not assigned to other links during this period, rendering those links unavailable for data exchange.

Wi-Fi 7 standardizes the procedure of transitioning between multi-link simultaneous channel snooping state and single-link data interaction state, as illustrated in Fig. 3.42.

(1) The non-AP MLD continuously listens to and monitors all its connected channels. It identifies a special initialization frame sent by the AP MLD, which is either a reutilized MU-RTS (Multi-User Request-to-Send) or BSRP (Buffer Status Report Polling) frame from Wi-Fi 6 technology. It is up to the chip manufacturer and device manufacturer to select which frame type as an initialization signal.
(2) Upon receiving the Initialization frame on one of its links, the non-AP MLD responds with an ACK frame. Subsequently, the hardware configuration is adjusted, assigning all antennas to the designated link for high-throughput data transmission.
(3) Following the initialization phase, the AP MLD and the non-AP MLD engage in data transmission over the selected link, while the other links remain inactive and are not available for data transfer.
(4) Once the data transmission process is complete, the non-AP MLD eMLSR returns to the multi-link simultaneous channel snooping state, resuming its monitoring role across all the links.

For the upstream direction, when a non-AP MLD eMLSR needs to send data to the AP MLD, it moves all its antennas to an idle channel and then sends data to the AP MLD.

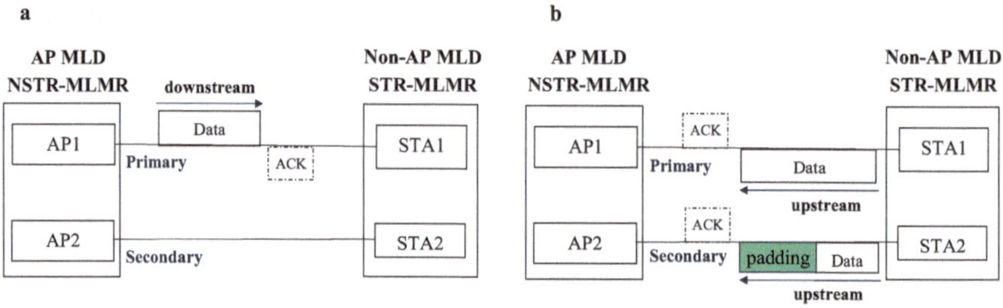

Fig. 3.43 (**a**) Downlink transmission on primary link only, (**b**) uplink transmission on both links

5. **Data Transmission Between an AP MLD NSTR-MLMR and a Non-AP MLD STR-MLMR**

A NSTR mobile AP MLD is an instance of an AP MLD NSTR-MLMR, which possesses a primary link and a secondary link. The secondary link cannot be utilized independently; instead, it is designed to work in conjunction with the primary link to enhance throughput and reduce power consumption by enabling simultaneous data transmission. In this setup, both the AP MLD NSTR-MLMR and the non-AP MLD STR-MLMR have the flexibility to transmit data on either the primary link alone or on both links simultaneously.

As shown in Fig. 3.43, an AP MLD NSTR-MLMR and a non-AP MLD STR-MLMR are connected over two links.

In Fig. 3.43a, the AP MLD sends data to the non-AP MLD solely through the primary link; In Fig. 3.43b, the non-AP MLD sends data to the AP MLD across both the primary and secondary links concurrently.

To mitigate the cross-link interference at the AP MLD NSTR-MLMR side, the non-AP MLD must ensure that its transmission on both links concludes at same time using the padding field within the transmitted data frames.

3.2.4 Discovery, Authentication, and Association Procedure of MLD

For multi-link devices, multiple links are utilized for data transmission to enhance the overall throughput. Nevertheless, the discovery, authentication, and association processes are conducted through a single link for connection efficiency, rather than repeating the same process on each individual link.

Figure 3.44 shows the Wi-Fi 7 MLD discovery, authentication, and association procedure.

Network discovery procedure: The non-AP MLD discovers an AP MLD and the information for all the links through Beacon frames or Probe Response frames from any of the links. It then exchanges multi-link Probe Request and Response

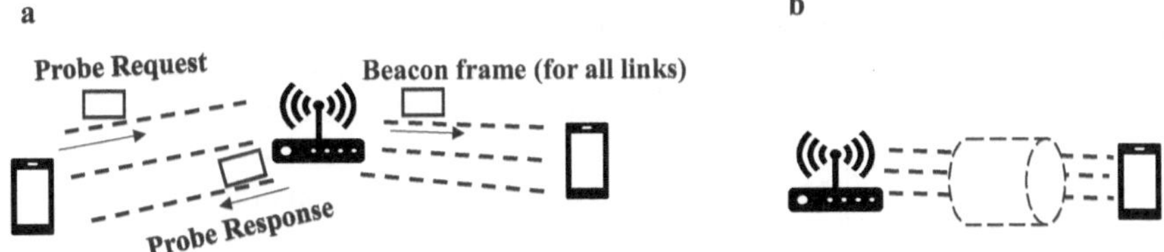

Fig. 3.44 (**a**) Network discovery of MLDs, (**b**) authentication and association of MLDs processed on one of the links

frames with the AP MLD to obtain comprehensive information about all the links, ultimately establishing an MLO connection.

- **Passive snooping mode:** The non-AP MLD receives the Beacon frame broadcasted periodically by the AP MLD. The Beacon frame carries the basic information of the multiple links.
- **Active scanning mode**: The non-AP MLD sends a multi-link Probe Request frame on a link, obtains the information about all the links of the AP MLD from the multi-link Probe Response frame.

MLD Authentication and Association Procedure Prior to Wi-Fi 7, the authentication and association process were applied to one link. However, in Wi-Fi 7, multiple links can be handled simultaneously during one authentication and association procedure.

3.2.4.1 Discovery Procedure of MLDs

To facilitate the discovery of AP MLD, Wi-Fi 7 introduces updates to the frame format of Beacon frames, Probe Response frames for the AP MLD, and Probe Request frames for non-AP MLD, along with enhancements to the discovery procedure.

1. **Beacon Frame of AP MLD**

As depicted in Fig. 3.45, a multi-link field has been added to the Beacon frame, encompassing the common information of the AP MLD. Additionally, another new field, named Reduced Neighbor Report (RNR), has been introduced to indicate the information of the other links, including details such as the channel, bandwidth, SSID, link index, and so on.

2. **Probe Request and Response Frames of MLDs**

The multi-link Probe Request frame contains a multi-link field, which the non-AP MLD uses to request the information about the AP MLD links. Once the AP MLD receives the multi-link Probe Request frame on one of its links, it responds with a multi-link Probe Response frame.

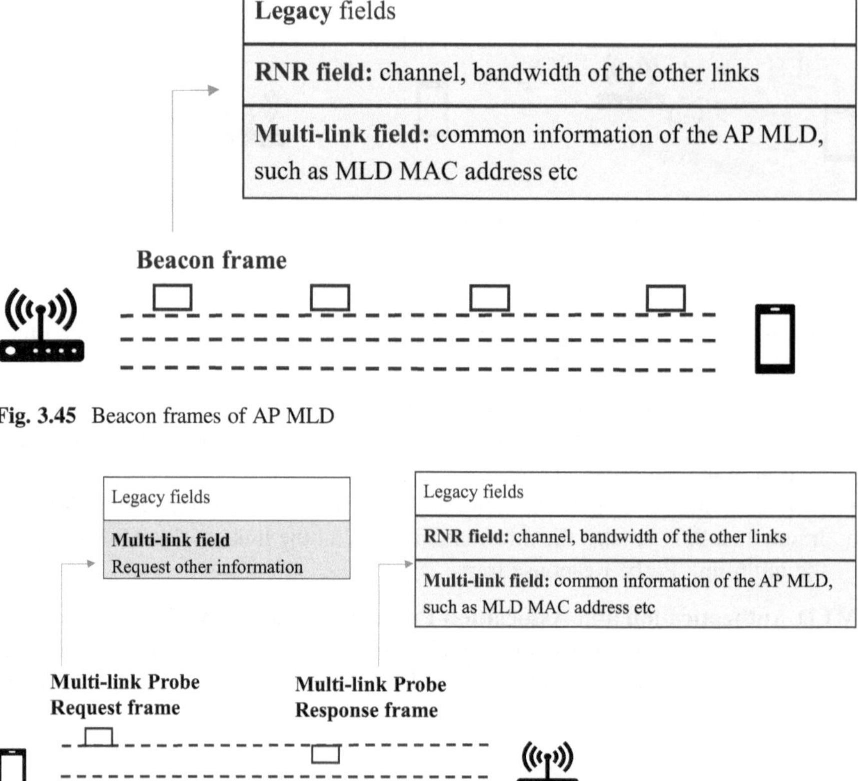

Fig. 3.45 Beacon frames of AP MLD

Fig. 3.46 Multi-link probe request and probe response frames

Similar to the Beacon frame format, Wi-Fi 7 also adds the same fields to the multi-link Probe Response frame, that is, the multi-link field contains the common information of the AP MLD, while the RNR field contains the basic information of other links.

As Fig. 3.46, the multi-link Probe Request frame consists of the legacy STA information set and capability set. Additionally, it incorporates a multi-link field for requesting multiple links. In response, the AP MLD sends a multi-link Probe Response frame which contains the multi-link and RNR fields with the information of the other links.

3. **Discovery Process of MLD**

The MLO discovery procedure includes passive snooping mode and active scanning mode.

In the case of passive snooping mode, a non-AP MLD discovers the AP MLD through the Beacon frames on one link and acquires information about all links from the RNR field.

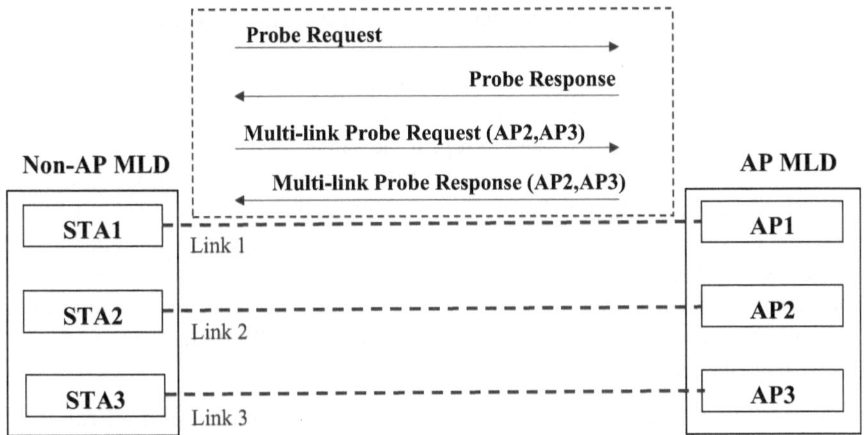

Fig. 3.47 Multi-link discovery via active scanning mode

For active scanning mode, there are two ways to implement it:

(1) The non-AP MLD sends a Probe Request frame on a specific link and receives the Probe Response frame containing the link IDs of all affiliated Aps. Subsequently, the non-AP MLD sends a multi-link Probe Request frame carrying the link IDs and receives the multi-link Probe Response frame containing the details about all affiliated Aps.
(2) The non-AP MLD sends Probe Request frames on each link and receives Probe Response frames with detailed link information from each affiliated AP.

Figure 3.47 illustrates an example of active scanning process for AP MLD.

STA1, STA2, and STA3 are the affiliated STAs of the non-AP MLD, while AP1, AP2, and AP3 are affiliated Aps of the AP MLD.

(1) STA1 sends a Probe Request frame to AP1.
(2) AP1 responds with a Probe Response frame, which carries the basic information of AP2 and AP3 in the RNR field.
(3) Upon receiving the Probe Response frame, STA1 obtains the basic information of AP2 and AP3. It then sends a multi-link Probe Request frame to AP1, specifying the link ID of AP2 and AP3 in the multi-link field.
(4) After AP1 receives the multi-link Probe Request frame from STA1, it puts the complete information of AP2 and AP3 in the multi-link field of a multi-link Probe Response frame and send it to STA1.
(5) The non-AP MLD obtains all the information about the multi-links of the AP MLD (AP1, AP2, and AP3). It can proceed to initiate authentication and association requests to establish the multi-link connection.

3.2.4.2 Authentication and Association of Multi-Link Operation

The MLDs handles authentication and association procedure on one of the links, with the management frames carrying information about all affiliated Aps and STAs. This approach eliminates the need to repeat the same steps on each link.

In Fig. 3.48, the AP MLD and non-AP MLD establish a connection through the 2.4 GHz link, and all three links are set up simultaneously for data transmission.

In the following section, we will discuss the frame format of multi-link Authentication Request and Response frames, as well as the multi-link Association Request and Response frames. Additionally, we will explore the procedure for multi-link authentication and association. Furthermore, Sect. 3.5 will introduce the multi-link 4-way handshake.

1. **Multi-link Authentication Request and Authentication Response Frame**

As shown in Fig. 3.49, the non-AP MLD sends an Authentication Request frame to the AP MLD, which carries the information about the affiliated STA of the current link and a multi-link field with the MLD MAC address of the non-AP MLD, indicating that it is a multi-link Request frame.

Upon receiving the multi-link Authentication Request frame, the AP MLD sends a multi-link Authentication Response frame to the non-AP MLD. This response frame carries a multi-link field containing the MLD MAC address of the AP MLD.

2. **Multi-link Association Request and Association Response Frame**

The non-AP MLD sends an Association Request frame to the AP MLD. This frame not only includes information about the current affiliated STA but also incorporates the multi-link field containing the MLD MAC address of the non-AP MLD. Additionally, it carries the capability set and information set of the other affiliated STAs that will be set up simultaneously.

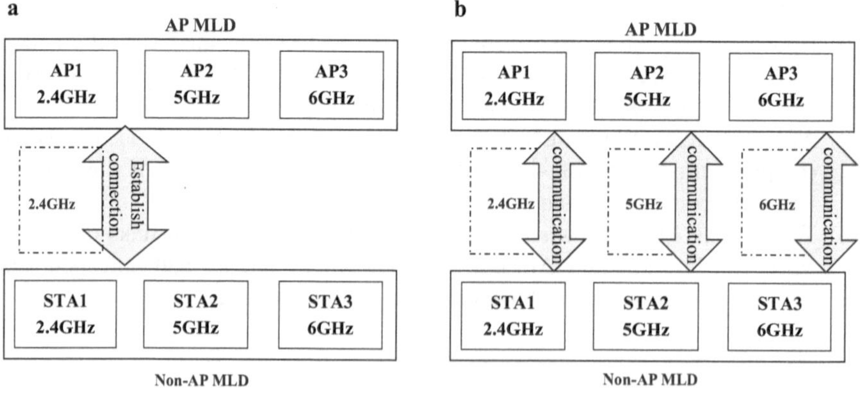

Fig. 3.48 (**a**) MLO connection established on 2.4GHz, (**b**) data transmission over three links

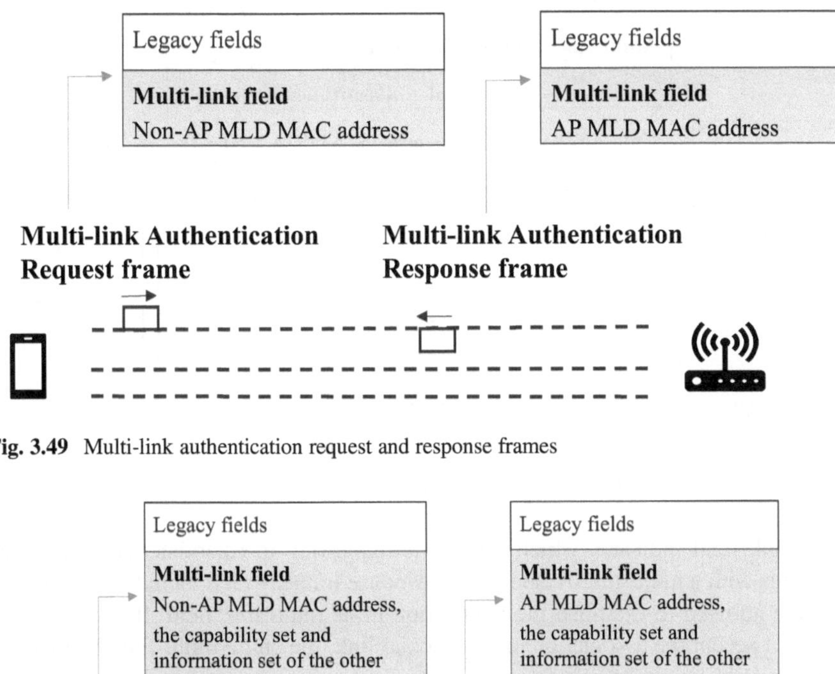

Fig. 3.49 Multi-link authentication request and response frames

Fig. 3.50 Multi-link association request and response frames

After receiving the multi-link Association Request from the non-AP MLD, the AP MLD sends a multi-link Association Response frame including the information about the current affiliated AP, as well as the multi-link field containing the MAC address of the AP MLD. Additionally, it carries the capability set, the information set, and the status of the other affiliated STAs.

The status field of the affiliated Aps is used to indicate whether the corresponding link is allowed to establish a connection. Figure 3.50 provides a visual representation of the Multi-link Association Request and Response frames.

3. **MLD Authentication and Association Procedure**

The multi-link device Authentication and Association procedure involves the exchanges of multi-link Authentication Request frame and Authentication Response frame, as well as multi-link Association Request and multi-link Association Response frame. In the Association Request frame sent by the non-AP MLD, the

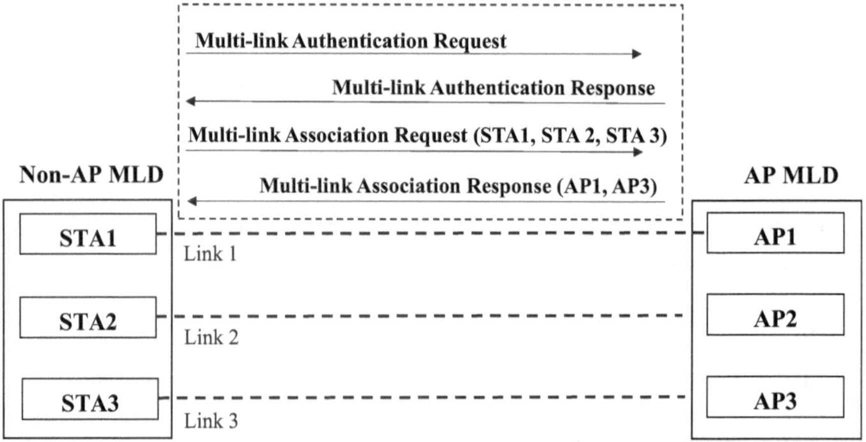

Fig. 3.51 Multi-link authentication and association

multi-link field indicates which links it is requesting to establish. The AP MLD responds with a multi-link Association Response frame, which includes the link IDs that are allowed to establish the connection in its multi-link field. If the AP MLD does not accept the association of a particular link, the entire multi-link Association Request fails.

Figure 3.51 provides an example of the multi-link Authentication Association frame exchange. In this example, there are 3 affiliated Aps of the AP MLD and 3 affiliated STAs of the non-AP MLD.

(1) The non-AP MLD initiates the multi-link authentication process by sending a multi-link Authentication Request frame to the AP MLD over link 1.
(2) AP1, upon receiving the Authentication Request, responds by sending a multi-link Authentication Response frame to the non-AP MLD over link 1.
(3) Upon receiving the Authentication Response frame, STA1 sends a multi-link Association Request to establish a connection over the three links. The multi-link field in the Association Request frame contains the MLD MAC address of the non-AP MLD and the capability set of all affiliated STAs.
(4) AP1 responds to the STA1 with a multi-link Association Response. However, based on the scheduling policy, only connections on AP1 and AP3 are allowed. Therefore, in the Association Response frame, the AP MLD marks the link state of AP1 and AP3 as successful, while rejecting the link of AP2.
(5) Finally, the non-AP MLD successfully establishes a dual-link connection with the AP MLD.

3.2.5 *Multiple Resource Unit Further Enhancing Spectrum Efficiency*

Channel bonding is one of the pivotal technologies integrated into Wi-Fi standards. Prior to Wi-Fi 6, earlier iterations of the Wi-Fi standards permit the aggregation of consecutive 20 MHz channels, and data is transmitted on the bonded channel only when all contiguous sub-channels are free.

Wi-Fi 6 introduced Preamble Puncturing to facilitate the bundling of noncontiguous channels. In case one of the subchannels within the bundled spectrum is busy, the AP or STA punctures the unavailable subchannel, and then bundles the remaining discontinuous subchannels for data transmission. This Preamble Puncturing enhances channel utilization and throughput.

However, it is important to note that Wi-Fi 6 only supports the Preamble Puncturing technology for the downlink direction. After the AP establishes a connection with the STA, it dynamically bundles the noncontiguous channels based on their respective states.

Compared with the previous standards, Wi-Fi 7 brings the following significant improvements to the channel bundling technology, enabling more efficient use of the frequency spectrum and higher data rates.

(1) **Support for Multiple Resource Unit (MRU):** Building upon Wi-Fi 6's capability to allocate OFDMA Resource Units (RUs) to individual clients devices, Wi-Fi 7 advances this functionality by allowing the aggregation of non-contiguous RUs into a unified MRU. This means that STAs can be assigned an MRU or multiple STAs can share MRUs using MU-MIMO.
(2) **Support Preamble Puncturing of MRU for uplink direction:** Wi-Fi 7 enables preamble puncturing on MRUs specifically for uplink transmission. An AP sends a Trigger frame to instruct STAs about which RUs within an MRU are punctured and allocated for their transmission use.
(3) **Support static Preamble Puncturing of MRU:** Wi-Fi 7 also supports static configuration of preamble puncturing. The AP broadcasts the channel bonding information and details about punctured MRUs through Beacon frames. This information is available when a STA connects to the AP, so it can start using these punctured MRUs or channels from the beginning of the connection.

3.2.5.1 Comparison of Preamble Puncturing and MRU

Figure 3.52 depicts examples that illustrate the disparities between Wi-Fi 6 Preamble Puncturing and Wi-Fi 7 MRU.

Operating specifically at the level of an individual 20 MHz channel, Preamble Puncturing in Wi-Fi 6 involves puncturing one such channel, whereas the other three non-contiguous 20 MHz channels are aggregated and dedicated to a single STA.

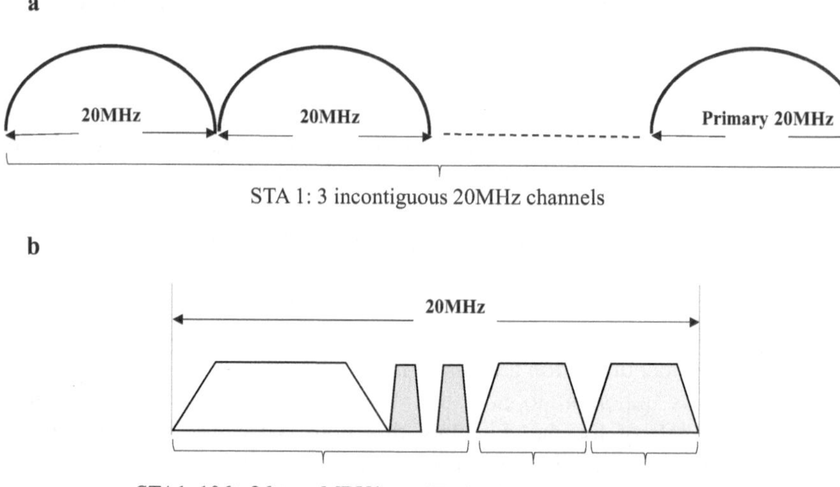

Fig. 3.52 (**a**) Wi-Fi 6 preamble puncturing, (**b**) Wi-Fi 7 multiple resource unit

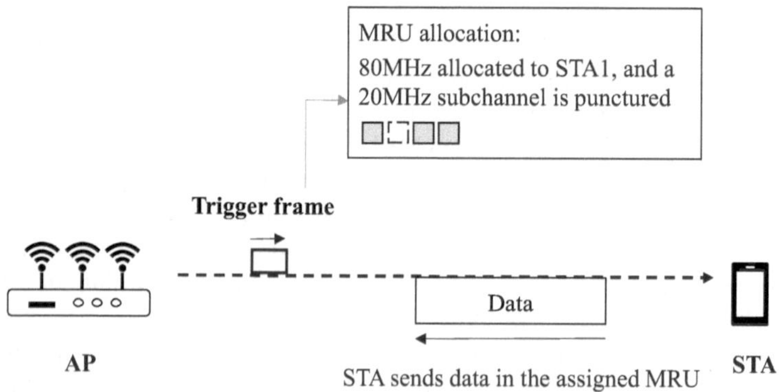

Fig. 3.53 Preamble puncturing of uplink direction

On the other hand, with Wi-Fi 7, it becomes possible to split a single 20 MHz channel to multiple Resource Units (RUs) and assign them to multiple STAs. As shown in the example, a 106-tone RU and a 26-tone RU are grouped as MRU1, which is subsequently allocated to serve STA1. Evidently, MRU technology offers greater flexibility and higher channel utilization compared to the Preamble Puncturing in Wi-Fi 6.

In this Wi-Fi 7 scenario depicted in Fig. 3.53, the AP employs Preamble Puncturing during uplink transmissions to maximize the efficient usage of channel bandwidth. Specifically, the AP allocates an 80 MHz channel for a given STA's transmission. However, one of the four constituent 20 MHz subchannels has its

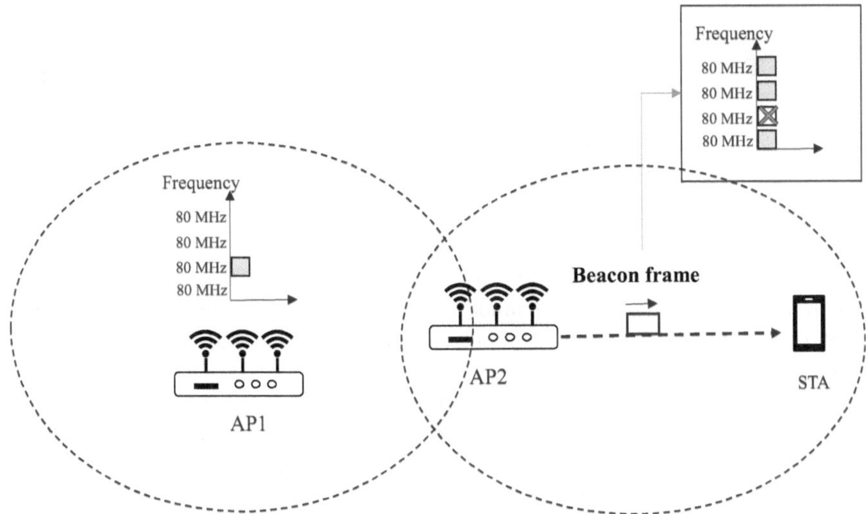

Fig. 3.54 Wi-Fi 7 static preamble puncturing

Disabled Subchannel Bitmap marked, indicating that this particular subchannel is punctured and hence not accessible for the transmission purposes.

The STA, upon receiving the Trigger frame from the AP with these allocation details, understands which specific RUs within the non-punctured 60 MHz are assigned to it. The STA then transmits its uplink data using only those allocated RUs.

Figure 3.54 illustrates another use case where Wi-Fi 7's Preamble Puncturing technique, in conjunction with channel bonding, is employed to facilitate effective coexistence between two adjacent Aps.

AP1 operates on a single, non-overlapping 80 MHz channel. Meanwhile, AP2 takes advantage of a cutting-edge channel bonding strategy exclusive to Wi-Fi 7. In this configuration, AP2 combines three non-contiguous 80 MHz channels into a broader 240 MHz channel for enhanced transmission capabilities.

AP2 broadcasts the information regarding the bundled, non-continuous channels via Beacon frames. As a result, all STAs within BSS2—operating under the coverage of AP2—comply with the designated channel configuration.

Thus, both AP1 and AP2 are able to transmit data simultaneously without causing collisions or degrading each other's performance. This approach profoundly enhances the spectral efficiency and overall capacity of the wireless environment.

As mentioned in the beginning of this section, Static Preamble Puncturing in Wi-Fi 7 typically refers to pre-configured puncturing that is broadcasted by the AP through Beacon frames and remains unchanged until reconfigured. This indicates that Wi-Fi 7 is equipped with mechanisms allowing the AP to adjust its channel usage based on the current state of the subchannels. If a specific subchannel becomes busy or occupied by another BSS, the AP has the option to exclude (or "puncture") this subchannel from the MRU allocation.

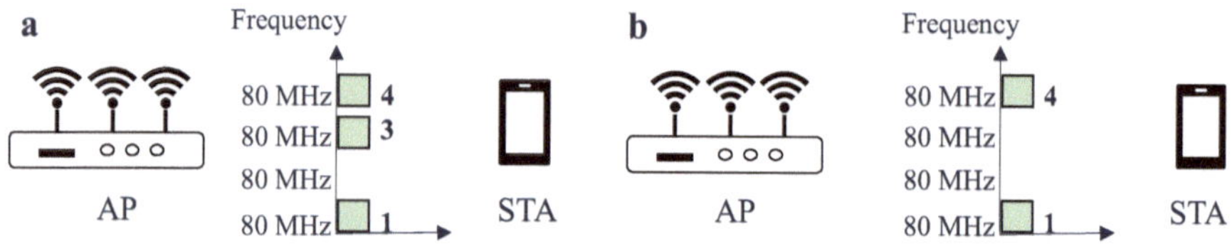

Fig. 3.55 (**a**) static preamble puncturing, (**b**) static + run-time preamble puncturing

In Fig. 3.55a, an AP and STAs are operating with a 320 MHz bandwidth, in which the second 80 MHz subchannel has been statically punctured due to interference or other considerations, leaving an effective bandwidth of 240 MHz for communication.

If a situation arises where the third 80 MHz subchannel gets occupied or experiences significant interference from another BSS, the AP can dynamically change the MRU configuration. This modification would involve excluding the third 80 MHz subchannel from the grouping. In Fig. 3.55b, this revised MRU now comprises the first and fourth 80 MHz subchannels, effectively creating a new bundled channel of 160 MHz. This adjustment enables the AP and STA to maintain their communication without interference from the occupied subchannel.

3.2.5.2 Multiple Resource Unit Allocation

A Wi-Fi 7 AP can assign one or multiple noncontiguous RUs to a single STA. Each RU is uniquely identified by two main parameters:

- **RU Index:** This index indicates the specific location of the RU within the entire available spectrum, which could span up to a channel bandwidth of 320 MHz.
- **RU Type:** The type defines the size of the RU in terms of the number of subcarriers it encompasses. For instance, an RU might consist of a certain number of tones (subcarriers), such as 26-tone, 52-tone, etc., reflecting the OFDMA capability of the standard.

In Wi-Fi 6, the allocation was typically limited to one RU per STA. However, in Wi-Fi 7, AP allocates either a RU or an MRU to each STA.

The RU types of Wi-Fi 6 and Wi-Fi 7 are Table 3.5. For Wi-Fi 7, given its capability to support channels as wide as 320 MHz, one new RU type (4 × 996-tone) has been introduced to better exploit this increased bandwidth.

The Wi-Fi 7 standard dictates that RUs with 242-tone or more tones are designated as large size RUs, while RUs with fewer than 242-tone are categorized as small size RUs. According to the Wi-Fi 7 standard, small size RUs can only be combined with small size RUs to form small size MRUs. Large size RUs, on the other hand, can only be combined with large size RUs to form large size MRUs.

Table 3.5 The RU types of Wi-Fi 6 and Wi-Fi 7

RU type	Number of RUs of Wi-Fi 6 (160 MHz)	Number of RUs of Wi-Fi 7 (320 MHz)
26-tone RU	74	148
52-tone RU	32	64
106-tone RU	16	32
242-tone RU	8	16
484-tone RU	4	8
996-tone RU	2	4
2x996 tone RU	1	2
4x996 tone RU	N/A	1

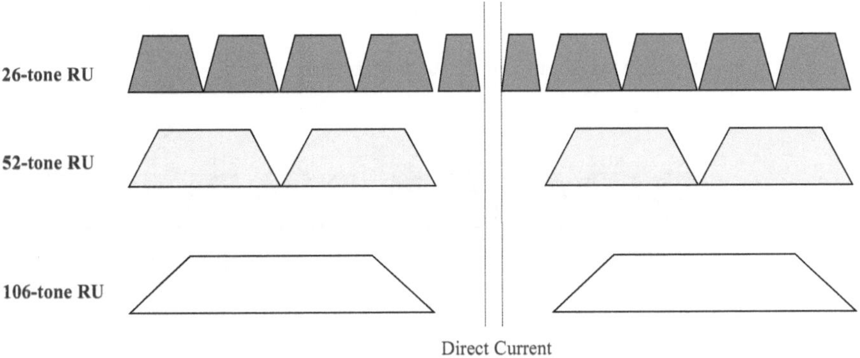

Fig. 3.56 RU location within a 20 MHz channel

1. **Small Size MRUs**

RUs within 20 MHz can be 26-tone, 52-tone, or 106-tone. A small size MRU must be a combination of adjacent small size RUs. Therefore, for a 20 MHz channel, there can be a 52 + 26 tone MRU or a 106 + 26 tone MRU, but not a 106 + 52 tone MRU. This is because there are Direct Current (DC) subcarriers in the central of the channel that separates the 52-tone from the 106-tone RU.

Figure 3.56 illustrates the location of RUs within a 20 MHz channel. The MRU is identified based on the location of the RUs that it comprises. In the example depicted in Fig. 3.57, there are two 106 + 26-tone MRUs within a 20 MHz channel: the 102 + 26-tone MRU 1 comprises 106-tone RU 1 and 26-tone RU 5, while the 102 + 26-tone MRU 2 comprises 106-tone RU 2 and 26-tone RU 5.

Wi-Fi 7 allows for the allocation of MRU and RU in a mix mode, with the caveat that none of them should overlap. In the example Fig. 3.58, the AP allocates a 106 + 26-tone MRU 1 to STA1, a 52-tone RU 3 to STA2, and a 52-tone RU 4 to STA3. The AP transmits data simultaneously to the STAs within the 20 MHz channel.

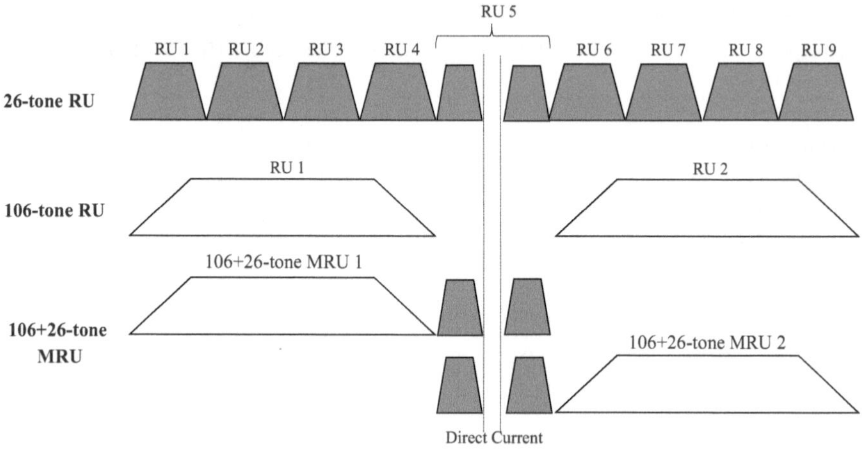

Fig. 3.57 106 + 26 tone MRU location within a 20 MHz channel

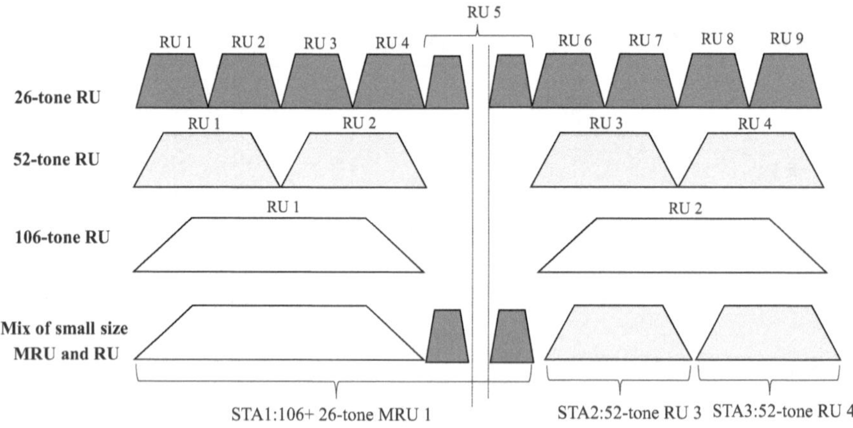

Fig. 3.58 Mix of MRU and RU allocation within a 20 MHz channel

2. Large Size MRUs

Large size MRU is composed of multiple large size RUs, which have a bandwidth of 20 MHz or more, such as the RUs of 242-tone, 484-tone, 996-tone, and 2 × 996 tone. The large size MRU is also identified by the RU type and RU location. Figure 3.59 shows different combinations of 996 + 484-MRUs at 160 MHz, which are:

- 996 + 484-tone MRU 1: consists of 996-tone RU 2 and 484-tone RU 2.
- 996 + 484-tone MRU 2: consists of 996-tone RU 2 and 484-tone RU 1.
- 996 + 484-tone MRU 3: consists of 996-tone RU 1 and 484-tone RU 3.
- 996 + 484-tone MRU 4: consists of 996-tone RU 1 and 484-tone RU 4.

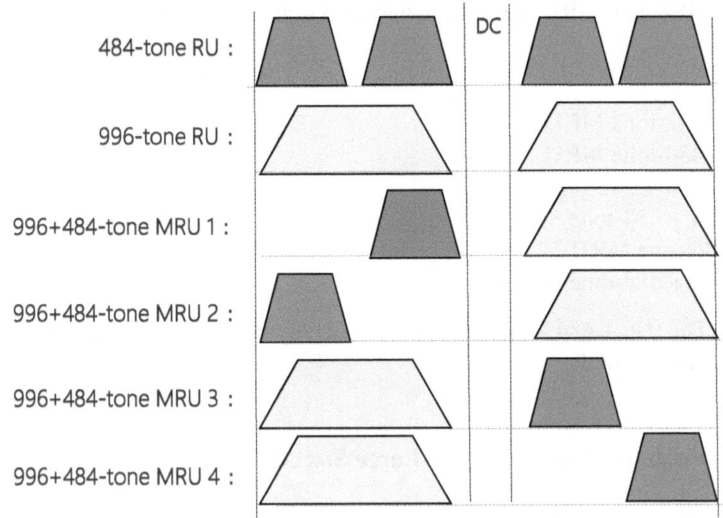

Fig. 3.59 996 + 484-tone MRU location in a 160 MHz channel

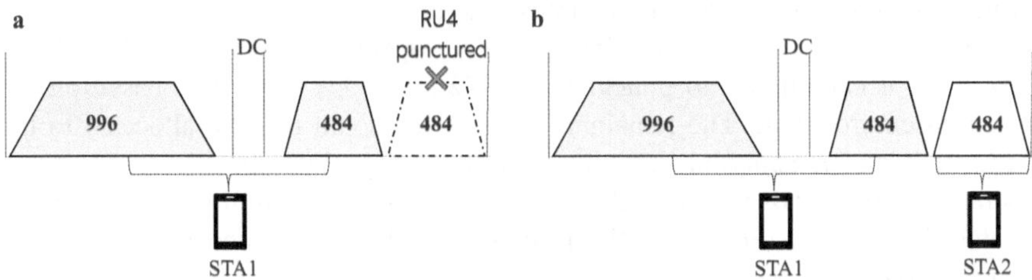

Fig. 3.60 (**a**) MRU allocation of non-OFDMA mode, (**b**) MRU allocation of OFDMA mode

A large size MRU can be assigned to a STA, or to multiple STAs in the MU-MIMO scenario.

As discussed in Sect. 2.2.2.1, if the entire spectrum resource is allocated as an RU to a single STA, it is referred to as non-OFDMA mode. If the spectrum is divided into multiple RUs and allocated to different STAs, it is known as OFDMA mode.

In terms of MRU technology, if only one MRU is available across the entire spectrum, with other RUs being unavailable, this mode is referred to as the non-OFDMA mode of MRU allocation. On the other hand, if the spectrum allows for a mix of MRU and RU allocation to multiple STAs, this mode is called OFDMA mode MRU allocation.

In the Fig. 3.60, the example of MRU allocation in non-OFDMA and OFDMA modes are provided for illustrative purpose. In the non-OFDMA mode in Fig. 3.60a, the 996 + 484-tone MRU 3 is allocated to STA1, and the 484-tone-RU4 is punctured and cannot be allocated. Conversely, in the OFDMA mode depicted in Fig. 3.60b, the 996 + 484-tone MRU 3 is allocated to STA1, and the 484-tone RU 4 is allocated to STA2.

In the Wi-Fi 7 standard, the following types of large size MRUs are defined:

- 484 + 242-tone MRU
- 996 + 484-tone MRU
- 996 + 484 + 242-tone MRU
- 2 × 996 + 484-tone MRU
- 3 × 996-tone MRU
- 3 × 996 + 484-tone MRU

Note: The 996 + 484 + 242 tone MRU can only be utilized for data transmission in non-OFDMA mode.

3.2.5.3 Preamble Puncturing for Large Size MRU

As mentioned earlier, the Preamble Puncturing technology is utilized to bundle discontinuous RU resources to enhance channel utilization and throughput. This technology operates in unit of 20 MHz, and the punctured channel cannot be assigned to a STA nor used for data transmission.

When it comes to large size MRUs, if an AP operates at 80 MHz, 160 MHz, or 320 MHz, it can choose to puncture any 242-tone RUs (20 MHz) based on the spectrum environment. The remaining multiple RUs can then be allocated to the STAs for data transmission. As the example in Fig. 3.61 illustrates, the AP is operating at 160 MHz, but the 242-tone RU 2 is punctured, resulting in no preamble on this channel. The remaining RUs form a 996 + 484 + 242 tone MRU 1 for data transmission.

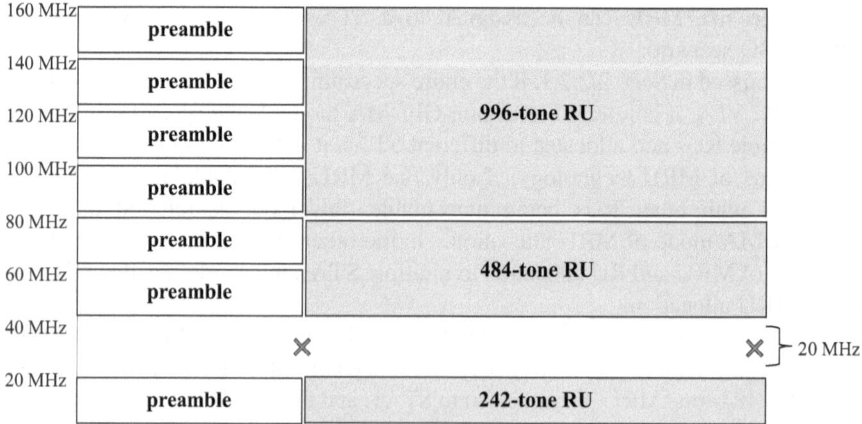

Fig. 3.61 Example of preamble puncturing over 160 MHz

Table 3.6 Rule of preamble punctured channels

Channel bandwidth	Punctured subchannel bandwidth	Location of the punctured subchannels
80 MHz	20 MHz	Any of the 20 MHz subchannels
	40 MHz	Not supported
160 MHz	20 MHz	Any of the 20 MHz subchannels
	40 MHz	Any of the 40 MHz subchannels
	80 MHz	Not supported
320 MHz	20 MHz	Not supported
	40 MHz	Any of the 40 MHz subchannels
	80 MHz	Any of the 80 MHz subchannels
	40 MHz+ 80 MHz	40 MHz: Any of the 40 MHz subchannels 80 MHz: Only the first or the last 80 MHz subchannel can be punctured
	160 MHz	Not supported

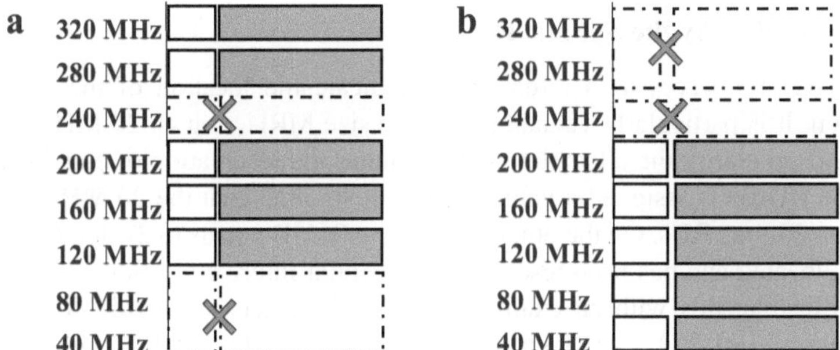

Fig. 3.62 (**a**) Puncture incontiguous 40 MHz + 80 MHz, (**b**) puncture continuous 40 MHz + 80 MHz

In theory, Preamble Puncturing technology can accommodate the puncturing of multiple discontinuous subchannels. However, to simplify the actual design process and ensure compatibility, Wi-Fi 7 defines a specific set of rules of the permissible sizes and locations of subchannels for Preamble Puncturing, as shown Table 3.6. These rules ensure that the system can effectively manage and allocate resources while maintaining a reasonable level of complexity.

In addition to the rule presented in Table 3.6, Wi-Fi 7 requires that channel bonding must commence with the initial subchannel. For example, when working with an 80 MHz bandwidth, the first two 20 MHz subchannels are grouped together to form a 40 MHz channel, while the last two 20 MHz are bundled into another 40 MHz channel. The two 20 MHz subchannels in the middle cannot be combined into a 40 MHz channel.

Figure 3.62 shows examples of an MRU on a 320 MHz bandwidth with 40 MHz + 80 MHz punctured. As illustrated in the figure, only the first or the last

80 MHz subchannel can be punctured, and the 40 MHz can be at located anywhere within the spectrum.

3.2.5.4 RU Reservation

When an AP allocates MRU or RU resources to STAs, there may exist reserved RUs that are not currently allocated to any STA. For instance, if an AP operating at 160 MHz bandwidth allocates RUs of 996-tone, 484-tone, and 242-tone to STA1, STA2, and STA3 respectively, it may also reserve a 242-tone RU for potential dynamic allocation in the future.

Although no data transmission on the reserved RU, the physical layer preamble is still transmitted so that other devices can detect the Wi-Fi signal and recognize that the channel is unavailable for their use.

Due to the flexibility of RU and MRU allocation in Wi-Fi 7, there are two ways to reserve the RU.

1. **Reserve RUs by the Specific RU ID**

The RU ID serves as a reference to indicate the location of the RU on the spectrum. It is particularly valuable for large size MRU, that is, 20 MHz or above, as it helps to clarify the allocation and facilitates the reservation of certain RUs.

If the RU ID is assigned a value of zero, it signifies that the 20 MHz is divided into nine 26-tone RUs. On the other hand, if the RU ID equals to 27, it means the RU is not allocated and has been reserved for potential future allocation.

To illustrate this with an example, Fig. 3.63 depicts a scenario where an AP operating at 160 MHz bandwidth allocates RUs to STA1, STA2, and STA3 for downstream transmission. Specifically, a 996-tone RU is allocated to STA1, a 484-tone RU is allocated to STA2, a 242-tone RU allocated to STA3, and a 242-tone RU is reserved which RU ID of 27. The preamble of the reserved 242-tone RU signals its occupation.

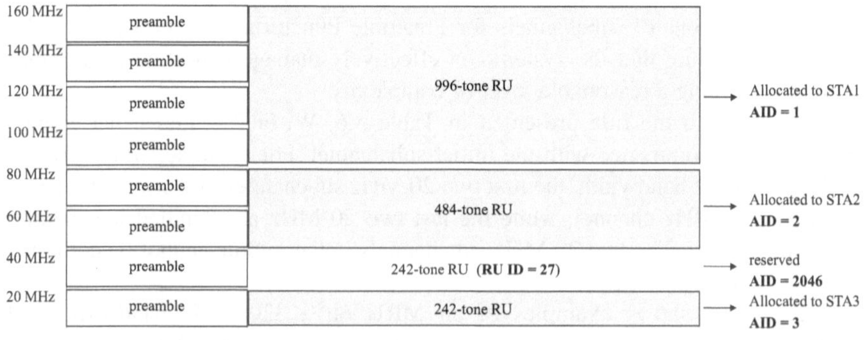

Fig. 3.63 RU reserved on 160 MHz bandwidth

2. **Reserve RUs by the AID**

The RU ID cannot be used to reserve small size RUs less than 20 MHz, so Wi-Fi 7 leverages the AID as an alternative mechanism. If a small size RU is allocated to a specific AID of 2046, it signifies that the RU is reserved and not assigned to any STA. This approach allows for more flexibility in managing the allocation of resources for different sizes of RUs, providing better support for various STA requirements and traffic patterns.

3.2.6 MU-MIMO Technology Update in Wi-Fi 7

Compared to Wi-Fi 6, Wi-Fi 7 has introduced enhancements to MU-MIMO, including changes to the channel sounding and uplink spatial stream transmission mode. These enhancements support Preamble Puncturing for uplink transmission and also facilitate the use of MRUs.

3.2.6.1 Channel Sounding

Wi-Fi 6 allows bundling of noncontiguous channels for downlink transmission, but not for uplink. In contrast, Wi-Fi 7 enables APs and STAs to utilize bundled noncontiguous channels for both uplink and downlink transmission. Furthermore, the channel sounding process in Wi-Fi 7 differs slightly from that in Wi-Fi 6.

1. **Channel Sounding Excludes the Punctured Subchannel**

The Channel Sounding procedure in non-triggered mode, as shown in Fig. 3.64, compares the approaches taken by Wi-Fi 7 and Wi-Fi. In Wi-Fi 6, the NDPA control frame is duplicated on each 20 MHz subchannel, while the NDP data frame and Compressed Beamforming frame are transmitted across the entire spectrum. However, in Wi-Fi 7, the NDPA frame is only duplicated on the available subchannels, while NDP frames and Compressed Beamforming frames are transmitted on the

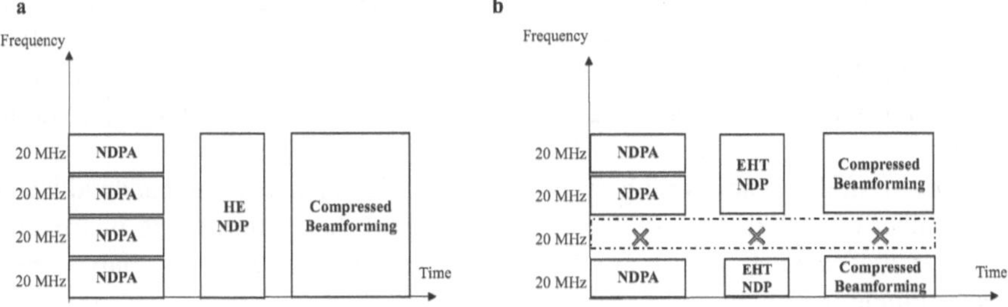

Fig. 3.64 (**a**) Wi-Fi 6 channel sounding over the entire channel, (**b**) Wi-Fi 7 channel sounding over the non-contiguous channel

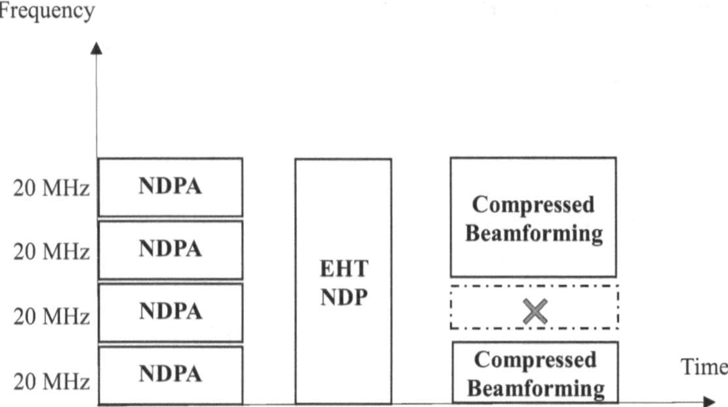

Fig. 3.65 Feedback partial of the beamforming matrix

bundled noncontiguous subchannels. Notably, the channel sounding procedure only occurs over the noncontiguous channels.

2. **Partial Feedback to Reduce the Size of Beamforming Matrix**

The maximum allowable size for a Compressed Beamforming frame is 11,454 bytes. If the frame size exceeds this limit, the Beamforming matrix will be divided and transmitted across two or more frames.

The determination of the Beamforming matrix is influenced by three factors: bandwidth, the number of spatial streams, and the compression level. The compression algorithm is not the focus of this book. Our discussion will be limited to the first two factors only.

The size of the uncompressed Beamforming matrix can be calculated as Eq. 3.1:

$$\textbf{The size of the uncompressedBeamforming matrix} = Nc \times 8 + Ns \times (2 \times Nb \times Nc \times Nr) \tag{3.1}$$

where *Nc* represents the number of spatial streams, *Ns* represents the number of subcarriers, *Nr* represents the number of transmitting antennas, and *Nb* represents the number of bits determined by the Coefficients Size field of the MIMO Control field.

Let's assume a Wi-Fi network operating with 8 spatial streams and a 320 MHz bandwidth. There are 1024 subcarriers. The amount of uncompressed Beamforming matrix information = 8 × 8 + 1024× (2 × 8 × 8 × 8) = 1,048,640bits, or 131,080 bytes.

The size of the Beamforming matrix increases with an increase of bandwidth and the number of spatial streams. To reduce the size of the Beamforming matrix and improve the channel utilization, Wi-Fi 7 allows STAs to feedback only partial beamforming matrix.

In the example of Fig. 3.65, the NDPA frames and the EHT NDP data frames sent by AP are transmitted over the entire 80 MHz bandwidth, while the Compressed

Beamforming matrix is transmitted using a MRU of at 484 + 242 tone. According to Eq. 3.1, the size of Beamforming matrix, when transmitted over the MRU, is reduced by a quarter in comparison to its size when transmitted over the full-band channel.

3.2.6.2 Spatial Streams for Uplink Transmission

In the uplink direction, a Wi-Fi 7 STA can transmit upstream data simultaneously through multiple spatial streams over an MRU or RU. By contrast, a Wi-Fi 6 STA supports upstream MIMO transmission only over a single RU.

Figure 3.66 demonstrates the operation of MU-MIMO for both RU and MRU in the context of Wi-Fi 7 uplink transmission. In this example, the AP operates on a 160 MHz bandwidth and supports two spatial streams. STA1 and STA2 are allocated the 996 + 484 + 242-tone MRU for MU-MIMO transmission, enabling them to transmit data over two spatial streams within this larger MRU. This allocation allows STA1 and STA2 to utilize the spatial diversity offered by MU-MIMO, improving overall network throughput and efficiency.

On the other hand, STA3 is allocated a 242-tone RU. Within this RU, STA3 transmits data frames on both spatial streams, utilizing the full bandwidth of the RU to maximize its uplink transmission capacity. This allocation ensures that STA3 can achieve its maximum potential in terms of data transmission, even though it is not participating in MU-MIMO transmission.

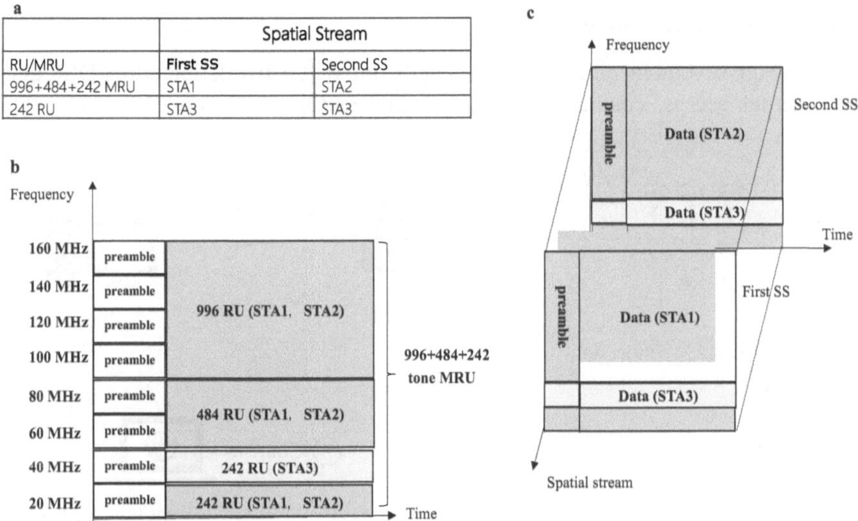

a

	Spatial Stream	
RU/MRU	First SS	Second SS
996+484+242 MRU	STA1	STA2
242 RU	STA3	STA3

Fig. 3.66 (a) RU/MRU allocation, (b) frequency domain, (c) spatial domain

3.2.7 *Low Latency Technology in Wi-Fi 7*

Latency refers to the time interval between when a user issues an instruction and when he receives a response from the server. For instance, it is the delay experienced from when a user clicks on a URL of a website until the server fully loads the corresponding web page for him. If the entire process takes an extended period, the user perceives network lag.

As shown in Fig. 3.67, the following factors contribute to latency: propagation distance, network type, the content of the webpage, and the method by which the device accesses the network:

(1) **Propagation Delay**

Propagation delay is one of the key contributors to latency. Information travels at the speed of light through a medium, such as optical fiber. If the server is located far away from the user, the bi-directional exchange of information takes longer. For instance, when a user in Shanghai accesses an Internet website hosted on a server in Chicago USA. The physical distance between the two places is 11,385 kilometers. The minimum propagation delay T would be approximately calculated as $T = \frac{11385*2}{3\times10^6}$ = 75 milliseconds(ms). Moreover, numerous switches and gateways along the transmission paths introduce additional processing delay, thereby making the overall delay significantly higher than the theoretical value of 75 ms. Conversely, if the server and the user within same local network, the propagation delay becomes negligible.

To mitigate the delay caused by physical distance, large companies often deploy servers in multiple locations, allowing end-users to access nearby servers more efficiently.

(2) **Network Infrastructure**

There are several methods for accessing the Internet network, including DSL dial-up Internet access, coaxial cable, fiber-optic, and satellite communication. The

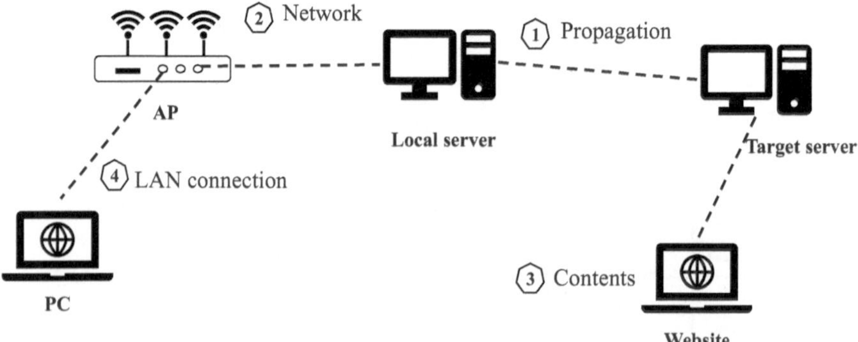

Fig. 3.67 Factors contributing to network delay

inherent delay of different network media varies. When traveling the same distance, data transmission through optical fiber communication can take 10–15 milliseconds, whereas satellite communication can incur a delay of about 600 milliseconds.

(3) **Contents**

The content loaded by the target website influences how long the destination server takes to process and transmits information. For example, when a site contains a substantial number of large files, such as image, audio, or video content, the server requires more time to deliver these contents to users. Furthermore, if the target website needs to retrieve information from third-party servers—like when loading third-party advertising content—it will take extra time to collect that information and then forward it to the user.

In order to reduce delay caused by website content loading, the client often utilizes local caching method for frequently visited websites.

(4) **LAN**

In a typical home or office environment, user devices are usually connected to the network through Ethernet or Wi-Fi. When accessing Internet via a Wi-Fi network, latency includes the channel access delay based on the CSMA/CA mode and queuing delay when AP dispatches traffic between multiple stations within the Wireless Local Area Network (WLAN).

This chapter focuses on the principle underlying latency generated when clients connect to networks via Wi-Fi, and how Wi-Fi 7 technology enhances latency improvements for latency-sensitive services.

3.2.7.1 Latency Caused by Wi-Fi Communication

The transmission delay in Wi-Fi communication is a result of both the channel access delay based on CSMA/CA and the delay incurred by the AP when scheduling multiple STAs.

1. **Channel Access Delay**

As previously introduced in Chap. 1, Wi-Fi devices utilize the CSMA/CA mechanism for channel access, which essentially means "listen before send." If the channel is free, a Wi-Fi device can immediately seize the channel to transmit data. However, if the channel is occupied, the Wi-Fi device must wait until the other device's transmission concludes and the channel becomes idle. Following this, it competes with other STAs for channel access until its transmission is successful initiated. The process introduces a notable delay, particularly in crowded environments where contention for the channel is high.

Figure 3.68 illustrates a network topology that can be utilized to measure the channel access delay in various environments. In this setup, a laptop with an IP address 192.168.18.3 is connected to an AP through a Wi-Fi connection operating on the 2.4 GHz frequency band. Concurrently, a desktop computer with an IP

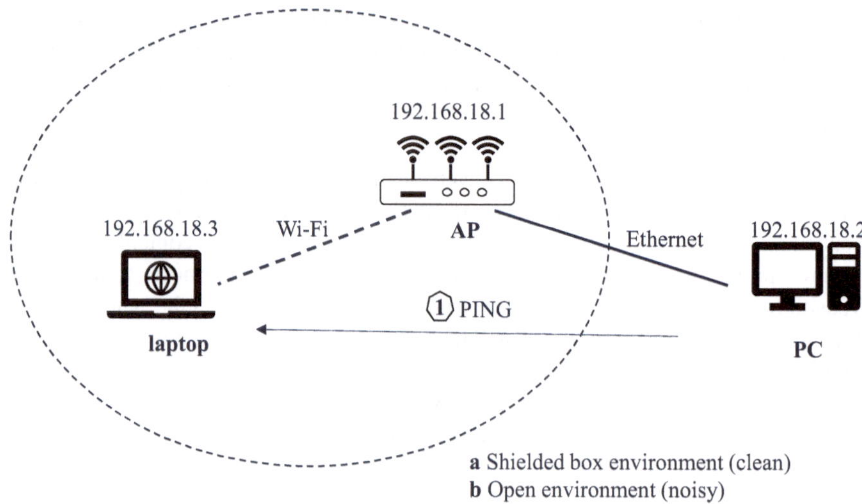

Fig. 3.68 Network topology for latency measurement

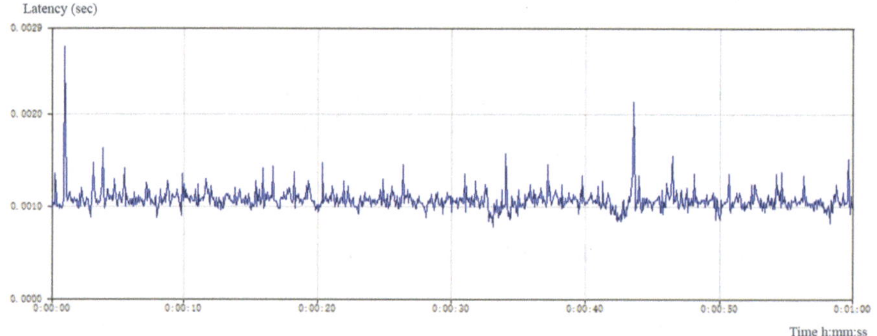

Fig. 3.69 Latency at a shielded box environment

address of 192.168.18.2 connects to the AP via Ethernet connection. The desktop sends PING requests to the laptop and subsequently receives the response. The latency is measured by analyzing the response time of these Ping command.

Figures 3.69 and 3.70 display the test results comparing a clean environment with a noisy one. When the laptop and AP work operate within a shielded box environment, devoid of competition from other Wi-Fi devices, the average delay is less than 1 millisecond and exhibits minimal variance. Conversely, when functioning in a noisy environment, the latency fluctuates over a much broader range, with the average delay increasing to as high as 12 milliseconds.

2. **The Delay of Scheduling**

When multiple devices attempt to access the channel simultaneously, the AP schedules the STAs for data transmission, and those STAs that are not scheduled

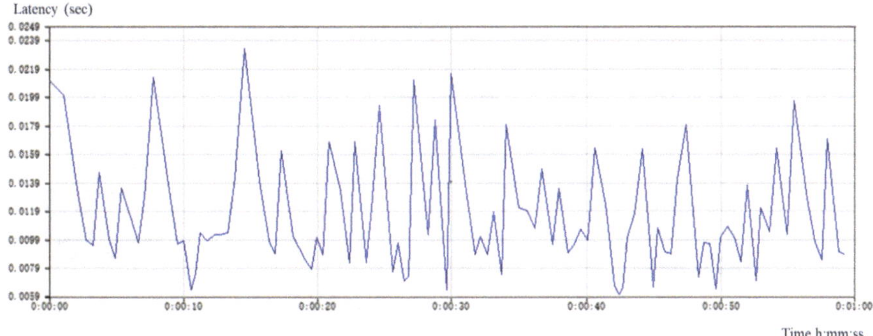

Fig. 3.70 Latency at a noisy Wi-Fi environment

must wait for the AP to assign a Transmission Opportunity (TXOP) for them. Such scheduling process introduces delays.

The Wi-Fi technology optimizes the scheduling of multi-STA scenario by employing OFDMA and MU-MIMO technologies, which help in reducing the delay of scheduling.

In situations where a device is running multiple services concurrently, latency tends to increase. Figure 3.71 depicts the delay in a multiple service scenario. In this case, while continuously sending Ping commands, the desktop also sends UDP traffic at a rate of 90Mbps to the laptop. From the test result, it is observed the average delay of the UDP data stream is 10 milliseconds, while the average delay of Ping commands is 6 milliseconds. Comparing these results with Fig. 3.69, the latency of PING increases from 1 ms to 6 ms, indicating that it is affected by the flow of other service due to the scheduling process.

3.2.7.2 The Improvements on Latency by Wi-Fi 6

The Wi-Fi 6 standard aims to enhance the Wi-Fi performance in dense environment, addressing the interference issues stemming from multiple STAs connected to the same AP or adjacent BSS. In summary, the latency can be improved through the following strategies:

- The Trigger frame scheme reduces the competition delay for channel access.
- The OFDMA scheme improves concurrency and minimizes the delay associated with waiting for channel access.
- The Spatial Reuse scheme mitigates interference from neighboring BSS.

Figure 3.72 [4] presents test result illustrating the service latency improvement achieved by OFDMA technology in a home environment. With all traffics streams active in the table, we assume the BSS is experiencing interference from four adjacent BSSs, each running a 50 Mbps data flow. According to the test result, when OFDMA is enabled, there is a significant improvement in latency for both downlink and uplink directions.

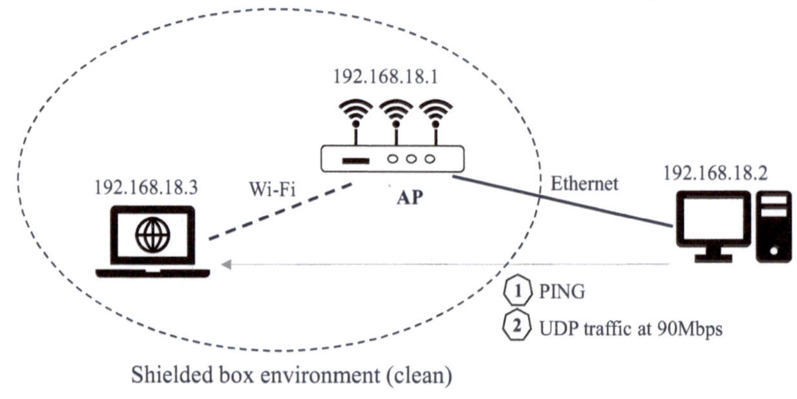

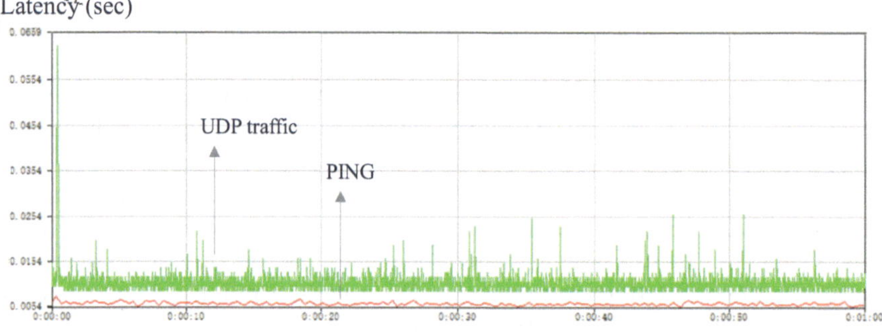

Fig. 3.71 Latency of UDP traffic and PING at shielded box environment

Traffic	Data rate (Mbps)
4 High-resolution video calls	4×3
4 interactive gaming	4×1.5 (downlink)
5 video surveillance cameras	5×3
3 Internet browsing services	3×2 (not mentioned in test results; assumed 2 Mbps each)
2 FTP upload	2×6 (uplink)
1 email (SMTP/POP3)	1 (not mentioned in test results; assumed 1 Mbps)
4 interference from adjacent BSSs	4×50

Fig. 3.72 Example of latency improvement by OFDMA

3.2.7.3 The Improvements in Latency Achieved by Wi-Fi 7

With the proliferation of Virtual Reality, online gaming services, streaming video platforms, home office setups, and cloud computing applications, latency has emerged as a critical factor that can ultimately undermine user experience. As an example, in the context of online gaming, latency must typically be less than 5 milliseconds to ensure a satisfactory user experience.

The IEEE Wi-Fi 7 task force, from its inception, has set low latency as one of its primary objectives. Latency improvements are pursued through several key approaches:

(1) **Higher Bandwidth**

Not surprisingly, the higher bandwidth allows for more data to be transmitted in a TXOP and results in fewer data frames in the queue. As shown in Fig. 3.73, there are fewer data frames queued for transmission in an 80 MHz channel compared to a 20 MHz channel.

Wi-Fi 7 supports up to 320 MHz channel bandwidth, which doubles the data transmission capacity on top of the 160 MHz channel bandwidth offered by Wi-Fi 6. This reduction in channel congestion leads to a decrease in both the average waiting time and scheduling delay, thereby contributing to reduced transmission latency between the AP and the STAs.

(2) **More Concurrent Users**

As Fig. 3.74 illustrates, OFDMA and MU-MIMO technologies enable concurrent transmissions, which effectively reduces scheduling latency. Wi-Fi 7 builds upon these enhancements from Wi-Fi 6 and further increases the capacity for supporting multiple concurrent users.

In the frequency domain, Wi-Fi 7 supports up to 148 26-tone RUs when operating at a 320 MHz bandwidth, compared to 74 RUs with Wi-Fi 6 using a 160 MHz bandwidth. Each RU can be allocated to an individual STA, meaning Wi-Fi 7 can theoretically accommodate up to 148 concurrent users, thus significantly reducing scheduling delay in scenarios involving a large number of STAs.

MU-MIMO is a spatial division multiple access technique that allows independent data transmission over multiple spatial streams. Both Wi-Fi 6 and Wi-Fi 7 support up to eight spatial streams, enabling the capability to serve up to eight concurrent users simultaneously.

(3) **New Wi-Fi 7 Technologies**

Wi-Fi 7 introduces several new technologies aimed at enhancing latency performance. The multi-link operation technology has been detailed in Sect. 3.2.3. In the subsequent sections, we will delve into two other technologies: QoS Characteristics and r-TWT technology.

Fig. 3.73 Latency improved by higher bandwidth

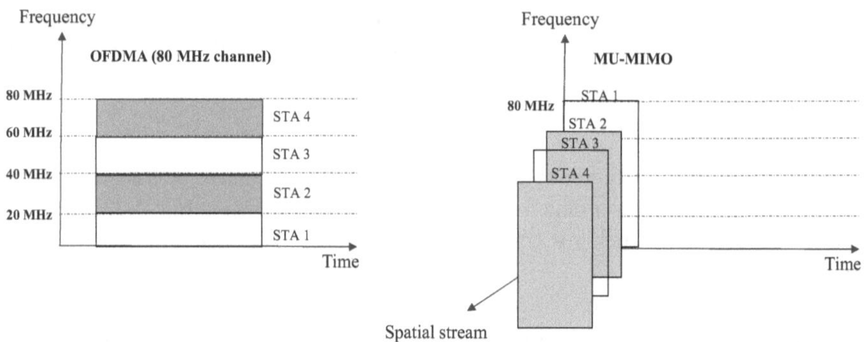

Fig. 3.74 Latency improved by more current users

3.2.7.4 QoS Characteristics

According to the Enhanced Distributed Channel Access (EDCA) introduced in Chap. 1, data services are classified into four traffic types: background (BK), best effort (BE), video (VI), and voice (VO). The AP schedules them according to their priority. For instance, when both data and voice streams reach the MAC layer of the AP simultaneously, it prioritizes voice traffic over data traffic to meet the stringent latency requirements for voice service.

Each service type has its specific latency specifications. For example, AR/VR demands a latency under 10 milliseconds, while online gaming requires less than 50 milliseconds. However, the EDCA traffic type-based scheduling method based may not suffice to meet the latency requirements of many emerging applications.

In 2012, the IEEE 802.11aa standard introduced the **Stream Classification Service**. Building upon this, Wi-Fi 7 introduces **QoS Characteristics** that empower APs to discern the unique attributes of each service flow, such as start and end time, maximum delay, transmission rate, and maximum packet error rate. This allows AP to schedule services more efficiently, thereby ensuring Quality of Service for latency-sensitive applications. It is worth noting that this technology doesn't universally improve latency across the entire Wi-Fi network but rather optimizes specific services with stringent latency requirements.

In this section, we will introduce both Stream Classification Service technology and the QoS Characteristics technology, along with their respective use cases.

1. **Stream Classification Service**

To meet the latency requirements for audio and video streams, IEEE defines the Stream Classification Service (SCS) technology within 802.11aa standard. As depicted in Fig. 3.75, prior to the data transmission, the STA informs AP about the stream's characteristics, including the source MAC address, destination MAC address, the IP five-tuple < source IP address, source port, destination IP address, destination port, and the transport layer protocol>. Upon receipt of data packets, the

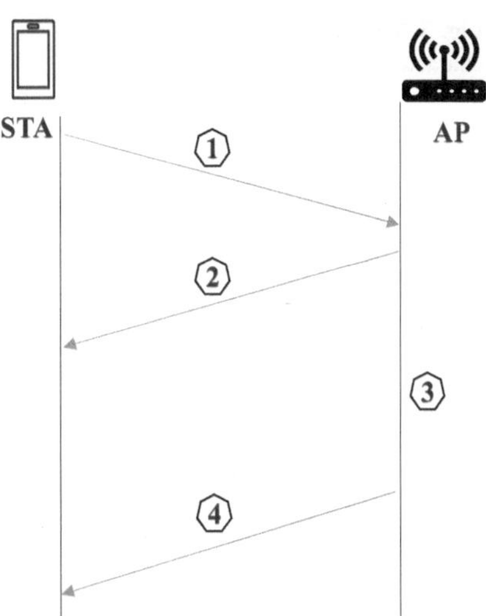

Fig. 3.75 Stream classification service

AP compares their characteristics against the pre-registered information. If a match is found, the corresponding data stream is placed into the high-priority queue and scheduled accordingly to guarantee priority handling.

(1) The STA sends an Action frame to request Stream Classification Service, which encapsulates both the IP layer information and the MAC layer address details pertaining to the service flows.
(2) Upon accepting the Stream Classification Service request, the AP stores the stream information locally and responds by transmitting a confirmation Action frame.
(3) When the AP receives the packets from the network side, it compares their MAC layer headers and IP headers with the local records. If the packet's information matches the registered stream classification information, the corresponding data frames are assigned to a high-priority queue for scheduling. Conversely, if there is no match, the data frames are scheduled based on the default traffic type.
(4) Subsequently, the AP schedules the data frames according to the priority of their respective queues and forwards the data streams to the STA accordingly.

2. **QoS Characteristics**

Based on the Stream Classification Service technology in 802.11aa, Wi-Fi 7 defines the QoS Characteristics technology specifically for latency-sensitive services. As illustrated in Fig. 3.76, the STA sends the QoS Characteristics related to the latency-sensitive service, along with the stream information and the MAC layer address, among other details, to the AP. Subsequently, the AP processes the information as follows:

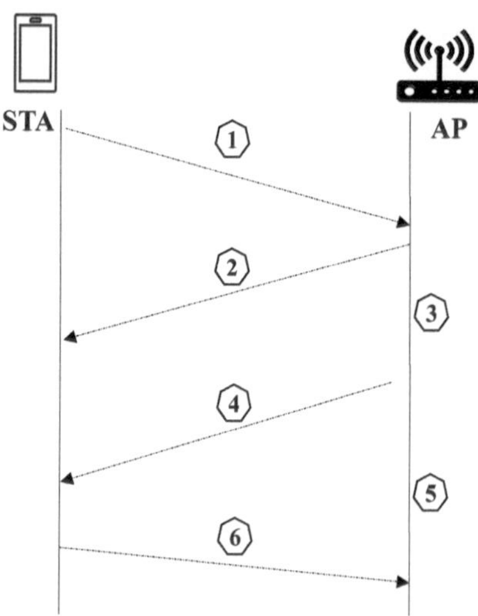

Fig. 3.76 QoS characteristic

- **In the downlink direction**, the AP receives data packets on the network side, compares their IP headers against the QoS characteristic of the latency-sensitive data stream, and then schedules them accordingly.
- **In the uplink direction,** the AP schedules data transmission based on the QoS characteristic request from STAs to effectively meet the latency requirements of upstream data effectively.

The QoS Characteristic process mirrors the functionality of the Stream Classification Service, yet it extends its scope to cater to both the uplink and downlink directions, ensuring optimized quality of service in both directions of data transmission.

(1) STA sends an Action frame to the AP, requesting the QoS Characteristic service. This frame contains the QoS Characteristic such as minimum service interval, maximum service interval, minimum data rate, delay bound, maximum MSDU size, and other relevant parameters. The format of the QoS Characteristic element is depicted in Fig. 3.77, where the parameters listed in the second row are optional.

(2) The AP responses with an Action frame, accepting the QoS Characteristic service of STA, and records QoS Characteristic locally.
(3) Upon receiving the downlink data stream, the AP compares both the MAC layer and IP layer header against the locally stored QoS characteristics. If a match is found, the AP schedules the stream according to the parameters to meet the requirements for latency, channel access, and packet error rates.
(4) The AP schedules the latency-sensitive traffic and sends the downlink data frames to the STA accordingly.

Octets:	1	1	1	4	4	4	3	3
	Element ID	Length	Element ID Extension	Control Info	Min Service Interval	Max Service Interval	Min Data Rate	Delay Bound

Octets:	0 or 2	0 or 4	0 or 1	0 or 3	0 or 4	0 or 2	0 or 1	0 or 1	0 or 2
	Max MSDU Size	Service Start Time	Service Start Time LinkID	Mean Data Rate	Burst Size	MSDU Lifetime	MSDU Delivery Ratio	MSDU Count Exponent	Medium Time

Fig. 3.77 QoS characteristic element format

(5) Based on the service interval and the MSPD size specified in the QoS characteristics, the AP periodically sends Trigger frames to schedule the uplink data transmission from the STA.
(6) The STA gains channel access via the Trigger frames and then sends its upstream data to the AP.

3.2.7.5 Restricted TWT

As introduced in Chap. 2, the Broadcast TWT(b-TWT) technology operates as follows: The AP subdivides a Beacon frame interval into multiple Service Periods (SP), assigns these SP to distinct b-TWT groups, and broadcasts the corresponding b-TWT group ID within Beacon frames. The STA joins a b-TWT group through either a negotiation or semi-negotiation procedure and thereafter wakes up during its designated service periods. During these periods, the STA fetches its buffered data from AP or transmits data within the allocated RU. By employing this method, the STA avoids the need to wake up periodically for snooping the Beacon frames or competing for channel access, thereby effectively optimizing the power consumption.

In a manner akin to b-TWT, the Wi-Fi 7 r-TWT scheduling AP splits the Beacon frame interval into dedicated service periods and assigns these periods to various r-TWT groups. Traffic that demands stringent QoS for latency is arranged to be transmitted periodically based on those requirements. The r-TWT enhancement provides protection to ensure that all STAs refrain from occupying the medium during r-TWT service periods.

Figure 3.78 illustrates the difference between b-TWT and r-TWT.

(1) **Traffic Types**

The b-TWT does not differentiate between the traffic type of the STAs. Instead, the STAs negotiate with the b-TWT scheduling AP to join a b-TWT group and thereby secures a transmission schedule suitable for their data transmission of the traffic types.

In contrast, the r-TWT offers support at the level of individual traffic types, particularly designed to accommodate and prioritize latency-sensitive traffic streams. During the negotiation procedure, the STA informs the r-TWT scheduling AP about the stream information pertaining to its latency-sensitive traffic. This allows the AP to reserve the resource and schedule the traffic accordingly.

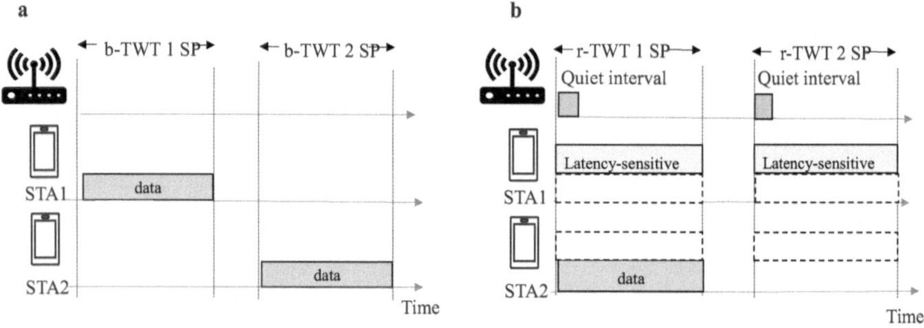

Fig. 3.78 (**a**) b-TWT, (**b**) r-TWT

(2) **Frequency of SPs**

Unlike b-TWT, where STAs wake up periodically during the service period allocated to their respective b-TWT groups without considering traffic types, r-TWT allows the scheduling AP to prioritize the latency-sensitive services. It does this by scheduling the services across multiple SPs, thereby increasing the frequency of channel access for priority services.

(3) **Enhanced Medium Access Protection**

Since the AP acquires channel resource through a CSMA/CA channel snooping process, the actual service start time for b-TWT may be later than anticipated.

Wi-Fi 7 has introduced Quiet Element to address this issue. The AP incorporates a Quiet Element within its Beacon frames, informing STAs not to compete for the channel during the specified quiet interval. Furthermore, STAs are required to complete their data transmission before the quiet interval commences. To minimize the impact on channel utilization, the quiet interval is defined to be 1 millisecond in duration.

During these quiet intervals, since no STA competes for channel, Aps can effectively schedule latency-sensitive traffics to meet the strict service start time requirements.

Figure 3.79 illustrates an example of a r-TWT service period. In this instance, Wi-Fi 6 STA1 terminates the TXOP before the quiet interval begins, and subsequently, Wi-Fi 7 STA2 transmits its latency-sensitive data within the scheduled SP. The quiet interval is positioned at the beginning of the r-TWT service period, thereby preventing non-r-TWT group STAs from interfering with or contending for the channel during scheduled transmissions.

3.2.7.6 A Use Case of QoS Characteristics and r-TWT

In the example depicted in Fig. 3.80, STA1 operates an AR/VR real-time service, while STA2 is an IoT device that periodically enters a dormant state and wakes up to exchange information with an Internet server.

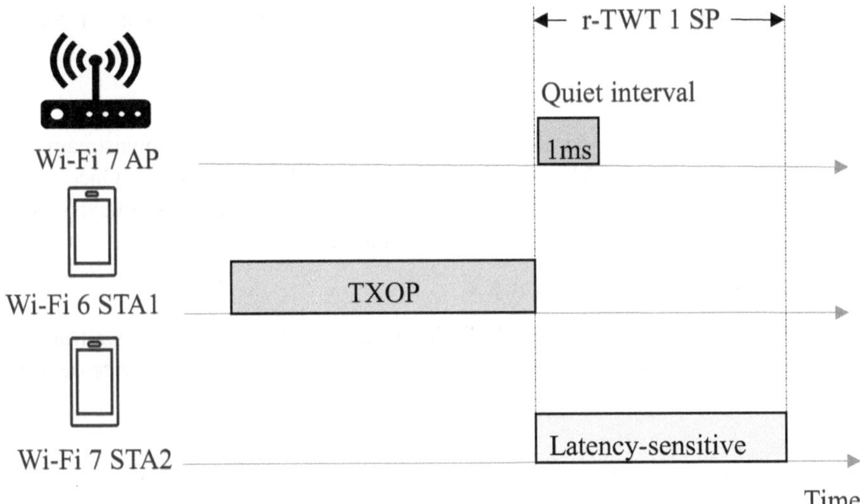

Fig. 3.79 r-TWT service period

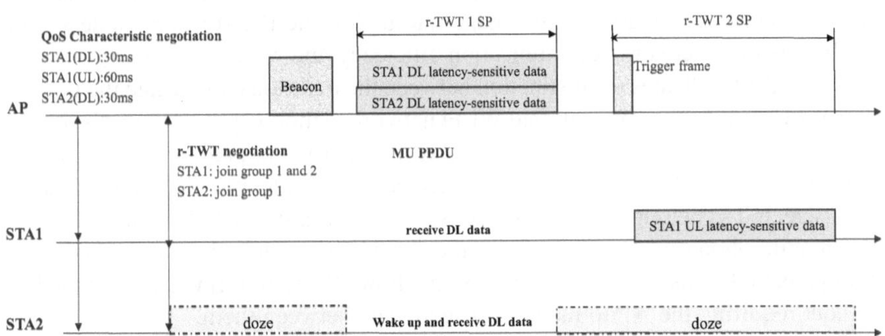

Fig. 3.80 Example of QoS Characteristics and r-TWT

(1) **Negotiation of QoS Characteristics**

In this scenario, STA1 and STA2, both connected to the AP, engage in negotiations with it to determine the QoS characteristics for their latency-sensitive data streams. The agreed-upon service start times are 30 milliseconds for the downstream traffic and 60 milliseconds for the upstream traffic of STA1, while the downstream traffic for STA2 has a service start time of 30 milliseconds. The AP acknowledges these requirements and records these specific characteristics locally.

(2) **Establishing r-TWT Membership**

The service period of r-TWT group 1 and r-TWT group 2 is set at 30 milliseconds. STA1 negotiates with the AP to join both r-TWT group 1 and r-TWT group 2, while STA2 negotiates to only join r-TWT group 1. Upon successful negotiation, STA2 enters a dormant mode to save power and wakes up before the start of r-TWT 1 service period.

(3) **Scheduling for r-TWT Group 1**

During the service period of r-TWT group 1, the AP schedules downstream data transmission for both STA1 and STA2 using MU-MIMO technology. Once STA2 receives its buffered data, it enters the dormant state and awaits the next service period. Meanwhile, STA1 remains active to run real-time services.

(4) **Scheduling for r-TWT Group 2**

At the designated time for r-TWT Group 2, the AP sends a Trigger frame to schedule STA1 for upstream data transmission during this group's service period.

3.2.8 Enhanced Peer-to-Peer Communication

The Wi-Fi Peer-to-Peer (P2P) communication refers to a scenario where two STAs establish a direct connection and transmit data to one another, independent of any AP involvement. In comparison with traditional modes, the Peer-to-Peer mode significantly enhances network communication efficiency and reduces delay.

Figure 3.81 indicates the distinction between the traditional mode and the Peer-to-Peer Wi-Fi mode. In a conventional Wi-Fi network, a mobile phone sends the data to the AP along path 1, which then forwards it to a TV via path 2, and vice versa. Conversely, in a Wi-Fi Peer-to-Peer network, both the mobile phone and the touchscreen TV belong to the same BSS and create a direct link with each other. The mobile phone mirrors its screen onto the TV and sends the data directly to it through path 3. This Peer-to-Peer capability allows STAs to form direct connections without requiring the AP to mediate or relay data between them.

The Wi-Fi Peer-to-Peer (P2P) technologies encompass two distinct modes: the Tunneled Direct Link Setup (TDLS) technology, as defined by IEEE 802.11 standard, and P2P technology, which is specified by Wi-Fi Alliance. In the Wi-Fi

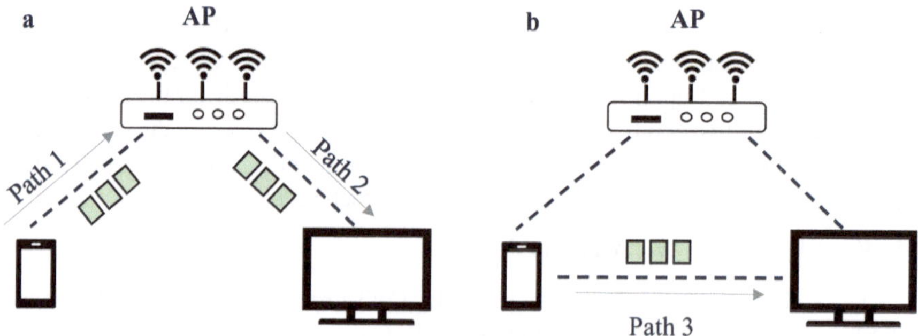

Fig. 3.81 (**a**) Traditional data flow, (**b**) peer-to-peer data flow

7 standards, the Peer-to-Peer mode has been further extended to support multi-link operation.

In Chap. 2, we delved into channel access technology based on Trigger mode, where an AP grants TXOP (Transmission Opportunity) to STAs via a Trigger frame for uplink data transmission, thus eliminating the overhead of STAs competing for channel access. Wi-Fi 7 extends this Trigger mode to incorporate TXOP sharing, enhancing the channel access method specifically for Peer-to-Peer communication.

In this section, we will explore the Peer-to-Peer technology four dimensions: the background and characteristics of Peer-to-Peer technology, the establishment of TDLS connection between the MLDs, the establishment of P2P connection among the MLDs, and the application of TXOP sharing technology.

3.2.8.1 Background of the Wi-Fi Peer-to-Peer Communication

The Peer-to-Peer communication employs two distinct modes: Tunneled Direct Link setup (TDLS) and Wi-Fi Alliance's P2P. In the TDLS mode setup, both STAs must initially establish a connection with the same AP, with the management frames for the TDLS discovery and TDLS setup procedure being relayed through the AP. On the other hand, in the WFA P2P mode, the two STAs have the flexibility to associate with different APs, and they directly exchange the management frames between themselves. The distinction is graphically represented in Fig. 3.82.

1. **The P2P TDLS Mode**

In 2010, IEEE ratifies the 802.11z, which defines the TDLS mode to improve channel utilization and throughput for transmission between the STAs within the same BSS.

Before establishing a TDLS connection, messages between two STAs can only be forwarded by the AP. The STA encapsulates TDLS Discovery and TDLS Setup request in data frames and sends them to the AP. The AP then forwards the data frames to the destination STA based on the address information in the header. However, the AP does not parse the TDLS information and is not involved in the TDLS connection establishment process.

Figure 3.83 illustrates an example of a mobile phone and a touchscreen TV establishing a TDLS connection.

(1) The user initiates screen casting from the mobile phone, and the device searches for available screens to display. The phone sends a TDLS Discovery request to the smart TV based on its local ARP information. The request is encapsulated within a data frame which the destination MAC address (DA) set as the smart TV's address.
(2) The AP relays the TDLS Discovery request data frame to the smart TV, where the receiver MAC address (RA) corresponds to the smart TV' s address, and the source MAC address (SA) is that of the mobile phone.

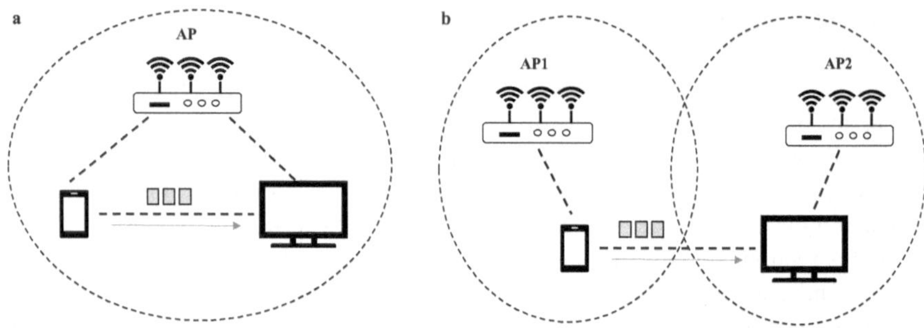

Fig. 3.82 (a) TDLS P2P mode, (b) WFA P2P mode

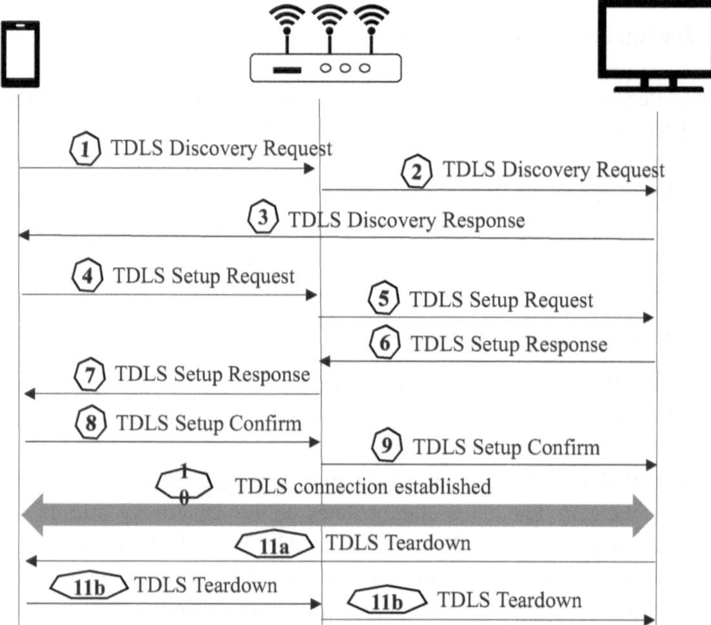

Fig. 3.83 Procedure of establishing and tearing down a TDLS connection

(3) The smart TV responds directly to the mobile phone with a TDLS Discovery response, bypassing the AP. At this stage, the smart TV appears in the list of available screens on the phone. The user is notified that the search process has completed and can choose to cast the screen onto the TV.

(4) Through (9) Subsequent TDLS Setup requests, responses and confirmation frames are processed as data frames and forwarded by the AP. The mobile phone and the smart TV negotiate an encryption key for secure data communication.

(10) After exchanging the necessary management frames, both devices establish the TDLS connection and begin transmitting data directly over this connection.

(11a)/(11b) Once the mobile phone and the smart TV finish data transmission, either party may terminate the TDLS connection by sending a TDLS Teardown frame. If they remain within the same BSS and can communicate directly, the Teardown request is sent to the other party directly, as illustrated in step 11a of Fig. 3.83. However, if they cannot communicate directly, the Teardown frame must be relayed through the AP, following the procedure outlined in steps 11b.

2. **The Wi-Fi P2P Defined by WFA**

The TDLS technology is confined to supporting only two STAs under the same Access Point, which does not accommodate scenarios involving p2p communication among more than two STAs or those where STAs are associated with different Aps.

In 2010, Wi-Fi Alliance introduced P2P technology as an extension of these capabilities. The Wi-Fi P2P technology, as defined by Wi-Fi Alliance, has been widely embraced by smart terminals, exemplified by the Wi-Fi Direct of Android systems and the AirDrop functionality in iOS systems.

P2P technology goes beyond one-on-one connection, also supporting group configurations in a one-to-many relationship. Within a P2P network, there are two distinct roles:

- **Group Owner (GO):** This role performs similarly to an AP within an infrastructure BSS, responsible for establishing a P2P group that can connect multiple devices.
- **Group Client (GC):** Acting akin to a STA within an infrastructure BSS, a Group Client connects to a Group Owner.

In the P2P network, each STA creates a new logical STA for itself, which is utilized to establish P2P connections with other STAs. These newly created logical STAs share the channel resource with their original STAs through time-division multiplexing.

Figure 3.84 illustrates a P2P group composed of three STAs that belong to separate BSSs. Each STA consists of two logical STAs. In this scenario, the mobile phone establishes a P2P connection with both smart TV 1 and smart TV 2, functioning as the GO, while the TVs functioning as the GCs. The mobile phone can simultaneously screen cast content to the two TVs.

The P2P connection and disconnection procedure are illustrated as Fig. 3.85.

(1)–(2) P2P Discovery: Both the mobile phone and the smart TV are P2P devices, with either of them capable of initiating Probe Request data frame to discover other P2P devices. As depicted in Fig. 3.85, the mobile phone sends a Probe Request and subsequently receives a Probe Response from the smart TV, thus enabling both devices to discover each other; as a result, the smart TV is displayed as a “detected devices” on the mobile phone.

(3)–(5) GO Negotiation: Upon the user’s selection to screen cast from the phone to the smart TV, the mobile phone initiates a GO negotiation request. Through the

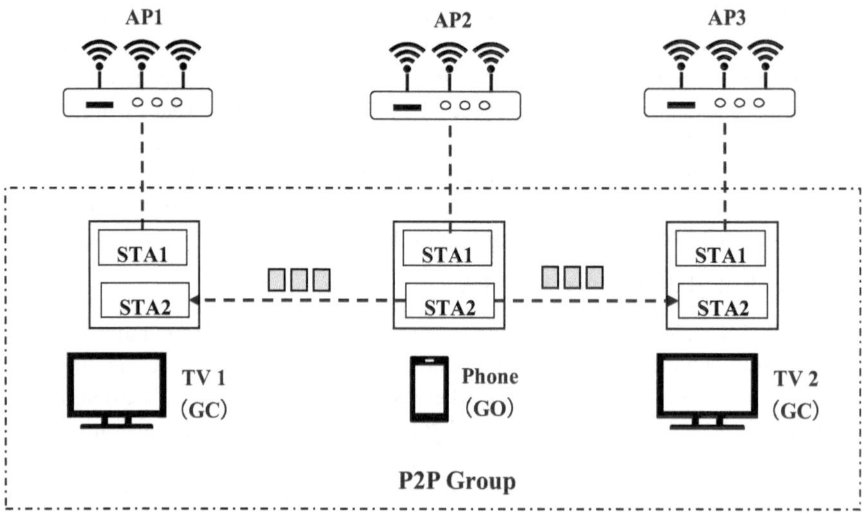

Fig. 3.84 P2P Communication between multiple STAs

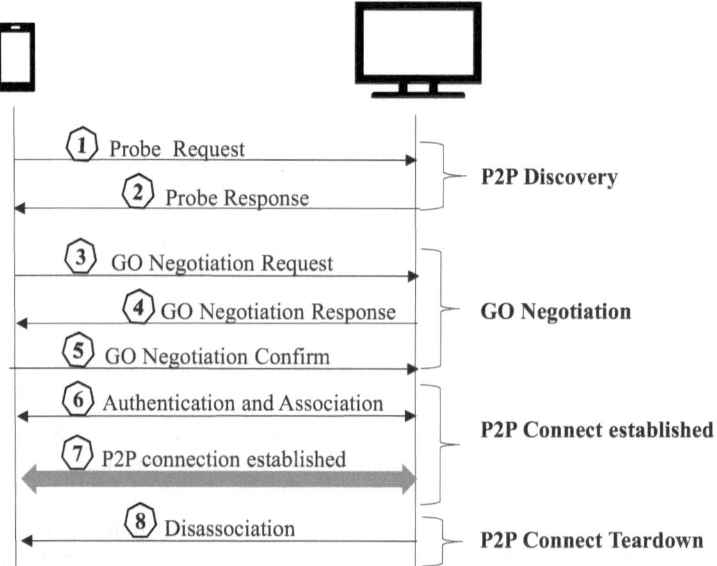

Fig. 3.85 Procedure of establishing and tearing down a P2P connection

GO negotiation process, the P2P devices determine their respective roles and exchange capability sets. In this example, the mobile phone assumes the role of GO, while the smart TV becomes the GC of the P2P connection.

(6)–(7) P2P Connection Establishment: Following a successful negotiation, the GC sends both GO Authentication and Association Requests to establish the P2P connection. Once the P2P connection is established, the GO periodically broadcasts Beacon frames on the channel, akin to an AP in an infrastructure BSS. The GC receives these Beacon frames and synchronizes its time with the GO, much like a STA would.

(8) P2P Connection Teardown: After the completion of P2P communication, either party can initiate the disconnection by sending a Disassociation Request to the other party.

3.2.8.2 TDLS for Non-AP MLD in Wi-Fi 7

The Wi-Fi 7 Multi-link Operation technology brings additional options to the P2P communication. A P2P non-AP MLD can engage in communication with another P2P non-AP MLD over any of the available links, or communicate with a legacy STA.

(1) **Data Path of the TDLS Connection Between Two Non-AP MLDs**

Figure 3.86 illustrates a network topology consisting of two non-AP MLDs and an AP MLD. Each non-AP MLD establishes two links with the AP MLD, thereby creating four potential paths for the TDLS connection between non-AP MLD-a and non-AP MLD-b.

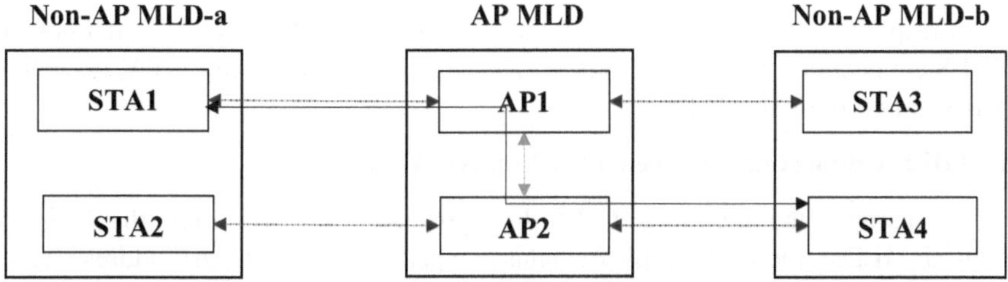

Four possible paths for the TDLS connection

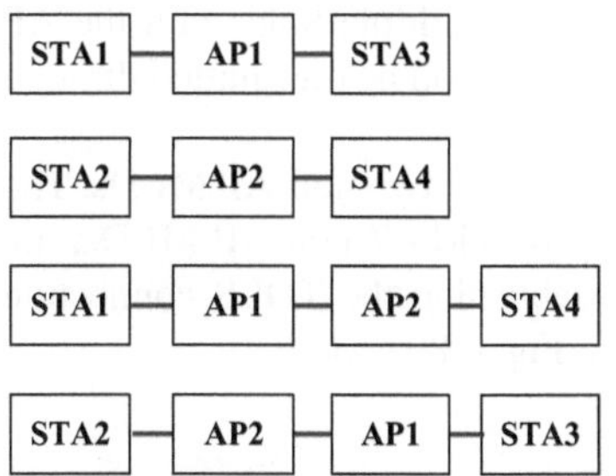

Fig. 3.86 TDLS connection between two non-AP MLDs

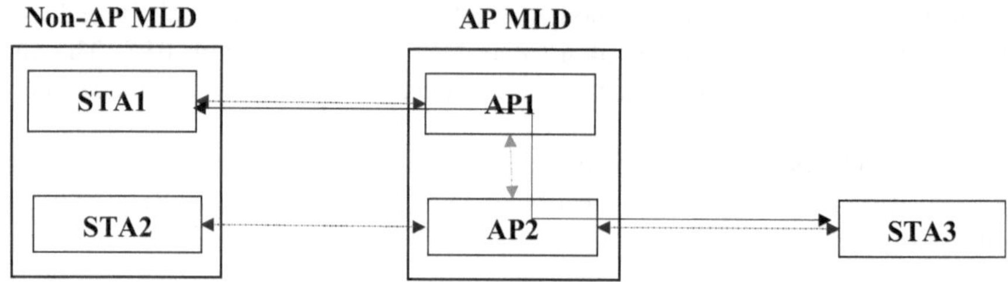

Two possible paths for the TDLS connection

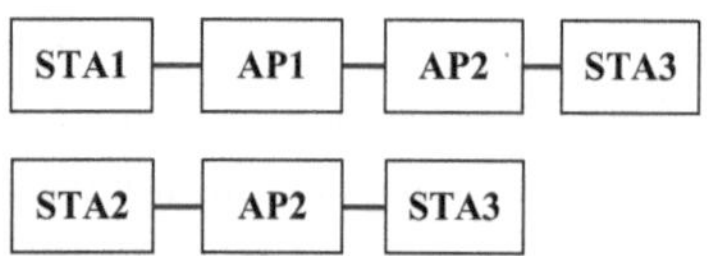

Fig. 3.87 TDLS connection between a non-AP MLD and a legacy STA

(2) Data Path of TDLS Connection Between a Non-AP MLD and a Legacy STA

Figure 3.87 presents an illustration featuring a non-AP MLD, an AP-MLD, and a legacy STA. The non-AP MLD establishes a dual-link connection with the AP MLD, while the legacy STA sets up a single-link connection with the affiliated AP2. Consequently, there exist two possible paths for the TDLS connection between the non-AP MLD and the legacy STA.

In response to changes in the data path for non-AP MLDs, Wi-Fi 7 defines the TDLS connection between non-AP MLDs and a legacy single-link STA, as well as between two non-AP MLDs.

1. TDLS Connection Between Two Non-AP MLDs

Compared to the traditional TDLS discovery and setup procedure, the TDLS of non-AP MLDs supports multiple transmission paths. The MLD MAC address serves as the unique identifier for the non-AP MLD, with the source and destination address being the MLD MAC addresses of the transmitter and receiver non-AP MLDs, respectively.

Furthermore, since both non-AP MLDs established multiple links with the AP MLD, the messages of establishing the TDLS connection can be transmitted through any of these links.

Figure 3.88 illustrates the TDLS connection topology of two non-AP MLDs. The mobile phone and the notebook, both functioning as Wi-Fi 7 non-AP MLDs, are connected to the AP MLD. The procedure for establishing the TDLS connection between the phone and the notebook is depicted in Fig. 3.89a and b.

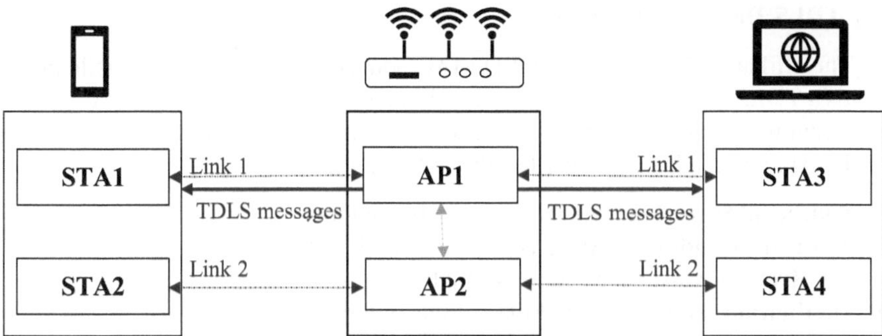

Fig. 3.88 Network topology of the TDLS connection between two non-AP MLD

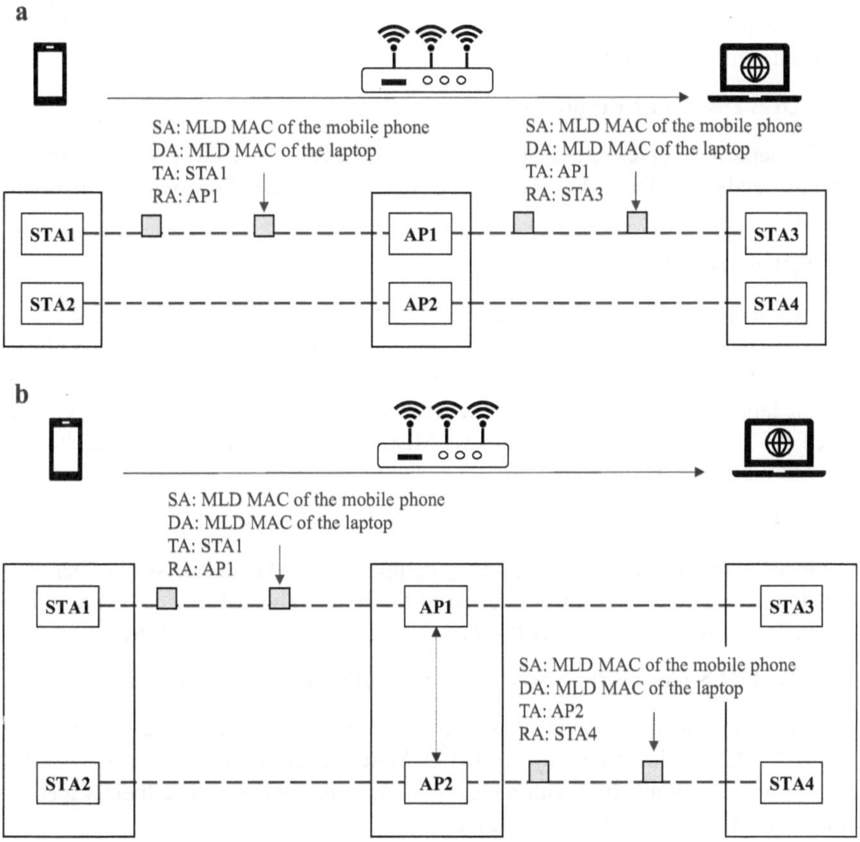

Fig. 3.89 (**a**) TDLS message through the affiliated AP1, (**b**) TDLS message through the affiliated AP1 and AP2

(1) **TDLS Discovery Request**

The affiliated STA1 with its MLD MAC address representing the mobile phone sends a TDLS Discovery request to the affiliated STA3 with its MLD MAC address representing the laptop. The message is encapsulated within a data frame addressed to the AP, and the MAC header has the following layout:

- **Source address:** MLD MAC of the mobile phone
- **Transmitter address:** MAC address of STA1
- **Receiver address:** MAC address of AP1
- **Destination address:** MLD MAC of the laptop

AP1 receives and updates the MAC header before forwarding the TDLS Discovery request to the laptop. The transmitter address is changed to AP1, and the receiver address is changed to STA3.

If the request is transmitted via AP2, then the addresses are modified accordingly. The transmitter address becomes AP2, and the receiver address becomes STA4 as depicted in the Fig. 3.89b.

(2) **TDLS Discovery Response**

The laptop receives the TDLS Discovery request from the affiliated AP and directly sends the TDLS Discovery response to the mobile phone without involving the AP.

(3) **TDLS Setup Request, Response, and Confirm**

The subsequent TDLS Setup Request, Response, and Confirm frames are encapsulated in data frames and forwarded through either AP1 or AP2, which are affiliated with the AP MLD. Following the TDLS message exchange procedure, the phone and the laptop establish the TDLS connection and successfully negotiate the encryption key. As a result, the two non-AP MLDs can communicate with each other without requiring AP intervention.

(4) **TDLS Teardown**

Once the mobile phone and the laptop complete the data transmission, either party can initiate a TDLS Teardown Request to the other. The TDLS Teardown request can be transmitted directly over the TDLS connection or via the AP MLD.

2. **The TDLS Connection Between a Non-AP MLD and a Legacy STA**

A legacy Wi-Fi device is identified by its unique MAC address, whereas a non-AP MLD is identified by its MLD MAC address. When a non-AP MLD establishes communication with a legacy STA, both devices utilize their respective unique MAC address for identification.

Figure 3.90 illustrates the network topology consisting of a non-AP MLD Wi-Fi 7 phone, a Wi-Fi 6 laptop, and a Wi-Fi 7 AP MLD. In the depicted scenario, STA1, which is affiliated with the non-AP MLD, establishes a TDLS connection with the laptop, as depicted in Fig. 3.91a.

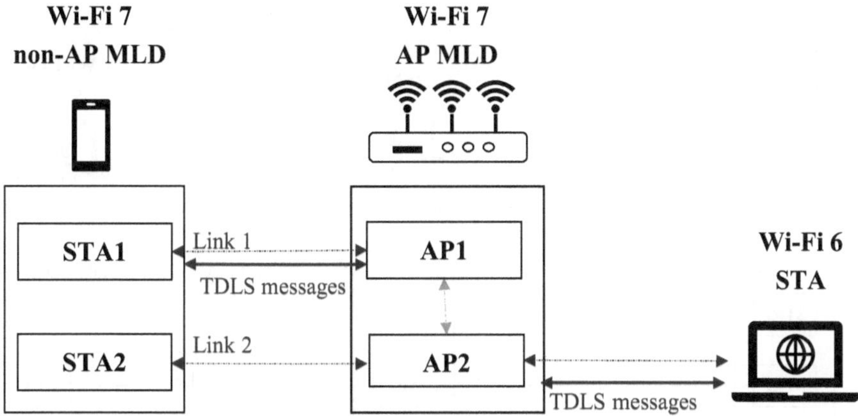

Fig. 3.90 Network topology of the TDLS connection between a non-AP MLD and a legacy STA

(1) **TDLS Discovery Request**

The phone initiates a TDLS Discovery Request to the laptop. The request is sent by the affiliated STA1 and encapsulated in a data frame. The following addresses are used:

- **Source address:** MLD MAC address of the mobile phone
- **Destination address:** MAC address of the laptop (STA)
- **Transmitter address:** MAC address of STA1
- **Receiver address:** MAC address of AP1

The affiliated AP1 receives the TDLS Discovery Request and then forwards it to the laptop through the affiliated AP2. In this case, the following addresses are used:

- **Transmitter address:** MAC address of AP2
- **Receiver address:** MAC address of the laptop (STA)

If the request is initiated from STA2, the Transmitter Address (TA) and Receiver Address (RA) are updated accordingly to AP2 and the laptop (STA), respectively, as illustrated in Fig. 3.91b.

(2) **TDLS Discovery Response**

Once the laptop receives the TDLS Discovery Request from the AP, it sends the TDLS Discovery Response directly to the mobile phone without involving the AP. The transmitter address is the MAC address of the laptop, and the receiver address is the MLD address of the mobile phone.

(3) **TDLS Setup Request, Response, and Confirm**

The subsequent TDLS Setup request, Response, and Confirm frames are encapsulated in the data frames and forwarded through either AP1 or AP2. This enables

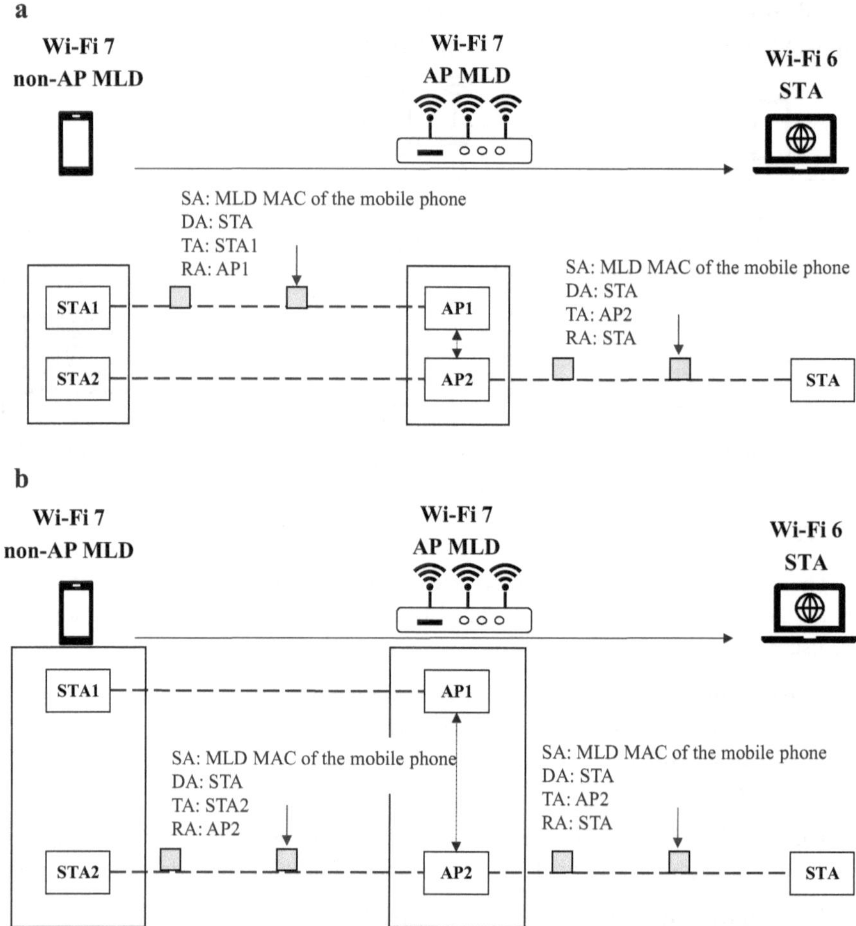

Fig. 3.91 (**a**) TDLS message through the affiliated AP1 and AP2, (**b**) TDLS message through the affiliated AP2

the establishment of a TDLS connection between the mobile phone and the laptop. Once the connection is established, the two devices can transmit data to each other without the need for the AP's intervention.

(4) **TDLS Teardown**

After the mobile phone and the laptop have finished their data transmission, either device can initiate a TDLS Teardown Request directly to the other device over the TDLS connection, or through the AP MLD.

3.2.8.3 P2P Connection Between Wi-Fi 7 Non-AP MLDs

To enable Wi-Fi 7 multi-link operation capabilities in Wi-Fi P2P connection, Wi-Fi Alliance established a new group in June 2022 to explore extending P2P for multi-link support with the aim to commence product certificate testing in 2024.

The multi-link P2P topology resembles the traditional single-link P2P connection. Each Wi-Fi 7 non-AP MLDs create a new non-AP MLD and utilizes it to establish a P2P connection with the peer. The two logical non-AP MLDs share the channel resources in a time division manner.

Figure 3.92 illustrates a P2P connection between a Wi-Fi 7 non-AP MLD mobile phone and a laptop. The Wi-Fi 7 phone connects to the Wi-Fi 7 AP-A via dual links, while the Wi-Fi 7 laptop has a dual-link connection with the Wi-Fi 7 AP-B. The user activates the screen casting on both the mobile phone and the laptop, leading to the creation of the non-AP MLD STA-c on the mobile phone, which includes the affiliated STA5 and STA6. Similarly, the laptop creates the STA-d containing affiliated STA7 and STA8. The STA-c and STA-d establish a P2P multi-link connection through the P2P multi-link discovery, negotiation, and connection procedure.

3.2.8.4 TXOP Sharing for Wi-Fi 7 P2P

In Wi-Fi 6, the AP supports transferring the TXOP to one or multiple STAs through Trigger frames, and then these STAs utilize the TXOP to send upstream data.

The Wi-Fi 7 AP possesses a similar function of allocating a portion of its TXOP to the STAs for uplink transmission. This is realized by employing the Triggered TXOP Sharing (TXS) Mode specified in **MU-RTS** Trigger frame. When the Triggered TXOP Sharing Mode subfield within an MU-RTS Trigger frame is set to a non-zero value, it is then designated as an MU-RTS TXS Trigger frame. When the TXOP is transferred, the STAs can use it to send upstream data to the AP, or facilitate Peer-to-Peer data transmission, as illustrated in Fig. 3.93.

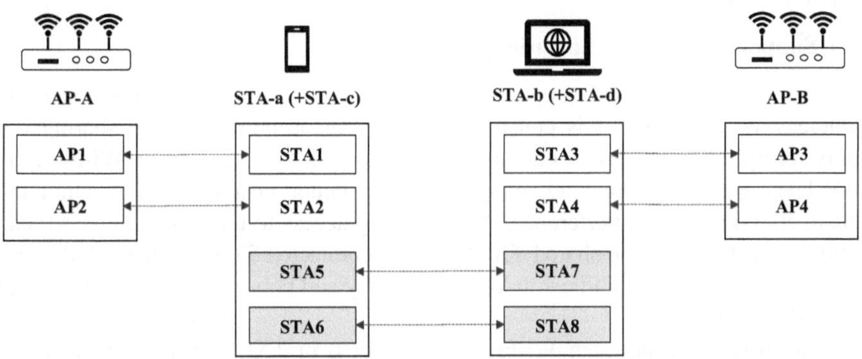

Fig. 3.92 Network topology of the P2P connection between non-AP MLDs

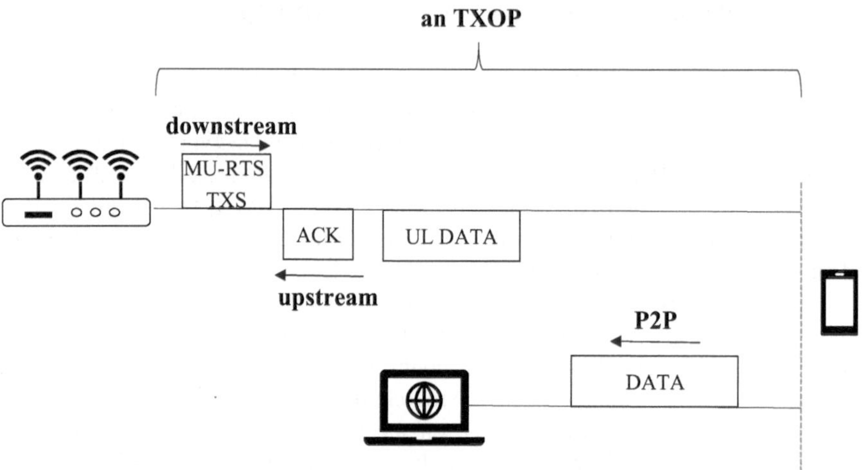

Fig. 3.93 Wi-Fi 7 TXOP sharing

Compared to the TXOP sharing technology employed in Wi-Fi 6, Wi-Fi 7 introduces advancements in the following aspects:

(1) **TXOP Sharing Parameters Controlled by the AP**

In Wi-Fi 6, an AP is responsible for defining several crucial parameters in the Trigger frames sent to STAs. These parameters include the transmission power of the STAs, the Modulation and Coding Scheme (MCS), and the RU allocation for efficient uplink transmission. However, it can be quite challenging for the AP to accurately determine and optimize these settings for all STAs in real-world scenarios. Wi-Fi 7 introduces an improvement to the process of TXOP sharing by simplifying the contents of the Trigger frame. Specifically, the AP now only specifies the RU allocation for TXOP sharing purposes, leaving out the transmit power and MCS settings. Instead, each STA autonomously determines its own transmit power level, MCS, and any other relevant parameters according to its current conditions and actual requirements.

(2) **Support P2P Communication**

The Wi-Fi 6 standard supports TXOP sharing for uplink transmission only, whereas Wi-Fi 7 takes this concept further by incorporating TXOP sharing not only for uplink transmission but also for Peer-to-Peer transmission. In Wi-Fi 7, the AP leverages its inherent advantage of being better positioned to preempt the channel and mitigate interference. After gaining access to the channel, the AP can effectively distribute the shared TXOP among connected STAs for their P2P activities. This innovation significantly reduces latency and boosts the overall throughput of P2P communication.

The differences between Wi-Fi 7 and Wi-Fi 6 in TXOP sharing are listed in Table 3.7.

Table 3.7 Difference of the TXOP sharing between Wi-Fi 7 and Wi-Fi 6

Difference	Wi-Fi 6 TXOP sharing	Wi-Fi 7 TXOP sharing
Type of trigger frame	Basic trigger frame, MU-RTS trigger frame	MU-RTS TXS trigger frame
TXOP sharing parameters in the trigger frame	Uplink transmission rate, transmission power, PPDU size, MCS, and RU allocation	RU allocation
Data frame type	TB PPDU based on OFDMA	Non-TB PPDU based on non-OFDMA
Transmission	Only for uplink transmission	Mode1: Support uplink transmission Mode2: P2P
Concurrent users	Frequency division multiplexing	Time division multiplexing

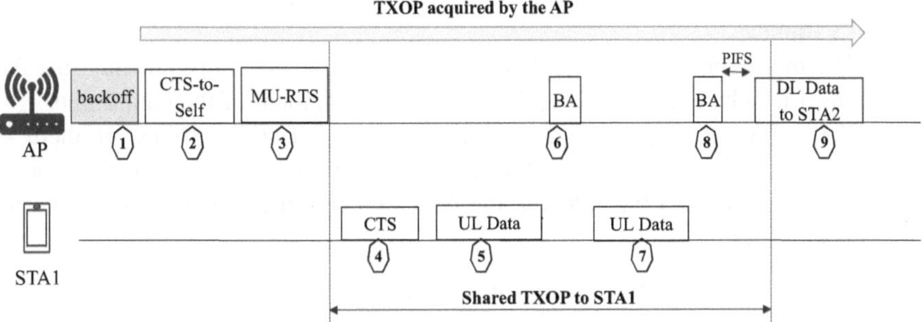

Fig. 3.94 TXOP sharing for uplink transmission

Next, we will discuss the Wi-Fi 7 TXOP sharing technology for uplink transmission and Peer-to-Peer data transmission in details.

1. **Wi-Fi 7 TXS for Uplink Transmission**

The AP transfers a TXOP to the STAs via MU-RTS Trigger frame, and the STAs transmit the uplink data during this TXOP duration. If the remaining TXOP is not sufficient for a STA to send a data frame, the AP utilizes the remaining TXOP to send downstream data to other STAs after a PIFS interval.

As shown in the example illustrated in Fig. 3.94, STA2 are connected to the AP via Wi-Fi, and STA1 requests TXOP sharing to transmit upstream data. The interaction steps are as follows:

(1) APs obtain a TXOP through the CSMA/CA mechanism.
(2) The AP sends a CTS-to-Self frame which asserts the TXOP duration.
(3) The AP sends an MU-RTS TXS Trigger frame to STA1 and transfer the TXOP to STA1. In this case, the Mode field is set to 1 and the shared TXOP duration must be less than or equal to the total TXOP duration acquired by the AP.

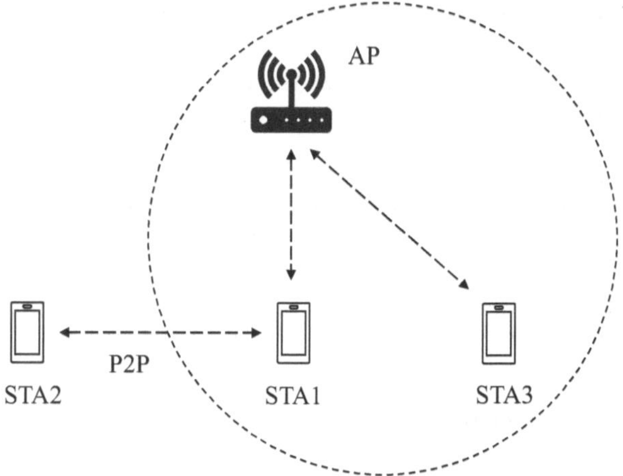

Fig. 3.95 Example of a mix mode TXOP sharing

(4) Upon receiving the MU-RTS TXS Trigger frame, STA1 responds by sending a CTS frame.
(5) STA1 then sends a non-TB PPDU data frame to the AP. Subsequently, the AP sends a Block ACK frame to STA1 in acknowledgment of the data frame.
(6) (7)/ (8) Repeat steps 5 and 6 until the shared TXOP expires. If there is insufficient remaining time in the shared TXOP for STA1 to transmit another data frame, after a PIFS interval, the AP can utilize the residual TXOP to send data to STA2.

2. **Wi-Fi 7 TXS for Mix Uplink and P2P Transmission**

The Wi-Fi 7 TXOP sharing can be utilized by the STA for both uplink transmission as well as P2P transmission.

Figure 3.95 illustrates the network topology of this mixed mode transmission. In this case, STA1 and STA3 are connected to the AP, while STA2 resides in a different BSS and has established a Peer-to-Peer connection with STA1. Using TXOP sharing technology, STA1 requests permission to transmit upstream as well as Peer-to-Peer data as described in Fig. 3.96.

(1) The AP obtains a TXOP through the CSMA/CA mechanism.
(2) The AP sends a CTS-to-Self frame which contains the TXOP duration.
(3) The AP sends a MU-RTS TXS Trigger frame to STA1 to transfer the TXOP to STA1. The mode field is set to 2, and the duration is set to the TXOP shared with STA1, which must be less than or equal to the TXOP duration obtained by the AP.
(4) Upon receiving the MU-RTS TXS Trigger frame, STA1 responds by sending a CTS frame to the AP.
(5) STA1 then sends an uplink transmission data frame to the AP in a non-TB PPDU format.

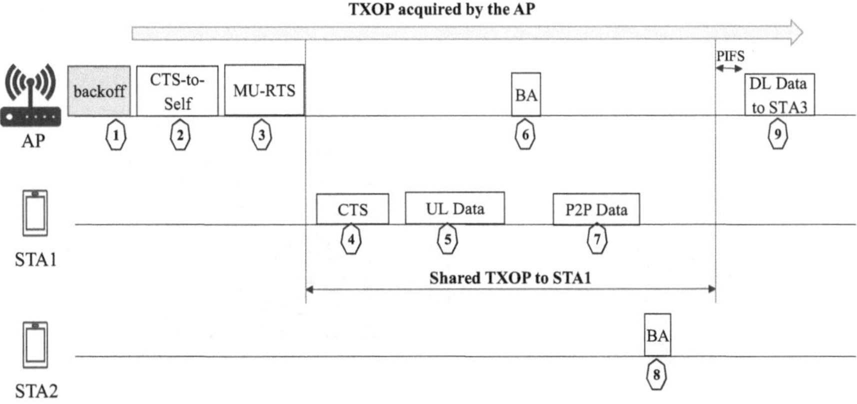

Fig. 3.96 TXOP sharing for uplink and P2P transmission

(6) Subsequently, the AP sends a Block ACK frame in acknowledgment of the data frame.
(7) STA1 sends a non-TB PPDU data frame to STA2 for the P2P transmission.
(8) STA2 sends a Block ACK frame to STA1 to acknowledge the data frame. Repeat step 5 and 6 or step 7 and 8 until the data transmission completes, or the remaining TXOP is insufficient for STA1 to transmit another data frame.
(9) Once the shared TXOP expires, the AP can continue to send data frames to STA3 after a PIFS interval.

For the mode 1 with uplink transmission only, the AP is allowed to leverage any remaining shared TXOP, since only AP and STA1 are involved. In this scenario, if STA1 does not send a frame after a PIFS interval, the AP can assume that STA1's transmission has concluded.

However, in case of the mode 2 operation where mixed transmissions are involved, the AP may not be able to detect the P2P traffic transmitted by STA2, especially if STA2 belongs to another BSS and situated at a distance from the AP. To preclude the possibility of collisions affecting STA1, the AP is prohibited from utilizing any residual portion of the shared TXOP. Instead, it must hold off on transmitting data frames until the shared TXOP has fully expired and an extra PIFS interval has transpired.

3.3 Emergency Preparedness Communications Services

With Wi-Fi networks being widely available in millions of households and across community and public areas, it presents a new opportunity for Emergency Preparedness Communications Services (EPCS) to disseminate emergency messages to the public.

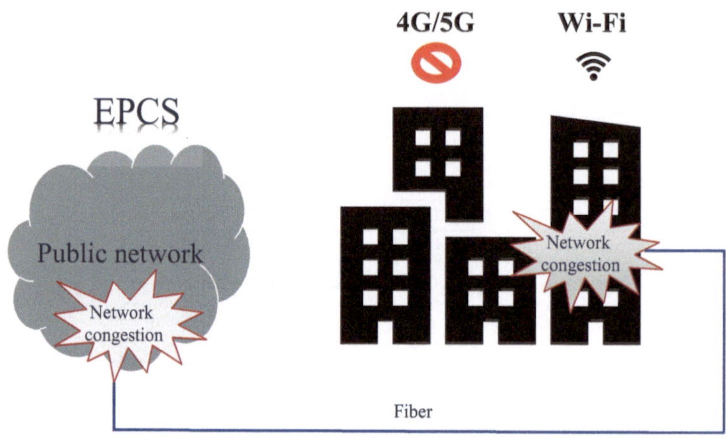

Fig. 3.97 Emergency preparedness communications services

As illustrated Fig. 3.97, during an emergency where the 4G/5G cellular network may be out of service due to network congestion, the management office of an apartment complex can utilize this technology. In such cases, when an emergency occurs, the office would need to promptly inform all residents to evacuate and proceed to a designated safe location.

In general, the EPCS is unpredictable, bursty, and of high priority. As more and more smart devices are connected to the Internet via Wi-Fi networks, the Wi-Fi technology is expected to manage emergency service through the challenges such as network congestion, latency.

To meet the QoS of the EPCS in the event of natural disasters, wars, and other emergencies, Wi-Fi 7 supports prioritizing the scheduling and transmission of emergency services, thereby reducing the transmission delay of emergency communications. With the Emergency Preparedness Communication Services, the government or the property operator can publish the evacuation information to the public in a timely manner through the existing wireless infrastructure.

As introduced in Sect. 1.2.5.4, the traffic is classified into four Access Categories according to the QoS requirements, with each Access Category having corresponding EDCA parameters for accessing the wireless medium, such as the Arbitrated Interframe Space Number, Cwmin and Cwmax, and TXOP Limit. The first three parameters determine the priority of the data in accessing the channel. By adjusting these parameters, the Wi-Fi 7 ensures a higher priority for the EPCS.

3.3.1 Feature Procedure of New Service

The Action frames are extended in Wi-Fi 7 with EPCS specific fields to support the EPCS. These are EPCS Priority Access Enable Request, Priority Access Enable

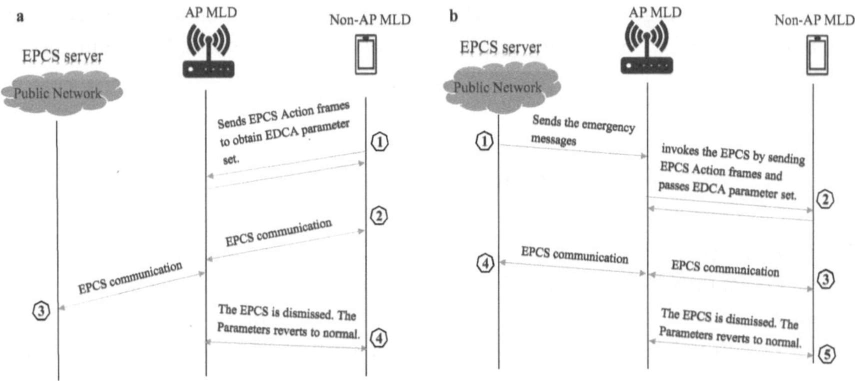

Fig. 3.98 (**a**) EPCS initiated by STA, (**b**) EPCS initiated from the network

Response, and EPCS Priority Access Teardown frame. Figure 3.98 shows the EPCS message exchange procedure initiated by the STA or from the Internet.

The procedure for a non-AP MLD to initiate the EPCS is described as follows:

(1) The non-AP MLD sends an EPCS Priority Access Enable Request to the AP MLD, and the AP MLD authorizes it based on locally cached information previously obtained in advance from the EPCS service provider, or online interaction through the service provider's authorization infrastructure. The non-AP MLD obtains the EDCA parameters for EPCS priority access.
(2) The non-AP MLD competes for the channel access with the designated parameters and sets up the EPCS communication channel. All traffic to and from the non-AP MLD shall be treated as highest priority.
(3) The AP MLD forwards the emergency communication data to the server at the public network server.
(4) After the emergency condition is resolved, the AP MLD or non-AP MLD tears down the EPCS, and reverts to the normal medium access parameters.

The procedure of EPCS initiated from the Internet is as follows:

(1) The service provider transmits the emergency information to the target AP MLD through the public network.
(2) The AP MLD initiates the EPCS by sending an unsolicited EPCS Priority Access Enable Request to the non-AP MLD. The non-AP MLD then acknowledges the request by sending an EPCS Priority Access Enable Response and obtains the EDCA parameters for the EPCS priority access.
(3) The AP MLD then transmits the emergency messages to the non-AP MLD. The non-AP MLD competes the channel access with the designated EDCA parameters and transmits the uplink emergency information to the AP MLD as required.
(4) Throughout the emergency period, the AP MLD forwards the EPCS communication traffic between the non-AP MLD and the wide network.

(5) Once the emergency is resolved, either the AP MLD or the non-AP MLD releases the EPCS priority access and reverts to its normal medium access parameters.

3.3.2 *Service Setup Approaches with Parameters*

To serve the EPCS, Wi-Fi 7 defines two approaches for setting up the EPCS priority access so that the EPCS authorized terminals can easily obtain the channel. Either the EDCA parameters are predefined by the service provider, or the AP and the STA can utilize the action frames to transmit the channel access parameters of the emergency communication service.

(1) **Predefined EDCA Parameters for EPCS Priority Access**

Similar to the generic services. The Wi-Fi 7 EPCS authorized terminals use the generic mechanism to acquire the channel access, either through a Trigger frame or the CSMA/CA mechanism. To ensure that the authorized terminals have the privilege to obtain the channel, the service provider can choose the channel access parameters for them, such as a small backoff window and a small inter-frame interval. If the network is congested, such specific EDCA parameters make it easier for the EPCS terminals to obtain priority access.

(2) **Passing EDCA Parameters via Action Frames for EPCS Priority Access**

Non-AP MLDs or AP MLDs can enable EPCS via EPCS Priority Access Enable Request frame and EPCS Priority Access Enable Response frame, which contains the relevant EDCA channel access parameters. Thus, non-AP MLDs can easily acquire channel access for EPCS communication.

The Priority Access Multi-link field of the EPCS priority access Action frames is defined as shown in Fig. 3.99.

Only when an emergency happens, National Security and Emergency Preparedness (NS/EP) service provider authorizes the users to enable the EPCS. When the

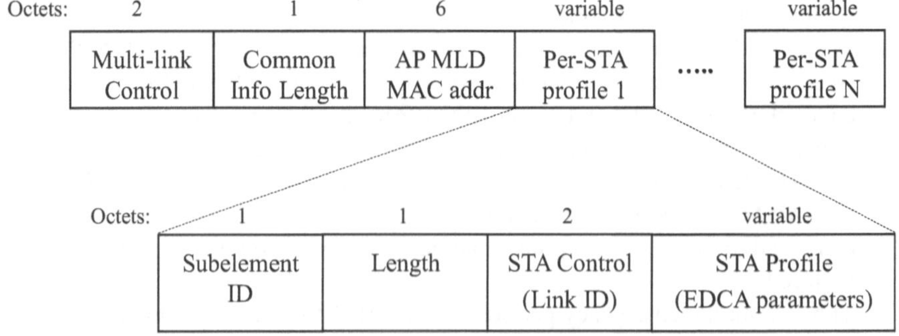

Fig. 3.99 Priority access multi-link field of the EPCS priority access action frames

emergency is cleared, either the AP MLD or the non-AP MLD can tear down EPCS priority access by transmitting an EPCS Priority Access Teardown frame.

3.4 The Updates on Physical Layer by Wi-Fi 7

The Wi-Fi 7 standard introduces several significant updates to the physical layer, aiming to enhance Wi-Fi performance and concurrent communications capabilities. These typically include the implementation of 4096-QAM (4 K-QAM) MCS, support for a 320 MHz channel bandwidth, and the adoption of MRU technology, as illustrated in Fig. 3.100.

(1) Wi-Fi 7 supports up to 4096-QAM, which signifies that each symbol can convey 12 bits of information, compared to Wi-Fi 6's 1024-QAM where each symbol carries 10 bits. Consequently, this results in a 20% improvement in modulation efficiency.
(2) Wi-Fi 7 supports up to a 320 MHz bandwidth in the 6 GHz band, compared to a maximum of 160 MHz bandwidth for the Wi-Fi 6. Consequently, this doubles the potential maximum throughput when using the highest available bandwidth.
(3) Wi-Fi 7 enables the allocation of multiple non-contiguous RUs to a STA for upstream data transmission, whereas Wi-Fi 6 only supports allocating one RU per STA at any given time. The MRU technology enhances channel utilization and, when combined with MU-MIMO, offers increased flexibility in RU allocation to accommodate diverse use cases.
(4) The MRU has been discussed extensively in Sect. 3.2.5. In this section, our focus will shift to the introduction of 4 K-QAM, the 320 MHz bandwidth, and the new PPDU format as features implemented by Wi-Fi 7.

3.4.1 New 4 K-QAM Modulation

The 4 K-QAM constellation diagram comprises 4096 distinct constellation points, each denoting a different modulation state. The boundary of the points of 4 K-QAM

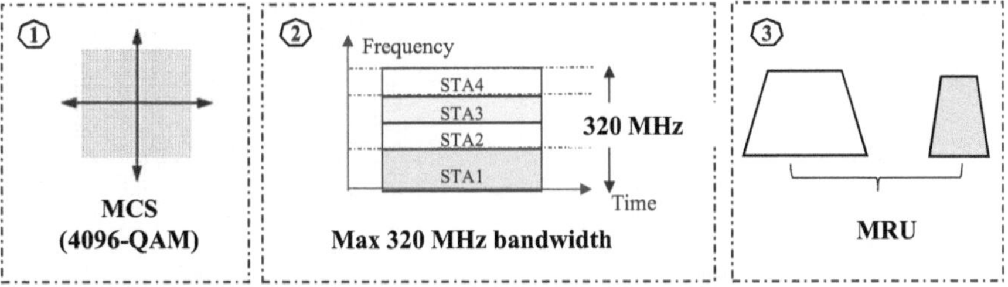

Fig. 3.100 The improvements on physical layer of Wi-Fi 7

is half of that of 1024-QAM constellation utilized in Wi-Fi 6 as illustrated in Fig. 3.101. Compared with 1024-QAM, 4 K-QAM possesses a higher number of points and correspondingly smaller distances between adjacent points.

4 K-QAM defines two modulation and coding schemes, namely, MCS 12 and MCS 13. Table 3.8 shows the specifications of MCS 12 and MCS 13 at different channel bandwidths. For a channel bandwidth of 80 MHz and an OFDM Guard Interval of 0.8us, the MCS 13 can reach up to 720.6 Mbps in the case of a spatial stream.

The higher modulation order, the lower the Error Vector Magnitude (EVM) tolerance. For Wi-Fi 6, 1024-QAM, the EVM_{db} must be less than -32dbm, or EVM% less than 1.77%, in order to have correct demodulation. For Wi-Fi 7, 4096-QAM, the EVM_{db} must be less than -38dbm, or say1.2%. To improve performance when using higher order modulation schemes, it is crucial to keep the EVM as low as possible. Practically speaking, several strategies can be employed to increase the Signal-to-Noise Ratio (SNR), thereby optimizing the performance. Here are some typical methods:

(1) Shortening the Distance Between APs and STAs

In practical scenarios, the Bit Error Rate (BER) typically worsens as the distance between the AP and STAs increases. This is due to the attenuation of the signal strength over longer distances, which can cause a reduction in SNR.

In day-to-day experiences, when a STA encounters a weak or unstable connection with the AP, users often instinctively move the STA closer to the AP. By doing so, they are essentially shortening the transmission distance and thereby amplifying the received signal. Consequently, the SNR improves because the signal becomes relatively stronger compared to the background noise. As a result, the BER decreases, translating into a more reliable and higher quality wireless connection.

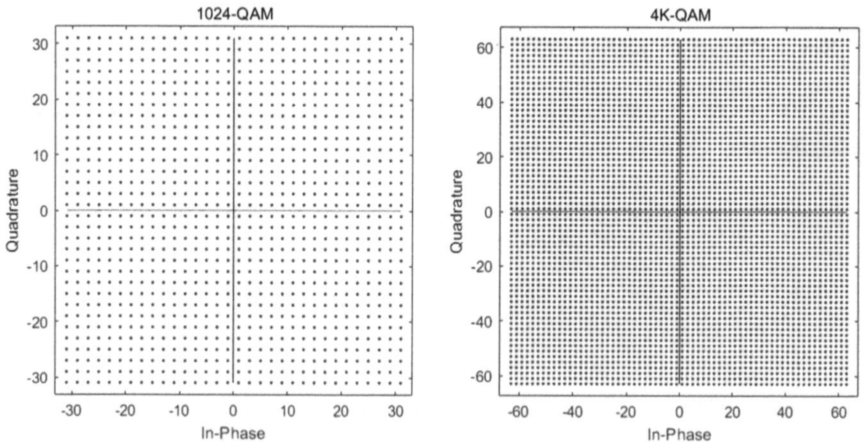

Fig. 3.101 Constellation diagram of 1024-QAM and 4096-QAM

Table 3.8 MCS and data rate of 4 K-QAM

Data rate at physical layer (Mbps)										Coding	Modulation
MCS	80 MHz			160 MHz			320 MHz				
GI (us)	0.8	1.6	3.2	0.8	1.6	3.2	0.8	1.6	3.2		
12	648.5	612.5	551.3	1297	1225	1102	2594	2450	2205	3/4	4 K-QAM
13	720.6	680.6	612.5	1441	1361	1225	2882	2722	2450	5/6	4 K-QAM

(2) **Enhancement of Multi-antenna Gain**

Typically, an AP is equipped with a larger number of antennas than individual STA. During single-user transmissions, the AP capitalizes on multi-antenna technologies, including beamforming, to augment the SNR. Furthermore, the deployment of multiple antennas at the AP facilitates spatial diversity, which helps to reduce the impacts of multipath interference and, in turn, further fortifies the SNR.

3.4.2 320 MHz Channel Bandwidth

The 320 MHz bandwidth consists of two consecutive 160 MHz channels in the 6 GHz band. The Confederation of European Posts and Telecommunications approves 480 MHz of spectrum in the 6 GHz band for unlicensed services. Hence, there is only one 320 MHz channel available in Europe. The FCC authorizes a total of 1.2 GHz of bandwidth in the 6 GHz band, as shown Fig. 3.102 [5]. Therefore, in the United States, Wi-Fi 7 has 3 non-overlapping 320 MHz channels.

The 320 MHz channel bandwidth brings the following changes to the Wi-Fi standard:

(1) **MRU Size**

With 320 MHz support in Wi-Fi 7, the AP is able to allocate an MRU to a STA of up to 280 MHz bandwidth, or 3x996 + 482-tone. For high-throughput services, the larger MRU increases throughput and reduces latency.

(2) **Bandwidth Query Report**

Wi-Fi 6 introduces the Bandwidth Query Report Poll (BQRP) Trigger frame, which is used to query the STAs about their subchannel states. The AP then allocates the RU resources to the STAs accordingly.

Figure 3.103 illustrates channel bitmap of the BQR subfield defined by Wi-Fi 6 and Wi-Fi 7. Each individual bit within this bitmap signifies a 20 MHz subchannel. In Wi-Fi 6, the field consists of 8 bits, thereby representing a 160 MHz channel. Wi-Fi 7 expands upon this by introducing two separate BQR subfields, each of

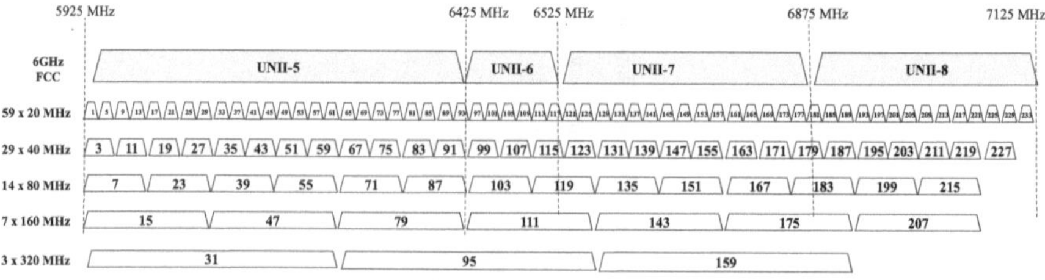

Fig. 3.102 FCC 6GHz Wi-Fi channel definition

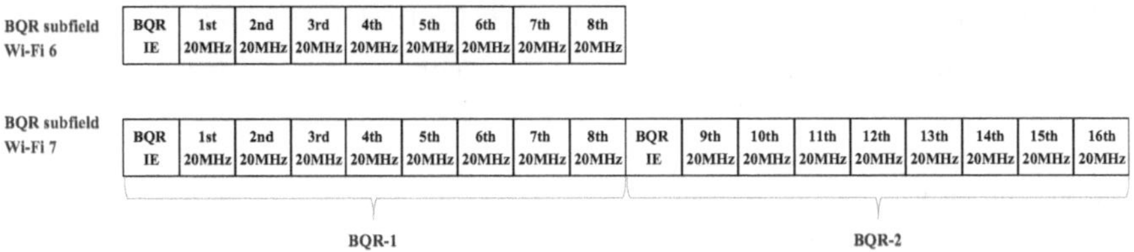

Fig. 3.103 BQR subfield format

Table 3.9 Theoretical maximum transmission rate of a single-link Wi-Fi 7 device

Physical layer technology	6GHz (maximum capability)
Number of spatial streams	8
Bits per symbol	12 bits for 4 K-QAM
Coding efficiency	5/6
Number of data subcarriers	980 × 4 (320 MHz bandwidth)
Symbol duration (us)	12.8us + 0.8us GI
Maximum data rate (Mbps)	23.05Gbps

which denotes the state of every 20 MHz subchannel within the initial 160 MHz segment and the subsequent 160 MHz segment.

(3) **Data Rate of a Single Link Wi-Fi 7 Device**

Wi-Fi 7 significantly increases the data rate by supporting 320 MHz bandwidth and 4 K-QAM. According to Eq. 1.1, with a single link of 320 MHz in the 6 GHz band, the theoretical maximum transmission rate of a Wi-Fi 7 device reaches 23Gbps using the transmit parameters as shown in Table 3.9.

$$\textbf{\textit{data rate}} = \frac{\textbf{\textit{number of information bits per symbol}} \times \textbf{\textit{coding efficiency}} \times \textbf{\textit{number of data subcarriers}} \times \textbf{\textit{number of spatial streams}}}{\textbf{\textit{a symbol period}}}$$

(4) **Data Rate of MLD**

Assuming that a Wi-Fi 7 device consists of 3 links at 2.4 GHz, 5 GHz, and 6 GHz, operating at 40 MHz, 80 MHz, and 320 MHz bandwidths respectively, and assuming that all of them have 8 spatial streams, the Wi-Fi 7 MLD can achieve a theoretical maximum transmission rate of 31.56 Gbps as shown in Table 3.10.

3.4.3 Wi-Fi 7 New Physical Layer Data Unit Frame Format

Wi-Fi 7 defines new preamble fields U-SIG, EHT-SIG, EHT-LTF, and EHT-STF to support the new physical layer technology. The new EHT PPDUs containing these

Table 3.10 Theoretical maximum transmission rate of a Tri-band Wi-Fi 7 MLD

Physical layer technology	2.4GHz	5GHz	6GHz
Number of spatial streams	8	8	8
Bits per symbol	12	12	12
Coding efficiency	5/6	5/6	5/6
Number of data subcarriers	468 (40 MHz bandwidth)	980 (80 MHz bandwidth)	980 × 4 (320 MHz bandwidth)
Symbol duration (us)	12.8us + 0.8us GI	12.8us + 0.8us GI	12.8us + 0.8us GI
Maximum data rate per link (Mbps)	2.75 Gbps	5.76 Gbps	23.05 Gbps
The total data rate (Gbps)	1.75 Gbps+5.75 Gbps+23.05 Gbps = 31.56 Gbps		

Table 3.11 The EHT PPDUs and EHT preambles

EHT PPDU	EHT preamble fields	Physical layer
EHT MU PPDU	U-SIG EHT-SIG EHT-LTF EHT-STF	Downlink OFDMA transmission Uplink and downlink MU-MIMO OFDMA transmission
EHT TB PPDU	U-SIG EHT-LTF EHT-STF	Uplink OFDMA transmission

new preamble fields are called EHT MU PPDU and EHT TB PPDU which are listed in Table 3.11.

(1) **U-SIG Field**

The U-SIG field carries the basic physical layer information such as channel bandwidth, coding rate, BSS coloring and other information required for the receiver to interpret EHT PPDUs. The U-SIG extends the Wi-Fi 6 HE-SIG field to support the new MCS12/MCS13 and 320 MHz bandwidth. The U-SIG field consists of two parts: U-SIG-1 and U-SIG-2. There are slight differences when it appears in an EHT MU PPDU compared to an EHT TB PPDU. Table 3.12 describes what the U-SIG field represents, using the example of U-SIG in an EHT MU PPDU Table 3.12.

(2) **EHT-SIG Field**

The EHT-SIG is similar to the HE-SIG-B field in Wi-Fi 6 but extends it to support preamble puncturing, MRU, and RU allocation at 320 MHz bandwidth, and so on. It includes both the common field and the user specific field, providing RU and spatial stream allocation information for multiple users, as shown in Fig. 3.104.

Table 3.12 U-SIG field in an EHT MU PPDU

U-SIG field	Description	Bit	Remark
U-SIG-1	PHY version identifier	B0-B2	0 represents for EHT PHY
	Bandwidth	B3-B5	Indicates the channel bandwidth of the PPDU, such as 20 MHz, 40 MHz, etc
	UL/DL	B6	Indicates whether the PPDU is sent in UL or DL 1: UL transmission 0: DL transmission
	BSS color	B7-B12	An identifier of the BSS
	TXOP	B13-B19	Indicate TXOP duration
	Disregard and validate	B20-B25	Reserved
U-SIG-2	PPDU type and compression mode	B0-B1	Indicate the EHT PPDU transmission types, OFDMA, NPD or etc.
	Validate	B2	Reserved
	Punctured channel information	B3-B7	Indicate which subchannel has preamble puncturing
	Validate	B8	Reserved
	HE-SIG MCS	B9-B10	Indicates the modulation scheme used for EHT PPDU
	Number of EHT-SIG symbols	B11-B15	Indicates the number of EHT-SIG symbols.
	CRC	B16-B19	CRC for the bit 0-41 of the U-SIG field.
	Tail	B20-B25	Sets to 0 and used to terminate the trellis of the convolutional decoder

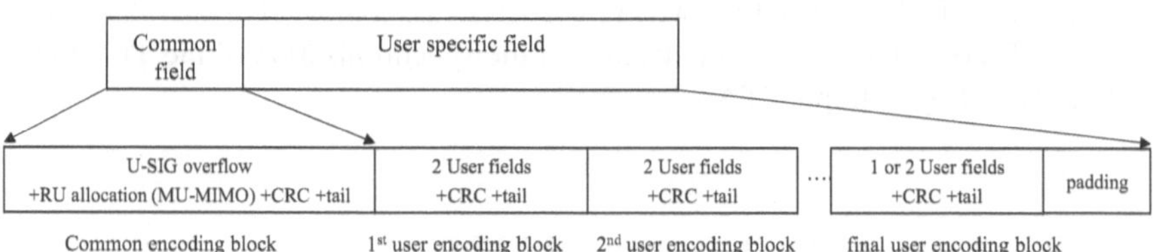

Fig. 3.104 EHT-SIG field

- **Common field:** Provides information that is common to all users.
- **User specific field:** Contains multiple user blocks followed by padding. Each user block contains the RU allocation information for individual STAs, allowing them to identify the location and size of the RU allocated to them.

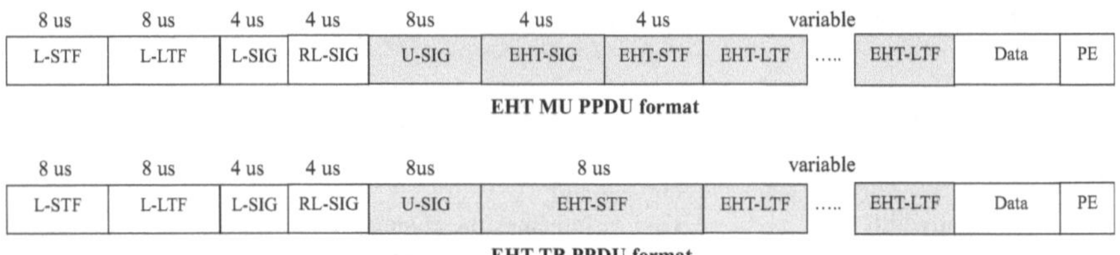

Fig. 3.105 EHT MU PPDU and EHT TB PPDU format

To ensure compatibility with IoT devices that are restricted to operating within a 20 MHz bandwidth, Wi-Fi 7 employs the standard preamble encoding format in its U-SIG and EHT-SIG fields, which are tailored for 20 MHz bandwidth units. If the channel bandwidth exceeds 20 MHz, these U-SIG and EHT-SIG fields are duplicated across multiple 20 MHz subchannels.

(3) **EHT-LTF and EHT-STF**

The EHT-LTF and the EHT-STF fields are similar to the HE-LTF and HE-STF defined by Wi-Fi 6. They contain channel fading and automatic gain control information, respectively. The EHT-LTF extends the channel fading to support MRU, while the EHT-STF extends the automatic gain control to support a 320 MHz bandwidth.

(4) **EHT PPDUs**

The EHT MU PPDU and EHT TB PPDU are defined in Wi-Fi 7 for the data frames for multi-user and single-user transmission respectively, as shown in Fig. 3.105. As stated, there is a minor difference between EHT MU PPDU and EHT TB PPDU:

- EHT MU PPDU contains the EHT-SIG field, which indicates MRU allocation information for MU-MIMO communication.
- The EHT-STF field in an EHT MU PPDU lasts 4us, compared to 8us when it is in an EHT TB PPDU. The extra 4us aids in the synchronization of the TB PPDUs transmitted by multiple STAs.

3.5 The Security Evolution for Wi-Fi 7

Information security is a paramount concern in the realm of telecommunication technologies. As Wi-Fi is the predominant solution for indoor short-range communication, it must ensure robust security measures for end-users, regardless of whether it is being used for home connectivity or public hotspot services.

Wi-Fi communication is the data transmission that occurs between the STAs and the AP through a wireless connection. Consequently, ensuring Wi-Fi security entails several key aspects: authorized connections between the router and STAs,

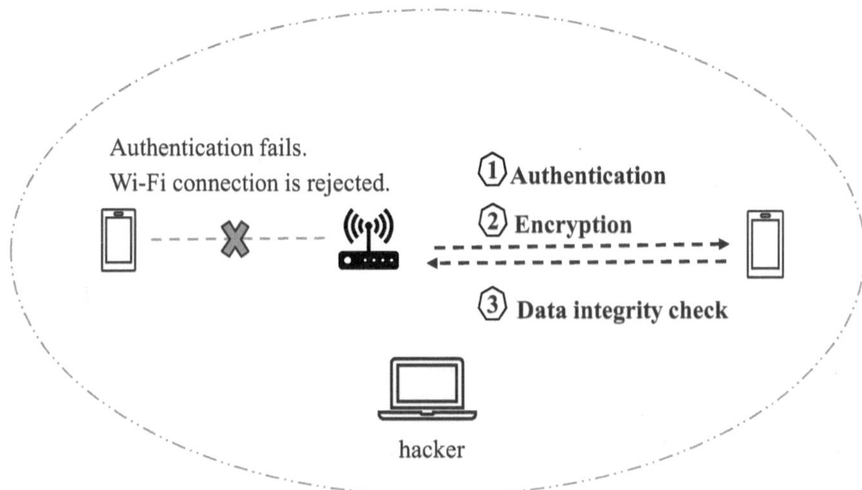

Fig. 3.106 Security in Wi-Fi communication

prevention of data interception during transmission, and guaranteeing that the original data reaches the recipient without any tampering. To this end, Wi-Fi security incorporates authentication, data encryption, and data integrity, as depicted in Fig. 3.106.

If a Wi-Fi network fails to provide a right level of security, hackers could potentially log into the network using a falsified identity, hijack or eavesdrop on sessions, violate user privacy, and inject forged frames, etc., resulting in serious security issues for end users. Therefore, ensuring robust security is always a pivotal technical consideration in the development of every Wi-Fi standard.

This section provides a comprehensive overview of the evolution of Wi-Fi security, subsequently detailing the key Wi-Fi security technologies, as well as the changes introduced by Wi-Fi 7.

3.5.1 Typical Wi-Fi Security Standards

The robust security of Wi-Fi network has significantly contributed to the widespread acceptance and large-scale deployment of Wi-Fi technology. Throughout the evolution of Wi-Fi standards, security measures have been consistently fortified, with vulnerabilities in previous generations addressed through the introduction of enhanced encryption algorithms and new security mechanisms.

The evolutionary path of Wi-Fi security standards is illustrated in Fig. 3.107, while Table 3.13 presents an overview of the authentication methods, encryption, and the data integrity check algorithms employed across these standards.

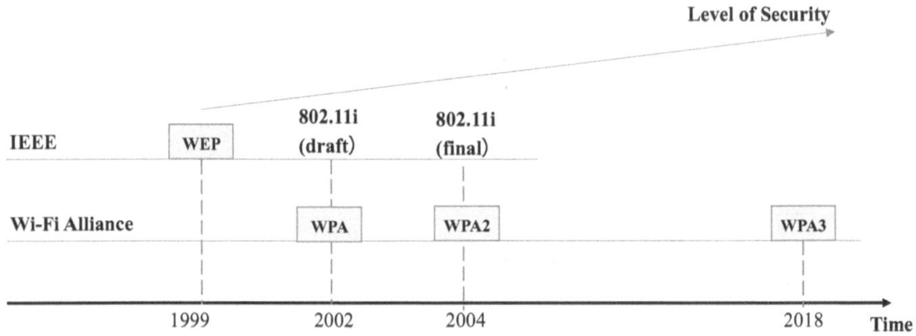

Fig. 3.107 Evolution of Wi-Fi security standards

Table 3.13 Overview of Wi-Fi security standards [6]

Security standards	Year	Level of security	Encryption algorithm	Data integrity	Link authorization	Authentication
WEP	1999	Low	RC4	CRC-32	Open system authentication; shared key authentication	None
WPA	2002	Medium	TKIP/RC4	MIC	Open system authentication	Pre-shared key or 802.1X authentication
WPA2	2004	High	CCMP/ AES	CCMP-MIC	Open system authentication	
WPA3	2018	Highest	GCMP/ CNSA	GCMP-MIC	Open system authentication	Simultaneous authentication of equals (SAE)

The first Wi-Fi security specification, known as **Wired Equivalent Privacy, WEP**), is an integral part of the IEEE 802.11 standard ratified in 1999, which aims to achieve a security level comparable to that of wired connection. It relies on the RC4 algorithm developed by RSA Security©. WEP supports data encryption and employs the 32-bit Cyclic Redundancy Check (CRC-32) to ensure the data integrity during the transmission. In terms of link authentication mechanisms, WEP offers two methods: Open System Authentication and Shared Key Authentication.

However, WEP was reported to have weakness in both the encryption algorithm and key management. Therefore, a new IEEE security standard **IEEE 802.11i** was ratified in July 2004, which defines Robust Security Network (RSN) and the encryption algorithms including Temporal Key Integrity Protocol(**TKIP**), Counter-Mode/CBC-MAC Protocol(**CCMP**), and Wireless Robust Authenticated Protocol(**WRAP**). The standard mandated the use of 802.1x authentication to achieve secure wireless LAN authentication and robust key management.

It took 4 years for the 802.11i standard to be completed. In order to accelerate the commercialization of Wi-Fi technology, Wi-Fi Alliance adopted the draft 802.11i standard in 2002 and subsequently published the Wi-Fi Protected Access specification (WPA). The WPA standard implements most of the contents from 802.11i, such as TKIP that is compatible with RC4 encryption, and the Message Integrity Check (MIC) for ensuring data integrity. WPA served as an interim solution before the introduction of WPA2.

In September 2004, Wi-Fi Alliance introduced Wi-Fi Protected Access 2 (WPA2), which was based upon the full IEEE802.11i Standard. In WPA2, the Advanced Encryption Standard (AES) replaces TKIP, and the CCMP (Counter Mode with Cipher Block Chaining Message Authentication Code Protocol) supersedes the MIC as the method for securing data transmission. Since then, WPA2 has become the standard configuration for Wi-Fi network security.

In 2017, Belgian researchers released a study on WPA2 Key Reinstallation Attacks, showing that hackers could exploit a weakness allowing them to reuse the discarded encryption keys, thereby enabling them to penetrate Wi-Fi networks and potentially eavesdrop on or tamper with user data. This research garnered considerable public attention concerning Wi-Fi security.

In June 2018, the Wi-Fi Alliance published the new security standard Wi-Fi Protected Access 3(WPA3), incorporating numerous enhancements over WPA2. For instance, the encryption algorithm has been upgraded from a 128-bit cryptographic algorithm to the 192-bit Commercial National Security Algorithms (CNSA) to cater to the enterprise scenario. In the case of home networks, the new handshake retransmission method supersedes WPA2's four-way handshake. For open-space Wi-Fi network, the data communication of each device is encrypted, enhancing complexity to safeguard the Wi-Fi network against dictionary-based password cracking. Additionally, if the password is entered incorrectly multiple times, the connection will be blocked. Moreover, the WPA3 supports parallel computation of MIC using the Galois/Counter Mode Protocol (GCMP), enhancing encryption and decryption efficiency compared to CCMP serial computation.

3.5.2 Key Features in Wi-Fi Security

Wi-Fi security technology has evolved over the past years. WPA3 is the latest standard that addresses the vulnerabilities of previous generations and will be elaborated in Sect. 3.5.3. In this section, we will first discuss the previous generation of Wi-Fi security technology in more detail and understand its main features and the weaknesses.

3.5.2.1 Wired Equivalent Privacy (WEP)

WEP, the first generation of Wi-Fi security standard, relies on the RC4 stream cipher algorithm. RC4 is a symmetric encryption algorithm, meaning it uses the same key for bitwise XOR operation with the data stream during both encryption and decryption processes.

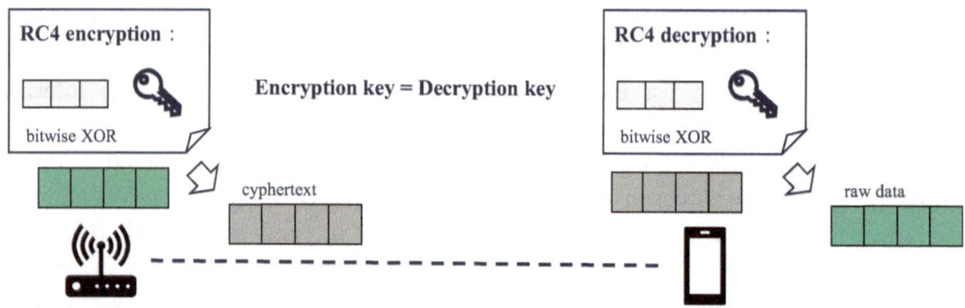

Fig. 3.108 WEP RC4 stream cipher algorithm

Table 3.14 Features in the WEP standard and the vulnerability

Feature	Vulnerability	Attacks
Initialization vector	The limited length of IV results in the same ciphertext appearing after a small number of frames	The **initialization vector attack:** The hacker can predict the IV and pseudo-random number generator and then break the encryption
Keystream	Same key used by the BSS and never updated	High risk for long-term usage of same cypher key
CRC-32	The CRC is weak for data integrity verification; for instance, the message is tampered by bit flip	Data tampering

The RC4 key is a pseudo-random string of a fixed length, either 64 bits or 128 bits. As depicted in Fig. 3.108 at the transmitter's end, the raw data stream is XORed with the pseudo-random RC4 key stream to produce ciphertext. The receiver then employs the identical pseudo-random keystream to XOR with the received ciphertext, thereby reconstructing the raw data. In a Wi-Fi LAN network employing the WEP method, all STAs and the AP within BSS utilize the same RC4 keystream for both encrypting and decrypting data.

Since the header of the data frames follow regular patterns, the key could be easily derived from the encrypted data frame headers. To disrupt this regularity in the ciphertext, the WEP standard introduces the concept of an Initialization Vector (IV). The Initialization Vector is a 24-bit pseudo-random string preset by the device manufacturer. It varies for each data frame and is used alongside the RC4 key to generate a pseudo-random key stream. This ensures that the same RC4 key can produce different keystreams.

However, it is important to note that WEP's use of RC4 is considered a weak algorithm and can be hacked within a matter of minutes. Table 3.14 outlines WEP vulnerability and the methods by which they could be exploited.

In addition, a hacker can intercept encrypted packets and deliberately resend them to the receiver in an attempt to deceive it. This tactic is referred as a replay attack.

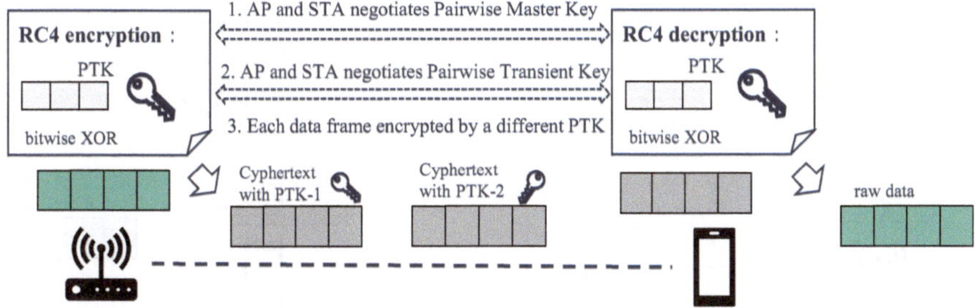

Fig. 3.109 WPA encryption and decryption

3.5.2.2 Wi-Fi Protected Access (WPA)

To address the weakness of WEP, Wi-Fi Alliance introduced the WPA standard in 2003. As illustrated in Fig. 3.109, WPA is also based on the RC4 algorithm, same as WEP. However, instead of using the key negotiated between the AP and the STA directly, it defines the Temporal Key Integrity Protocol (TKIP), which employs a 4-way handshake process to negotiate the PTK for each pair of AP and STA, and the key is dynamic for every data frame.

Since the encryption keys differ for each data frame, cracking the TKIP key becomes significantly challenging, requiring a large number of operations and thereby imposing a high computational cost.

On the other hand, to prevent from malicious modification on the encrypted data, WPA introduces a Message Integrity Code (MIC) field at the end of the data frames to verify data integrity. The MIC uses the Michael algorithm, replacing the CRC-32 in WEP. If the receiver detects a mismatch in the MIC field, it assumes that the data frames have been tampered with maliciously. The WPA standard defines a series of countermeasures, such as re-negotiating the Group Transient key, suspending the current transmission for 60 seconds, etc., to protect the communication from attack.

3.5.2.3 WPA2

Wi-Fi Alliance ratified the WPA2 standard in 2004, incorporating the **Counter Mode with Cipher Block Chaining Message Authentication Code Protocol** (CCMP) and **Advanced Encryption Standard (AES)** cipher to replace the TKIP protocol and the RC4 algorithm used in the WPA standard, respectively. As shown in Fig. 3.110 WPA2 splits the data into 128-bit blocks and encrypts each data block with a 128-bit AES keystream.

The frame format is shown in Fig. 3.111, indicating the difference between the unencrypted data frame and the encrypted data frames according to WEP/WPA/WPA2. WPA2 adds the CCMP and MIC subfields to the MSDU, where the MIC is

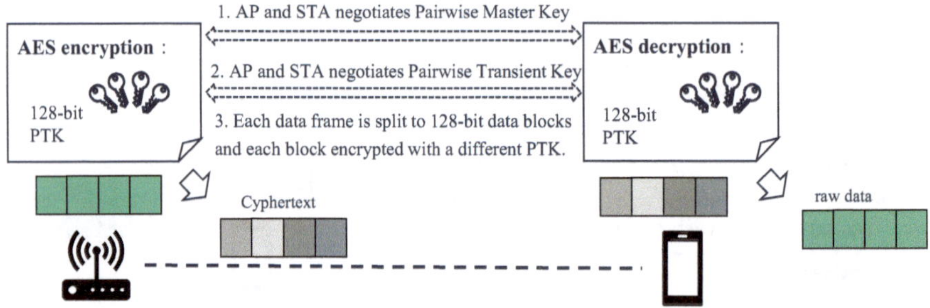

Fig. 3.110 WPA2 encryption and decryption

Raw data	MAC Header	MSDU				
WEP encrypted	MAC Header	Initialization Vector	MSDU	CRC-32	FCS	
WPA encrypted	MAC Header	TKIP	MSDU	MIC	CRC-32	FCS
WPA2 encrypted	MAC Header	CCMP	MSDU	MIC (encrypted)	FCS	

Fig. 3.111 Data frame format of WEP, WPA, and WPA2

encrypted alongside the payload data in 128-bit data blocks. The CCMP header and the MIC field contain information from the MAC header information such as the frame sequence number. This design allows WPA2 to effectively protect devices from Replay Attacks.

3.5.2.4 Pre-shared Key Authentication

In addition to data encryption methods, authentication represents another crucial technology in Wi-Fi security. Its purpose is to verify that the STA is a legitimate 802.11 device before it is allowed to connect to the BSS. This process is akin to plugging an Ethernet cable into an 802.3 device's Ethernet port. The 802.11 authentication represents the initial step in establishing a connection between the AP and the STA. As Wi-Fi security standards have progressed, authentication has also evolved from basic to more robust security measures.

WEP supports both **Open System authentication** and Shared Key authentication. In Shared-key authentication, the STA must be configured with the same key as the AP, as illustrated in Fig. 3.112.

The AP compares the received data with the original data. If there is a match, it sends the Authentication Response to confirm that the authentication process has

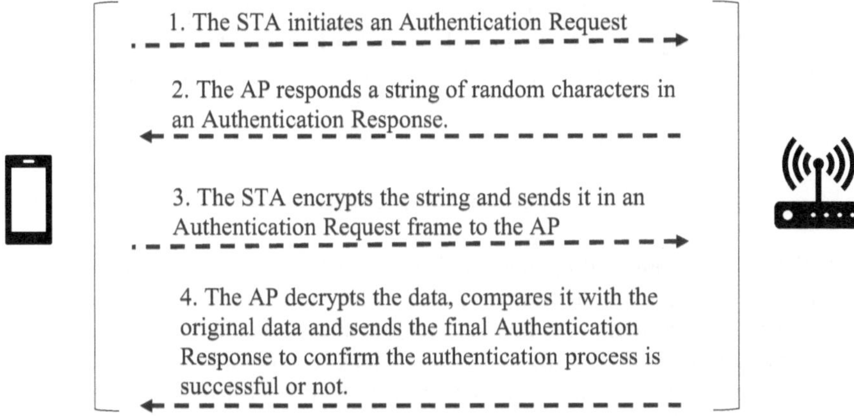

Fig. 3.112 Shared key authentication of WEP

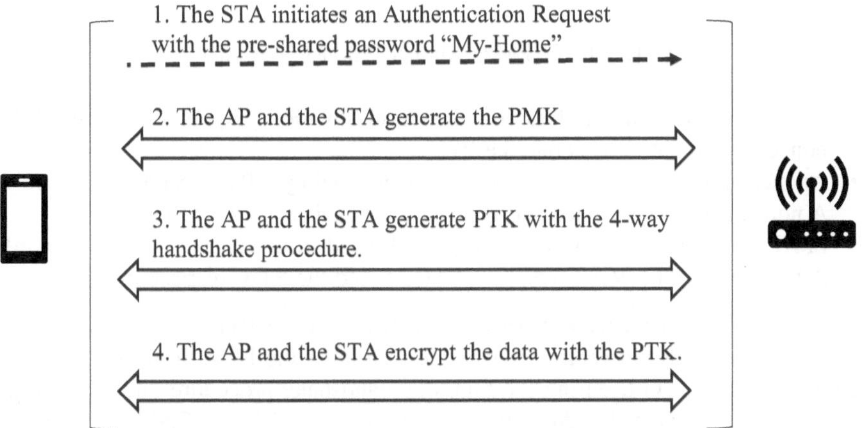

Fig. 3.113 Pre-shared key authentication

been successful; otherwise, it issues a negative response. The same key employed during WEP authentication is also used for encrypting the data.

The shared key authentication method is relatively straightforward. However, it is noteworthy that the static WEP key can be easily compromised by capturing and analyzing the Authentication Request and Response frames.

Evolved from the Shared Key authentication method, both WPA and WPA 2 support the Pre-shared key (PSK) and 802.1x authentication protocols. The Pre-shared key authentication method is widely adopted in home and small enterprise networks.

Figure 3.113 illustrates the Pre-shared Key procedure. The AP configures a password that is shared to STAs. When a STA initiates an Authentication request to the AP, it includes the pre-shared password in the request and then generates the

Pairwise Master Key (PMK). Followed by a 4-way handshake procedure, the AP and the STA finally generate a pair of keys called Pairwise Transient Key (PTK), which are used to encrypt unicast data. Each pair of an AP and a STA possesses a unique PTK for unicast transmissions between them.

The PMK is generated as Eq. 3.2

$$\text{PMK} = \text{PBKDF2}\ (\text{password}, \text{SSID}, \text{SSID length}, 4096, 256) \tag{3.2}$$

- PBKDF2: A pseudorandom function that takes a password and a random string of characters as input and iteratively applies a hash function to generate the key.
- Password: A minimum of 8 characters configured on the AP.
- SSID and SSID length: SSID string and its length configured on the AP .
- 4096: Represents the number of times the password is hashed during the process, specifically 4096 iterations.
- 256: Indicates the resulting master key is 256 bits in size.

The PTK is generated as Eq. 3.3

$$\text{PTK} = \text{PRF}\ (\text{PMK}, \text{Anonce}, \text{Snonce}, \text{AA}, \text{SPA}) \tag{3.3}$$

- PRF: A pseudorandom function that hashes various inputs including PMK, nonces to ultimately generate the PTK.
- Anonce and Snonce: Random numbers generated by AP and STA, respectively. A nonce is used only once and is never used again with the PMK.
- PMK: The Pairwise Master Key already derived from a shared secret password.
- AA and SPA: The MAC address of the AP and the STA, respectively.

The four-way handshake process guarantees that the PTK is both unique and random, effectively preventing reverse derivation of the PMK from the PTK. As depicted in Fig. 3.114, during the four-way handshake procedure, the AP and the STA utilize the Extensible Authentication Protocol Over LAN (EAPOL) frames to negotiate and establish the PTK.

(1) **The First Handshake**

The AP sends the A-Nonce to the STA. The STA which possesses the PMK, A-Nonce, its own S-Nonce, and the MAC addresses of both the AP and the STA, can then generate the PTK.

(2) **The Second Handshake**

The STA sends its S-Nonce to the AP. Using the PMK, S-Nonce, A-Nonce, and the MAC addresses of both parties, the AP generates the PTK.

The PTK comprises the EAPOL-Key confirmation key (KCK), the EAPOL-Key Encryption Key (KEK), and the Temporal key (TK). The KCK and the KEK are utilized for encryption and verification during the four-way handshake process, while the TK is employed for the encryption of unicast traffic. In addition, the AP

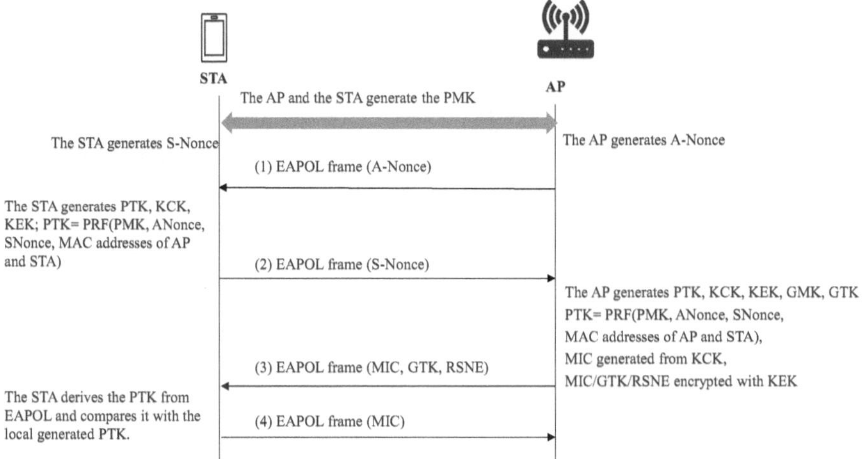

Fig. 3.114 4-Way handshake

generates a Group Master Key (GMK) and a Group Transient key (GTK), which are utilized for the encryption of multicast data.

(3) **The Third Handshake**

The AP employs KCK to generate MIC field**.** Subsequently, it encrypts the GTK, MIC, along with Robust Security Network Element (RSNE) using KEK. Once this encryption process is completed, the AP proceeds to transmit this securely encapsulated information to the STA.

(4) **The Fourth Handshake**

The STA decrypts the frames received from the AP using the locally generated KEK and further validates the integrity of the message by examining the MIC field. Subsequently, the STA derives the PTK based on KEK and KCK. It then compares the RSNE from the handshake message with its own locally stored RSNE. If the locally derived PTK matches the one derived from the handshake message, and the RSNEs are identical, the STA sends an acknowledgment to the AP. This acknowledgment includes a MIC generated using the locally derived KCK.

The AP restores the KCK from the MIC of the STA's data frame and verifies whether it corresponds to the key generated locally. If there is a match, the handshake process is considered successfully completed.

3.5.2.5 802.1x Authentication for WPA/WPA2

The 802.1x is a port-based client/server access control standard, widely implemented in enterprise wired or wireless LANs. As shown in Fig. 3.115 the server authenticates the Wi-Fi stations at the port level using the Extensible Authentication Protocol

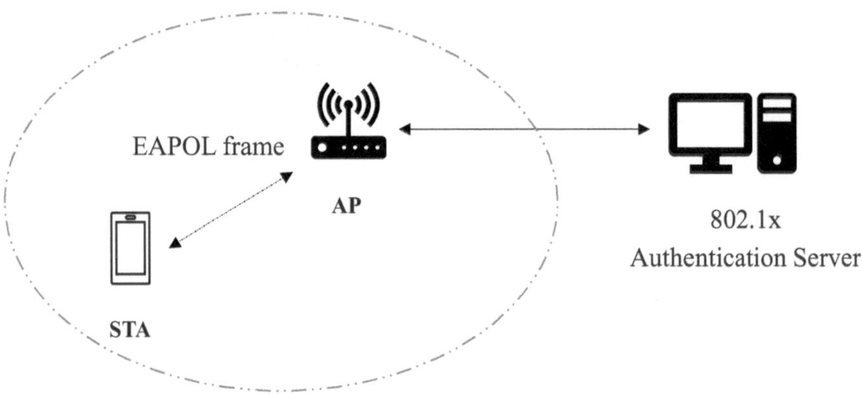

Fig. 3.115 802.1x authentication

(EAP), with the AP acting as an intermediary to relay authentication messages between the clients and the authentication server.

In this system, ports are categorized as either controlled or uncontrolled. Controlled port blocks traffic until the supplicant has been successfully authenticated; conversely, uncontrolled port allows only EAP authentication traffic to pass through. Once the authentication is successful, the controlled port opens, enabling network traffic to flow through it and granting access to the network.

802.1x supports various authentication methods. The authentication can be based on unique user credentials, digital certificates pre-installed on the stations, or even the SIM card of the terminal device. Ultimately, it is up to the 802.1x network service provider to decide which authentication method to employ.

Regarding encryption key generation of 802.1x authentication, the procedure is akin to that used in Pre-shared Key authentication. After a station successfully completes the 802.1x authentication, each device generates a unique Master Session Key (MSK), from which it then derives a PMK. This differs from WPA-PSK and WPA2-PSK, where the PMK is generated directly from a Pre-shared Key authentication method.

3.5.2.6 The Encryption Key Generation Tree

In the previous subsection, we discussed several different keys used within the 802.1x and pre-shared key authentication mechanisms. Each of these keys can be traced back to a common initial key, which forms the basis of a concept known as a key generation tree, as shown in Fig. 3.116.

1. **Unicast Key Generation**

The generation tree of unicast keys is depicted in the right half of Fig. 3.117. The top level key for the 802.1x authentication method is the Master Session Key (MSK), while for Pre-shared Key method, it is the Pre-shared Key (PSK). The

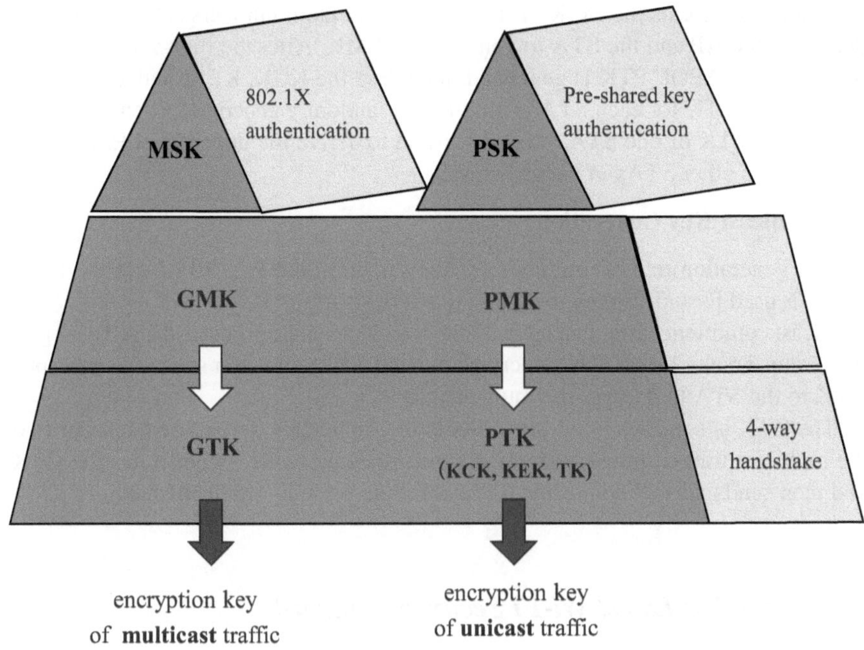

Fig. 3.116 Encryption key generation tree

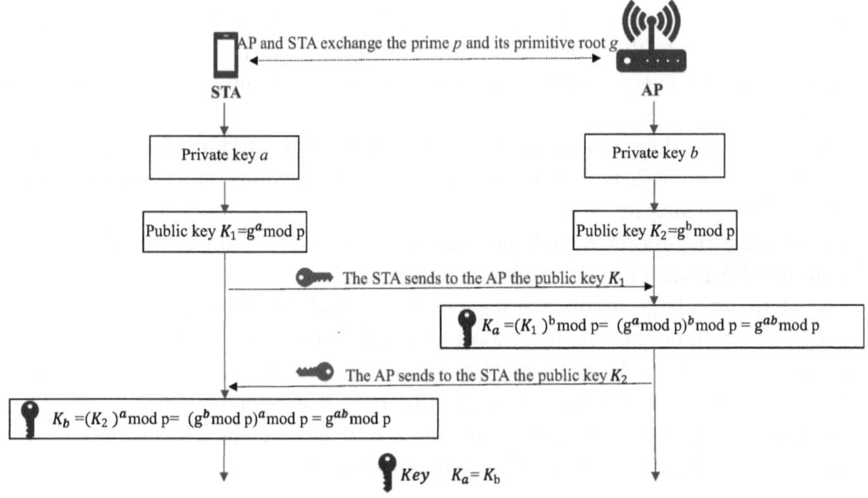

Fig. 3.117 Diffie-Hellman key exchange procedure

algorithm transforms the MSK or the PSK with random numbers selected independently by the AP and the STA to generate the PMK. After the four-way handshake process, the EAPOL PTK is generated, including the KCK, KEK, and TK.

Since the PTK for each STA is unique and randomly generated, even if a hacker obtains the PTK of one STA, it is impossible to derive the upper level PMK or the PTKs of the other STAs in the same BSS.

2. **Multicast Key Generation**

The generation tree of multicast keys is shown in the Fig. 3.117. Unlike PMK, which is used for unicast key negotiation, a Group Master Key (GMK) is utilized for multicast communication. During the four-way handshake process, the AP generates the Group Transit Key (GTK), encrypts it using KEK, and then sends the encrypted GTK to the STA to decrypt the multicast data.

The GTK is common to all the STAs in the same BSS. To ensure the security of the multicast traffic, the AP periodically refreshes the GMK, regenerates the GTK, and then sends it to all connected STAs through the four-way handshake.

3.5.3 WPA3: Latest Wi-Fi Security Standard

The WPA3 standard [7] was ratified by Wi-Fi Alliance in June 2018. It is built upon the Simultaneous Authentication of Equals (SAE) protocol, where both the AP and the STA exchange public keys with each other. Following this, each party computes a hash of the received public key using its local private key, and subsequently sends these hash values to the other for verification purposes. This process generates a unique PMK for every connection established between an associated STA and the STA.

The SAE algorithm was initially proposed by Dan Harkins for the 802.11s standard back in 2012, with the aim of securing connections and communications between APs. In later revisions, the discrete logarithm and elliptic curve based SAE protocol were incorporated into the standard, effectively addressing vulnerability found in WPA2, such as offline dictionary attacks.

As there are a large number of legacy devices that do not support WPA3, these legacy STAs will not be able to connect to an AP if it is WPA3 only. To facilitate a smooth network upgrade and maintain compatibility with such devices, the AP is often configured in a hybrid mode supporting both WPA2 and WPA3.

In the subsequent section, we will delve into the technical characteristics of WPA3 and outline the interaction mechanism within the SAE protocol.

3.5.3.1 Key Features of WPA3

WPA3 has already become the next-generation security standard that strengthens the security protection across a wide range of Wi-Fi networks, including public Wi-Fi hotspots, home networks, and 802.1x-enabled enterprise networks alike.

(1) **WPA3 for Home Network**

The WPA3 SAE method ensures that a unique PMK is created for each connection made by a STA. When a STA is authenticated with the AP through the four-way handshake procedure, it generates a distinct PMK for each association. Additionally, the elliptic curve algorithm prevents the reverse derivation of the AP's keys from a STA's PMK.

Conversely, with the WPA2 Pre-shared Key method, all STAs utilize the same password to connect to the AP, resulting in the generation of an identical PMK. If a hacker obtains the PMK of a STA, they can deduce the AP's keys and, as a result, compromise the entire BSS.

(2) **WPA3 for Enterprise Network**

During the four-way handshake, the MIC is generated using the EAPOL-KCK, which originates from both the PTK and the PMK. A hacker could perform an offline dictionary attack by trying different PMKs until a matching MIC is found; if successful, they could then derive the PTK based on the cracked PMK.

According to the WPA2, the KCK length is 128 bits. However, for WPA3 in 802.1x authenticated enterprise networks, the KCK is increased to 192 bits. This extension increases the complexity of a dictionary attack from 2^{128} operations to 2^{192} operations, providing improved protection for enterprise networks using WPA3.

(3) **WPA3 for a Public Wi-Fi**

Many public Wi-Fi networks do not require the STAs to type in any password to get connected. For example, with public Wi-Fi in hospitals, airports, and coffee shops, users connect directly to Wi-Fi hotspots and are then prompted to authenticate via a webpage using their mobile phone number and a dynamic verification code. In this way, the Wi-Fi network doesn't provide any encryption on the traffic.

WPA3 supports the same user experience as the legacy Wi-Fi, but WPA3 does support encryption of traffic to enhance data security for public Wi-Fi. The AP and STAs generate both the PMK and the PTK through the four-way handshake process and encrypt the traffic using the PTK.

3.5.3.2 SAE Protocol

With the WPA2 Pre-Shared Key method, once a hacker has obtained the password of an AP, they can derive the PMK and, by subsequently eavesdropping on the four-way handshake, obtain the PTKs. This would allow them to decrypt all traffic within the BSS.

However, SAE technology allows unique PMKs to be generated for each STA through negotiation. This means that even if a hacker were to gain access to the AP's password, they would be unable to determine the PTKs.

The SAE handshake is also known as the Dragonfly protocol [8], which is based on Diffie-Hellman Key Exchange (DHKE) invented by American cryptographers

Whitfield Diffie and Martin Hellman in 1976. DHKE has been widely adopted in many computer communication protocols, including SSH, VPN, HTTPS, and others, and is considered a cornerstone of modern cryptography. The following is a brief overview of the Diffie-Hellman and SAE key exchange protocols.

1. **Diffie-Hellman Key Exchange Protocol**

We will first discuss the concepts of the primitive root and the discrete logarithm, which are fundamental to the operation of the Diffie-Hellman key exchange protocol, followed by an examination of the key exchange process itself.

(1) **Primitive Root**

The integer g is a primitive root of a prime number *p* if the values of $g^x \ mod \ p$ are different. So for every number *k* coprime to $p\ (k < p)$, there exists an integer *x* such that $k \equiv g^x \ mod \ p$, where x is in the range [0, *p*-2].

For example, g = 3 is the primitive root of the prime number p = 7, since

$$K_0 = 3^0 \ mod \ 7 = 1,$$

$$K_1 = 3^1 mod \ 7 = 3,$$

$$K_2 = 3^2 \ mod \ 7 = 2,$$

$$K_3 = 3^3 \ mod \ 7 = 6,$$

$$K_4 = 3^4 \ mod \ 7 = 4,$$

$$K_5 = 3^5 \ mod \ 7 = 5.$$

(2) **Discrete Logarithm**

If the integer g is a primitive root of a prime number *p,* for an integer *K*, $K = g^i \ mod \ p$,where $k < p$, and i€ [0,(*p*-2)].

The exponent i is called the **discrete logarithm** of K to the base g modulo p.

It is easy to generate K if the primitive root g, discrete logarithm i, and the prime number p are known. But for a large prime number p, it takes an incredible amount of computation to derive the discrete logarithm i, even if K, the primitive root g and p are given. This is how the Diffie-Hellman key exchange protocol ensures the security.

(3) **Diffie-Hellman Key Exchange Procedure**

Figure 3.117 shows the Diffie-Hellman key exchange procedure.

(a) The STA and the AP obtain the public parameters p and g, where g is a primitive root of p.
(b) The STA and the AP locally generate the private keys a and b, respectively, and then generate the public keys as $K_1 = g^a \ mod \ p$, $K_2 = g^b \ mod \ p$.
(c) The STA and the AP exchange the public key K_1 and K_2 with each other.

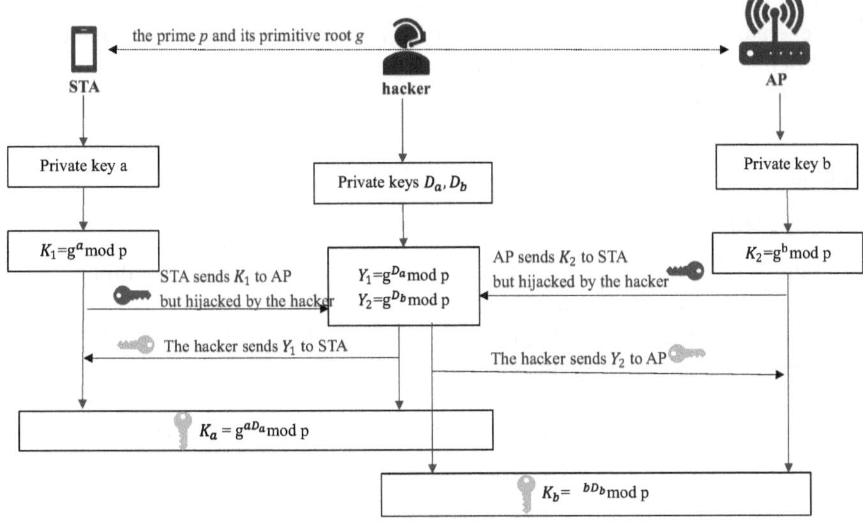

Fig. 3.118 Man-in-the-middle attack on Diffie- Hellman protocol

(d) The AP receives K_1, and generates the local key with the formula $K_a = (K_1\ )^b\ mod\ p = (g^a\ mod\ p)^b\ mod\ p = g^{ab}\ mod\ p$. Similarly, the STA uses K_2 to generate $K_b = (K_2\ )^a\ mod\ p = (g^b\ mod\ p)^a\ mod\ p = g^{ab}\ mod\ p$. Hence the $Key = K_a = K_b$, and it is to be used as the encryption key for the traffic between the AP and the STA.

(4) **Vulnerability of Diffie-Hellman Protocol**

Since the sniffer cannot derive the keys from the prime number p, primitive root g, and the public keys K_1 and K_2, the Diffie- Hellman key exchange protocol is resistant to the sniffing attacks. However, it is vulnerable to the Man-in-the-Middle (MITM) attack as indicated in Fig. 3.118. The AP and the STA do not verify each other when transmitting p and g, so the hacker could play in the middle, sniff p and g, replace the public keys K_1 and K_2 with the forged keys and then hijack the communication.

(1) The hacker intercepts the prime number p, the primitive root g, and the public key K_1 sent by the STA, and he generates a forged public key Y_2 based on his private key D_b and sends Y_2 to the AP.
(2) Similarly, the hacker intercepts the public key K_2 sent by the AP and, using his own private key D_a, the prime number p, and the primitive root g, to generates a forged public key Y_1, and sends it to STA.

(3) The STA and the hacker locally generate K_a, and the AP and the hacker locally generate K_b, where K_a and K_b are different because they were generated with different public keys sent by the hacker.

2. **SAE Key Exchange Protocol**

The SAE protocol is also based on discrete logarithms. Compared with Diffie-Hellman key exchange, it introduces the following enhancements:

(1) **Generate the Primitive Root**

In the SAE protocol, the primitive root g is a unique point on the elliptic curve, generated from the pre-shared password of the AP according to Eq. 3.4.

Hashed_password = H(Max(AP_MAC, STA_MAC)| Min(AP_MAC, STA_MAC| Passphrase | counter)

$$x = ((\text{KDF}(\text{hashed\_password}, \text{len})) \bmod (p-1)) + 1;$$
$$y = \text{sqrt}(\text{E}(x))$$
$$P = (x, y) \tag{3.4}$$

Where H represents the hash algorithm, STA_MAC is the MAC address of the STA, and AP_MAC is the MAC address of the AP, Passphrase is the preconfigured password of the AP, and counter represents the number of iterations of the hash operations.

KDF is a predefined function, p is a prime number.

Sqrt(E(x)) represents the vertical axis value on the elliptic curve corresponding to the horizontal axis value x.

P represents the point on the elliptic curve with the coordinate (x,y). In other words, it represents the primitive root g. As required by the SAE protocol, the primitive root is not transmitted in plain text.

(2) **Improvement on the Key Generation and Exchange**

The key exchange procedure of SAE is illustrated in Fig. 3.119.

(a) The private keys of the AP and the STA are split into a_1、 a_2 and b_1、 b_2 respectively where a=a_1+a_2, b=b_1+ b_2. a_1 and b_1 are stored locally.
(b) The STA sends the private key a and the public key $K_1 = g^{-a_2}\ mod\ p$ in the first frame.
(c) The AP sends its private key b and the public key $K_2 = g^{-b_2}\ mod\ p$ in the second frame.
(d) The STA has g and a_1 which are generated locally, and obtains b and K_2 from the AP, the key is generated as $K_a = (g^b \text{ mod p} \times K_2)^{a_1} mod\ p = (g^b \times g^{-b_2})^{a_1} mod\ p = (g^{b-b_2})^{a_1} mod\ p = (g^{b_1})^{a_1} mod\ p$.
(e) Similarly, the AP has generated g, b_1 and obtains a and K_1 from the STA, then it generates the key

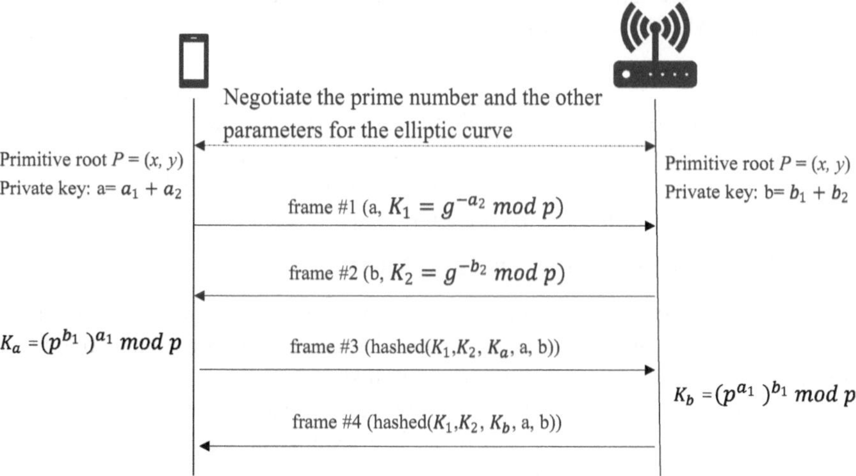

Fig. 3.119 Key exchange of SAE protocol

$$K_b = (g^a \bmod \mathrm{p} \times K_1)^{b_1} mod\ p = (g^a \times p^{-a_2})^{b_1} mod\ p = (g^{a-a_2})^{b_1} mod\ p$$
$$= (g^{a_1})^{b_1} mod\ p.$$

(f) Therefore, the AP and the STA generate the same key $K_a = K_b$ to be used as the PMK.

(3) **The Verification of the Keys**

The STA and the AP independently hash the key and exchange the hashed value in the third and the fourth frames for verification. If the verification is successful on both sides, it indicates that the keys generated on both sides are indeed identical. This mutual authentication method further enhances the security for the SAE protocol.

3.5.4 *Updates on the Security Protocols in Wi-Fi 7*

The Wi-Fi 7 standard adapts the security protocol to accommodate multi-link operation, such as the key generation process and the 4-way handshake procedure. This section describes the characteristics of the MLD unicast and multicast data encryption, outlines the key exchange procedure specific to MLDs and details the modifications made to the CCMP protocol.

3.5.4.1 Characteristics of Encryption Keys for MLD Unicast and Multicast Traffic

As discussed in 3.2.3, the unicast traffic of multi-link devices can be transmitted and retransmitted across any of the multiple links, whereas the multicast traffic is replicated and transmitted over all links. As a result, for unicast traffic, the multi-link device employs the same encryption keys across all links, while for multicast traffic, it utilizes a specific key for each individual link.

1. **The Encryption of Unicast Traffic of MLD**

After a Wi-Fi transmitter sends a data frame, it waits for the acknowledgment from the receiver. If no ACK is received, or if it receives a response indicating failed transmission, the data frame will be retransmitted.

For the Wi-Fi 7 MLDs, data frames can be transmitted and retransmitted not only on the current link, but also on other links. This requires all links to utilize the same PTK to encrypt and decrypt unicast data frames. Therefore, if unicast data frames are retransmitted on other links, only the corresponding link information in the header of the PSDU needs to be updated, without the need to reprocess the encryption.

An example of the retransmission of a unicast frame over two links is shown in Fig. 3.120. The retransmission procedure is described below:

(1) The non-AP MLD encrypts the unicast data frame with the PTK and adds MAC addresses for link 1 to the header; specifically, the receiver's MAC address is that of AP1, and the transmitter's address is that of STA1. The frame is then transmitted over link 1. Upon receiving the data frame, AP1 sends the ACK. However, the ACK frame is lost during transmission.
(2) The non-AP MLD substitutes the MAC1 address in the data frame with the MAC addresses for link 2 and retransmits it over link 2. This process does not require decryption and re-encryption of the MSDU. Upon successful receipt of the frame, the AP MLD sends an ACK in response.
(3) After the non-AP MLD receives the ACK frame, it confirms the successful transmission of the unicast data.

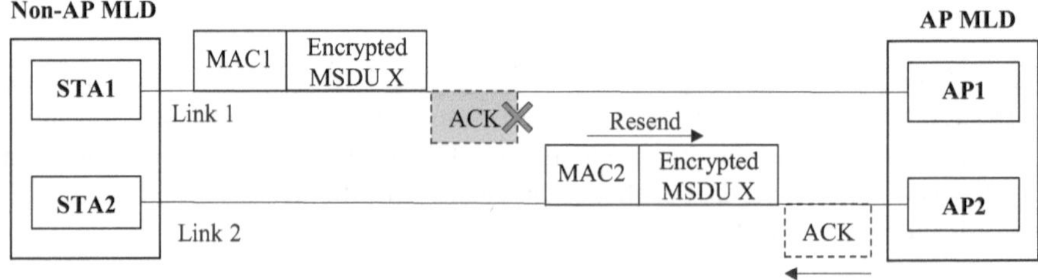

Fig. 3.120 Encrypted unicast traffic retransmission over multi-links

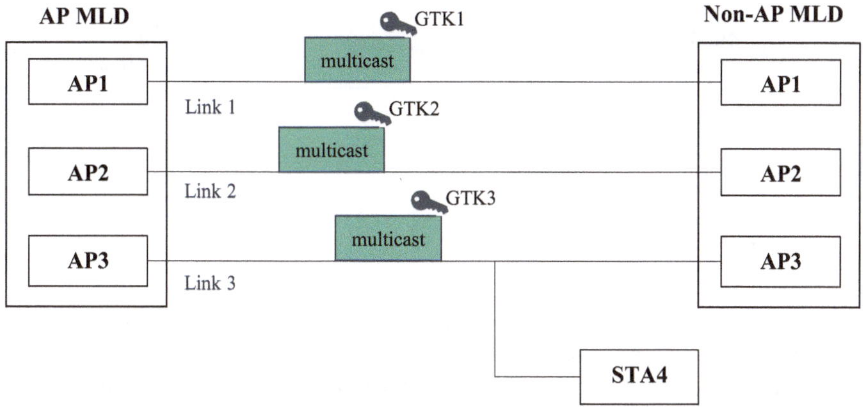

Fig. 3.121 Encrypted multicast traffic transmission over multi-links

2. **The Encryption of Multicast Traffic of MLD**

The AP MLDs transmit the multicast data frames across all links. Non-AP MLD can opt to receive these data frames on any single links or across multiple links. They then check the frame sequence number to eliminate duplicates. Multicast data frames are encrypted with different GTKs for each link.

As shown in Fig. 3.121, the AP MLD establishes a multi-link connection with a non-AP MLD and a single-link connection with STA4 over the 6 GHz band. The multicast data is encrypted respectively with GTK1, GTK2, and GTK3, and transmitted to both the affiliated STAs of the non-AP MLD and STA4.

Because each link has a different channel state, and some STAs may be in dormant mode, multicast data frames are transmitted independently on each link and are not necessarily synchronized with those on other links.

If a non-AP MLD opts to receive multicast traffic through multiple links, it decrypts the data using the respective the GTK for each link, reorders the frames by sequence number, removes any duplicates, and then forwards them to the upper-layer applications.

If a non-AP MLD chooses to receive multicast traffic through a single link, the process is same as that for traditional single-link STAs.

3.5.4.2 The Key Exchange Procedure for MLD

The WPA3 authentication for MLD is similar to that of single-link devices using WPA3. Initially, the PMK is generated based on SAE protocol, followed by the generation of the PTK through the 4-way handshake procedure. As illustrated in Fig. 3.122, the MAC addresses of the MLD are utilized for key generation, rather than the MAC addresses of each individual link. Consequently, the PTK is shared

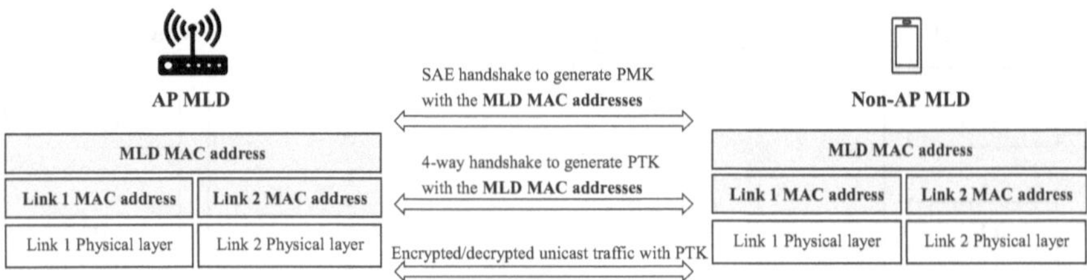

Fig. 3.122 PTK exchange procedure for MLDs

among all the links and is employed for the encryption and decryption of unicast traffic.

Regarding multicast, each link of the AP MLD has its own individual GTK for encryption and decryption of multicast traffic. The AP-MLD passes all the GTKs to the non-AP MLD, and the non-AP MLD uses the GTKs to decrypt the multicast traffic. It also compares the RSNE element in the data frames with its local RSNE to verify validity.

1. **Changes in the SAE Protocol for PMK Generation**

The SAE protocol requires that the MAC addresses of the AP MLD and the non-AP MLD be used to generate the keys. For example, when generating the hashed_password for the primitive root P(x,y) on the elliptic curve in the Eq. 3.4, the AP_MAC is the MLD MAC address of the AP MLD, and the STA_MAC is the MLD MAC address of the non-AP MLD.

2. **Changes in the 4-way Handshake Procedure for PTK/GTK Generation**

In the 4-way handshake procedure, the changes for MLD support includes adapting the MLD MAC addresses, the MLO RSNE, and the MLO GTK.

(1) **MLD MAC Address Used for PTK Generation**

After the SAE handshake, the AP and the STA negotiate and generate the PTK through the 4-way handshake procedure according to Eq. 3.3, i.e.,

$$\text{PTK} = \text{PRF (PMK, ANonce, SNonce, AA, SPA)}$$

For MLD devices, AA here is the MLD MAC address of the AP MLD, while the SPA is the MLD MAC address of the non-AP MLD.

(2) **MLO RSNE**

During the 4-way handshake, the AP MLD sends the MLO RSNE element to the non-AP MLD for verification. This element contains the link number and RSNE information for each link, including Authentication Key Management Suite, Pairwise Cipher Suite, Group Data Cipher, Group Management Cipher Suite, etc. For an MLD, the authentication key management, the PTK and GTK generation algorithms for unicast and multicast traffic are same for all links. However, it is not

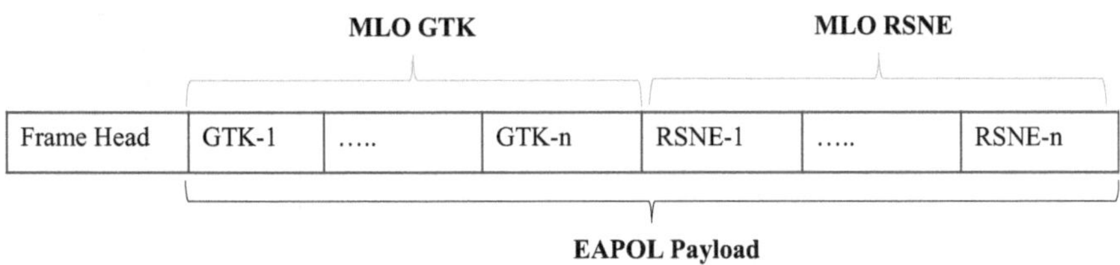

Fig. 3.123 The EAPOL frame format with MLO GTK and MLO RSNE

mandatory for each link to encrypt the management frames, so the RSNE could differ for each link.

For example, on the 2.4 GHz and 5 GHz bands, an AP MLD may be configured to non-forced management frame encryption mode to ensure backward compatible and interoperability with STAs that do not support management frame encryption. However, on the 6 GHz band, the AP MLD can be configured in forced management frame encryption mode.

3. **MLO GTK for Multicast Traffic**

Each link of the AP MLD uses its own individual GTK to encrypt and decrypt multicast traffic. During the four-way handshake, the AP MLD sends the MLO GTK to the non-AP MLD, which specifies the link number and the corresponding GTK for each link. The non-AP MLD then uses the GTK to decrypt the multicast traffic and compares the RSNE element in the data frames to its local RSNE to verify their validity.

The format of the third EAPOL frame, which contains the GTK and the RSNE for MLD is illustrated in Fig. 3.123. The MLO GTK element and MLO RSNE element are located within the payload body of the EAPOL frame.

3.5.4.3 The CCMP Encryption and the Updates in Wi-Fi 7

This section describes the principle of the CCMP encryption and what has been updated in the Wi-Fi 7 standard to support MLD.

1. **The Principle of CCMP**

As introduced in the previous sections, to counteract replay attacks where sniffers resend duplicate packets to the receiver by altering header information fields, data frames encrypted using CCMP include not only the original upper-layer data but also a CCMP header field and a Message Integrity Code (MIC) field. The generation of these fields is related to the MAC header fields and the frame number of the data frame.

As shown in Fig. 3.124, the CCMP encrypts the payload of a plain-text MPDU using the following input parameters:

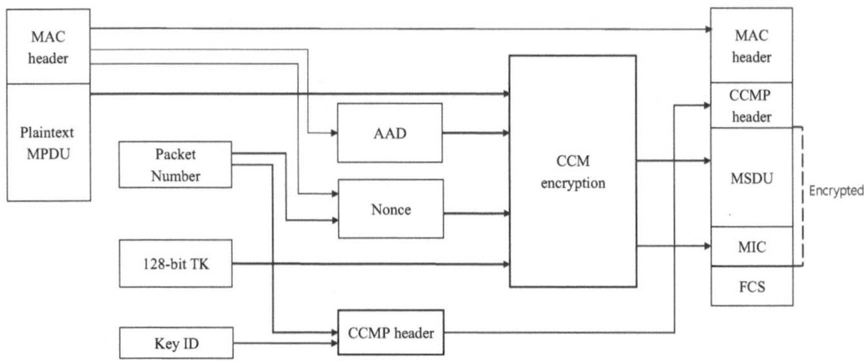

Fig. 3.124 CCMP encapsulation diagram

(1) The Additional Authentication Data (AAD), which is derived from the MAC addresses, frame sequence number, and QoS control in the MAC header. This information is used for data integrity of MAC header fields.
(2) A nonce, which is generated based on the combination of the packet number (PN) and the transmitter address, and priority data used in the QoS.
(3) 128-bit Temporal Key (TK), as part of the PTK.
(4) Key ID combined with TK to construct CCMP header.

The encapsulated CCMP MPDU consists of the original MAC header, CCMP header, the MSDU upper-layer payload, and the MIC. The CCMP does not encrypt the Packet Number and Key Id, which allows the receiver to extract these values directly from the CCMP header. Subsequently, the receiver derives the Nonce and the Additional Authentication Data (AAD) based on the information contained in the MAC header.

Once the receiver has obtained the AAD, the Nonce, and the 128-bit Temporal Key (TK), it uses these parameters to decrypt the encrypted MSDU (MAC Service Data Unit) and the Message Integrity Check (MIC). By verifying the Key Confirmation Key (KCK) derived from the MIC field, the receiver ensures the authenticity and integrity of the decrypted data.

2. **The Updates of CCMP for MLD**

Since the unicast data frame may be transmitted and retransmitted across any of the multiple links, so in case of a retransmission occurring on another link, the MAC address in the header shall be replaced with the MAC address corresponding to the new link.

To support the multi-link devices, the CCMP is adapted as follows:

(1) The nonce does not depend on the MAC address of any specific links; instead, it is generated using either the MLD MAC address of the AP MLD or the non-AP MLD.

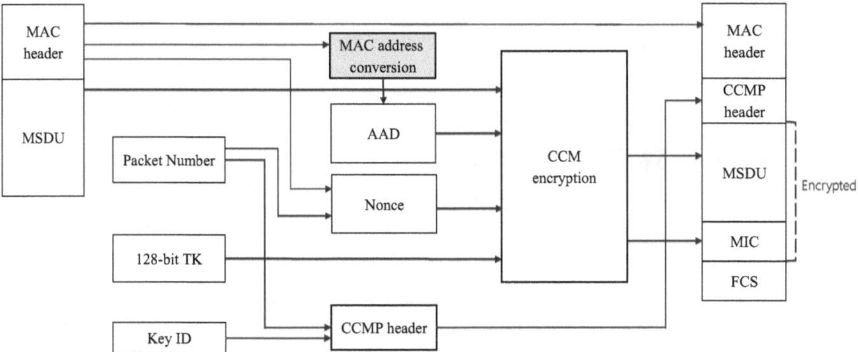

Fig. 3.125 CCMP encapsulation for MLD

(2) The unicast data frames in the MLD system are consistently numbered at the upper MLD MAC layer. The sequence number remains unique and continuous across all links.
(3) The AAD field is derived based on the MLD MAC address and does not refer to the individual links specifically.

As an example, consider the AAD field: In Fig. 3.125, multi-link device's CCMP implementation features an extra MAC address conversion module. This module maps the transmitter and the receiver MAC address to their corresponding MLD MAC addresses to generate the AAD. The same MAC address conversion process is required at the receiver side for decrypting the data frames.

3.6 Mesh Networking with Wi-Fi 7

The transmission power of the wireless signal is subject to national or regional regulations. For instance, in many countries, the maximum transmission power of the 2.4 GHz band is limited to 20dbm, which confines the Wi-Fi signal to a limited space. Additionally, indoor environment can cause the Wi-Fi signal to be attenuated by the walls, the furniture, and other obstacles.

To enhance Wi-Fi signal coverage, one straightforward solution is the installation of a Wi-Fi repeater. As depicted in Fig. 3.126, a repeater can connect to the AP router through a wired or wireless connection, relaying communications between the AP router and the STA. When a STA moves to an area with weak connection to the AP router, the STA switches to a repeater that offers a stronger signal quality.

The repeater can expand the coverage of home wireless network. However, it typically operates independently without real-time coordination with the AP router. Essentially, it creates a second BSS within the home. The choice of which network device (AP or repeater) to connect to is determined by the STA based on factors such as signal strength and network configuration. This may sometimes lead to a STA

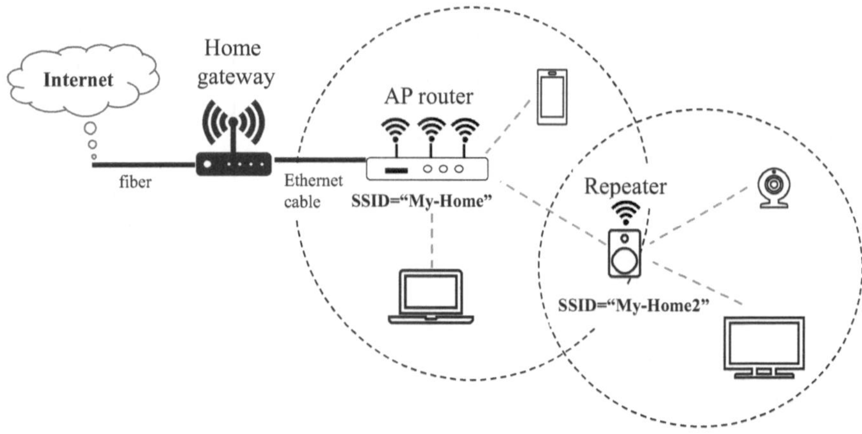

Fig. 3.126 A home network with a Wi-Fi repeater

remaining connected to a suboptimal BSS—even when a better connection is available with another BSS. In addition, if a repeater is improperly positioned, it could potentially worsen network performance rather than improve it.

The technology designed to overcome the shortcomings of Wi-Fi repeater is known as whole-home Wi-Fi. There is a growing demand to deploy multiple APs within homes to create a cohesive indoor wireless network. These APs communicate and coordinate with each other to provide comprehensive coverage and enable seamless roaming. When a STA moves from one room to another within the home, it remains connected to the network through the AP that offers the strongest signal, ensuring an uninterrupted connection.

To facilitate Wi-Fi networking, IEEE defines the 802.11s Wireless Mesh Network (WMN) protocol, as a supplement to the 802.11 MAC layer. The 802.11s standard specifies the framework for constructing a mesh network using the existing 802.11a/b/g/n protocols. In this mesh network, each AP has the capability to receive, forward data, and communicate with other APs within the network.

The 802.11s protocol is utilized in enterprise Wi-Fi environments, which typically require a large array of APs to provide extensive coverage across office spaces and public areas, ensuring high performance for commercial applications. The Enterprise APs are commonly installed on ceiling and connected to the switches by Ethernet cables, as depicted in Fig. 3.127.

Compared to enterprise network, home networks are relatively simple. Typically, a small number of APs are sufficient to cover the living spaces. These APs are often setup in either a tree or a star topology and managed by a single root AP, rather than having each AP communicate directly with each other.

Home network AP routers typically do not support the more complex 802.11s standard, largely due to cost considerations. Before Wi-Fi Alliance ratifies a multi-AP standard, APs use proprietary messaging and management models to set up the

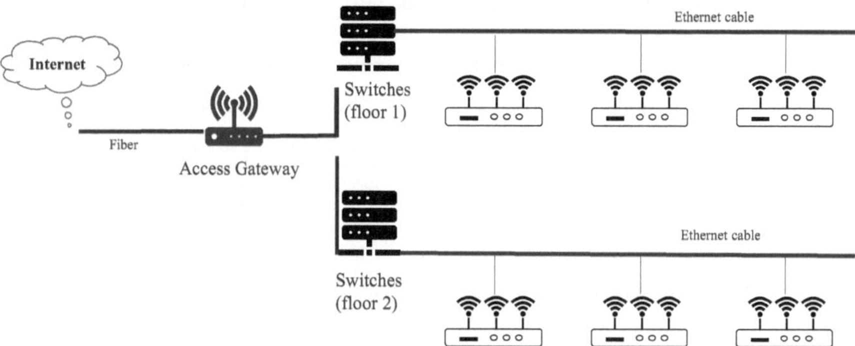

Fig. 3.127 Enterprise Wi-Fi network

Wi-Fi networks. Consequently, APs from different manufacturers could not interoperate with each other and form a network.

In 2018, Wi-Fi Alliance ratified the multi-AP specification, which enables interoperability across Wi-Fi APs from various vendors within a single Wi-Fi network. The WFA also defines a certification program to ensure compliance with the Multi-AP specification.

EasyMesh™ is Wi-Fi Alliance's trademark for its certification program, which validates implementations of the Multi-AP specification. EasyMesh certification is granted to devices that perform either mesh controller or agent roles. When AP products are EasyMesh certified, they are capable of interoperating with one another to form an EasyMesh network. In this section, we will explore multi-AP technology and its adaption to support Wi-Fi 7 multi-link operation.

3.6.1 Overview on Wi-Fi Multi-AP Technology

The Multi-AP specification defines the control protocols between multiple APs along with the essential data objects required to facilitate onboarding, provisioning, control, and management of the multi-AP network. Additionally, the specification outlines the mechanism for routing traffic between the APs within a multi-AP network. The evolution of the WFA Multi-AP standards is illustrated as Fig. 3.128.

(1) The Multi-AP Release 1 (R1) specification, ratified in 2018, establishes the fundamental framework for mesh interoperability, covering essential functions such as device onboarding, client steering, and Wi-Fi backhaul optimization.
(2) The Multi-AP Release 2(R2) specification ratified in 2019 introduces advanced functionality to enhance network management capabilities and user experience. These include VLAN traffic separation, refined client steering, channel management, and diagnostic support.

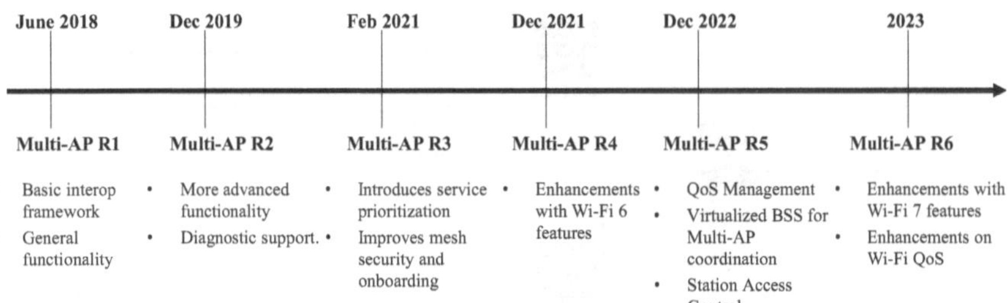

Fig. 3.128 Evolution of Wi-Fi Alliance Multi-AP specifications

(3) The Multi-AP Release 3 (R3) specification further enhances the ecosystem by introducing service prioritization and improving the security of control messages between multiple APs as well as the onboarding process. All features in R3 are optional.
(4) The WFA consolidated previous iterations into the Multi-AP Release 4(R4), incorporating Wi-Fi 6 features such as BSS Coloring with Spatial Reuse Groups, etc.
(5) In 2022, the Release 5(R5) was ratified, bringing in the traffic QoS management, station access control, and Virtualized BSS (VBSS) technology to improve coordination between multiple APs and enhance the roaming experience. All features included in R5 features are optional.
(6) In 2023, the Multi-AP Release 6 (R6) was ratified, adapts to Wi-Fi 7 features, including multi-link operation and static puncturing. It also bolsters the diagnosis capabilities and Wi-Fi QoS Management stream classification service.

3.6.1.1 EasyMesh Network Topology

The EasyMesh network is structured as a tree topology, consisting of a Multi-AP Controller at the root, several Multi-AP agents and various Wi-Fi stations. Controller and Agent designate the distinct roles that multi-AP devices plan with a Wi-Fi EasyMesh network. A multi-AP device acting as the Multi-AP controller is referred as the root AP, whereas a Multi-AP device functioning solely as an agent is known as the extender AP. Typically a root AP incorporates both the controller and the agent. However, it is possible for a root AP to be a device that lacks Wi-Fi function; in such cases, it contains only the controller module and not the agent.

1. **EasyMesh Controller**

The controller is a logical entity that operates on a home gateway or an AP router with a WAN connection to the access network. It functions as the central intelligence of the entire EasyMesh network, overseeing network configuration, control, and management.

- **WAN interface:** The controller aggregates the traffic from all nodes in the EasyMesh network and routes it to the access network.
- **Network control and management:** The controller is responsible for managing the device onboarding and the backhaul, as well as coordinating the agents to optimize the mesh network's performance.
- **Network provisioning:** Network configuration is managed by the user or the network administrator through the controller. The controller ensures that settings such as channel settings, SSID, the credentials are consistently synchronized across all agents.

2. **EasyMesh Agent**

The EasyMesh agents are also logical entities operating on all Wi-Fi AP nodes. Both the controller and agent can be hosted on the same AP router, which possesses a WAN connection to the Internet.

Within the EasyMesh network, there are two types of connections:

- **Backhaul**: This is either a wired or wireless connection between the controller and an agent, or between the agents.
- **Fronthaul:** The connection exists between an agent and a Wi-Fi station.

If an extender AP is distant from the root AP, it will initially connect to a neighboring AP that has a direct connection to the root AP. Some extender APs may require multiple hops to reach the root. In scenarios where there are multiple paths for the backhaul connection, the root AP determines the optimal path for the extender AP to take in order to enhance the network performance. At given time, only one active backhaul link is permitted between any two Multi-AP devices.

An agent connects to the Controller either directly or indirectly via a wired or wireless backhaul connection. The wired connection can include Ethernet, coaxial cable, power line communication, etc. Typically, Wi-Fi backhaul incurs more latency compared with an Ethernet backhaul.

The agent executes the instructions received from the EasyMesh Controller, reports measurements and capabilities to the Controller and other Agents within the EasyMesh network, and provides the fronthaul connection to the stations.

An example of an EasyMesh network topology is depicted as Fig. 3.129. In this scenario, the Wi-Fi AP with a WAN connection to the Internet serves as the controller, comprising an agent role itself along with three additional APs in the network. Agent 1 and Agent 3 connect to the controller through Wi-Fi backhaul, and Agent 2 utilizes an Ethernet backhaul. All agents provide the fronthaul connection to their respective stations.

The EasyMesh specification integrates, reuses, and extends various mature technologies to define how multiple APs can cooperatively establish a Wi-Fi network. Considering that the backhaul within an EasyMesh network may span different mediums, in order to accommodate the diverse MAC layer standards, the IEEE 1905 protocol is introduced as the intermedium layer positioned between the MAC layer and the logical link layer, as depicted in Fig. 3.130.

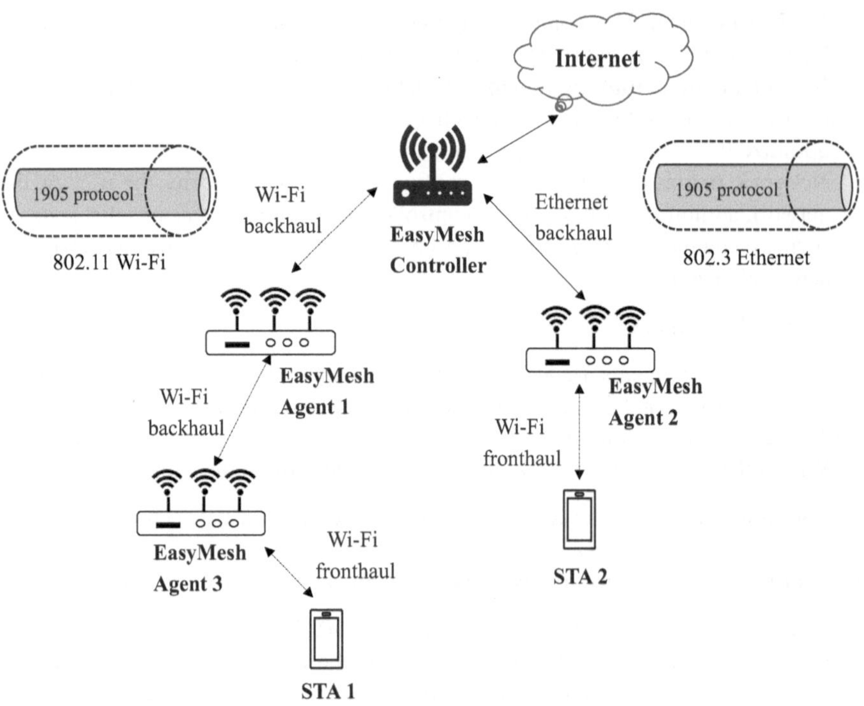

Fig. 3.129 Backhaul and fronthaul of EasyMesh network

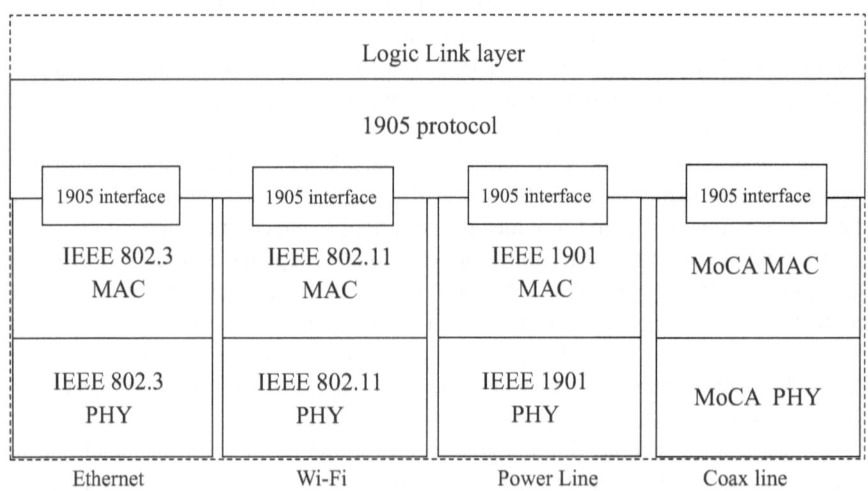

Fig. 3.130 IEEE 1905 protocol

3.6.1.2 EasyMesh Control Messages

The EasyMesh specification outlines a control protocol for the onboarding, provisioning, management, and control of multiple APs.

1. **AP Capability Report**

Within an EasyMesh network, mesh agents may originate from various vendors and possess different capabilities regarding operational frequency bands, maximum bandwidth, the number of antennas, data rate, etc. As an EasyMesh agent joins the network, it reports its capability to the controller. The controller then compiles the capabilities of each agent to dynamically optimize the EasyMesh network topology. This includes adjusting the operating channel, managing client roaming and implementing load balancing to enhance the overall performance of the EasyMesh network.

2. **Channel Selection and Transmit Power Control**

The controller is tasked with managing the operating channel and the transmit power for each agent. If agents are operating on different channels, the controller may set each node to the maximum permissible transmission power to boost signal strength and coverage. Conversely, if nodes are working on the same channel, the controller will determine an appropriate transmission power for each node to minimize interference among the mesh nodes.

3. **Link Metrics Report**

Wi-Fi signal strength can fluctuate in response to changes in the environment changes. The link state between mesh nodes, as well as between a node and the client, is quantified and periodically reported to the controller. This enables the controller to adapt to these variations. For instance, if the controller identifies that a mesh agent is experiencing from significant signal interference, it will direct the agent to switch to a cleaner channel immediately.

4. **Client Steering and Load Balancing**

The controller issues instruction to the agents to direct client stations to roam from one node to another, achieving network load balancing. Additionally, the controller can steer a client to a mesh node with fewer hops to the WAN to provide services that require high bandwidth and low latency.

5. **Backhaul Optimization**

The controller dynamically adjusts the network topology based on node status and link metrics. For instance, if a mesh node's Ethernet connection encounters a problem, the controller will switch the backhaul from Ethernet to Wi-Fi, enabling the mesh network to self-heal. When the Ethernet connection is restored, the controller will revert the node to Ethernet backhaul to ensure optimal connectivity.

3.6.1.3 Features of EasyMesh

The EasyMesh specification outlines the mechanism through which multiple APs can onboard and collaborate with each other. It employs a self-optimized architecture designed to deliver high-performance services for stations roaming within home or enterprise Wi-Fi networks. The specification includes the following features:

1. **Self-organized and Self-learning**

The EasyMesh controller learns the environment by collecting the link metrics, AP capability, and client metrics from the agents and adapts autonomously. Should the 2.4 GHz band experience severe interference, the controller would steer the dual-band STAs to the clean 5 GHz band to have a stable performance, and leave only the single-band STAs operating at 2.4 GHz. The network configurations are synchronized to the agents whenever the changes happen. When the user modifies the configurations of the EasyMesh network through the web UI or mobile App, such as renaming the SSID or changing the password, the controller applies the new configuration and synchronizes it among all the agents in the network.

2. **Self-healing**

The EasyMesh network is capable of optimizing the backhaul connection and recovering from node failures. For instance, if an extender AP is relocated from the bedroom to the kitchen, the controller optimizes the topology without requiring intervention from the end user. If an agent fails, the other nodes can proactively reconnect and restore their connection to the root AP, as the exemplified in Fig. 3.131. When Agent 2 goes out of service, the backhaul of Agent 3 is disrupted. Agent 3 then switches to Agent 1 to reestablish the backhaul connection and continue serving the client stations. The controller updates the network topology and reports the state of Agent 2 to network management in real time.

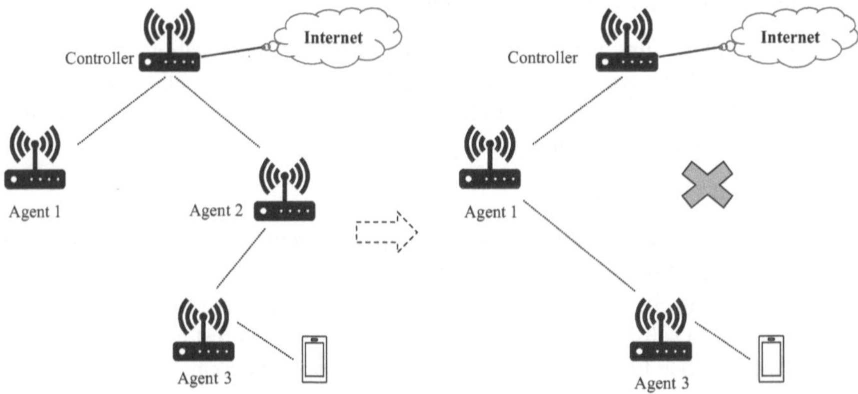

Fig. 3.131 Self-healing of EasyMesh network

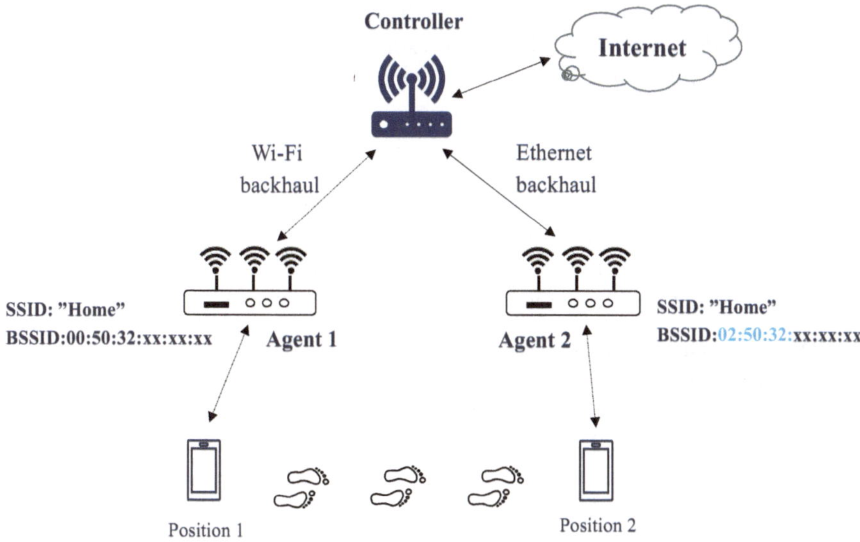

Fig. 3.132 Client roaming of EasyMesh network

3. **Client Roaming**

The EasyMesh controller continuously monitors the signal strength of client stations and determines the optimal time for a client to roam from one node to another to maintain the best possible connection. If a client's RSSI falls below a predefined threshold, the controller steers it toward the most suitable AP. The EasyMesh controller decides to steer the clients to another node in case many clients are connected to the same node and degrade the overall performance, which is referred as load balancing.

As Fig. 3.132, within an EasyMesh network, when a STA moves from position 1 to position 2, it gets further from the Agent 1 and the signal becomes weak. To prevent any degradation in Wi-Fi performance, the controller selects Agent 2 based on signal strength and traffic load data, and then steers the STA to disconnect from Agent 1 and reconnect with Agent 2 automatically. The user doesn't have to manually select or reconnect to the network; instead, they are unaware that their device has seamlessly roamed to another AP within the EasyMesh network.

In the EasyMesh network, while multi-APs share the same SSID, each has a different BSSID. When a STA roams to the AP2, it must regenerate the encryption keys using the MAC address of the new AP. It is worth noting that this key negotiation process may cause a brief interruption in data transmission, potentially affecting the user experience, particularly for services requiring ultra-low latency.

4. **Virtualized BSS**

In 2022, the EasyMesh R5 standard was ratified, introducing the Virtualized BSS (vBSS) feature for the first time, aimed at delivering a seamless roaming user experience.

The vBSS technology creates a virtualized BSS for each STA, where each virtualized BSS serves a specific STA exclusively. The controller dynamically creates or instantiates the vBSS on an agent, complete with its security context tailored to the STA, without necessitating a conventional association/authentication procedure. Additionally, it can delete the vBSS on an agent even with or without disassociation.

The vBSS management employs a "make before break" methodology, ensuring that as the STA roams between different physical APs, it remains continuously connected to its dedicated vBSS and thereby avoids packet loss during handovers.

The Virtualized BSS technology has the following features:

A vBSS Serves a Dedicated STA
The controller establishes a virtualized BSS for each STA. The EasyMesh agent interacts with the STA using existing Wi-Fi management and control frames to facilitate support vBSS. Notably, Beacon frames are sent as a unicast message directly to the target STA, which means that other STAs are unable to detect or discover the virtualized BSS.

vBSS Transfer Along with the Client Roaming
When the controller detects the signal strength of a STA has dropped below a predetermined threshold and identifies another agent capable of providing better signal coverage, it will instantiate a vBSS on the alternative agent while synchronizing the configuration from the previous agent, such as the connection status, encryption key, and other relevant settings on. The new vBSS instance then takes over the client connection. Subsequently, the vBSS on the original agent is deleted.

Band Steering and Channel Selection
The APs in the EasyMesh network may possess varying capabilities, including supported frequency bands, bandwidth, and operating channel. For adjacent APs that share the same frequency band, the controller might configure them to operate on different channels to prevent channel competition and interference. Consequently, during the transition of the virtualized BSS from one agent to another, it might switch to utilizing another band, channel, or channel bandwidth. As a result, prior to transitioning to the new agent, the virtualized BSS directs the STA to switch to the new band or channel. Subsequently, the STA adheres to the new channel of the new agent.

Ultra-Low Latency
The client stations remain connected to the vBSS when they roam within the coverage of the EasyMesh network, resulting in minimum latency and even zero-latency. This ensures a superior user experience for services that demand ultra-low latency, such as AR/VR applications used with headsets.

An example illustrating how the Virtualized BSS operates is provided in Fig. 3.133.

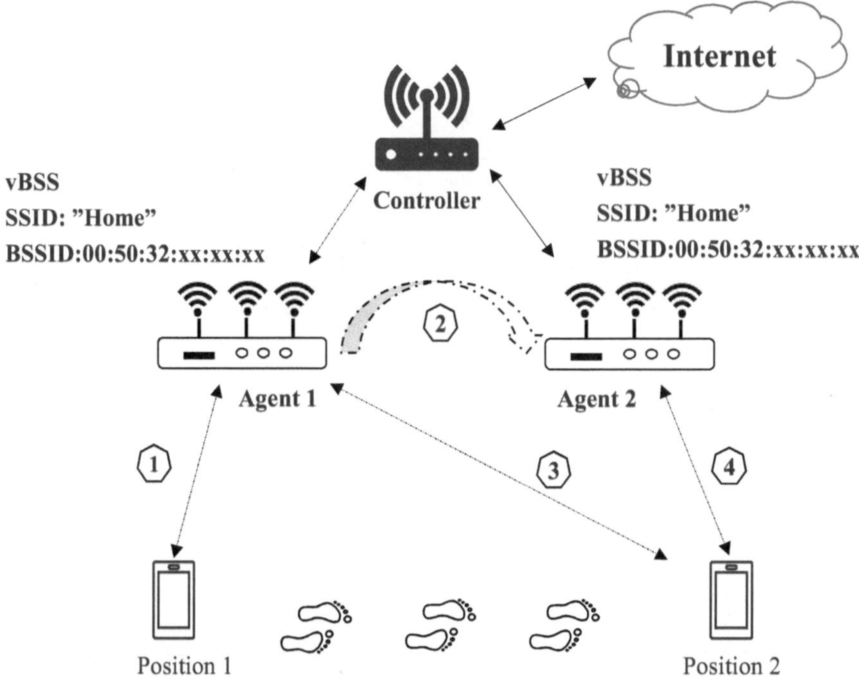

Fig. 3.133 Client roaming in a vBSS

(1) The controller creates a Virtualized BSS for the mobile phone on Agent 1. The phone receives the unicast Beacon frames and maintains time synchronization just like it would with a normal BSS.
(2) When the mobile phone moves from position 1 to position 2, the controller detects that its RSSI has fallen below a predefined threshold. Simultaneously, it recognizes that Agent 2 is closer to phone. Therefore, the controller duplicates the Virtualized BSS information and creates an identical instance at Agent 2.
(3) The Virtualized BSS of Agent 1 sends an instruction to the STA to switch to the new channel of Agent 2, after which the controller removes the vBSS instance on the Agent 1.
(4) The STA switches to the new operating channel of Agent 2 and begins receiving the unicast Beacon frames from the new vBSS instance. Throughout the entire roaming process, the STA remains connected to the same SSID/BSSID and is not aware that it has switched between multiple APs.

In EasyMesh R5, the specification of a Virtualized BSS is designed to accommodate only one STA at any given time. This approach aims to ensure compatibility with existing AP devices and minimize the impact on Wi-Fi chipset designs, thereby making the vBSS technology more readily adoptable by manufacturers across the industry. In the current specification, the Virtualized BSS technology does not support features such as OFDMA and MU-MIMO, nor does it facilitate peer-to-

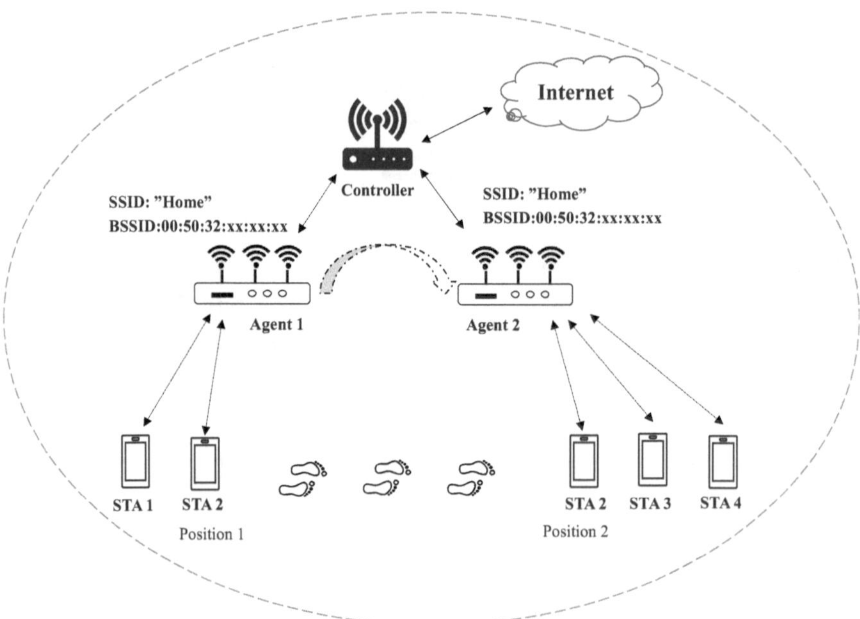

Fig. 3.134 A proprietary implementation of fast roaming within the EasyMesh network

peer communication through TDLS technology. If these advanced capabilities, specifically OFDMA and MU-MIMO, were to be incorporated into the vBSS technology, there would be significant improvements in throughput, latency, and roaming performance. The evolution of the vBSS technology is expected to continue in subsequent EasyMesh specifications,

Apart from the vBSS technology, some vendors have proprietary solutions aimed at optimizing roaming performance. One such option is illustrated in Fig. 3.134. In this scenario, the agents share the same BSSID within the EasyMesh network. When a STA establishes a connection to one of the agents, the controller synchronizes the encryption keys with other nodes. This allows the STA to roam between different agents without having to reconnect. Subsequently, when the controller detects that the RSSI of the STA2 is below the threshold, it synchronizes the information of the STA2 from Agent 1 to Agent 2 and then instructs Agent 2 to take over the connection to the STA2.

Similar to the vBSS technology, in this case, the STA2 is unaware that the connection has passed from Agent 1 to Agent 2. As the BSS is not dedicated to any STA, so the Beacon frames are broadcast to all STAs.

3.6.2 *Mesh Networking Update with Wi-Fi 7 Support*

In a Wi-Fi 7 EasyMesh network, the EasyMesh controller, agents, and STAs could be multi-link devices or a combination of legacy single-link devices and multi-link devices, which introduces additional complexity to the EasyMesh control and management protocols. In the year 2023, Wi-Fi Alliance ratified EasyMesh Release 6(R6) [9], incorporating support for Wi-Fi 7 multi-link operation as well as Preamble Puncturing features.

3.6.2.1 The EasyMesh Network Consists Only Wi-Fi 7 MLDs

The Wi-Fi 7 multi-link operation can effectively enhance the throughput of an EasyMesh network. The EasyMesh controller, as a Multi-Link Device (MLD), establishes multi-link connections with agent MLDs, and these agents also connect to the non-AP MLDs over multi-links.

This section describes the networking topology of Wi-Fi 7 MLDs within EasyMesh and discuss the roaming of Wi-Fi 7 non-AP MLDs within this context.

1. **EasyMesh Network Topology of Wi-Fi 7 MLDs**

Figure 3.135 presents an example of an EasyMesh networking topology of Wi-Fi 7 MLDs. The controller, Agent 1, and Agent 2 are all Wi-Fi 7 AP MLDs. Specifically, Agent 1 connects to the controller using a Wi-Fi backhaul link, while Agent 2 employs an Ethernet backhaul connection. The STA1 and STA2 are non-AP

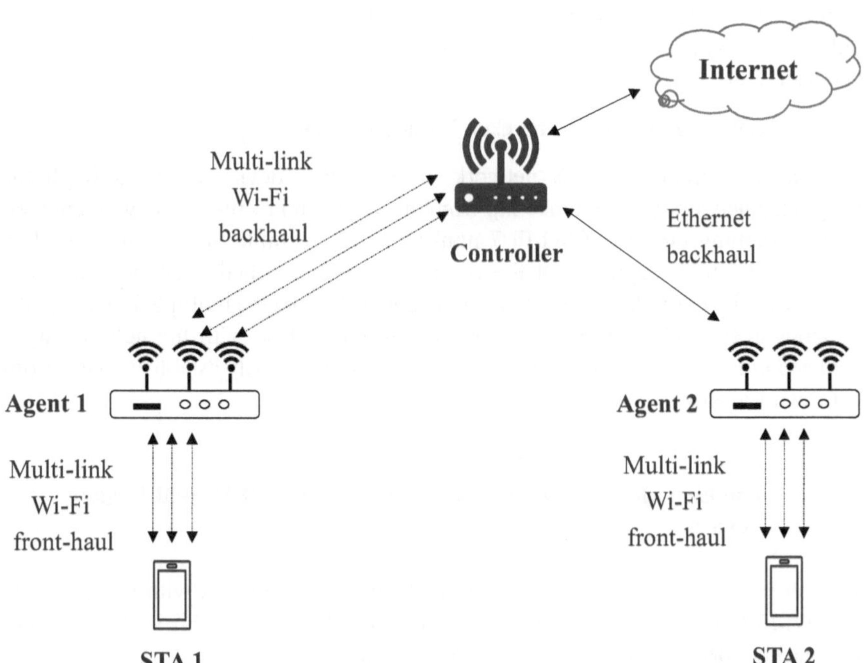

Fig. 3.135 An EasyMesh network of Wi-Fi 7 MLDs

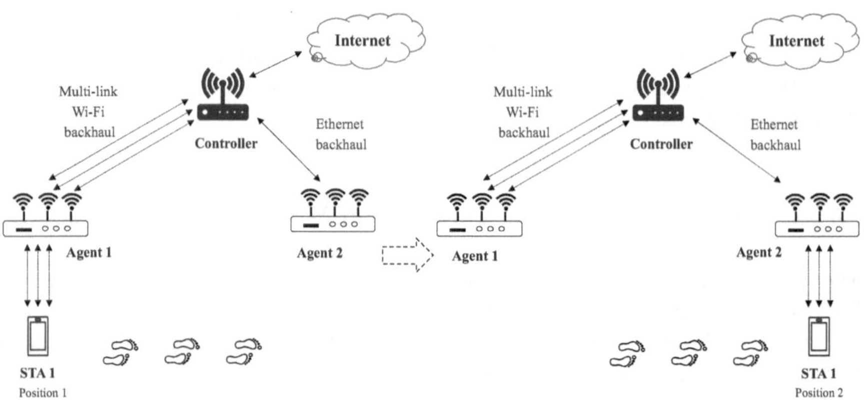

Fig. 3.136 An example of a non-AP MLD roam at an EasyMesh network

MLDs, and their fronthaul connections with the agents are established through multi-link Wi-Fi links.

If the Controller, agents and STAs possess different MLO capabilities, then the backhaul and the fronthaul connections can only be established on links that are mutually supported by both entities involved. For instance, if both the Controller and Agent 1 each support three links, but STA1 only supports 2.4 GHz and 5 GHz links. In such a scenario, STA1 would establish a dual-link connection with Agent 1. Similarly, if the Controller supports three links while an Agent supports two links, the backhaul connection would be configured over those two common links between them.

2. **Non-AP MLD Roam in the EasyMesh Network**

In a non-Virtualized BSS network, a single-link device roams through the EasyMesh network by disconnecting from one agent and reconnecting with another.

The roaming process of Wi-Fi 7 non-AP MLD is similar to that of single-link device, with the exception that the connection is established over multiple links. When a Wi-Fi 7 non-AP MLD roams, it disconnects from the multiple links with the previous agent and re-establishes a multi-link connection with the new agent, as depicted in Fig. 3.136. A non-AP MLD cannot simultaneously establish connections with two EasyMesh agents.

3.6.2.2 The EasyMesh Network Consists of Wi-Fi 7 MLDs and Legacy Devices

The Wi-Fi 7 multi-link devices can be deployed in conjunction with legacy Wi-Fi 5 or Wi-Fi 6 devices to establish a hybrid EasyMesh network. This section outlines various network scenarios and the roaming behavior of STAs.

1. **Network Scenarios**

The Wi-Fi 7 multi-link operation offers a higher bandwidth connection and introduces much more flexible topology for an EasyMesh network. A hybrid EasyMesh network consists of a hybrid fronthaul network and a hybrid backhaul network.

- **Hybrid fronthaul network:** This can involve either a Wi-Fi 7 agent AP MLD connection to a Wi-Fi 6 STA or a Wi-Fi 6 agent connecting to a Wi-Fi 7 non-AP MLD.
- **Hybrid backhaul network:** This can involve either a Wi-Fi 7 controller AP MLD connecting to a Wi-Fi 6 agent or a Wi-Fi 6 controller connecting to a Wi-Fi 7 agent AP MLD.

2. **Fronthaul Connection Between a Wi-Fi 7 AP MLD and a Wi-Fi 6 STA**

When an EasyMesh agent AP MLD connects to a legacy single-link STA, it behaves the same as a legacy AP. The STA establishes a connection with the agent AP MLD over one of the links. As illustrated in Fig. 3.137, a tri-band Wi-Fi 7 AP MLD and a dual-band Wi-Fi 7 AP MLD forms an EasyMesh network utilizing the 5 GHz and 6 GHz dual-link backhaul. The throughput of the backhaul can reach 4.3 Gbps. Simultaneously, the dual-band AP MLD has the fronthaul with a Wi-Fi 6E client over the 6 GHz link, both operating at a 160 MHz bandwidth, resulting in the fronthaul throughput of 2.4 Gbps.

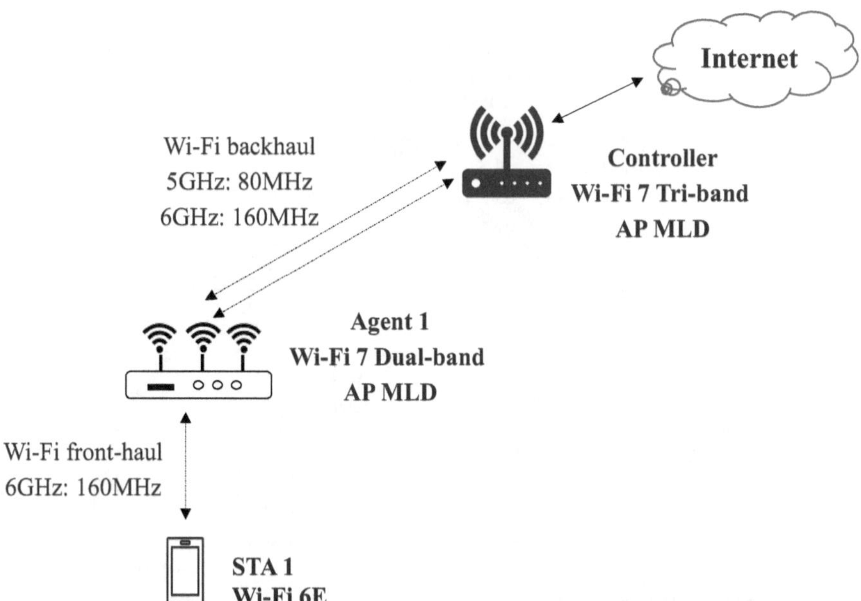

Fig. 3.137 Fronthaul connection between a Wi-Fi 7 AP MLD and a Wi-Fi 6 STA

3. **Fronthaul Connection Between a Wi-Fi 6 EasyMesh Agent and a Wi-Fi 7 Non-AP MLD**

A Wi-Fi 6 multi-band AP can be considered as multiple APs coexisting on the same physical wireless router. Even though it supports multiple bands, it does not allow connecting with a non-AP MLD over multiple bands. Therefore, the Wi-Fi 7 non-AP MLD can only establish a connection over one link with the Wi-Fi 6 AP.

4. **Backhaul Connection Between a Wi-Fi 7 AP MLD Controller and a Wi-Fi 6 Multi-band Agent**

A Wi-Fi 6 multi-band agent is not permitted to establish a connection over multiple links with a Wi-Fi 7 AP MLD Controller; instead, the connection must be maintained over a single link only.

Figure 3.138 illustrates three network scenarios mentioned above. The Controller, Agent 1, STA1, and STA4 are all multi-link devices, while Agent 2, STA2, and STA3 are Wi-Fi 6 devices which support multiple bands. The EasyMesh network tree consists of two branches:

- **Left branch 1:** The Controller establishes a multi-link backhaul connection with Agent 1 in channel 11 in the 2.4 GHz band, channel 149 in the 5GHz band, and channel 101 in the 6 GHz band. Agent 1 has the fronthaul connection with STA1 on the same channels of 3 links, as well as a single-link fronthaul connection with STA2 on channel 101 in the 6GHz band.

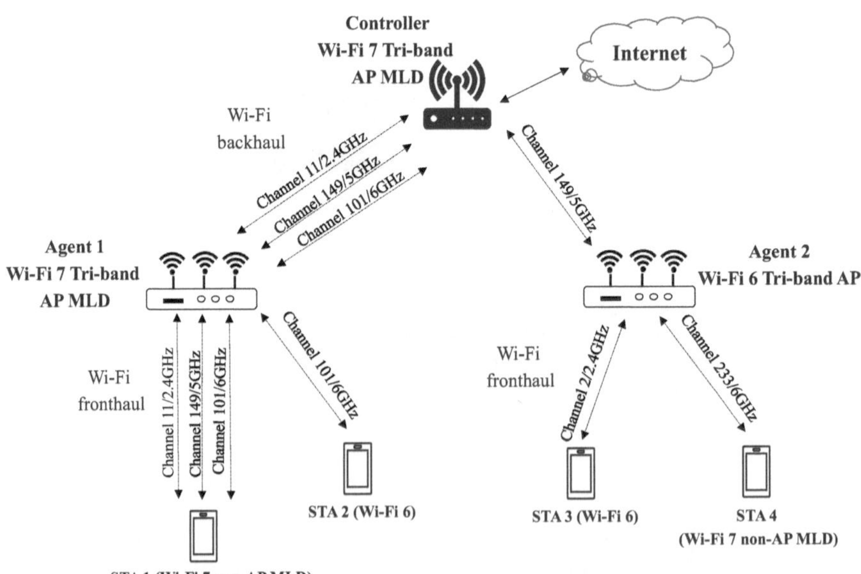

Fig. 3.138 A hybrid Wi-Fi 7 and Wi-Fi 6 EasyMesh network

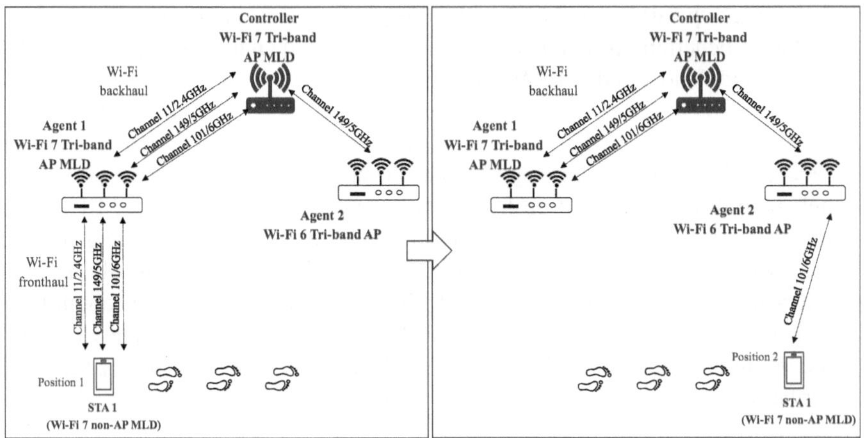

Fig. 3.139 Non-AP MLD roams in a hybrid EasyMesh network

- **Right branch 2:** Agent 2 establishes the backhaul connection with the Controller on channel 149 in the 5 GHz, and simultaneously, it has the fronthaul connection with STA3 in the 2.4 GHz band and with STA4 in the 6 GHz band.

5. **Wi-Fi 7 STA Roam Within a Hybrid EasyMesh Network**

A Wi-Fi 7 non-AP MLD can establish multi-link connections with Wi-Fi 7 AP MLD agents and single-link connections with Wi-Fi 6 agents, no matter whether they are single-band or multi-band. Consequently, when a Wi-Fi 7 non-AP MLD roams within a hybrid EasyMesh network from the coverage of a Wi-Fi 7 AP MLD Agent to that of a Wi-Fi 6 Agent, it transitions between multi-link and single-link operational modes accordingly.

An example is presented Fig. 3.139 The Controller, Agent 1, and STA1 are MLDs, while Agent 2 is a tri-band Wi-Fi 6 AP. As STA1 relocates from position 1 to position 2, it disconnects the multi-link fronthaul connection with Agent 1 and then re-establishes a new connection with Agent 2 on channel 101 of the 6 GHz band. Should the STA navigate back to position 1, it will revert its connection from single-link to multi-link, re-engaging with the multi-link capabilities of Agent 1.

3.7 Summary

The Wi-Fi 7 standard brings a multitude of innovative technologies to meet the demands of emerging application services that require ultra-high speed, massive concurrency, and ultra-low latency.

- **Ultra-high speed:** Wi-Fi 7 is capable of supporting a data transmission rate up to 36 Gbps, benefiting from the key technologies include multi-link operation, 4 K-QAM modulation, and 320 MHz bandwidth.
- **Massive concurrency:** Wi-Fi 7 can accommodate up to 148 concurrent OFDMA users within the 320 MHz bandwidth on the 6 GHz band. The introduction of Preamble Puncturing technology enables the aggregation of noncontiguous channels both downstream and upstream communications. Furthermore, MRU technology facilitates the bundling of multiple RUs, significantly enhancing support for a vast number of concurrent user operations with exceptional flexibility.
- **Ultra-low latency:** technologies in Wi-Fi 7, such as multi-link operation, QoS Characteristics, restricted TWT, TXOP sharing, and MRU, collectively contribute to reducing transmission latency, which is crucial for latency-sensitive services.

(1) **Multi-link operation:** The multi-link operation enables Wi-Fi 7 multi-link devices to transmit data across multiple combined bands, significantly enhancing bandwidth and throughput. Depending on the connection characteristics of various multi-link devices, the operation can be either synchronous or asynchronous. The Wi-Fi 7 standard has adapted network discovery, authentication, association process, and security protocols to support the MLO. Importantly, multi-link operation can also be utilized to boost the throughput of a TDLS or P2P Peer-to-Peer connection between two non-AP MLDs.

(2) **4 K-QAM modulation:** Wi-Fi 7 enhances the modulation scheme to 4096-QAM, with each symbol encoding 12 bits of information. The 4 K-QAM technology contributes to a 20% increase in throughput compared to Wi-Fi 6.

(3) **320 MHz bandwidth:** Wi-Fi 7 supports a maximum of 320 MHz bandwidth in the 6GHz band, effectively doubling the bandwidth and, consequently the throughput compared to Wi-Fi 6.

(4) **Restricted TWT:** Building on the b-TWT technology from Wi-Fi 6, Wi-Fi 7 specifies dedicated service periods for latency-sensitive services and introduces the Quiet Element to ensure priority access for APs.

(5) **TXOP sharing:** Wi-Fi 6 defines the channel access mode based on Trigger frame for OFDMA data transmission in the uplink direction. Wi-Fi 7 extends this to Peer-to-Peer transmission between two STAs, thereby achieving low latency in P2P scenarios.

(6) **MRU:** While Wi-Fi 6 supports transmitting downstream data on noncontiguous channels, Wi-Fi 7 extends this capability to support uplink direction as well. Moreover, this technology has been expanded from channel level to Resource Unit (RU) level. Wi-Fi 7 enables bundling of multiple RUs for data transmission.

This chapter also introduces the evolution of EasyMesh based on WFA multi-AP protocol. To enhance the user experience with seamless roaming and to support Wi-Fi 7 multi-link devices, Wi-Fi Alliance introduced the Virtualized BSS feature in EasyMesh R5 and the multi-link mode in EasyMesh R6.

References

1. IEEE (2023) Draft Standard for Information technology--Telecommunications and information exchange between systems Local and metropolitan area networks--Specific requirements - Part 11: Wireless LAN Medium Access Control (MAC) and Physical Layer (PHY) Specifications Amendment: Enhancements for Extremely High Throughput (EHT) (IEEE P802.11be/D5.0). November. pp. 1-1045
2. Cheng G, Yang ZJ (2020) New Wi-Fi technology survey after Wi-Fi6. Application of Electronic Technique, 46(4), 19-23. doi:https://doi.org/10.16157/j.issn.0258-7998.191372
3. Lopez-Perez D, Garcia-Rodriguez A, Galati-Giordano L, Kasslin M, Doppler K (2019) IEEE 802.11be Extremely High Throughput: The Next Generation of Wi-Fi Technology Beyond 802.11ax. IEEE Communications Magazine, 57(9), 113–119
4. Qualcomm (2021) The Benefits of OFDMA for Wi-Fi 6
5. FCC (2020) FCC Opens 6 GHz Band to Wi-Fi and Other Unlicensed Uses [online]. Available at: https://www.fcc.gov/document/fcc-opens-6-ghz-band-wi-fi-and-other-unlicensed-uses-0
6. IEEE (2020) IEEE Standard for Information Technology—Telecommunications and Information Exchange between Systems - Local and Metropolitan Area Networks—Specific Requirements - Part 11: Wireless LAN Medium Access Control (MAC) and Physical Layer (PHY) Specifications (Revision of IEEE Std 802.11-2016). IEEE Std 802.11-2020. pp. 1-4379. doi: https://doi.org/10.1109/IEEESTD.2021.9363693
7. Wi-Fi Alliance (2020) WPA3™ Specification (Version 3.0)
8. Harkins D (2015) RFC 7664: Dragonfly Key Exchange [S]. Internet Research Task Force (IRTF).
9. Wi-Fi Alliance (2023) Marketing Requirements Document for Wi-Fi EasyMesh™ Release 6 (R6) Program [Z]

References

Chapter 4
Wi-Fi 7 Product Development and Test Methods

Abstract Building upon the Wi-Fi fundamentals and the introduction of new Wi-Fi 7 technologies covered in previous chapters, this chapter offers a thorough overview of the Wi-Fi 7 Access Point (AP) product development process, touching on elements such as product specifications, key performance indicators, and the transformative implications of Wi-Fi 7 technology. It explores the general development practices for Wi-Fi products, which encompass system design and software development methodologies, and concludes with an examination of testing methodologies unique to Wi-Fi 7 products. Within the comprehensive development cycle, software implementation stands as a crucial phase in the realization of a Wi-Fi 7 AP. The chapter highlights principal software development focal points, including connection management, data forwarding, performance optimization, wireless channel management, as well as the development guidelines to support EasyMesh and network management. This approach aims to provide readers with profound insights into AP development from a software perspective.

4.1 Overview of Wi-Fi 7 Product Development

To develop Wi-Fi products, it is crucial to start with a comprehensive design based on system requirements analysis. This analysis should be driven by market demand for Wi-Fi services and involve identifying deployment scenarios the product must support, outlining essential functions it should provide, and establishing specifications it must adhere to.

Upon completing the product definition, the development process commences. This process typically involves crafting the system architecture, developing the product hardware and software, and rigorously testing the product's functionality and performance. An illustration of the product development process is depicted in Fig. 4.1.

G. Cheng et al., *Wi-Fi 7*, https://doi.org/10.1007/978-981-97-9026-5_4

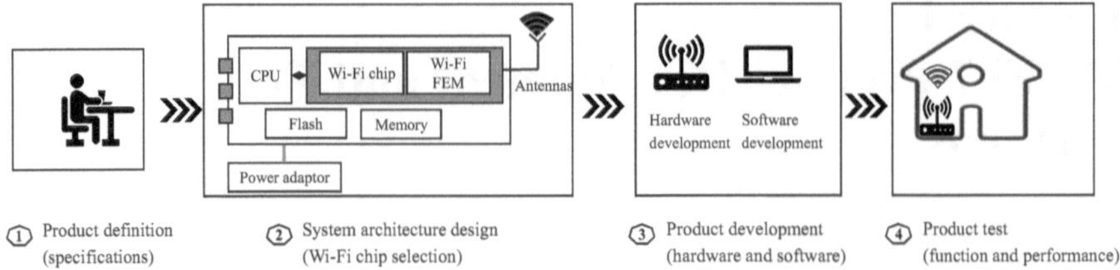

Fig. 4.1 Development process of Wi-Fi products

4.1.1 Wi-Fi 7 Product Definition and Specifications

4.1.1.1 The Demand for Wi-Fi Technology and Products in the Market

The global demand for Wi-Fi APs is primarily driven by operators' applications for broadband access and home wireless routers. Residential gateways (RGWs), which are equipped with Wi-Fi, typically support fiber or 5G uplink network interfaces, while home wireless routers often support Ethernet or Wi-Fi uplink network interfaces. The APs discussed in this book encompass a variety of residential gateways and home wireless routers.

Residential gateways and wireless routers are often categorized by the number of frequency bands they support. The common types include:

- **Single-band products**: Operate on the 2.4 GHz frequency band.
- **Dual-band products**: Operate on both the 2.4 GHz and 5 GHz frequency bands.
- **Tri-band products**: Combine the 5 GHz high band (5.8 GHz) and 5 GHz low band (5.1 GHz) with the 2.4 GHz band. With the introduction of Wi-Fi 6E, the standard that supports the 6 GHz frequency band, it is expected that tri-band products will support the 2.4 GHz, 5 GHz, and 6 GHz frequency bands.

The demand for Wi-Fi technology varies significantly from one region to another worldwide. Since around 2020, there has been an acceleration in Wi-Fi technology upgrades, particularly among telecom operators, who not only upgrade residential gateways for broadband access but also increasingly purchase and deploy wireless routers, which are considered vital for extending home networks. The following paragraphs outline the trends in the adoption of Wi-Fi technology by operators.

(1) **Wi-Fi 6 products have become mainstream in the market**

The demand for Wi-Fi 6 products varies across regions worldwide. In North America, operators are increasingly deploying high-end Wi-Fi 6 gateways or wireless routers, normally equipped with four antennas per band.

Operators in South America, Southeast Asia, and Europe mainly deployed Wi-Fi 5 dual-band gateways or wireless routers before 2022, with dual-band Wi-Fi 6 products now gradually gaining traction.

In the Chinese market, Wi-Fi 6 dual-band gateways have become standard products offered by operators. The transition from Wi-Fi 5 to Wi-Fi 6 products is

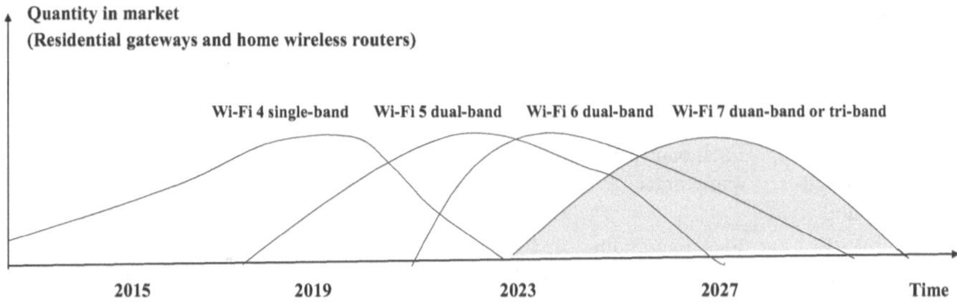

Fig. 4.2 Evolution of Wi-Fi products in the market

expected to be ongoing in 2024, indicating a continued shift toward the newer technology.

(2) **Promotion of Wi-Fi 6E products that support 6 GHz band**

The deployment of Wi-Fi 6E products, which support the 6 GHz band, has been available on the market since 2022. North America is the leading market for Wi-Fi 6E, followed by Europe and other regions.

(3) **The beginning of products that support Wi-Fi 7 technology**

Wi-Fi 7 chipset samples were demonstrated in 2022, with Wi-Fi 7 AP and STA products available in 2023 and 2024 on a limited scale. The market for Wi-Fi 7 products is projected to grow rapidly starting in 2025, positioning Wi-Fi 7 as a key technology in wireless networking for the next 5 years.

Figure 4.2 illustrates the evolution of products with different generations of Wi-Fi technology in the market, providing a reference for understanding market trends.

It can be observed that the evolution of products with different generations of Wi-Fi technology occurs every 3–4 years in the market. Additionally, there is a noticeable differentiation between low-end and high-end products within the same generation of Wi-Fi technology. For instance, in the case of Wi-Fi 5 technology, low-end AP products are typically dual-band AP products with two antennas for data transmission per band, whereas the high-end AP products are dual-band devices equipped with four antennas per band.

Similarly, with the advent of Wi-Fi 7 technology, it is expected that there will be various types of AP products available in the market, catering to both low-end and high-end segments. Refer to Table 4.1 for examples of different AP product types.

In this chapter, the introduction of Wi-Fi 7 development and testing will use the tri-band AP product listed in item 4 and the dual-band AP product listed in item 5 of Table 4.1 as basic reference models.

Table 4.1 Wi-Fi 7 AP product types

Index	Product types	Frequency bands and antennas	Description	Application scenarios
1	Wi-Fi 7 quad-band	Each band with 4 antennas	4x4 2.4 GHz,4x4 5 GHz low,4x4 5 GHz High,4x4 6 GHz	High-end residential gateway, Wi-Fi 7 AP
2	Wi-Fi 7 tri-band	Each band with 4 antennas	4x4 2.4 GHz,4x4 5 GHz,4x4 6 GHz	High-end residential gateway, Wi-Fi 7 AP
3	Wi-Fi 7 dual-band	Each band with 4 antennas	4x4 2.4 GHz,4x4 5 GHz	Mid-to-high end residential gateway, Wi-Fi 7 AP
4	Wi-Fi 7 tri-band	Each band with 2 antennas	2x2 2.4 GHz,2x2 5 GHz,2x2 6 GHz	Mid-to-low end residential gateway, Wi-Fi 7 AP
5	Wi-Fi 7 dual-band	Each band with 2 antennas	2x2 2.4 GHz,2x2 5 GHz	Low-end residential gateway, Wi-Fi 7 AP

Table 4.2 Wi-Fi 7 AP product specifications

Categories	Specifications	Dual-band product BE3600	Tri-band product BE9300
Wi-Fi parameters	Maximum physical rate	3600 Mbps	9300 Mbps
	Wi-Fi frequency bands	2.4 GHz, 5 GHz	2.4 GHz, 5 GHz, and 6 GHz
	Multiple-input multiple-output (MIMO)	2x2 for 2.4 GHz and 5 GHz bands	2x2 for 2.4 GHz, 5 GHz, and 6 GHz bands
	Maximum bandwidth	40 MHz for 2.4 GHz band, 160 MHz for 5 GHz band	40 MHz for 2.4 GHz band, 160 MHz for 5 GHz band, 320 MHz for 6 GHz band
	EasyMesh	Supported	Supported
Other parameters	Ethernet ports	Uplink Ethernet port: 2.5 Gbps; Ethernet LAN ports: One with 1 Gbps capability and one with 2.5 Gbps capability	Uplink Ethernet port: 10 Gbps; Ethernet LAN ports: One with 1 Gbps capability and one with 10 Gbps capability
	Flash storage	256 MB	256 MB
	Memory	512 MB	512 MB

4.1.1.2 Wi-Fi 7 AP Product Definition

Table 4.2 presents the product specifications of two Wi-Fi 7 AP products as examples, highlighting the key parameters that the end user and operators consider when selecting Wi-Fi products.

Product names like BE3600 or BE9300 indicate the Wi-Fi 7 technology and the product's maximum physical rate. In the case of Wi-Fi 6 APs, the product name of AX3000 is commonly seen in the market. Here, "AX" represents the IEEE 802.11ax

Table 4.3 The examples of Wi-Fi AP product names

AP product name	AX3000	BE3600	BE9300
The origin of AX or BE	AX is the name of the IEEE 802.11ax standard	BE is the name of the IEEE 802.11be standard	BE is the name of the IEEE 802.11be standard
Description of the performance	The physical rate at 2.4 GHz is 574 mbps	The physical rate at 2.4 GHz is 688 mbps	The physical rate at 2.4 GHz is 688 mbps
	The physical rate at 5 GHz is 2402 mbps	The physical rate at 5 GHz is 2882 mbps	The physical rate at 5 GHz is 2882 mbps
	No 6 GHz band support	No 6 GHz band support	The physical rate at 6 GHz is 5764 mbps
The sum of the physical rates	2976 mbps	3570 mbps	9334 mbps

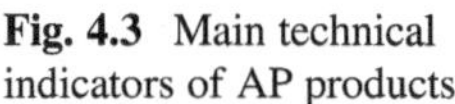

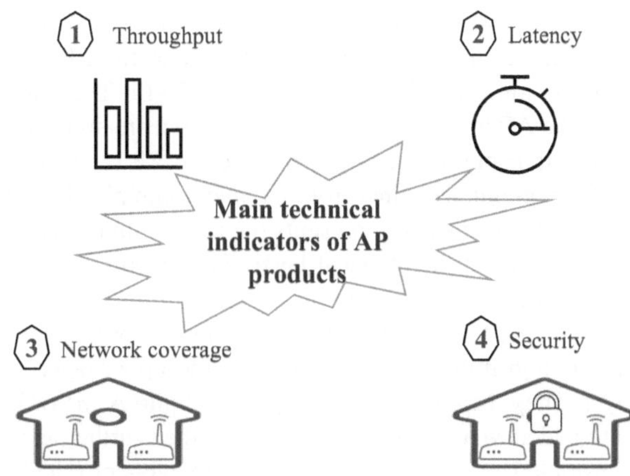

Fig. 4.3 Main technical indicators of AP products

standard, and the number represents the product's maximum physical rate. Table 4.3 illustrates examples of Wi-Fi AP product names and their descriptions.

Similarly, **BE7200** represents the Wi-Fi 7 dual-band AP (4x4 2.4 GHz, 4x4 5 GHz), and **BE19000** represents the Wi-Fi 7 tri-band AP (4x4 2.4 GHz, 4x4 5 GHz, 4x4 6 GHz).

4.1.1.3 Technical Specification of the Wi-Fi 7 AP

The product specifications of Wi-Fi 7 AP products, as listed in Table 4.2, serve as a reference for product introduction in the market. However, for developers and vendors designing the product, a more comprehensive set of technical indicators primarily includes throughput, latency, network coverage, and security, as illustrated in Fig. 4.3.

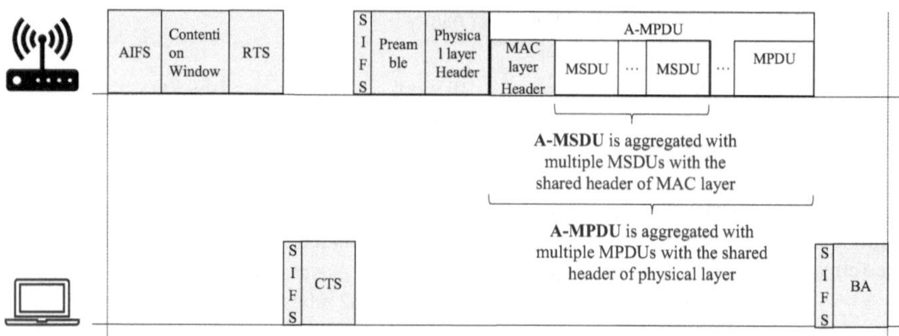

Fig. 4.4 Diagram of Wi-Fi data transmission procedure

1. **Throughput**

Throughput denotes the maximum data rate of user service data transmission between AP and STA over a Wi-Fi connection. It measures the user service data transmission capability of an AP over Wi-Fi. The throughput of data transmission from the AP to the STA is called the downstream throughput, while the throughput of data transmission from the STA to the AP is called the upstream throughput.

Throughput is distinct from the maximum physical rate, which is specified in the AP product name and represents the maximum bit rate at which the AP product can transmit data at the physical layer. This maximum physical rate is higher than the actual throughput achieved by the AP.

Referring to the Wi-Fi data transmission procedure [1] in Fig. 4.4, user service data is transmitted as MSDUs from the upper-layer software to the Wi-Fi MAC layer. These MSDUs are first aggregated into A-MSDUs, encapsulated into MPDUs with added MAC layer frame headers, then further aggregated into A-MPDUs, and transmitted over the Wi-Fi connection with physical layer frame headers added during the transmission opportunities. Due to the overhead of the frame headers of the Wi-Fi MAC layer and physical layer, as well as the overhead of the data transmission procedure at the Wi-Fi MAC layer, such as the collision avoidance contention window, frame intervals, data frame acknowledge and retransmission, etc., the time taken for the transmission of user service data is part of the time spent in the entire data transmission procedure, and the actual throughput is lower than the maximum physical rate.

The expected throughput is approximately 65% of the maximum Wi-Fi physical rate, as per the TR-398 Wi-Fi performance test specification from Broadband Forum [2]. For example, considering the BE9300 product with a maximum physical rate of 9334 Mbps, the expected throughput would be around 6067 Mbps.

Throughput primarily depends on the physical rate and the efficiency of wireless medium utilization of the AP product. Table 4.4 outlines key Wi-Fi technologies that contribute to throughput improvement.

Table 4.4 Wi-Fi technologies with throughput improvement

Categories	Wi-Fi key technologies	Increasing physical rate	Increasing throughput
Physical layer coding and modulation techniques	4 K-QAM modulation in Wi-Fi 7	Yes	Yes
Wireless channel bandwidth	5 GHz band with 160 MHz bandwidth and 6 GHz band with 320 MHz bandwidth in Wi-Fi 7	Yes	Yes
Wireless channel utilization	Multi-link operation in Wi-Fi 7	No	Yes
Wireless channel utilization	A-MSDU and A-MPDU aggregation in traditional Wi-Fi	No	Yes
Wireless channel utilization	MU-MIMO multiple-input multiple-output in traditional Wi-Fi	No	Yes
Wireless channel utilization	OFDMA technology introduced from Wi-Fi 6	No	Yes

2. **Latency**

Wi-Fi latency refers to the time taken for data packets to be successfully sent from the AP to the STA or vice versa over the Wi-Fi connection. The latency of data transmission from the AP to the STA is called downstream latency, while the latency of data transmission from the STA to the AP is called upstream latency. As introduced in Chap. 3, Wi-Fi latency mainly includes the delay of wireless channel access and AP data transmission scheduling with multiple STAs and multiple services.

Latency is a crucial performance indicator for AP product development and testing. The Wi-Fi Enhanced Distributed Channel Access (EDCA) mechanism in traditional Wi-Fi increases the wireless medium access opportunities of high-priority services, based on the priority level of the service data packets, thereby improving the latency performance of these services. In addition, the higher physical rate and throughput provided by Wi-Fi 7 technology can enhance Wi-Fi latency. Features such as low-latency service recognition and r-TWT in Wi-Fi 7 further enhance latency performance. Table 4.5 describes the key Wi-Fi technologies that improve Wi-Fi latency performance.

3. **Network coverage**

Network coverage refers to the capability of AP products to provide Wi-Fi signal coverage. Due to the attenuation of Wi-Fi wireless signal propagation in the air, the wireless signal of Wi-Fi products covers only a certain range. Generally, the higher the transmission power of the AP, the larger the wireless network coverage. The actual range an AP can cover depends on the environment. In an open space, an AP provides a good Wi-Fi signal within a range of 50 m or more, but in an indoor environment, the actual coverage of the AP will be significantly affected by the

Table 4.5 Wi-Fi technologies with latency improvement

Categories	Wi-Fi key technologies	Improving latency
Wireless channel access	Enhanced distributed channel access (EDCA) mechanism in traditional Wi-Fi	Yes
Wireless channel access	r-TWT in Wi-Fi 7	Yes
Data transmission scheduling	Low-latency services recognition in Wi-Fi 7	Yes
Data transmission scheduling	OFDMA technology introduced from Wi-Fi 6	Yes

attenuation of Wi-Fi signals caused by obstacles like walls and interference from other household appliances, such as microwaves.

Network coverage is typically indicated by the Received Signal Strength Indication (RSSI) of Wi-Fi signals over different distances. This can also be measured using the Rate vs Range (RVR) test, which measures Wi-Fi throughput over varying distances.

- **RSSI:** The unit is dBm. The larger the RSSI value, the higher the received signal strength. The measured RSSI value gradually decreases when the distance from the AP increases.
- **RVR test:** RVR tests are usually performed with test instruments, which simulate different distances with the controlled attenuation of signal. Higher signal attenuation leads to lower Wi-Fi throughput.

Figure 4.5 illustrates an RVR test result for a tri-band Wi-Fi 7 AP. The first three charts represent the test result for each frequency band of 2.4 GHz, 5 GHz, and 6 GHz, and the fourth chart represents the test result for the simultaneous transmission with all three frequency bands.

There is almost no change in throughput result when the signal attenuation is lower than 20 dBm, while it begins to decrease rapidly when the signal attenuation is higher than 30 dBm, and it becomes almost zero when the signal attenuation reaches 70 dBm. The RVR test results represent the relationship between the network coverage supported by the AP and the throughput.

The main factors affecting network coverage include the Wi-Fi transmission power of AP products and the transmission and reception capabilities of the antennas. Since network coverage depends on various indoor environments, it's difficult to specify the network coverage in AP product specifications. However, it is an essential indicator in product development and testing.

4. **Security**

Wi-Fi security involves the security of data transmission over Wi-Fi connections. From the initial WEP technology to the latest WPA3 standard, Wi-Fi security standards aim to provide comprehensive security for Wi-Fi networks. Wi-Fi 7 AP

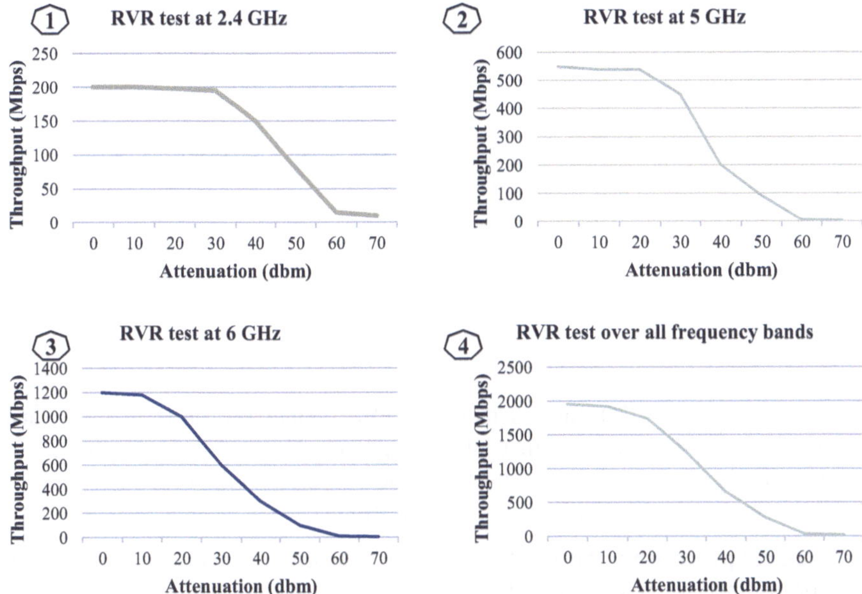

Fig. 4.5 RVR test for Wi-Fi 7 AP

products are expected to support the latest WPA3 security standard for enhanced security.

4.1.2 *Wi-Fi 7 Product Development Process*

Following the product requirements analysis and specification definition, the product development process can commence. This section provides an overview of the development and testing of Wi-Fi products.

4.1.2.1 System Architecture Design

The system architecture design involves conducting feasibility studies based on product requirements, specifications, and cost considerations. It encompasses the system framework definition and chipsets selection according to the product's feature list, performance targets, and key resource requirements, including memory and flash.

Taking the Wi-Fi 7 tri-band AP product BE9300 as an example, Fig. 4.6 illustrates the system framework, which also serves as the schematic diagram of the product's hardware construction. The system framework, similar between the Wi-Fi 7 multi-link APs and traditional single-link APs, includes central processing units,

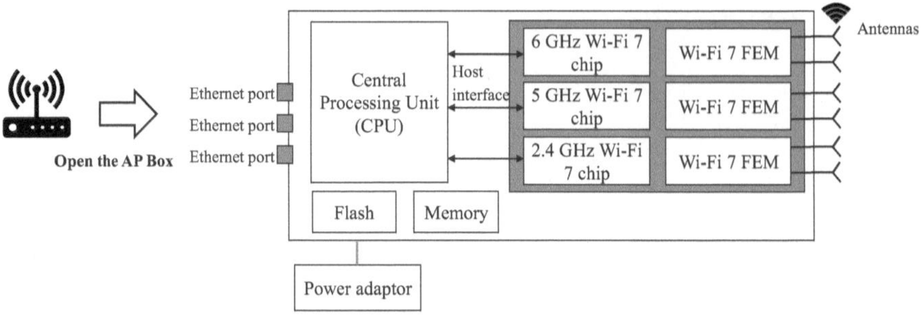

Fig. 4.6 System framework of Wi-Fi 7 AP

Wi-Fi 7 chips, Wi-Fi 7 front-end modules (FEM), antennas, flash, memory, and other components, along with their interconnections. The system framework is the input for the product hardware and software development in the next stage.

The key components in Fig. 4.6 are listed below:

(1) **Central processing unit (CPU):** Provides the software execution environment for loading and running the AP product software.
(2) **Wi-Fi 7 chip:** Core component for communication over Wi-Fi, implementing functions defined by the Wi-Fi 7 standard, such as multi-link operation, etc.
(3) **Host interface:** Hardware interface between the Wi-Fi chipset and CPU for data packet transmission and configuration.
(4) **Wi-Fi 7 Front-End Module (FEM):** Used for power amplification of RF signals in the transmission direction, and for amplifying received signals and suppressing noise in the receiving direction, thereby improving the signal-to-noise ratio and reception sensitivity of the received signal.
(5) **Wi-Fi antenna:** Passive component responsible for sending and receiving radio frequency signals.
(6) **Flash memory:** Provides storage functions for firmware images, configuration, data files, and logs.
(7) **Memory:** Provides software storage and operational data reading/writing functions.

In the system design, the selection of key components such as CPU, Wi-Fi chip, front-end module, and antenna is crucial for meeting performance requirements.

Typically, AP product designers opt for system on chip (SoC) solutions designed for wireless routers and AP products. SoCs integrate CPU, main functional components, and peripheral interfaces, such as Ethernet MAC/PHY, USB controllers, serial ports, and peripheral component interconnect express (PCIe) interfaces. Some SoCs also integrate the Wi-Fi functionality, providing the highly integrated SoC solutions for AP products. In order to meet the high throughput requirements of AP products, some SoCs integrate a hardware acceleration engine to forward packets from Wi-Fi and other LAN interfaces to the WAN interface and vice versa.

Table 4.6 Key components of Wi-Fi 7 AP product

Index	Component types	Quantity
1	SoC	1
2	Wi-Fi chips	3
3	Wi-Fi front-end modules	3
4	Wi-Fi antennas	6
5	Flash (256 M bytes)	1
6	Memory (512 M bytes)	1
7	Ethernet chips	3

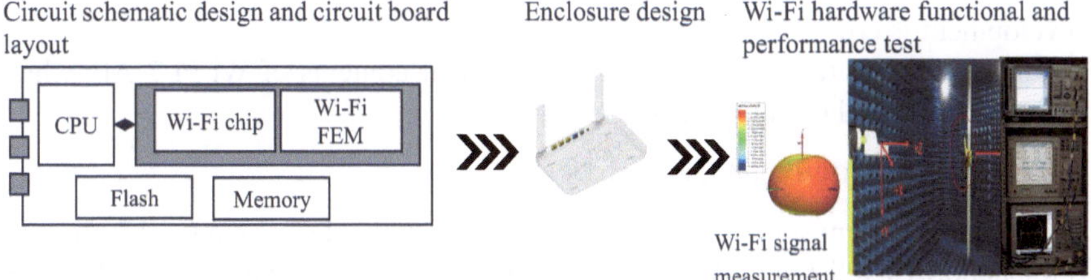

Fig. 4.7 Hardware development for Wi-Fi 7 AP

The Wi-Fi 7 solutions provided by Wi-Fi chip vendors range from single-chip solutions to multi-chip solutions. In the single-chip solution, a single Wi-Fi 7 chip implements the functions of multi-link operation and multiple frequency bands. Conversely, the multi-chip solution utilizes multiple Wi-Fi 7 chips, with each chip dedicated to one frequency band, and multi-link operation is either distributed across multiple chipsets or done in the processor (in software).

The host interface between the Wi-Fi 7 chip and the SoC typically utilizes a PCIe interface, which is a high-speed serial bus interface capable of meeting the data transmission requirements of Wi-Fi 7 technology. PCIe has evolved to its latest version PCIe 6.0, with PCIe 3.0 being the current mainstream version. PCIe 3.0 supports a data transmission rate of 8 Gbps with a single lane, and it supports double data rate with dual lanes.

For instance, in the case of a Wi-Fi 7 chip designed with a multi-chip solution, the primary components included in the multi-link AP product BE9300 can be referenced in Table 4.6.

4.1.2.2 Hardware Development

The hardware development of Wi-Fi 7 AP involves designing circuit schematics and circuit board layouts according to the system framework, designing product enclosures, and conducting relevant functional and performance tests to meet the radio frequency specifications of Wi-Fi 7. Relevant certification tests for different regions are conducted in third-party laboratories. Figure 4.7 illustrates the typical hardware development flow.

4.1.2.3 Software Development

Software development entails designing and implementing necessary software based on the system architecture. Mostly, chipset vendors provide software development kits (SDKs) and corresponding chip firmware with basic Wi-Fi 7 standard functions implemented. Developers leverage these SDKs for further enhancement and hardening of the product instead of starting from scratch to implement the protocol specifications in the Wi-Fi 7 standard.

For developers working on AP product software, understanding the service handling processes of Wi-Fi chip software and the main contents of AP software development is crucial.

Figure 4.8 illustrates the software development contents of Wi-Fi 7 AP, which primarily include the following five aspects:

(1) **Wi-Fi connection management**

The initial and most important software function to be developed for AP products is to support establishing a Wi-Fi connection between the AP and the STA. Wi-Fi 7 introduces the multi-link connections between multi-link STA and multi-link AP through one of the links, thereby introducing new methods of Wi-Fi connection management.

(2) **Wi-Fi data forwarding and performance optimization**

Wi-Fi data forwarding refers to the forwarding from the Wi-Fi STAs to the uplink port and vice versa, which constitutes the fundamental function of the Internet service provided by AP products. With Wi-Fi 7, data forwarding involves multi-link operation, where multiple links between the AP and the STA simultaneously transmit and receive data. The AP must manage the state of multi-link connections and support optimized performance and high service quality.

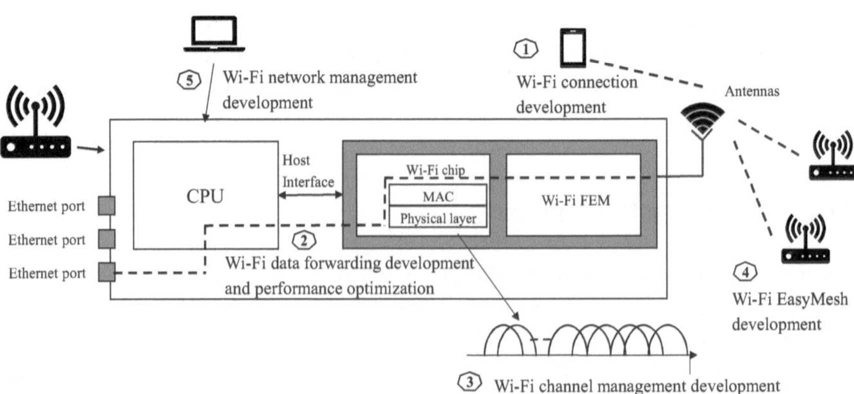

Fig. 4.8 Software development contents of Wi-Fi 7 AP

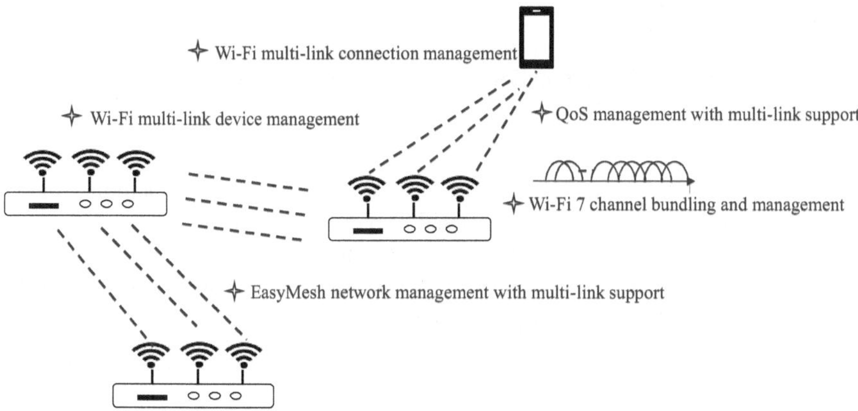

Fig. 4.9 Main differences of software development for Wi-Fi 7 AP

(3) **Wi-Fi wireless channel management**

Wi-Fi wireless channel management refers to the optimization of Wi-Fi wireless channels, supporting automatic channel selection to enhance the performance of Wi-Fi networks. APs need to implement wireless channel optimization, considering the supported wireless channels, bandwidth, and channel bundling capability.

(4) **Wi-Fi Mesh network management**

Wi-Fi Mesh network management refers to the software implementation of EasyMesh network functions for Wi-Fi 7 APs, considering the characteristics of the Wi-Fi 7 multi-link feature. EasyMesh facilitates the creation of a unified, seamless Wi-Fi network with multiple APs.

(5) **Wi-Fi network management**

Wi-Fi network management refers to the software implementation of network management functions, including network configuration, monitoring, and fault detection. This chapter introduces the software design of Wi-Fi network management, including Wi-Fi 7 multi-link management based on Wi-Fi network management protocols.

Figure 4.9 outlines the main differences in software development between Wi-Fi 7 APs and previous generation APs. With the introduction of multi-link operation in Wi-Fi 7, the key distinctions in Wi-Fi 7 AP software development include Wi-Fi multi-link connections, configuration management of multi-link devices, QoS management, and EasyMesh network management linked with multi-link. Additionally, the software development involves new methods for channel bundling and channel resource management associated with Wi-Fi 7.

4.1.2.4 Product Test

Product testing verifies the function and performance of the Wi-Fi 7 AP products after the hardware and software development is completed. Broadly, the testing can be categorized as follows:

- **Functional test**: Verifies the functionality of key technologies, including multi-link operation, OFDMA, and Restricted Target Wake Time.
- **Performance test**: Validates throughput, latency, and network coverage in typical deployment scenarios of Wi-Fi 7 AP products. This part also describes the test setups and steps used for performance testing.

4.2 Wi-Fi 7 AP Product Software Development

This section begins by outlining the software architecture design of Wi-Fi 7 AP products, followed by an introduction to the primary aspects of software development.

4.2.1 Software Architecture for Wi-Fi 7 AP Products

Software development for Wi-Fi 7 products begins with the design of the corresponding software architecture. The design process involves analyzing product requirements and decomposing the product software into functional software modules with clear responsibilities, interfaces, and relationships between software modules. Software architecture design will be the guidance for the subsequent development stages.

4.2.1.1 Software Hierarchical Model

Typically, software architectures follow a bottom-up *hierarchical model*, which also maps to the current product system framework comprising the CPU core and other functional components. Figure 4.10 illustrates the layered structure of Wi-Fi AP software.

- **Lower layer**: Comprises the Operating System (OS) and Wi-Fi driver software responsible for initialization and configuration of Wi-Fi chips.
- **Middle layer**: Built on top of the operating system, it contains the Wi-Fi-related modules, such as connection management, data forwarding, wireless channel management, as well as AP device management and Wi-Fi EasyMesh network functions, etc.

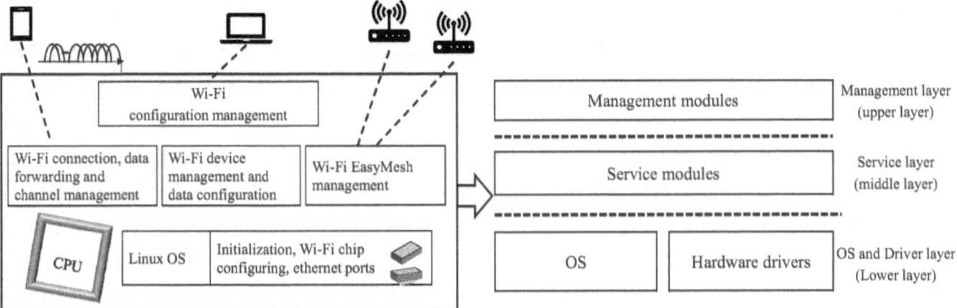

Fig. 4.10 Software architecture of Wi-Fi 7 AP

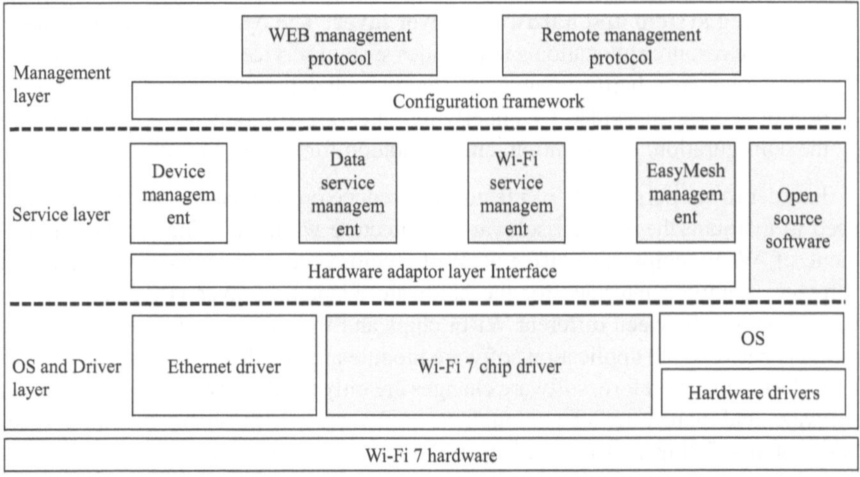

Fig. 4.11 Software modules of Wi-Fi 7 AP

- **Upper layer houses**: Software modules for Wi-Fi management through web pages and remote network management protocols, etc.

The right side of Fig. 4.10 illustrates the abstraction of the actual software structure into a layered model, including the operating system and hardware driver layer, service layer, and management layer. Each layer implements corresponding software functions and defines abstract application programming interfaces for upper-layer modules.

Software module division and responsibility definition should consider the realization of product functions on the one hand and adaptability to potential requirement changes, ensuring module cohesion and clear functionality. This approach facilitates software scalability and reduces the complexity of the software.

While the abstracted software architecture remains consistent across Wi-Fi 7 and previous APs, the implementation of individual modules requires adjustments due to new Wi-Fi 7 technologies. Figure 4.11 highlights (grayed area) modules requiring modification due to innovations in Wi-Fi 7.

- **Management layer:** This layer provides the configuration interface for the product, such as the local web-based management and the remote management protocols of operators like the TR-069 protocol defined by the Broadband Forum (BBF). These management methods need to be extended to support multi-band and multi-link connections for Wi-Fi 7.
- **Service layer:** Responsible for implementing AP product service functions, including the device management module, data forwarding service management module, Wi-Fi service management, and EasyMesh network management module. With the introduction of Wi-Fi 7 new technologies such as multi-link and low latency, software development within this layer is essential to accommodate changes related to data service processing, Wi-Fi service management, and EasyMesh network management.
- **Operating system and hardware driver layer:** The operating system manages hardware resource allocation and provides system services. The driver software is a bridge between hardware and software to realize the initialization and abstraction of services provided by underlying hardware components and implements the configuration, initialization, and adaptation for the Wi-Fi 7 chip.

In order to support new Wi-Fi features or reduce product costs, AP products may need to maintain the original software architecture while allowing for the replacement of Wi-Fi chips. As different Wi-Fi chip vendors provide varying driver software, a unified interface for the hardware adaptation layer is crucial to mask the differences between different Wi-Fi chips and their driver software. This interface sits between the application software module and the driver software and needs to be designed. Therefore, software changes are only needed in the underlying driver software and hardware adaptation layer software, which shield the differences between Wi-Fi chips, ensuring compatibility when replacing Wi-Fi chips.

Additionally, to ensure the application software of AP products remains independent of different configuration management methods, a unified configuration management framework module is introduced between the management protocol module and the application software module. The management protocol module handles protocol processing and manages configuration parameters between the management protocol module and the application software module. Should there be a need to change the configuration management protocol, the modification of the software is done solely on the configuration management protocol module only.

4.2.1.2 The Operating System of the Wi-Fi AP

Wi-Fi AP product development typically adopts the Linux operating system. Most of the Wi-Fi chipset vendors provide their drivers and SDK based on Linux. As a free and open-source operating system, Linux has been widely used in various hardware platforms. Thanks to contributions from the vast community of programmers, Linux continues to evolve, adhering to the POSIX portable operating system programming interface specification. It supports multiuser and multitask capabilities over diverse

Table 4.7 Operating System options for Wi-Fi 7 AP products

Categories	Linux	Openwrt
Network drivers and protocols	Linux kernel provides the network driver development framework and drivers for various chipsets and supports rich network protocols	Openwrt incorporates a modified version of the Linux kernel and reuses the same network drivers and protocols
Application layer software modules	Application layer software modules of AP products are developed by the AP product vendors	Openwrt implements some application layer software modules of AP products, such as network service management, Wi-Fi service management, management by web pages, and configuration management framework, serving as a baseline for AP product vendors to develop new features
Open source software modules and software packages	Linux supports various open source software modules applicable to AP products, such as network protocols, Wi-Fi authentication management, etc.	Openwrt supports various open source software modules; in addition, it offers support for a large number of software packages developed within the Openwrt community
Wi-Fi chip support	The software packages of Wi-Fi chip vendors typically support Linux by default	Many prominent chip vendors offer support for Openwrt within their SDK

CPU architectures and drivers for multiple chips, and it has made significant strides in terms of stability, security, and debuggability.

In addition, Linux boasts a robust network subsystem that supports various network protocols and data forwarding functions, aligning well with the requirements of network driver and data forwarding service development for network devices.

In the industry, several flavors of operating systems based on Linux have emerged, catering to specific applications and use cases. Examples include the Android operating system for smartphones and the Openwrt operating system for wireless routers and AP products.

Openwrt is an open-source operating system based on the Linux kernel, integrating wireless router application services and providing rich network functionalities. The Openwrt community provides a vast array of software packages, enhancing the functionality of Openwrt.

In the broadband service provider market, many overseas broadband operators have shown high interest in Openwrt-based Wi-Fi APs. In the retail market, routers developed based on Openwrt have seen widespread adoption.

Wi-Fi AP products can be developed based on Linux or Openwrt, the comparison between these two alternatives can be found in Table 4.7.

4.2.1.3 Driver Module for Wi-Fi 7

The software development kits (SDK) and accompanying firmware offered by Wi-Fi 7 chip vendors constitute the Wi-Fi driver package. Although these driver packages vary in code among vendors, they all collaborate with the chip hardware to execute Wi-Fi frame processing at the physical layer, wireless media access, and primary functions of the MAC layer.

The Wi-Fi driver package provides the initial configuration for the chip and encapsulates the configuration parameters and data packets of the chip into a generic software interface. The interface is independent of the specific hardware, which can be utilized to implement the service data transmission and chip configuration during the Wi-Fi AP software development.

Let's delve into the framework and key functions of the Wi-Fi driver package, along with the generic software interface catered to upper-layer applications.

1. **Framework and Main Functions of the Wi-Fi Driver Package**

The Wi-Fi driver package, shown in Fig. 4.12, comprises firmware executing within the Wi-Fi chip and driver software running on the host CPU. The division of responsibilities between them varies depending on the implementation.

The firmware is the software running in the Wi-Fi chip, which is between the host CPU and the chip hardware. It acts as an intermediary between the chip and the host CPU and provides the main functions listed below:

- Configuration management of the chip from the CPU.
- Transmission of management frames, control frames, and data packets between the chip and CPU.
- Scheduling of data packets sent by the driver software.
- Wireless media access control.

The driver software is the set of software modules provided by chip vendors to product developers of Wi-Fi AP products. It provides the host communication

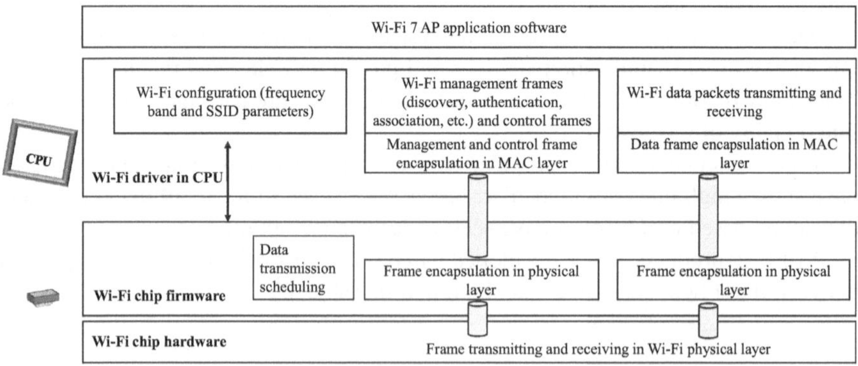

Fig. 4.12 Framework of Wi-Fi driver package

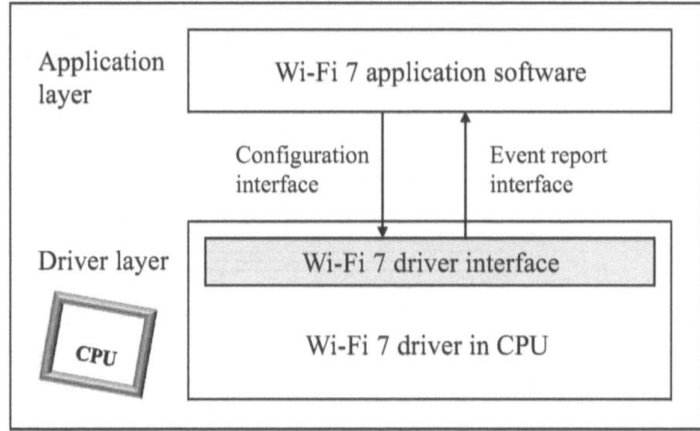

Fig. 4.13 Interface of Wi-Fi 7 driver package

interface between the CPU and the Wi-Fi chip and implements the generic software interface defined by Linux for upper-layer application software. In addition to this, its main functions include:

- Chip initialization, firmware downloading, and Wi-Fi chip-related configuration.
- Processing of MAC layer management frames and control frames.
- Transmission and reception of MAC layer data packets.

Although the main functions of driver software for Wi-Fi 7 chips and previous generations of Wi-Fi chips are similar, adaptations are necessary for handling management frames, control frames, and data packets of the MAC layer due to new Wi-Fi 7 technologies like multi-link operation.

2. **Generic Software Interface for Upper-Layer Applications**

The Wi-Fi driver provides a software interface for upper-layer applications, enabling configuration, management, and event reporting, as shown in Fig. 4.13.

In order to provide consistent software interfaces for upper-layer applications from the Wi-Fi driver software of different Wi-Fi chip vendors, Linux provides a generic Wi-Fi driver software module that defines the generic Wi-Fi driver software interfaces. Wi-Fi chip vendors can take this generic Wi-Fi driver software module as a base to implement the Wi-Fi driver package according to the specific hardware design of the Wi-Fi chip.

The framework of the generic Wi-Fi driver software module is described in Fig. 4.14. The cfg80211 software module implements two sets of driver software interfaces: *WEXT* (Wireless Extensions) interfaces based on Linux IOCTL and *NL80211* interfaces based on Linux NETLINK.

IOCTL and *NETLINK* are two communication mechanisms in Linux. The Linux environment comprises of user space and kernel space, each with its own independent memory address space. Applications typically run in user space, while drivers operate in kernel space. Linux employs these mechanisms to facilitate communication between applications and Wi-Fi driver software. IOCTL is the communication mechanism based on control commands over the Linux device file descriptor, while

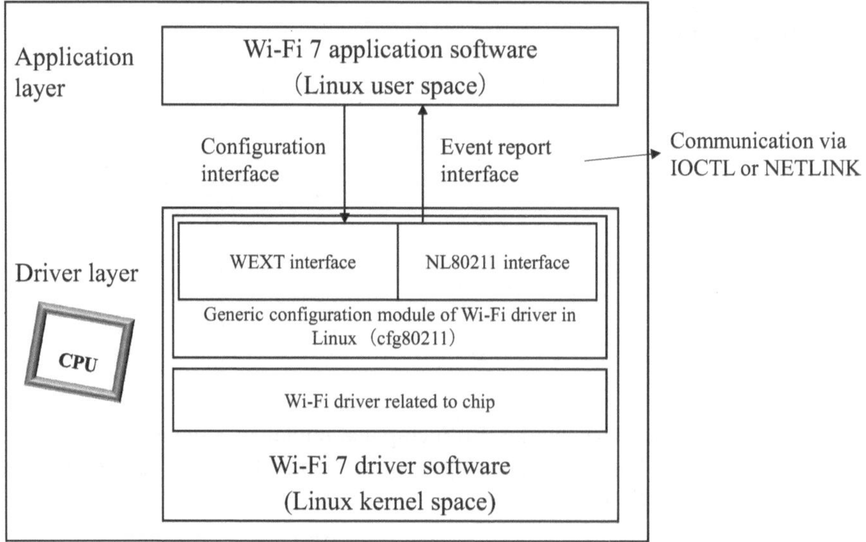

Fig. 4.14 Framework of generic Wi-Fi driver software module

NETLINK is the communication mechanism based on messages over the Linux socket interface.

(1) **WEXT (Wireless Extension)**

This is the first generation of generic Wi-Fi interfaces integrated into Linux. It implements the configuration management interface based on Linux IOCTL and implements the event reporting interface based on Linux NETLINK.

(2) **NL80211**

This is the new generation of generic Wi-Fi interfaces that implements both the configuration interface and the event reporting interface based on Linux NETLINK. NL80211 supports all interfaces defined by WEXT and has better scalability than WEXT. NL80211 provides comprehensive Wi-Fi driver interfaces for applications, encompassing Wi-Fi chip configuration, SSID configuration, STA association authentication, STA key configuration, and event reporting.

4.2.1.4 Wi-Fi Management Model

The Wi-Fi management model encompasses the basic elements of a Wi-Fi network, including APs, STAs, Wi-Fi frequency bands, and BSS (Basic Service Set), with corresponding associations between them. Wi-Fi product development involves implementing the configuration and management of these basic elements in a Wi-Fi network, such as displaying network information in a graphical format, including details like Wi-Fi frequency band information, BSS information, and the

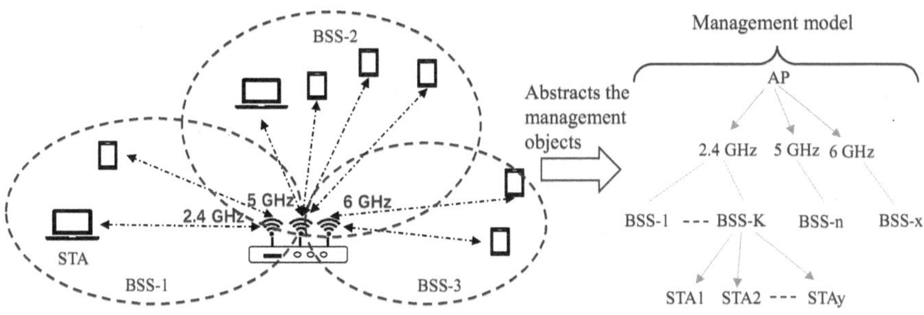

Fig. 4.15 Wi-Fi 6 management objects and management model

number of connected STAs. These basic elements are called *Wi-Fi management objects*, and their association between them forms the *Wi-Fi management model.*

As shown on the left side of Fig. 4.15, Wi-Fi 6 APs typically have three frequency bands: 2.4 GHz, 5 GHz, and 6 GHz. Each band can be configured with multiple SSIDs to establish their own BSS networks, with the corresponding STAs connected to each BSS network, respectively. On the right side of Fig. 4.15, the basic elements of the Wi-Fi network are abstracted into corresponding management objects, forming a coherent management model.

The management objects in a Wi-Fi network include APs, Wi-Fi frequency bands, BSS, and Wi-Fi STAs connected to APs. The relationships between these management objects are outlined below:

- **APs and Wi-Fi frequency band:** An AP supports one or more Wi-Fi frequency band objects. Each Wi-Fi band management object defines configuration parameters such as Wi-Fi channel, bandwidth, transmit power, channel scanning, and statistics at the Wi-Fi band level.
- **Wi-Fi frequency bands and BSS networks:** One Wi-Fi frequency band supports one or more BSS objects. BSS networks are identified by SSIDs. Each BSS management object defines configuration parameters, such as SSID name, authentication method, encryption method, password, EDCA access category parameters, and statistics at the BSS level.
- **BSS networks and Wi-Fi STAs:** Each BSS supports Wi-Fi connections to one or more Wi-Fi STAs. Each Wi-Fi STA management object defines parameters such as MAC address, physical layer data rate, RSSI, and statistics at the STA level.

With Wi-Fi 7's support for multi-link operation technology, a Wi-Fi 7 AP with multi-link support is called a multi-link AP, and the Wi-Fi 7 STA with multi-link support is called a multi-link STA. Figure 4.16 is an example of the management objects and management model of a Wi-Fi 7 network. As a result, new configuration management parameters are needed:

- For the BSS management object, to indicate the association relationship with one or more Wi-Fi frequency bands.

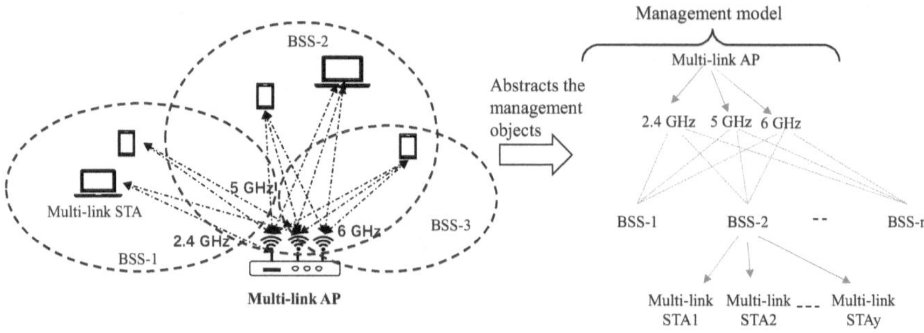

Fig. 4.16 Wi-Fi 7 management objects and management model

- For the multi-link STA management object, to indicate the multiple links established over different frequency bands between the multi-link STA and the multi-link AP.

The Wi-Fi management model serves as an abstracted data model for managing Wi-Fi services. In software development, this model handles the association relationships and parameters of these management objects to implement the corresponding product configuration, database storage, and user interface presentation.

The Wi-Fi network management system communicates with the AP device through the management protocol. This protocol delineates the management data model and the operational methods of the management objects. The network management system executes configuration management operations on the management objects and parameters to realize the Wi-Fi service management of the AP.

To ensure standardized management of AP Wi-Fi services and to facilitate interoperability between network management systems and APs from different vendors, the Broadband Forum standards organization has defined the standard management data model specifications for devices like home gateways and wireless routers. Notably, TR-098 and TR-181 are among these specifications, and they will be elaborated upon in the section on Wi-Fi 7 Network Management.

4.2.2 Wi-Fi 7 Connection Management

The Wi-Fi connection management module is primarily responsible for handling the processes of association and disassociation between the Wi-Fi station and the AP. The main change in Wi-Fi 7 connection management, compared to the previous Wi-Fi technologies, is the support for multi-link, which allows the establishment of Wi-Fi connections across multiple links between a multi-link STA and a multi-link AP.

To implement the software functionality of Wi-Fi connection management, it is essential to understand the state machine of the Wi-Fi connection process and the

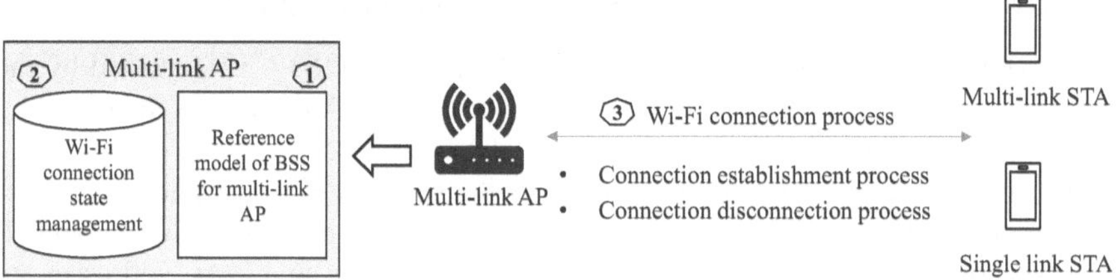

Fig. 4.17 Main contents of Wi-Fi connection management development

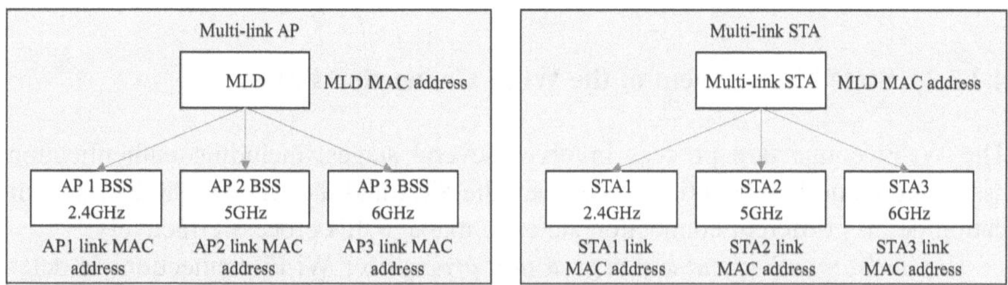

Fig. 4.18 Reference model of BSS and STA for multi-link device in Wi-Fi driver

reference model of BSS of multi-link AP devices in the Wi-Fi driver. Figure 4.17 outlines the primary components of Wi-Fi connection management. This section begins by elucidating the state management of the Wi-Fi connection process and the reference model of BSS for multi-link AP devices in the Wi-Fi driver. Subsequently, it delves into the software implementation of Wi-Fi connection management accordingly.

4.2.2.1 Reference Model of BSS for Multi-Link AP in Wi-Fi Driver

In the previous section, we explained the management model of Wi-Fi 7, in which a BSS management object is associated with one or more Wi-Fi frequency band management objects. The service management software module configures the Wi-Fi driver module according to the configuration parameter information of the BSS management object.

(1) **Reference model of BSS for multi-link AP in Wi-Fi driver**

As shown on the left side of Fig. 4.18, each BSS management object corresponds to a multi-link MLD object in the Wi-Fi driver.

The MLD object is identified by the MLD MAC address and represents the logical object of the multi-link BSS, and the BSS object is identified by the MAC address of each link (e.g., AP1, AP2, AP3).

(2) **Reference model of multi-link STA in station Wi-Fi driver**

As shown on the right side of Fig. 4.18, the multi-link STA is identified by the MLD MAC address of the multi-link STA, while the STA per link is identified by the MAC address of each link (e.g., STA1, STA2, STA3).

In summary, this reference model outlines the structure and identification mechanisms for multi-link BSS and multi-link STA in a Wi-Fi driver environment. It clarifies how BSS management, MLD objects, BSS objects, and MAC addresses are utilized to manage and differentiate between multiple links in both AP and STA configurations.

4.2.2.2 State Management of the Wi-Fi Connection Process

The Wi-Fi connection process involves several stages, including authentication, association, and key negotiation between the STA and the AP. The 802.11 specification defines different connection states to manage this process effectively.

The *authentication and key negotiation process* for Wi-Fi connections is determined by the security standards configured on the Wi-Fi network. Wi-Fi network access security standards have evolved from the WEP standard to WPA, WPA2, and the latest WPA3, as defined by the 802.11i specification.

WPA and later security standards meet the definition of 802.11i Robust Security Network (RSN), and the Wi-Fi connections between STAs and APs based on WPA and later security standards are called Robust Secure Network Association (RSNA) Wi-Fi connections. The RSNA Wi-Fi connection procedure consists of a four-way handshake in which both the STA and AP confirm that the peer has the same PMK, generate the PTK and GTK temporary keys, and complete the key negotiation for Wi-Fi connections.

Figure 4.19 shows the state transition of the RSNA Wi-Fi connection process.

The connection process between a multi-link AP and a multi-link STA or a single-link STA follows a standardized state transition procedure. Here is an explanation of the states involved in this process:

(1) **State 1, unauthenticated state**: This is the initial state of the Wi-Fi connection process, in which the STA initiates an authentication request, and the connection state transits to state 2 if the authentication procedure is successful.
(2) **State 2, authenticated unassociated state**: In this state, the STA initiates an association request to start the association procedure of the Wi-Fi connection, and the connection state transits to state 3 if the association procedure is successful.
(3) **State 3, authenticated associated state**: In this state, the AP initiates a four-way handshake procedure between the AP and the STA, and the connection state transits to state 4 if the four-way handshake procedure is successful.
(4) **State 4, authenticated associated state with RSNA established**: This is the final state of a successful Wi-Fi connection, in which the AP and the STA start transmitting encrypted data.

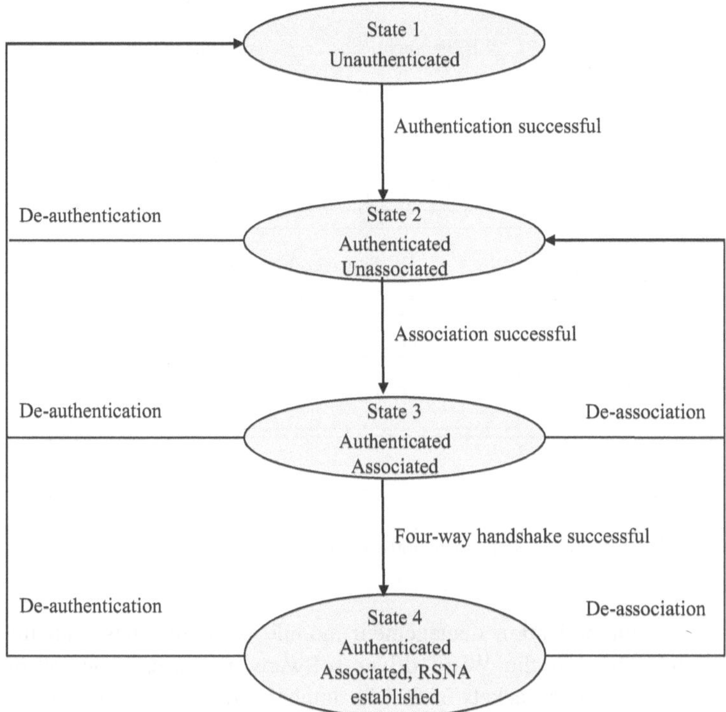

Fig. 4.19 State transition of the Wi-Fi connection process

4.2.2.3 Software Implementation of the Wi-Fi Connection Process

The software modules related to the Wi-Fi connection management function include the Wi-Fi authentication management software module of the service layer and the Wi-Fi connection management software module of the driver layer, as shown in Fig. 4.20.

The Wi-Fi connection management software module is responsible for handling of authentication and association management frames in the Wi-Fi connection process and is responsible for the management of the connection state during the Wi-Fi connection process.

Wi-Fi authentication management module facilitates the authentication and key negotiation procedures in the Wi-Fi connection process. The open source software module *hostapd* is widely used for authentication management, which offers the below functions:

- 802.11 Authentication procedure with open system authentication mode and SAE authentication mode
- 802.1x Extended Certification Procedure
- The four-way handshake procedure

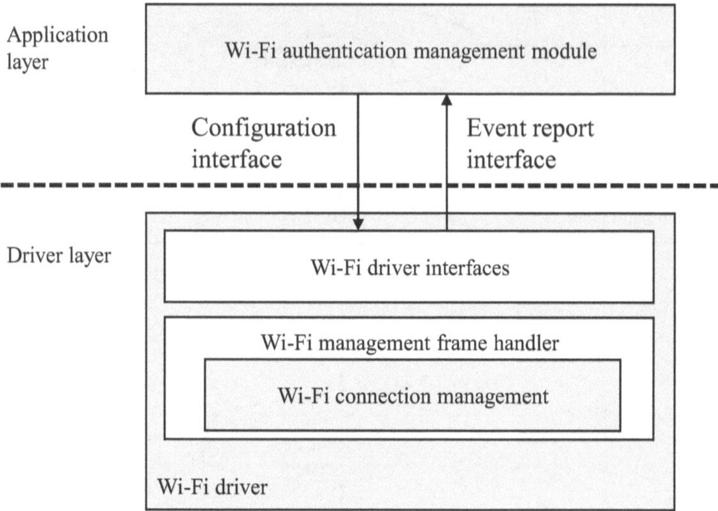

Fig. 4.20 Wi-Fi connection management software modules

The Wi-Fi authentication management module communicates with the Wi-Fi driver module through the Wi-Fi driver software interfaces. The Wi-Fi driver module reports the data packets of 802.11 authentication and association management frames, 802.1x authentication, and four-way handshake to the Wi-Fi authentication management module. Subsequently, the Wi-Fi authentication management module returns the authentication result and the keys generated from the four-way handshake procedure to the Wi-Fi driver module.

1. **Connection establishment process between the multi-link AP and the multi-link STA**

Figure 4.21 illustrates the Wi-Fi connection process between a multi-link AP and a multi-link STA, based on the WPA3 security standard and pre-shared key authentication method.

Authentication Procedure The multi-link AP and the multi-link STA perform authentication interactions using the Simultaneous Authentication of Equals (SAE) protocol. This is done through authentication request frames and authentication response frames, which contain two pairs of authentication messages. The first pair of authentication messages completes the negotiation of the key, and the second pair of authentication messages completes the confirmation of the key. The authentication request and authentication response management frames carry multi-link information elements that contain the MLD MAC address.

The Wi-Fi authentication management module is responsible for implementing the SAE protocol, completing the authentication based on the pre-shared key, and generating a paired master key (PMK).

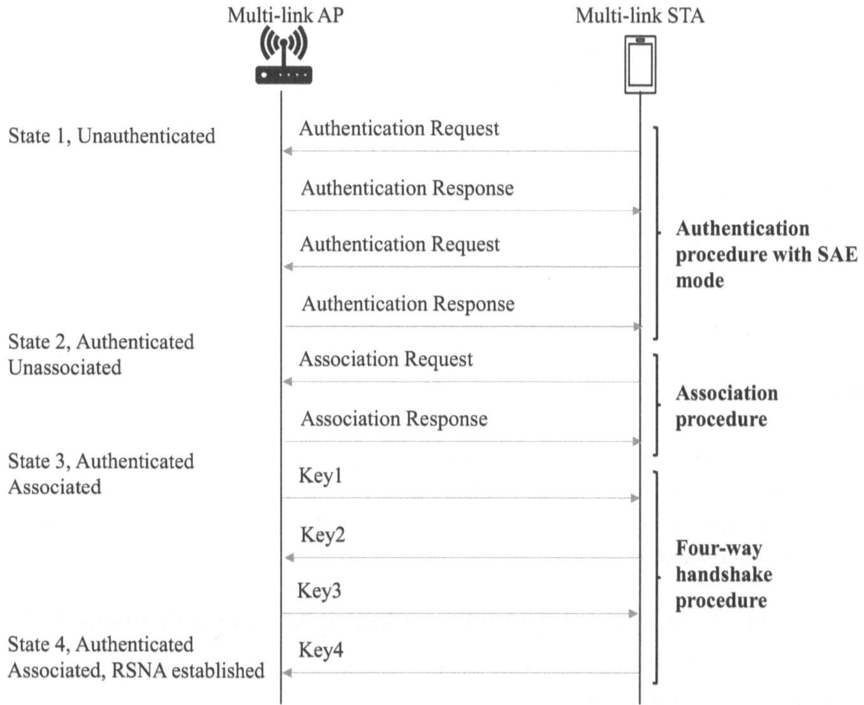

Fig. 4.21 Wi-Fi connection establishment process

The Wi-Fi driver module is responsible for the state management of the Wi-Fi connection, changing the Wi-Fi connection state to the authenticated unassociated state after the authentication procedure is completed.

Association Procedure The multi-link AP and the multi-link STA perform association interactions through association request frames and association response frames. These frames carry multi-link information elements containing the MLD MAC address and the link information to establish the multi-link connection.

The Wi-Fi driver module is responsible for handling the association request frames and completes the negotiation of the Wi-Fi capability set and connection parameters of each link according to the multi-link information carried in the association request frame. After the association procedure is successful, the Wi-Fi driver module changes the Wi-Fi connection state to the authenticated association state.

Four-Way Handshake Procedure The Wi-Fi authentication management module is responsible for the protocol processing of the four-way handshake procedure. The four-way handshake protocol packets contain the MLD MAC address and the link information, requesting the establishment of a multi-link connection. The Wi-Fi authentication management module generates a Pairwise Transient Key (PTK) shared among multiple links and generates a Group Temporal Key (GTK) for each

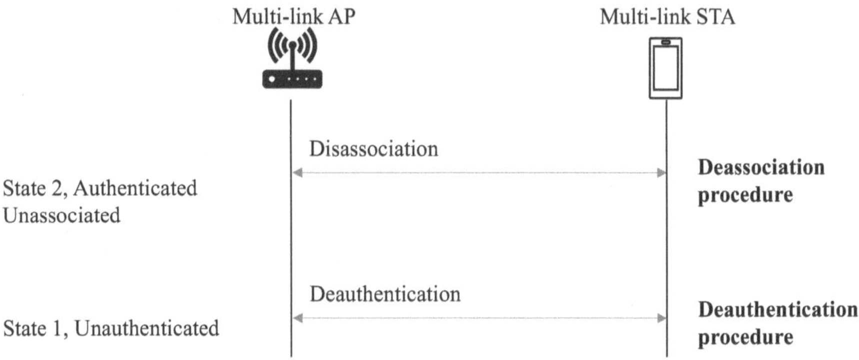

Fig. 4.22 Wi-Fi disconnection process

link. It sends the GTK to the multi-link STA in a four-way handshake protocol packet. The Wi-Fi driver module changes the Wi-Fi connection state to the authenticated associated with RSNA established state after the successful completion of the four-way handshake.

2. **Disconnection process between the multi-link AP and the multi-link STA**

Figure 4.22 illustrates the disconnection process, including disassociation and deauthentication procedures.

The disassociation and deauthentication procedures can be initiated by a multi-link AP or multi-link STA on any link that has established a connection so as to complete the multi-link disconnection process.

The Wi-Fi authentication management module is responsible for deleting the keys of all previously established multi-link connections, and the Wi-Fi driver module changes the Wi-Fi connection state to unauthenticated after the disconnection process has been completed.

3. **Wi-Fi connection establishment and disconnection process between multi-link AP and single-link STA**

The Wi-Fi 7 connection and disconnection process between multi-link APs and single-link STAs is the same as in previous Wi-Fi technologies.

The single-link STA completes the single-link connection process with the multi-link AP on its operating frequency band, including Wi-Fi authentication, association, and the four-way handshake procedure. If the connection process succeeds, the Wi-Fi connection state changes to the authenticated and RSNA established state.

The single-link STA completes the single-link disconnection process with the multi-link AP on its operating frequency band, including Wi-Fi disassociation and deauthentication procedures. Once the disconnection process is completed, the Wi-Fi connection state changes to the unauthenticated state.

4.2.3 Wi-Fi 7 Data Forwarding

The Wi-Fi data forwarding function in a Wi-Fi 7 AP implements the forwarding of data packets between the Wi-Fi network interface and other network interfaces of the AP.

The AP device supports Wi-Fi network interfaces and one or more Ethernet ports. One of the Ethernet ports is used for the AP's uplink network interface, which is called the Wide Area Network (WAN) port. The remaining Ethernet ports serve as Local Area Network (LAN) ports.

Using data forwarding between the Wi-Fi interface and the WAN port as an example, Fig. 4.23 illustrates the pathway through which a STA accesses the WAN-side network via the Wi-Fi connection established between the multi-link STA and the multi-link AP.

Depending on the system design of the AP product and the capabilities of the SoC, the data forwarding path between the Wi-Fi interface and the WAN port is realized in two approaches. One is the data forwarding path based on CPU software, and the other is the data forwarding path based on the SoC hardware acceleration engine. With the increasing physical rate of Wi-Fi, it is difficult to meet the throughput requirements in the CPU software-based data forwarding path. Hence, more AP products are adopting the SoC hardware acceleration engine to realize data forwarding paths to meet high throughput requirements.

In the data forwarding path based on CPU software, data transmission and reception of packets from Wi-Fi and Ethernet are handled by the software driver, and the data forwarding is implemented in the CPU software.

Data forwarding based on hardware involves direct processing by the hardware acceleration engine of the SoC, bypassing the need for CPU software intervention. This hardware-based approach enables efficient data transmission between the Wi-Fi chip and the Ethernet chip.

Compared with the previous Wi-Fi technologies, the primary distinction of the data forwarding path in Wi-Fi 7 lies in its support for multi-link operation within the

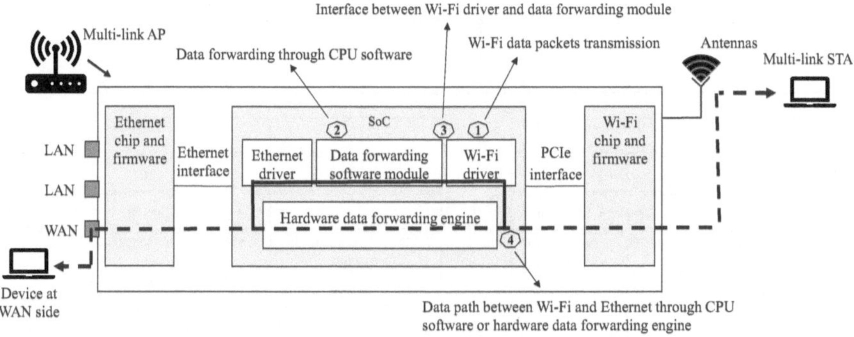

Fig. 4.23 Wi-Fi data forwarding path

Wi-Fi driver module or hardware forwarding engine of multi-link Access Points (APs). This section delves into the data forwarding function from four aspects:

- Multi-link data forwarding in the Wi-Fi 7 MAC layer.
- Data Forwarding Module of the CPU software.
- Interface between the Wi-Fi driver and the Data Forwarding Software Module.
- Data Forwarding Path Based on CPU Software and Hardware.

4.2.3.1 Multi-Link Data Forwarding in Wi-Fi 7 MAC Layer

The upper MAC layer and lower MAC layer of multi-link APs are described in the multi-link operation section of the third chapter.

In the MAC layer implementation of multi-link APs, the link-specific lower MAC layer and upper MAC layer are pivotal components described in the multi-link operation section of the third chapter. Specifically, a link-specific upper MAC layer for each link is implemented to facilitate data transmission over the single-link connections with single-link STAs. In addition, an upper MAC layer common to multi-link is implemented to support data transmission over the multi-link connection with the multi-link STAs.

Figure 4.24 illustrates the process of MAC layer multi-link data transmission processing. The upper MAC layer common to multi-link is responsible for the common part of the multi-link data transmission processing. The lower MAC

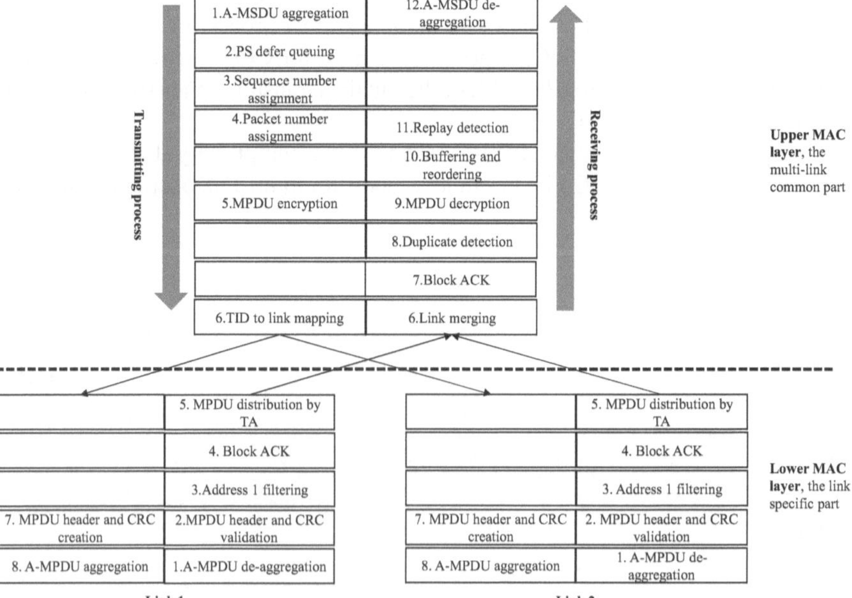

Fig. 4.24 Wi-Fi MAC layer multi-link data transmission process

layer of each link is responsible for the link-specific part of the multi-link data transmission processing.

In the transmit direction, the multi-link common upper MAC layer is responsible for several processes:

- MSDU aggregation to efficiently combine multiple MSDUs.
- Data packet caching in power-saving mode.
- Sequence number allocation for MAC layer data frames.
- Encryption of MPDU packets, along with packet number allocation for the encryption process.
- Multi-link scheduling based on the mapping between TID and multi-link, which directs encrypted MPDU packets to the appropriate transmission links.

In the transmit direction, upon receiving the encrypted MPDU packet from the upper MAC layer, the lower MAC layer:

- Updates the MAC layer frame header.
- Calculates the MPDU checksum.
- Performs A-MPDU aggregation.
- Sends the packets to the physical layer to complete the transmission process.

In the receive direction, the lower MAC layer:

- Performs A-MPDU de-aggregation.
- Checks the MPDU header and CRC.
- Conducts receiving address filtering.
- Processes Block ACKs.
- Distributes MPDU packets to the upper MAC layer based on the transmission address of the MPDU packets.

In the receive direction, after receiving MPDU packets from the lower MAC layer, the multi-link common upper MAC layer:

- Merges and caches received MPDU packets from multiple links.
- Synchronizes multi-link Block ACK information.
- Detects duplicate packets.
- Decrypts MPDU packets.
- Sorts packets according to the MAC layer data frame sequence numbers.
- Conducts packet replay detection using packet numbers.
- De-aggregates A-MSDUs, completing the MAC layer receiving process.

The data transmission process in the MAC layer is similar between multi-link and single-link. The main difference for multi-link is that the multi-link common upper MAC layer handles the common part of multi-link data transmission and performs the scheduling of downstream data packets, while the link-specific lower MAC layer performs the distribution of upstream data packets.

Scheduling of Downstream Data Packets The upper MAC layer common to multi-link performs multi-link scheduling of downstream data transmission according to the mapping between TID and multi-link, also considering the load of each link.

Distribution of Upstream Data Packets The lower MAC layer distributes MPDU packets according to the transmitting address of MPDU packets. If the transmitting address corresponds to a single-link STA, the MPDU packet is sent to the link-specific upper MAC layer for single-link data receiving processing. If the transmitting address corresponds to a multi-link STA, the MPDU packet is sent to the multi-link common upper MAC layer for multi-link data reception processing.

4.2.3.2 The Data Forwarding Module of the CPU Software

Data forwarding between the Wi-Fi interface and WAN port of AP products is facilitated by two distinct forwarding models: the bridge forwarding model and the route forwarding model.

- **Bridge forwarding model:** Bridge forwarding is the data forwarding based on the Layer 2 MAC address and VLAN information of 802.3 Ethernet data frames. This model is employed for data forwarding between different network interfaces within the LAN and also between LAN and WAN, as shown in Fig. 4.25.
- **Route forwarding model:** Route forwarding is the data forwarding based on network layer IP address information. This model is utilized for data forwarding between different network interfaces across IP network segments, as shown on the right side of Fig. 4.25.

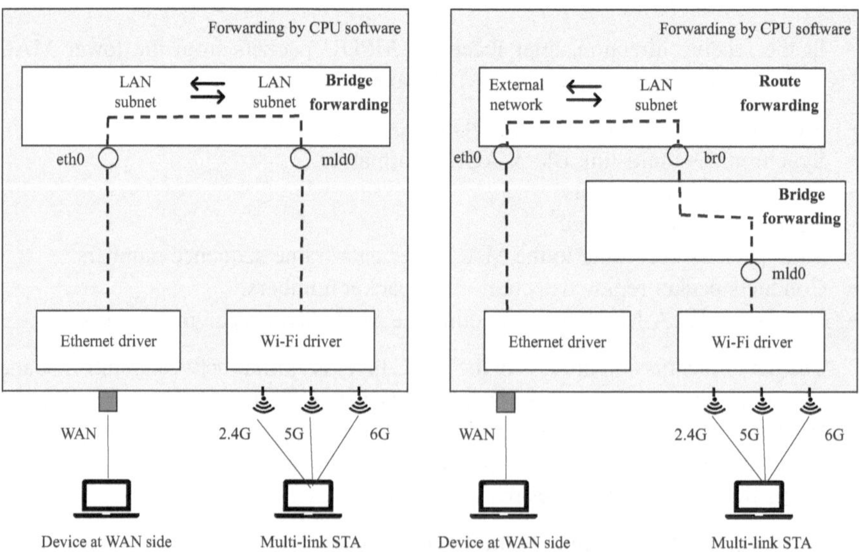

Fig. 4.25 Data forwarding models

The key components of the data forwarding in software are:

1. **Network interface**

Within the CPU software's data forwarding module, the network interface serves as a representation of a network device, corresponding to either an Ethernet physical interface or a Wi-Fi wireless interface. In Fig. 4.25, the network interface "eth0" corresponds to the Ethernet WAN port, while the network interface "mld0" corresponds to the Wi-Fi interface of the Wi-Fi driver module.

The network interface encapsulates the specifics of different network devices at the lower layer hardware and provides a standardized set of interfaces for the upper-layer data forwarding module. These interfaces are utilized for handling data packet transmission and network device configuration management. Both the Ethernet driver and Wi-Fi driver modules create network interface objects, allowing the upper-layer data forwarding module to operate seamlessly across different hardware interfaces without needing to distinguish between them.

2. **Bridge forwarding software module**

The bridge forwarding software module is responsible for implementing Layer 2 forwarding based on the Layer 2 MAC address and VLAN information of 802.3 Ethernet data frames. This functionality is supported within the Linux network subsystem.

In the Linux network subsystem, the bridge device objects can be created and associated with network interface objects. These bridge devices manage the Layer 2 forwarding function of data packets between network interfaces.

3. **Route forwarding software module**

The route forwarding software module implements the data forwarding function based on IP address information of the network layer, which is supported in the Linux network subsystem.

As depicted in the right side of Fig. 4.25, the route forwarding software module forwards data packets between the network interfaces, such as "eth0" and "br0," which correspond to the Ethernet WAN port and the bridge device object created by the bridge forwarding software module, respectively. The IP address of eth0 is typically assigned by the service provider, and the IP address of br0 is in the IP segment of the local area network.

The route forwarding software module performs network address translation (NAT) when performing data forwarding between the local area network and the external network. In this scenario, the WAN IP address is global IPv4, and LAN address belongs to a private subnet.

- **Data packet transmitting with NAT support:** When transmitting data packets to the external network (WAN), the NAT function translates the source IP address of data packets from the IP address of the Wi-Fi station within the LAN segment to the IP address of the eth0 interface (WAN).

- **Data packet receiving with NAT support**: When receiving data packets from the external network, the NAT function translates the destination IP address of data packets from the IP address of the eth0 interface to the IP address of the Wi-Fi station.

4.2.3.3 Interface Between the Wi-Fi Driver and the Data Forwarding Software Module

The upper MAC layer of the multi-link AP includes the upper MAC layer specific for each link and the upper MAC layer common to the multi-link. These layers work in tandem to ensure efficient transmission between the upper MAC layer and the data forwarding software module.

The upper MAC layer specific for each link creates a network interface for each BSS object, which is used for data packets transmission of the single-link STAs. The upper MAC layer common to multi-link creates a network interface for each BSS object, which is used for data packets transmission of the multi-link STAs.

Figure 4.26 illustrates the network interface "mld0," which is created for the BSS object by the upper MAC layer common to the multi-link and is used for data packets transmission of the multi-link STAs connected with this BSS.

In the direction of receiving Wi-Fi data packets, the lower MAC layer distributes the MPDU packets received from the multi-link STA to the multi-link common upper MAC layer based on the transmitting address of the MPDU packet. Subsequently, the multi-link common upper layer executes the data packet receiving process, identifying the corresponding network interface mld0 associated with the BSS object connected to the multi-link STA. The MSDU data packets are then transmitted to the data forwarding software module through this network interface.

Conversely, during Wi-Fi data packet transmission, the data forwarding software module identifies the corresponding network interface mld0 according to the destination MAC address. It transmits the MSDU data packet through the network interface to the multi-link common upper MAC layer. The multi-link common upper MAC layer completes the data packet transmission process, dispatching the MPDU data packet to the lower MAC layer of a specific link according to the decision of the multi-link scheduling.

4.2.3.4 Data Forwarding Path Based on CPU Software and Hardware

Figure 4.27 illustrates the data forwarding paths based on CPU software and hardware between the Wi-Fi interface and the WAN port. The AP device in this example is based on a SoC that supports a hardware acceleration engine alongside three Wi-Fi 7 chips.

For the processing of multi-link data forwarding in the MAC layer, the work split between the Wi-Fi driver and firmware depends on the Wi-Fi chip implementation. The functions of the lower MAC layer are usually implemented in the firmware

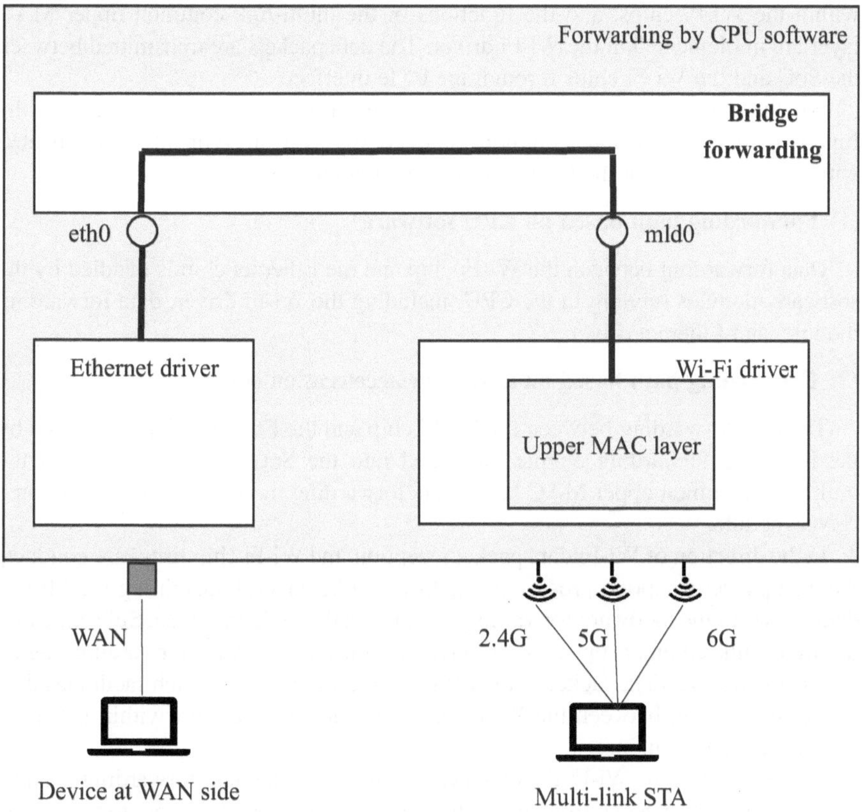

Fig. 4.26 Interface between Wi-Fi driver and data forwarding module

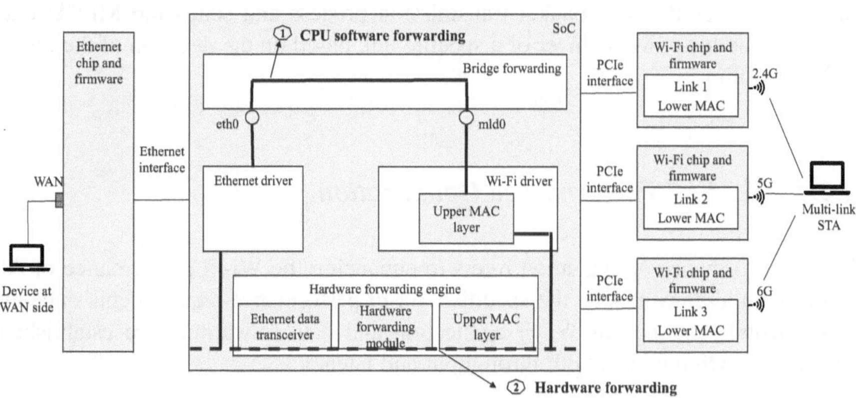

Fig. 4.27 AP software and hardware data forwarding paths

within the Wi-Fi chips, and the functions of the multi-link common upper MAC layer are implemented in the Wi-Fi driver. The data packets are transmitted between the SoC and the Wi-Fi chips through the PCIe interface.

For the data forwarding path based on the hardware acceleration engine, the functions of the multi-link common upper MAC layer are typically implemented within the processor of the hardware acceleration engine.

(1) **Forwarding path based on CPU software**

Data forwarding between the Wi-Fi chip and the Ethernet chip is handled by the software modules running in the CPU, including the Wi-Fi driver, data forwarding module, and Ethernet driver.

(2) **Forwarding path based on hardware acceleration engine**

The data forwarding between the Wi-Fi chip and the Ethernet chip is handled by the hardware forwarding engine integrated into the SoC, which implements the multi-link common upper MAC layer, data forwarding module, and Ethernet transceiver module.

In the direction of Wi-Fi data packet reception, the Wi-Fi chip firmware conducts the data packet reception process of the lower MAC layer, transmitting the MPDU data packet to the hardware forwarding engine via the PCIe interface. Subsequently, the multi-link common upper MAC layer within the hardware forwarding engine directs the MSDU data packet to the data forwarding module, which facilitates data packet forwarding between the Wi-Fi interface and Ethernet port within the hardware acceleration engine.

In the direction of Wi-Fi data packet transmission, the data forwarding module receives the data packet from the Ethernet transceiver module and forwards the MSDU data packet to the multi-link common upper MAC layer based on the destination MAC address. Following this, the multi-link common upper MAC layer completes the data packet transmission process and sends the MPDU data packet to the lower MAC layer of a specific link based on the decision of the multi-link scheduling.

4.2.4 Wi-Fi 7 Performance Optimization

Wi-Fi performance optimization refers to enhancing the Wi-Fi performance of AP products in alignment with the specified Wi-Fi performance requirements once the fundamental functions of Wi-Fi connection and data forwarding are established. This optimization covers both throughput and latency.

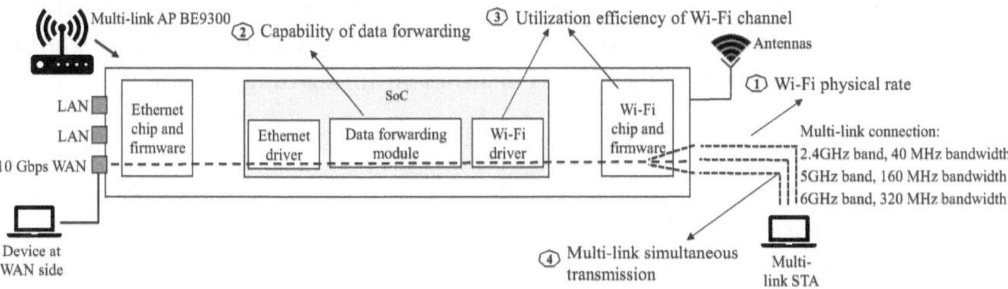

Fig. 4.28 Throughput performance optimization

4.2.4.1 Throughput Performance Optimization

Figure 4.28 illustrates the primary factors affecting the throughput between the multi-link STAs connected over Wi-Fi and the WAN side devices, including the physical rate of the Wi-Fi connection, data forwarding capability, and Wi-Fi channel utilization efficiency. Additionally, Wi-Fi 7 multi-link operation technology, which supports upstream and downstream data transmission on multiple links, enhances throughput.

1. **Physical rate of Wi-Fi connection**

The stable physical rate of the Wi-Fi connection is essential for throughput optimization. The first step involves verifying the physical rate to ensure it remains stable at the highest value. The EHT-SIG field in the Wi-Fi 7 physical layer frame header indicates the physical rate at which the data packet is transmitted. The physical rate can usually be viewed with the commands provided by the Wi-Fi driver or via information in the data frame header of captured Wi-Fi packets.

After Wi-Fi connection establishment, the multi-link AP device performs a dynamic rate adjustment based on signal quality, packet loss, and retransmissions. For AP products that meet the requirements of the corresponding hardware test specifications, the physical rate of the Wi-Fi connection is usually stable at the highest value when performing throughput tests in an interference-free environment.

2. **Capability of data forwarding**

The capability of data forwarding refers to the ability of the data forwarding module to forward data packets between the Wi-Fi interface and the Ethernet port. This capacity depends on the processing speed of the CPU and the memory availability for the data forwarding path for CPU software-based forwarding. It also depends on the processing speed of the hardware forwarding engine and the memory availability for the data forwarding path based on the hardware acceleration engine. The evaluation of the performance of the CPU-based forwarding or hardware engine-based forwarding in the system design stage is key to meeting the requirements of the product's data forwarding capability.

To optimize throughput performance, it is essential to monitor packet loss statistics of the CPU software or hardware forwarding engine's data forwarding module to ensure no packet loss due to insufficient forwarding capability.

3. **Utilization efficiency of Wi-Fi channel**

Wi-Fi channel utilization efficiency indicates the proportion of time spent on user service data transmission within the Wi-Fi transmission procedure.

Transmission procedure overhead, including Wi-Fi MAC layer and physical layer frame header overhead, wireless media access procedure overhead, and MAC layer data frame confirmation and retransmission process overhead, affects channel utilization efficiency. The higher the proportion of time spent on user service data transmission, the higher the utilization efficiency of the wireless channel.

Wi-Fi MAC layer frame aggregation technology is one of the most important technologies to improve channel utilization efficiency, including A-MSDU and A-MPDU. This technology aggregates multiple MSDU data units into one physical layer frame and transmits the frame after gaining access to the wireless media. This method reduces the overhead of the frame header of the MAC layer and the physical layer, improving the efficiency of wireless media access and data frame transmission, and improving the utilization efficiency of the Wi-Fi channel and throughput.

The degree of throughput improvement from frame aggregation technology is directly related to the number of MSDUs that are aggregated into the A-MSDU and A-MPDU aggregation frames. A higher number of aggregated MSDUs leads to increased Wi-Fi channel utilization efficiency and throughput. The number of MSDUs that can be aggregated depends on the maximum size of MPDU and PSDU defined in the 802.11 specification, along with the aggregation capability of the Wi-Fi chip.

This section outlines A-MSDU and A-MPDU frame aggregation in Wi-Fi 7, along with the throughput performance improvements facilitated by frame aggregation technology.

(1) **Maximum Length of A-MSDU and A-MPDU Aggregation Frame in Wi-Fi 7**

Table 4.8 displays the maximum length of A-MSDU and A-MPDU according to the Wi-Fi 7 specification [1].

(2) **Negotiation of A-MSDU and A-MPDU Aggregation Frame Length in Wi-Fi 7**

The AP and STA negotiate the aggregation frame length during the Wi-Fi connection establishment stage according to the EHT capability information element carried by the association request and association response frames. These frames contain the maximum length of MPDU and A-MPDU that the Wi-Fi device supports. Table 4.9 outlines the length parameters defined in EHT capability within this negotiation process [1].

Table 4.8 Maximum length of Wi-Fi 7 aggregation frame

Frame aggregation technology	Maximum length	Wi-Fi 6	Wi-Fi 7
A-MSDU	The maximum length of an A-MSDU is indirectly constrained by the maximum MPDU size, which is defined in Wi-Fi specification	Subtract the size of MAC layer header from the maximum MPDU size (11,454 bytes)	Subtract the size of MAC layer header from the maximum MPDU size (11,454 bytes)
A-MPDU	The maximum length of an A-MPDU equals to the maximum PSDU size, which is defined in Wi-Fi specification	6,500,631 bytes	15,523,200 bytes

Table 4.9 Aggregation frame length negotiation for Wi-Fi 7 products

EHT capability information element	Description
Maximum MPDU length	0 indicates 3895 bytes 1 indicates 7991 bytes 2 indicates 11,454 bytes
Maximum A-MPDU length exponent extension	This field is the extension of the exponential value when the maximum A-MPDU length is expressed as an exponential form with base 2 If the value is not 0, the maximum A-MPDU length is calculated using the following formula and does not exceed the maximum A-MPDU length defined in Wi-Fi specification $\min(2^{(23\ +\ \text{exponent extension of maximum A-MPDU length})}, 15523200)$ If the value is 0, the maximum A-MPDU length refers to the definition of VHT and HE capability elements in Wi-Fi specification.

(3) **Throughput Improvement from A-MPDU**

Throughput can be improved by setting the maximum length of the A-MPDU aggregation frame in each frequency band of the Wi-Fi product according to the capability of the Wi-Fi product. Increasing the length of A-MPDU aggregation frames leads to higher throughput, with greater aggregation enabling the transmission of more MSDUs within a frame.

Considering the BE9300 product as an example, Fig. 4.29 displays the throughput variations with different A-MPDU aggregation settings. This test was conducted in the 5 GHz frequency band with a physical rate of 2882 Mbps and a data packet size of 1500 bytes. The throughput is very low when the A-MPDU is off, and the throughput increases through the higher number of aggregated MSDUs. The throughput is close to 65% of the expected physical rate when the number of aggregated MSDUs reaches 64, and the throughput exceeds the expected value when the number of aggregated MSDUs reaches 256.

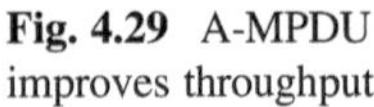

Fig. 4.29 A-MPDU improves throughput

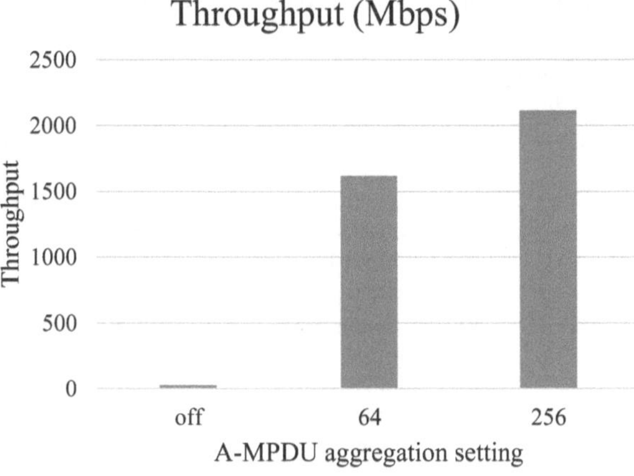

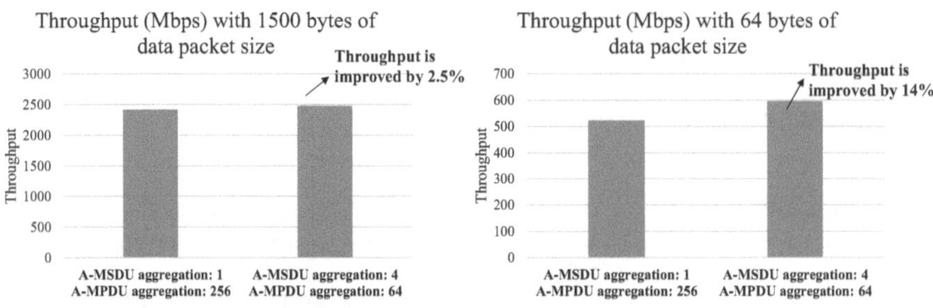

Fig. 4.30 A-MSDU improves throughput

(4) **Throughput Improvement from A-MSDU**

Multiple MSDUs are aggregated into a single A-MSDU, which shares the MAC layer frame header and reduces the overhead of the MAC layer frame header accordingly. This optimization is particularly beneficial for small-sized of user data packets.

Let's consider the BE9300 product as an example. Figure 4.30 shows the throughput variations under different A-MSDU aggregation settings according to the theoretical analysis in the 5 GHz frequency band with a physical rate of 2882 Mbps.

The benefits of A-MSDU aggregation become more pronounced when considering scenarios with small-sized data packets. Even while the number of MSDUs aggregated in one A-MPDU remains constant, enabling A-MSDU aggregation further enhances throughput. On the left side of Fig. 4.30, for a 1500 bytes packet size, the throughput improved by 2.5% when there are four MSDUs aggregated into one A-MSDU. On the right side of Fig. 4.30, for the scenario of a 64 bytes packet size, the throughput improved by 14% when there are four MSDUs aggregated into one A-MSDU.

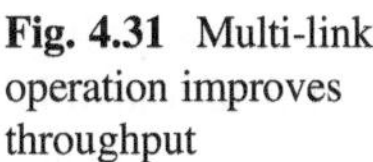

Fig. 4.31 Multi-link operation improves throughput

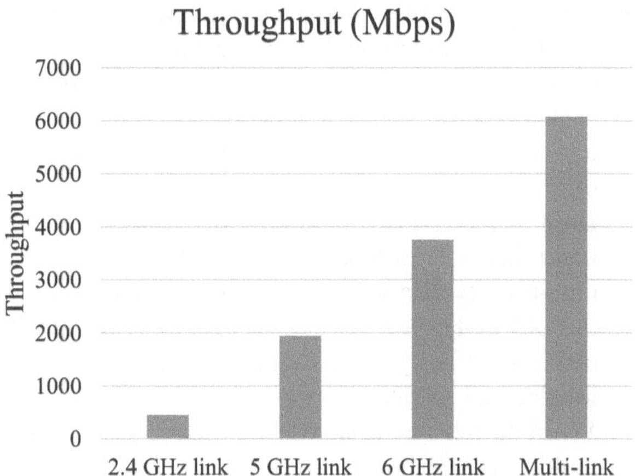

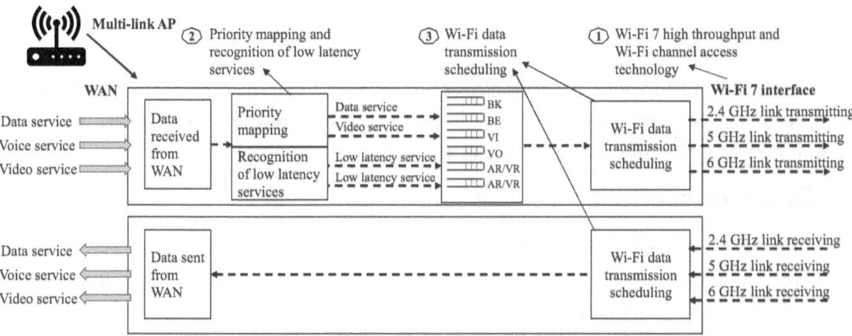

Fig. 4.32 Latency performance optimization

4. **Throughput improvement with multi-link operation technology**

This technology offers significant throughput improvement by enabling simultaneous data transmission across multiple links between the multi-link AP and the multi-link STA. Figure 4.31 shows the theoretical throughput result of the BE9300 product, where the throughput over a multi-link Wi-Fi connection is the sum of the throughput of single-link Wi-Fi connections for each link. However, the actual throughput attained over a multi-link Wi-Fi connection is based upon the performance of multi-link scheduling.

4.2.4.2 Latency Performance Optimization

Figure 4.32 illustrates the key factors affecting the latency of data transmission between the WAN interface and the Wi-Fi interface of the multi-link AP device, including throughput and wireless channel access technology, handling of data packets prioritization, and Wi-Fi data transmission scheduling.

- **Throughput and Wi-Fi channel access technology:** The extremely high throughput brought by Wi-Fi 7 technology reduces the latency of data transmission through Wi-Fi networks. In addition, the restricted Target Wake Time technology of Wi-Fi 7 supports the scheduling of the data transmission of low-latency services at the target time, ensuring the real-time data transmission of low-latency services.
- **Data packets prioritization:** The downstream priority mapping function in multi-link APs differentiates the data packets, effectively reducing latency for high-priority data services. Moreover, the technology for identifying characteristics of low-latency services ensures swift recognition and directs such traffic to dedicated priority queues. This approach ensures real-time data transmission for low-latency services.
- **Wi-Fi data transmission scheduling:** The Wi-Fi data transmission scheduling in multi-link APs includes the scheduling of multi-link transmission and the scheduling of OFDMA and MU-MIMO transmission. The multi-link AP performs the scheduling with consideration of the data packet's priority, which reduces the latency of the high-priority traffic and the low-latency services.

The following introduces more about the topics of downstream priority mapping, the characteristics recognition of low-latency services, and the Wi-Fi data transmission scheduling for latency optimization.

1. **Downstream priority mapping**

In the IP-based network, the priority of the data packet is defined separately at the IP layer, Ethernet layer, and Wi-Fi MAC layer. The multi-link AP implements priority mapping between the IP layer or Ethernet layer and the 802.11 MAC layer. Data forwarding in Wi-Fi is then executed based on the priority of the 802.11 MAC layer. Figure 4.33 illustrates the priority mapping within the 802.11 MAC layer.

The first chapter introduced the 802.11 MAC layer, which defines eight traffic types ranging from 0 to 7, corresponding to the 802.11 priority levels of data frames within the MAC layer. Additionally, it outlines four radio access categories (AC)—VO, VI, BE, and BK—corresponding to priorities from highest to lowest. A clear mapping between these categories is established.

At the Ethernet layer, priorities are identified using an 802.1D priority tag, ranging from 0 to 7, aligning with the eight priorities designated for Ethernet data frame forwarding at Layer 2. This results in a direct and one-to-one mapping between the priority of the Ethernet Layer and the traffic types of the 802.11 MAC Layer.

Meanwhile, at the IP layer, priority is marked by the Differentiated Services Code Point (DSCP) value in the IP frame header, ranging from 0 to 63, which identifies the service type of the data packet. For the mapping between the DSCP value and the 802.11 MAC layer traffic type, a common practice is to map the upper three bits of the DSCP to the 802.11 MAC layer traffic type. However, it is worth noting that this mapping is not perfectly aligned with the priorities defined by the DSCP values

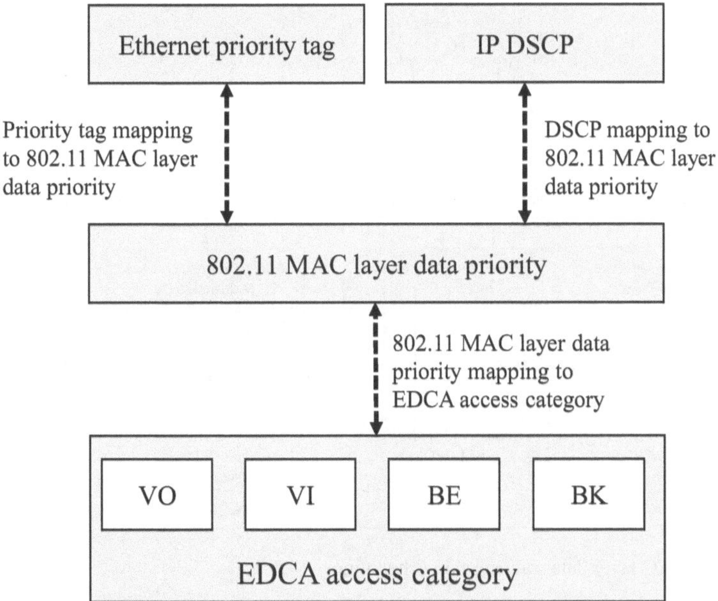

Fig. 4.33 Priority mapping

defined by the Internet Engineering Task Force (IETF). As a result, the IETF has defined a reference mapping between DSCP values and 802.11 MAC layer traffic types to serve as a guideline for implementation.

2. **The characteristics recognition of low latency services**

Wi-Fi 7 extends Stream Classification Service (SCS) technology by introducing the QoS Characteristics information element to delineate the QoS characteristic parameters of SCS streams. Key components of this recognition process include:

- **SCS capability:** In the Extended Capabilities information element of the Beacon frame, a value of 1 at bit 54 indicates that the multi-link AP supports SCS. Conversely, a value of 0 indicates a lack of support.
- **QoS characteristics capability:** In the EHT Capabilities information element of the Beacon frame, a value of 1 at bit 5 of the EHT MAC capability field indicates that the multi-link AP supports the QoS characteristics information element. Conversely, a value of 0 indicates a lack of support.

With supporting SCS and QoS characteristics, the multi-link AP completes the characteristics recognition process for specific low-latency services with STAs. Subsequently, it orchestrates downstream and upstream data transmission scheduling based on the priority and the QoS characteristics to meet the latency requirements of low-latency services.

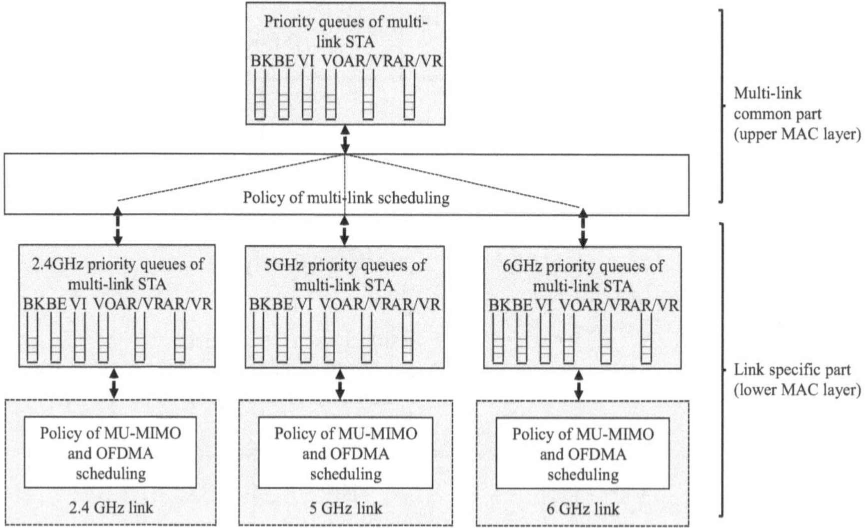

Fig. 4.34 MAC layer data transmission scheduling

3. **The Wi-Fi data transmission scheduling**

Figure 4.34 illustrates the MAC layer data transmission scheduling model. Within both the upper and lower MAC layers, *priority queues* are designated for each multi-link STA connected to the multi-link AP. The multi-link scheduling module schedules the transmission of data packets from the priority queues of the upper MAC layer to the corresponding priority queues of a specific link in the lower MAC layer. At each link level, the MU-MIMO and OFDMA scheduling module facilitates multiuser data transmission scheduling in both downstream and upstream directions, leveraging MU-MIMO and OFDMA technologies.

Here's an elaboration on the multi-link scheduling module and the MU-MIMO and OFDMA scheduling modules:

(1) **Multi-link scheduling module**

The multi-link scheduling module schedules data transmission with consideration of the load balancing of multiple links and the priority of data packets.

- **Load balancing:** Performs the transmission scheduling according to the load on each link to achieve the multi-link load balancing and improve the utilization efficiency of wireless channel.
- **Priority of data packets:** Data transmission scheduling is also influenced by the priority of the data packets. Mapping from TID to the corresponding link of the multi-link AP and multi-link, STA is considered. If there is no mapping for the TIDs, the data packets with higher priority can be scheduled to links with higher physical rates and lower interference, ensuring lower latency.

(2) **MU-MIMO and OFDMA scheduling module**

For scenarios involving multiple users with low-latency services, the multi-link AP allocates MRUs based on the volume of data packets in different priority queues of each STA. Data transmission then occurs bidirectionally using OFDMA, effectively reducing latency for low-latency services.

In cases with multiple users requiring high-throughput services, the multi-link AP allocates larger MRU resources based on the amount of data packets in various priority queues of each STA. Data transmission then occurs bidirectionally using a combination of OFDMA and MU-MIMO, enhancing overall throughput performance.

4.2.5 Wi-Fi 7 Wireless Channel Management

Wi-Fi networks operate in the unlicensed wireless frequency bands. In the actual deployment environment of a Wi-Fi network, there are various interference factors that impact the AP wireless channel access and data transmission. This interference includes interference generated by other Wi-Fi devices operating in the same frequency band, as well as interference generated by non-Wi-Fi devices in the same frequency band. Selecting a wireless channel with minimal interference as the working channel of the AP is crucial for optimizing Wi-Fi network performance and the reliability of the Wi-Fi network.

4.2.5.1 Channel Selection Overview

AP devices support both manual and automatic modes for configuring the working channel. In manual configuration mode, users manually configure the working channel of the AP through the AP's configuration page. In automatic configuration mode, the AP automatically selects the channel with the least interference based on the interference levels.

Wi-Fi channel management involves automatic channel selection (ACS) when the AP is configured in the automatic mode.

For example, in a Wi-Fi network deployment scenario shown in Fig. 4.35, the AP of neighbor network 1 operates on channel 1 with a channel bandwidth of 20 MHz in the 2.4 GHz band, and the AP of neighbor network 2 operates on channel 11 with a channel bandwidth of 20 MHz in the 2.4 GHz band. In order to avoid interference from the neighbor networks, the AP of Home network selects channel 6, ensuring optimal network performance by operating on a different channel than the neighboring networks.

The functions of wireless channel management encompass the following three aspects:

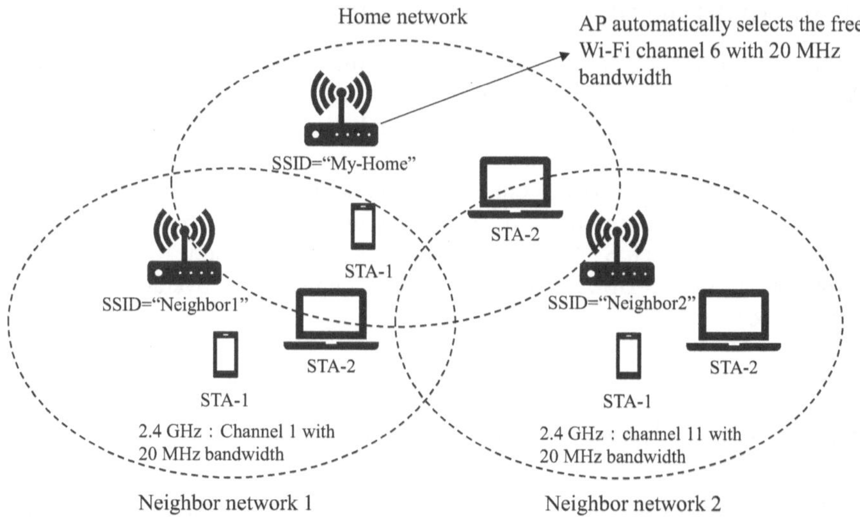

Fig. 4.35 Deployment scenario of Wi-Fi channel optimization

(1) **Support automatic channel selection for different Wi-Fi frequency bands**

The available channels in a frequency band include basic channels with a 20 MHz bandwidth, as well as channels with higher bandwidths bundled from multiple adjacent 20 MHz channels, such as 40 MHz, 80 MHz, etc. Each channel is identified by its primary 20 MHz channel ID and its bandwidth. The wireless channel management facilitates the automatic selection of the optimal wireless channel among all available channels in different frequency bands.

(2) **Automatic channel selection during the initialization stage**

During the initialization stage following the AP reboot, the AP scans all available channels. Based on the results of this channel scan, the system selects the optimal channel with the least interference as the working channel of the AP.

(3) **Automatic channel selection at runtime**

During the operation of the AP, the AP continuously monitors the interference on the current working channel and all other available channels. When certain conditions specified by the automatic channel selection algorithm are met, the AP triggers the automatic channel selection and switches to a new channel.

The functions of wireless channel management are realized by the wireless channel management module and the Wi-Fi driver module. As shown in Fig. 4.36, the wireless channel management module retrieves the list of available channels and triggers the channel scanning to assess the interference conditions on each channel. Based on the scan results, it automatically selects the optimal channel. On the other hand, the Wi-Fi driver module maintains the list of available channels and executes

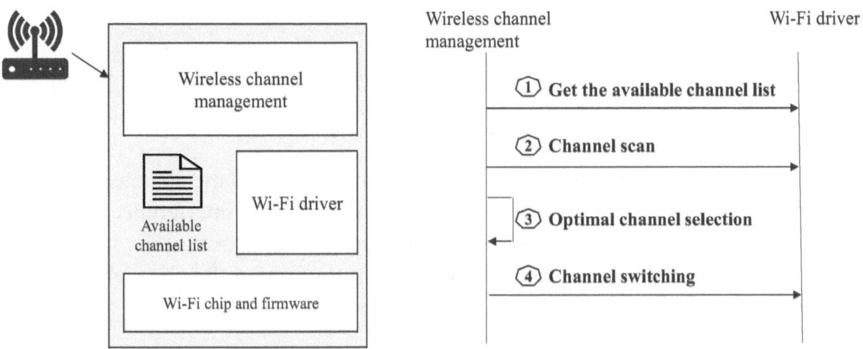

Fig. 4.36 Wi-Fi channel management software module

the actions of channel scanning and channel switching as directed by the wireless channel management module.

The difference in wireless channel management for Wi-Fi 7 mainly includes the following four aspects.

(1) **Support for wireless channels with higher bandwidth**

Wi-Fi 7 supports wireless channels with 320 MHz bandwidth as an optional requirement in the 6 GHz frequency band.

(2) **Impact of channel bundling technology in Wi-Fi 7**

Wi-Fi 7 employs preamble puncturing technology, which masks the subchannels with interference and supports data transmission over discontinuous bundled channels. This influences the channel selection algorithm to prefer bundled channels with higher bandwidth and selects the 20 MHz channel with the least interference in the bundled channel as the primary 20 MHz channel.

(3) **Influence of Wi-Fi 7 multi-link technology**

The multi-link operation technology supports data transmission and retransmission across multiple links. This capability helps mitigate potential packet loss caused by the channel scanning procedure.

(4) **Channel switching process in Wi-Fi 7**

The 802.11 specification includes a seamless channel switching process based on Channel Switch Announcement (CSA). Wi-Fi 7 enhances the sending of CSA messages for channel switching of a single link over multiple links, thereby improving the reliability of the seamless channel switching process.

The following sections introduce the wireless channel management function from three aspects: channel scanning, the automatic channel selection process, and channel switching.

4.2.5.2 Channel Scanning

Wireless channel management is responsible for initiating channel scanning and gathers statistics information on each wireless channel to assess interference levels of the channel.

The statistics information of the wireless channel includes the channel utilization within the Wi-Fi network, the channel utilization of external interference, the power levels of background noise, and the information on neighboring APs in the same operating channel. The total channel utilization is the sum of the channel utilization of the Wi-Fi network and the external interference.

- **Current working channel**: The AP collects the statistics information on the current working channel during normal transmission and reception by monitoring the Wi-Fi physical layer carrier and MAC layer beacon frames.
- **Nonworking channel:** For nonworking channels, the AP conducts off-channel scans to collect relevant statistics. This procedure involves temporarily switching to the nonworking channel to be scanned and collects relevant statistics information by monitoring the Wi-Fi physical layer carrier listening and MAC layer beacon frames.

Figure 4.37 describes the channel scan procedure for nonworking channels. This procedure involves temporarily switching to the nonworking channel, monitoring it for relevant data, and then returning to the current working channel.

To mitigate service impact from possible packet loss during the channel scanning procedure, the policies for triggering channel scanning are described as follows:

- **Define the period of off-channel scan:** Scans are conducted sequentially with specific intervals, ensuring that each channel scan's duration remains within tens of milliseconds to about 100 milliseconds, thereby reducing the service impact from the off-channel scan. Additionally, the multi-link AP performs off-channel scans in only one frequency band at a time. In this way, the multi-link supports data packet transmission on other links during the off-channel scanning process to minimize service impact.

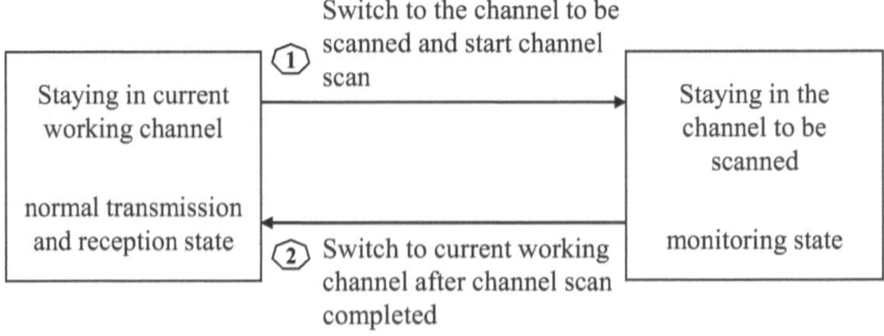

Fig. 4.37 Wi-Fi channel scan procedure

- **Define the trigger conditions of off-channel scan:** Scans are initiated only when no data is being transmitted or received on the current working channel, or when the interference level of the current channel is higher than a certain threshold.

4.2.5.3 Automatic Channel Selection Process

Figure 4.38 illustrates the channel selection process. It evaluates the channel score based on the scan results of the current working channel and the nonworking channels, then selects the preferred channel according to the channel selection policy and decides whether to initiate channel switching.

1. **Channel Score Evaluation**

For each channel with 20 MHz bandwidth, the channel score is evaluated according to the channel scan results of interference level, background noise, and neighboring APs in the channel. Channels exhibiting lower interference, minimal noise, and fewer neighboring APs receive higher channel scores. For bundled channels with higher bandwidth, the channel scores are computed by considering the weighted scores of each 20 MHz subchannel. The primary 20 MHz channel carries more weight, influencing the overall score of the bundled channel.

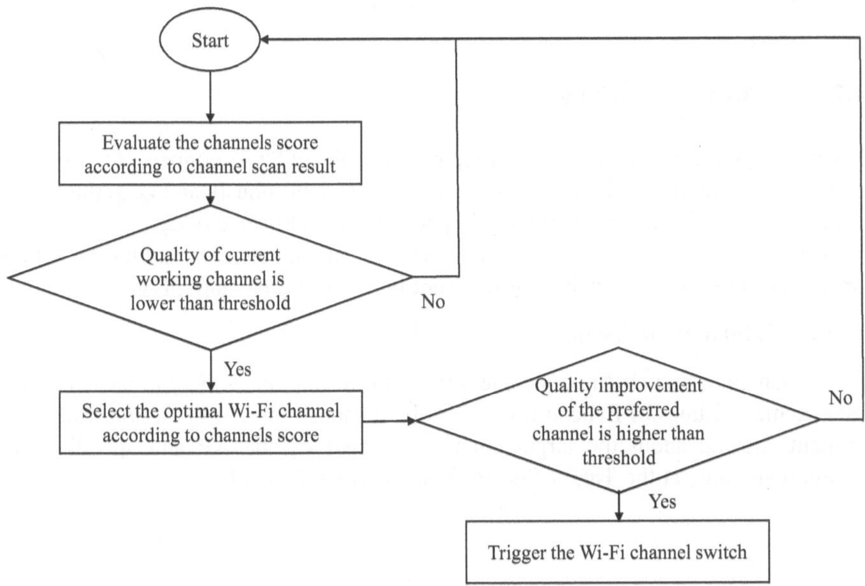

Fig. 4.38 Wi-Fi channel selection process

2. **Channel Selection Preference**

The optimal channel is selected according to the channel score; additionally, below rules are defined for channel selection based on the characteristics of the Wi-Fi frequency band.

- Channels with higher transmission power are preferred to improve the coverage of the Wi-Fi network.
- Considering the heavy congestion in the 2.4 GHz frequency band, channels with 20 MHz bandwidth are preferred.
- For the 6 GHz band with numerous channels, channels defined as preferred scanning channels are prioritized as the primary 20 MHz channels of the bundled channels, enhancing network discovery efficiency.

3. **Trigger Conditions of Channel Switching**

Considering the service impact of Wi-Fi channel switching (e.g., packet loss or Wi-Fi disconnection and reconnection), the trigger conditions for channel switching need to be well defined to avoid frequent channel switching. The following thresholds are defined for the trigger conditions of channel switching.

- **Threshold of current channel quality:** Channel switching is allowed only when the interference, background noise, or number of APs on the current channel surpasses predefined thresholds.
- **Channel quality of the preferred channel:** Channel switching is allowed only if the quality score of the preferred channel exceeds that of the current channel by a certain margin. This ensures that channel switching occurs only when there's a significant improvement in channel quality score.

4.2.5.4 Channel Switching

When the AP initiates channel switching on one link, all STAs connected to this link need to be notified to switch to the same channel synchronously and keep the Wi-Fi connections established to avoid any impact on the end-user services.

The 802.11 specification defines the CSA information element and the operating procedure for channel switch advertisement between the AP and STAs.

1. **CSA Information Element**

The Channel Switch Announcement (CSA) information element is carried in the management frames of Beacon frames, Probe response frames, or Action frames. It contains details about the target channel selected by the AP and specifies the countdown value at the Target Beacon Transmission Time (TBTT) interval.

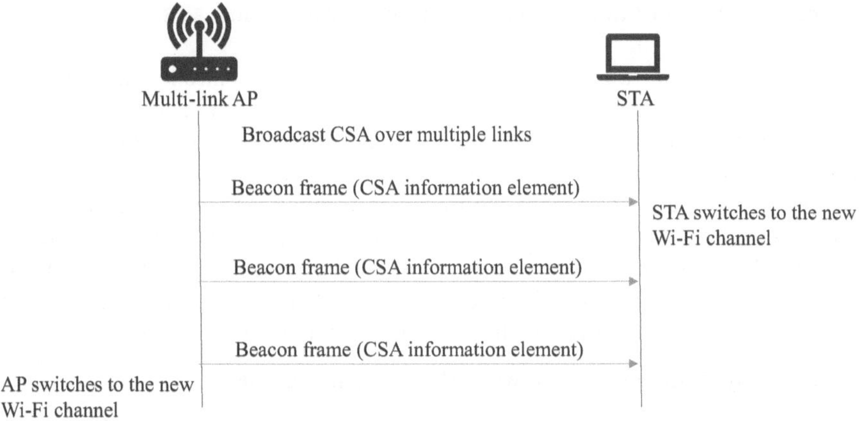

Fig. 4.39 Wi-Fi channel switching procedure

2. **Channel Switch Advertisement Procedure**
   - The multi-link AP disseminates management frames containing the CSA information element to all connected STAs, so that the STAs synchronously switch to the target channel according to the CSA received.
   - Additionally, the multi-link AP broadcasts the CSA information element to the multi-link STAs over other links as well, so that the multi-link STAs can perform the channel switch according to the CSA received over other links.

Figure 4.39 illustrates an example of the channel switching procedure between the multi-link AP and the STA. Here, the multi-link AP broadcasts the CSA information element with Beacon frames across multiple links, specifying the number of TBTT interval countdowns. Upon the countdown reaching zero, the AP performs a channel switch at the physical layer.

4.2.6 Wi-Fi 7 EasyMesh Network

The Wi-Fi Alliance's EasyMesh specification has garnered wide industry support. APs from different vendors equipped with EasyMesh technology can seamlessly interconnect to form an EasyMesh network with each other, extending the Wi-Fi coverage.

This section delves into the integration of EasyMesh features within Wi-Fi 7 multi-link AP products, including the functional requirements of EasyMesh, the protocol framework, software design, and the implementation of key EasyMesh functions.

4.2.6.1 The Main Functions of EasyMesh for Multi-Link APs

An EasyMesh network is a Wi-Fi network consisting of a controller AP and one or more proxy APs. Figure 4.40 shows the main functions of the EasyMesh network.

The main functions of EasyMesh for multi-link APs include the *proxy AP onboarding* to join the EasyMesh network, *wireless backhaul link optimization* of the proxy AP, the *Wi-Fi connection switching* between different Wi-Fi frequency bands and STA *Roaming* between APs. Table 4.10 describes each of these features.

Considering the tri-band multi-link AP BE9300 and the dual-band multi-link AP BE3600 as examples, Table 4.11 describes the onboarding components of the multi-link APs, including the backhaul links and network topologies.

1. **The EasyMesh network between BE9300 and BE9300**

Figure 4.41 illustrates the EasyMesh network consisting of two BE9300.

Backhaul Link The controller and proxy AP establish a tri-band multi-link wireless backhaul with a physical rate of up to 9.3 Gbps.

Fronthaul Link For the physical rate of the fronthaul link between the AP and STAs with two spatial streams, it reaches up to 9.3 Gbps with the Wi-Fi 7 tri-band STA, 2.4 Gbps with the Wi-Fi 6E STA in the 6 GHz frequency band, and up to 1.2 Gbps with the Wi-Fi 6 STA in the 5 GHz frequency band.

2. **The EasyMesh network between BE9300 and Wi-Fi 6E AP**

Figure 4.42 illustrates the EasyMesh network consisting of the BE9300 as the controller and the Wi-Fi 6E AP (AX5400) as the proxy.

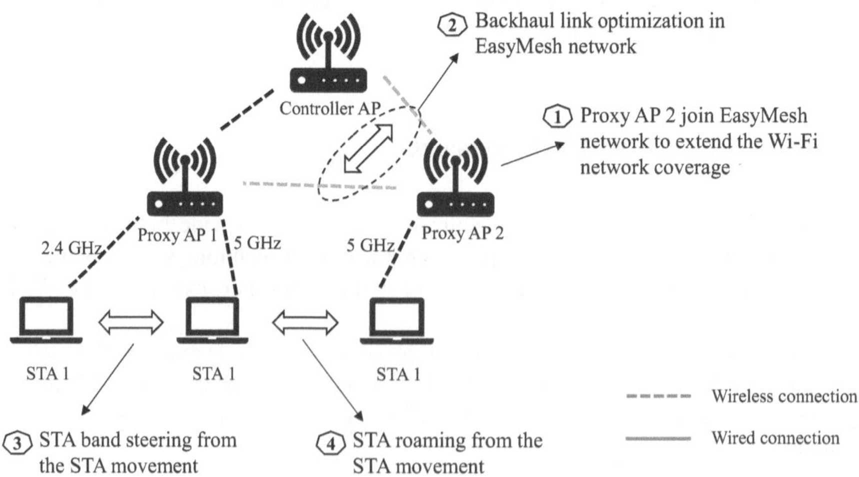

Fig. 4.40 Main functions of the EasyMesh network

Table 4.10 Main features of EasyMesh

Features	Description	Specifications
Onboarding	Form EasyMesh network with multiple Wi-Fi 7 multi-link APs with wired or Wi-Fi backhaul links. EasyMesh network can be formed between Wi-Fi 7 AP and Wi-Fi 6 APs. Support the EasyMesh network topology of tree or chain. The Wi-Fi backhaul link can be multi-link or single-link Wi-Fi connection over a frequency band of 2.4 GHz, 5 GHz, and 6 GHz. Support the onboarding method of push button defined in the EasyMesh specification.	The automatic onboarding procedure without manual configurations needed
Wi-Fi backhaul link optimization	Support backhaul link metrics collection defined in the EasyMesh specification and select the optimal Wi-Fi backhaul link according to backhaul link metrics.	The period of Wi-Fi backhaul link switching is less than 1 s
Wi-Fi connection switching (Band steering)	Support STA link metrics collection and establish Wi-Fi connection between STA and AP at the optimal frequency band according to STA link metrics. For single-link STA, Wi-Fi connection switching between different Wi-Fi frequency bands of the multi-link AP is supported. For multi-link STA, it prefers the multi-link Wi-Fi connection instead of band steering between different frequency bands of the multi-link AP.	The period of Wi-Fi connection switching is less than 1 s
Roaming	Support STA link metrics collection and establish a Wi-Fi connection between STA and the target AP with optimal performance according to STA link metrics. Support Wi-Fi connection switching between STA and different APs.	The period of Wi-Fi connection switching is less than 1 s

Backhaul Link The wireless backhaul link prioritizes the 6 GHz frequency band, where the physical rate of the backhaul link reaches up to 2.4 Gbps. Since the Wi-Fi signal attenuation is quicker in the 6 GHz than in the 5 GHz frequency band, in scenarios with longer distances, the wireless backhaul switches to the alternative 5 GHz frequency band if the physical rate of the backhaul link becomes too low due to weak Wi-Fi signals in the 6 GHz frequency band.

Fronthaul Link For the physical rate of the fronthaul link between the proxy AP and STAs with two spatial streams, it achieves up to 2.4 Gbps with the Wi-Fi 6E STA in the 6 GHz frequency band and up to 1.2 Gbps with the Wi-Fi 6 STA in the 5 GHz frequency band.

Table 4.11 Onboarding functions of BE9300 and BE3600

Onboarding component	BE9300	BE3600
Wired backhaul link	10 Gbps	2.5 Gbps
Wi-Fi backhaul link	Support multi-link Wi-Fi connection as Wi-Fi backhaul link over all frequency bands of 2.4 GHz, 5 GHz, and 6 GHz	Support multi-link Wi-Fi connection as Wi-Fi backhaul link over all frequency bands of 2.4 GHz and 5 GHz
Network topologies	Tree and chain	Tree and chain
Wi-Fi backhaul link preference with different proxy APs	(1) Prefer multi-link Wi-Fi connection over frequency bands of 2.4 GHz, 5 GHz, and 6 GHz when forming an EasyMesh network with another BE9300 (2) Prefer 6 GHz frequency band and take 5 GHz frequency band as backup when forming an EasyMesh network with Wi-Fi 6E tri-band AP	(1) Prefer multi-link Wi-Fi connection over frequency bands of 2.4 GHz and 5 GHz when forming an EasyMesh network with another BE3600 (2) Prefer 5 GHz frequency band when forming an EasyMesh network with Wi-Fi 6 dual-band AP

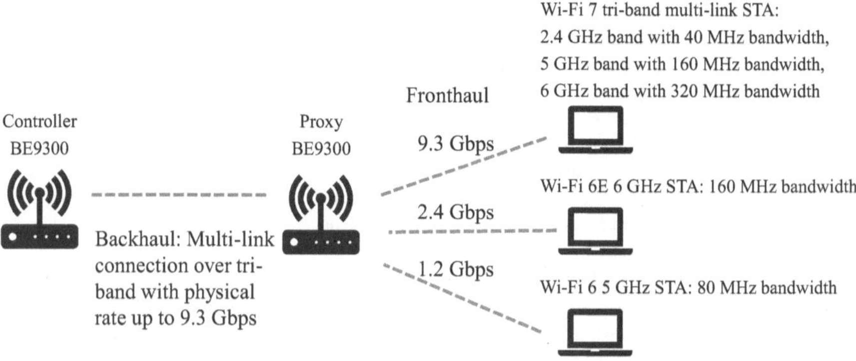

Fig. 4.41 EasyMesh network formed by BE9300

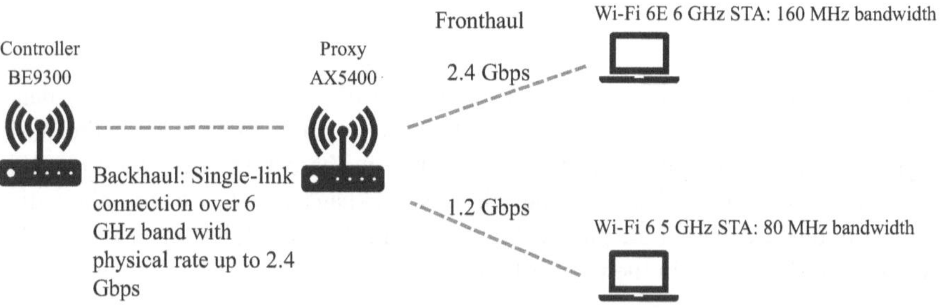

Fig. 4.42 EasyMesh network formed by BE9300 and Wi-Fi 6E AP

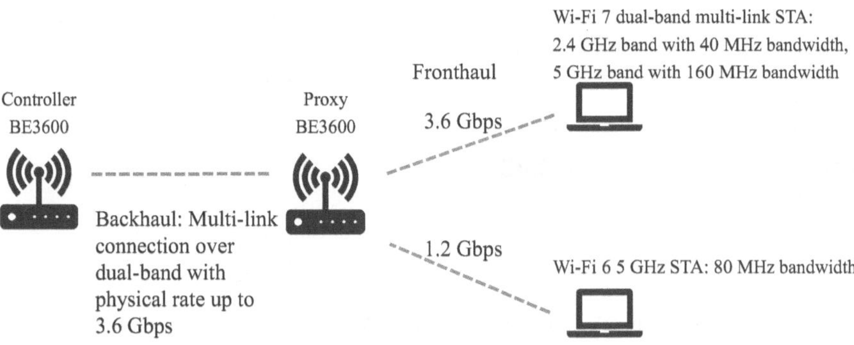

Fig. 4.43 EasyMesh network formed by BE3600

3. **The EasyMesh network between BE3600 and BE3600**

Figure 4.43 illustrates the EasyMesh network consisting of two BE3600.

Backhaul Link The wireless backhaul link prioritizes the multi-link Wi-Fi connection of the 5 GHz and 2.4 GHz frequency bands, with a physical rate of up to 3.6 Gbps.

Fronthaul Link For the physical rate of the fronthaul link between the AP and STAs with two spatial streams, it reaches up to 3.6 Gbps with the Wi-Fi 7 dual-band STA and up to 1.2 Gbps with the Wi-Fi 6 STA in the 5 GHz frequency band.

4. **The EasyMesh network between BE3600 and Wi-Fi 6 AP**

Figure 4.44 illustrates the Easy Mesh network consisting of the BE3600 as controller and the Wi-Fi 6 AP as proxy.

Backhaul Link The wireless backhaul link prioritizes the Wi-Fi connection in the 5 GHz frequency band, with a physical rate up to 2.4 Gbps. The dedicated backhaul link in the 2.4 GHz frequency band is not considered due to its low bandwidth and physical rate.

Fronthaul Link For the physical rate of the fronthaul link between the proxy AP and STAs with two spatial streams, it reaches up to 2.4 Gbps with the Wi-Fi 6 STA in the 5 GHz frequency band and up to 0.6 Gbps with the Wi-Fi 6 STA in the 2.4 GHz frequency band.

4.2.6.2 EasyMesh Protocol Framework and Software Design

The EasyMesh specification outlines the EasyMesh network architecture and the control message protocol between APs within the EasyMesh network. This section provides an overview of the network architecture, control message protocol [3], and software design of EasyMesh.

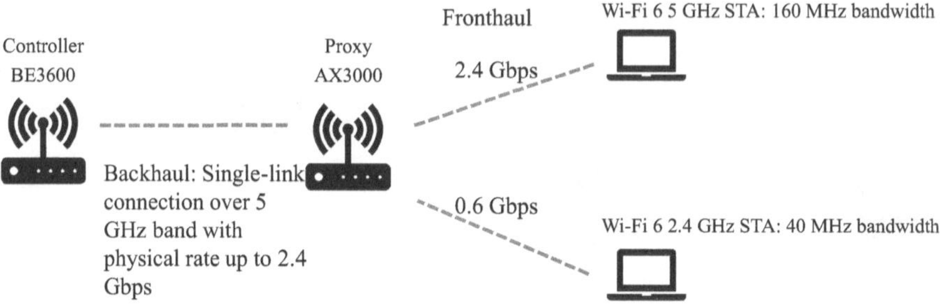

Fig. 4.44 EasyMesh network formed by BE3600 and Wi-Fi 6 AP

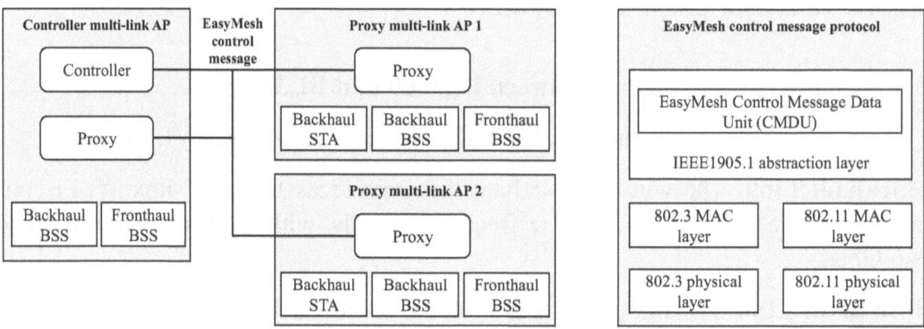

Fig. 4.45 EasyMesh network architecture and control message protocol

1. **Network Architecture and Control Message Protocol**

Figure 4.45 illustrates the EasyMesh network architecture and control message protocol.

The controller multi-link AP implements the controller logical entity and the proxy logical entity, as well as the backhaul BSS and fronthaul BSS. The proxy multi-link AP implements the proxy logical entity and creates the backhaul BSS, fronthaul BSS, and backhaul STA.

- **Backhaul BSS:** The controller or proxy multi-link AP device creates the backhaul BSS, to which other proxy AP devices establish the Wi-Fi backhaul link and join the EasyMesh network.
- **Fronthaul BSS:** Also created by the controller or proxy multi-link AP, the fronthaul BSS enables Wi-Fi STAs to establish connections and access the Wi-Fi network.
- **Backhaul STA:** Created by the proxy multi-link AP, the backhaul STA facilitates the establishment of the Wi-Fi backhaul link to the backhaul BSS of other multi-link AP devices in the EasyMesh network and joins the EasyMesh network.

The multi-link APs in the EasyMesh network communicate with each other through control messages transmitted over the wired or wireless backhaul link.

Table 4.12 Control message types

Control messages	Message type	Description
Controller AP discovery	0x0007	AP autoconfiguration search message used to search for the controller AP
	0x0008	A message to respond to the AP autoconfiguration search message
AP autoconfiguration synchronization	0x0009	AP autoconfiguration message used to synchronize Wi-Fi configuration
	0x000A	AP autoconfiguration message used to renew Wi-Fi configuration
Backhaul link metrics	0x0005	Link metrics query message
	0x0006	A message to respond to the link metrics query message
Backhaul link steering	0x8019	Backhaul link steering request
	0x801A	A message to respond to the backhaul link steering request message
STA link metrics	0x800D	STA link metrics query for associated STAs
	0x800E	A message to respond to the STA link metrics query for associated STAs
	0x800F	STA link metrics query for unassociated STAs
	0x8010	A message to respond to the STA link metrics query for unassociated STAs
STA connection steering	0x8014	STA connection steering request
	0x8015	A message to provide the result of the STA connection steering request message

The controller multi-link AP manages the EasyMesh network using these control messages.

The EasyMesh control message protocol is depicted on the right side of Fig. 4.45. Based on the IEEE 1905.1 abstraction layer protocol, which provides a common interface to various underlying communication technologies, such as 802.3 Ethernet and 802.11 Wi-Fi, the EasyMesh control messages extend the IEEE 1905.1 control messages. These messages facilitate the controller multi-link AP device in managing the EasyMesh network.

The EasyMesh control messages include all aspects of EasyMesh network management, including controller AP discovery, AP autoconfiguration synchronization, backhaul link metrics query, backhaul link steering, STA link metrics query, and STA connection steering, etc. Table 4.12 provides a brief overview of these control message types defined in the EasyMesh specification, aiding in the comprehension of subsequent content related to EasyMesh development.

2. **The software design of EasyMesh**

Figure 4.46 illustrates the software design of EasyMesh, aligning with the EasyMesh network architecture. It includes the software modules of the 1905 protocol, EasyMesh controller, and EasyMesh proxy.

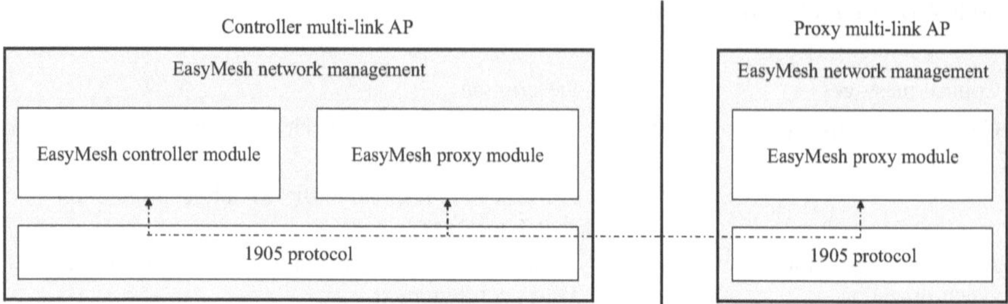

Fig. 4.46 EasyMesh software modules

- **1905 protocol software module**: Implements the functionalities of the IEEE 1905.1 abstraction layer protocol.
- **EasyMesh controller software module**: The controller software module is the control unit for the EasyMesh function, which runs on the controller AP device. It implements the functions of EasyMesh network management tasks, including configuration synchronization of proxy APs, collecting backhaul link metrics and STA link metrics, managing backhaul link optimization, and controlling STA connection steering, etc.
- **EasyMesh agent software module:** The agent software module, executing on each AP device in the EasyMesh network, is responsible for reporting the AP device's capabilities and the link metrics associated with backhaul and STA connections. Additionally, it executes instructions based on the control messages received from the controller AP device.

4.2.6.3 EasyMesh Onboarding Process

The EasyMesh network onboarding process encompasses both wired and wireless methods. The wired onboarding process of the EasyMesh network is shown in Figs. 4.47 and 4.48 depicts the wireless onboarding process.

1. **Wired Onboarding Process**

Fig. 4.47 outlines the wired onboarding process, which initiates by connecting the new proxy multi-link AP to the EasyMesh network via a wired cable. Subsequently, the controller multi-link AP completes the configuration synchronization of the newly added proxy multi-link AP.

2. **Wireless Onboarding Process**

The wireless onboarding process of the EasyMesh network is illustrated in Fig. 4.48. This process first configures the EasyMesh backhaul BSS access information for the new proxy multi-link AP. Following this, the proxy multi-link AP joins the EasyMesh network through the backhaul BSS, after which the controller

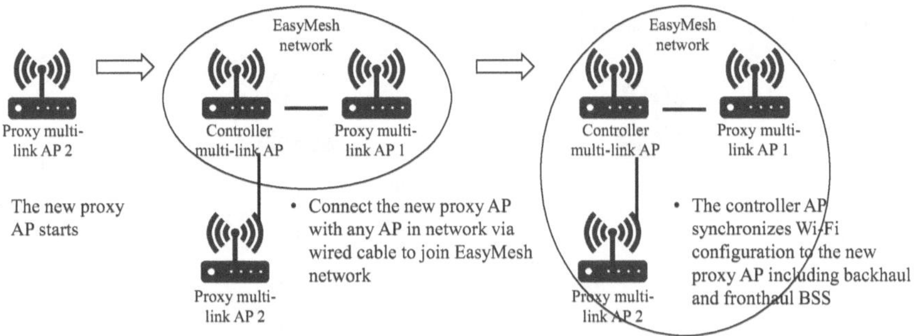

Fig. 4.47 EasyMesh wired onboarding process

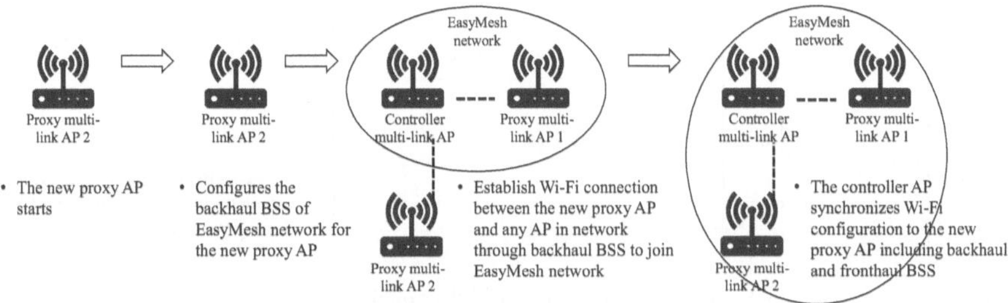

Fig. 4.48 EasyMesh wireless onboarding process

multi-link AP completes the configuration synchronization of the newly added proxy multi-link AP.

The main difference between the wireless and wired onboarding is that the wireless onboarding process requires the backhaul BSS access information to be configured for the new proxy multi-link AP. Once the new proxy multi-link AP joins the EasyMesh network via a wired or wireless connection, the configuration synchronization process remains consistent regardless of the onboarding method.

Figure 4.49 illustrates the detailed wireless onboarding procedure utilizing the Push Button Configuration (PBC) method defined in the EasyMesh specification [3].

(1) **Configuration of backhaul BSS access information**

By triggering the PBC button simultaneously on the multi-link AP 2 and multi-link AP 1, the backhaul STA of the multi-link AP 2 establishes a Wi-Fi connection to the fronthaul BSS of multi-link AP 1. This connection is established with the encryption key negotiated based on the MAC address of the backhaul STA. Subsequently, over this Wi-Fi connection, the multi-link AP 1 sends the backhaul BSS access information to multi-link AP 2.

Table 4.13 shows the contents of the backhaul BSS access information, which includes the SSID name, the authentication type, the encryption method, and password of the backhaul BSS.

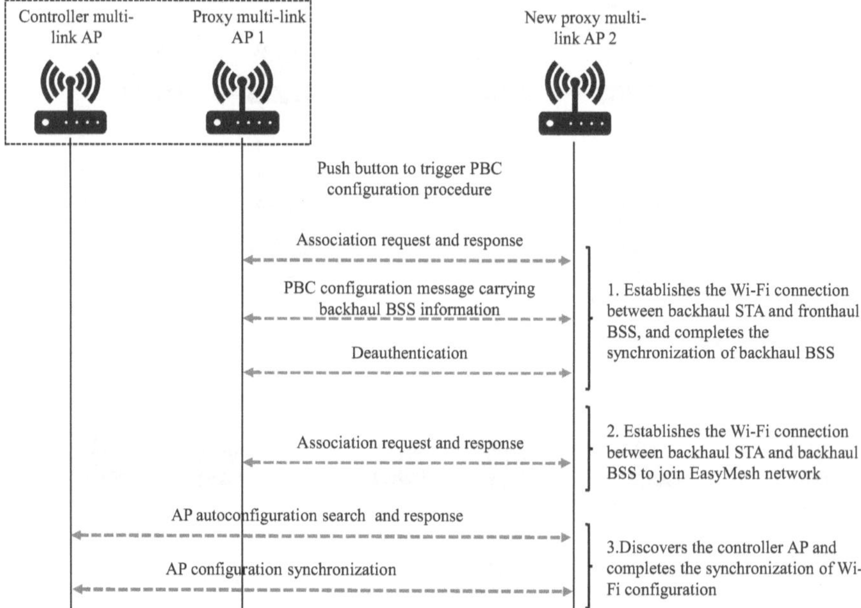

Fig. 4.49 EasyMesh onboarding process based on PBC method

Table 4.13 Backhaul BSS access information

Parameters	Description
SSID	SSID name of the backhaul BSS
Authentication type	The authentication type of the BSS
Encryption method	The encryption method of the BSS
Password	The password to connect to the BSS

(2) **Establishing the Wi-Fi connection to the backhaul BSS**

After receiving the backhaul BSS access information, multi-link AP 2 establishes a Wi-Fi connection to the backhaul BSS of the target AP via the backhaul STA and joins the EasyMesh network.

(3) **Controller AP discovery and Wi-Fi configuration synchronization**

Once multi-link AP 2 has joined the EasyMesh network, it initiates the controller AP discovery control message to identify the controller multi-link AP. Once discovered, the controller multi-link AP performs the AP autoconfiguration synchronization with the agent multi-link AP 2. Figure 4.50 illustrates the AP autoconfiguration synchronization process and the BSS configuration content defined in the EasyMesh specification.

Multi-link AP 2 sends an autoconfiguration request to the controller multi-link AP for each frequency band, and the controller multi-link AP responds with an

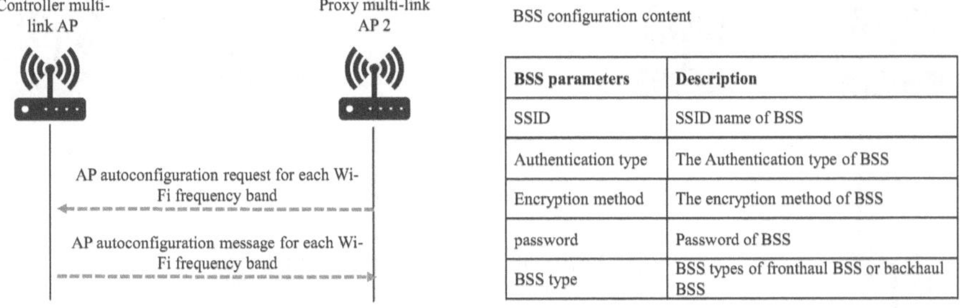

BSS parameters	Description
SSID	SSID name of BSS
Authentication type	The Authentication type of BSS
Encryption method	The encryption method of BSS
password	Password of BSS
BSS type	BSS types of fronthaul BSS or backhaul BSS

Fig. 4.50 AP autoconfiguration synchronization

autoconfiguration message containing the BSS configuration content for that frequency band.

In the case of Wi-Fi 7 multi-link APs, the BSS configuration content must be extended to denote one or more Wi-Fi frequency bands associated with the BSS Additionally, the AP autoconfiguration message will be extended to denote one or more Wi-Fi frequency bands associated with the backhaul STA. This enhancement is outlined in the latest iteration of the EasyMesh specification, version R6.

4.2.6.4 Backhaul Link Optimization

The new proxy multi-link AP selects the target multi-link AP in the EasyMesh network according to the level of the Wi-Fi signal. It then establishes the wireless backhaul link toward the target AP during the wireless onboarding process. After the onboarding process is completed, the controller AP monitors the link metrics of the backhaul link and selects the preferred backhaul link for optimization. Figure 4.51 illustrates the scenario of backhaul link optimization.

The process of wireless backhaul link optimization is shown in Fig. 4.52, which includes the backhaul link metrics query, optimization policy, link steering, and backhaul link switching.

1. **Backhaul Link Metrics Query**

The controller multi-link AP collects the link metrics of the current backhaul link and all candidate backhaul links through the backhaul link metrics query control message. Key parameters include link type and physical rate of the link. Figure 4.53 shows the key parameters of backhaul link metrics for a proxy multi-link AP device in the EasyMesh network.

2. **Policy of Backhaul Link Optimization**

The controller multi-link AP selects the preferred backhaul link according to the policy of backhaul link optimization, which mainly includes the following aspects.

(1) Preference for wired backhaul links.
(2) Preference for higher physical rates in wireless backhaul links.

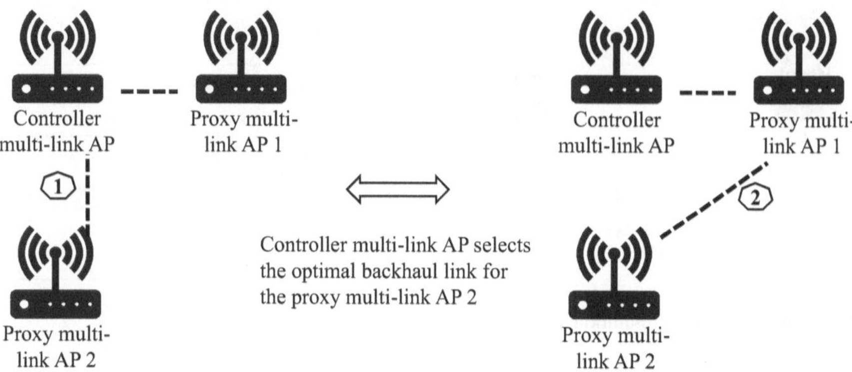

Fig. 4.51 Backhaul link optimization scenario

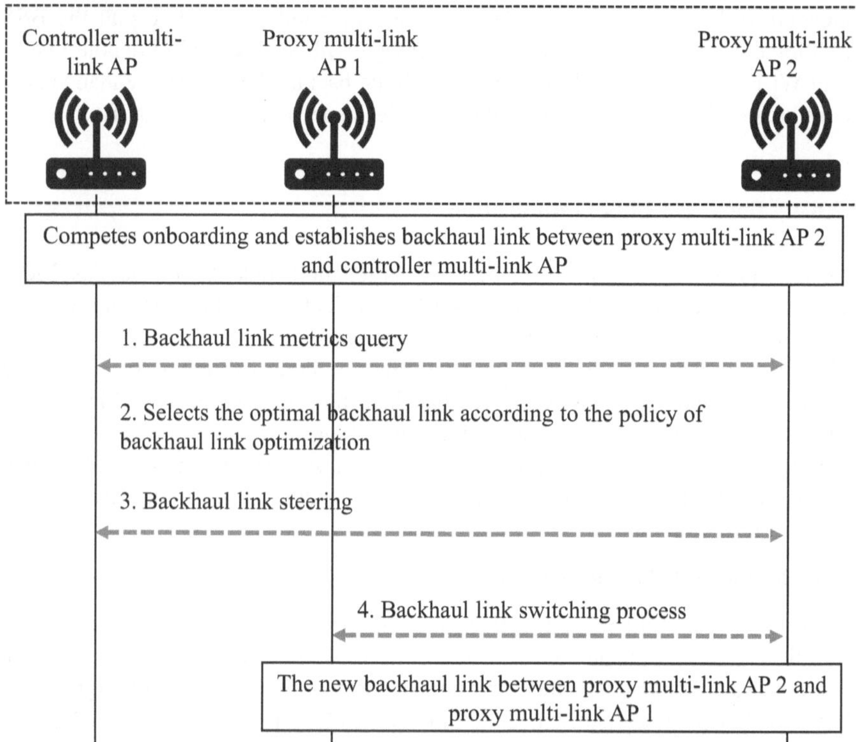

Fig. 4.52 Wireless backhaul link optimization process

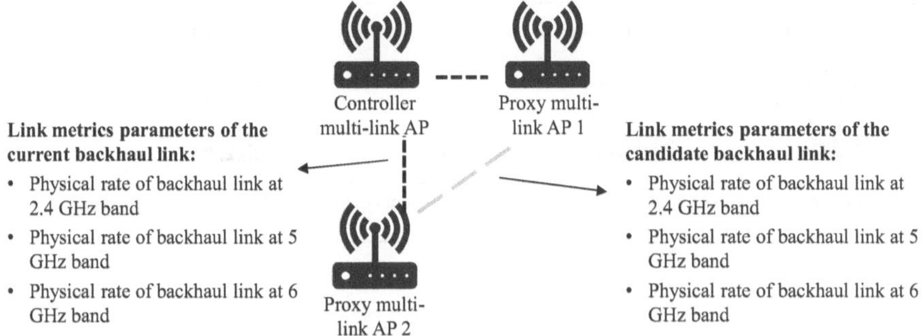

Fig. 4.53 Key parameters of wireless backhaul link metrics

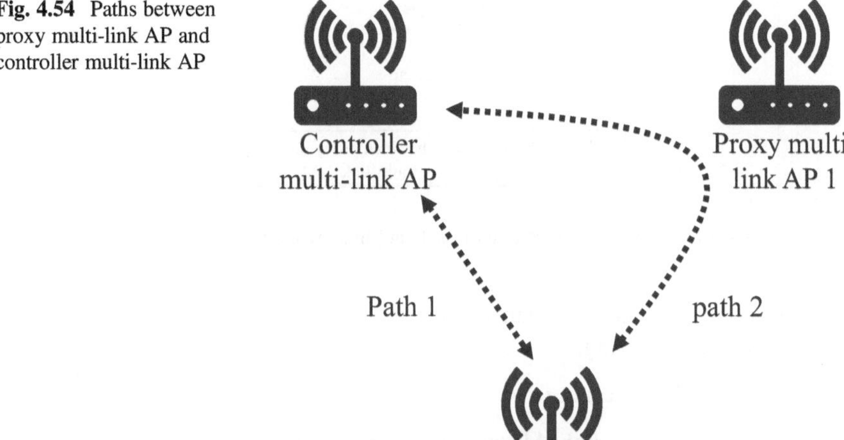

Fig. 4.54 Paths between proxy multi-link AP and controller multi-link AP

(3) Calculation of quality scores for different paths between proxy multi-link APs and controller multi-link APs, the path with the highest quality score is preferred. Figure 4.54 shows the two paths available between the proxy AP 2 and the controller AP.

- The quality score of path 1 is determined by the link metrics of the backhaul link between the proxy AP 2 and the controller AP.
- The quality score of path 2 is determined by the link metrics of the backhaul link between the proxy AP 2 and the proxy AP 1, as well as the backhaul link between the proxy AP 1 and the controller AP.

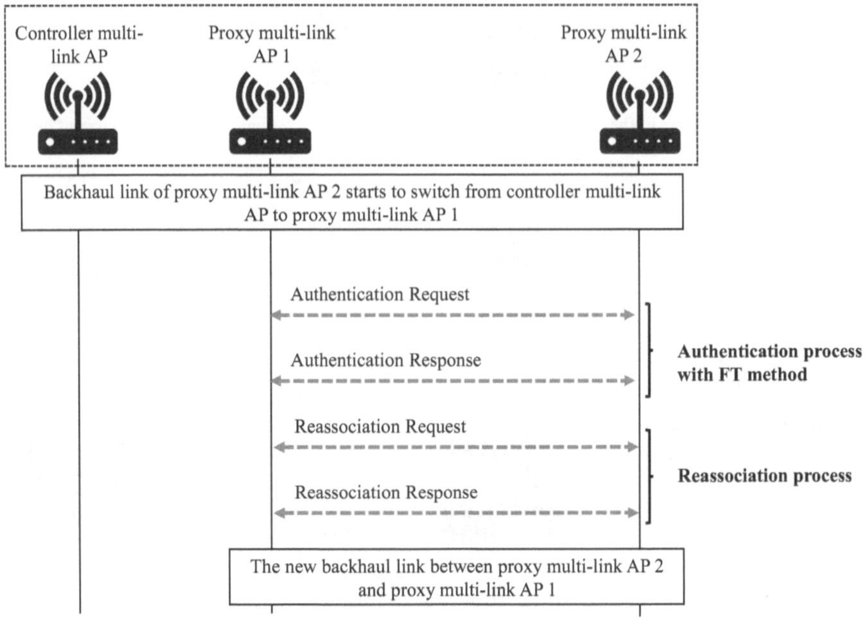

Fig. 4.55 Fast BSS Transition procedure of backhaul link switching

(4) Threshold for candidate path quality score improvement to prevent frequent backhaul link steering.

3. **Backhaul Link Steering**

The controller multi-link AP triggers the backhaul link steering by sending a backhaul link steering control message to the proxy multi-link AP, which contains the MAC address of the backhaul STA, the BSSID of the backhaul BSS, and the Wi-Fi channel of the backhaul BSS.

To steer the backhaul link over multiple links in Wi-Fi 7, the backhaul link steering control message needs to be extended with new parameters of MLD MAC address of the backhaul BSS and the BSSID of multiple links. This depends on the extension in the subsequent version of the EasyMesh specification.

4. **Process of Backhaul Link Switching**

In the process of backhaul link switching, the current backhaul link will be released, and the new backhaul link will be established, which may cause an interim service interruption. Adopting the Fast BSS Transition (FT) procedure for backhaul link switching will shorten the period of the service interruption, which is illustrated in Fig. 4.55.

The FT procedure to establish the backhaul link between the multi-link APs includes the authentication procedure and the reassociation procedure, in which the generation of the PMK and the usual four-way handshake are not needed. To support the FT procedure, the PMK was distributed among multi-link AP devices in the EasyMesh network when the PMK was generated during the initial establishment of the backhaul link between the backhaul STA and the backhaul BSS in the EasyMesh network.

Authentication Procedure This includes the authentication request and authentication response frames, which carry the multi-link information element and the MLD MAC address. The PTK will be generated based on the PMK during the exchange of the authentication frames.

Reassociation Procedure This includes the reassociation request and the reassociation response frames, which carry the multi-link information element, the MLD MAC address, and the link information to establish the multi-link connection. The reassociation procedure completes the negotiation of the multi-link connection parameters and generates the GTK for each link, which is sent to the backhaul STA that initiates the multi-link connection.

4.2.6.5 Wi-Fi Band Steering Between Frequency Bands and Roaming Between Multi-Link APs

Figure 4.56 shows the scenarios in which the STA performs band steering between different Wi-Fi frequency bands and performs roaming between different multi-link APs in the EasyMesh network.

The single-link STA may perform band steering or roaming as it moves through the network, and the roaming could happen between the different Wi-Fi frequency bands of the different multi-link APs. The multi-link STA prefers to maintain the Wi-Fi connection over multiple links. It may perform roaming between different multi-link APs instead of band steering between different frequency bands of the same multi-link AP while moving through the network.

After the Wi-Fi STA is connected to the EasyMesh network, the controller multi-link AP collects the link metrics of the STA and the link metrics of the backhaul links It then selects the optimal target BSS for the STA according to the metrics collected.

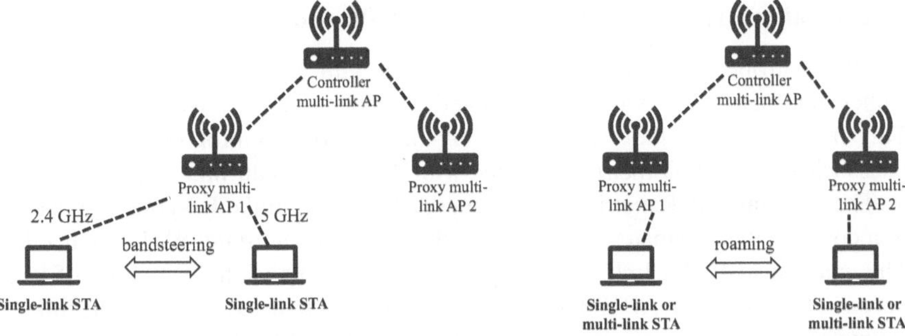

Fig. 4.56 Switching between Wi-Fi bands and roaming between APs

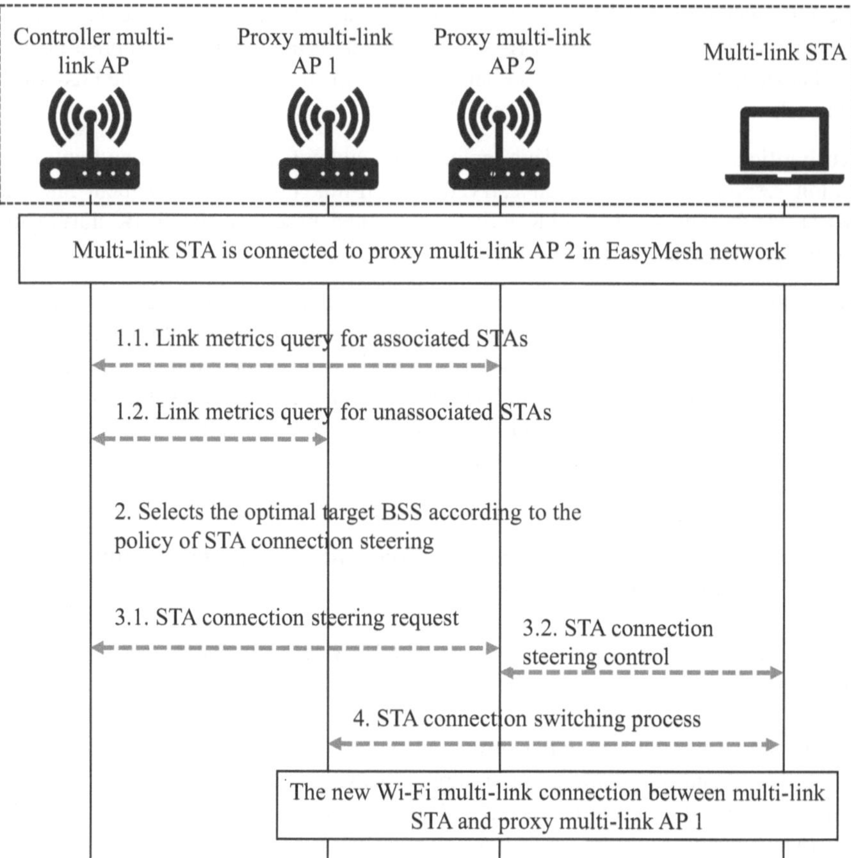

Fig. 4.57 Wi-Fi connection steering process

The controller multi-link AP controls the band steering or roaming of the STA by sending the STA connection steering control message to the STA. Figure 4.57 illustrates the Wi-Fi connection steering process of the multi-link STA.

1. **The link metrics query of the associated STA and unassociated STA**

The controller multi-link AP communicates with the proxy multi-link APs to gather link metrics for both associated and unassociated STAs within the network. This involves using the associated STA link metrics control message and the unassociated STA link metrics message with the proxy multi-link APs.

The associated link metrics control message defined in the EasyMesh specification contains the parameters of RSSI and the physical rate of the Wi-Fi connection. The unassociated STA link metrics query message contains the parameter of RSSI between the multi-link AP and the STA, based on which the controller multi-link AP estimates the physical rate according to the capability of the STA.

2. **The policy of the STA connection steering**

The multi-link AP selects the preferred target BSS for the STA according to the policy of STA connection steering, which mainly considers the following aspects.

(1) The frequency band with higher bandwidth is preferred for the single-link STAs.
(2) The BSS that supports multi-link is preferred for the multi-link STAs.
(3) Target multi-link APs with higher RSSI are preferred.
(4) Similar to the backhaul link optimization, there are multiple paths between the STA and the controller multi-link AP, and the path with the highest quality score is preferred. The path score is calculated based on the physical rate of the STA's Wi-Fi connection and the physical rates of the multiple backhaul links of this path.
(5) The threshold for candidate path quality score improvement: the STA connection steering is allowed only when the quality score improvement of the candidate path exceeds the threshold compared to the quality score of the current path, which avoids the possible frequent STA connection steering.

3. **The STA connection steering**

The controller multi-link AP requests the proxy multi-link AP to initiate the process of STA connection switching via sending the STA connection steering control message, which contains the MAC address of the STA, as well as the BSSID and Wi-Fi channel information of the target BSS.

In the case of connection steering for Wi-Fi 7 multi-link STAs, the STA connection steering control message specifies the MLD MAC address of the target multi-link AP and the Wi-Fi channel information corresponding to one link of the multiple links, based on which the proxy multi-link AP sends a BSS transition request action frame carrying the multi-link information to the STA and triggers the STA to start the multi-link connection process over that link.

4. **The process of the STA connection switching**

During the STA connection switching process, the multi-link STA releases the multi-link connection with the current BSS and establishes a multi-link connection with the target BSS. Similar to the fast BSS transition procedure of the backhaul link switching, the FT procedure can be adopted in the STA connection switching process for STAs with FT capability, which shortens the period of service interruption caused by the STA connection switching process.

4.2.7 Wi-Fi 7 Network Management

To implement Wi-Fi network management functions, the usual solution is to support the Wi-Fi management via local web access or a remote management protocol. This ensures that both end users and network operators can effectively manage and control the Wi-Fi network. As shown in Fig. 4.58, the local web management system

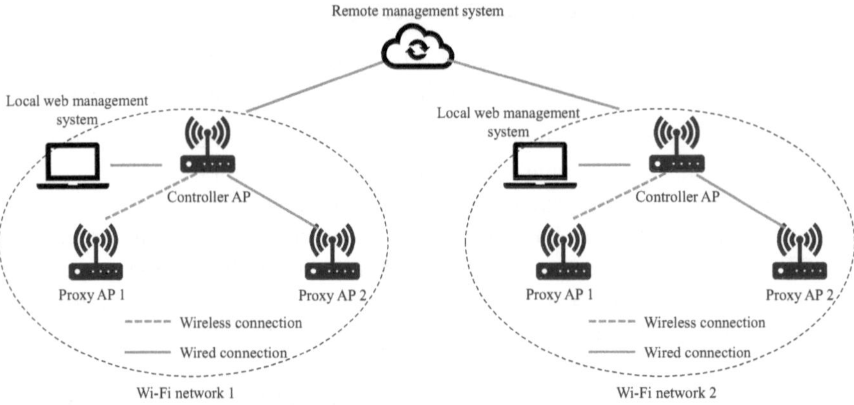

Fig. 4.58 Wi-Fi network management topology

provides Wi-Fi network management functions for end users through the local management IP address of the controller AP. The remote management system provides Wi-Fi network management capabilities for network operators by accessing the public network management IP address of the controller AP through the external network.

Wi-Fi network management encompasses two primary functions: Wi-Fi service configuration and Wi-Fi network information query.

(1) **Wi-Fi service configuration**

It involves the configuration of Wi-Fi physical layer and MAC layer parameters of different frequency bands, such as Wi-Fi channel and bandwidth, transmission power, etc. Additionally, BSS parameters need to be configured, such as SSID name, authentication and encryption method, etc.

(2) **Wi-Fi network information query**

It includes information about Wi-Fi network topology, connected Wi-Fi STAs, and Wi-Fi channels, etc. The information about Wi-Fi network topology contains the multiple AP devices in the network, the link type and physical rate of the backhaul link between AP devices, and the RSSI of the wireless backhaul link, etc. The information about connected Wi-Fi STAs contains the list of connected STA devices, the physical rate, RSSI, and packet statistics for each STA, etc. The information about Wi-Fi channels contains a list of available wireless channels, the channel utilization, interference, and neighboring BSS for each wireless channel, etc.

The introduction of Wi-Fi 7 brings changes primarily related to the support of multi-link operation technology. These changes include:

- Enhanced Wi-Fi service configuration to support the configuration of multiple affiliated links for a BSS object.

- Updates to Wi-Fi network information query to support information queries for each link of the multi-link connection between a multi-link STA and a multi-link AP, including the physical rate, RSSI, and packet statistics, etc.

In the subsequent sections, we will delve into the management protocols for Wi-Fi network management, highlight the changes related to Wi-Fi 7, and present the software design for Wi-Fi network management.

4.2.7.1 Wi-Fi Network Management Protocol

The controller AP communicates with the proxy APs to achieve configuration synchronization and network information collection within the Wi-Fi network. The local management system or remote management system communicates with the controller AP in the Wi-Fi network via management protocols to realize the network management function, as illustrated in Fig. 4.59.

1. **Local management protocol**

The local management system manages the Wi-Fi network via the web pages that are based on the HTTP(S) protocol. The end users access the web pages of the AP through a web browser to perform the Wi-Fi network management.

The contents of the web pages provided by the controller AP are defined according to product specifications and local configuration management requirements. Primarily, these include Wi-Fi frequency band configuration, BSS configuration, network topology queries, connected STAs queries, and Wi-Fi channel queries, etc.

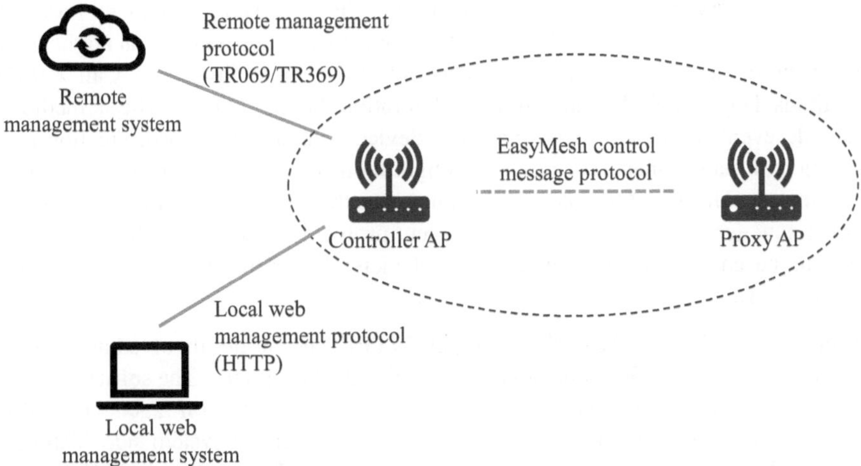

Fig. 4.59 Wi-Fi network management protocol

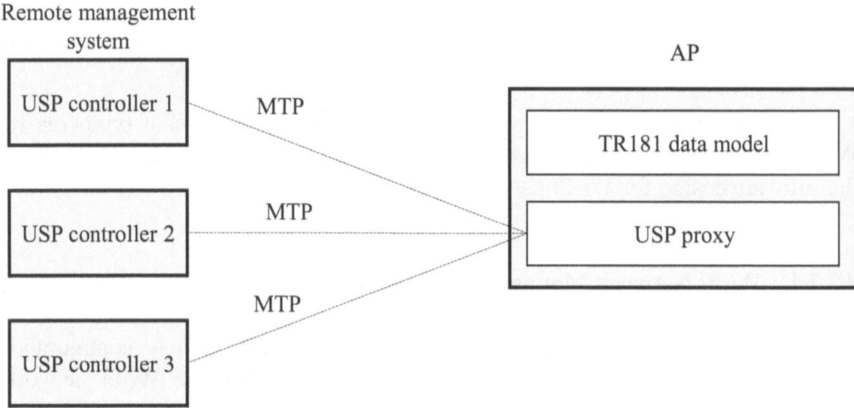

Fig. 4.60 TR-369 protocol architecture

2. **Remote management protocol**

The remote management system oversees Wi-Fi network operations via standard remote management protocols and standard Wi-Fi management models. The standardization of remote management protocols and management models ensures interoperability between remote management systems and AP devices from different vendors, facilitating network operators to manage those AP devices through a set of Wi-Fi network remote management systems.

The Broadband Forum has defined remote management protocols for customer premises equipment (CPE) and data models for CPE management, applicable to the management of user-side access gateway devices, AP devices, and STA devices in the local area network. The main remote management protocols include the TR-069 and TR-369 protocols, while the standard data models include TR-098 and TR-181.

The TR-069 protocol, also known as the CPE WAN Management Protocol (CWMP), is widely employed for remote management. It operates as an application layer protocol carried over HTTP and defines Remote Procedure Call (RPC) methods between CPE and Auto Configuration Server (ACS). These methods include event notification and reporting, device software download, creation and deletion of management objects, and configuration and query of management object parameters. The TR-369 protocol, also known as the User Services Platform (USP), is the new generation of remote management protocol developed by the Broadband Forum based on TR-069. Figure 4.60 depicts the architecture of the TR-369 protocol [4].

Lightweight Message Transfer Protocol (MTP) The entities involved in communication with the TR-369 protocol are called the USP endpoints. The software entity engaged in communication on the AP side is known as the USP agent. It is also referred to as the USP controller on the remote management system side. Through the MTP connection established between them, the USP controller and USP agent exchange TR-369 management messages in real time, facilitating functions such as

Wi-Fi network information queries and event reporting. Additionally, the USP agent has the capability to establish connections with multiple USP controllers concurrently, enabling support for various applications on the remote management system.

Extended TR-181 Data Model The TR-369 management protocol uses the extended TR-181 data model for Wi-Fi network management. It supports the management capabilities of the TR-069 protocol, and supports the message transfer mechanisms and the extended RPC methods of the TR-369 protocol.

4.2.7.2 TR-098 and TR-181 Standard Data Models

The TR-098 data model was published in 2005 and is the first version of the CPE management data model defined by the Broadband Forum. The TR-181 data model is the second version of the CPE management data model released by the Broadband Forum based in 2010. TR-181 defines the new management objects for devices, network interfaces, network protocols, and different applications, etc., which covers the content of TR-098 and delivers higher flexibility for user-side device and service management.

The Wi-Fi management objects defined by the TR-181 data model include Wi-Fi frequency band management objects, SSID management objects, Access Point management objects, and End Point management objects. In addition, revision 15 of the TR-181 data model adds the latest Wi-Fi Data Elements defined by the Wi-Fi Alliance, which enhances the capability of EasyMesh network management.

Figure 4.61 illustrates the data model of Wi-Fi network management defined in the latest version of the TR-181 data model [5].

The left side diagram shows the Wi-Fi data model defined by TR-181, which is mainly used for the configuration of basic Wi-Fi services of the AP. The right side diagram shows the Wi-Fi data elements supported by TR-181, which are mainly used for EasyMesh network management, including EasyMesh network topology, backhaul link optimization, and the policy of Wi-Fi band steering and roaming, etc.

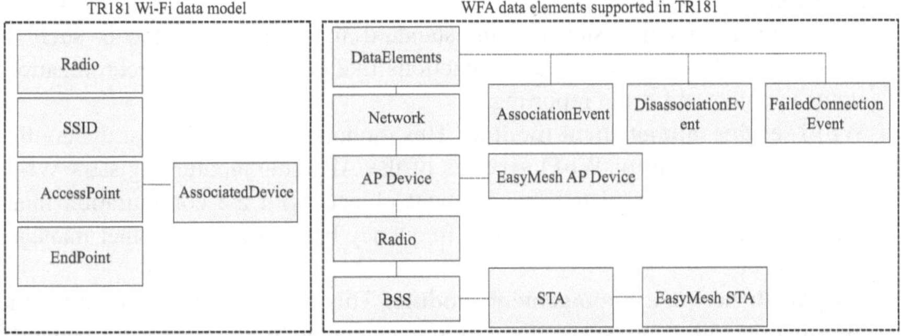

Fig. 4.61 TR-181 Wi-Fi data model

Table 4.14 TR-181 data model impact from Wi-Fi 7

Management objects	Changes brought by Wi-Fi 7
The SSID management object in the Wi-Fi data model, and the BSS management object in the WFA data element	New management objects or management parameters will be defined to denote one or more Wi-Fi frequency bands associated with BSS.
The associated device management object in the Wi-Fi data model, and the associated device management object in the WFA data element	New management objects or management parameters for Wi-Fi 7 capability, physical rate, signal strength and packets statistics of each associated device.
The frequency band management object in the WFA data element	New parameters for Wi-Fi 7 capability of each Wi-Fi frequency band.
The EasyMesh network AP device management object in the WFA data element	New management objects or management parameters for physical rate, signal strength, and packets statistics of each backhaul link.
The event management objects in the WFA data element	New parameters for Wi-Fi 7 capability and multi-link information of multi-link STA events.

The TR-181 data model needs to be extended according to the Wi-Fi 7 capability set and multi-link technology for Wi-Fi 7 network management. Table 4.14 describes the impact of Wi-Fi 7 on the TR-181 data model. The details of the TR-181 data model extension depend on the definition in the subsequent version of the TR-181 data model by the Broadband Forum.

4.2.7.3 Wi-Fi Network Management Software Design

Wi-Fi network management software modules are responsible for implementing Wi-Fi network service configuration and information query functions for the AP based on the network management protocols. Figure 4.62 illustrates the software design of Wi-Fi network management for the AP.

The software design consists of the following modules:

- **Management protocol module:** This module handles communication with remote management systems using standard management protocols such as TR-069 and TR-369. It facilitates functions like configuration synchronization, status updates, and event reporting.
- **Wi-Fi service management module:** This module is responsible for the configuration management of Wi-Fi services of the AP. This module registers Wi-Fi service configuration-related management objects with the configuration management framework, including Wi-Fi frequency band, SSID, and other management objects.
- **EasyMesh network management module:** This module is responsible for the information collection and configuration management of the EasyMesh network.

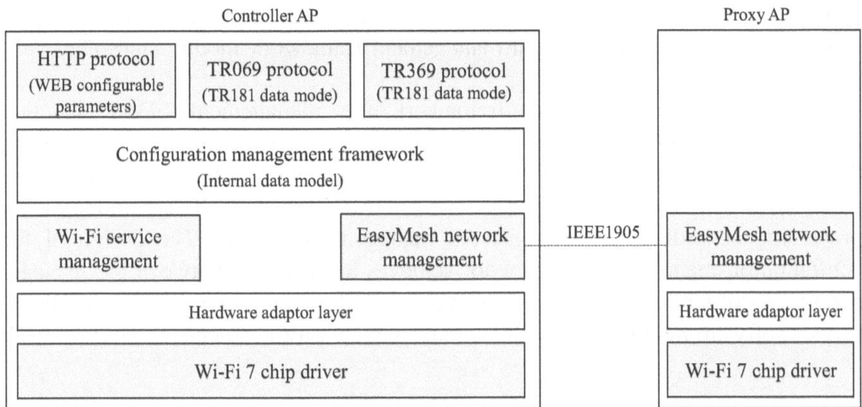

Fig. 4.62 Wi-Fi network management software design

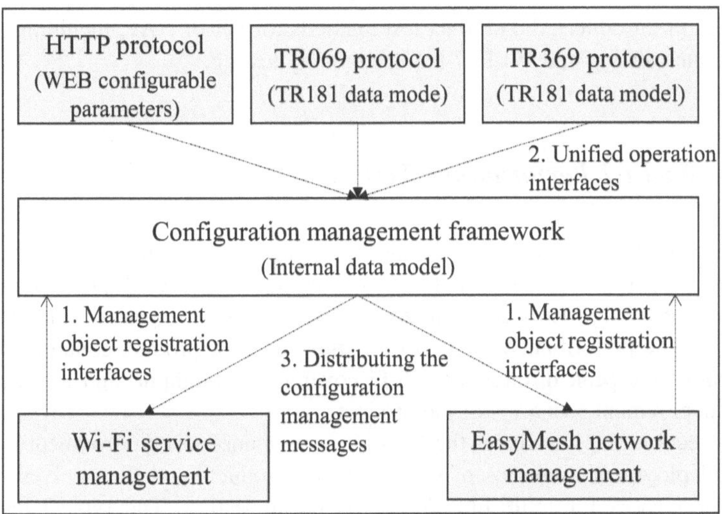

Fig. 4.63 Configuration management message distribution

This module registers the Wi-Fi data element management objects with the configuration management framework.

- **Configuration management framework:** This module defines the internal data model of the AP and provides unified operation interfaces based on the internal data model for the management protocol module. In addition, this module distributes the configuration management messages according to the registered management objects. It calls the interface of the Wi-Fi service management module and the EasyMesh network management module to complete the configuration management operation.

Figure 4.63 illustrates the configuration management message distribution procedure between the configuration management framework module and other software modules.

The configuration management framework offers management object registration interfaces for the service software modules and unified operation interfaces based on the internal data model for the management protocol modules. It distributes the configuration management messages to different service software modules for processing according to the registered management objects. The design of the configuration management framework achieves a separation between the management protocol modules and the service modules, eliminating the need to modify the service software modules when a new management protocol needs to be supported.

4.3 Wi-Fi 7 AP Product Testing

This section introduces the product test methods for Wi-Fi 7 AP, including product performance testing and Wi-Fi 7 key technology testing.

4.3.1 Wi-Fi 7 Performance Testing

Performance testing is a critical component of the Wi-Fi 7 multi-link AP product evaluation. Such testing is crucial to ensure that the multi-link AP product meets the performance requirements and delivers a satisfactory user experience in real-world scenarios. The performance testing of the multi-link AP product contains the measurement of the peak throughput, Wi-Fi coverage, throughput, and latency in the typical deployment scenarios of the product.

This section first introduces the Wi-Fi 7 performance test environment based on typical deployment scenarios of multi-link AP products and then delves into the typical test cases for multi-link AP performance testing. The typical test cases include:

- RVR throughput test.
- Throughput and latency test in scenarios with multiple STAs and multiple services.
- Performance test in the EasyMesh network.

4.3.1.1 Typical Deployment Scenarios for Multi-Link AP Product

Figure 4.64 **a** shows a deployment scenario of a single multi-link AP that provides network access services for multiple STAs with different service types. Figure 4.64 **b** shows a deployment scenario of an EasyMesh network formed by three multi-link

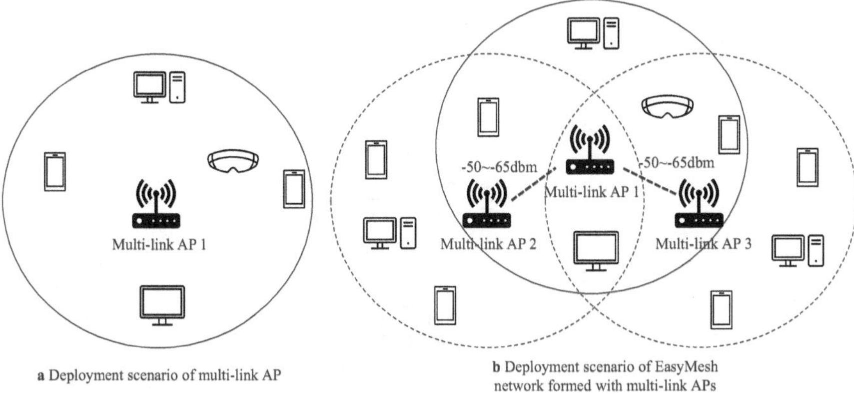

Fig. 4.64 (**a**) Deployment scenario of multi-link APs, (**b**) Deployment scenario of EasyMesh network formed with multi-link APs

APs, which expands the coverage of the Wi-Fi network and provides network access services for more STAs.

For the Wi-Fi network deployment scenario with multiple STAs, the requirements for the multi-link AP product performance test are described as follows:

(1) **Throughput test within the Wi-Fi coverage range:** This is to validate the maximum throughput reached according to the Wi-Fi signal strength and the physical rate at different locations within the Wi-Fi coverage range.
(2) **Throughput test with different priorities of services:** This is to validate the AP's ability to fairly schedule among multiple STAs and give preference to scheduling for higher-priority services, ensuring overall throughput across various locations while maintaining the throughput and latency requirements for higher-priority services.
(3) **Throughput test in a congested environment:** This is to validate the AP's transmission scheduling capability to prioritize higher-priority services, ensuring that their throughput and latency requirements are met within a congested environment.

4.3.1.2 Wi-Fi 7 Performance Test Environment

Considering the typical deployment scenarios of multi-link APs and the characteristics of Wi-Fi 7 technologies, such as multi-link operation, OFDMA, and MU-MIMO, the Wi-Fi 7 performance test environment needs to cover the following three aspects.

1. **Controllable test environment**

The controllable test environment supports controlling the position and signal strength among the multi-link AP and STAs, as well as the interference signal level.

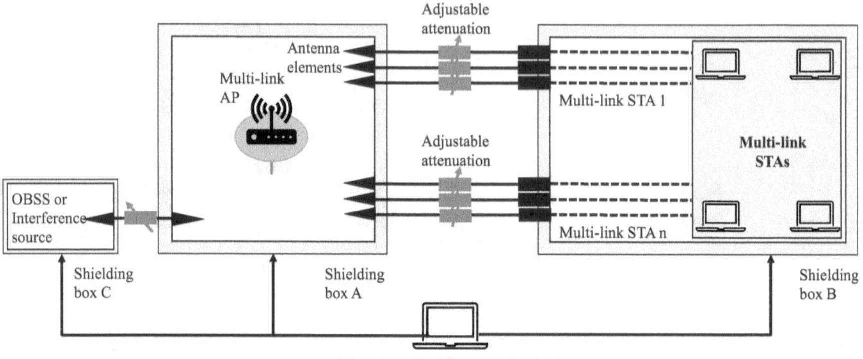

Fig. 4.65 Wi-Fi 7 performance test environment

It simulates typical deployment scenarios and is designed to ensure the consistency and repeatability of performance test results. The environment commonly includes shielding rooms or boxes.

2. **Support multiple multi-link STAs with independent physical layer**

In traditional Wi-Fi performance testing, traffic generation equipment simulates multiple STAs with independent MAC layers, utilizing a single physical STA device. However, this approach is not sufficient for testing Wi-Fi 7's advanced features, such as MU-MIMO or OFDMA. For Wi-Fi 7 performance testing in multi-STA environments, traffic generation equipment must be employed, featuring multiple multi-link STAs that support independent physical layers.

3. **Support traffic generation of multiple service types**

To simulate the typical deployment scenario with multiple STAs and multiple service types, the traffic generation equipment in the Wi-Fi 7 performance test environment needs to generate traffic of different service types and flexibly control the traffic parameters of protocol type, packet length, traffic size, and packet priority, etc.

Figure 4.65 describes the typical Wi-Fi 7 performance test environment, which includes a multi-link AP, multi-link STAs, a console and traffic generation tool, an OBSS or interference source, adjustable attenuators, shielding boxes, and turntables, etc.

(1) **Shielding box A**

It is used to place the multi-link AP, which is assembled with multiple antenna components. These components are used to connect with Wi-Fi STAs in another shielding box to form the working environment for wireless communication between the multi-link AP and STAs. A turntable is assembled in shielding box A to control the angle of the multi-link AP during testing.

(2) **Shielding box B**

It is used to place multiple STAs, which are connected to the antenna components assembled in shielding box A by cables.

(3) **Shielding box C**

It is used to place OBSS or interference source equipment, which is connected to the antenna components assembled in shielding box A by cables, to simulate the interference in the same or adjacent channels of the multi-link AP.

(4) **Adjustable attenuator**

The adjustable attenuators are connected to cables between the shielding boxes, which are used to control the attenuation on each cable and simulate the different distances between the multi-link AP and STAs in the shielding boxes.

(5) **Console and traffic generation tool**

The console can be integrated with the traffic generation tool, which connects with the multi-link AP and other test equipment to perform test operations, generate and analyze traffic for performance testing, and generate the performance test results, including throughput and latency.

Different types of traffic can be generated according to different scenarios of Wi-Fi performance testing. Table 4.15 shows the typical traffic types used in different performance test scenarios.

4.3.1.3 RVR Test

RVR test is the throughput test over different distances between AP and STA. The throughput test with a short distance is used to measure the maximum throughput result of the AP product, and the throughput test with a long distance is used to measure the network coverage capability of the AP product. Also, the RVR test is performed at different angles between the AP and STA to measure the Wi-Fi coverage capability of the AP at various angles.

The RVR test of the multi-link AP includes the throughput test of each Wi-Fi frequency band with a single-link Wi-Fi connection and the throughput test over multiple frequency bands with a multi-link Wi-Fi connection between the multi-link AP and multi-link STA.

1. **Test topology**

Taking BE9300 as an example, the RVR test topology is shown in Fig. 4.66. The BE9300 is placed on the turntable of shielding box A, and the turntable is used to control the angle of the multi-link AP. The multi-link STA is placed in shielding box B, which supports 2x2 2.4 GHz frequency band with 40 MHz bandwidth, 2x2 5 GHz frequency band with 160 MHz bandwidth, and 2x2 6 GHz frequency band with 320 MHz bandwidth.

Table 4.15 Data traffic types for Wi-Fi performance test

Traffic types	Description	Wi-Fi performance test scenarios
Normal UDP data traffic	The data traffic attributes include the number of data traffic flows, size of data packet in bytes, and size of data traffic in mbps	Applicable for Wi-Fi throughput test in the scenario of single service: The throughput result is the rate at which the UDP data traffic is successfully received. Record the throughput result under the condition of zero packet loss in the clean test environment without interference.
Normal TCP data traffic	The data traffic attributes include the number of data traffic flows, size of data packet in bytes, and size of data traffic in mbps	Applicable for Wi-Fi throughput test in the scenario of single service: The throughput result is the rate at which the TCP data traffic is successfully received. The throughput result of TCP is related to packet loss and latency of data transmission, which is better to measure the performance of data transmission in a Wi-Fi network.
Data traffic with multiple services	The data traffic contains the following types of services: Voice service: UDP data traffic with high priority and traffic size of 1 mbps HD video: TCP data traffic with high priority and traffic size of 10 mbps 4 K video: TCP data traffic with high priority and traffic size of 35 mbps AR/VR: TCP data traffic with high priority and traffic size of 80 mbps Normal data service: TCP data traffic with normal priority and without size limit of data traffic	Applicable for Wi-Fi throughput and latency test in the scenario of multiple STAs and multiple services Measure the throughput result of normal data service and the throughput and latency of services with high priority

The shielding boxes are connected by cables, and the attenuation of Wi-Fi signals is controlled by the adjustable attenuator between the shielding boxes to simulate different distances between the multi-link AP and multi-link STAs.

The throughput test is performed with normal TCP data traffic generated by the traffic generator tool.

2. **Test steps**

   (1) **Configure multi-link AP:** Configure the 2.4 GHz frequency band with 40 MHz bandwidth, the 5 GHz frequency band with 160 MHz bandwidth, and the 6 GHz frequency band with 320 MHz bandwidth.

   (2) **2.4 GHz frequency band RVR test:** Create a single-link BSS at the 2.4 GHz frequency band and establish a single-link Wi-Fi connection at the 2.4 GHz frequency band between the multi-link STA and BE9300.

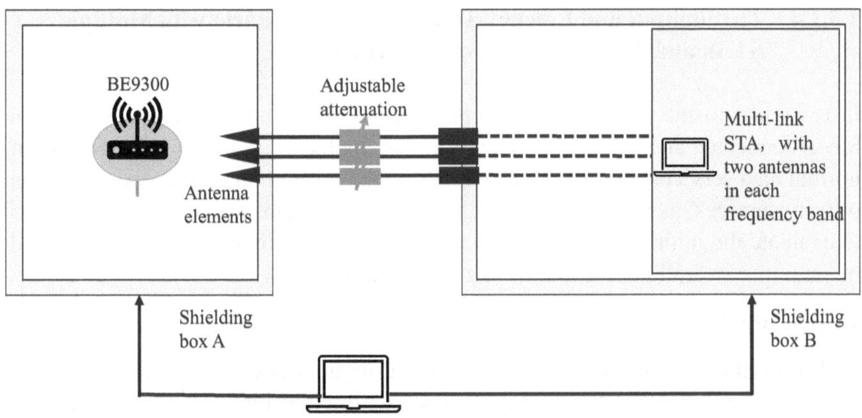

Fig. 4.66 Multi-link AP RVR test

(a) Set the initial value of attenuation and angle: Set the controllable attenuation to 0 dB and set the turntable to the angle of 0°.
(b) Measure the throughput at different attenuations: Gradually increase the attenuation at 3 db intervals until the Wi-Fi connection is disconnected. At each interval, measure the throughput for both downstream and upstream directions.
(c) Measure the throughput at different angles: Gradually increase the angle at 30° intervals until it reaches the initial angle of 0°, and repeat step (b) at each angle setting.

(3) **5 GHz frequency band RVR test:** Create a single-link BSS at the 5 GHz frequency band and establish a single-link Wi-Fi connection at the 5 GHz frequency band; repeat the steps (a) through (c) for the 5 GHz frequency band throughput test.
(4) **6 GHz frequency band RVR test:** Create a single-link BSS at the 6 GHz frequency band and establish the single-link Wi-Fi connection at the 6 GHz frequency band; repeat the steps (a) through (c) for the 6 GHz frequency band throughput test.
(5) **RVR test over multiple frequency bands:** Create a multi-link BSS with tri-bands of 2.4 GHz, 5 GHz, and 6 GHz frequency bands and establish the multi-link Wi-Fi connection over tri-bands; repeat the steps (a) through (c) for the multiple frequency bands throughput test.

3. **Test results**

Record the throughput results at the different attenuation and angle settings for single-link over each frequency band and multi-link over tri-bands.

It is expected that the throughput result of multi-link over tri-bands is the sum of the throughput results of single-link over each frequency band.

4.3.1.4 Throughput and Latency Test Under the Scenario with Multiple STAs and Multiple Types of Services

In reference to the typical deployment scenario of a multi-link AP with multiple STAs connected and different services running, including voice, video, AR/VR, and normal data services, this test aims to measure the throughput and latency of higher-priority services, as well as the throughput of normal data services. The objective is to evaluate the multi-link AP's ability to prioritize the higher-priority services while maintaining overall throughput in this test scenario.

1. **Test topology**

Taking the BE9300 as an example, the throughput and latency test topology is shown in Fig. 4.67. The BE9300 is enclosed within the shielding box A, while four multi-link STAs are placed within shielding box B. The traffic generation tool is used to generate data traffic of different service types for throughput and latency testing. Specifically, one STA generates traffic for 4 K video service, another for AR/VR service, and the remaining two STAs generate traffic for normal TCP data service without size limitations. Inside the multi-link AP, the traffic of video and AR/VR services is mapped to the VI access category, and the traffic for normal TCP data services is mapped to the BE access category.

2. **Test steps**

   (1) **Configure multi-link AP:** Configure the 2.4 GHz frequency band with 20 MHz bandwidth, the 5 GHz frequency band with 160 MHz bandwidth, and the 6 GHz frequency band with 320 MHz bandwidth. Create the multi-link BSS with all three frequency bands affiliated.

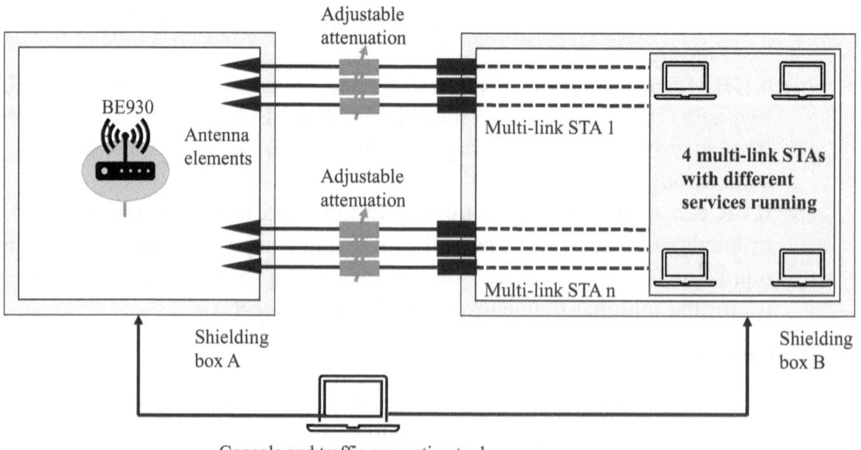

Fig. 4.67 Throughput and latency test of multi-link AP

(2) **Establish multi-link Wi-Fi connections:** Establish the multi-link Wi-Fi connections between the multi-link AP and all multi-link STAs over tri-bands.
(3) **Throughput and latency test:** Run the traffic of the corresponding services on all STAs at the same time and measure the throughput and latency of each STA.

3. **Test results**

The throughput and latency results of the higher-priority services, such as video and AR/VR services, are recorded to ensure they meet the specified throughput and latency requirements. Additionally, the throughput result of the normal TCP data services is recorded to ensure that the overall throughput of all STAs reaches the expected value.

4.3.1.5 Performance Test in the EasyMesh Network

The performance test in the EasyMesh network includes the throughput test of the backhaul link and the throughput and latency tests of higher-priority services and normal data services in the scenario with multiple STAs and multiple types of services.

1. **Test topology**

Taking the EasyMesh network with two BE9300 AP devices as an example, the test topology is shown in Fig. 4.68. The controller AP is placed in the shielding box A, and the proxy AP is placed in the shielding box C. Four multi-link STAs are placed in the shielding box B. The traffic generation tool is used to generate data traffic of different types of services for the throughput and latency test; it is the traffic of AR/VR service for two STAs as well as the traffic of normal TCP data service without size limits for the remaining two STAs. Inside the multi-link AP, the traffic of AR/VR services is mapped to the VI access category, and the traffic of normal TCP data services is mapped to the BE access category.

2. **Test steps**

(1) **Configure the controller multi-link AP:** Configure the 2.4 GHz frequency band with 20 MHz bandwidth, the 5 GHz frequency band with 160 MHz bandwidth, and the 6 GHz frequency band with 320 MHz bandwidth. Create the multi-link BSS with all three frequency bands affiliated.
(2) **Onboarding the proxy AP to form the EasyMesh network:** Form the EasyMesh network by adding the proxy AP and setting the RSSI of the backhaul link between the controller AP and proxy AP to a value between −50 dBm and −65 dBm to simulate the signal strength of the backhaul link in a typical deployment scenario via the adjustable attenuator.
(3) **Establish multi-link Wi-Fi connections:** Establish the multi-link Wi-Fi connections between two multi-link STAs and the controller AP with

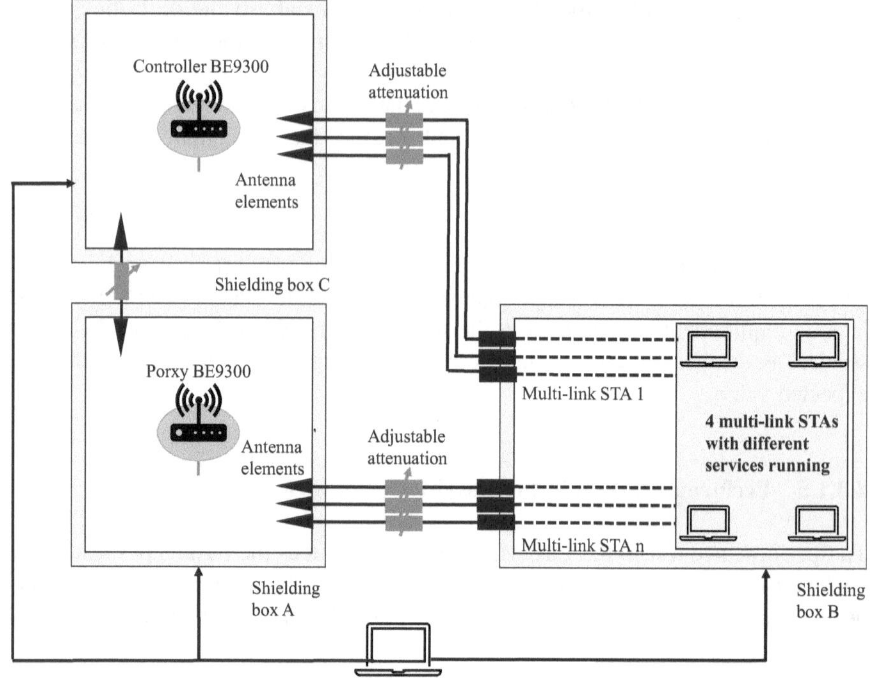

Fig. 4.68 EasyMesh network performance test

different services, and establish multi-link Wi-Fi connections between the other two multi-link STAs and the proxy AP with different services.

(4) **Throughput test over backhaul link:** Run the traffic of TCP normal data services without size limits between the 10 Gbps LAN ports of the controller and proxy APs and measure the throughput in both directions of upstream and downstream of the backhaul link.

(5) **Throughput and latency test:** Run the traffic of the corresponding service on all STAs at the same time and measure the throughput and latency of each STA.

3. **Test results**

Record the throughput result of the backhaul link; it is expected that the throughput result of the backhaul link reaches the expected throughput of the multi-link Wi-Fi connection according to the RSSI and physical rate of the backhaul link.

Record the throughput and latency results of higher priority services, ensuring they meet the throughput and latency requirements of the higher priority services.

Record the throughput result of the normal TCP data services, ensuring that the overall throughput result of all STAs reaches the expected value.

4.3.2 Wi-Fi 7 Key Technologies Test

This section describes the tests for key features in Wi-Fi 7. The main features of the Wi-Fi 7 technologies test include:

- Multi-link operation technology test.
- OFDMA and MRU allocation technology test.
- Restricted target wake time technology test.

4.3.2.1 Multi-Link Operation Technology Test

Chapter 3 introduces two types of multi-link AP devices and five types of multi-link STA devices. The multi-link APs include asynchronous multi-link simultaneous transmission and synchronous multi-link simultaneous transmission, while the multi-link STAs include asynchronous multi-link simultaneous transmission, enhanced asynchronous multi-link simultaneous transmission, synchronous multi-link simultaneous transmission, multi-link single radio mode, and enhanced multi-link single radio mode.

Taking the asynchronous multi-link AP devices as an example, this section describes the testing of the following two different multi-link transmission technologies:

- Validate the multi-link data transmission function over the multi-link Wi-Fi connection between the asynchronous multi-link AP and the asynchronous multi-link STA.
- Validate the multi-link data transmission function over the multi-link Wi-Fi connection between the asynchronous multi-link AP and the enhanced multi-link single-radio STA.

The test topology and test steps are described as follows.

1. **Test topology**

The test topology of multi-link operation technology is shown in Fig. 4.69. The asynchronous multi-link AP is placed in the shielding box A, while the asynchronous multi-link STA and enhanced multi-link single-radio STA are placed in the shielding box B. The traffic generation tool is used to generate normal TCP data traffic without size limits between the multi-link AP and STA to validate the multi-link simultaneous transmission function. Additionally, the interference source equipment is placed in the shielding box C, which is used to simulate wireless interference on a link for the multi-link AP to validate the impact on the multi-link data transmission from interference.

2. **Test steps and results**

   (1) **Configure multi-link AP:** Configure the 2.4 GHz frequency band with a 20 MHz bandwidth, the 5 GHz frequency band with a 160 MHz bandwidth,

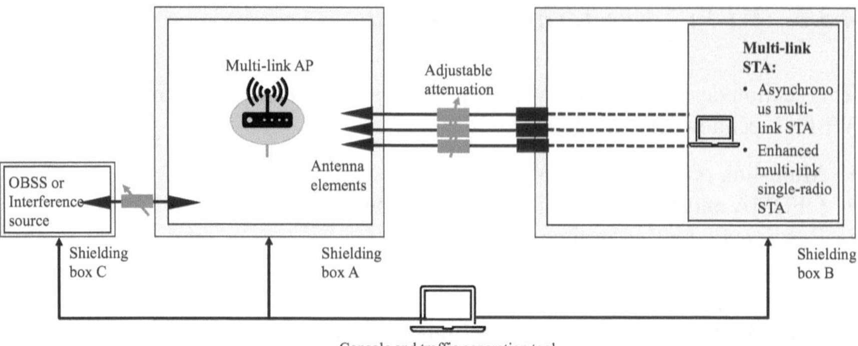

Fig. 4.69 Multi-link operation technology test

and the 6 GHz frequency band with a 320 MHz bandwidth. Create the multi-link BSS with all three frequency bands affiliated.

(2) **Check multi-link AP capability:** Check the multi-link capability of the multi-link AP based on the Beacon management frames sent from the multi-link AP.

   (a) Check the Enhanced Multi-Link (EML) capabilities in the multi-link information element carried by the Beacon frame. A value of 1 at the first bit of the EML capabilities indicates that the multi-link AP supports multi-link data transmission with the enhanced multi-link single-radio STA.
   (b) Check the Multi-link Device (MLD) capabilities in the multi-link information element carried by the Beacon frame. The value at bits 0 to 3 of the MLD capabilities indicates the maximum number of simultaneous links that the multi-link AP supports. It is the value of the maximum number of simultaneous links minus 1. For example, a value of 2 indicates that the multi-link AP supports three links for asynchronous multi-link simultaneous transmission.

(3) **Validate the multi-link simultaneous transmission function between the asynchronous multi-link STA and the multi-link AP:** Establish the multi-link Wi-Fi connection between the asynchronous multi-link STA and the multi-link AP.

   (a) Configure the mapping between TID and multiple links using the Wi-Fi driver command lines of the multi-link AP or STA, and validate the multi-link data transmission according to the mapping between TID and multiple links.

      • Map the VI access category to the link of the 6 GHz frequency band in both upstream and downstream directions. Run bidirectional TCP data

traffic with VI priority, measure the throughput, and validate that the data traffic is transmitted over the link of the 6 GHz frequency band.
- Similarly, map the VI access category to the link of the 5 GHz frequency band, measure the throughput, and validate that the data traffic is transmitted over the link of the 5 GHz frequency band.
- Similarly, map the VI access category to the link of the 2.4 GHz frequency band, measure the throughput, and validate that the data traffic is transmitted over the link of the 2.4 GHz frequency band.

(b) Configure the default mapping between TID and multiple links using the Wi-Fi driver command lines of the multi-link AP or STA to allow traffic of each access category to be transmitted over either link.

- Run TCP data traffic without size limit in the downstream direction, measure throughput, and validate that the data traffic is transmitted over links of all frequency bands.
- Run TCP data traffic without size limit in the upstream direction, measure throughput, and validate that the data traffic is transmitted over links of all frequency bands.

(4) **Validate the multi-link simultaneous transmission function between the enhanced multi-link single radio STA and the multi-link AP:** Establish the multi-link Wi-Fi connection between the enhanced multi-link single radio STA and the multi-link AP.

(a) Configure the mapping between TID and multiple links using the Wi-Fi driver command lines of the multi-link AP or STA, and validate the multi-link data transmission according to the mapping between TID and multiple links.

- Map the VI access category to the link of the 6 GHz frequency band in both upstream and downstream directions, run bidirectional TCP data traffic with VI priority, measure the throughput, and validate that the data traffic is transmitted over the link of the 6 GHz frequency band.
- Similarly, map the VI access category to the link of the 5 GHz frequency band, measure the throughput, and validate that the data traffic is transmitted over the link of the 5 GHz frequency band.
- Similarly, map the VI access category to the link of the 2.4 GHz frequency band, measure the throughput, and validate that the data traffic is transmitted over the link of the 2.4 GHz frequency band.

(b) Configure the default mapping between TID and multiple links using the Wi-Fi driver command lines of the multi-link AP or STA to allow traffic of each access category to be transmitted over either link.

- Run TCP data traffic without size limit in the downstream direction, measure throughput, and validate that the data traffic is transmitted over one idle link at any time. Adding interference across the entire bandwidth of the Wi-Fi channel of a link, measure throughput, and validate that the data traffic is transmitted over another idle link.
- Run TCP data traffic without size limit in the upstream direction, measure throughput, and validate that the data traffic is transmitted over one idle link at any time. Adding interference across the entire bandwidth of the Wi-Fi channel of a link, measure throughput, and validate that the data traffic is transmitted over another idle link.

4.3.2.2 OFDMA and MRU Allocation Technology Test

Based on OFDMA and MRU allocation technologies, the multi-link AP dynamically allocates RU or MRU for different STAs and performs data traffic transmission simultaneously with multiple STAs, improving the efficiency of the Wi-Fi channel spectrum and the latency performance in multiple STA scenarios.

When interference occurs within subchannels that are 20 MHz in bandwidth, the multi-link AP masks the subchannels with interference using the preamble puncturing technology and performs data traffic transmission with multiple STAs over the remaining subchannels, including the primary 20 MHz subchannel.

This section introduces the test topology and test steps for validating the OFDMA and MRU allocation technology. These tests cover the preamble puncturing function and OFDMA function under the scenario with multiple STAs.

1. **Test topology**

   The test topology for testing OFDMA and MRU allocation technology is shown in Fig. 4.70. The multi-link AP is placed in shielding box A, and four multi-link STAs are placed in shielding box B. A traffic generation tool is used to generate data traffic for different types of services. It includes the traffic of higher priority service for three STAs as well as the traffic of normal TCP data service without size limits for the remaining one STA. Additionally, the interference source equipment is placed in the shielding box C, which is used to simulate wireless interference in the Wi-Fi channel.
2. **Preamble puncturing function test**

   (1) **Configure multi-link AP:** Configure the 2.4 GHz frequency band with 20 MHz bandwidth, the 5 GHz frequency band with 160 MHz bandwidth, and the 6 GHz frequency band with 320 MHz bandwidth. Create the multi-link BSS with all three frequency bands affiliated.

   (2) **Preamble puncturing function test at 5 GHz frequency band.**

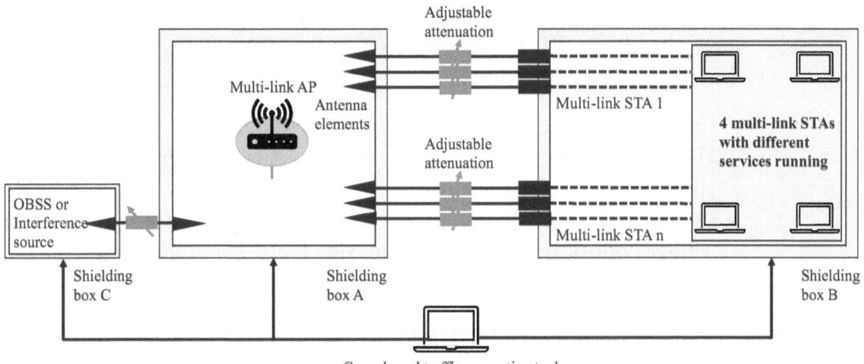

Fig. 4.70 OFDMA and MRU allocation technology test

(a) Establish a single-link Wi-Fi connection between an STA and the multi-link AP at the 5 GHz frequency band, and run bi-directional normal TCP data traffic without size limits.
(b) Add interference on the subchannels with 20 MHz or 40 MHz bandwidth other than the primary 20 MHz subchannel. It is expected that the multi-link AP masks the preamble on the subchannels with interference and performs bi-directional data transmission over the other subchannels.
(c) Check the punctured channel information or MRU allocation information carried in Wi-Fi packets to validate that the subchannels with interference are masked and not used for data traffic transmission.

- In the downstream direction, the punctured channel information of the U-SIG field in the preamble of the data packets indicates the subchannels masked.
- In the upstream direction, the MRU allocation information in the trigger control frame indicates the subchannels not allocated.

(3) **Preamble puncturing function test at 6 GHz frequency band**

(a) Establish the single-link Wi-Fi connection between a STA and the multi-link AP on the 6 GHz frequency band, and run bi-directional normal TCP data traffic without size limits.
(b) Add interference on the subchannels with 40 MHz, 80 MHz, or 40 MHz plus 80 MHz bandwidth, other than the primary 20 MHz subchannel. It is expected that the multi-link AP masks the preamble on the subchannels with interference and performs bi-directional data transmission over the other subchannels.

(c) Check the punctured channel information or MRU allocation information carried in Wi-Fi packets to validate that the subchannels with interference are masked and not used for data traffic transmission.

- In the downstream direction, the punctured channel information of the U-SIG field in the preamble of the data packets indicates the subchannels masked.
- In the upstream direction, the MRU allocation information in the trigger control frame indicates the subchannels not allocated.

3. **OFDMA function test based on MRU**

(1) **Configure multi-link AP:** Configure the 2.4 GHz frequency band with 20 MHz bandwidth, the 5 GHz frequency band with 160 MHz bandwidth, and the 6 GHz frequency band with 320 MHz bandwidth. Create the multi-link BSS with all three frequency bands affiliated.

(2) **OFDMA function test at 2.4 GHz frequency with multiple STAs**

(a) Establish a single-link Wi-Fi connection on the 2.4 GHz frequency band between four STAs and the multi-link AP. Run bidirectional higher priority data traffic of 20 Mbps for three STAs, and run bidirectional normal TCP data traffic without size limits for the remaining one STA.

(b) Validate that the multi-link AP performs data traffic transmission in both upstream and downstream with multiple STAs based on OFDMA multiplexing technology and prioritizes the transmission for higher priority data traffic.

(c) In the downstream direction, the EHT-SIG field in the preamble of the data packet carries the MRU allocation information for the current 20 MHz bandwidth and the user information corresponding to each MRU allocated.

- In each EHT MU PPDU data frame, the multi-link AP dynamically allocates RU to multiple STAs, with the size of the RU allocated being 26 tones, 52 tones, 106 tones, 52 plus 26 tones, or 106 plus 26 tones. The RUs of 52 plus 26 tones and 106 plus 26 tones are MRUs allocated.
- The RU allocation and transmission scheduling can be checked via the command lines of the Wi-Fi driver or based on the Wi-Fi packets captured. It is expected that the multi-link AP prioritizes the RU allocation and transmission scheduling for higher priority data traffic. When there are not enough data packets in the transmitting queues for the STAs with higher priority data traffic, the multi-link AP allocates the entire 20 MHz bandwidth to the STA, which is running with normal TCP data traffic. It is expected that the multi-link AP makes full use of the frequency band resource of the Wi-Fi channel.

(d) In the upstream direction, the trigger control frame sent by the multi-link AP carries the MRU allocation information for the current 20 MHz bandwidth and the user information corresponding to each MRU allocated. The STAs transmit the upstream EHT TB PPDU data packets according to the MRU allocation information carried in the trigger control frame received.

- In the Trigger control frame, the multi-link AP dynamically allocates RU to multiple STAs, with the size of RU allocated being 26 tones, 52 tones, 106 tones, 52 plus 26 tones, or 106 plus 26 tones. The RUs of 52 plus 26 tones and 106 plus 26 tones are MRUs allocated.
- The RU allocation and transmission scheduling can be checked via the command lines of the Wi-Fi driver or based on the Wi-Fi packets captured. It is expected that the multi-link AP prioritizes the RU allocation and transmission scheduling for higher priority data traffic. When there are not enough data packets to be transmitted by the STAs with higher priority data traffic, the multi-link AP allocates the entire 20 MHz bandwidth to the STA, which is running with normal TCP data traffic for upstream data traffic transmission. It is expected that the multi-link AP makes full use of the frequency band resource of the Wi-Fi channel.

(3) **OFDMA function test at 5 GHz frequency band under the scenario with multiple STAs**

(a) Establish the single-link Wi-Fi connection on the 5 GHz frequency band between four STAs and the multi-link AP. Run bidirectional higher priority data traffic of 200 Mbps for each of three STAs, and run bidirectional normal TCP data traffic without size limits for one STA.
(b) Validate that the multi-link AP performs data traffic transmission in both upstream and downstream with multiple STAs based on OFDMA multiplexing technology and prioritizes the transmission for higher priority data traffic.
(c) Repeat the steps (c) and (d) of the 2.4 GHz frequency band test to validate the OFDMA function on the 5 GHz frequency band. There are 8 subchannels of 20 MHz bandwidth, and the size of RU can be 26 tones, 52 tones, 106 tones, 52 plus 26 tones, or 106 plus 26 tones, where the RUs of 52 plus 26 tones and 106 plus 26 tones are MRUs allocated. The RU can also be a large RU with a size of 242 tones, 484 tones, 996 tones, or a combination of the above large RUs.

(4) **OFDMA function test at 6 GHz frequency band under the scenario with multiple STAs**

(a) Establish the single-link Wi-Fi connection on the 6 GHz frequency band between four STAs and the multi-link AP. Run bidirectional higher priority data traffic of 200 Mbps for each of three STAs, and run bidirectional normal TCP data traffic without size limits for one STA.

(b) Validate that the multi-link AP performs data traffic transmission in both upstream and downstream with multiple STAs based on OFDMA multiplexing technology and prioritizes the transmission for higher priority data traffic.

(c) Repeat the steps (c) and (d) of the 2.4 GHz frequency band test to validate the OFDMA function on the 6 GHz frequency band. There are 16 subchannels of 20 MHz bandwidth, and the size of RU can be 26 tones, 52 tones, 106 tones, 52 plus 26 tones, or 106 plus 26 tones, where the RUs of 52 plus 26 tones and 106 plus 26 tones are MRUs allocated. The RU can also be a large RU with a size of 242 tones, 484 tones, 996 tones, 2 × 996 tones, or a combination of the above large RUs.

4.3.2.3 Restricted Target Wake Time Technology Test

Based on the Restricted Target Wake Time (r-TWT) technology, the multi-link AP and STAs negotiate the target wake time and perform downstream and upstream data transmission of low-latency services within the period of the target wake time, which improves the latency performance of low-latency services.

This test is used to validate the wireless media access and low-latency services data transmission capabilities of the multi-link AP based on r-TWT technology.

1. **Test topology**

The test topology of r-TWT technology is shown in Fig. 4.71. The multi-link AP is placed in shielding box A, and two multi-link STAs that support the r-TWT feature are placed in shielding box B. The traffic generation tool is used to generate data traffic of different types of services; traffic of low-latency service is generated for one STA, and the traffic of normal TCP data service without size limit is generated for another STA.

2. **Test steps and results**

(1) **Configure multi-link AP:** Configure the 2.4 GHz frequency band with 20 MHz bandwidth, the 5 GHz frequency band with 160 MHz bandwidth, and the 6 GHz frequency band with 320 MHz bandwidth. Create the multi-link BSS with all three frequency bands affiliated.

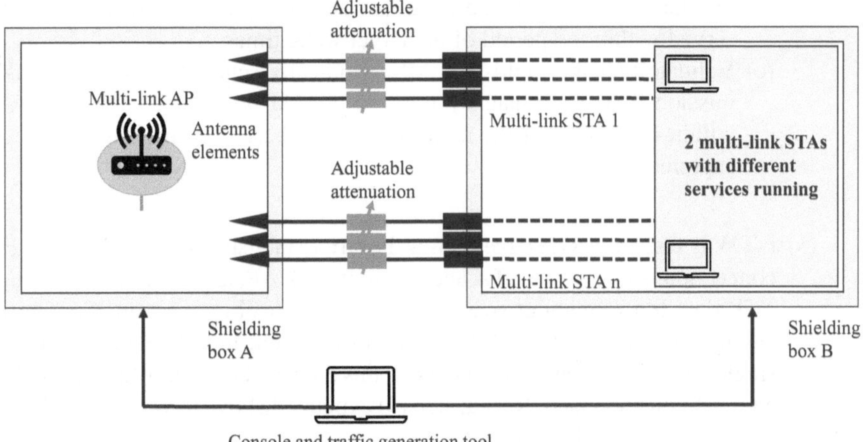

Fig. 4.71 Restricted target wake time technology test

(2) **Check AP capability:** Check the multi-link AP capability of the r-TWT feature based on the Beacon management frame sent from the multi-link AP at each frequency band. The value of 1 at the fourth bit of the EHT MAC capability information element in the Beacon frame indicates that the multi-link AP supports the r-TWT feature.

(3) **Set parameters of r-TWT:** Set the parameters of the r-TWT feature by command lines of the Wi-Fi driver for the multi-link BSS. This includes the r-TWT group ID, target wake time interval, and target wake duration, and check that the TWT information element in the Beacon frame carries the configured parameters of each r-TWT group.

(4) **r-TWT test at 2.4 GHz frequency band:** Establish the multi-link Wi-Fi connection between one STA and the multi-link AP, and execute the normal TCP data traffic without size limit over this Wi-Fi connection. Configure another STA to join the r-TWT group of the multi-link AP and establish a single-link Wi-Fi connection between this STA and the multi-link AP at the 2.4 GHz frequency band to validate the r-TWT function at the 2.4 GHz frequency band.

   (a) Check that the r-TWT information element is carried in the association request and association response frames during the connection process. This element should contain the r-TWT group ID to be joined and the traffic ID (TID) of the low-latency traffic to be served in both upstream and downstream directions within the period of the target wake time.

   (b) If the r-TWT information element is not included in the association response frame, the STA may join the r-TWT group via action frames. Check the r-TWT information element carried in the action frame, which contains the r-TWT group ID to be joined and the TID of the low-latency traffic in the upstream and downstream directions to be served within the period of the target wake time.

(c) Validate that the multi-link AP periodically schedules the data transmission of the low-latency traffic indicated by the TID for the STA within the period of the target wake time based on the Wi-Fi packets captured.

(5) **r-TWT test at 5 GHz frequency band:** Establish the multi-link Wi-Fi connection between one STA and the multi-link AP, and execute the normal TCP data traffic without size limit over this Wi-Fi connection. Configure another STA to join the r-TWT group of the multi-link AP and establish a single-link Wi-Fi connection between this STA and the multi-link AP at the 5 GHz frequency band. Repeat step (4) explained above to verify the r-TWT feature at the 5 GHz frequency band.

(6) **r-TWT test at 6 GHz frequency band:** Establish the multi-link Wi-Fi connection between one STA and the multi-link AP, and execute the normal TCP data traffic without size limit over this Wi-Fi connection. Configure another STA to join the r-TWT group of the multi-link AP and establish a single-link Wi-Fi connection between this STA and the multi-link AP at the 6 GHz frequency band. Repeat step (4) explained above to verify the r-TWT feature at the 6 GHz frequency band.

4.4 Summary

This chapter provides a comprehensive overview of the development of Wi-Fi 7 AP products, covering their specifications, performance indicators, software development, and product testing. Readers gain insights into the definition of Wi-Fi 7 AP products, the development process, and the impact of Wi-Fi 7 technology on AP product development and testing.

Product Specifications Wi-Fi 7 products are expected to gain prominence in the market from 2025. Tri-band Wi-Fi 7 AP products will dominate in regions with 6 GHz spectrum availability, while dual-band Wi-Fi 7 AP products will be prevalent in regions without 6 GHz spectrum. Key performance indicators include throughput, latency, network coverage, and security.

Development Process The development process encompasses system architecture design, hardware development, software development, and product testing. System architecture design involves chipset selection and structural planning based on product specifications and cost considerations. Hardware development includes circuit schematics, circuit board design, and hardware testing. Software development involves architecture design and the implementation of Wi-Fi 7-related functions. Product testing ensures functionality and performance compliance with specifications and Wi-Fi 7 technologies.

Software Development With a focus on Wi-Fi 7's multi-link technology, software development covers network management, connection management, data forwarding, EasyMesh network support, and channel management. Throughput and latency performance optimization methods are discussed, considering key factors influencing performance.

Product Test Typical deployment scenarios guide product performance testing, including RVR tests and throughput/latency tests with multiple STAs and services. Key technology testing includes multi-link operation, OFDMA, MRU allocation, and r-TWT technologies.

References

1. IEEE (2023) Draft Standard for Information technology--Telecommunications and information exchange between systems Local and metropolitan area networks--Specific requirements - Part 11: Wireless LAN Medium Access Control (MAC) and Physical Layer (PHY) Specifications Amendment: Enhancements for Extremely High Throughput (EHT) (IEEE P802.11be/D5.0). November. pp. 1–1045
2. Broadband Forum (2024) TR-398 Wi-Fi Residential & SOHO Performance Testing, Issue 3
3. Wi-Fi Alliance (2024) Wi-Fi EasyMesh Specification, Version Draft 6.0
4. Broadband Forum (2022) TR-369 User Services Platform (USP), Issue 1, Amendment 2
5. Broadband Forum (2024) TR-181 Device Data Model, Issue 2, Amendment 17

Chapter 5
Wi-Fi Industry Alliance Promoting Technologies and Products

Abstract The standards organizations and industry alliances have played a pivotal role in the great success of Wi-Fi commercialization and its wide popularity. First and foremost, as introduced in previous chapters, the IEEE 802.11 committee serves as the cornerstone for Wi-Fi technology specifications. Then, the Wi-Fi Alliance (WFA) offers testing and certification services, ensuring that wireless products from suppliers adhere not only to the IEEE 802.11 standard but also emphasize interoperability, security, user-friendliness, and the advancement of innovative technologies. In the telecommunications sector, the Broadband Forum (BBF) views Wi-Fi as an extension of broadband access, defining specifications focused on effectively managing Wi-Fi within home networks. The Wireless Broadband Alliance (WBA), with participation from numerous renowned operators and manufacturers, actively engages in discussions on market demands and commercial advancements in Wi-Fi. This chapter provides an overview of the contributions made by the WFA, BBF, and WBA.

5.1 The Success of Wi-Fi Alliance in the Age of Technology

As depicted in Fig. 5.1, various standards organizations and industry alliances contribute to the widespread adoption of Wi-Fi as it is today. The IEEE defines and releases technology specifications every 4 or 5 years. The Wi-Fi Alliance (WFA) provides a bridge between IEEE standards and commercial products through testing and certification services. The Broadband Forum (BBF) ratifies specifications for effectively managing Wi-Fi within home networks as an extension of broadband access. The Wireless Broadband Alliance (WBA) guides and promotes the evolution and application of Wi-Fi technology, leveraging industry studies and discussions involving many well-known operators and manufacturers. Additionally, the 3rd Generation Partnership Project (3GPP) recognizes the importance of integrating Wi-Fi access networks into the 5G standards framework. Given Wi-Fi's broad applicability across various scenarios, these entities prioritize Wi-Fi technology in their specifications and initiatives.

G. Cheng et al., *Wi-Fi 7*, https://doi.org/10.1007/978-981-97-9026-5_5

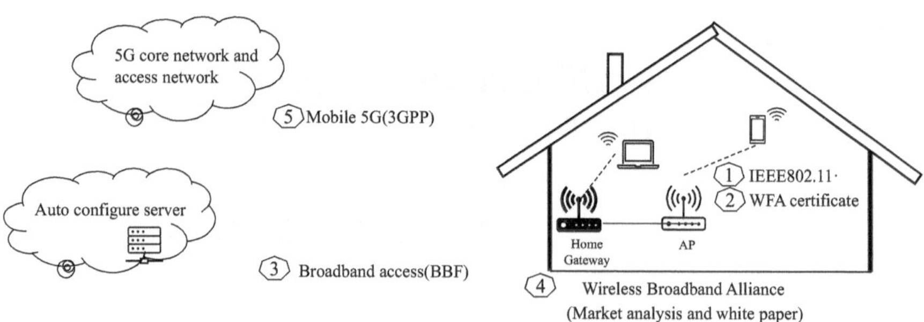

Fig. 5.1 Wi-Fi-related standards organizations and industry alliances

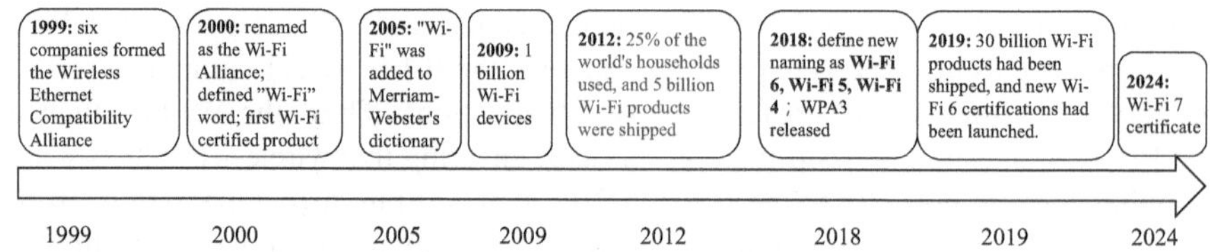

Fig. 5.2 Evolution of Wi-Fi Alliance and commercialization

The Wi-Fi Alliance, headquartered in Austin, Texas, United States, has been instrumental in driving the development and rapid adoption of Wi-Fi products. Its evolution and impact can be succinctly illustrated in Fig. 5.2 [1]. The Wi-Fi Alliance's roots trace back to 1999 when six companies joined to establish the Wireless Ethernet Compatibility Alliance (WECA). The main purpose of this alliance was to promote the commercialization of the IEEE 802.11 standard. The alliance underwent a significant transformation in October 2002, being rebranded as the Wi-Fi Alliance. In 2005, the word "Wi-Fi" was added to Merriam-Webster's dictionary. With the increasing use of Wi-Fi products, the name of Wi-Fi has gradually become a household name.

In 2012, a quarter of households worldwide embraced Wi-Fi, marking the shipment of 5 billion Wi-Fi products. Fast forward to 2019, 30 billion Wi-Fi products had been shipped, and new Wi-Fi 6 certifications were launched. In 2023, the Wi-Fi Alliance completed the development of Wi-Fi 7 certification specifications. It is expected that Wi-Fi 7 certified products will be available in the market in 2024.

Today, Wi-Fi technology has seamlessly integrated into daily life and work routines, standing out as one of the greatest success stories of the technological era. Wi-Fi's global economic value is expected to reach $5 trillion by 2025, with an annual delivery of 1 billion devices delivered each year.

5.1.1 *Wi-Fi Alliance Testing and Certification Methods*

Without the 802.11 standard developed by the IEEE, there would be no core technology for the Wi-Fi Alliance. But without the interoperability certification of the Wi-Fi Alliance and the development of new usability specifications, Wi-Fi products would not be as widespread and adopted as they are today.

In 2018, the Wi-Fi Alliance introduced a mapping system that correlates the IEEE 802.11 standard with numerical serial numbers, as shown in Table 5.1. For instance, 802.11n corresponds with Wi-Fi 4, 802.11ac corresponds to Wi-Fi 5, 802.11ax corresponds to Wi-Fi 6, and 802.11be corresponds to Wi-Fi 7. This transition eliminated the use of numeric ordinal numbers for standards predating Wi-Fi 4.

The emergence of digital serial numbers simplifies the understanding and recognition of Wi-Fi technology for the general public. Similar to the simplicity of identifying mobile communication standards like 4G and 5G, this approach aids in promoting Wi-Fi and popularizing it to the public.

Users can easily determine the current Wi-Fi standard through a visual user interface on a mobile phone or other terminal with a screen, such as the Wi-Fi identifier shown in Fig. 5.3. An identifier with 6 indicates that the current wireless connection is Wi-Fi 6.

The Wi-Fi Alliance has established a set of testing requirements for products that support Wi-Fi technology. Products that pass these interoperability tests meet the Wi-Fi Alliance certification requirements and may include computers, smartphones, home appliances, network equipment, and consumer electronics, etc. The Wi-Fi CERTIFIED logo is granted to products that have passed the certification test, provided by device suppliers who are members of the Wi-Fi Alliance.

Device suppliers reach out to the Wi-Fi Alliance's Authorized Test Laboratory (ATL) to certify the Wi-Fi features of their products, such as Wi-Fi CERTIFIED 6™ or previous Wi-Fi standards. Products can also be certified for specific applications, such as multi-access Wi-Fi systems and seamless connectivity experiences while in motion.

Wi-Fi Alliance certification [2] is offered through three avenues:

Table 5.1 Wi-Fi names vs IEEE standards

Name definition	Technical specifications
Wi-Fi 7	802.11be
Wi-Fi 6	802.11ax
Wi-Fi 5	802.11ac
Wi-Fi 4	802.11n

Fig. 5.3 Visual identifiers defined by the Wi-Fi Alliance (from www.wi-fi.org)

1. **FlexTrack**: Tailored for sophisticated product designs developed from scratch, allowing for a high degree of flexibility in Wi-Fi product design. Testing is conducted in an Authorized Test Laboratory.
2. **QuickTrack:** Tailored to products based on components that have already undergone full Wi-Fi functionality testing in a Qualified Solution. This facilitates targeted modifications to Wi-Fi components and functionality. Testing can be carried out at an Authorized Test Laboratory or a member testing site.
3. **Derivatives:** Geared toward copies of a Wi-Fi CERTIFIED device, such as those utilizing the same chipset for multiple products. Members may seek certification for derivative products without the need for additional testing.

5.1.2 Certification Specifications Developed by Wi-Fi Alliance

The Wi-Fi Alliance consistently introduces new certification programs every year, aimed at promoting interoperability verification of products supporting the IEEE 802.11 core standard, IoT applications, product security, and user experience enhancements. Listed below are some of the major certification programs, indicated in Table 5.2.

5.1.3 Wi-Fi Alliance Certification for QoS Management

The Wi-Fi Alliance, through certifications like WMM and QoS, exemplifies its commitment to advancing innovative technologies in the Wi-Fi domain, thereby enhancing industry development and improving user experiences.

Historically, IEEE 802.11 standards [3] mainly focused on performance improvements such as spectral efficiency, channel bandwidth expansion, and concurrency. However, prioritizing quality of service (QoS) has not been a primary concern. To address this, IEEE introduced 802.11e [4] in 2004, offering new operational methods and parameter configurations to enhance QoS support at the MAC layer. This standard defines four access categories (AC) to prioritize data streams: Voice, Video, Best Effort, and Background. Data flows are assigned to these access categories according to their User Priority. Each access category contends for the wireless medium using distinct channel access parameters.

To ensure QoS interoperability across different products, the Wi-Fi Alliance introduced Wi-Fi Multimedia (WMM) certification, based on the 802.11e standard, starting in December 2004. A successful WMM certification test for a Wi-Fi AP signifies its capability to map various service flows to different access categories.

Referring to Fig. 5.4, downstream traffic flows to the Wi-Fi AP, where the Wi-Fi MAC layer classifies the service flow and maps it to the corresponding AC queue before transmitting it to the station. In this process, a crucial prerequisite is that the

Table 5.2 Examples of Wi-Fi Alliance certifications

Index	Certificate feature	Core technology	Technical characteristics and application scenarios
1	Wi-Fi CERTIFIED HaLow™	IEEE 802.11ah	Operates in the sub-1 GHz band, enabling long-range and low-power connectivity. Applications include IoT and industrial IoT environments, as well as markets such as retail, agriculture, healthcare, smart homes, smart cities, etc.
2	Wi-Fi CERTIFIED WPA3™	Technical enhancements based on WPA2	WPA3 provides a new level of security for both personal and enterprise networks. WPA3-personal provides more robust password-based authentication, while WPA3-Enterprise builds upon the foundation of WPA2-Enterprise with the additional requirement of using protected management frames on all WPA3 connections.
3	Wi-Fi CERTIFIED 6®	IEEE 802.11ax	Compared with previous Wi-Fi specifications, Wi-Fi 6 provides higher data rates, increased capacity, performance in environments with many connected devices, and improved power efficiency.
4	Wi-Fi CERTIFIED WiGig™	IEEE 802.11ad	Enabling gigabit speeds per second in the 60 GHz band, it expands enterprise applications for virtual reality, multimedia, gaming, wireless docking, and high-speed connectivity. Multiband Wi-Fi CERTIFIED products supporting 2.4 GHz, 5 GHz, and 60 GHz allow handoff between frequency bands.
5	Wi-Fi CERTIFIED EasyMesh™	IEEE 802.11 k/v/u/r	Multiple access points form a unified network that extends Wi-Fi coverage for indoor and outdoor spaces, including basic diagnostics, channel and band changes, and the ability to steer stations to a different associated AP as needed.
6	Wi-Fi CERTIFIED Wi-Fi Direct®	IEEE 802.11 standards	Without joining a Wi-Fi network, Wi-Fi devices can be directly connected to each other, making it convenient to print, share content, and play games.
7	Wi-Fi Multimedia™ (WMM®)	IEEE 802.11 standards	WMM adopts quality of service enhancements defined in the IEEE 802.11e standard, including four access categories: Voice, video, best effort, and background.
8	Wi-Fi CERTIFIED QoS Management™	IEEE 802.11 standards	It builds upon and extends WMM with new technologies that enable clients and APs to negotiate and request that identified IP flows be assigned to specific access categories defined by WMM.

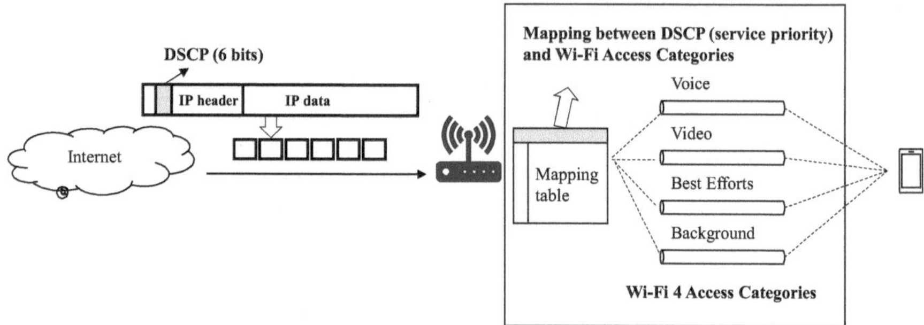

Fig. 5.4 QoS support from WMM defined by WFA

priority of the data packets has been set in the Differentiated Services Code Point (DSCP) field in the IP packet header, aligning with the MAC layer's data priority settings.

However, in real-world industry deployments, there is often inconsistency between DSCP values and WMM User Priorities. Many applications are beginning to set DSCP fields, but numerous Internet servers still use the default DSCP fields in downstream datagrams. Additionally, Internet service providers' devices may reset the DSCP field of the original datagram in the network, and some devices may have DSCP fields that do not match the network service requirements. Therefore, when a Wi-Fi AP receives a data packet from the Internet, it cannot effectively forward the data to the station through the priority queue of the WMM.

To address these industry-wide inconsistencies in how DSCP is mapped to WMM User Priorities, the Wi-Fi Alliance introduced its first QoS management certification in December 2020 [5, 6].

Wi-Fi QoS management certification extends WMM by enabling access points (APs) and client devices to negotiate and/or request that identified IP flows be assigned to particular access categories. This certification encompasses several key technologies:

1. **Stream Classification Service (SCS):** Facilitates the classification and Wi-Fi QoS processing of specific IP flows, including data flows to and from the 5G core network. This allows traffic such as games, voice, and video to take precedence over other types of traffic.
2. **Mirrored Stream Classification Service (MSCS)**: Allows stations to request that the AP use QoS mirroring to apply specific QoS treatment to downstream IP flows.
3. **Differentiated Service Code Point Policy**: Enables unified QoS treatment across Wi-Fi and wired networks, empowering network administrators to configure specific QoS policies.
4. **Differentiated Service Code Point Policy:** Enables stations to dynamically configure DSCP policies for specific upstream IP traffic, allowing them to be

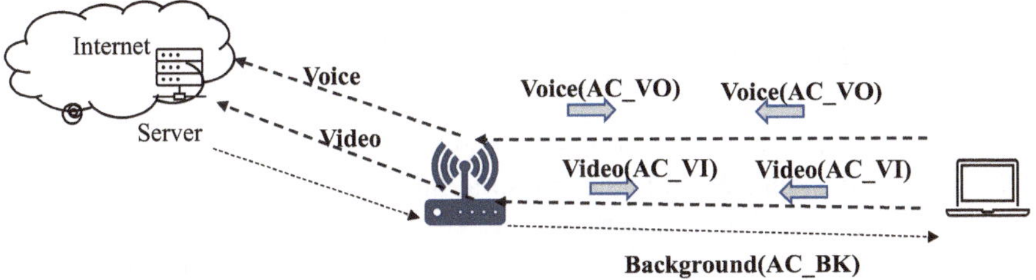

Fig. 5.5 The station and AP cooperate to implement QoS treatment of downstream traffic

marked with different DSCP values. This enhances the experience of low-latency applications like eXtended Reality (XR).

While the original WMM technology only classifies traffic flows into four categories, the new QoS management technology requires collaboration and negotiation between APs and stations to identify and classify traffic flows for specific services. With high-priority treatment of specific data streams in Wi-Fi networks, it enhances the performance of interactive cloud and edge services and provides users with a superior real-time application experience.

Figure 5.5 illustrates an example of a station requesting a Mirrored Stream Classification Service from an AP. Upon accepting the request, the AP copies the corresponding priority for upstream voice or video traffic sent by the station and applies the same priority to downstream traffic. This ensures that bidirectional service flows are handled with high-priority transmission in Wi-Fi networks.

The Wi-Fi Alliance's QoS management certification doesn't directly correspond with specific IEEE 802.11 standards. However, the technical advancements in Wi-Fi 7 technology aimed at improving low-latency performance, combined with the Wi-Fi Alliance's QoS management certification, are expected to greatly enhance overall low-latency processing in Wi-Fi networks.

5.2 Contribution of Wireless Broadband Alliance to Wi-Fi Industry

The Wireless Broadband Alliance (WBA) was established in 2003, comprising major operators, service providers, industry players, and other companies worldwide within the global wireless ecosystem. Members include AT&T in the United States, T-Mobile in Germany, BT in the United Kingdom, and DoCoMo in Japan, along with chip vendors like Intel and device vendors like Cisco. Every year, the WBA conducts research on the latest Wi-Fi topics in the industry through working groups or task forces. The results of the research are usually published in white papers.

5.2.1 Wireless Broadband Alliance Working Groups and Task Groups

Figure 5.6 illustrates the main working groups and task groups in 2022, including Wi-Fi 6/6E, expanding Wi-Fi in the industrial Internet, and enhancing user experience in various scenarios such as rural areas, etc. [7].

In addition, the integration of mobile 5G and Wi-Fi enterprise networks has also become a significant focus for the Wireless Broadband Alliance (WBA). The working group examines requirements, scenario use cases, technical solutions, and more to provide solution references for 5G enterprise private networks.

5.2.2 Promote the Development of Wi-Fi Sensing Technology

Detecting and sensing human activity through Wi-Fi signal propagation is a promising innovation in Wi-Fi technology. With Wi-Fi APs radiating Wi-Fi signals in almost every corner of the home, the potential for commercializing Wi-Fi signal recognition of human behavior is significant, offering numerous applications for smart homes.

Various schemes exist for recognizing human behavior through Wi-Fi signals, all based on leveraging signal characteristics altered by the movement of objects during signal propagation. These signals, traveling from transmitter to receiver, undergo changes due to factors such as direct emission, diffraction, and reflection. By analyzing the final received signal, human motion can be recognized based on its unique characteristics.

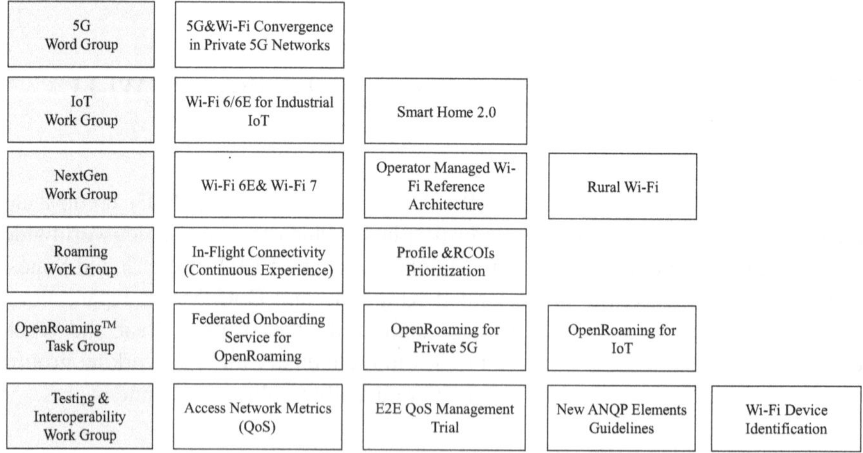

Fig. 5.6 Working groups and task groups of the Wireless Broadband Alliance

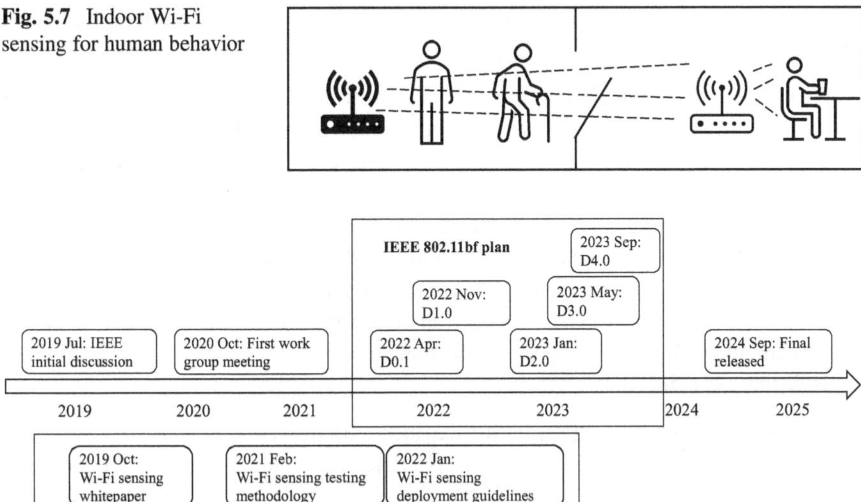

Fig. 5.7 Indoor Wi-Fi sensing for human behavior

Fig. 5.8 Wi-Fi sensing technology development promoted by WBA

Currently, using Wi-Fi Channel State Information (CSI) from each OFDM subcarrier is a novel method for environment sensing and human motion recognition. Figure 5.7 shows two Wi-Fi APs exchanging data while there are people standing, walking, or sitting in the same room. Through sophisticated algorithms, the Wi-Fi APs analyze received Wi-Fi signals to extract information about human behavior.

To standardize Wi-Fi sensing technology on the unlicensed spectrum, the IEEE is developing the 802.11bf standard, as shown in Fig. 5.8. In October 2020, the IEEE 802.11 Working Group initiated a new Task Group BF (TGbf) to develop a new amendment for WLAN sensing to support Wi-Fi sensing in both sub-7 GHz bands, including the 2.4 GHz, 5 GHz, and 6 GHz bands, as well as the 60 GHz millimeter-wave. There was a draft version D0.1 released in April 2022, with a further release in September 2023 for Version D4.0, targeted for final approval in 2024. The Wireless Broadband Alliance developed a Wi-Fi sensing white paper in 2019, providing an overview of Wi-Fi sensing technology. The WBA published a test methodology in 2021 and released deployment guidance in 2022 [8], continuing to promote the development of sensing technology in the industry.

Below are some key points from the deployment guidance for sensing technologies. Despite abundant information on Wi-Fi network deployments and Wi-Fi AP placement for optimal performance, there is a notable absence of documentation on Wi-Fi sensing performance in such deployments. The deployment guidance provided by the WBA aims to ensure the performance of Wi-Fi sensing technology within home environments. It addresses how environmental factors and device characteristics can affect sensing performance. The deployment guidance includes relevant experiments to provide real data as reference points. Following are some examples:

1. **Environmental factors:** Signal attenuation of 2.4 GHz, 5 GHz, and 6 GHz by different building materials, room layout influencing electromagnetic wave propagation, and the impact of mechanical and electrical interference on Wi-Fi sensing, etc.
2. **Device factors**: The frequency band and channel bandwidth supported by the device; the impact of legacy power-saving modes and not actively transmitting or receiving data affects their involvement in Wi-Fi sensing; the impact of Wi-Fi network topology on Wi-Fi perception functionality; and the impact of device placement on Wi-Fi perception performance, etc.
3. **Related experiments:**

   - **Motion detection region identification**: Utilizing two devices to measure and pinpoint areas where motion is detected within the Wi-Fi network environment.
   - **Impact of AP placement in multi-floor buildings:** Analyzing the consequences of positioning access points (APs) in various locations within multi-floor buildings, with particular emphasis on the wireless backhaul channel.
   - **Influence of user control on sensing testing**: Evaluating how user control and interaction impact the testing procedures and outcomes of Wi-Fi sensing experiments.

In conclusion, the deployment guidance offered by the Wireless Broadband Alliance provides a reference for end users seeking to leverage Wi-Fi sensing technology. It includes network deployment methods, Wi-Fi AP placement, network topology, sensing system settings, and environmental considerations. Despite being a subject of extensive university research, Wi-Fi sensing technology remains in its nascent stage of commercialization. The series of white papers published by the Wireless Broadband Alliance plays a pivotal role in advancing the evolution and development of this technology within the industry.

5.3 Contribution of Broadband Forum to Wi-Fi Management

The Broadband Forum, originating from the Digital Subscriber Line (DSL) forum, initially focused on formulating new standards for DSL communication products, such as provisioning. In 2008, it was renamed as the "Broadband Forum." This rebranding expanded its scope beyond DSL-related specifications to encompass fiber broadband access as well. The forum broadens its focus to address architecture, device and service management, and the definition of software data model interoperability and certification specifications.

5.3.1 *Support TR-069 Protocol for Broadband Network Devices*

Chapter 4 introduces TR-069 as a network management protocol for Wi-Fi devices. This protocol is a specification published by the Broadband Forum, officially known as CPE WAN management protocol (CWMP) [9]. It defines an application layer protocol for the remote management of end-user devices, referred to as customer-premises equipment (CPE). In this architecture, the CPE functions as the client, while an Auto Configuration Server (ACS) acts as the server. Communication between the CPE and ACS occurs over the Hypertext Transfer Protocol (HTTP) or Simple Object Access Protocol (SOAP) over HTTP, as shown in Fig. 5.9.

With support from over 1 billion installed units, the TR-069 protocol has become foundational for large-scale broadband deployment and shaping the broadband experience worldwide.

With the rise of the Internet of Things, the evolution of smart homes, and the increasing focus on new security challenges and implementing cloud-based business models, etc., the industry is undergoing a reevaluation of how to deliver and measure broadband experiences within households.

Particularly, Wi-Fi is an important extension of broadband access to the home. If there is a problem with Wi-Fi Internet access, normally users are not able to distinguish between Wi-Fi problems and broadband access problems. Consequently, for service providers, enhancing the broadband access experience involves efficient management and investigation of potential Wi-Fi-related issues.

In recent years, managing Wi-Fi within home networks has emerged as a key focal point for operators and has become a primary area of focus for new specifications from the Broadband Forum. This shift has paved the way for the emergence of the TR-369 protocol.

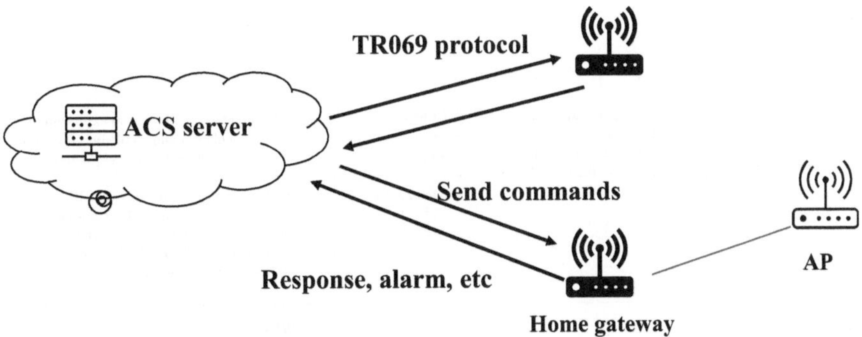

Fig. 5.9 Remote management via TR-069 protocol

5.3.2 *TR-369 Protocol for All Aspects of Home Network Management*

TR-369 [10], also referred to as the User Services Platform (USP), is an evolution of TR-069, offering broader support for various home network management scenarios. Unlike TR-069, TR-369 caters to a wider range of deployment scenarios and accommodates an expanded array of devices. Importantly, TR-369 is designed to coexist with TR-069 and offers an easy migration pathway from TR-069 to TR-369. Figure 5.10 illustrates the evolutionary progression from TR-069 to TR-369.

From the perspective of the services provided by TR-369, the main capabilities of the CPE will include:

- **Management and monitoring network interfaces:** This includes overseeing physical interfaces such as Ethernet, Wi-Fi, and Zigbee, as well as managing protocol interfaces like IPv6, IPv4, and Dynamic Host Configuration Protocol (DHCP).
- **Management and monitoring network services and clients**: This involves managing firewalls, Quality of Service (QoS), routing policies, connected hosts, and application layer connection interfaces such as Message Queuing Telemetry Transport (MQTT), among others.
- **Performance measurement and diagnosis:** TR-369 supports performance measurement, such as download and upload speeds, as well as diagnostic tools like packet capture to identify and troubleshoot network issues.
- **Container and application management:** This facilitates the installation, monitoring, and lifecycle management of software modules. It also supports the management of containers on the USP agent through defined objects and parameters.

One of the main objectives of the TR-369 standard is to assist operators in enhancing the management of home Wi-Fi networks. Wi-Fi networks are highly susceptible to environmental factors, leading to fluctuations in performance and connectivity status. Consequently, managing Wi-Fi networks poses numerous challenges for operators compared to traditional telecom networks.

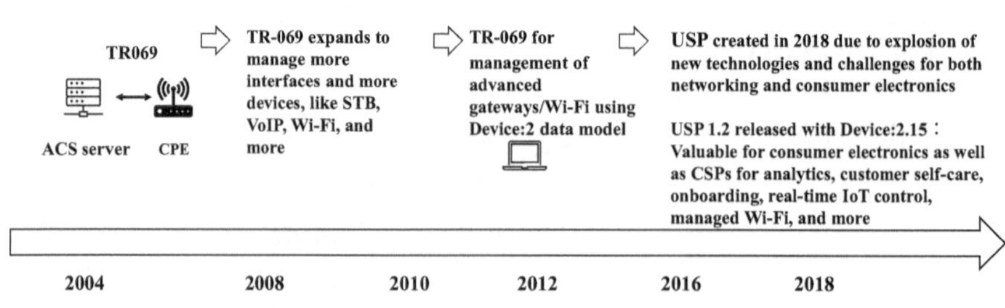

Fig. 5.10 TR-369 protocol evolution

The key to Wi-Fi management lies in the Device:2 Data Model for USP, which has been utilized for Wi-Fi network setup and monitoring for over a decade and is continuously maintained and updated. TR-369 introduces several Wi-Fi management features:

- **Enhanced daily operation and maintenance of Wi-Fi:** Supports the dynamic collection of various Wi-Fi statistics and operational data, including Wi-Fi mesh networks based on the Wi-Fi Alliance Data Elements standard. This data is analyzed for Wi-Fi network optimization and can be managed remotely.
- **Support for network optimization using algorithms such as machine learning:** USP bulk data collection facilitates data aggregation and uploading to the cloud in a scheduled manner. Machine Learning techniques automate the management and optimization of home networks with Wi-Fi.
- **Support for network management functions in software module mode:** Support Software Module Management (SMM) facilitates the installation, upgrades, and uninstallation of container applications. This capability allows for the flexible deployment of additional Wi-Fi management functions.

With the advent of Wi-Fi 7 products in the market, new features such as multi-link operation in Wi-Fi 7 will inevitably impact the data model of TR-369. It is anticipated that Wi-Fi management for TR-369 will continue to evolve and expand to accommodate these changes.

References

1. Wi-Fi Alliance. https://www.wi-fi.org/sites/default/files/public/Infographic_20_years_of_Wi-Fi.pdf. Accessed 6 Aug 2024
2. Wi-Fi Alliance. https://www.wi-fi.org/certification. Accessed 6 Aug 2024
3. IEEE (2020) IEEE Standard for Information Technology--Telecommunications and Information Exchange between Systems - Local and Metropolitan Area Networks--Specific Requirements - Part 11: Wireless LAN Medium Access Control (MAC) and Physical Layer (PHY) Specifications (Revision of IEEE Std 802.11-2016). IEEE Std 802.11-2020. pp. 1–4379. https://doi.org/10.1109/IEEESTD.2021.9363693
4. IEEE (2005) IEEE Standard for Information technology–Local and metropolitan area networks–Specific requirements–Part 11: Wireless LAN Medium Access Control (MAC) and Physical Layer (PHY) Specifications - Amendment 8: Medium Access Control (MAC) Quality of Service Enhancements. IEEE Std 802.11e-2005
5. Wi-Fi Alliance (2020) Wi-Fi QoS Management Technical Specification. https://www.wi-fi.org/file/wi-fi-qos-management-specification
6. Wireless Broadband Alliance (2023) E2E QoS Improvement: Optimizing QoS Over Wi-Fi. https://wballiance.com/e2e-qos-improvement-optimizing-qos-over-wi-fi/
7. Wireless Broadband Alliance (2022) WBA Industrial Report 2023
8. Wireless Broadband Alliance (2022) Wi-Fi Sensing Deployment Guidelines
9. Broadband Forum (2018) CPE WAN Management Protocol [R]. Retrieved from broadband-forum.org
10. Broadband Forum (2019) Realizing the Promise of the Connected Home with User Services Platform (TR-369)

Chapter 6
Wi-Fi 7 Technology Applications and Experience Upgrades

Abstract Wi-Fi 7 builds upon the foundation of Wi-Fi 6 technology and represents a significant performance leap from its predecessor. With this advancement, Wi-Fi 7 further enhances the application scenarios that have evolved from the earliest versions of Wi-Fi technology, including high-density connections and business applications requiring high bandwidth and low latency. This chapter explores the current state of Wi-Fi technology in home environments, urban public areas, and key industry areas. It highlights the changes and new user experiences introduced by Wi-Fi 7's high-performance technical characteristics. Readers will gain insights into how Wi-Fi 7, with its high bandwidth and low latency, meets the need for high-speed data transmission and real-time services over short distances. This chapter also provides an overview of effective Wi-Fi network design across different application scenarios. It outlines Wi-Fi 7 product functional specifications, demonstrating Wi-Fi 7's ability to meet the growing demands for faster, more robust, and low-latency wireless communication across diverse environments and applications.

6.1 Enhancing Entertainment Experiences in the Comfort of Your Home

6.1.1 Exploring AR/VR User Experience and Advancements in Wi-Fi Technology

In the international landscape, the AR/VR virtual reality industry marked its inception in 2016, while 2018 witnessed the emergence of the cloud VR sector, and 2019 witnessed the dawn of the 5G cloud VR era. Globally, AR/VR technology is experiencing a period of accelerated development and growth, with significant expansion across education, entertainment, medical, and other sectors. The global virtual reality industry is anticipated to maintain an impressive average annual growth rate of 54% from 2020 to 2024.

Referring to Fig. 6.1, AR/VR technology has undergone a remarkable evolution, prioritizing immersive user experiences. It all began with products focusing on primary immersion in 2016, gradually expanding to include partial immersion and

G. Cheng et al., *Wi-Fi 7*, https://doi.org/10.1007/978-981-97-9026-5_6

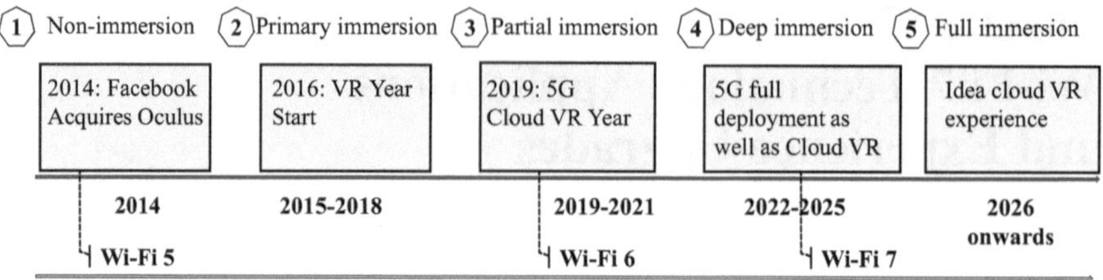

Fig. 6.1 Development route of virtual reality

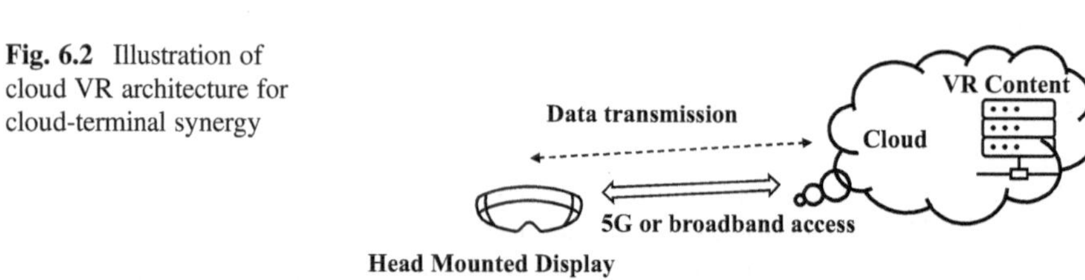

Fig. 6.2 Illustration of cloud VR architecture for cloud-terminal synergy

eventually aiming for deep immersion by the years 2025 and 2026, ultimately leading to a fully immersive experience. In virtual reality, immersion is achieved by utilizing advanced computer technology to create three-dimensional stereoscopic images, transporting users into a virtual environment that feels remarkably real.

Interestingly, this development journey closely aligns with the evolution of Wi-Fi technology. Wi-Fi 6 corresponds to a state of partial immersion, while the emergence of Wi-Fi 7 perfectly caters to the demand for deep immersion, matching the ever-evolving needs of AR/VR experiences. The seamless integration of Wi-Fi advancements with the progression of AR/VR demonstrates their synergistic growth in providing enhanced user experiences.

6.1.1.1 Technical Requirements for Cloud VR

As of now, the AR/VR product chain, which includes application services, terminal products, network platforms, and content production, has attained a stable state and continues to evolve. Technological development has centered around the collaboration between cloud and terminal architecture, garnering significant attention from the industry. This approach involves moving VR/AR content to the cloud, thus separating application processing from terminal presentation. The cloud takes charge of business computing, and the results are transmitted to the terminal via 5G or broadband wired networks. This approach offers various benefits, such as reducing terminal costs, enhancing user mobility, and enabling more convenient and flexible terminal use. Refer to Fig. 6.2 for a visual representation of this architecture.

The rise of the cloud VR industry chain, complemented by the 5G or broadband networks from network providers, has fostered a collaborative environment where each manufacturer can focus on its specific areas of expertise. Cloud resource providers and content platform distributors offer a rich repository of AR/VR content

Table 6.1 Performance-index requirements for VR experiences

Stage		Start-up phase	Comfort phase	Ideal experience phase
Immersion mode		Primary immersion	Partial immersion	Deep immersion
Estimated commercial time (year)		2016–2018	2019–2021	2022–2026
VR video business	Bandwidth	Greater than 60 Mbps	Greater than 75 Mbps	Greater than 230 Mbps
	Network round-trip latency	Less than 20 ms	Less than 20 ms	Less than 20 ms
	Packet loss rate	9×10^{-5}	1.7×10^{-5}	1.7×10^{-6}
VR strong interactive business	Bandwidth	Greater than 80 Mbps	Greater than 260 Mbps	Greater than 1 Gbps
	Network round-trip latency	Less than 20 ms	Less than 15 ms	Less than 8 ms
	Packet loss rate	1.0×10^{-5}	1.0×10^{-5}	1.0×10^{-6}

resources and streamlined content distribution. Network providers, on the other hand, ensure high-bandwidth, low-latency data transmission networks, while hardware equipment manufacturers optimize terminal product designs. By collectively enhancing and improving various aspects, the industry aims to deliver a seamless user experience, ultimately realizing the full potential of virtual reality.

Network providers primarily focus on transferring data from the cloud to the user's home. From there, Wi-Fi takes over the responsibility of ensuring high bandwidth and low latency for the last tens of meters in wireless transmission. However, if there is packet loss or significant delay in Wi-Fi transmission, it can result in a negative user experience, causing issues like freezing, jumping, or lagging. Wi-Fi technology has advanced from Wi-Fi 5 to Wi-Fi 6 and Wi-Fi 7, providing effective technical solutions for AR/VR short-range wireless data connections within the room. These advancements in Wi-Fi technology ensure a smooth and immersive user experience in AR/VR applications.

Referring to Table 6.1 [2, 4], VR mainly includes video services and strong interaction services. "Video services" refer to the delivery of immersive video content that allows users to experience virtual environments and scenes as if they were present in them. This content can include 360° videos, virtual tours, and other visual experiences that provide a sense of presence and immersion. On the other hand, "strong interaction services" in VR pertain to experiences that enable users to actively engage and interact within the virtual environment. This goes beyond passive video consumption and involves user input and responses that affect the virtual world. Strong interaction services often include virtual games, simulations, and interactive experiences where users can manipulate objects, explore virtual spaces, and interact with characters or elements in the virtual world. The evolution process of cloud VR can be divided into three stages based on performance

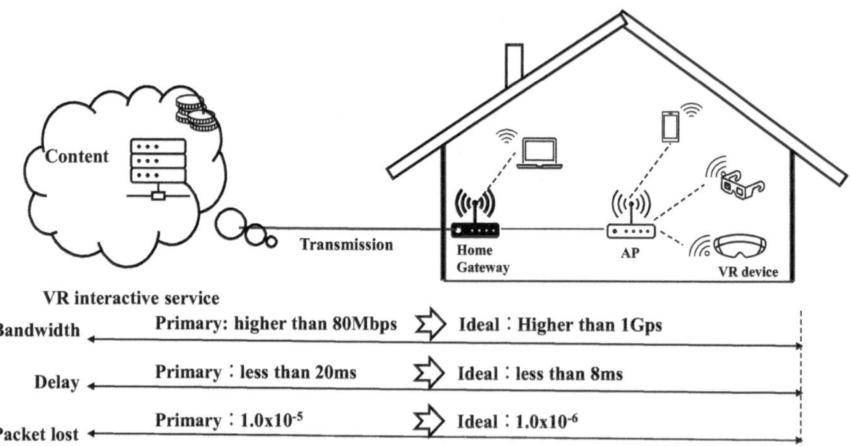

Fig. 6.3 Illustration of the end-to-end network of cloud VR's strong interactive service

indicators. The initial stage spans from 2016 to 2018, followed by the comfort experience stage around 2020. After 2022, cloud VR gradually enters the ideal experience stage.

The VR strong interaction business in Table 6.1 mainly consists of VR online games. These games demand real-time operation and action-based interactions between users and servers, which places high requirements on both bandwidth and low latency. This is crucial to ensure a smooth and responsive gaming experience, as any delays or lags can disrupt the sense of immersion and hinder gameplay.

Figure 6.3 depicts the end-to-end data transmission process of cloud VR strong interaction, along with the bandwidth, network delay, and packet loss data presented in Table 6.1. In the ideal stage, the network round-trip delay should be less than 8 ms, referring to the round-trip latency between the cloud server and the VR headset. Meeting such strict latency requirements poses a significant challenge for the deployment of cloud VR networks.

6.1.1.2 Wi-Fi Technology Standards Supporting VR Services

For end-to-end data transmission, the Wi-Fi network plays a critical role as one of the key links. It involves the short-range wireless connection between the wireless router in the user's home and the VR headset. The performance of the Wi-Fi network should ideally surpass the overall technical indicators of the end-to-end network, meeting more stringent requirements.

To elaborate, when considering network latency, it can be broken down into different segments, such as metro networks, broadband access networks, and home Wi-Fi networks. In an optimal scenario, the transmission latency on the Wi-Fi network should be lower than the end-to-end delay. This ensures that the Wi-Fi

Table 6.2 Wi-Fi technology standards support VR services

Stage		Start-up phase	Comfort phase	Ideal experience phase
VR video business	Bandwidth	Wi-Fi 5	Wi-Fi 5	Wi-Fi 6
	Network round-trip latency	Wi-Fi 6	Wi-Fi 6	Wi-Fi 6
	Packet loss	Not applicable	Not applicable	Not applicable
VR strong interactive business	Bandwidth	Wi-Fi 5	Wi-Fi 6	**Wi-Fi 7**
	Network round-trip latency	Wi-Fi 6	Wi-Fi 6 or **Wi-Fi 7**	**Wi-Fi 7**
	Packet loss	Not applicable	Not applicable	Not applicable

Table 6.3 Latency indicators for VR strong interaction services

	Basic experience phase	Comfort experience	Ideal experience
Network round-trip latency	Less than 20 ms	Less than 15 ms	Less than 8 ms
Home Wi-Fi network latency	Less than 10 ms	Less than 7 ms	Less than 5 ms
Wi-Fi technology is recommended	Wi-Fi 6	**Wi-Fi 7**	**Wi-Fi 7**

network contributes positively to reducing overall latency and maintaining a smooth and responsive VR experience.

To achieve such high-quality data transmission, the Wi-Fi network needs to provide low-latency connections and high-bandwidth capabilities, especially in the context of VR strong interaction services, where real-time responsiveness is crucial. Advances in Wi-Fi technology, such as Wi-Fi 6 and Wi-Fi 7, aim to enhance network performance, reduce latency, and deliver a seamless VR experience by effectively managing data transmission within the home network environment.

Table 6.2 presents the suggested Wi-Fi standards based on both VR video services and VR strong interaction services, as outlined in Table 6.1. This table also encompasses the performance metrics associated with each Wi-Fi standard. Notably, packet loss is contingent upon both the Wi-Fi network environment and the efficacy of product processing services. As such, there exists no direct quantifiable correlation with the Wi-Fi standard, rendering it an unsuitable metric for recommending Wi-Fi standards.

In Table 6.2, Wi-Fi 7 emerges as the superior choice for enhanced user experiences in strong interaction VR services. This advantage can be attributed to its technical attributes of high bandwidth and low latency.

In Table 6.3, we use the latency index of VR strong interaction services to explain Wi-Fi network latency requirements and their corresponding Wi-Fi standards. When we compare the delay at various stages of deployment—basic experience, comfortable experience, and ideal experience—it is best for the Wi-Fi network at home to have a latency that is 50% of the total network delay. This helps ensure that VR strong interactive services don't suffer from frustrating delays. To meet this goal, we recommend using Wi-Fi 6 and Wi-Fi 7, as shown in Table 6.3. Among these, Wi-Fi 7 really shines, especially for the comfortable and ideal experience phases, thanks to its advanced technical features.

6.1.1.3 Wi-Fi 7 AP that Implements Strong Interactive Services for Cloud VR

To make cloud-based VR strong interactive services meet comfortable and ideal experiences, we have laid out the specifications for Wi-Fi 7 APs in Table 6.4. These specs include support for a 320 MHz channel bandwidth in the 6 GHz band or 160 MHz in the 5 GHz band. The APs also handle service quality control and prioritize service traffic, especially for low-latency services, which is crucial for smooth VR strong interactive experiences.

6.1.2 Wi-Fi 7 Technology Supporting Ultra HD Video Services

Video technology is moving from high-definition to ultra-high-definition television (UHDTV), such as 4K and 8K Ultra HD TVs. Ultra HD means resolutions higher than 3840 × 2160 pixels, including 4K (3840 × 2160) and 8K (7680 × 4320) Ultra HD TVs.

To put it in perspective, HDTV has about 2 million pixels, 4K UHD TV has around 8.3 million pixels, and 8K UHD TV goes even further with a massive 33 million pixels. You can find the details in Table 6.5. To compare, 4K Ultra HD TVs have 4 times the pixels of HDTVs, and 8K Ultra HD TVs have 16 times more pixels than HDTVs.

Table 6.4 Wi-Fi 7 AP specifications

AP selection	Functional specifications
Hardware requirements	Wi-Fi 7 AP BE7200, or Wi-Fi 7 AP BE19000
	Wi-Fi 7 dual-band, or Wi-Fi 7 tri-band
	Multi-antenna 4 × 4 2.4 GHz, 4 × 4 5 GHz Or multi-antenna 4 × 4 2.4 GHz, 4 × 4 5 GHz, 4 × 4 6 GHz
	Maximum bandwidth support of 160 MHz (for 5 GHz) or 320 MHz (for 6 GHz)
Software requirements	Multi-link simultaneous transmit and receive technology supported in Wi-Fi 7
	Supports Wi-Fi 7 multi-resource unit (MRU) technology
	Supports Wi-Fi 7 recognition of low-latency service feature
	Supports QoS with high-priority processing of video or voice

Table 6.5 Summary of video technologies and definition

Video type	Resolution (horizontal pixels× vertical pixels)	Pixels (points)
Standard definition (SD)	720 × 576	About 410,000
High definition (HD)	1280 × 720	About 920,000
Full HD	1920 × 1080	About 2 million
4K Ultra HD	3840 × 2160	About 8.3 million
8K Ultra HD	7680 × 4320	About 33 million

Table 6.6 Service indicators of 8K video network transmission

8K service type	Network bandwidth	Network latency	Packet loss rate
Video on demand	Greater than 280 Mbps	Less than 10 ms	10^{-5}
Live streaming	Greater than 216 Mbps	Less than 100 ms	10^{-6}

8K Ultra HD TVs are impressive, with 12-bit depth for colors and a high frame rate of 120 frames per second. This creates a big leap in visual quality. In comparison, older analog TVs like NTSC or PAL ran at 30 or 25 frames per second, HDTV increased it to 60 frames per second, and now 8K UHD TV goes up to 120 frames per second. This higher frame rate means that fast-moving objects on the screen appear much smoother. Ultra-high-definition TVs don't just stop at sharper images. They also greatly enhance colors, brightness, and the range of colors they can display, making for a more vibrant and lifelike viewing experience.

The incredibly detailed images and rich information offered by ultra-high-definition videos aren't just about enhancing home entertainment. They find diverse applications in fields like medicine, education, manufacturing, and transportation. For instance, in 2021, China Central Radio and Television Station broadcasted the Spring Festival Gala in 8K live through a trial channel. The Gala's 8K Ultra HD TV feed reached over 30 cities, including Beijing, Shanghai, Shenzhen, Chengdu, and Haikou. This simultaneous broadcast on 8K large screens and TVs shows that 8K video streaming is becoming a common practice. As a result, 8K video is gaining familiarity among the public and becoming widely adopted across various industries.

6.1.2.1 Technical Requirements for 8K UHD Video

8K Ultra HD TV introduces new benchmarks for network transmission performance. Looking at network bandwidth, latency, and packet loss, as outlined in Table 6.6 [3] for transmitting 8K videos, a single 8K video live broadcast necessitates over 216 Mbps. Besides network bandwidth, video transmission must also meet specific standards for network delay and packet loss. Otherwise, viewers might frequently encounter issues like pixelation, disruptions, and buffering during viewing. These problems directly impact the quality of the user's viewing experience.

Currently, the assurance of smooth UHD video transmission across networks predominantly rests in the hands of operators. This provides them significant

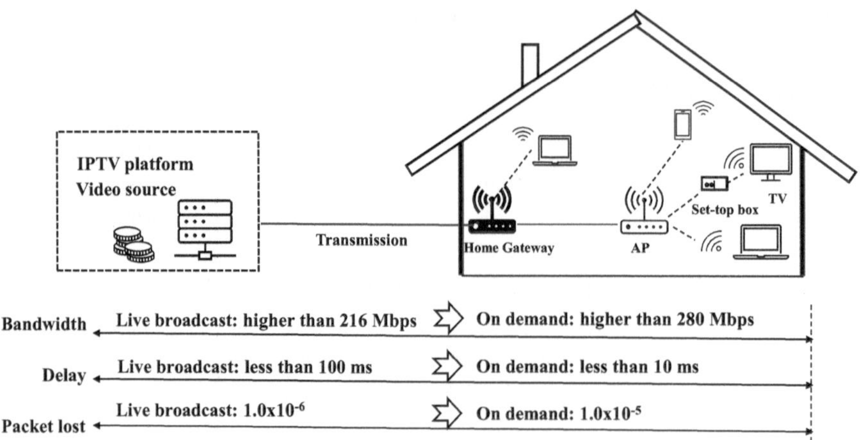

Fig. 6.4 Network transmission requirement for 8K ultra-high video

influence over the network metrics pertinent to UHD video. Figure 6.4 provides a visualization of end-to-end transmission for 8K video-on-demand and live streaming.

In comparison to cloud-based VR, the performance requirements for 8K Video On Demand (VOD) are closely aligned with the optimal experience stage of cloud VR video services. For instance, the bandwidth should exceed 230 Mbps, the network delay should remain under 20 ms, and the packet loss rate should reach a value as low as 1.7×10^{-6}. This illustrates that the quality of 8K VOD mirrors the high standards set by cloud VR video services' ideal experience stage.

6.1.2.2 Introduction to Video Transmission over the Network

Video transmission over networks involves two main methods based on different encoding techniques and stream types.

1. **Carrier-based IPTV broadcasting**

IPTV stands for Internet Protocol Television, which offers video services through IP-based networks, using on-demand or multicast modes. IPTV is often referred to as interactive TV due to its interactive menu-based program selection. The IPTV system includes streaming media services, program editing, storage, certification, and billing. The core video content transmitted to users typically uses MPEG-4/H.264 as the primary streaming media format.

The video sources of IPTV mainly come from radio and television providers. The system employs an operator-optimized virtual private network, ensuring high network transmission reliability. This method requires fixed bit rate (CBR) encoding and UDP-based RTSP real-time streaming to maintain network Quality of Service

(QoS) and provide reliable operational and maintenance services. In-home setups involve set-top boxes provided by operators, allowing users to access TV content.

2. **OTT TV methods**

OTT (Over the Top) refers to content providers utilizing operator networks to provide services independently. Home users purchase dedicated network set-top boxes from the market or the content provider, connecting them to home networks to access video content from the Internet.

OTT TV employs video coding standards such as MPEG-4/H.264, often utilizing variable bit rate (VBR) encoding. This method uses buffering at the terminal to adapt to varying Internet-based video sources and network conditions. OTT TV relies on TCP-based HTTP downloads for on-demand video services. It often uses lower bit-rate high-definition formats to ensure smooth video playback over IP networks.

Carrier IPTV and OTT service providers support various ways to transmit video to TVs through home gateways:

- Connecting the home gateway to the set-top box via a network cable, then connecting the set-top box to the TV using a cable
- Linking the home gateway and set-top box via Wi-Fi, then connecting the set-top box to the TV using a cable (common for OTT content providers)
- Directly transmitting video from the home gateway to the TV via Wi-Fi (common for OTT content providers)

6.1.2.3 Wi-Fi Technology for Supporting 8K Ultra HD Video

Wi-Fi networks play a pivotal role as data transmission links in end-to-end video delivery, influencing factors such as bandwidth, network latency, and packet loss rate. Notably, Wi-Fi performance must exceed the specifications of the overall end-to-end network, meaning Wi-Fi network transmission delays should be even lower than the total delay.

Considering the network bandwidth required for 8K video on demand or live broadcasts, Wi-Fi networks should provide a bandwidth of at least 280 Mbps or 216 Mbps. Both Wi-Fi 6 and Wi-Fi 7 can fulfill these requirements. However, as the demand for transmitting multiple 8K videos simultaneously may grow in the future, Wi-Fi 7 emerges as the more suitable choice for ultra-high-definition home video.

Consulting Table 6.7, let's examine the latency of live and on-demand 8K UHD video streaming. To prevent video transmission delays from becoming an issue, it is

Table 6.7 Latency metrics supported by Wi-Fi technology

Stage	Live video	Video on demand
Network RTT	Less than 100 ms	Less than 10 ms
Home Wi-Fi network latency	Less than 50 ms	Less than 5 ms
Wi-Fi technology	Wi-Fi 5 or Wi-Fi 6	**Wi-Fi 7**

suggested that the latency of the home Wi-Fi network be maintained at 50% of the end-to-end network delay. As seen in the table, live video broadcasts can be efficiently handled by Wi-Fi 5 or Wi-Fi 6 technologies, while video-on-demand scenarios benefit from Wi-Fi 7. Given the potential demands of households for multiple UHD services in the future, Wi-Fi 7 is the recommended and forward-looking solution.

6.1.2.4 Wi-Fi 7 AP for 8K UHD Services

To make sure 8K UHD videos flow smoothly, Wi-Fi 7 Access Points (APs) need specific features, as mentioned in Table 6.8. These APs should support a channel width of 320 MHz in the 6 GHz band or 160 MHz in the 5 GHz band. They should also manage service quality and data flow priority for low-latency tasks, which is a key requirement for 8K content. In addition, APs should be great at handling the TV provider's multicast data for IPTV. Wi-Fi 7 APs are the backbone of top-notch 8K UHD services.

6.1.3 Elevating Home Wi-Fi Technology: Enhancing the Experience

Beyond the demands of AR/VR and ultra-high-definition video with their bandwidth and latency requirements, the expansion of broadband access has propelled home Wi-Fi networks to prominence. Like essential public resources—water, electricity, and gas—Wi-Fi has ingrained itself in our lives.

However, challenges remain. Inconsistent signal strength and varying speeds across different rooms disrupt the user experience. For working from home and remote learning scenarios, people encounter disruptions like frequent disconnections

Table 6.8 Wi-Fi 7 AP specifications

AP selection	Functional specifications
Hardware requirements	Wi-Fi 7 AP BE7200, or Wi-Fi 7 AP BE19000
	Wi-Fi 7 dual-band, or Wi-Fi 7 tri-band
	Multi-antenna 4 × 4 2.4 GHz, 4 × 4 5 GHz Or multi-antenna 4 × 4 2.4 GHz, 4 × 4 5 GHz, 4 × 4 6 GHz
	Maximum bandwidth support of 160 MHz or 320 MHz
Software requirements	Multi-link operation technology supported in Wi-Fi 7
	Supports Wi-Fi 7 multi-resource unit (MRU) technology
	Supports Wi-Fi 7 low-latency service feature recognition
	Supports Quality of Service framework, prioritizing video and IPTV multicast streams

or sluggish responses, often uncertain if Wi-Fi is unstable. Wi-Fi, as a life infrastructure, beckons for greater stability and an improved user experience.

6.1.3.1 Home Wi-Fi: Enhancing Coverage and Minimizing Interference

When using Wi-Fi at home, there are common challenges that arise within buildings. First, indoor Wi-Fi signal coverage can be an issue [5]. Additionally, dense deployment of Wi-Fi APs can lead to channel congestion, causing interference between different Wi-Fi networks.

1. **Wi-Fi signal coverage issues**

Typically, home broadband gateways and Wi-Fi APs are placed near entrances or in living rooms. Even though the entire room might only be a few tens of meters in length or width, variations in positioning and the presence of obstacles—whether stationary or movable—can impact the path that Wi-Fi signals take. Consequently, this results in an uneven distribution of Wi-Fi signal strength across the room. Signal measurements across different parts of a room often reveal areas with stronger signals alongside weaker ones. Factors influencing Wi-Fi signal coverage include the placement of Wi-Fi APs, their transmission power, and the physical properties of the materials blocking the signal.

Fig. 6.5 illustrates an example of indoor Wi-Fi signal attenuation and coverage. Materials such as glass, wood, doors, and concrete walls can lead to signal losses; for instance, concrete walls might attenuate Wi-Fi signals by 20 dB. In the given scenario, the Wi-Fi AP located in the living room exhibits a signal strength of −45 dBm. However, when trying to access the Internet from the bedroom, the signal strength drops below −60 dBm. This discrepancy in signal strength often translates to reduced Internet speeds and a less satisfactory user experience.

Illustrating the scenario in Fig. 6.5, if a user moves indoors (Bedroom, Kitchen) with a Wi-Fi device, the video playback on that device might become choppy due to

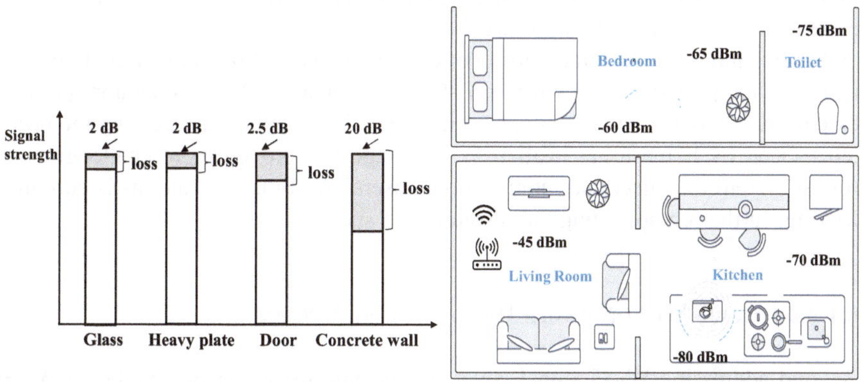

Fig. 6.5 Example of indoor Wi-Fi signal loss

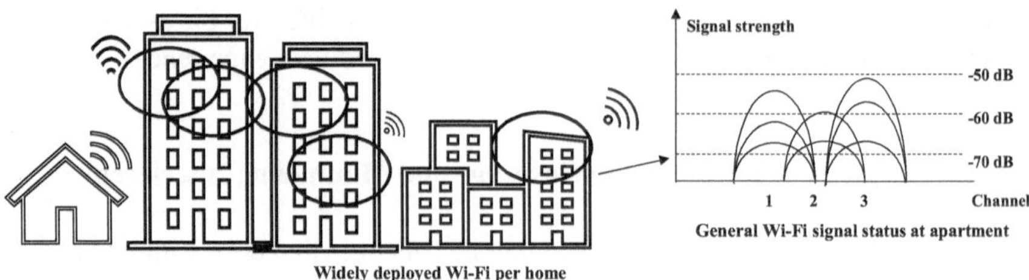

Fig. 6.6 Channel interference of home Wi-Fi

fluctuations in signal strength. This can lead to frozen audio and voice interruptions. When individuals utilize Wi-Fi within their homes, the expectation is to maintain a consistent Internet speed throughout every corner of the room.

2. **Wi-Fi signal interference challenges**

As Wi-Fi devices become ubiquitous within households and residential areas, a new issue arises: the mutual interference of Wi-Fi signals. In communities, Wi-Fi signals from neighbors both upstairs, downstairs, and next door can congest the limited wireless channels available. This congestion leads to increasingly crowded Wi-Fi channels, impacting data speed and the user experience.

Consider Fig. 6.6, which showcases a depiction of multiple Wi-Fi devices occupying channels within a building. In this example, the Wi-Fi 2.4 GHz channels 1, 2, and 3 are already occupied by multiple devices. However, in real-world scenarios, even more Wi-Fi devices occupy the same or neighboring channels, leading to inevitable interference between them. As a result, APs and terminals from different Wi-Fi networks compete for wireless channels through mechanisms like conflict avoidance and fallback. Unfortunately, this competition ultimately culminates in a reduction of the Wi-Fi data transmission rate.

Frequently, users remain unaware that the sluggishness of their home Wi-Fi can be attributed to congested channels. Not many users resort to advanced diagnostic tools to assess this issue. Home users naturally anticipate consistent, reliable Wi-Fi experiences within their living spaces.

Significantly, a substantial portion of complaints voiced by home users to broadband service providers stems from Wi-Fi-related matters. While operators possess extensive experience in maintaining communication channels, addressing the problems faced by home users in their Wi-Fi usage has proven more challenging. A robust system to collect and monitor home users' Wi-Fi usage patterns is currently lacking, further complicating the resolution of such issues.

6.1.3.2 Home Wi-Fi Network Deployment and Planning

Beyond addressing Wi-Fi signal coverage and interference concerns, home Wi-Fi encounters diverse bandwidth demands. These include bandwidth-hungry

Table 6.9 Home Wi-Fi network design scheme

Network scenarios	Design goals
Bandwidth and performance	Minimum 100 Mbps coverage throughout the entire room; and the maximum access rate of 1 Gbps for a single terminal
Latency requirements	Supporting low latency for specific services; prioritizing video and voice services
Networking and overlay	Indoor networking supported by a minimum of 3 APs; maintaining signal strength above −60 dBm in all areas
Capacity design	Up to 64 concurrent terminals supported per home; each AP accommodating up to 32 concurrent terminals, each with a minimum rate of 10 Mbps
Seamless roaming	In-room terminals switch between APs within 100 ms
Secure access	Family members authenticate using credentials provisioned in the AP; guest access through a separate SSID
Anti-interference	APs employ distinct frequency bands for backhaul communication and terminal connections

applications like online gaming and ultra-high-definition video, alongside real-time services such as video conferencing and distance learning. Furthermore, the surge in wireless device connections at home adds to the complexity. Table 6.9 showcases a comprehensive design solution catering to these requirements, transforming a 100-square-meter home environment into a hub of seamless connectivity.

Examining the home Wi-Fi network design scheme in Table 6.9, upgrading Wi-Fi technical standards to support high bandwidth, low latency, and accommodate numerous concurrent terminals emerges as a foreseeable trajectory in the evolution of home Wi-Fi networks over the upcoming years.

Referencing the example of home Wi-Fi networking shown in Fig. 6.7, each living room, bedroom, and dining room features a Wi-Fi AP interconnected through Mesh. This Wi-Fi AP can be either a Wi-Fi-enabled home gateway or a dedicated Wi-Fi AP linked to a home gateway. Via Wi-Fi mesh networking, comprehensive Wi-Fi signal coverage within the room can be achieved, ensuring a minimum Wi-Fi signal strength of −60 dBm from every angle.

6.1.3.3 Functional Specifications for Advanced Home Wi-Fi 7 APs

When considering the landscape of home Wi-Fi, the prevalent choice currently is the dual-band Wi-Fi 5 AP, with Wi-Fi 6 dual-band gaining traction in the market. However, casting an eye toward the home user experience beyond 2024, Wi-Fi 7 APs, promising enhanced performance, emerge as the favored option. Table 6.10 outlines the recommended selection criteria for home Wi-Fi APs, necessitating support for multiband Wi-Fi 7, EasyMesh networking capabilities, robust security with WPA3, and the ability to identify and prioritize low-latency services.

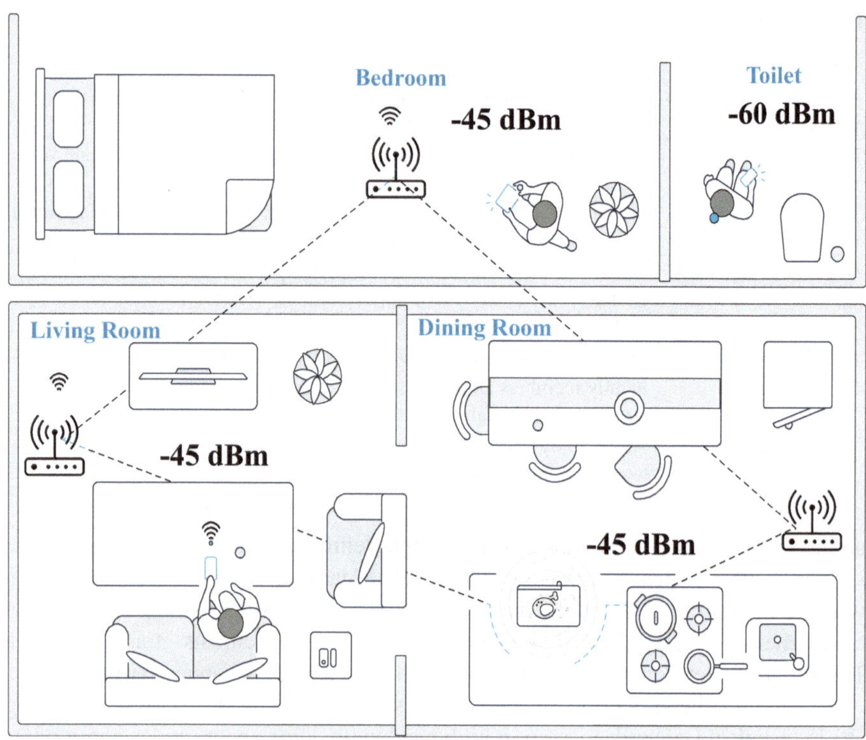

Fig. 6.7 Home Wi-Fi mesh networking configuration

Table 6.10 Functional specifications of Wi-Fi APs

AP selection	Functional specifications
Hardware requirements	Horizontal or vertical Wi-Fi AP
	Wi-Fi 7 AP BE7200, or Wi-Fi 7 AP BE19000
	Wi-Fi 7 dual-band, Wi-Fi 7 tri-band
	Supports 4 or 8 spatial streams
	Multi-antenna configuration of 4 × 4 2.4 GHz, 4 × 4 5 GHz Multi-antenna configuration of 4 × 4 2.4 GHz, 4 × 4 5 GHz, 4 × 4 6 GHz
	Supports bandwidths of 160 MHz or 320 MHz
Software requirements	Support Wi-Fi 7-based Easy Mesh wireless networking
	Multi-link operation technology supported in Wi-Fi 7
	Multi-resource unit technology that supports Wi-Fi 7
	Supports WPA3 security level
	Supports Wi-Fi 7 low-latency service features
	Enables QoS control for services, prioritizing video and voice processing

6.2 Wi-Fi 7 Applications in Various Industries

6.2.1 Wi-Fi Applications in Educational Multimedia Classrooms

The modern classroom landscape has undergone a transformation, with multimedia classrooms becoming a cornerstone of contemporary education. These classrooms boast a range of equipment, including projectors, screens, digital control systems, power amplifiers, speakers, computers, wireless screen projectors, interactive electronic whiteboards, and even virtual reality (VR) setups. Leveraging specialized teaching software, these facilities harness the power of multimedia elements like graphics and videos, empowering teachers to effectively fulfill their teaching responsibilities.

Integral to these multimedia classrooms are wired or wireless networks. The latter, with its inherent convenience and mobility, is garnering increasing attention. Refer to Fig. 6.8 for insights into the array of devices within a multimedia classroom and the wireless network connections in play. Typically, a ceiling-mounted AP is installed, allowing seamless connectivity. Through the AP's Wi-Fi, computers, projectors, screens, and other devices interact, facilitating functions such as data transmission and projection within the classroom.

6.2.1.1 Wireless Network Requirements for Multimedia Classrooms

Multimedia classrooms, often limited in space with areas ranging from 70 to 100 square meters, host dozens of students simultaneously accessing the network for classes. This high-density, high-concurrency environment poses unique challenges. As highlighted in Table 6.11, besides traditional Internet and audio services, the advent of bandwidth-intensive offerings like desktop sharing in online meetings, high-definition video, and even VR experiences introduces significant demands on network resources. These simultaneous bandwidth needs present a substantial challenge for networking capabilities.

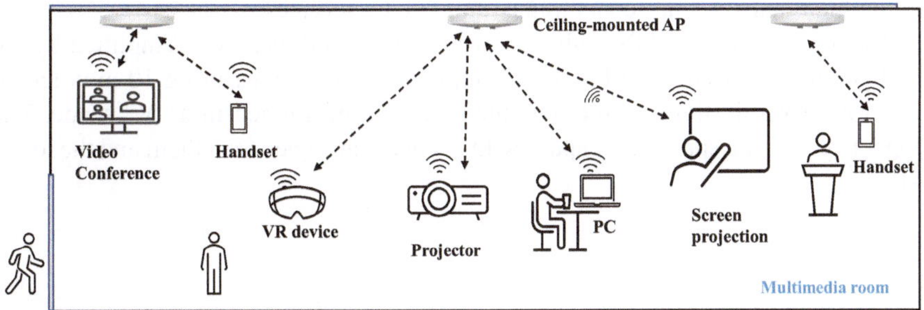

Fig. 6.8 Application of Wi-Fi in multimedia classrooms

Table 6.11 Bandwidth requirements for multimedia classrooms

Business type	Online meetings for desktop sharing	HD video	VR video (Basic)	VR strong interaction (Basic)
Bandwidth requirements per person	2 Mbps	4 Mbps	60 Mbps	80 Mbps
Bandwidth requirement for 20 people	40 Mbps	80 Mbps	1200 Mbps	1600 Mbps

In addition to network bandwidth, multimedia classrooms also have the following requirements for wireless networks:

- **Network coverage:** Ensuring uniform wireless signal coverage devoid of dead zones or blind spots, capable of accommodating the concurrent data usage of numerous users
- **Access terminal type**: Catering to a diverse array of devices such as desktop computers, laptops, tablets, projectors, wireless screen projectors, and electronic whiteboards
- **Seamless roaming**: Facilitating seamless roaming for mobile devices within the multimedia classroom
- **Security measures:** Verifying access terminals to thwart unauthorized device access and packet attacks
- **Management and maintenance:** Enabling the visualization and management of network traffic, terminal access, and network issues

Contrasted with wireless network setups predating Wi-Fi 5, the contemporary landscape demands enhanced support for bandwidth-intensive services, an influx of concurrent terminal connections, and smooth classroom-wide roaming—all of which are integral to the present-day Wi-Fi network deployment.

6.2.1.2 Designing Effective Wireless Networks

Tailoring wireless networks to the demands of modern multimedia classrooms can be achieved through the guidelines presented in Table 6.12. This design blueprint is tailored for classrooms spanning less than 100 square meters, efficiently accommodating high-density, high-concurrency multimedia services.

The arrangement of APs within the wireless network can be exemplified by the configuration showcased in Fig. 6.9. Within a classroom measuring 10 m in length and 8 m in width, three ceiling-mounted APs are positioned in a "V" shape. The upper two APs are spaced 5 m apart, with a 4 m distance between them and the lower AP.

Table 6.12 Design scheme of Wi-Fi network

Network scenarios	Design goals
Bandwidth and performance	Minimum 100 Mbps coverage throughout the entire classroom; individual user access reaching up to 1 Gbps
Latency requirements	Supporting low latency for specific services; prioritizing video or voice services
Networking and overlay	Indoor networking supported by a minimum of 3 APs; maintaining signal strength above −50 dBm in all areas
Capacity design	Supporting up to 64 terminals concurrently within the classroom; each AP accommodating up to 32 concurrent terminal connections with a minimum rate of 10 Mbps
Seamless roaming	Terminals within the classroom switch between APs within 50 ms
Secure access	External devices entering the classroom network require wireless network authentication and verification
Anti-interference	Backhaul communication between APs employs a distinct frequency band, while terminals use separate frequency bands for connections

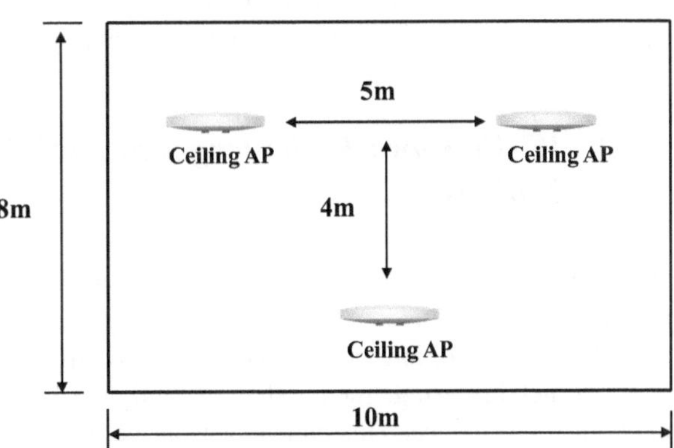

Fig. 6.9 Example of wireless network layout for multimedia classroom APs

6.2.1.3 Functional Specifications of the Wi-Fi 7 AP for Multimedia Classroom

Table 6.13 presents a recommended Wi-Fi 7 AP selection specification. For the evolving demands of multimedia classrooms and the intricacies of high-density, high-concurrency network design, Wi-Fi 7 APs must exhibit an array of capabilities. These include support for multiband Wi-Fi 6 or Wi-Fi 7, EasyMesh networking, 802.1× authentication, and the enhanced security of WPA3. Notably, Wi-Fi 7 introduces multi-link operation technology that significantly enhances concurrent terminal capacity and low-latency service performance.

Table 6.13 Functional specifications of Wi-Fi APs

AP selection	Functional specifications
Hardware requirements	Ceiling-mounted AP
	Wi-Fi 7 AP BE7200, or Wi-Fi 7 AP BE19000
	Wi-Fi 7 dual-band, or Wi-Fi 7 tri-band
	Multi-antenna configuration of 4 × 4 2.4 GHz, 4 × 4 5 GHz multi-antenna configuration of 4 × 4 2.4 GHz, 4 × 4 5 GHz, 4 × 4 6GHz
	Supports eight spatial streams under MU-MIMO technology to enhance multiuser connection performance
	Supports bandwidths of 160 MHz or 320 MHz
Software requirements	Easy Mesh wireless networking with Wi-Fi 7 support
	Incorporates Wi-Fi 7's multi-link operation technology and load balancing technology
	Multi-resource unit (MRU) technology that supports Wi-Fi 7
	Supports Portal authentication, or 802.1× authentication, and supports WPA3 security level
	Supports Wi-Fi 7 low-latency service feature
	Enables QoS control for services, prioritizing video and voice processing

6.2.2 Wi-Fi Network Challenges in High-Density Stadium Settings

Wi-Fi deployment within stadiums hosting high-density connections presents a unique set of challenges. With varying stadium sizes accommodating thousands to tens of thousands of individuals, the surge of simultaneous Wi-Fi usage for activities like Internet browsing, media sharing, and live video streaming strains wireless network performance. This endeavor is at the intersection of public space network optimization and the capabilities of the latest Wi-Fi standards.

6.2.2.1 Wireless Network Requirements for the Stadium

The stadium environment is characterized by spacious, semi-closed spaces where audiences frequently engage with smartphones. During sports events, activities include photo uploads, video sharing, voice calls, messaging, and online browsing. The challenge lies in maintaining a large number of wireless connections over extended periods, often requiring high-density concurrent services. Table 6.14 offers insights into the bandwidth demands for various user activities.

In addition to bandwidth occupation, the interplay of wireless signals from multiple APs within the open stadium can lead to channel conflicts and interference, hindering data forwarding. Addressing this issue through strategic AP installation and interference reduction is pivotal for effective wireless network design.

The stadium wireless network prerequisites encompass:

Table 6.14 Bandwidth requirements for a stadium

Business type	Web surfing	Video	Image sharing	Voice	Instant messaging
Bandwidth requirements per person	1 Mbps	2 Mbps	2 Mbps	0.128 Mbps	0.256 Mbps
3000 people bandwidth requirements	3000 Mbps	6000 Mbps	6000 Mbps	384 Mbps	768 Mbps

Table 6.15 Design scheme of Wi-Fi network

Network scenarios	Design goals
Network performance	Minimum 20 Mbps coverage across the entire stadium, with individual user access reaching up to 100 Mbps
Networking and overlay	Support for Mesh networking; maintaining signal strength above −60 dBm in all areas
Capacity design	Scaling according to stadium size; accommodating up to 3000 concurrent terminal connections; each AP supporting up to 128 concurrent terminal connections with a minimum rate of 10 Mbps per terminal
Secure access	External device entry into the stadium network requires wireless network authentication and verification
Anti-interference	Adjacent APs staggered through channels or spatial directions to minimize signal interference

- **Network coverage:** Uniform wireless signal coverage without dead spots
- **High concurrent services:** Supporting thousands of concurrent connections and data transfers, proportional to the venue size
- **High-density connections:** Enabling a minimum of 1 user per square meter and at least 100 users per 100 square meters
- **Access terminal type:** Predominantly smartphones, potentially including a limited number of other smart devices like tablets
- **Security requirements:** Verifying access terminals to counteract unauthorized access and packet attacks
- **Management and maintenance:** Enabling the visualization and management of network traffic, terminal access, and network issues

Traditionally, users in stadiums often encounter issues such as slow Internet speeds, sluggish media transmission, and weak signal strength. These problems underscore the necessity of proper wireless network design to accommodate high-density scenarios.

6.2.2.2 Wireless Network Design

Tailored to stadium requirements, Table 6.15 presents a reference design blueprint. Its key focus is ensuring robust network performance within high-density and high-

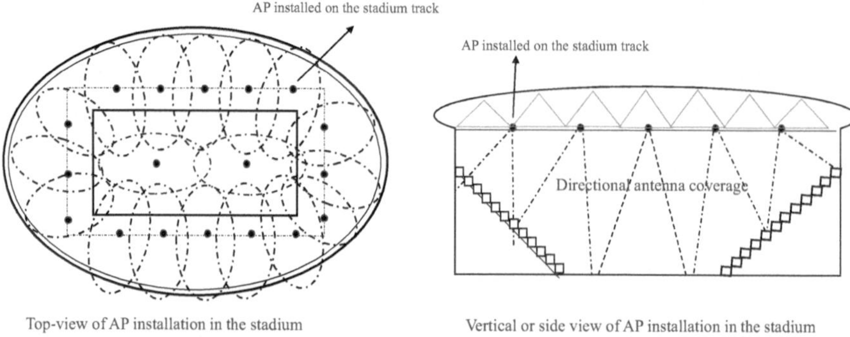

Fig. 6.10 Illustration of Wi-Fi deployment in a stadium

concurrency environments while mitigating interference between multiple APs. This design scheme prioritizes network security, stability, and reliability.

AP installation in a stadium is typically done in a horse track fashion. To mitigate interference between APs, external small-angle directional antennas are employed. For instance, the antenna angle for the 2.4 GHz channel is less than 50°, and less than 20° for the 5 GHz channel. The installation specifics are determined by the venue's spatial layout and the elevation of the horse track from the seats.

Figure 6.10 [6] illustrates the top view and longitudinal view of an AP installed along the stadium's horse track, featuring small-angle directional antennas. Equidistant placement of APs minimizes overlapping signal areas and spatially reduces Wi-Fi interference. Additionally, neighboring APs are configured with nonoverlapping channels to avert same-channel interference. For example, if the 2.4 GHz channel of an AP is 1, the channel of the AP on either side of it is set to 6 or 11.

6.2.2.3 Functional Specifications for the Wi-Fi 7 AP

For stadiums grappling with high-density and high-concurrency scenarios, the Wi-Fi 7 APs must cater to specific requirements. These APs necessitate support for multiband Wi-Fi 6 or Wi-Fi 7, Portal authentication, WPA3 security level, and QoS service quality control features. Furthermore, to manage potential load and rate degradation due to heavy user traffic, Wi-Fi 7's multi-link operation technology becomes instrumental for effective load balancing (Table 6.16).

6.2.3 *Wi-Fi Network Design for Hotel Buildings: Meeting Modern Guest Connectivity Needs*

In the era of seamless connectivity, Wi-Fi has become an indispensable amenity for hotels and hotel-managed apartments. Ensuring effective Wi-Fi access is not only a

Table 6.16 Functional specifications of Wi-Fi APs

AP selection	Functional specifications
Hardware requirements	Ceiling-mounted AP
	Wi-Fi 7 AP BE7200, or Wi-Fi 7 AP BE19000
	Wi-Fi 7 dual-band, or Wi-Fi 7 tri-band
	Multi-antenna configuration of 4 × 4 2.4 GHz, 4 × 4 5 GHz (domestic) Multi-antenna configuration of 4 × 4 2.4 GHz, 4 × 4 5 GHz, 4 × 4 6 GHz
	Directional antenna design enhancing coverage in specific directions and minimizing interference from neighboring APs
	Supports eight spatial streams with MU-MIMO technology to improve multiuser connection performance
	Supports bandwidths of 160 MHz or 320 MHz
Software requirements	Easy Mesh wireless networking with Wi-Fi 7 support
	Harnesses Wi-Fi 7's multi-link operation technology and load balancing technology
	Multi-resource unit (MRU) technology that supports Wi-Fi 7
	Support Portal authentication and WPA3 security level
	Supports QoS control of services, prioritizing video or voice processing

convenience but also a crucial factor impacting guest satisfaction and reservation rates. This overview focuses on the Wi-Fi access network planning and schemes tailored for small and medium-sized hotels.

6.2.3.1 Wi-Fi Requirements for Hotel Apartments

Hotel apartments encompass diverse spaces, including rooms, conference halls, restaurants, corridors, and more. Guests carry devices throughout the premises, requiring reliable Wi-Fi coverage for tasks ranging from emails and conference calls to video streaming and social media sharing. The network must accommodate peak usage periods like rest and meal times while ensuring secure and authorized access.

Hotel Wi-Fi networks face demands similar to high-density scenarios like stadium venues. However, unique factors specific to hotels contribute to their design and optimization:

- **Peak usage cycles**: Guest Wi-Fi usage often aligns with daily routines such as rest and meals. This can result in concentrated periods of high usage, especially during peak times.
- **Extended video streaming**: Guests may engage in extended video streaming, making uninterrupted video quality crucial. This calls for a network capable of sustaining high-quality video services for prolonged periods.
- **Authentication and authorization**: Hotel networks typically require guest authentication through room numbers or check-in identities. This process ensures

Table 6.17 Bandwidth requirements of hotel apartments

Business type	Web surfing	Video	Image sharing	Voice	Instant messaging
Bandwidth requirements per person	1 Mbps	2 Mbps	2 Mbps	0.128 Mbps	0.256 Mbps
Bandwidth requirement for 600 people	600 Mbps	1200 Mbps	1200 Mbps	76.8 Mbps	153.6 Mbps

authorized access and allows the hotel to manage each guest's network experience.

- **Customized data allocation**: Hotels can allocate varying levels of wireless data traffic to different guests based on their needs. This flexibility ensures fair usage and meets the preferences of individual guests.

Table 6.17 takes 300 standard rooms as an example, assuming 600 guests, and counts the bandwidth requirements of the Wi-Fi network of a hotel apartment.

From Table 6.17, if the video of the hotel apartment is throttled, the total bandwidth on the Wi-Fi network is not particularly high, and one or two Wi-Fi 7 APs can support such traffic. However, the challenges of the Wi-Fi network in hotel apartments come more from the coverage of Wi-Fi signals in all venues, the number of concurrent wireless connections within a specific time range, the roaming of terminals in different venues as guests move around, and the access authentication of Wi-Fi terminals.

The requirements for wireless networks in hotel apartments are as follows:

- **Network coverage:** Comprehensive and uniform Wi-Fi signal coverage throughout the premises
- **High concurrent services:** Support simultaneous connections and data transfers for hundreds of users
- **High-density connection:** Enable dense connections, such as 1 user per square meter and 100 users per 100 square meters in specific areas like restaurants or conference rooms
- **Roaming needs:** Facilitate automatic terminal switching between different Wi-Fi networks
- **Access terminal type:** Primarily smartphones, alongside other smart devices like tablets
- **Security requirements:** Authenticate access terminals to prevent unauthorized access or attacks
- **Management and maintenance:** Monitor network traffic, terminal access, and address network issues

Among these requirements, Wi-Fi signal strength and service data transmission rates are more affected by guest experience, which is related to factors such as network coverage, the number of terminals connected at the same time, and environmental interference. These factors need to be paid attention to designing Wi-Fi networks.

6.2.3.2 Wireless Network Design

In line with the Wi-Fi requirements and design goals for hotel apartments, the wireless network design scheme is proposed in Table 6.18.

For effective Wi-Fi coverage within the hotel apartment, the following deployment strategy [4] is recommended:

- **Standard rooms**: Install a Wi-Fi AP in each standard room. These APs can be either wall-mounted panels or horizontally positioned APs under TV cabinets.
- **Suites**: For larger spaces such as suites, consider adding ceiling-mounted APs to enhance Wi-Fi signal coverage.

Figure 6.11 illustrates this approach.

Figure 6.12 depicts an alternate approach for deploying Wi-Fi network access points in a hotel apartment environment. The design involves strategically positioning ceiling-mounted Wi-Fi APs in the corridors of the building. In this arrangement, APs are not installed directly within standard rooms, which can reduce the overall number of APs needed. Instead, additional APs are placed within suites to enhance coverage in these larger spaces.

Benefits of this approach:

- Cost-effective: Reduced AP deployments in standard rooms can lead to cost savings in terms of equipment and installation.
- Roaming facilitation: This setup supports the roaming requirements of guests moving around the room with their devices.
- Centralized coverage: Ceiling-mounted APs in corridors can provide central coverage, optimizing signal distribution throughout the hotel apartment.

Table 6.18 Design scheme of Wi-Fi network in hotel apartments

Network scenarios	Design goals
Bandwidth and performance	Ensure a minimum coverage of 10 Mbps across all areas of the hotel apartment Support a maximum access rate of 100 Mbps for each individual user
Networking and overlay	Support mesh indoor networking to create a seamless coverage mesh Maintain a signal strength of no less than −60 dBm in all regions
Capacity design	Tailor the network capacity to the scale of the hotel apartment Accommodate up to 600 simultaneous terminals accessing the network Each AP should handle up to 128 concurrent terminals Guarantee a minimum terminal data rate of 10 Mbps
Seamless roaming	Facilitate smooth terminal roaming between APs within the hotel apartment Ensure a seamless transition with a switching time of less than 1000 ms
Secure access	Enforce wireless network authentication and authorization for external devices Authenticate devices entering the hotel apartment's network
Anti-interference	Employ separate frequency bands for backhaul communication between APs and separate frequency bands for connections to terminals

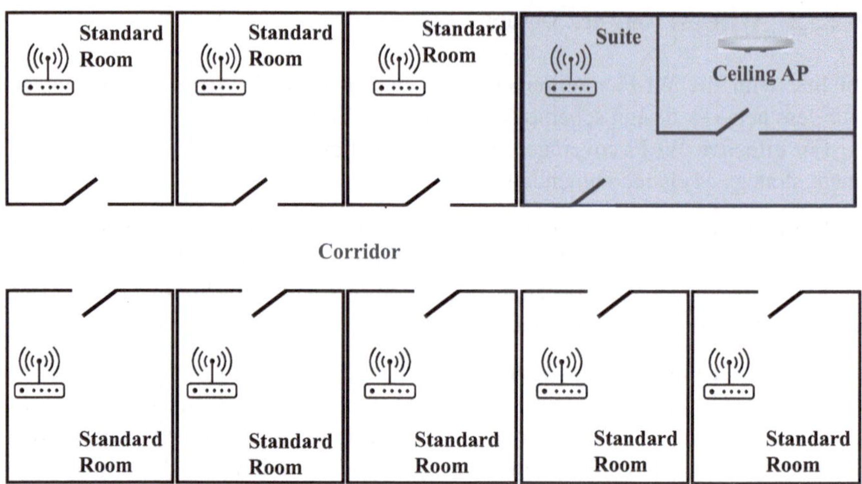

Fig. 6.11 Example of deploying a Wi-Fi network in a hotel apartment

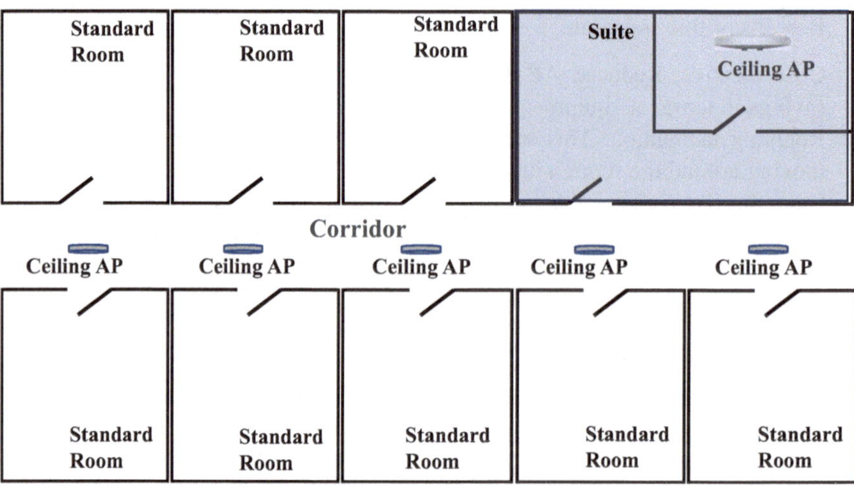

Fig. 6.12 Example of a hotel apartment deploying a Wi-Fi network in a corridor

- Space efficiency: Placing APs in corridors can free up valuable space within guest rooms.
- Coverage enhancement: Additional APs within suites ensure comprehensive coverage in larger spaces, preventing dead zones.
- Guest experience: Guests can experience seamless connectivity while moving within their rooms and across common areas.

To achieve optimal coverage and performance when deploying APs in the corridor, it is recommended to position them near the door of each guest room.

This positioning allows the AP's signal to directly transmit into the room through the door, enhancing signal strength and quality within the rooms.

6.2.3.3 Functional Specifications of the Wi-Fi AP

Table 6.19 presents the recommended functional specifications for selecting Wi-Fi access points (APs) that cater to the specific needs of hotel apartments. To support the demands of high density and concurrency in certain areas and during specific time periods, APs should possess the following features.

In addition, in the case of high concurrency, load and rate degradation of data transmission may occur in a single AP. Thus, it is necessary to use Wi-Fi 7's multi-link operation technology to achieve the effect of load balancing.

6.2.4 Wi-Fi Usage in Enterprise Offices: Enhancing Workplace Efficiency

Wi-Fi in the enterprise office has become an indispensable tool for daily work. Employees rely on Wi-Fi access in various spaces, such as offices, conference rooms, and multifunction halls, to connect directly to the corporate network. This wireless connectivity trend is gradually supplanting traditional wired Ethernet

Table 6.19 Functional specifications of Wi-Fi APs

AP selection	Functional specifications
Hardware requirements	APs can be panel, tabletop, or ceiling-mounted for versatile deployment options
	Wi-Fi 7 AP BE7200, or Wi-Fi 7 AP BE19000
	Wi-Fi 7 dual-band, or Wi-Fi 7 tri-band
	Multi-antenna 4 × 4 2.4 GHz, 4 × 4 5 GHz. Multi-antenna 4 × 4 2.4 GHz, 4 × 4 5 GHz, 4 × 4 6 GHz
	Directional antenna design to improve coverage in the specified direction and reduce interference from other neighboring APs
	Supports eight spatial streams with MU-MIMO technology to improve multiuser connection performance
	Supports bandwidths of 160 MHz or 320 MHz
Software requirements	Easy Mesh wireless networking with Wi-Fi 7 support
	Supports Wi-Fi 7's advanced features, including multi-link operation technology and load balancing
	Multi-resource unit technology (MRU) supported in Wi-Fi 7
	Support Portal authentication and WPA3 security level
	Supports Wi-Fi 7 low-latency service feature recognition
	Supports QoS control of services, with high-priority processing for video and voice

connections. Enterprise environments vary, encompassing small offices with around ten individuals to larger spaces like conference rooms or multifunctional halls accommodating over 50 people. These spaces can range from compact 20-square-meter zones to expansive areas spanning hundreds of square meters. Consequently, Wi-Fi deployment strategies must align with the indoor layout and the specific needs of the office setting.

6.2.4.1 Wireless Network Requirements for Corporate Offices

In the corporate office context, Wi-Fi networks play a pivotal role in facilitating various online tasks. Employees rely on these networks for tasks like sending and receiving emails, sharing documents, browsing information, and participating in online meetings. Unlike entertainment scenarios, the focus here is on maintaining consistent connection rates for efficient online work. This includes real-time voice communication and low-resolution video transmission during virtual meetings.

For example, let's consider an office with 50 people or an enterprise with 500 employees. In Table 6.20, we outline the bandwidth requirements for the Wi-Fi network of such an enterprise office.

From Table 6.20, it is evident that the primary concern isn't just the total bandwidth but rather the ability to support a moderate number of concurrent connections while ensuring low latency for seamless collaborative work and real-time interactions. This is especially critical in larger office spaces, where Wi-Fi signal coverage and potential attenuation effects come into play.

Hence, while the overall bandwidth demand might not be exceptionally high, the strategic deployment of multiple Wi-Fi access points (APs) can help distribute concurrent connection loads and ensure comprehensive signal coverage. Apart from bandwidth, fulfilling wireless network requirements for corporate offices also involves coverage, roaming capabilities, security measures, and effective management.

Key wireless network requirements for corporate offices encompass:

- **Network coverage:** Comprehensive signal coverage across all office areas
- **Number of concurrency:** Supporting 30–50 simultaneous connections during regular working hours.

Table 6.20 Bandwidth requirements for enterprise office environments

Business type	Sending and receiving mail	Document sharing	Information browsing	Online meetings	Instant messaging
Bandwidth requirements per person	2 Mbps	2 Mbps	1 Mbps	3 Mbps	0.256 Mbps
Bandwidth requirement for 50 people	100 Mbps	100 Mbps	50 Mbps	150 Mbps	12.8 Mbps
Bandwidth requirement for 500 people	1000 Mbps	1000 Mbps	500 Mbps	1500 Mbps	128 Mbps

- **High-density connections:** Facilitating at least 1 user per square meter or 100 users per 100 square meters, particularly in shared spaces and conference
- **Roaming requirements:** Enabling smooth automatic transitions between different Wi-Fi APs as employees move around.
- **Access terminal type:** Mainly catering to work computers and smartphones
- **Security requirements:** Implementing access device verification, enterprise-level security protocols, and authorization mechanisms to prevent unauthorized access
- **Management and maintenance:** Establishing systems for monitoring network traffic, terminal access, and promptly addressing network issues

Given the significance of maintaining secure internal communications and resources, ensuring the security of the Wi-Fi network is paramount for corporate entities. The network serves as a crucial gateway for employees to access vital internal resources, necessitating robust security measures to prevent unauthorized access and potential breaches.

6.2.4.2 Wireless Network Design

To cater to the Wi-Fi wireless network needs of enterprise offices, the design scheme presented in Table 6.21 focuses on ensuring comprehensive Wi-Fi coverage across office spaces, meeting the bandwidth demands and concurrent connections of employees during work hours, and guaranteeing the network's security.

The wireless network architecture involving APs can be illustrated using the example shown in Fig. 6.13.

In an office measuring 50 m long and 20 m wide, multiple ceiling APs are installed in a "V" shape, with a distance of 20 m between the two APs horizontally and 16 m between them and the APs deployed in the bottom layer.

Table 6.21 Office Wi-Fi network design

Network scenarios	Design goals
Bandwidth and performance	Ensure a minimum of 10 Mbps coverage throughout the office, supporting a maximum access rate of 100 Mbps for individual users
Networking and overlay	Enable mesh indoor networking, ensuring a signal strength of at least −60 dBm across all areas
Capacity design	Tailor the design to match the office's size, accommodating up to 100 terminals for concurrent network access; each access point (AP) supports up to 64 terminals, each with a minimum rate of 10 Mbps
Seamless roaming	Enable mobile roaming for terminals within the office, ensuring smooth transitions between APs with switching times under 1000 ms
Secure access	Mandate wireless network authentication and authorization for any external devices entering the office environment
Anti-interference	Utilize separate frequency bands for backhaul communication between APs and connections between APs and terminals

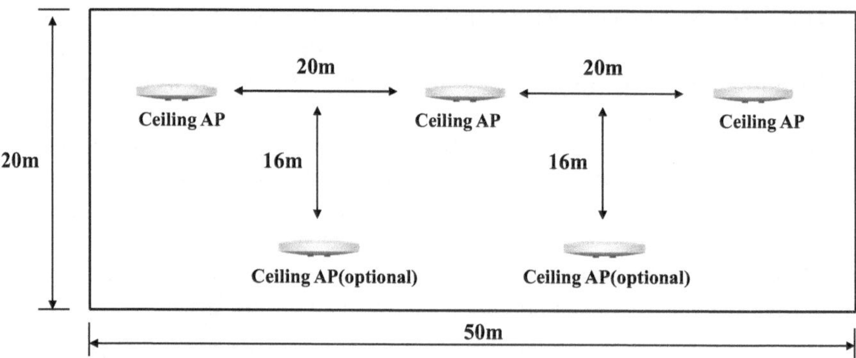

Fig. 6.13 Example of AP networking scheme for office Wi-Fi network

Table 6.22 Functional specifications of Wi-Fi APs

AP selection	Functional specifications
Hardware specifications	Ceiling-mounted AP
	Wi-Fi 7 AP BE7200, or Wi-Fi 7 AP BE19000
	Wi-Fi 7 dual-band, or Wi-Fi 7 tri-band
	Multi-antenna configuration of 4 × 4 2.4 GHz, 4 × 4 5 GHz Multi-antenna configuration of 4 × 4 2.4 GHz, 4 × 4 5 GHz, 4 × 4 6GHz
	Support of MU-MIMO technology to support eight spatial streams, enhancing multiuser connectivity
	Supports bandwidths of 160 MHz or 320 MHz
Software requirements	Support for Easy Mesh wireless networking with Wi-Fi 7 compatibility
	Supports Wi-Fi 7's multi-link simultaneous interpretation technology and load balancing technology
	Multi-resource unit technology (MRU) that supports Wi-Fi 7
	Support for the 802.1x authentication method and WPA3 security level
	Supports QoS control of services, with high-priority processing of video and voice services

6.2.4.3 Functional Specifications of the Wi-Fi Access Points for Offices

To address the demands of high density and concurrent usage within office and conference room environments during working hours, Wi-Fi access points (APs) must be equipped with specific capabilities. Table 6.22 outlines the recommended specifications for these APs.

References

1. IEEE (2023) Draft Standard for Information technology--Telecommunications and information exchange between systems Local and metropolitan area networks--Specific requirements - Part

11: Wireless LAN Medium Access Control (MAC) and Physical Layer (PHY) Specifications Amendment: Enhancements for Extremely High Throughput (EHT) (IEEE P802.11be/D5.0). November. pp. 1–1045

2. Huawei (2018) Cloud VR Network Solution White Paper
3. Huawei (2021) White Paper on 8K Ultra-High-Definition Video Full Optical Quality Bearing Technology
4. Tang H, Lin G, Wang P, Zhang A, Song X, Ye H (2021) Wi-Fi 6: From Introduction to Application. Beijing: Posts and Telecom Press
5. Cheng G (2020) Smart Home Technology Survey. Beijing: China Machine Press
6. Xiao M, Xu T, Shu J et al (2020) Wireless Network Design of Gymnasium Based on Wi-Fi 6. Modern Information Technology, 4(03), 42–46+49. https://doi.org/10.19850/j.cnki.2096-4706.2020.03.014

Chapter 7
Convergence of Wi-Fi 7 and Mobile 5G Technology

Abstract This chapter explores the convergence of mobile 5G and Wi-Fi access, with a particular focus on the emerging Wi-Fi 7 technology. It begins by examining the technological characteristics of 5G, Wi-Fi 6, and Wi-Fi 7. Following this, the chapter illustrates the framework and architecture of the converged network, which incorporates relevant 3GPP standards. Afterwards, it presents a summary of convergence technologies, including, but not limited to, Wi-Fi terminal device registration within mobile networks, data security, quality-of-service assurance, and seamless roaming between mobile networks and Wi-Fi access. Subsequently, the chapter describes end-to-end network slicing within a converged 5G and Wi-Fi access network. It outlines the requirements and network management scheme for network slicing and analyzes the feasibility of incorporating Wi-Fi 7 and Wi-Fi Mesh technologies into the 5G end-to-end network slicing strategy. Moreover, the chapter delves into the application scenarios of network slicing in the converged 5G and Wi-Fi 7 access network, such as enterprise deployments or campus environments.

7.1 Technology Comparison Between Wi-Fi 7 and Mobile 5G

In 2018, the mobile 5G R15 standard was finalized, coinciding with the release of the Wi-Fi 6 standard. Following this, the commercial rollout of both 5G mobile communication and Wi-Fi 6 began around 2020, introducing high-bandwidth, low-latency features to the technology. The release and rollout of 5G and Wi-Fi 6 have sparked industry discussions comparing these two technologies. The central question revolves around whether the rapid deployment of 5G will eventually supplant indoor Wi-Fi. The prevailing consensus is that both 5G and Wi-Fi possess distinct application scenarios, making them suitable for different purposes. The ongoing progression of communication technology doesn't necessitate an either-or choice; rather, it emphasizes the coexistence of these technologies.

Figure 7.1 depicts the timeline of evolution between the 5G standards and Wi-Fi generations.

G. Cheng et al., *Wi-Fi 7*, https://doi.org/10.1007/978-981-97-9026-5_7

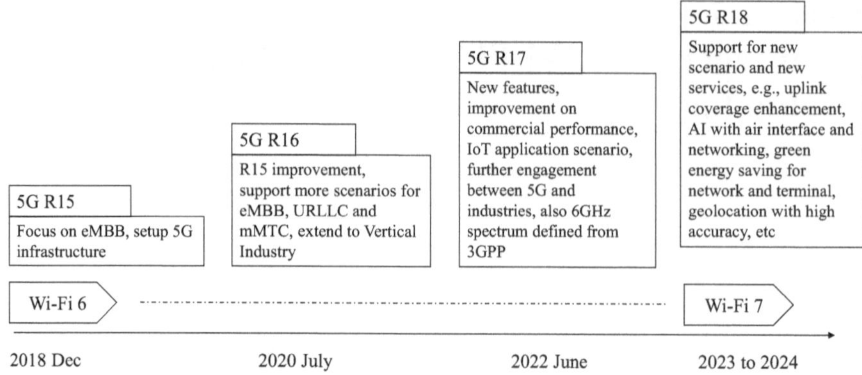

Fig. 7.1 Evolution of mobile 5G standards

Mobile 5G's R15 version set the foundational framework for 5G, with Enhanced Mobile Broadband (eMBB) serving as a pivotal feature for high-bandwidth mobile transmission. The R16 version, frozen on July 16, 2020, represents the first comprehensive standard for 5G, extending its application into various industries through the integration of massive Machine-Type of Communication (mMTC) and Ultra-Reliable Low-Latency Communications (uRLLC). This integration empowers 5G to be a transformative technology for societal applications.

An upgraded iteration, the R17 version, standardized in June 2022, introduced improvements to the network's core capabilities and explored novel applications such as medium and low-speed Internet of Things (IoT), extended reality, and more. Anticipated to debut in 2024, the 5G R18 standard will mark the second phase of technical standards, spanning R18 to R20. Coincidentally, 2024 will also see the gradual emergence of Wi-Fi 7 products.

It is evident that the coexistence and synergy between mobile 5G, Wi-Fi 6, and Wi-Fi 7 across various industries and scenarios will remain the dominant theme in wireless data communication from 2024 to 2030. A comparison of the key technologies in 5G networks, Wi-Fi 6, and Wi-Fi 7 can be found in Table 7.1 [1].

From Table 7.1, it is evident that the transition from Wi-Fi 6 to Wi-Fi 7 standards hasn't shifted the focus or core patterns of key technologies. Let's explore the advantages of Wi-Fi 6 and Wi-Fi 7 in indoor scenarios, as well as the strengths of mobile 5G in outdoor situations:

(1) **Technical Advantages of Wi-Fi 6 and Wi-Fi 7 in Indoor Scenarios**

Wi-Fi 7 can achieve an impressive indoor user experience rate of 10 Gbps. This is a crucial technology for high-bandwidth services like video streaming, online gaming, and virtual reality within short indoor distances.

After more than 20 years of widespread adoption, Wi-Fi has served as a basic backbone for a myriad of home devices, facilitating data transmission over short indoor distances. Even with the emergence of 6th generation (6G) mobile communication, manufacturers of existing household terminals are inclined to enhance their

Table 7.1 Technical comparison between mobile 5G, Wi-Fi 6, and Wi-Fi 7

Technical comparison		Mobile 5G	Wi-Fi 6	Wi-Fi 7
Technical characteristics	Theoretical rate	20 Gbps	9.6 Gbps	36 Gbps
	Average user experience rate	1 Gbps	1 Gbps	1Gbps–10 Gbps
	Operating spectrum	Licensed	Unlicensed	Unlicensed
	Modulation techniques	Maximum support for 256-QAM	Maximum support is 1024-QAM	Maximum support 4096-QAM
	Channel bandwidth	100 MHz	Maximum 160 MHz	Maximum 320 MHz
	Channel access	OFDMA	OFDMA and CSMA/CA	OFDMA and CSMA/CA
	Multiple Input Multiple Output (MIMO).	Outdoor: 64 spatial streams Indoors: 4 spatial streams	8 spatial streams	8 spatial streams
	Delay	eMBB:4 ms uRLLC:0.5 ms	10 ms to 20 ms (depending on indoor environment)	Less than 10 ms (depending on indoor environment)
	The number of terminals connected simultaneously	Supports 100,000	Up to 74 terminals	Up to 148 terminals
Product comparison	Terminal type	Mainly mobile phones	All kinds of smart terminals, mobile phones, computers, etc. equipped with Wi-Fi chips	All kinds of smart terminals, mobile phones, computers, etc. equipped with Wi-Fi chips
	Security	High wireless transmission security	Supports WPA3	Supports WPA3

products with new Wi-Fi standards rather than switching to 6G technology. This underscores the preference for Wi-Fi's unlicensed spectrum approach over mobile communication technologies based on licensed spectrum. In addition, while Wi-Fi APs are stationary, the ongoing support for EasyMesh networking in the Wi-Fi standard enhances indoor coverage.

(2) **Technical Advantages of Mobile 5G in Outdoor Scenarios**

Mobile 5G boasts the capability to connect over 100,000 devices and serves as a foundational communication technology for IoT in vast public spaces. Its low power consumption makes it a suitable solution for basic communication needs in IoT. Mobile 5G's millisecond-level low latency is particularly valuable in domains like the Internet of Vehicles and the Industrial Internet. Both personal and industrial applications leverage 5G's high-bandwidth mobility, making it a standout technology for wireless communication, especially in outdoor contexts. This mobility advantage is unique to mobile communications, setting it apart from Wi-Fi.

In summary, Wi-Fi 6 and Wi-Fi 7 continue to excel in indoor settings, while mobile 5G shines in outdoor environments. Each technology plays to its strengths, ensuring a well-rounded approach to wireless communication across various scenarios.

Conversely, the exploration of collaboration between mobile 5G and Wi-Fi technologies in specific application scenarios is equally intriguing. This involves questions like whether Wi-Fi terminals can effectively communicate with those in the 5G network via wired connections, or if the 5G network can expand its reach to encompass Wi-Fi access points. These topics delve into the technical aspects of integrating Wi-Fi access networks with mobile 5G, and we will delve into them in the following discussion.

7.2 The Continuous Integration of Wi-Fi Networks and Mobile 5G

One basic application for integrating Wi-Fi access networks and mobile networks revolves around how mobile devices can fulfill their intended applications using Wi-Fi networks. In Fig. 7.2, the illustration demonstrates this concept: mobile phones, initially connected to mobile networks for calls and Internet access, may switch to Wi-Fi connections in situations where the mobile network experiences issues like service failures, congestion, limited signal coverage, or high tariffs. By

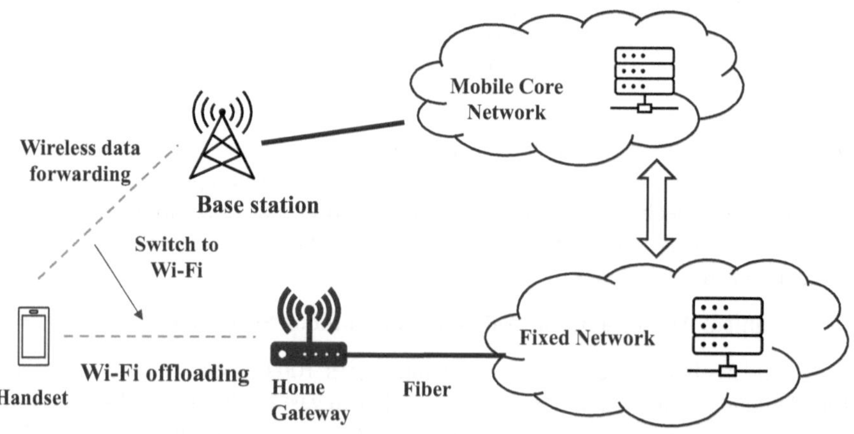

Fig. 7.2 Convergence of mobile and Wi-Fi access networks

connecting to the mobile network through a wired connection, the desired functions are still completed.

As depicted in Fig. 7.2, merging Wi-Fi access networks and mobile networks necessitates alterations to the 3GPP mobile network framework. The essential task is to identify and support mobile devices that connect to the network via Wi-Fi. This topic traces back to 2004, when 3GPP, starting with the R6 version, began defining an architecture for the convergence of mobile networks and wireless LANs. This innovation allowed operators to channel traffic from mobile networks through indoor wireless LANs. Subsequent iterations of the 3GPP specification have seen continued evolution and enhancement.

The era of mobile 4G presented an opportunity for 3GPP to blend Wi-Fi access, prompting improved planning for the convergence [2]. However, the integration of 4G and Wi-Fi networks did not find significant favor with operators, resulting in limited commercial deployment. For many, the convergence of 4G and Wi-Fi might be an unfamiliar concept. The core consideration for convergence lies in the potential benefits for customers and the feasibility of network investments, encompassing aspects of demand and technical solutions [3].

1. **Essential criteria for mobile network and Wi-Fi access convergence**

During the period of 4G network and Wi-Fi access integration, the aim was to leverage Wi-Fi's spectrum resources for routing mobile data traffic and enhancing the data bandwidth for wireless user services. In simple terms, the goal was to avoid constraining 4G networks, allowing people to utilize Wi-Fi for online activities whenever available.

Nonetheless, 4G itself provided robust indoor coverage and didn't rely on Wi-Fi to extend its reach. Furthermore, with operators actively promoting high-traffic services on their rapidly expanding 4G networks, the fusion of 4G networks and Wi-Fi access didn't yield substantial value.

2. **Technical approach to mobile network and Wi-Fi access integration**

The integration of Wi-Fi access into the 4G system required changes within the 4G core network and radio access network nodes (eNBs). Traditional 4G network architecture featured intricate interfaces and gateways, intricate connections between core network and radio access network nodes, and various solutions for integrating core and radio access networks to accommodate non-3GPP Wi-Fi networks. Consequently, this led to heightened technical complexities.

Without compelling scenario-driven necessities and efficient solutions, the extensive commercial viability of integrating mobile 4G and Wi-Fi access networks remained elusive.

However, in the era of mobile 5G, the convergence of mobile and Wi-Fi networks presents a fresh opportunity. To begin, the gradual construction of 5G base stations and enhancements to indoor coverage are ongoing, representing medium- to long-term engineering advancements. Moreover, the progression of 5G technology into millimeter-wave technology necessitates robust indoor data transmission solutions.

Furthermore, leveraging service modular architecture and network function virtualization technology, the 5G core network distinguishes control and data planes, making it easier to integrate and adapt to Wi-Fi access networks compared to the mobile 4G framework. Additionally, mobile 5G introduces support for network slicing. Enabling slicing in mobile networks requires support from the 5G Radio Access Network (RAN), core networks, and terminal equipment. To ensure comprehensive end-to-end coverage for 5G network slicing, a seamless solution involves connecting Wi-Fi and including slicing support within 5G network management. This naturally becomes part of the convergence of mobile and Wi-Fi networks, enabling Wi-Fi access networks to seamlessly integrate with 5G's management, configuration, and service operations, thereby supporting network slicing.

From the Wi-Fi technology perspective, Wi-Fi 6 and Wi-Fi 7 standards have taken a leap into the realm of carrier-grade data transmission. This means they can handle high amounts of data swiftly and with minimal delays. The merging of Wi-Fi access networks and the dynamic world of mobile 5G results in a win-win situation for both technologies, boosting their performance together. As we look ahead to Wi-Fi 7's arrival, we anticipate it will further improve the Quality of Service (QoS) for directing 5G traffic, leading to even better results. This exciting journey showcases how Wi-Fi and mobile 5G are joining forces to reshape the wireless technology landscape.

The convergence of the Wi-Fi access network and mobile 5G mainly includes two parts. First, it is about setting up the way 5G traffic moves through indoor wireless LAN and wired networks to reach the mobile core network. Second, it is about making sure 5G end-to-end services work with the required performance well within this setup.

7.2.1 3GPP Convergence Standard Evolution with Wi-Fi Technology Support

The 3GPP R15 and R16 versions have taken thorough steps in defining Wi-Fi access. For enabling Wi-Fi access, R15 introduces a convergence framework for untrusted non-3GPP networks, while R16 focuses on the trusted non-3GPP access convergence architecture [3–6]. This section uses these two versions as a reference to introduce the framework specifications guiding the convergence of 5G networks and Wi-Fi access and the direction of standard evolution.

7.2.1.1 5G R15's Convergence Framework for Mobile Network and Wi-Fi Network

Figure 7.3 illustrates the convergence depicted in the 3GPP R15 standard, centered on untrusted non-3GPP networks. The existing Wi-Fi access network, referred to as untrusted non-3GPP networks, becomes the avenue through which Wi-Fi terminals link with the 3GPP-defined mobile core network.

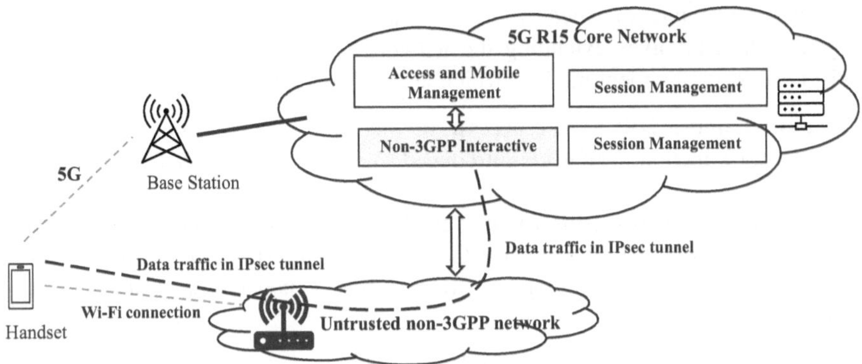

Fig. 7.3 Untrusted non-3GPP network convergence architecture in 5G R15 version

The key definitions and technologies included in the converged architecture of 3GPP R15 are as follows:

(1) **Standardization of network architectures**

A new non-3GPP interactive function unit (N3IWF) is introduced to the original 5G core network. Wireless terminals access the untrusted non-3GPP network via Wi-Fi, and N3IWF takes on responsibilities such as processing terminal registration and authentication requests, as well as setting up a data channel. This ensures seamless data forwarding between the 5G core network and the Wi-Fi access network.

(2) **Device compatibility of end devices**

Terminal hardware need not be altered; only a software upgrade is required to support N3IWF network discovery and Internet Protocol Security (IPsec) secure channel capabilities. This facilitates the network convergence services defined in the 3GPP R15 standard.

(3) **Channel reliability**

Control messages and data between the terminal and N3IWF are securely transmitted through IPsec tunneling. Upon successful authentication and registration with the 5G core network via the Wi-Fi network, an IPsec tunnel is established between the terminal and N3IWF. This facilitates the transmission of subsequent control messages, alongside the creation of IPsec sub-channel security associations for data transmission.

7.2.1.2 5G R16's Convergence Framework for Mobile Networks and Wi-Fi Network

The 3GPP R16 standard, ratified in July 2020, further advances the integration of 5G core networks with Wi-Fi access, building upon the foundation laid by R15. The network architecture specified in the R16 standard is illustrated in Fig. 7.4. R16's key alteration involves extending the network architecture to accommodate two Wi-Fi access deployment models, which are detailed below:

- **Trusted non-3GPP Wi-Fi access:** In this scenario, the Trusted Non-3GPP Gateway Function (TNGF) is introduced to supplant the N3IWF function from R15.
- **Wi-Fi access in Residential Gateway (RG) or Cable Modem (CM):** Another novel addition is the Fixed Access Gateway Function (FAGF), facilitating Wi-Fi access in situations involving Residential Gateway or Cable Modem configurations.

In Fig. 7.4, the mobile phone establishes a connection with the trusted non-3GPP network through Wi-Fi, and it is the responsibility of TNGF to manage authentication requests, establish data channels, and meet the service needs of mobile devices accessing the network via Wi-Fi. This evolution in the R16 standard amplifies the seamless interaction between mobile networks and Wi-Fi access.

7.2.1.3 Wi-Fi Paving the Path for 5G Network Convergence

Wi-Fi technology plays a pivotal role in underpinning the convergence framework that propels mobile 5G forward. This fusion, whether stemming from R15's untrusted non-3GPP network or R16's trusted non-3GPP network, necessitates robust Wi-Fi terminal and AP support. Figure 7.5 [7] showcases a spectrum of key technologies, spanning from Wi-Fi terminal device discovery and registration authentication within mobile networks to data security, quality-of-service assurance, and seamless roaming between mobile networks and Wi-Fi access.

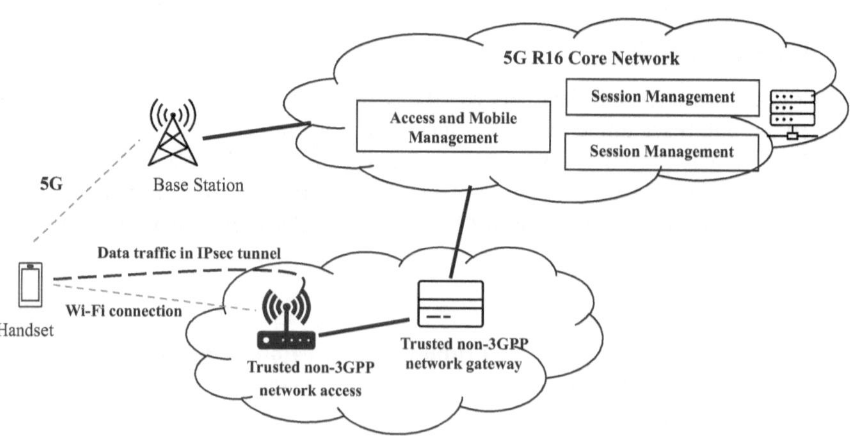

Fig. 7.4 Trusted non-3GPP network convergence architecture in 5G R16 version

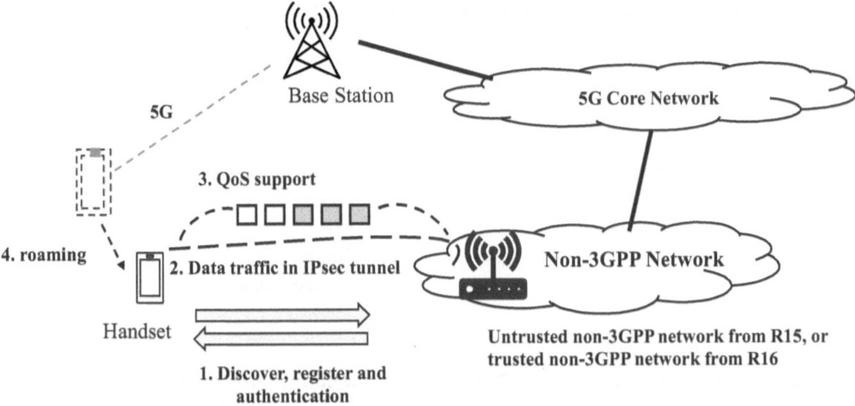

Fig. 7.5 Technologies enabling Wi-Fi's role in mobile network convergence

(1) **Wi-Fi Terminal Devices Registration in Mobile Networks**

The 5G network convergence architecture builds upon the separation of the core network and the access network. Here, terminal devices execute authentication and registration processes for both 3GPP and non-3GPP networks through a unified approach. This authentication status is shared within the core network unit.

In version 3GPP R16, pure Wi-Fi end devices don't utilize mobile network-defined signaling for registration. Instead, they rely on the non-3GPP Extended Extensible Authentication Protocol-Transport Layer Security (EAP-TLS) and Tunneled Transport Layer Security (EAP-TTLS) authentication methods. These methods facilitate authentication. Additionally, the trusted non-3GPP gateway functional unit takes on the responsibility of managing the registration and service for the 5G network.

(2) **Security Measures for Data Forwarding in Converged Networks**

The 5G network establishes a uniform data forwarding protocol for both trusted and untrusted non-3GPP networks. It ensures data forwarding security by leveraging Wi-Fi security mechanisms and IPSec tunneling technology.

In the context of R15's untrusted non-3GPP network access, an encrypted IPSec tunnel is formed between the endpoint and N3IWF, secured with a matching key. For R16's trusted non-3GPP network access, a secure Layer 2 link is established between the terminal and the Wi-Fi access point. Subsequently, an IPSec tunnel is set up over this link to ensure data forwarding security. The data forwarding protocol remains consistent with that of the untrusted non-3GPP network.

(3) **Ensuring Quality of Service (QoS) for Data Services in Converged Networks**

The 5G air interface specification dictates a user access rate of 10 Gbps and ultra-low latency in milliseconds. Comparatively, traditional Wi-Fi 6, prevalent indoors,

Table 7.2 Comparison between 5G network indicators and Wi-Fi performance

Technical indicators	User experience rate	Peak rate	Delay	Connection density
4G network	10 Mbps	1 Gbps	10 ms	10^5/km^2
5G network	1 Gbps	10 Gbps	1 ms	10^6/km^2
Wi-Fi 6	1 Gbps	9.6 Gbps	10 ms	Usually 64–128 (per 100 m^2; dependent on access devices)
Wi-Fi 7	10 Gbps	30 Gbps	<10 ms	Usually 128–256 (per 100 m^2; dependent on access devices)

provides connection rates in the hundreds of megabits and latency in the tens of milliseconds. However, Wi-Fi 7 technology significantly bolsters the technical foundation for seamless 5G service transition. This enhances the efficiency of service traffic bypass within 5G networks and guarantees a high Quality of Service (QoS) for 5G services.

Refer to Table 7.2 for a comprehensive overview of mobile network metrics and Wi-Fi experience performance.

(4) **Roaming Technology Between 5G Networks and Wi-Fi Networks**

Roaming between 5G networks and Wi-Fi networks is a crucial technology in the evolution of 5G networks supporting Wi-Fi access. This enhances user experience by allowing seamless transitions between networks.

Roaming can be initiated by the terminal device, often based on factors such as wireless signal quality, Wi-Fi bandwidth, and service quality. Additionally, 5G networks can provide network policies to terminals, aiding in network selection based on user preferences and policies.

The 3GPP specification outlines the roaming process between 5G and Wi-Fi networks. Core network units share authentication status and user data channel information, enabling smooth roaming and uninterrupted services. This technology ensures uninterrupted connectivity as users move between networks.

7.2.2 5G Network Slicing Requirements Incorporating with Wi-Fi Technology

Within the realm of integrating 5G networks with Wi-Fi access, the capabilities and service standards of 5G can be extended to Wi-Fi networks. The following sections describe the standard specifications for 5G network slicing and the technical requirements for related Wi-Fi access.

The essence of 5G network slicing lies in its ability to virtually divide a physical network into several software-defined virtual networks, tailored to various applications or services. Each network slice has its own distinct topology, resource

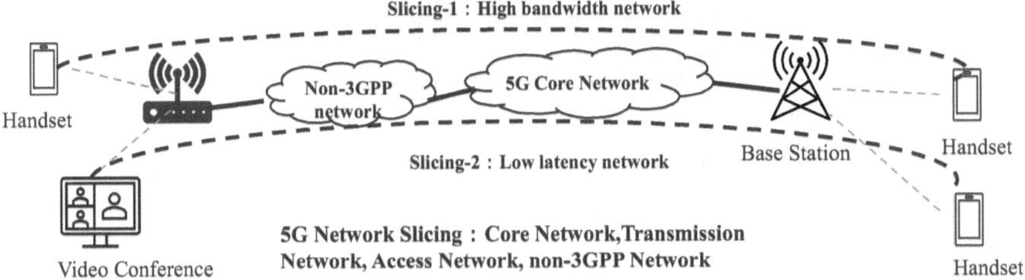

Fig. 7.6 Example of end-to-end 5G network slicing

allocation, traffic management, and configurations. This enables 5G networks to cater to diverse user needs and application scenarios effectively.

Customized requirements arise across different industries and scenarios, such as priority, security, mobility, and transmission performance. 5G network slicing accommodates these differences by establishing multiple independent logical networks within the same physical network framework.

Figure 7.6 presents an illustration of two slices within the convergence of 5G and Wi-Fi networks. One slice focuses on high-bandwidth data transmission, while the other emphasizes low-latency connections suitable for tasks like video conferencing.

As can be seen in the figure, the 5G network slicing structure encompasses radio access networks, core networks, transmission networks, and non-3GPP networks. The radio access network slice utilizes wireless spectrum resources and hardware for diverse access functionalities. Through software-defined control functions in radio access network slicing, different slices effectively share wireless spectrum resources.

In the context of 5G-Wi-Fi network convergence, realizing the potential of 5G network slicing involves Wi-Fi networks supporting slicing in management and service operation. Current Wi-Fi technologies can align with certain 5G slicing specifications, while new Wi-Fi solutions may be necessary to meet other specifications.

7.2.2.1 Development of 5G Network Slicing Specifications

The formulation of 5G network slicing standards has undergone extensive deliberations within 3GPP. In 3GPP TR23.799 [9], three distinct network slicing scenarios are introduced. These scenarios encompass various aspects, such as fully slicing all core network functions, including user and control planes, slicing core network control planes while keeping user planes unsliced, and scenarios where only user plane slicing is relevant.

These scenarios emphasize the need for user plane slicing, especially in the context of Wi-Fi access network and mobile network integration. As Wi-Fi access network integration progresses, the focus on slicing requirements for Wi-Fi access networks becomes paramount.

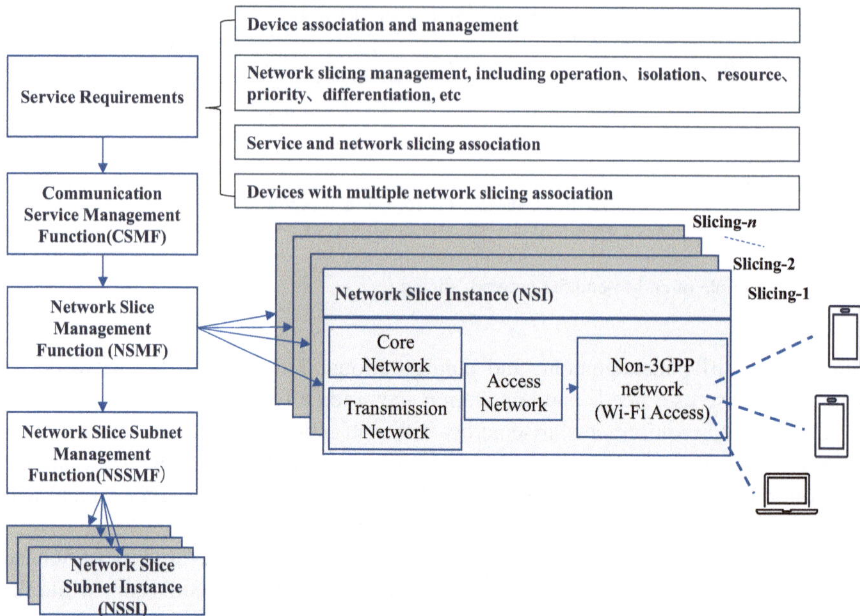

Fig. 7.7 Management architecture for 3GPP network slices

TS22.261 [8] defines the framework for slice requirements. This framework encompasses aspects such as device association and management within network slices, service-to-slice associations, and device-to-multiple-slice associations. These aspects address diverse requisites, including priority, billing, policy management, security, mobility, and transmission performance.

3GPP TR28.801 [11] defines the network slice management and operation framework. This framework encompasses key components such as the Communication Service Management Function (CSMF), Network Slice Management Function (NSMF), Network Slice Instances (NSI), Network Slice Subnet Management Function (NSSMF), and Network Slicing Subnet Instances (NSSI). However, it is worth noting that the current framework doesn't yet encompass non-3GPP network slice management.

Figure 7.7 [12] illustrates the service requirements for slice management, presenting a holistic view of TR28.801 network slice management integrated with Wi-Fi access. This amalgamation results in a unified framework for managing 5G networks, including non-3GPP access. Wi-Fi terminals interface with segmented virtual networks via non-3GPP networks, facilitating the realization of specific service scenarios.

7.2.2.2 Wi-Fi Technology's Role in 5G Network Slicing

Before diving into slicing technology for 5G networks, let's explore a scenario that's quite familiar—supporting various user needs on a Wi-Fi access network. Think about it: on a single Wi-Fi network, we have regular users and heavy data users coexisting, and in enterprise Wi-Fi, it handles both employees and visitors. It turns out the Wi-Fi access network has already paved the way for some of the slicing concepts that 5G networks demand. This interplay is depicted in Table 7.3 [10].

Looking at Wi-Fi from a technical lens, device association, management, slice control, and isolation are doable with existing Wi-Fi tech. However, resource allocation, priorities, differentiation, and business linkage demand custom solutions from manufacturers. Notably, standard bodies like the Wi-Fi Alliance haven't addressed these aspects yet. The arrival of Wi-Fi 7 or Wi-Fi mesh could spark conversations about these topics.

Table 7.3 Wi-Fi technology supports 5G network slices

Serial number	Category	The requirement entry for the slice	Current status
1	Device affinity and management in network slices	**Device association:** Wi-Fi APs use VLAN port bonding, BSSID, and SSID to associate devices with slices	Existing technology
2		**Device management:** Hotspot 2.0 and enterprise Wi-Fi support device mobility across slices	Existing technology
3	Management of network slices	**Slice management:** VLANs, SSIDs, and BSSIDs create and maintain slices	Existing technology
4		**Slice isolation:** Logical isolation of slices' traffic via multiple VLANs, SSIDs, and BSSIDs	Existing technology
5		**Slice resources:** Manufacturers to develop resource allocation mechanisms, such as utilizing SSIDs or air resources	Manufacturer development
6		**Slice priority:** There is no Wi-Fi standard support, and it needs to be developed by manufacturers, such as using the proportion of air interface resources and traffic rate limiting to achieve priority differentiation	Manufacturer development
7		**Slice differentiation:** Without Wi-Fi standard support, manufacturers need to develop varied policy controls and functions	Manufacturer development
8	Service association	**Service association:** Without Wi-Fi standard support, manufacturers define mechanisms to link services with slices	Manufacturer development
9	Multi-slice support	**Multi-slice support:** Wi-Fi 6 lacked multi-slice support until now	There is no traditional scheme

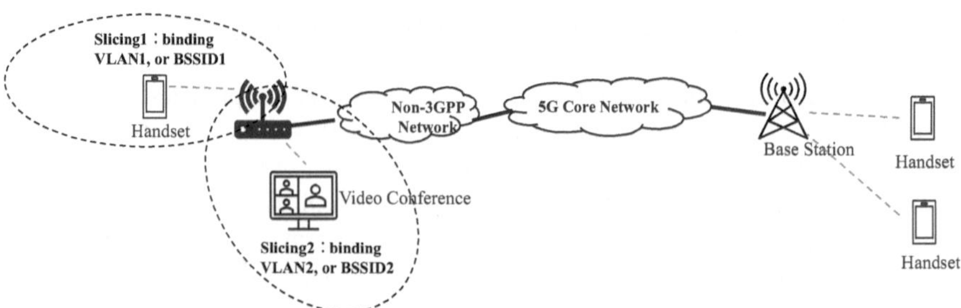

Fig. 7.8 Wi-Fi network slicing scheme for device management and service differentiation

Device Association and Slice Management Referring to Fig. 7.8 [12], in a Wi-Fi access network, VLAN1 is associated with a specific BSSID, and the terminals are associated with that slice. Similarly, other sets of terminals are connected over the same BSSID and associated with VLAN2. These configurations isolate the traffic between VLAN1 and VLAN2, enabling the creation of network slicing in the Wi-Fi access network.

In addition, Wi-Fi APs can work their magic using multiple BSSIDs and SSIDs—typically, 1 SSID per 1 BSSID. Look at Fig. 7.8 again. BSSID1 and BSSID2 each accompany one of the Wi-Fi endpoints. BSSID1 serves regular Internet access, while BSSID2 rolls out high-speed, low-latency services. This setup answers network slicing's call for diverse devices and distinct business needs.

7.2.2.3 Enabling Network Slicing with Wi-Fi 7 Technology

Wi-Fi access networks are stepping up to support the realm of 5G network slicing. The crux lies in how we logically carve up the physical Wi-Fi resources to build distinct virtual networks. In Wi-Fi 6, the physical layer employed OFDMA technology to split subcarriers into separate clusters, each functioning as an independent Resource Unit (RU). These RUs were assigned to various devices for data transmission, birthing a fresh spectrum-driven resource setup that catered to the needs of slices.

Wi-Fi 7 advances this capability further with its multi-link operation, introducing another way to segment network resources—this time based on physical links. The flexibility of managing multiple resource units further refines the management of spectrum resources, making it an even better fit for various application scenarios. Plus, Wi-Fi 7 steps up in the low-latency game, bringing in a capability to identify specific service features. This introduces the technical avenue for aligning "service and network slicing."

In Fig. 7.9, we delve into three pivotal technologies of Wi-Fi 7 [1] that rally behind network slicing.

(1) **Multi-Link Operation (MLO) technology**: Different slices, diverse services from one device, or varied terminals can choose to transmit on a specific link

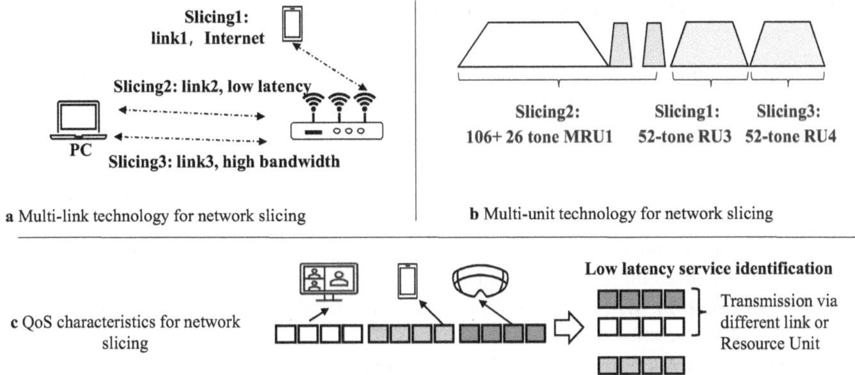

Fig. 7.9 (**a**) Multi-link technology for network slicing, (**b**) Multi-unit technology for network slicing, and (**c**) QoS characteristics for network slicing

within the multi-link connectivity to the AP. The mapping of services to links is provided by the AP to the client. In Fig. 7.9a, Link 2 and Link 3 mapped to slices 2 and 3, respectively, fulfilling the "device association with multiple network slices" requirement.

(2) **Multi-Resource Unit (MRU) technology:** In Fig. 7.9b, each slice is assigned an MRU, the size of the MRU determined by the particular slice requirement. This feature is quite remarkable for enabling slicing and is adaptable to different business needs.
(3) **Low-latency service feature recognition:** In Fig. 7.9c, the spotlight is on recognizing services that need quick responses. Services that can't tolerate delays, such as virtual reality and network video services. Once these are identified, they're easily connected to their respective slices for smooth operation.

It is evident that Wi-Fi 7's advanced technology in segmenting and managing network resources positions the Wi-Fi 7 standard as a more suitable candidate for achieving comprehensive network slicing alongside 5G networks slicing. For details about slice management techniques specific to Wi-Fi 7, refer to Table 7.4.

7.2.2.4 Wi-Fi EasyMesh Technology and Network Slicing in the 5G Framework

Wi-Fi-based EasyMesh (Mesh) networks have gained prominence in the home network market. To achieve end-to-end network slicing within the 5G framework, the network slicing of Wi-Fi mesh plays a pivotal role. The crux of mesh network slicing lies in establishing data connections between Wi-Fi Access Points (APs), specifically through the backhaul channel, to enable slicing.

Table 7.4 Connection between Wi-Fi 7 technology and slicing requirements

S·No	Slice requirement	Wi-Fi 7 technology
1	**Device association:** Wi-Fi 7 uses multi-link and multi-resource unit management; this allocates sliced resources to different terminals for seamless data transmission	Fully supported
2	**Device management**: Wi-Fi 7 facilitates switching Wi-Fi devices between slices through link or resource unit reassignment	Fully supported
3	**Slice management**: Wi-Fi 7 empowers the creation and maintenance of sliced links or resource units	Fully supported
4	**Slice isolation:** Wi-Fi 7-based distinct slices ensure effective isolation of traffic and services	Fully supported
5	**Slice resources**: Wi-Fi 7 flexibly slices links or resource units based on capacity	Fully supported
6	**Slice priority:** While not natively supported by Wi-Fi 7, manufacturers can tailor it as per their product needs; for instance, differentiating priority using air interface resources and traffic rate limits	Manufacturer development
7	**Slice differentiation:** Similar to priority, Wi-Fi 7 lacks direct support, but manufacturers can adapt policy controls, functions, and performance to their product needs	Manufacturer development
8	**Service association**: Wi-Fi 7 supports low-latency service feature identification, and manufacturers can at least associate low-latency-related services to slices	Partial support
9	**Multi-slice support**: Multi-Link Operation technology permits associating distinct services of the same terminal with various links; this empowers terminals to support multiple network slices concurrently	In the tank

For multiple network slices to coexist on a shared backhaul channel, Wi-Fi 7 technology can classify data streams smartly using VLANs or SSIDs. However, Wi-Fi lacks a standardized approach for managing resources and adjusting the priorities of diverse data streams. This gap requires attention from manufacturers. The multi-link operation technology of Wi-Fi 7 can assign distinct links within the backhaul channel to different slices. Additionally, Wi-Fi 7's capability to identify low-latency services aligns well with associating low-latency slices and their corresponding service data streams.

In Fig. 7.10, the backhaul linking Wi-Fi APs is ingeniously divided into two slices using the multi-link approach. Slice 1 caters to operator network management, handling control and management messages with high reliability, albeit with limited bandwidth. On the other hand, Slice 2 caters to high-bandwidth, low-latency needs, accommodating home video streaming or network gaming. This illustration demonstrates how network slicing within the Wi-Fi mesh, guided by technologies like multi-link associations and low-latency recognition, can effectively meet the slicing requirement for 5G-Wi-Fi convergence.

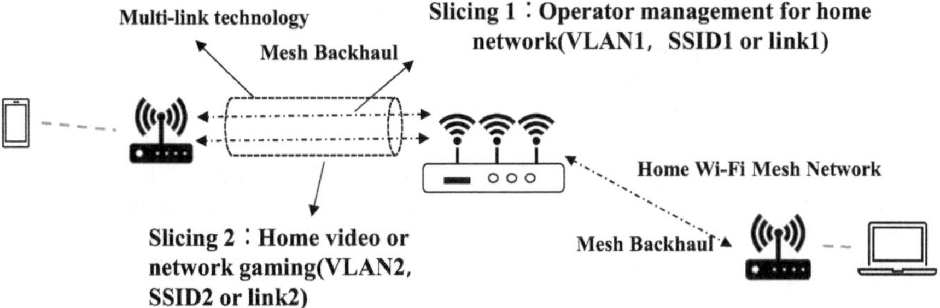

Fig. 7.10 Slice scheme for a Wi-Fi Mesh network

7.3 Application Scenarios for Wi-Fi Network and 5G Convergence

Bringing together the benefits of 5G mobile networks and Wi-Fi access networks finds relevance in various contexts such as smart cities, industrial Internet, hospitality, enterprise spaces, and smart homes. While certain key technologies remain to be thoroughly addressed for their seamless fusion, and standards organizations continue to refine specifications, the inevitable union of these two technologies is bound to provide support across multiple scenarios.

7.3.1 Types of Scenarios Applied by 5G and Wi-Fi Network Convergence

Drawing insights from earlier discussions on the pivotal technologies of 5G networks and Wi-Fi, as well as the essence of network slices, let's delve into the distinctive demands of 5G networks in Wi-Fi access convergence. Refer to Table 7.5 for a comprehensive view of these scenarios, including performance indices and the corresponding focus on key technology design.

7.3.2 Application Examples of Convergence Network

Let's look at an illustration in Fig. 7.11, showcasing a 5G private network and a converged Wi-Fi network in an enterprise campus or community setting. The 5G private network, aligned with the 3GPP 5G standard, can be established in collaboration with the public 5G network or independently. Either way, the convergence of 5G networks and Wi-Fi access networks is similar.

In the example of Fig. 7.11, a Wi-Fi 7 gateway collaborates with diverse standard Wi-Fi APs to create a wireless LAN. This LAN integrates with the 5G mobile core

Table 7.5 Scenarios of 5G and Wi-Fi network convergence

Scene type	Network convergence parameters and performance	Key technologies for convergence	Network slicing requirements
Public Wi-Fi Hotspots (e.g., airports, stadiums)	**Access density:** 128 terminals/wireless access points	5G and Wi-Fi 6 or Wi-Fi 7 access convergence, terminal authentication, QoS and registration, data service QoS assurance, roaming between mobile networks and Wi-Fi networks, and other key technologies	Slicing distinguishes the traffic requirements and service assurance of different users
Industrial areas, telemedicine, IoT, etc.	**Access density:** 32–64 terminals/wireless access points **User rate:** 200 Mbps–600 Mbps **Low latency:** Supports 1–10 ms latency	5G and Wi-Fi 6 or Wi-Fi 7 access convergence, terminal authentication, data forwarding security, QoS assurance for data service, and other key technologies	Slicing distinguishes between low-latency services and common services
Homes, communities, hotel apartments, office environments, etc.	**Access density**: 32–64 terminals/wireless access points **User rate:** 200 Mbps–1 Gbps **Medium and high latency:** Supports 10–50 ms latency	5G and Wi-Fi 6 or Wi-Fi 7 access convergence, terminal authentication and registration, QoS assurance for data service, roaming between mobile networks and Wi-Fi networks, and other key technologies	Slicing distinguishes between high-bandwidth and low-latency services, between internal devices and guest devices

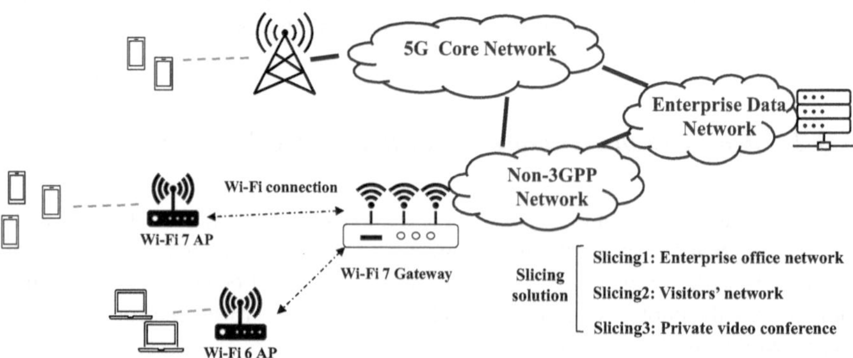

Fig. 7.11 5G and Wi-Fi convergence in corporate campuses or communities

Table 7.6 Wi-Fi network slicing examples in application scenarios

Quantity	The slice type	Requirements for slicing
Slice-1	Office network access for enterprise employees	**Functions**: Support terminal authentication and registration, QoS guarantee of data services, end-to-end data encryption, and reserved enterprise bandwidth **Performance**: High slicing priority, low transmission delay, and high access reliability
Slice-2	Temporary access by external visitors	**Function**: Support terminal authentication, basic Internet access, no billing, and adequate bandwidth **Performance**: Low slicing priority, average transmission delay, and average reliability
Slice-3	High-bandwidth, low-latency enterprise-specific video conferencing	**Functions**: Support terminal authentication, QoS guarantee for data services, end-to-end data encryption, and reserved enterprise bandwidth **Performance**: High slicing priority, low transmission delay, and high access reliability

Table 7.7 Hardware specifications for Wi-Fi 7 broadband gateways and APs

AP selection	Wi-Fi 7 gateway specifications	Wi-Fi 7 AP specifications
Hardware requirements	Wi-Fi 7 gateway BE19000	Wi-Fi 7 AP BE19000 or BE7200
	Wi-Fi 7 tri-band	Wi-Fi 7 tri-band
	Multi-antenna 4 × 4 2.4 GHz, 4 × 4 5 GHz, 4 × 4 6 GHz	Multi-antenna 4 × 4 2.4 GHz, 4 × 4 5 GHz, 4 × 4 6 GHz
	Supports 320 MHz bandwidth	Supports 320 MHz bandwidth

network through trusted or untrusted non-3GPP networks, thereby establishing a comprehensive enterprise private network in tandem with the enterprise data network.

This converged network, beyond meeting the stipulated requirements of access density, user rates, and latency, also showcases three end-to-end network slicing instances, encompassing Wi-Fi 7 and Wi-Fi Mesh. These slices cater to various needs, including employee office network access, temporary external visitor Internet access, and high-bandwidth, low-latency enterprise-specific video conferencing.

Each network slice occupies distinct resources, configurations, and connections within the enterprise private network. These diverse slicing requirements and types are outlined in detail in Table 7.6.

In the converged 5G and Wi-Fi access network, the software and hardware specifications and functions of the Wi-Fi 7 broadband gateway and AP are mentioned in Tables 7.7 and 7.8. Remember, not all Wi-Fi 7 devices have every standard feature, and they might not achieve the best possible performance defined in the Wi-Fi 7 standard. So, when talking about product specs, focus on the unique technologies that match the specific scenario.

Table 7.8 Software function requirements for Wi-Fi 7 broadband gateways and APs

AP selection	List of Wi-Fi 7-related software features for gateways and APs
Functional requirements	Supports EasyMesh networking based on Wi-Fi 7
	Supports Wi-Fi 7's multi-link operation technology and load balancing technology
	Multi-resource unit technology that supports Wi-Fi 7
	Support 802.1x authentication methods, WPA3 security level
	Supports low-latency service feature recognition
	Support QoS control of services, prioritizing video or voice

7.3.3 The Future of 5G and Wi-Fi Network Convergence Evolution

The evolution of network convergence for Wi-Fi access after 3GPP R15 has been more comprehensive compared to the 4G era. However, practical concerns about end-to-end service quality, data security, and network management for mobile and pure Wi-Fi devices in converged networks remain vital topics for years ahead.

(1) **End-to-End Service Quality of Converged Networks**

In 5G, network slicing supports end-to-end service quality management. Yet, integrating Wi-Fi access network operations into slice management lacks detailed specifications. Air interface resource priority and delay control in Wi-Fi remain separate from 5G's deployment. Achieving unified management of service quality parameters across 5G and Wi-Fi is a technical challenge for effective network convergence. On a positive note, Wi-Fi 7's multi-link operations, multi-resource management, and low-latency service features bring opportunities and support to network slicing technology.

(2) **Data Security for 5G Terminals Switching to Wi-Fi**

Wi-Fi networks function within unlicensed frequency bands, allowing diverse terminals to connect to the same gateway. When 5G terminals switch to ordinary Wi-Fi nodes for data forwarding, and after the relevant authentication procedure, end-to-end network security still needs to be reassessed. Currently, no research or discussion exists on ensuring end-to-end security in such scenarios.

(3) **Converged Network Operations and Maintenance**

Generally, the operation and management of Wi-Fi-based broadband access gateways focus on the parameters of the network interface and lack effective management methods for the performance and service quality parameters of Wi-Fi access. As 5G and Wi-Fi access networks merge, not only is unified network operation essential, but also enhanced maintenance and supervision of 5G terminal access to Wi-Fi networks. This becomes a central concern for operators and equipment vendors in their plans for network convergence.

References

1. IEEE (2023) Draft Standard for Information technology--Telecommunications and information exchange between systems Local and metropolitan area networks--Specific requirements - Part 11: Wireless LAN Medium Access Control (MAC) and Physical Layer (PHY) Specifications Amendment: Enhancements for Extremely High Throughput (EHT) (IEEE P802.11be/D5.0). November. pp. 1–1045
2. Rajavelsamy R, Choudhary M, Das D (2016) A Review on Evolution of 3GPP Systems Interworking with WLAN. Journal of ICT Standardization, 3(2), 133–156. https://doi.org/10.13052/jicts2245-800X.322
3. Jiang YM, Cheng G (2021) Fixed Wireless Convergence Evolution Analysis between 5G and Wi-Fi Access. Mobile Communications, 45(5), 135–139
4. Wireless Broadband Alliance and NGMN Alliance (2019) RAN convergence paper. September 2019
5. 3GPP (2021) Technical specification group services and system aspects; system architecture for the 5G system; Stage 2 (3GPP TS 23.501 V16.1.0) [EB/OL]. [2021-03-20]. http://www.3gpp.org/DynaReport/23501.htm
6. 3GPP (2021) Study on the wireless and wireline convergence for the 5G system architecture (3GPP TS 23.716) [EB/OL]. [2021-03-20]. http://www.3gpp.org/DynaReport/23716.htm
7. 3GPP TS 23.402 V17.0.0 (2021) Architecture enhancements for non-3GPP accesses
8. 3GPP (2021) Service requirements for next generation new services and markets (3GPP TS 22.261) [EB/OL]. [2021-03-18]. http://www.3gpp.org/DynaReport/22261.htm
9. 3GPP (2021) Study on Architecture for next generation system (3GPP TR 23.799) [EB/OL]. [2021-03-20]. http://www.3gpp.org/DynaReport/23799.htm
10. Cheng G, Jiang YM (2021) Analysis for 5G network slicing with Wi-fi access convergence. Communications Technology, 54(08), 1930–1936
11. 3GPP (2021) Study on management and orchestration of network slicing for next generation network (3GPP TR 28.801) [EB/OL]. [2021-03-20]. http://www.3gpp.org/DynaReport/28801.htm
12. WBA (2018) Network slicing - understanding Wi-Fi capabilities (WBA 5G workgroup V1.0) [EB/OL]. [2018-03-27]. https://extranet.wballiance.com

References

Chapter 8
Outlook for Wi-Fi Technology Development

Abstract In general, IEEE releases a new Wi-Fi standard every 4–5 years. Wi-Fi 7 is the latest Wi-Fi generation in 2024. It is foreseeable that the Wi-Fi 8 specification will be completed around 2027, and Wi-Fi 8 products will start to hit the market by 2028. Wi-Fi 8 originated from the Ultra-High Reliability Study Group (UHR SG), established by IEEE in July 2022. This group aims to focus on improving the reliability of Wi-Fi connections, further reducing latency, improving Wi-Fi manageability, optimizing throughput across varying signal-to-noise ratios, and minimizing power consumption. This chapter begins by providing insights into the evolving broadband access and mobile communication technologies, which coincide with the development period of Wi-Fi 8. Subsequently, the chapter discusses the latest developments in the Wi-Fi 8 standard, such as further advancements in traditional key Wi-Fi technologies and technical solutions for multi-AP collaboration. Additionally, the chapter briefly introduces new Wi-Fi technology topics, including those related to Millimeter-wave Bands and Artificial Intelligence/Machine Learning.

8.1 Turning on Ultra-High Broadband Networks

The ability to access the Internet via Wi-Fi at home relies on the connection between Wi-Fi routers and either wired broadband access networks or mobile communication networks. Broadband access and mobile communication network operators expect high-performance Wi-Fi technologies that align with advancements in their end-to-end communication networks.

Figure 8.1 depicts a conceptual mapping between Wi-Fi, wired broadband access networks, and the evolution of mobile communications. While there is no concrete timeline for the commercialization of next-generation broadband access and mobile 6G, this figure offers a prediction, as detailed below.

1. **Broadband access**

Gigabit-Capable Passive Optical Network (GPON) access gateways have been deployed with Wi-Fi 4 and Wi-Fi 5 for quite some years. Recently, 10 Gbps PON with Wi-Fi 6 has emerged among operators worldwide. It is foreseeable that both

G. Cheng et al., *Wi-Fi 7*, https://doi.org/10.1007/978-981-97-9026-5_8

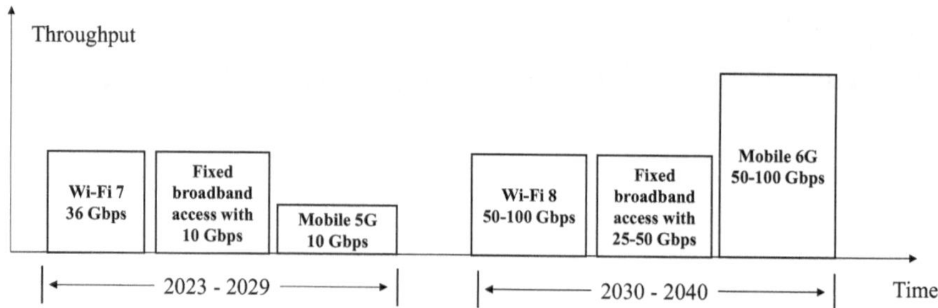

Fig. 8.1 Wi-Fi technology evolution and broadband access

Wi-Fi 6 and Wi-Fi 7 will be deployed by operators in the coming years as indoor extensions of 10 Gbps broadband access.

As the next-generation technology solutions for broadband access, GPON or 10G GPON are projected to be upgraded to 25 Gbps or 50 Gbps PON around 2030. Concurrently, Wi-Fi gateways or access points will also be upgraded to support Wi-Fi 8 speeds probably above 50 Gbps. This advancement is expected to provide an end-to-end solution for ultra-high broadband access.

2. **Mobile networks**

As the mass deployment of mobile 5G is in full swing around the world, 3GPP's new standard R18 for 5G is set to be finalized in 2024. The commercialization of this new mobile 5G standard is expected to occur over the next 5 years. In parallel, the expansion of 5G to indoor coverage and the enhancement of indoor performance will be supported by Wi-Fi 6 and possibly Wi-Fi 7, offering higher performance.

While mobile 5G remains a significant focus in the industry, attention has swiftly shifted toward the key technology of mobile 6G across different vendors. Emerging technologies such as artificial intelligence, network perception, extreme performance experience, space-space-ground integrated networking, perception communication, and computing integration are under exploration. Presently, it is challenging to predict which key technologies will be incorporated into the 6G standard. However, based on historical trends of each generation of mobile communications introduced roughly every 10 years, a draft timeline for the release of the 6G standard is anticipated around 2030.

Mobile 6G is expected to surpass 5G in terms of user experience. For example, it is expected to achieve a peak rate of Tbps, a user experience rate of 10–100 Gbps, and a sub-millisecond latency. From the perspective of Wi-Fi technology, performance indicators such as user experience rates and latency of 6G align with the objectives of Wi-Fi 8. Around 2030, Wi-Fi 8, serving as an indoor complement and extension of 6G communication, will contribute to forming a comprehensive solution for wireless ultra-broadband networks.

Combined with the advancement of broadband access and mobile communications, it is anticipated that after 2030, the infrastructure of ultra-wideband networks,

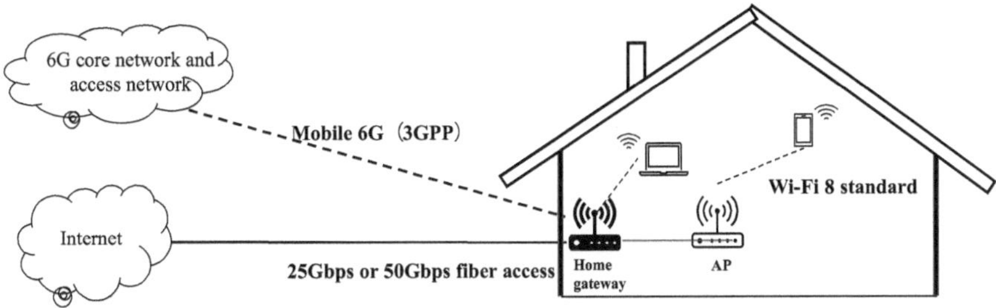

Fig. 8.2 Illustration of Home Wi-Fi 8 with broadband access and mobile network

as shown in Fig. 8.2, will emerge. This will lead to a significant leap in user experience when utilizing such networks.

8.2 Looking Ahead to Key Technologies of Next-Generation Wi-Fi

In each iteration of Wi-Fi standards, there is a significant advancement in physical layer technology, such as improving the modulation, channel bonding, channel bandwidth expansion, and MU-MIMO. As the Wi-Fi 8 standard is formulated, there will be a reexploration of these key technologies for further improvement.

The UHR group aims to provide high stability for Wi-Fi data transmission in the channel. Multi-AP collaboration technology, which reduces mutual interference between BSS and improves channel utilization and data transmission stability, aligns well with UHR objectives. While Wi-Fi 7 initially considered multi-AP collaboration technology, its complexity led to its deferral. However, this technology is expected to be revisited for Wi-Fi 8.

In the mobile 5G R15 standard, AI/ML has already been utilized in network data collection, analysis, and network automation. In mobile 6G networks, AI/ML will have broader applications, including load balancing, user data management, and optimization at the MAC and PHY layers.

It can be expected that the design goal of the IEEE AI/ML group will align with the targets defined for the AI/ML applications in mobile 6G networks. Combined with the characteristics of Wi-Fi networks, the AI/ML function will further enhance the overall performance of Wi-Fi communication systems.

8.2.1 Upgrades to Traditional Key Technologies

Looking back at the history of Wi-Fi standard evolution, Wi-Fi 4 and Wi-Fi 6 stand as significant milestones.

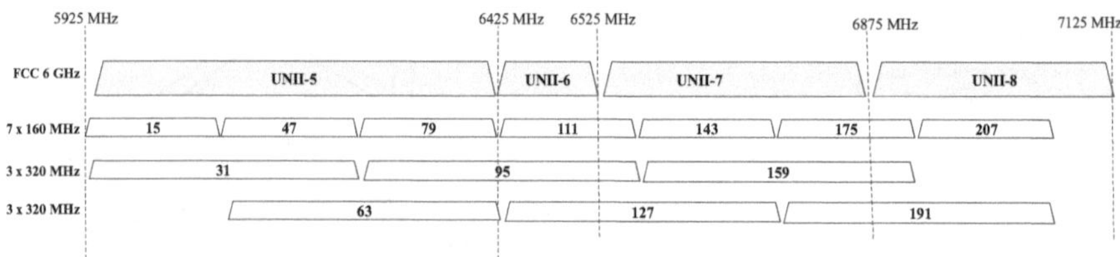

Fig. 8.3 320 MHz channel on 6 GHz

Wi-Fi 4 introduced support for MIMO technology and channel bonding, while Wi-Fi 6 expanded to the 6 GHz band and supported Orthogonal Frequency Division Multiple Access (OFDMA). These standards enhanced the foundation of traditional Wi-Fi technologies, focusing on spectrum efficiency and leveraging spatial and spectrum multiplexing to drive Wi-Fi networks toward higher bandwidth and efficiency.

With the significant performance improvements brought by the Wi-Fi 7 standard [1], the potential for further advancements in traditional key Wi-Fi technologies remains a topic of discussion [2].

1. **Channel bandwidth**

As depicted in Fig. 8.3, Wi-Fi 7 supports up to six 320 MHz channels on the 6 GHz band, but only three of these channels can operate simultaneously without overlapping. Considering the available spectrum resources in the 6 GHz band, Wi-Fi 8 is unlikely to introduce a new breakthrough in channel bandwidth beyond Wi-Fi 7, that is, it may continue to support up to 320 MHz channels rather than focusing on expanding to 640 MHz channels as a priority in the new standard.

2. **Modulation efficiency**

Wi-Fi 7 introduced 4096-QAM, also known as 4 K QAM ($4096 = 2^{12}$), representing a 20% improvement in data rate compared to Wi-Fi 6. With Wi-Fi 8, there is speculation that the modulation target could be 16 K QAM, $16\text{ K} = 2^{14}$, bringing a 16.66% increase in data rate. However, higher-order modulation brings increased implementation complexity, and the rate of improvement becomes more limited. Therefore, whether to adopt 16 K QAM as a standard for Wi-Fi 8 will be subject to discussion within the standards organization.

3. **Multiple input and multiple output**

In the development of Wi-Fi 7, the IEEE group considered including 16 spatial streams in the standard. But due to time constraints, this was deferred to Wi-Fi 8 for further discussion.

However, the necessity of 16 spatial streams for home networks and devices is debatable. While increasing spatial streams can enhance performance, it also raises concerns about antenna count, complexity, appearance, power consumption, and cost. Manufacturers need to carefully evaluate the cost-effectiveness of supporting more than eight antennas on a Wi-Fi AP device. Additionally, efficiently managing data transmission and control between APs and stations with 16 spatial streams presents technical challenges for implementation.

8.2.2 Evolution of New Key Technologies

8.2.2.1 Multi-AP Collaboration Technology

Wi-Fi 6 introduced OFDMA to address performance challenges in densely populated areas. With more APs deployed, there arises a need for effective collaboration between neighboring APs. While Wi-Fi 7 began discussions on technical solutions for dense AP deployment scenarios, the overlap of wireless signals between APs remains a significant challenge. Besides minimizing mutual interference between APs, maximizing the utilization of limited time-frequency and air resources is crucial for improving system efficiency and data forwarding performance in multi-AP environments. Because of the technical complexity, the technical solution for multi-AP collaboration [3, 4] was deferred from Wi-Fi 7 to Wi-Fi 8.

Efficient multi-AP cooperation hinges on leveraging spectrum multiplexing, spatial multiplexing, and other technologies in individual Wi-Fi APs. This enables different APs to negotiate and cooperate, but without interfering with each other at the same time, thereby reducing the latency and performance issues caused by interference.

Referring to Fig. 8.4, multi-AP collaboration includes OFDMA, beamforming, and distributed MIMO-based collaboration.

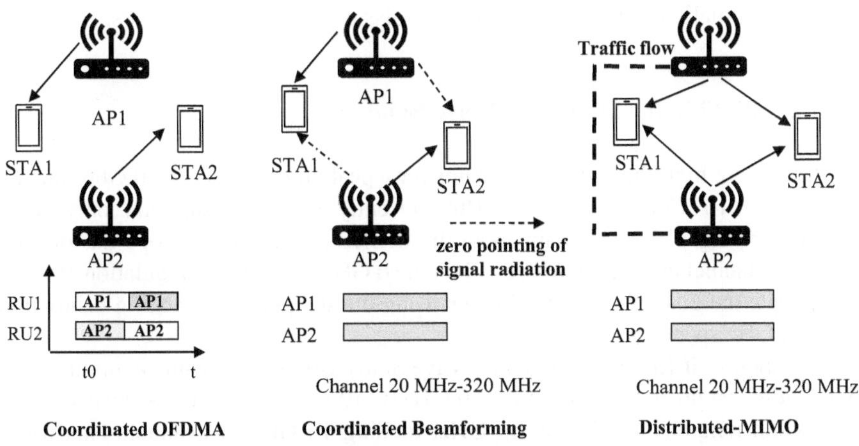

Fig. 8.4 Wi-Fi multi-AP cooperation mode

1. **OFDMA Collaboration (Coordinated OFDMA)**

Based on the OFDMA technology of 802.11ax, a new mode of collaboration enables different APs to utilize different Resource Units (RUs) for simultaneous data transmission at the same time through negotiation. This reduces the collision in the competition window between APs and maximizes the use of channel resources as much as possible. This approach, being the simplest form of multi-AP collaboration, is very beneficial for optimizing the latency of short packets.

2. **Beamforming based collaboration**

This collaboration is also known as Coordinated Null Steering or Coordinated Beamforming. The premise of cooperation relies on APs equipped with multiple pairs of antennas. Through space multiplexing technology, multiple APs provide beamforming gain to different devices simultaneously while directing zero signal radiation to other devices. This efficient use of space resources enhances data transmission.

Implementation involves APs cooperating via management messages. The APs acquire Channel State Information from nonassociated devices and adjust antenna direction accordingly to achieve zero radiation.

3. **Distributed MIMO collaboration (D-MIMO, Distributed-MIMO)**

This is a more complex mechanism within multi-AP cooperation. It transforms adjacent APs from sources of interference into collaborators for data transmission, thereby expanding spatial multiplexing and increasing coverage through beamforming.

The D-MIMO mechanism requires the optimization of the original collision avoidance mechanism (CSMA/CA) so that multiple APs can enhance the handling of channel access in overlapping signal areas. Even it may be necessary to establish the architecture of the master AP and the slave AP, where the master AP coordinates frequency domain resources and controls the transmission of management frames to facilitate mutual cooperation and data transmission among multiple APs.

8.2.2.2 Wi-Fi in the Millimeter-Wave Band

Wi-Fi's future high-throughput goal aims for a peak throughput of 100 Gbps and an average of 10 Gbps per device. But currently the FCC supports only three nonoverlapping 320 MHz channels in the 6 GHz band, while Europe has opened only one channel in the 320 MHz band on the 6 GHz band. These regulations further complicate the goal of significantly increasing throughput by expanding bandwidth in the 6 GHz spectrum.

In response, IEEE has set up a mmWave Study Group (SG) with attention on the bandwidth resources available in the 60 GHz mmWave band. This spectrum offers a bandwidth range of 45 GHz to 60 GHz, totaling 15 GHz of available bandwidth resources. Traditional 802.11ad/ay technology supports a minimum channel bandwidth of 2.16 GHz and can reach 8.64 GHz through channel bundling technology. Based on existing 802.11ad/ay technology, the mmWave SG group proposes a 60 GHz band with a bandwidth of 160 MHz to 1280 MHz. This wider bandwidth range can accommodate the needs of multi-AP deployments in dense environments across different channels without causing interference.

8.2.2.3 Artificial Intelligence and Machine Learning

The goal of integrating AI/ML into Wi-Fi networks is to enhance Wi-Fi performance and optimize channel utilization efficiency. As shown in Fig. 8.5, the application of AI/ML in Wi-Fi will be evident in the following six aspects:

1. **Channel access:** According to the channel status, the back-off window can dynamically adjust through AI/ML, replacing random back-off modes. This reduces channel idle time and conflict probability, enhancing channel utilization efficiency.
2. **Link adaptation:** AI/ML predicts the current channel state and automatically selects the optimal transmission rate to improve system throughput.
3. **PHY layer optimization:** The external non-Wi-Fi or Wi-Fi signal can be automatically identified by AI/ML, thereby reducing the interference generated by noise and improving the efficiency of decoding and modulation.
4. **Beamforming optimization:** Through the AI/ML prediction for channel characteristics, beamforming transmission bandwidth and transmission power can be automatically selected, thereby reducing the channel detection time and improving system throughput.
5. **Multiuser optimization:** AI/ML can be used to accurately allocate RU/MRU to each user to meet the requirements for high throughput and low latency in multiuser concurrent scenarios.

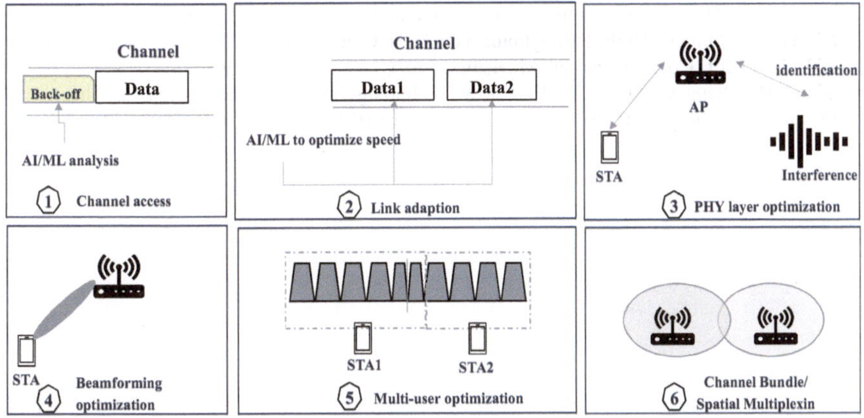

Fig. 8.5 AI/ML optimization for Wi-Fi communication systems

6. **Channel bonding/Spatial multiplexing:** According to the channel and sub-channel status, the number of channel bonding and transmit power can be automatically selected through AI/ML, and the CCA threshold can also be automatically adjusted, ensuring full use of channel resources and improving throughput.

8.3 Conclusion

Wi-Fi has emerged as one of the most successful wireless data transmission technologies. Over the past few decades, its evolution from an initial speed of 2 Mbps in 1997 to the latest speeds exceeding 30 Gbps in 2024, spanning seven generations, reflects a remarkable increase in speed by a factor of 15,000 in 26 years. Wi-Fi's global economic impact is projected to soar to almost $5 trillion by 2025, with an annual delivery of 1 billion devices. As Wi-Fi technology continues to advance, with enhancements such as higher throughput capabilities and reduced latency, its role in facilitating data communications across short distances is expected to remain pivotal across diverse scenarios in the coming decade.

References

1. IEEE (2023) Draft Standard for Information technology--Telecommunications and information exchange between systems Local and metropolitan area networks--Specific requirements - Part 11: Wireless LAN Medium Access Control (MAC) and Physical Layer (PHY) Specifications Amendment: Enhancements for Extremely High Throughput (EHT) (IEEE P802.11be/D5.0). November. pp. 1–1045
2. Reshef E, Cordeiro C (2022) Future Directions for Wi-Fi 8 and Beyond. IEEE Communications Magazine, 60(10), 50–55. October. https://doi.org/10.1109/MCOM.003.2200037
3. Lopez-Perez D, Garcia-Rodriguez A, Galati-Giordano L, Kasslin M, Doppler K (2019) IEEE 802.11be Extremely High Throughput: The Next Generation of Wi-Fi Technology Beyond 802.11ax. IEEE Communications Magazine, 57(9), 113–119. September
4. Qian ZH, Cheng G (2024) Wi-Fi 7 Key Technology Analysis and Survey. Application of Electronic Technique, 50(03), 13–18. https://doi.org/10.16157/j.issn.0258-7998.234435